Contents

List of Illustrations

Diagrams

Maps

Photographs

Acknowledgments for photographs

Cover photograph: NASA (JSC Digital Image Collection—Earth Observation Images). The satellite image shows East Anglia under 70 per cent cloud cover.

Celebrations: p. 1, Andrew Holt; pp. 2 and 3, Millennium—Millennium Festival, Clarion Communications, Derry City Council, Bristol Evening Post & Press, Glasgow City Council, City Repro, Newcastle City Council.

Inland Waterways: p. 1, compiled from information supplied by British Waterways/Waterways Ireland; p. 2, background and top left—British Waterways, bottom right—Kennet Horse Boat Company, centre left—Northern Ireland Tourist Board; p. 3, all images—British Waterways; p. 4, all images except bottom left—British Waterways, bottom left—Guthrie Hutton.

Cultural Life in Britain: p. 1, top left—DV8 Physical Theatre/Michael Rayner, Sydney 2000 Olympic Arts Festival, bottom right and inset—Cinemagic/Steve Thompson; p. 2, top left and right—British Library Board, bottom left and inset—Redundant Technology Initiative, www.lowtech.org; p. 3, top—Ingrid Pollard—Autograph, bottom—Hugh Russell; p. 4, top right and inset—Foreign & Commonwealth Office, bottom left and inset—Edinburgh Military Tattoo.

Crafts and Skills: p. 1, all images—Countryside Agency/Simon Warner/C. Ward; p. 2, all images—Countryside Agency/Andy Tryner/Toby Adamson/Edmund Glover/Graham Parish *except* middle right—Llechwedd Slate Caverns; p. 3, top right—Mike Hartwell, bottom centre —National Botanic Garden of Wales, remainder—Countryside Agency/Simon Warner/Archie Miles/Andy Tryner; p. 4, all images—Leon Downey, Llangoffan Farmhouse Cheese.

National Lottery Funded Projects: p. 1, all images—copyright Tate, London 2000/Marcus Leith *except* middle right—Corporation of London; p. 2, all images—Dulwich Picture Gallery; p. 3, top right—The Lowry/Len Grant, remainder—British Museum; p. 4, all images—Science Museum; p. 5, all images—Dynamic Earth; p. 6, all images—National Botanic Garden of Wales; p. 7, top centre and middle left—Simon Burt/Apex, middle right (aerial shot)—Eden Project, bottom centre—Odyssey Project; p. 8, National Lottery Charities Board/Zak Walters/Insight/Tegywn Roberts/Neil Walker.

Olympic Success: pp. 1–4, PA Photos.

National Cycle Network/Trams and Light Railways: p. 1, compiled from information supplied by Sustrans, www.nationalcyclenetwork.org.uk; p. 2, all images—Sustrans/Steve Morgan/Jonathan Bewley/Patrick Davies; p 3. all images—Blackpool Transport; p. 4, top left and middle right—Foreign & Commonwealth Office, bottom left—Tramtrack Croydon Limited.

Seaside Piers/Regeneration: p. 1, background image—City of Bangor Council, top left—The Fisher Family, bottom left—Clevedon Pier and Heritage Trust Limited/Charlotte Wood, bottom right—Paignton Pier; p. 2, top—Redcar and Cleveland Borough Council, bottom—Leisure Services Department of Southend Borough Council; p. 3, Glasgow, all images—Glasgow City Council, Cardiff, all images—Welsh Development Agency, except inset of Techniquest—Cardiff Marketing Ltd and bottom left—Foreign & Commonwealth Office; p. 4, Sheffield: top left/inset and top right—Sheffield City Council, middle right and inset—Gleeson Homes, Belfast: bottom right—Waterfront Hall, Belfast City Council, bottom left and inset—Belfast City Council.

The Queen's Awards 2000: p. 1, top left and right—King's College London, bottom left—DANDO Drilling; p. 2, top centre—Andergauge Limited, bottom left and inset—JCB; p. 3, top left and right—John Ross Jr (Aberdeen) Limited, middle centre and left—Macallan, bottom left—Cannon Avent Group plc; p. 4, top left—Power Generation Division of Hydra-Tight Sweeney, top right—Gripple Limited, bottom left—D W Windsor, bottom right—Ecotricity.

Symbols and Conventions

Units of Measurement. In most cases, metric measurements are used, although for certain measurements, such as for speed limits, the imperial measurement is given first.

Billion: 1 billion = 1,000 million.

Rounding of Figures. In tables where figures have been rounded to the nearest final digit, the constituent items may not sum to the total.

n.a. = not available

Foreword

Britain 2001 is the 52nd edition of an official annual reference book that was first published in the 1940s. Since 1997 it has been produced by the Office for National Statistics (ONS). Drawing on a wide range of official and other authoritative sources, *Britain 2001* provides a factual and up-to-date overview of the United Kingdom, while also covering the main aspects of current government policy. It is a widely used work of reference, both in the United Kingdom itself, and overseas, where it is an important element of the information service provided by British diplomatic posts.

The term 'Britain' is sometimes used as a short way of expressing the full title of the country: the United Kingdom of Great Britain and Northern Ireland (or, more simply again, the United Kingdom or the UK). 'Great Britain' comprises England, Wales and Scotland only. The adjectives 'British' and 'UK' are used interchangeably in this publication and cover the whole of the United Kingdom. As far as possible, the book applies to the UK as a whole, as the title suggests. However, sometimes the information given refers to just: Great Britain; England and Wales; or, in some instances, England, Scotland, Wales or Northern Ireland alone.

The 52nd edition has more charts and tables than ever before, and 40 colour pages including some new and redrawn maps. The text is 285,000 words long and has been fully updated and revised. Every effort is made to ensure that the information given in *Britain 2001* is accurate at the time of going to press. The text is generally based on information available up to the end of August 2000.

The five Parts of *Britain 2001* align with their equivalents in another ONS publication, the *Annual Abstract of Statistics*, so that the two books can be consulted as complementary volumes, painting a picture of the UK in words and figures. Readers who are interested in more detailed information about regions within the UK can find up-to-date statistics in another ONS publication, *Regional Trends*.

Sources

To help the reader seeking further information, at the end of each chapter there is a brief further reading section, which lists the main statistical publications and other important documents, such as recent White Papers. A selection of websites is included at the end of most chapters. The main government websites are included in the entry for Government Departments and Agencies in Appendix 1.

ONS issues a number of important statistical publications, many of which have been used in the compilation of *Britain 2001*, including:

Annual Abstract of Statistics
Business Monitors/Sector Reviews
Economic Trends
Family Spending
Labour Market Trends
Living in Britain: Results from the General Household Survey
Monthly Digest of Statistics
Population Trends
Regional Trends
Social Trends
Travel Trends
United Kingdom Balance of Payments—the Pink Book
United Kingdom National Accounts—the Blue Book

Details of these and other statistics can be found on the National Statistics website (www.statistics.gov.uk) or by contacting National Statistics Direct, Room 1.015, Office for National Statistics, Government Buildings, Cardiff Road, Newport NP10 8XG. Tel: 01633 812078. Fax: 01633 812762. E-mail: ns.direct@statistics.gov.uk

In compiling *Britain 2001*, information about particular companies has been taken from company reports and news releases, or from other publicly available sources. No information about individual companies has been taken from returns submitted in response to ONS statistical inquiries. Very strict arrangements operate within ONS to ensure that such data remain confidential.

Acknowledgments

Britain 2001 has been compiled with the full co-operation of around 250 organisations, including other government departments and agencies. The editor would like to thank all the people from these organisations who have taken so much time and care to ensure that the book's high standards of accuracy have been maintained. Their contributions and comments have been extremely valuable.

The book was researched, written and edited by a combination of in-house authors and freelances. The main in-house team comprised Jil Matheson, John King, Derek Tomlin, David Harper, Conor Shipsey, Christine Lillistone, Nina Mill, Dave Sharp, Carol Summerfield, Victoria Jackson, Jackie Jackson, Alistair Dent and John Chrzczonowicz. The freelance writers were Henry Langley (who also contributed to the production of the book), Richard German (who also compiled the index), John Collis and Oliver Metcalf. Picture research and design of colour sections were undertaken by Frances Riddelle. Freelance design work, including all diagrams, most colour and black and white maps, and layout of colour sections, was done by Ray Martin. Jane Howard, Jole Cosgrove and Rosemary Hamilton proofread the text. The cover was designed by The Stationery Office.

Reader's Comments

We welcome readers' comments and suggestions. These should be sent to: The Editor, *Britain Yearbook*, Room B5/02, Office for National Statistics, 1 Drummond Gate, London SW1V 2QQ, UK. E-mail: Britain.Yearbook@ons.gov.uk

About the Office for National Statistics

The Office for National Statistics (ONS) is the government agency responsible for compiling, analysing and disseminating many of the United Kingdom's economic, social and demographic statistics, including the retail prices index, trade figures and labour market data, as well as the periodic census of the population and health statistics. The Director of ONS is also the National Statistician and the Registrar General for England and Wales, and the agency administers the statutory registration of births, marriages and deaths there.

Official statistics bearing the National Statistics logo are produced to high professional standards set out in the National Statistics Code of Practice. They undergo regular quality assurance reviews to ensure that they meet customer needs. They are produced free from any political interference.

1 Introduction

The recent establishment of the Scottish Parliament, the National Assembly for Wales and the Northern Ireland Assembly is bringing about the most significant change in the constitution in the United Kingdom since its formation in 1801.[1] In addition, eight new Regional Development Agencies and the London Development Agency have been set up in England.

Physical Features

The United Kingdom (UK) constitutes the greater part of the British Isles. The largest of the islands is Great Britain, which comprises England, Scotland and Wales. The next largest comprises Northern Ireland, which is part of the UK, and the Irish Republic. Western Scotland is fringed by the large island chains known as the Inner and Outer Hebrides, and to the north east of the Scottish mainland are the Orkney and Shetland Islands. All these, along with the Isle of Wight, Anglesey and the Isles of Scilly, have administrative ties with the mainland, but the Isle of Man in the Irish Sea and the Channel Islands between Great Britain and France are largely self-governing, and are not part of the UK. The UK is one of the 15 member states of the European Union (EU).

With an area of about 243,000 sq km (93,000 sq miles), excluding inland water, the UK is just under 1,000 km (about 600 miles) from the south coast to the extreme north of Scotland and just under 500 km (around 300 miles) across at the widest point.

Channel Islands and Isle of Man

Although the Channel Islands and the Isle of Man are not part of the United Kingdom, they have a special relationship with it. The Channel Islands were part of the Duchy of Normandy in the 10th and 11th centuries and remained subject to the English Crown after the loss of mainland Normandy to the French in 1204. The Isle of Man was under the nominal sovereignty of Norway until 1266, and eventually came under the direct administration of the British Crown in 1765, when it was bought for £70,000. Its parliament, 'Tynwald', was established more than 1,000 years ago and is the oldest legislature in continuous existence in the world. Today the territories have their own legislative assemblies and systems of law, and their own taxation systems. The British

[1] When the UK was the United Kingdom of Great Britain and Ireland. The Irish Free State (now the Irish Republic) was created in 1922, leaving Northern Ireland in the Union. The devolution of political power is discussed in greater detail in chapters 2, 3, 4, 5 and 6.

Government is responsible for their international relations and external defence.

The relationship of the Channel Islands and the Isle of Man with the EU is limited to trading rights only. Rules on customs matters apply to the Islands under the same conditions as they apply to the UK. However, the free movement of people and services within the EU as a whole only extends to the Islanders if they have close ties with the UK, although they do still enjoy their traditional rights in the UK.

- Highest mountain: Ben Nevis, in the Highlands of Scotland, 1,343 m (4,406 ft)
- Longest river: the Severn, 354 km (220 miles) long, which rises in central Wales and flows through Shrewsbury, Worcester and Gloucester in England to the Bristol Channel
- Largest lake: Lough Neagh, Northern Ireland, 396 sq km (153 sq miles)
- Deepest lake: Loch Morar in the Highlands of Scotland, 310 m (1,017 ft) deep
- Highest waterfall: Eas a'Chual Aluinn, from Glas Bheinn, also in the Highlands of Scotland, with a drop of 200 m (660 ft)
- Deepest cave: Ogof Ffynnon Ddu, Wales, 308 m (1,010 ft) deep
- Most northerly point on the British mainland: Dunnet Head, north-east Scotland
- Most southerly point on the British mainland: Lizard Point, Cornwall
- Closest point to mainland continental Europe: Dover, Kent. The Channel Tunnel, which links England and France, is a little over 50 km (31 miles) long, of which nearly 38 km (24 miles) are actually under the English Channel.

Climate and Wildlife

The climate in the United Kingdom is generally mild and temperate. Prevailing winds are south-westerly and the weather from day to day is mainly influenced by depressions and their associated fronts moving eastwards across the Atlantic, punctuated by settled, fine, anticyclonic periods of a few days to weeks. In general, there are few extremes of temperature; it rarely rises above 32°C (90°F) or falls below –10°C (14°F).

Average annual rainfall is more than 1,600 mm (over 60 inches) in the mountainous areas of the west and north but less than 800 mm (30 inches) over central and eastern parts. Rain is fairly well distributed throughout the year but, on average, March to June are the driest months and September to January the wettest. During May, June and July (the months of longest daylight) the mean daily duration of sunshine varies from five hours in northern Scotland to eight hours in the Isle of Wight. During the months of shortest daylight (November, December and January) sunshine is at a minimum, with an average of an hour a day in northern Scotland and two hours a day on the south coast of England.

The UK is home to a great variety of wildlife, with an estimated 30,000 animal species, as well as marine and microscopic life; about 2,800 species of 'higher' plants; and many thousands of mosses, fungi and algae. However, as elsewhere in the world, urban development, changes in farming methods and other factors have put pressure on a number of species and plants. Action is being taken to halt the decline of species (see chapter 20), while the Millennium Seed Bank Project (see p. 446) is aiming to collect and conserve seeds of 24,000 species, including the seeds of the entire UK native seed-bearing flora by the end of 2000.

Population

The population of the UK increased from 38.2 million in 1901 to 59.5 million in 1999 (see Table 1.1). Official projections, based on mid-1998 population estimates, forecast that the population will reach nearly 60 million by 2001 and 61.8 million by 2011.

Selected population and other vital statistics for 1999 are given in Table 1.2 for England, Wales, Scotland and Northern

The Census of Population was first conducted in 1801 and it has been held every ten years ever since, with one exception, 1941.

The next Census is due to take place on 29 April 2001. For the first time it will be a resident-based count, so that people will be enumerated at the address where they are usually resident rather than where they are present on Census night. Questions in the Census cover a variety of topics, such as for residents, name, sex and date of birth; marital status; country of birth; ethnic group; usual address one year previously; qualifications; and a range of questions connected with work. For households, questions include the type and tenure of accommodation, availability of bath and toilet and of central heating, and number of cars or vans owned or available. New questions include those on religion (see p. 235), general health, the provision of unpaid personal care and the lowest floor level of accommodation (although this has previously been asked in Scotland).

Table 1.1: Population and Population Change,[1] United Kingdom *Thousands*

	Population at start of period	Average annual change				
		Births	Deaths[2]	Excess of births over deaths	Net migration and other adjustments	Overall annual change
1901–1911	38,237	1,091	624	467	–82	385
1911–1921	42,082	975	689	286	–92	194
1921–1931	44,027	824	555	268	–67	201
1931–1951	46,038	785	598	188	25	213
1951–1961	50,287	839	593	246	6	252
1961–1971	52,807	963	639	324	–12	312
1971–1981	55,928	736	666	69	–27	42
1981–1991	56,352	757	655	103	43	146
1991–1999	57,814	744	637	107	104	211
1999–2001	59,501	*716*	*627*	*88*	*140*	*228*
2001–2011	*59,954*	*701*	*614*	*87*	*95*	*182*
2011–2021	*61,773*	*712*	*620*	*92*	*95*	*187*

[1] Census-enumerated population up to 1951; mid-year estimates of resident population from 1961 to 1999, and mid-1998-based projections for population changes from 1999 to 2021.
[2] Including deaths of non-civilians and merchant seamen who died outside the UK.
Sources: Office for National Statistics, Government Actuary's Department, General Register Office for Scotland and Northern Ireland Statistics and Research Agency

Ireland. More detailed statistics, by region and by local authority, are given in the Office for National Statistics (ONS) publication *Regional Trends No 35*, published in September 2000, which also contains statistics on a wide range of economic and social subjects, and are available on the National Statistics website (see p. 6).

Historical Outline

The name 'Britain' derives from Greek and Latin names probably stemming from a Celtic original. Although in the prehistoric timescale the Celts were relatively late arrivals in the British Isles, only with them does Britain emerge into recorded history. The term 'Celtic' is often used rather generally to

Table 1.2: Population and Selected Statistics, 1999

	England	Wales	Scotland	Northern Ireland	United Kingdom
Population (thousands)	49,753	2,937	5,119	1,692	59,501
Per cent of population aged:					
under 5	*6.1*	*5.8*	*5.8*	*7.1*	*6.1*
5–15	*14.2*	*14.5*	*13.9*	*17.2*	*14.3*
16 to pension age[1]	*61.6*	*59.8*	*62.3*	*60.4*	*61.6*
above pension age[1]	*18.1*	*19.9*	*18.0*	*15.2*	*18.1*
Population density (people per sq km)	381	141	66	125	245
Per cent population change					
1981 to 1999	6.3	4.4	−1.2	9.6	5.6
Live births per 1,000 population	11.8	10.9	10.8	13.7	11.8
Deaths per 1,000 population	10.4	11.9	11.8	9.3	10.6

[1] Pension age is 65 for males and 60 for females.
Sources: Office for National Statistics, National Assembly for Wales, General Register Office for Scotland and Northern Ireland Statistics and Research Agency

distinguish the early inhabitants of the British Isles from the later Anglo-Saxon invaders.

After two expeditions by Julius Caesar in 55 and 54 BC, contact between Britain and the Roman world grew, culminating in the Roman invasion of AD 43. Roman rule was gradually extended from south-east England to include Wales and, for a time, the lowlands of Scotland. The final Roman withdrawal in 409 followed a period of increasing disorder during which the island began to be raided by Angles, Saxons and Jutes from northern Europe. It is from the Angles that the name 'England' derives. The raids turned into settlement and a number of small English kingdoms were established. The Britons maintained an independent existence in the areas now known as Wales and Cornwall.

Among the Anglo-Saxon kingdoms more powerful ones emerged, claiming overlordship of the whole of England, first in the north (Northumbria), then in the midlands (Mercia) and finally in the south (Wessex). However, further raids and settlement by the Vikings from Scandinavia occurred, although in the 10th century the Wessex dynasty defeated the invading Danes and established a wide-ranging authority in England. In 1066 England was invaded by the Normans (see p. 7), who then settled along with others from France.

Dates of some of the main events in Britain's history are given below. The early histories of England, Wales, Scotland and Northern Ireland are included in chapters 2 to 5.

Significant Dates

55 and 54 BC: Julius Caesar's expeditions to Britain
AD 43: Roman conquest begins under Claudius
122–38: Hadrian's Wall built
c.409: Roman army withdraws from Britain
450s onwards: foundation of the Anglo-Saxon kingdoms
597: arrival of St Augustine to preach Christianity to the Anglo-Saxons
664: Synod of Whitby opts for Roman Catholic rather than Celtic church
789–95: first Viking raids
832–60: Scots and Picts merge under Kenneth Macalpin to form what is to become the kingdom of Scotland
860s: Danes overrun East Anglia, Northumbria and eastern Mercia
871–99: reign of Alfred the Great in Wessex
1066: William the Conqueror defeats Harold Godwinson at Hastings and takes the throne

1086: *Domesday Book* completed: a survey of English landholdings undertaken on the orders of William I
c.1136–39: Geoffrey of Monmouth completes *The History of the Kings of Britain*
1215: King John signs Magna Carta to protect feudal rights against royal abuse
13th century: first Oxford and Cambridge colleges founded
1301: Edward of Caernarvon (later Edward II) created Prince of Wales
1314: Battle of Bannockburn ensures survival of separate Scottish kingdom
1337: Hundred Years War between England and France begins
1348–49: Black Death (bubonic plague) wipes out a third of England's population
1381: Peasants' Revolt in England, the most significant popular rebellion in English history
c.1387–c.1394: Geoffrey Chaucer writes *The Canterbury Tales*
1400–c.1406: Owain Glyndŵr (Owen Glendower) leads the last major Welsh revolt against English rule
1411: St Andrews University founded, the first university in Scotland
1455–87: Wars of the Roses between Yorkists and Lancastrians
1477: first book to be printed in England, by William Caxton
1534–40: English Reformation; Henry VIII breaks with the Papacy
1536–42: Acts of Union integrate England and Wales administratively and legally and give Wales representation in Parliament
1547–53: Protestantism becomes official religion in England under Edward VI
1553–58: Catholic reaction under Mary I
1558: loss of Calais, last English possession in France
1588: defeat of Spanish Armada
1558–1603: reign of Elizabeth I; moderate Protestantism established
c.1590–c.1613: plays of Shakespeare written
1603: union of the crowns of Scotland and England under James VI of Scotland
1642–51: Civil Wars between King and Parliament
1649: execution of Charles I
1653–58: Oliver Cromwell rules as Lord Protector
1660: monarchy restored under Charles II
1660: founding of the Royal Society for the Promotion of Natural Knowledge
1663: John Milton finishes *Paradise Lost*
1665: the Great Plague, the last major epidemic of plague in England
1666: the Great Fire of London
1686: Isaac Newton sets out his laws of motion and the idea of universal gravitation
1688: Glorious Revolution; accession of William and Mary
1707: Acts of Union unite the English and Scottish Parliaments
1721–42: Robert Walpole, first British Prime Minister
1745–46: Bonnie Prince Charlie's failed attempt to retake the British throne for the Stuarts
c.1760s–c.1830s: Industrial Revolution
1761: opening of the Bridgewater Canal ushers in Canal Age
1775–83: American War of Independence leads to loss of the Thirteen Colonies
1801: Act of Union unites Great Britain and Ireland
1805: Battle of Trafalgar, the decisive naval battle of the Napoleonic Wars
1815: Battle of Waterloo, the final defeat of Napoleon
1825: opening of the Stockton and Darlington Railway, the world's first passenger railway
1829: Catholic emancipation
1832: first Reform Act extends the franchise (increasing the number of those entitled to vote by about 50 per cent)
1833: abolition of slavery in the British Empire (the slave *trade* having been abolished in 1807)
1836–70: Charles Dickens writes his novels
1837–1901: reign of Queen Victoria
1859: Charles Darwin publishes *On the Origin of Species by Means of Natural Selection*
1868: founding of the Trades Union Congress (TUC)
1907: Henry Royce and C.S. Rolls build and sell their first Rolls-Royce (the Silver Ghost)
1910–36: during the reign of George V, the British Empire reaches its territorial zenith

1914–18: First World War
1918: the vote given to women over 30
1921: Anglo-Irish Treaty establishes the Irish Free State; Northern Ireland remains part of the United Kingdom
1926: John Logie Baird gives the first practical demonstration of television
1928: voting age for women reduced to 21, on equal terms with men
1928: Alexander Fleming discovers penicillin
1936: Jarrow Crusade, the most famous of the hunger marches in the 1930s
1939–45: Second World War
1943: Max Newman, Donald Michie, Tommy Flowers and Alan Turing build the first electronic computer, Colossus I, which was used for breaking enemy communications codes in the Second World War
1947: independence for India and Pakistan: Britain begins to dismantle its imperial structure
1948: the National Health Service comes into operation, offering free medical care to the whole population
1952: accession of Elizabeth II
1953: Francis Crick and his colleague James Watson of the United States discover the structure of DNA
1965: first commercial natural gas discovery in the North Sea
1969: first notable discovery of offshore oil in the North Sea
1973: the UK enters the European Community (now the European Union)
1979–90: Margaret Thatcher, the UK's first woman Prime Minister
1994: Channel Tunnel opened to rail traffic
1997: General Election: the Labour Party returns to power with its largest ever parliamentary majority
1999: Scottish Parliament, National Assembly for Wales and Northern Ireland Assembly assume their devolved powers

Further Reading

Annual Publications

Annual Abstract of Statistics, Office for National Statistics. The Stationery Office.
Regional Trends, Office for National Statistics. The Stationery Office.
Social Trends, Office for National Statistics. The Stationery Office.

Websites

National Statistics: www.statistics.gov.uk
The Meteorological Office: www.met-office.gov.uk

2 England

England is predominantly a lowland country, although there are upland regions in the north (the Pennine Chain, the Cumbrian mountains and the Yorkshire moors) and in the South West (Bodmin Moor, Exmoor, Dartmoor and the Mendip Hills). The greatest concentrations of population are in London and the South East, South and West Yorkshire, Greater Manchester and Merseyside, the West Midlands, and conurbations in the north-east on the rivers Tyne and Tees. England's population is expected to rise from 50.2 million in 2001 to 53.7 million in 2021.

Early History

The name 'England' is derived from the Angles, one of the Germanic tribes which established monarchies in lowland Britain in the 5th century, after the final withdrawal of the Romans in 409. The Anglo-Saxon kingdoms were initially fairly small and numerous, but gradually larger entities emerged. Eventually Wessex came to dominate, following its leading role in resisting the Danish invasions of the 9th century. Athelstan (who reigned from 924 to 939) used the title of 'King of all Britain', and from 954 there was a single Kingdom of England. The present Royal Family is descended from the old royal house of Wessex—a connection seen in June 1999 when the Queen's youngest son, Prince Edward, was created Earl of Wessex on his marriage.

In 1066 the last successful invasion of England took place. Duke William of Normandy defeated the English at the Battle of Hastings and became King William I. Many Normans and others from France came to settle; French became the language of the nobility for the next three centuries; and the legal and social structures were influenced by those prevailing across the Channel.

When Henry II, originally from Anjou, was king (1154–89), his 'Angevin empire' stretched from the river Tweed on the Scottish border, down through much of France to the Pyrenees. However, almost all the English Crown's possessions in France, after alternating periods of expansion and contraction, were finally lost during the late Middle Ages.

England and Wales were integrated administratively and legally in 1536–42 during the reign of Henry VIII, and the union of England and Scotland took place in 1707, when Queen Anne was Sovereign.

Government

In contrast to Wales, Scotland and Northern Ireland, England has no separate elected

England[1]: Counties and Unitary Authorities, 1 April 1998

Counties
Unitary Authorities
Northumberland
Tyne and Wear
Durham
Cumbria
North Yorkshire
York
East Riding of Yorkshire
Lancashire
West Yorkshire
Greater Manchester
Merseyside
South Yorkshire
North Lincolnshire
Cheshire
Derbyshire
Nottinghamshire
Lincolnshire
Staffordshire
Leicestershire
Norfolk
Shropshire
W. Midlands
Warwickshire
Northamptonshire
Cambridgeshire
Suffolk
Worcestershire
County of Herefordshire
Bedfordshire
Buckinghamshire
Hertfordshire
Essex
Gloucestershire
Oxfordshire
West Berkshire
Greater London
Wiltshire
Surrey
Kent
Somerset
Hampshire
W. Sussex
E. Sussex
Isles of Scilly
Devon
Dorset
Isle of Wight
Cornwall
D Darlington
H Hartlepool
M Middlesbrough
RC Redcar and Cleveland
ST Stockton-on-Tees
Bn Blackburn with Darwen
Bpl Blackpool
H Halton
W Warrington
S Stoke-on-Trent
T Telford and Wrekin
De Derby
KH City of Kingston upon Hull
Lr Leicester
NEL North East Lincolnshire
Nt Nottingham
Pe Peterborough
R Rutland
B City of Bristol
BS Bath and North East Somerset
NS North Somerset
SG South Gloucestershire
Sw Swindon
L Luton
MK Milton Keynes
Md Medway
SS Southend-on-Sea
Tk Thurrock
Bo Bournemouth
Pl Poole
Py Plymouth
Ty Torbay
BF Bracknell Forest
BH Brighton and Hove
Po Portsmouth
Re Reading
Sl Slough
So Southampton
W Wokingham
WM Windsor and Maidenhead

1 Local Government Structure

On 4 August, 2000 the Queen Mother celebrated her 100th birthday. A number of public engagements were held around the day to mark the occasion. The photograph shows Her Majesty driving in an open carriage down The Mall in London, accompanied by Prince Charles, en route to an event held in her honour on Horse Guards Parade.

Millennium Celebrations in the UK

New Year, London

New Year, Manchester

The Dragon Festival 2000

BBC Music Live

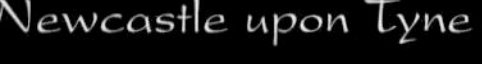

Newcastle upon Tyne

Yurts and traditional food from Asia

Storytelling, North West

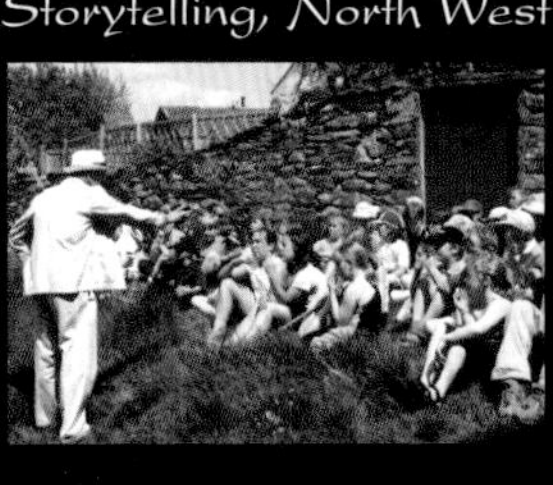

Bristol

Derry-Londonderry

Millennium Youth Games Final, Southampton

Sudanese Women's Festival

Millennium Youth Games Final, Cardiff

Glasgow

Samba Súlis, Bath Abbey

Population Density, 1998

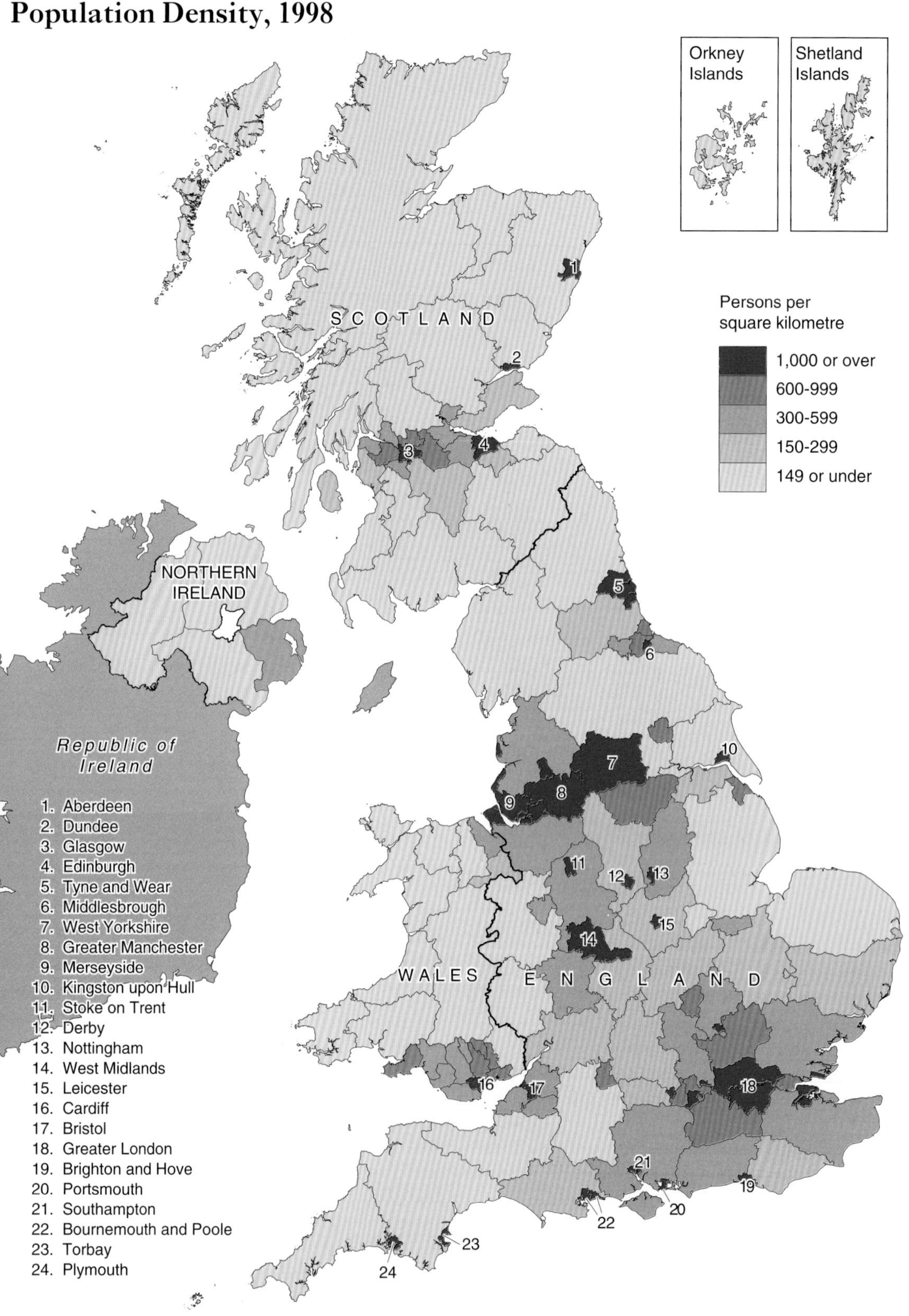

Sources: Office for National Statistics, General Register Office for Scotland, Northern Ireland Statistics and Research Agency

national body exclusively responsible for its central administration. Instead a number of government departments look after England's day-to-day administrative affairs (see Appendix 1) and a network of nine Government Offices for the Regions (GOs—see p. 11) is responsible for the implementation of several government programmes in the regions.

There are 529 English parliamentary constituencies represented in the House of Commons. After the General Election of May 1997, England had 328 Labour Members of Parliament (MPs), 165 Conservative, 34 Liberal Democrat, one held by the Speaker and one independent.[1] By August 2000 there had been nine by-elections in English constituencies, with the political party that had been representing the constituency retaining the seat in all but one case, Romsey, in Hampshire, which the Liberal Democrats gained from the Conservatives. Conservative support tends to be strongest in suburban and rural areas, and the party has a large number of parliamentary seats in the southern half of England. The Labour Party has tended in the past to derive its main support from the big cities and areas associated with traditional industry, but it won many seats in the last General Election that had previously been considered safe Conservative constituencies. The Liberal Democrats, who are traditionally strong in the South West, now have nearly a third of their 35 English seats in Greater London and the South East.

Local government is administered in many areas through a two-tier system of county and district councils. However, there are also a number of single-tier, or unitary, authorities—especially in the larger cities, and since July 2000 the capital has been run by the new Greater London Authority (see p. 63).

England elects 71 representatives (MEPs) to the European Parliament (see pp. 69–70). In the June 1999 election, the Conservatives won 33 seats, Labour 24, the Liberal Democrats nine, the UK Independence Party three and the Green Party two.

The English legal system comprises on the one hand a historic body of conventions known as 'common law' and 'equity', and, on the other, parliamentary and European Community legislation ('statute law'). In the formulation of common law since the Norman Conquest, great reliance has been placed on precedent. Equity law—law outside the scope of the common law or statute law—derives from the practice of petitioning the Lord Chancellor in cases not covered by common law.

The Church of England, which was separated from the Roman Catholic Church at the time of the Reformation in the early 16th century, is the Established Church (that is, the official religion of England). The Sovereign must always be a member of the Church and appoints its two archbishops and 42 other diocesan bishops (see p. 237).

London

In May 2000, Londoners voted for a directly elected Mayor for the capital, and a separately elected assembly of 25 members.[2] Subsequent elections will take place every four years. The Mayor and Assembly form the Greater London Authority (GLA), the first elected London-wide body since the Greater London Council was abolished in 1986. The GLA assumed its responsibilities in July 2000; at the same time, four other administrative bodies came into being and are accountable to it: a new Metropolitan Police Authority; the London Fire and Emergency Planning Authority; Transport for London; and the London Development Agency, one of nine regional agencies covering the whole of England (see p. 394).

[1] The Speaker of the House of Commons, who presides over the debates there (see p. 43), traditionally does not vote along party lines and so is not counted towards the strength of the party for which he or she was originally elected. The independent MP is the former journalist Martin Bell, who represents Tatton in Cheshire. In April 2000 the Labour MP Ken Livingstone gave up his Party's Whip and now sits in the House of Commons without party affiliation.

[2] Of the 25 members, 14 represent constituencies covering two or more London boroughs; the rest are 'London-wide Members' divided among the political parties according to their share of the vote for these 11 seats (see p. 10). The new arrangements do not affect the continuance of the separate post of Lord Mayor of London (first established in 1191), whose role is restricted to the City of London—the financial 'Square Mile' at the heart of the capital.

Mayor and Assembly for London—Election Results, May 2000

Mayor

Londoners chose the Member of Parliament Ken Livingstone, standing as an Independent candidate, as their first directly elected Mayor in May 2000.

Elections were held under the supplementary vote system, where voters mark both their first and second choices. If no candidate receives more than 50 per cent of first choices, only the two leading candidates remain in contention and second votes for these are added in to give an overall winner.

After the first count, the results were:

Party	*Number of votes cast*	*% of votes cast*
Independent	667,877	39.0
Conservative	464,434	27.1
Labour	223,884	13.1
Liberal Democrats	203,452	11.9
Others	154,515	8.9

After second choice votes were added to those first cast for the leading two candidates, the Independent had a total of 776,427 votes (58 per cent) and the Conservative 564,137 (42 per cent). The Independent candidate was duly elected, with a majority of 212,290 votes. From an electorate of 5,093,464 the turnout was 1,714,162 (33.7 per cent).

Assembly

For the purpose of electing the Assembly, London was divided into 14 constituencies whose members were elected on a 'first-past-the-post' basis. A further 11 seats were allocated on a 'top-up' basis, where votes were counted across London and shared among the political parties in proportion to the votes each party received.

The results for the Assembly were:

Party	*Number of constituency seats*	*Number of top-up seats*	*Total*
Labour	6	3	9
Conservative	8	1	9
Liberal Democrats	–	4	4
Green	–	3	3

Initially occupying offices near the Houses of Parliament, the GLA will eventually move to a new building being constructed on a previously developed site between London Bridge and Tower Bridge, on the south bank of the river Thames.

The Regions of England

Regional Development Agencies (RDAs) were launched in eight English regions in April 1999. The ninth, in London, followed in July 2000 on the establishment of the GLA. RDAs aim to provide co-ordinated regional economic development and regeneration, reduce the economic imbalances which exist within and between regions and enable the English regions to improve their competitiveness.

In April 2000 the Government established a Regional Co-ordination Unit, thus implementing a key conclusion from a Cabinet Office Performance and Innovation Unit report—*Reaching Out: The Role of Central Government at Regional and Local Level.*

The main functions of the new unit, which brings together the interests of a range of departments, are to:

- co-ordinate the delivery of central Government's regional initiatives, including those affecting local areas;
- promote the use of GOs by Whitehall departments;
- encourage better working between the GOs and other regional and local partners; and
- manage the shared functions of the GOs.

The economic performance of the nine English regions (see map opposite), and subregions within them, varies quite considerably. For example, Inner London has had the highest level of gross domestic product (GDP) per head in the European Union (EU) for a number of years, even

The Regions of England Covered by the GORs

though it also contains some of the worst pockets of deprivation in the UK. Under the new Objective 1 status for EU funding that came into force in January 2000 (see p. 396), three areas of England—Merseyside, South Yorkshire, and Cornwall and the Isles of Scilly—qualified for funding from 2000 to 2006. According to the latest figures, household disposable income per head in 1998 was above the England average in London, the South East and East; and the same three regions had the highest gross hourly earnings for full-time employees in 1999. The North East had the lowest household disposable income and GDP per head in 1998, as well as the lowest average hourly earnings in 1999.

Some of the consequences of economic success in the wealthier English regions are higher residential and industrial property prices, higher rental costs for offices and higher volumes of traffic. As people working in London tend to commute from further afield than those in other cities, average journey times to work are far longer in London than elsewhere, ranging from 30 minutes in Outer London to 55 minutes into Central London, compared with an average in Great Britain of just 25 minutes. In autumn 1998 the number of people entering Central London between 7.00 a.m. and 10.00 a.m. on each working day was nearly 1.1 million, a 3 per cent increase on the previous year. Public transport is used by 78 per cent of those working in Central London, compared with the average of 13 per cent for Great Britain as a whole.

The Labour Force Survey for March to May 2000 showed that 75.4 per cent of people of working age in England were in employment, compared with 74.6 per cent in the UK as a whole. Comparable rates for unemployment were 5.4 per cent and 5.6 per cent respectively.

Regional Development Agencies

RDAs are accountable through ministers to Parliament. Each RDA has a board of 13 or 14 members, including the chairman, and on each board a majority of members has business experience. The boards also include local councillors, and members with expertise in the fields of education, rural affairs, the voluntary sector and trade union issues. RDAs have been allocated some £1.2 billion of programme spending for 2000–01; this is scheduled to rise to £1.7 billion by 2003–04. Their initiatives are also expected to attract private finance.

From April 2002, the RDAs' funding programmes will be drawn together to allow them greater flexibility in allocating their resources.

Rural Areas

There are over 16,500 rural towns, villages and hamlets in England with populations of 10,000 or fewer.[3] According to this definition, one in five people live in a rural area. Over three-quarters of rural settlements have populations of under 500.

Car ownership is greater in rural households (83 per cent) than nationally (70 per cent), but the countryside often lacks services that urban dwellers take for granted. The closure of many rural post offices in

[3] The data in this section come from the Countryside Agency (see p. 314).

Table 2.1: England Area and Population, by Region,[1] 1999

	Population (thousands)	Population density (people per sq km)	Change in population 1981–99 (%)
North East	2,581	300	–2.1
North West	6,881	486	–0.9
Yorkshire and the Humber	5,047	327	2.6
East Midlands	4,191	268	8.8
West Midlands	5,336	410	2.9
East	5,419	283	11.6
London	7,285	4,611	7.0
South East	8,078	423	11.5
South West	4,936	207	12.7
England	**49,753**	**381**	**6.3**

[1] The region in England covered by each regional Government Office.
Source: Office for National Statistics

recent years is a notable example. Another is the comparative lack of public transport serving country areas. In 1998 the Government allocated an extra £150 million over three years to improve rural transport in the UK as a whole. A further £10 million a year for the next two years was announced in the 1999 Budget. This extra funding has led to the creation of 1,800 new or improved rural bus services in England.

The Environment

Despite its high population density and degree of urbanisation, England has many unspoilt rural and coastal areas. There are eight National Parks (including the Norfolk and Suffolk Broads), nine forest parks, 37 designated Areas of Outstanding Natural Beauty, 22 Environmentally Sensitive Areas, over 200 country parks recognised by the Countryside Agency, and more than 1,540 km (960 miles) of designated heritage coastline. At the end of March 2000, there were 202 National Nature Reserves, 635 Local Nature Reserves and 4,088 Sites of Special Scientific Interest. (See also chapter 20.)

Culture

London and the other large cities have a wealth of cultural centres, including major art galleries, renowned museums, theatres, ballet and opera houses, and concert halls. Many theatres outside London are used for touring by the national theatre, dance and opera companies. Popular culture also thrives in England, as elsewhere in Britain: there are numerous kinds of pop music, theatre styles such as pantomime and musicals, jazz festivals and performances by comedians. Safari, wildlife and theme parks all offer family activities and entertainment. A proportion of the proceeds from the National Lottery (see p. 117) is allocated to arts projects.

Many regions and towns have associations with great English writers, artists and musicians: such as Stratford-upon-Avon (William Shakespeare), the Lake District (William Wordsworth), Stoke-on-Trent (Arnold Bennett), Haworth (the Brontë sisters) and Dorset (Thomas Hardy); Essex and Suffolk (John Constable) and Salford (L. S. Lowry); and Worcestershire (Edward Elgar), Aldeburgh (Benjamin Britten) and Liverpool (The Beatles).

Further Reading

Regional Trends (annual publication), Office for National Statistics. The Stationery Office.

3 Northern Ireland

Northern Ireland is, at its nearest point, only 21 km (13 miles) from Scotland. It has a 488-km (303-mile) border with the Irish Republic. About half of its population of 1.7 million people live in the eastern coastal region, the centre of which is the capital, Belfast.

In December 1999 the Westminster Parliament devolved power to the Northern Ireland Assembly and its Executive Committee of Ministers (although the Assembly was briefly suspended in early 2000). Devolution followed endorsement of the Belfast (Good Friday) Agreement by the people of Northern Ireland in a referendum held in May 1998. The North/South Ministerial Council, North/South Implementation Bodies, British-Irish Council and British-Irish Intergovernmental Conference also became fully functioning institutions when devolution took place.

The Northern Ireland Continuous Household Survey (CHS)[1] reported in the late 1990s that 54 per cent of the population regarded themselves as Protestants and 42 per cent as Roman Catholics. Most of the Protestants are descendants of Scots or English settlers who crossed to north-eastern Ireland. Northern Ireland has a younger population, with proportionately more children and fewer pensioners, than any other region in the UK.

History

During the 10th century Ireland was dominated by the Vikings. In 1169 Henry II of England invaded Ireland, having been granted its overlordship by the English Pope Adrian IV, who was anxious to bring the Irish Church into full obedience to Rome. Although a large part of the country came under the control of Anglo-Norman nobles, little direct authority was exercised from England during the Middle Ages.

The Tudor monarchs showed a much greater tendency to intervene in Ireland. During the reign of Elizabeth I, a series of campaigns was waged against Irish insurgents. The main area of resistance was the northern province of Ulster. After the collapse of this resistance in 1607 and the flight of its leaders, Protestant immigrants from Scotland and England settled in Ulster.

The English civil wars (1642–51) led to further uprisings in Ireland, which were

[1] Northern Ireland Statistics and Research Agency: CHS sample 1995–96 to 1997–98.

Table 3.1: Northern Ireland Area and Population, by Board[1] and District, 1999

	Population (thousands)	Population density (people per sq km)	Change in population 1981–99 (%)
Eastern	673	385	5.0
Ards	71	188	23.1
Belfast	284	2,594	–10.1
Castlereagh	67	785	9.6
Down	64	98	18.7
Lisburn	111	249	30.6
North Down	76	936	13.1
Northern	428	105	13.5
Antrim	51	120	10.1
Ballymena	59	94	7.7
Ballymoney	26	62	12.5
Carrickfergus	38	469	32.0
Coleraine	56	115	18.8
Cookstown	32	62	11.6
Larne	31	92	6.2
Magherafelt	39	69	19.1
Moyle	15	31	6.5
Newtonabbey	81	539	12.2
Southern	309	101	12.8
Armagh	54	80	9.4
Banbridge	40	88	32.5
Craigavon	80	283	8.5
Dungannon	48	62	9.8
Newry and Mourne	88	98	13.1
Western	281	60	12.3
Derry	107	280	18.3
Fermanagh	58	34	10.3
Limavady	32	54	16.7
Omagh	48	42	6.8
Strabane	37	44	3.5
Northern Ireland	**1,692**	**125**	**9.6**

[1]Health and Social Services Board areas.

Sources: Office for National Statistics and Northern Ireland Statistics and Research Agency

crushed by Oliver Cromwell. More fighting took place after the overthrow of the Roman Catholic James II in 1688. During the Battle of the Boyne in 1690 the forces of James II, who was trying to regain the throne, starting in Ireland, were defeated by those of the Protestant William of Orange (William III).

Throughout most of the 18th century there was uneasy peace. In 1782 the Irish Parliament (dating from medieval times) was given legislative independence; the only constitutional tie with Great Britain was the Crown. The Parliament, however, represented only the privileged Anglo-Irish minority, and the Roman Catholic majority was excluded from it. Following the abortive rebellion led by Wolfe Tone's United Irishmen movement in 1798, Ireland was unified with Great

Northern Ireland: Districts, 1 April 1998

Britain under the 1800 Act of Union. The Irish Parliament was abolished in 1801 and Irish members sat in both Houses of the Westminster Parliament.

The Irish question was one of the major issues of British politics during the 19th century. In 1886 the Liberal Government introduced a Home Rule Bill designed to give a new Irish Parliament devolved authority over most internal matters while Britain maintained control over foreign and defence policy. This failed as did a second Bill introduced in 1893.

The issue returned to the political agenda in 1910 because the Liberal Government was dependent for its political survival on support from the pro-Home Rule Irish Parliamentary Party. The controversy intensified as unionists and nationalists in Ireland formed private armies. In 1914 Home Rule was approved in the Government of Ireland Act. Implementation, however, was suspended by the outbreak of the First World War.

A nationalist rising in Dublin in 1916 was suppressed and its leaders executed. Two years later the nationalist Sinn Féin party won a large majority of the Irish seats in the general election to the Westminster Parliament. Its members refused to attend the House of Commons and, instead, formed the Dáil Éireann in Dublin. A nationalist guerrilla force called the Irish Republican Army (IRA) began operations against the British administration in 1919.

In 1920 the Government of Ireland Act provided for separate Parliaments in Northern and Southern Ireland, subordinate to Westminster. The Act was implemented in Northern Ireland in 1921, giving six of the nine counties of the province of Ulster their own Parliament with powers to deal with internal affairs. However, the Act proved unacceptable in the South, and in 1922, following negotiations between the British Government and Sinn Féin, which led to the Anglo-Irish Treaty of 1921, the 26 counties of

Southern Ireland left the UK to become the Irish Free State (now the Irish Republic).

From 1921 until 1972 Northern Ireland had its own Parliament in which the Unionists, primarily representing the Protestant community, held a permanent majority and formed the regional government. The nationalist minority resented this persistent domination and their effective exclusion from political office and influence.

Between the late 1960s and early 1970s, the civil rights movement and responses to it led to serious inter-communal rioting. This led to the introduction in 1969 of British Army support for the police.

Because of increased terrorism and inter-communal violence, the British Government took over direct responsibility for law and order in 1972. The Northern Ireland Unionist Government resigned in protest at this decision, the regional government was abolished, and direct rule from Westminster began. A Secretary of State was appointed with a seat in the UK Cabinet and with overall responsibility for the government of the Province.

Political Change

The system of direct rule was never intended to be permanent. Over the years, successive British and Irish Governments have worked closely together to bring peace to Northern Ireland, recognising the need for new political arrangements acceptable to both communities in the Province.

In 1985, an Anglo-Irish Agreement provided a new basis for relations between the UK and the Irish Republic, creating an Intergovernmental Conference in which to discuss issues such as improved cross-border co-operation and security. During the early 1990s, the British Government continued bilateral talks with the Northern Ireland parties and separately with the Irish Government on matters of mutual interest under the auspices of the Anglo-Irish Intergovernmental Conference.

In 1993 the British and Irish Governments signed the Downing Street Declaration, setting out their views on how a future settlement might be achieved and restating the fundamental principle that any constitutional change would require the consent of a majority of people in Northern Ireland.

Following the British General Election in May 1997, the new Government confirmed its intention of making the talks process as inclusive as possible and maintained that any agreement reached would have to have the broad support of the parties representing each of the main communities.

Multi-party talks held in Belfast in April 1998 concluded with what became known as the 'Good Friday Agreement'. Legislation was passed at Westminster authorising a referendum on the settlement in Northern Ireland and permitting elections to a new Northern Ireland Assembly. The Irish Parliament also considered the Agreement and passed legislation authorising a concurrent referendum in the Irish Republic. In May 1998 referendums were held in both parts of Ireland, and the Agreement received a clear endorsement. Northern Ireland voted 71.1 per cent in favour and 28.8 per cent against, while in the Irish Republic the result was 94.3 per cent and 5.6 per cent respectively.

A new Northern Ireland Assembly of 108 members was elected by proportional representation (single transferable vote) in June 1998 and met for the first time the following month (see p. 17). Legislation to implement the whole settlement, and formally institute devolved administrative powers, was introduced in the Westminster Parliament in July 1998 and received Royal Assent in November that year. The Northern Ireland Act 1998 is intended to give legal effect to the Good Friday Agreement. It sets out the principle of consent to change in constitutional status and makes the detailed provision necessary for the future administration of Northern Ireland, and new arrangements on human rights and equality.

In December 1999, power was devolved by the Westminster Parliament to the Northern Ireland Assembly and its Executive Committee of Ministers. At the same time the North/South Ministerial Council, North/South Implementation Bodies, British-Irish Council and British-Irish Intergovernmental Conference became fully functioning institutions. However, in

February 2000, following publication of the report of the Independent International Commission on Decommissioning, the Secretary of State for Northern Ireland suspended the operations of the Assembly and the institutions, owing to a lack of substantive progress being made on decommissioning of illegally held arms. After further talks between all parties, a political settlement was reached and devolved powers were restored to the Assembly and the power-sharing institutions in May 2000.

Government

Following devolution, the Secretary of State for Northern Ireland remains responsible for Northern Ireland Office matters not devolved to the Assembly. These include matters such as policing, security policy, prisons and criminal justice. The Secretary of State represents Northern Ireland interests in the UK Cabinet.

Northern Ireland elects 18 Members of Parliament (MPs) to the House of Commons and, by proportional representation, three of the 87 UK representatives to the European Parliament.

Northern Ireland Representation in the House of Commons

Number of Seats: September 2000

Party	*Seats*
Ulster Unionist	9
Social Democratic & Labour	3
Democratic Unionist	3
Sinn Féin[1]	2
United Kingdom Unionist	1

[1]The Sinn Féin members have not taken their seats.

The first by-election in Northern Ireland since the General Election and the creation of the Northern Ireland Assembly took place in September 2000, when the Democratic Unionist Party gained the seat from the Ulster Unionist Party.

The Province's 26 local government district councils have limited executive functions. The councils nominate locally elected representatives to sit as members of the various statutory bodies set up to administer regional services, such as education and libraries, health and personal social services, drainage and fire services.

The Northern Ireland Assembly

The Assembly meets in Parliament Buildings at Stormont, Belfast and is the prime source of authority for all devolved responsibilities. It has full legislative and executive authority, which means it has the power to make laws and take decisions on all the functions of the new Northern Ireland Departments (see p. 18).

At its first meeting in July 1998, the Assembly elected, on a cross-community basis, a First Minister and a Deputy First Minister and appointed ten Ministers with responsibility for the new Northern Ireland Departments. Together, these 12 Ministers make up the Executive Committee, which meets to discuss and agree on issues which cut across the responsibilities of two or more Ministers. Its role is to prioritise executive business and recommend a common position where necessary.

Assembly Elections June 1998: Results by Party

Party	*Seats*
Ulster Unionist	28
Social Democratic & Labour	24
Democratic Unionist	20
Sinn Féin	18
Alliance	6
United Kingdom Unionist	5
Progressive Unionist	2
Northern Ireland Women's Coalition	2
Others	3

The Executive's main function is to plan each year, and review as necessary, a programme of government with an agreed budget. This is subject to approval by the Assembly, after scrutiny in Assembly Committees, on a cross-community basis.

The Assembly has ten Statutory Committees. Membership of Committees is in broad proportion to party strengths in the Assembly to ensure that the opportunity of Committee places is available to all Members. Each Committee has a scrutiny, policy development and consultation role in relation to its Department and a role in the initiation of legislation.

The New Northern Ireland Departments

The Office of the First Minister and Deputy First Minister is responsible for the strategic overview of the work of the Assembly. These Ministers have particular responsibility for economic policy; equality; liaison with the North/South Ministerial Council, British-Irish Council, British-Irish Intergovernmental Conference, Civic Forum and the Secretary of State for Northern Ireland; European affairs; international matters; community relations; public appointments policy; honours; freedom of information; victims and women's issues.

The other departments and their main responsibilities are:

Enterprise, Trade and Investment—economic development policy; industry; research and development; tourism; Health and Safety Executive; company regulation; consumer affairs; energy policy.

Regional Development—transport planning; public transport; roads; rail; ports and airports; water; strategic planning.

Culture, Arts and Leisure—arts and culture; sport and leisure; libraries and museums; inland waterways; inland fisheries; Ordnance Survey; Public Record Office; language policy; lottery matters; visitor amenities.

Social Development—housing policy; voluntary activity; urban renewal; community sector; Housing Benefit Review Boards; Social Security Agency; Child Support Agency; Lands Division; social legislation.

Environment—planning control; environment and heritage; protection of the countryside; waste management; pollution control; wildlife protection; local government; sustainable development; road safety; transport licensing and enforcement.

Finance and Personnel—finance; personnel; information technology; common services; accommodation; legal services; Northern Ireland Statistics and Research Agency; Land Registry; Rates Collection Agency; Government Purchasing Agency; Office of Law Reform.

Education—schools funding and administration; special education; school effectiveness; school planning and provision; Schools Inspectorate; pre-school education; Youth Service; teachers (numbers and remuneration).

Higher and Further Education, Training and Employment—higher education; further education; vocational training; employment services; employment law and labour relations; teacher training and teacher education; student support and postgraduate awards; training grants.

Health, Social Services and Public Safety—health; social services; public health and safety; health promotion; Fire Authority.

Agriculture and Rural Development—food; farming and environment policy; veterinary matters; Science Service; rural development; forestry; sea fisheries; rivers.

Intergovernmental Dialogue

The North/South Ministerial Council brings together those with executive responsibilities in Northern Ireland and the Irish Government to work on matters of mutual interest. The Council meets on a regular basis to develop consultation, co-operation and action on an all-island and cross-border basis.

Six new North/South Implementation Bodies, established by international agreement between the British and Irish Governments, came into effect in December 1999; their role is to implement policies agreed by Ministers in the North/South Ministerial Council. The new bodies are: the Food Safety Promotion Board; the Trade and Business Development Body; the Special European Union Programmes Body; the Foyle, Carlingford and Irish Lights Commission (dealing with marine matters); and the North/South Language Body.

The British-Irish Council has been set up to promote and develop good relationships among the peoples of the United Kingdom and Ireland. It comprises representatives of the British and Irish Governments, the Northern Ireland Assembly, the National Assembly for Wales and the Scottish Parliament, and delegates from the Channel Islands and the Isle of Man, who come together to address issues of mutual interest. As a priority, the Council has decided to examine and develop policies for co-operation on drugs, social exclusion, the environment and transport. Other areas for discussion will include agriculture, tourism, culture, health, education, approaches to EU issues, links between cities, towns and local districts, sporting activity, and minority and lesser used languages.

The British-Irish Intergovernmental Conference replaces the Anglo-Irish Intergovernmental Council and the Intergovernmental Conference established under the 1985 Anglo-Irish Agreement. Its role is to promote bilateral co-operation on matters of mutual interest between the two governments.

A Civic Forum, consisting of 60 members representative of the business, trade union, voluntary and other sectors of the Northern Ireland community, is to be established to act as a consultative mechanism on social, economic and cultural matters.

Human Rights and Equality

As in the rest of the United Kingdom, the European Convention on Human Rights and Fundamental Freedoms will become enshrined into Northern Ireland domestic law when the Human Rights Act comes into force in October 2000.

A commitment to the protection of human rights and the promotion of equality was central to the Good Friday Agreement. The Northern Ireland Act 1998, which followed the Agreement, established a new Equality Commission and a Human Rights Commission. The Act also strengthened the existing equality legislation by imposing a new statutory equality duty on all public authorities, requiring them to be alert to the need to promote equal opportunities and good community relations.

Northern Ireland Human Rights Commission

The Northern Ireland Human Rights Commission was created to advise government and the Northern Ireland Assembly on human rights issues, particularly on the need for legislation to protect human rights. As part of this work, the Commission has launched a major consultative exercise on the scope for a special Bill of Rights for Northern Ireland.

Equality Commission for Northern Ireland

The Equality Commission was formed following the amalgamation of the four former equality bodies (which were responsible for fair employment, equal opportunities, racial equality and disability issues) in a move to streamline the monitoring of equality issues in Northern Ireland. As well as taking over the work of its predecessors, the Commission is responsible for enforcing the new statutory equality duty.

The Parades Commission

The Parades Commission has full statutory powers to help implement the Public Processions (Northern Ireland) Act 1998 over contentious parades in Northern Ireland. In the absence of local agreement on contentious parades, the Commission may make legally binding determinations, such as imposing route conditions. The Commission imposed route conditions on 152 such parades in the year to 31 March 2000 out of a total of 3,403.

The vast majority of parades each year are organised by the Protestant/Unionist community, especially the 'Loyal Orders'. Most take place during the six months from around Easter to the end of September.

Victims of Violence Commission

The Victims of Violence Commission looks at possible ways of providing greater recognition of the suffering felt by victims of violence arising from the events of the last 30 years. Following its report in May 1998, the Government has announced a number of support measures for victims, including an independent review of criminal injuries compensation arrangements.

Security Policy

The authorities have exceptional powers to deal with and prevent terrorist activities, including special powers of arrest for those suspected of certain serious terrorist offences, non-jury courts to try terrorist offences (see p. 230) and the banning of terrorist organisations (see p. 215).

Under the Police (Northern Ireland) Act 1998, a new office of Police Ombudsman was established to provide an independent means of impartially investigating complaints against police officers in Northern Ireland and to react to incidents perceived to be in the public interest, even if no individual complaint has been made. The Police Ombudsman designate is expected to exercise full responsibilities towards the end of 2000.

Policing and Justice

During 1999 an independent Policing Commission under the chairmanship of the last Governor of Hong Kong and former Northern Ireland Minister, Chris Patten, reviewed the future policing needs in Northern Ireland. The Patten Commission was set up under the terms of the Good Friday Agreement and it published its report in September 1999. As a result of its recommendations, the Government brought forward the Police (Northern Ireland) Bill, which, when enacted, would, among other things:

- enhance accountability through a new Policing Board;
- create new district policing partnerships to enhance local accountability;
- redress the severe religious imbalance in the service between Protestants and Catholics; and
- implement a new name and badge for the Service.

In parallel with the work of the Patten Commission, the Government carried out a wide-ranging review of the criminal justice system in Northern Ireland. The review consulted political parties, interested bodies, organisations and individuals, and published its recommendations in March 2000. These recommendations are subject to further consultation.

The Economy

Throughout the 1990s the Northern Ireland economy performed well. Employment grew throughout the decade and unemployment has declined since 1993. However, the Labour Force Survey for March to May 2000 showed that 64.9 per cent of those people of working age in Northern Ireland were in employment, compared with 74.6 per cent in the UK as a whole. Comparable rates for unemployment were 7.0 per cent and 5.6 per cent respectively.

A substantial increase in new inward investment in growth industries such as computer software, telecommunications and network services contributed to the 2,500 new jobs generated by the Industrial Development Board in 1999–2000.

Northern Ireland's economic strategy has been reviewed to take account of changing needs by a largely private sector-led steering group which drew on the input of 18 working groups. The steering group report—*Strategy 2010*—has been presented to the Northern Ireland Assembly for its consideration.

The public expenditure allocation within the Northern Ireland Executive's responsibility for 2000–01 is £5.3 billion.

Economic Assistance

In 1986 the British and Irish Governments established the International Fund for Ireland. Some three-quarters of the fund is spent in Northern Ireland, the rest going to border areas in the Irish Republic. Programmes cover business enterprise, tourism, community relations, urban development, agriculture and rural development. Donors include the United States, Canada, New Zealand and the European Union. The Berlin EU summit at the end of March 1999 agreed a Special Programme for Northern Ireland in support of peace worth about £260 million between the years 2000 and 2004. It also confirmed the renewal for three years of EU support of approximately £10 million a year for the International Fund for Ireland.

Including funding from the new Special Programme, Northern Ireland will receive around £900 million under the EU Structural Funds Programmes for the period 2000–06 (see p. 396). The priority areas eligible for funding under the Community Support Framework (CSF), which has been agreed with the European Commission, are peace and reconciliation; economic growth and renewal; employment, human resource development and social inclusion; balanced regional, urban and rural development; and North/South and wider co-operation. An indicative allocation of 7.5 per cent of the funds in the Northern Ireland CSF has been set aside for North-South co-operation.

The Irish Language

In July 1998 a statutory duty was placed on the education authorities in Northern Ireland to encourage and facilitate Irish-medium education. In August 2000 there were eight grant-aided schools teaching 1,423 primary and secondary school pupils (out of a total of 334,000 in Northern Ireland) in Irish as the first language. In addition, there were 13 independent schools teaching a further 284 pupils.

A new branch within the Northern Ireland Civil Service has been established to develop policy on linguistic diversity. Estimates suggest that around 142,000 people in Northern Ireland have some ability to use Irish as a means of communication, either orally or in writing. A cross-border implementation body has been set up with responsibility for promoting the Irish language and facilitating and encouraging its use.

Further Reading

Northern Ireland Expenditure Plans and Priorities. The Government's Expenditure Plans 1999–2002. The Stationery Office, 1999.

Websites

Northern Ireland Executive: www.nics.gov.uk

Northern Ireland Assembly: www.ni-assembly.gov.uk

Northern Ireland Office: www.nio.gov.uk

4 Scotland

Scotland has a population of just over 5 million people, three-quarters of whom live in the central lowlands. Its chief cities are Edinburgh (the capital), Glasgow, Aberdeen and Dundee. The country contains large areas of unspoilt and wild landscape, and many of the UK's mountains, including its highest peak, Ben Nevis (1,343 m, 4,406 ft).

Scotland's first Parliament for almost 300 years was officially opened by the Queen in July 1999. The Scottish Executive, headed by the First Minister, is responsible for governing day-to-day Scottish affairs.

Early History

At the time of the Roman invasion of Britain, what is now Scotland was mainly inhabited by the Picts. Despite a long campaign, Roman rule never permanently extended to most of Scotland. In the sixth century, the Scots from Ireland settled in what is now Argyll, giving their name to the present-day Scotland.

War between the kingdoms of England and Scotland was frequent in the Middle Ages. Despite reverses such as the defeat of William Wallace's uprising in 1298, Robert the Bruce's victory over Edward II of England at Bannockburn in 1314 ensured the survival of a separate kingdom of Scotland.

The two crowns were eventually united when Elizabeth I of England was succeeded in 1603 by James VI of Scotland (James I of England), who was her nearest heir. Even so, England and Scotland remained separate political entities during the 17th century, apart from an enforced period of unification under Oliver Cromwell in the 1650s, until in 1707 the English and Scottish Parliaments agreed on a single Parliament for Great Britain.

Population

Scotland's population has changed relatively little in the last 50 years. In June 1999 the estimated population was 5.1 million (see Table 4.1), compared with 5.2 million in 1971 and 5.1 million in 1951. Population density averages 66 people per sq km, the lowest density in the UK.

Scottish Parliament and Executive

The Scotland Act 1998 provided the necessary statutory framework to establish a Scottish Parliament and Executive, which the majority of Scottish people had endorsed by referendum held in September 1997. Of those who voted in the referendum, 74 per cent supported the devolution proposition, and, on a second question—whether to give the new

Table 4.1: Scotland Area and Population, 1999

	Population (thousands)	Population density (people per sq km)	Change in population 1981–99 (%)
Cities			
Aberdeen	213	1,144	0.1
Dundee	144	2,217	–14.8
Edinburgh	452	1,722	1.3
Glasgow	611	3,493	–14.2
Least densely populated areas			
Argyll and Bute	90	13	–1.3
Eilean Siar[1]	28	9	–12.6
Highland	209	8	7.0
Orkney Islands	20	20	2.2
Scottish Borders	106	22	5.1
Shetland Islands	23	16	–13.7
Scotland	**5,119**	**66**	**–1.2**

[1] Formerly Western Isles

Sources: Office for National Statistics and General Register Office for Scotland

Parliament tax-varying powers—64 per cent of voters were in favour.

In May 1999, 129 Members of the Scottish Parliament (MSPs) were elected for a fixed four-year term: 73 MSPs for single-member constituencies and 56 MSPs representing eight regions, based on the European parliamentary constituencies, each with seven members. The latter were allocated so that each party's overall share of seats in the Parliament, including the constituency seats, reflected its share of the regional vote. Under the 'additional member system' of proportional representation (PR), each elector had two votes: one for a constituency MSP and a 'regional' vote for a registered political party or an individual independent candidate.

The Labour Party, which has traditionally done well in elections in Scotland, is the largest single party (see Table 4.2), with 55 MSPs, in 52 of the 73 constituency seats, including nearly all those in central Scotland. The Scottish National Party is the second largest party, with 35 MSPs. In the election, most of its seats came from the 'top-up' PR system, as did all the 18 seats won by the Conservative Party, the third largest party in the Parliament, although the latter subsequently won its first constituency seat in a by-election, taking the seat from the Labour Party.

Responsibilities

The Scottish Parliament's responsibilities include health; education and training; local government; housing; economic development; many aspects of home affairs and civil and criminal law; transport; the environment; agriculture, fisheries and forestry; and sport and the arts. In these areas, the Scottish Parliament is able to amend or repeal existing Acts of Parliament and to pass new legislation.

Responsibility for a number of other issues, including overseas affairs, defence and national security, overall economic and monetary policy, employment legislation and social security, remains with the UK Government and Parliament as 'reserved' matters under Schedule 5 of the Scotland Act 1998. The position of Secretary of State for Scotland, with a seat in the Cabinet, continues and carries responsibility for representing Scottish interests within the UK Government through the Scotland Office.

The Scottish Executive is responsible for all public bodies whose functions and services

Scotland: New Council Areas, 1 April 1998

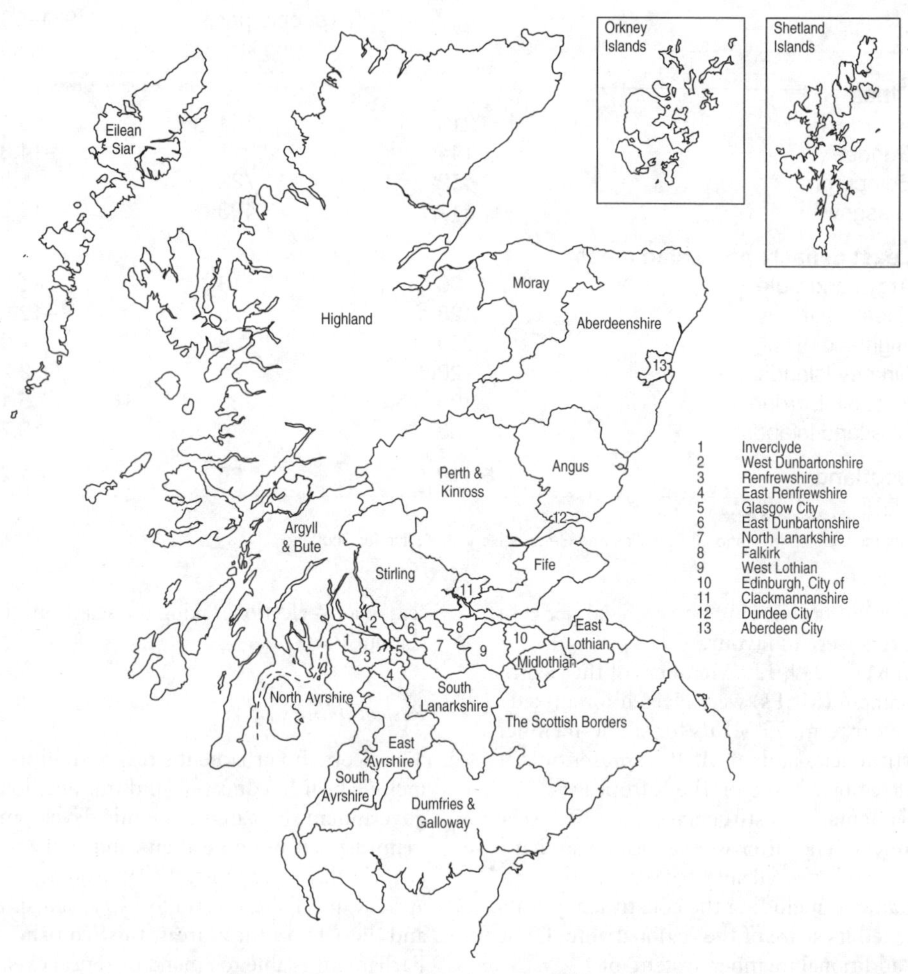

Table 4.2: Electoral Representation in Scotland, July 2000—Number of Seats

	Scottish Parliament			Westminster Parliament (MPs)	European Parliament (MEPs)
	Constituency MSPs	Additional MSPs	Total MSPs		
Labour	*52*	*3*	55	55	3
Scottish National Party	*7*	*28*	35	6	2
Conservative	*1*	*18*	19	—	2
Liberal Democrats	*12*	*5*	17	10	1
Independent	*1*	—	1	1	—
Scottish Socialist Party	—	*1*	1	—	—
Green	—	*1*	1	—	—
Total seats	*73*	*56*	129	72	8

have been devolved and is accountable to the Scottish Parliament for them. It also has an input into bodies such as the Forestry Commission (see p. 466), which operate in Scotland and elsewhere in the UK.

At present, the Parliament meets at the General Assembly Hall in Edinburgh's Old Town. A new permanent site for the Parliament is planned at Holyrood, at the other end of the Royal Mile—a street in the historic centre of Edinburgh and the location of Parliament House where the last Scottish Parliament met from 1640 to 1707. The new building is expected to be completed by the end of 2002.

The Scottish Executive is headed by a First Minister, normally the leader of the party able to command majority support in the Parliament. Following the 1999 election, the Executive is being run by a partnership between Labour and the Liberal Democrats, with the latter having two seats in the Cabinet, including that of Deputy First Minister. The Cabinet comprises 11 positions:

- First Minister;
- Deputy First Minister and Minister for Justice;
- Minister for Communities;
- Minister for Transport and the Environment;
- Minister for Health and Community Care;
- Minister for Rural Affairs;
- Minister for Children and Education;
- Lord Advocate;
- Minister for Parliament;
- Minister for Enterprise and Lifelong Learning; and
- Minister for Finance.

Finance

The Scottish Parliament has a budget of £16.9 billion in 2000–01, which is allocated, through the Secretary of State for Scotland, by the UK Parliament. Once the amount of the budget has been determined, the Scottish Parliament is free to allocate resources across the expenditure programmes.

> Work has begun on the production of a Gaelic Dictionary of Procedural Terms to be used in the Scottish Parliament, local authorities and other key institutions in Scotland. It will enable Gaelic to be more easily used as a language of public debate and administration, establishing a standard terminology which can be adapted and refined as necessary on a continuing basis. Financial assistance for the project has come from the Scottish Executive, Highlands and Islands Enterprise, the Gaelic Language Promotion Trust and the Gaelic Society of Inverness. The dictionary is expected to be ready for use early in 2001.

The Parliament has the power to increase or decrease the basic rate of income tax—22 pence in the pound—by a maximum of 3 pence. Liability to tax is based on residence: a person is considered resident if he or she is a UK resident for tax purposes and either spends 50 per cent or more of the tax year in Scotland or has his or her only or principal home there.

The Parliament is responsible for determining the form of local taxation and, if it wishes, is able to alter both the council tax and business rates.

Spending

The Budget Act 2000—an Act of the Scottish Parliament—gave statutory authority to the Scottish Executive to spend money out of the Scottish Consolidated Fund in the financial year 2000–01. It set out the purposes for which financial resources can be used and the maximum amounts which can be used for each of the Executive's spending programmes.

Priorities for spending include:

- the provision of nursery places for all four year olds and progress towards a target of places for all three year olds;
- £16 million to establish class sizes of 30 or under for primary school children under the age of seven;
- £29 million to increase enrolments in further education institutions;

- NHS Direct (see p. 189), more one-stop clinics, and electronic appointment booking systems;
- the establishment of a Drug Enforcement Agency;
- a new domestic violence fund to improve a range of services including more refuge spaces;
- proposals for two National Parks;
- improvements to living conditions of low-income householders, especially pensioners;
- five major trunk road schemes, with a total capital cost of £140 million over three years; and
- £30 million spending from the Public Transport Fund including the Edinburgh cross rail project and bus priority corridors in Glasgow.

The Economy

In the last 50 years the economy has moved away from the traditional industries of coal, steel and shipbuilding, with the establishment of the offshore oil and gas industry, growth in services and, more recently, developments in high-technology industries, such as chemicals, electronic engineering and information technology. Manufacturing remains important, and Scotland's manufacturing exports were provisionally estimated at £18.5 billion in 1999.

Notable features of the Scottish economy include:

- *Electronics.* Scotland has one of the biggest concentrations of the electronics industry in Western Europe, employing about 42,500 workers in 1997. Electrical and instrument engineering exports were provisionally worth £10 billion in 1999, 54 per cent of Scotland's manufacturing exports.
- *Oil and gas.* Offshore oil and gas production has made a significant contribution to the Scottish economy in the last 30 years. Many of the UK's 125 offshore oilfields are located to the east of Shetland, Orkney or the east coast of Scotland (see map at the back of the book).
- *Whisky.* Whisky continues to be one of Scotland's most important industries. There are 100 whisky distilleries in operation, mostly in the north-east. Whisky exports dominate exports by the drinks industry, which were provisionally valued at £1.5 billion in 1999.
- *Tourism.* Tourism is a major industry, supporting about 161,000 jobs. In 1999 expenditure by tourists in Scotland was valued at £2.5 billion; there were 12.4 million tourist trips, including those originating in Scotland.
- *Financial services.* Funds managed by financial institutions in Scotland were worth some £277 billion in 1999, of which £103.8 billion were in long-term life insurance funds and £93.9 billion in pension funds. Several financial institutions are based in Scotland, including insurance companies, fund managers, unit trusts and investment trusts. There are four Scottish-based clearing banks, which have limited rights to issue their own banknotes.
- *Forestry.* Scotland accounts for just under half of the UK's timber production. In the last ten years there has been significant international and local investment in wood-based panel production and in pulp and paper processing.
- *Fishing.* Fishing remains significant, particularly in the north-east and the Highlands and Islands. In 1999, Scotland accounted for 69 per cent by weight and 61 per cent by value of the fish landed in the UK by British vessels. Fish farming, particularly of salmon, has become much more important, and Scotland produces the largest amount of farmed salmon in the EU. However, some fish farms have recently been affected by a viral disease, Infectious Salmon Anaemia, and measures are being taken to eradicate it.

Support for industry and commerce is managed by two bodies: Scottish Enterprise and Highlands and Islands Enterprise (see p. 395). Inward investment is encouraged by Locate in Scotland, a joint operation between the Scottish Executive and Scottish Enterprise. In 1999–2000, 91 inward investment projects were recorded, which are expected to lead to investment of £650 million and the creation or safeguarding of over 19,000 jobs.

The Labour Force Survey for March to May 2000 showed that 72.3 per cent of those people of working age in Scotland were in employment, compared with 74.6 per cent in the UK as a whole. Comparable rates for unemployment were 7.6 per cent and 5.6 per cent respectively.

Legal System

The principles and procedures of the Scottish legal system (see p. 226) differ in many respects from those of England and Wales. These differences stem, in part, from the adoption of elements from medieval canon law and selective borrowing from other European legal systems, based on Roman law, during the 16th century. Preservation of Scots law and the Scottish Courts was provided for in the 1707 Treaty of Union. In addition to separate courts and a separate legal profession, Scotland has its own prosecution, prison and police services.

Education and Culture

The Scottish education system has a number of distinctive features (see chapter 10), including a separate system of examinations and differences in the curriculum. A new system of courses and awards for education after 16, 'Higher Still', started to be phased in from August 1999, and is expected to be fully implemented in 2003. Record numbers of students are entering post-compulsory education—about 546,000 students were enrolled in vocational, further or higher education in 1998–99.

The Adults with Incapacity Act 2000 became the first major piece of legislation to pass through the Scottish Parliament. When it comes into effect in 2001, it is estimated that it will provide greater protection for around 100,000 Scottish adults with incapacity—some of the most vulnerable members of society.

Gaelic, a language of ancient Celtic origin, is spoken by some 70,000 people, many of whom live in the Hebrides. The Scottish Executive is providing £12.5 million to support Gaelic in 2000–01. Broadcasting is the largest single area, accounting for £8.5 million. In 1999–2000 there were 1,831 children in Gaelic-medium education in 59 primary schools and 232 pupils in 13 secondary schools. Extra resources are being allocated to supporting Gaelic education and cultural organisations. (See also box on p. 25.)

The annual Edinburgh Festival is one of the world's leading cultural events. Held in August and September, it brings about £100 million into the Scottish economy each year, and the International Festival, Jazz Festival, Festival Fringe, Book Festival, Film Festival and Military Tattoo combine to make the Edinburgh Festival the largest arts festival in the UK. Scotland possesses several major collections of the fine and applied arts, such as the Burrell Collection in Glasgow and the Scottish National Gallery of Modern Art in Edinburgh. A new Museum of Scotland has been built in Edinburgh to house the National Museums' Scottish Collection.

Further Reading

Investing in You—The Annual Expenditure Report of the Scottish Executive. Scottish Executive, 2000.

Scotland Act 1998. The Stationery Office, 1998.

Scotland's Parliament. Cm 3658. The Stationery Office, 1997.

Websites

Scottish Executive: www.scotland.gov.uk

The Scottish Parliament: www.scottish.parliament.uk

The Scotland Office: www.scottishsecretary.gov.uk

5 Wales

Wales (or Cymru in the Welsh language) has a population of 2.9 million people, about two-thirds of whom live in the southern valleys and the lower-lying coastal areas. The chief urban centres are the capital, Cardiff (with a population of 324,000), Swansea and Newport in the south and Wrexham in the north. Much of Wales is hilly or mountainous with the highest peak being Yr Wyddfa (Snowdon) at 1,085 m (3,560 ft).

In July 1999 the National Assembly for Wales, set up to give the Welsh people greater control over their own affairs, took on virtually all the functions formerly exercised by the Welsh Office and the Secretary of State for Wales.

Early History

After the collapse of Roman rule (see p. 4), Wales remained a Celtic stronghold, although during Norman times often under the influence of England. In 1282 Edward I completed a successful campaign to bring Wales under English rule. The great castles that he built in north Wales remain among the UK's finest historic monuments. Edward I's eldest son—later Edward II—was born at Caernarfon in 1284 and was created Prince of Wales. The title has been given to the eldest son of successive reigning monarchs ever since.

Continued strong Welsh national feeling culminated in the unsuccessful rising led by Owain Glyndŵr at the beginning of the 15th century. The Tudor dynasty, which ruled England from 1485 to 1603, was of Welsh ancestry. The Acts of Union of 1536 and 1542 united England and Wales administratively, politically and legally.

National Assembly for Wales

In a referendum held in May 1997, government proposals for devolution in Wales were endorsed by a narrow majority of the Welsh people—50.3 per cent of those who voted were in favour and 49.7 per cent were against. The Government of Wales Act 1998 subsequently provided the necessary statutory framework to establish a National Assembly for Wales.

Electors had two votes in the first elections to the Assembly, which took place in May 1999: one for a candidate in their local constituency and one for a party list. The Assembly comprises 60 members: 40 from local constituencies (covering the same areas as those for Welsh seats in the House of Commons) and 20 elected by the additional member system of proportional representation from electoral regions—four for each of the five former European parliamentary constituencies in Wales.

Table 5.1: Wales Area and Population, 1999

	Population (thousands)	Population density (people per sq km)	Change in population 1981–1999 (%)
Blaenau Gwent	72	658	–5.2
Bridgend (Pen-y-bont ar Ogwr)[1]	132	535	4.3
Caerphilly (Caerffili)	170	612	–1.0
Cardiff (Caerdydd)	324	2,317	13.1
Carmarthenshire (Sir Gaerfyrddin)	169	71	2.3
Ceredigion (Sir Ceredigion)	72	40	17.2
Conwy	112	99	13.3
Denbighshire (Sir Ddinbych)	91	108	5.0
Flintshire (Sir y Fflint)	147	337	6.4
Gwynedd	116	46	4.1
Isle of Anglesey (Sir Ynys Môn)	65	92	–4.0
Merthyr Tydfil (Merthyr Tudful)	56	506	–7.2
Monmouthshire (Sir Fynwy)	87	102	13.2
Neath Port Talbot (Castell-nedd Port Talbot)	138	313	–3.1
Newport (Casnewydd)	138	728	4.5
Pembrokeshire (Sir Benfro)	114	72	5.9
Powys	126	24	12.6
Rhondda, Cynon, Taff (Rhondda, Cynon, Taf)	241	567	0.9
Swansea (Abertawe)	230	608	0.2
Torfaen (Tor-faen)	90	713	–0.1
Vale of Glamorgan (Bro Morgannwg)	121	362	7.1
Wrexham (Wrecsam)	125	252	5.3
Wales (Cymru)	**2,937**	**141**	**4.4**

[1] Welsh-language local authority names are given in parenthesis if there are differences between the English and Welsh names.

Sources: Office for National Statistics and National Assembly for Wales

Table 5.2: Electoral Representation in Wales, August 2000—Number of Seats

	National Assembly			Westminster Parliament (MPs)	European Parliament (MEPs)
	Constituency seats	Regional seats	Total seats		
Labour	*27*	*1*	28	34	2
Plaid Cymru	*9*	*8*	17	4	2
Conservative	*1*	*8*	9	—	1
Liberal Democrat	*3*	*3*	6	2	—
Total seats	*40*	*20*	60	40	5

Wales: Unitary Authorities, 1 April 1998

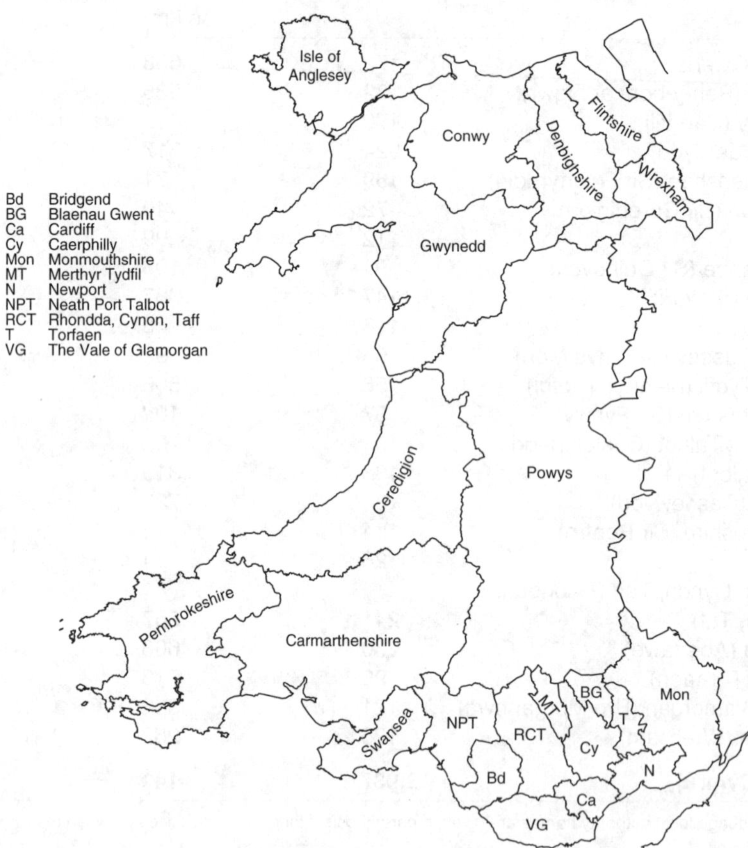

The Labour Party has traditionally had strong support in Wales. It has the largest number of seats in the Assembly (see Table 5.2)—although in the election it did not obtain an overall majority. Since October 2000 it has run the Assembly in partnership with the Liberal Democrats.

Responsibilities

In July 1999 the Assembly took over most of the functions formerly held by the Secretary of State for Wales. These include responsibilities for economic development; agriculture, forestry, fisheries and food; education and training; industry; local government; health and personal social services; housing; the environment; planning; transport and roads; arts, culture and the Welsh language; ancient monuments and historic buildings; and sport and recreation. Its budget for 2000–01 is £8 billion. Foreign affairs, defence, taxation, overall economic policy, social security and broadcasting are the main functions for which responsibility has remained with the Government in London. The office of Secretary of State for Wales continues, although his or her functions have changed considerably. The post holder retains a seat in the Cabinet and has responsibility for primary legislation, bidding for the Assembly's budget and representing Welsh interests in the Westminster Parliament. As part of the UK, Wales retains full constituency representation in the Parliament in London.

The Assembly has powers to make secondary legislation (see p. 49) to meet distinctive Welsh circumstances. It is based in Cardiff Bay, initially meeting in a temporary chamber until an adjacent new Chamber and associated facilities are opened in 2003.

The First Secretary heads the Assembly and in February 2000 he appointed a Cabinet of eight Assembly Secretaries. Their responsibilities are:

- local government and housing;
- education (of children up to age 16);
- health and social services;
- post-16 education and training, Welsh language and culture;
- agriculture and rural development;
- environment (incorporating transport and planning);
- trefnydd (business secretary); and
- finance.

The First Secretary is currently responsible for economic development, industry and European matters.

The Assembly is responsible for a number of public bodies. The organisations with the largest expenditure are:

- the Higher Education Funding Council for Wales (with planned gross expenditure in 2000–01 of £293 million);
- the Welsh Development Agency (WDA, see p. 355) (£179 million); and
- the Further Education Funding Council for Wales (£213 million).

Local Government

The 22 unitary authorities (see map opposite) have collective responsibility for spending over a third of the Assembly's budget. The National Assembly has a responsibility for setting the framework of policy and of

A Better Wales—The Assembly Cabinet's 10-year Strategy for Improving the Quality of Life in Wales

In January 2000, the Assembly Cabinet published its strategic plan for improving life in Wales: *A Better Wales.* The ten-year strategy is built round five key areas: opportunities for learning; a stronger economy; better health and wellbeing; quality of life; and better, simpler government.

As well as the long-term aims, *A Better Wales* set out more than 100 targets for achievement by the end of the current Assembly (2003), and the actions needed to achieve them. Among these targets are:

- no infant classes with more than 30 pupils, by September 2001;
- fewer than one-third of pupils leaving school without a qualification;
- at least seven out of eight adults having qualifications;
- a 10 per cent increase in the number of Welsh exporting companies;
- 40,000 net additional jobs;
- at least 50 per cent of Welsh companies using electronic commerce (e-commerce);
- a 5 per cent increase in the number of jobs in dairy, lamb and beef processing;
- 1 million more tourism trips;
- a cut in the death rate for breast cancer and in the rate at which invasive cervical cancer occurs;
- better management of hospital waiting times, within 12 months;
- a rail strategy for Wales, including better north–south links;
- a new, more co-ordinated approach to improving the most disadvantaged Welsh communities;
- a higher profile for Welsh culture, language, arts and sport;
- savings of at least £80 million through a more modern approach by the public sector to buying goods and services; and
- fairer funding arrangements for local government and the National Health Service.

secondary legislation within which local government operates. It also has a responsibility to ensure that local decision-making reflects the requirements of the law and, where appropriate, priorities determined by the National Assembly. Measures to modernise local authority management structures, strengthen local democracy and improve local financial accountability were contained in the Local Government Act 2000, which the Assembly will implement in Wales.

A Partnership Council has been set up comprising elected representatives of all sectors of local government (including representatives of the National Parks, police and fire authorities and community councils) and the National Assembly. It will enable local government to advise the National Assembly on all aspects of its functions, make representations to the National Assembly and assist in the preparation of guidance and advice to councils.

Welsh Language

In 1997, 21 per cent of the population in private households said that they spoke Welsh. In much of the rural north and west, Welsh remains the first language.

Welsh is now more widely used for official purposes, and is treated equally with English in the work of the Assembly. It is also quite extensively used in broadcasting, while most road signs are bilingual. Welsh-medium education in schools is encouraged. Welsh is taught—as a first or second language—to most pupils between the ages of 5 and 16, and from September 2000 will be taught to all pupils in this age group. In addition, other subjects are taught in Welsh in about 500 schools, in both the primary and secondary sectors.

The National Assembly has assumed the main responsibility for enhancing Welsh culture and developing greater use of the Welsh language. The Welsh Language Act 1993 established the principle that, in public business and the administration of justice in Wales, Welsh and English should have equal treatment. The Welsh Language Board aims to promote and facilitate the use of the Welsh language; in 2000–01 its gross expenditure will be £6 million.

Economy

Recent decades have seen fundamental changes in the Welsh economy, which traditionally used to be based on coal and steel. Wales now has a more diverse range of manufacturing industries, including many at the forefront of technology, and a growing number involved in e-commerce. However, the steel industry remains important, and crude steel production in Wales was around 6.1 million tonnes in 1998, accounting for 42 per cent of UK steel output.

The Labour Force Survey for March to May 2000 showed that 69.7 per cent of people of working age in Wales were in employment, compared with 74.6 per cent in the UK as a whole. Comparable rates for unemployment were 6.5 per cent and 5.6 per cent respectively. As part of the *Better Wales* strategic plan (see p. 31), the National Assembly has set a target for an additional 40,000 jobs to be created in Wales before the end of its first term of office (2003).

Manufacturing accounts for 28 per cent of gross domestic product (GDP) in Wales, well above the UK average. Wales is an important centre for consumer and office electronics, automotive components, chemicals and materials, aerospace, and food and drink. Around 30,500 people are employed in the optical and electrical industries, and 11,900 in the automotive components sector. In the service sector, tourism and leisure services are significant—estimates indicate that about 9.8 million tourist trips were made to Wales in 1998—while call centre activity is becoming more important and prevalent.

A key feature of the economy has been the volume of investment from overseas companies and from elsewhere in the UK. Since 1983, over 2,000 inward investment projects have been recorded in Wales, bringing in a total investment of £13.2 billion and promising the creation and safeguarding of nearly 204,000 jobs. Overseas-owned manufacturing companies in Wales employ in excess of 75,000 people.

The Welsh Development Agency (WDA) has been given broader functions and powers, so that it is now better placed to contribute to economic regeneration across the whole of Wales. Increased resources are being provided to support business development, and a new Entrepreneurship Action Plan for Wales is being co-ordinated by the WDA, to develop a stronger business culture.

Environment

Wales has a rich and diverse natural heritage. About one-quarter is designated as a National Park or Area of Outstanding Natural Beauty (see p. 315). As well as three National Parks—Snowdonia, the Brecon Beacons and the Pembrokeshire Coast—and five Areas of Outstanding Natural Beauty, there are two national trails, 36 country parks and large stretches of heritage coast. There are also 62 National Nature Reserves, over 900 Sites of Special Scientific Interest and a number of internationally important nature conservation sites in Wales. For example, 44 sites are proposed for designation as Special Areas of Conservation under the European Community (EC) Habitat Directive, 13 Special Protection Areas are classified under the EC Wild Birds Directive, and ten wetlands of international importance are designated under the Ramsar Convention (see p. 320). There are six Environmentally Sensitive Areas (see p. 459), representing about 25 per cent of the land in Wales, while a new scheme, Tir Gofal, introduced in 1999–2000, replaced most of the current agri-environment schemes. Tir Gofal aims to encourage agricultural practices that will help to protect and enhance the landscape and wildlife of the Welsh countryside.

The quality of bathing waters on the coastline of Wales has reached an all-time record for compliance with European standards. National standards for river quality in Wales showed that nearly 99 per cent of rivers were classified as 'good' or 'fair' in 1999.

Cultural and Social Affairs

Welsh literature has a long tradition and can claim to be one of the oldest in Europe. The Welsh people have strong musical traditions and Wales is well known for its choral singing, while both the Welsh National Opera and the BBC National Orchestra of Wales have international reputations. Special festivals, known as eisteddfodau, encourage Welsh literature and music. The largest is the annual Royal National Eisteddfod, consisting of competitions in music, singing, prose and poetry entirely in Welsh. Artists from all over the world come to Llangollen for the annual International Musical Eisteddfod. The biennial 'Cardiff Singer of the World' competition has established itself as one of the world's leading singing competitions.

The National Museums and Galleries of Wales include the Museum of Welsh Life at St Fagans, near Cardiff; and the recently rebuilt Welsh Slate Museum at Llanberis. The main building in Cardiff contains many paintings by Welsh artists, including Augustus John, Gwen John and Kyffyn Williams as well as a representative collection of other important artistic works. A new Industrial and Maritime Museum is to be built in Swansea. The National Library of Wales at Aberystwyth contains over 4 million books.

An active local press includes several Welsh and English language publications. The fourth television broadcaster, Sianel Pedwar Cymru (S4C), has recently been broadcasting in Welsh for 12 hours a day on its new digital channel.

Among many sporting activities, there is particular interest in rugby union football, which has come to be regarded as the Welsh national game. Wales staged the final of the Rugby World Cup in November 1999 at the Millennium Stadium in Cardiff.

Further Reading

A Better Wales. The National Assembly for Wales, 2000.

Government of Wales Act 1998. The Stationery Office, 1998

Websites

National Assembly for Wales: www.wales.gov.uk

Office of the Secretary of State for Wales: www.ossw.wales.gov.uk

6 Government

Britain's system of parliamentary government is not based on a written constitution, but is the result of gradual evolution over many centuries. The Monarchy itself can be traced back for more than a thousand years, while Parliament is one of the oldest representative assemblies in the world. The present Government is engaging in a wide-ranging programme to decentralise power, open up government, reform Parliament and increase individual rights.

A Scottish Parliament, a National Assembly for Wales and a Northern Ireland Assembly have taken up their devolved powers to govern their own domestic affairs. In May 2000 elections were held for a Mayor and Assembly for London and the new Greater London Authority came into being in July. The first stage of reforming the House of Lords has taken place and proposals have been made to hold a referendum on the voting system for the House of Commons.

The Constitution

The United Kingdom does not have a constitution set out in any single document. Instead its constitution is made up of statute law, common law and conventions.[1]

The constitution can be altered by Act of Parliament, or by general agreement, so it is adaptable to changing political conditions.

The UK Parliament is the legislature and the supreme authority. The *executive* consists of: the Government—the Cabinet and other ministers responsible for policies; government departments and agencies, responsible for national administration; devolved administrations in Scotland, Wales and Northern Ireland; local authorities, responsible for many local services; public corporations, responsible for operating particular nationalised industries; independent bodies responsible for regulating the privatised industries; and other bodies subject to ministerial control.

The *judiciary* (see chapter 14) determines common law and interprets statutes.

Origins of Government

The United Kingdom comprises England, Wales, Scotland and Northern Ireland, each with its own distinct culture and history.

[1] Conventions are rules and practices which are not legally enforceable but which are regarded as indispensable to the working of government.

England was united as a kingdom over a thousand years ago, and Wales became part of the kingdom during the reign of King Henry VIII (see p. 28). The thrones of England and Scotland were dynastically united in 1603, and in 1707 legislation passed in the two countries provided for the establishment of a single Parliament of Great Britain with supreme authority both in England and Wales, and in Scotland (see p. 22).

Ireland had links with the kingdom of England since the 13th century, and in 1801 the creation of the United Kingdom was completed by a union joining the Irish Parliament to that of Great Britain (see p. 15). In 1922 Southern Ireland (now the Irish Republic) became an entirely separate and self-governing country. The six counties of Northern Ireland had been given their own subordinate Parliament in 1920, and voted to remain within the United Kingdom.

Although the Scottish Parliament and assemblies in Wales and Northern Ireland are now operational (see below), the UK Parliament in Westminster still has an elected chamber comprising members from English, Scottish, Welsh and Northern Irish constituencies. It therefore represents people sharing very varied backgrounds and traditions, and retains ultimate authority for government and law-making in the UK (see p. 47).

Administration of Scottish, Welsh and Northern Ireland Affairs

England and Wales, Scotland and Northern Ireland have different systems of law, different judiciaries, different education systems and different systems of local government. Following devolution, the powers of the Secretaries of State for Scotland, for Wales and for Northern Ireland have been greatly reduced and now the main functions of these Cabinet members are to ensure that the reserved interests of the parts of the UK they represent are recognised and promoted in central government and that the devolution settlements work satisfactorily.

Background to Devolution

Referendums held in Scotland and Wales in 1997 endorsed proposals to devolve power from Parliament at Westminster to a Scottish Parliament (see p. 22) and a National Assembly for Wales (see p. 28). Legislation was passed in 1998 to establish these bodies, and elections were held in May 1999.

The Scottish Parliament has law-making powers, including defined and limited financial authority to vary tax revenue. It has taken democratic control over most of the responsibilities formerly exercised by The Scottish Office, including health, education, justice, local transport, agriculture and the environment. The National Assembly for Wales exercises democratic control over the former Welsh Office functions. It has secondary legislative powers and can reform and control the Welsh public bodies for which it is responsible. The National Assembly is responsible for a similar range of policy areas as the Scottish Parliament. The main difference is that justice matters in Wales remain the responsibility of the UK Government.

A comprehensive agreement on a political settlement for Northern Ireland—the Good Friday Agreement—was reached in 1998. Following a referendum endorsing the Agreement, elections to a new Northern Ireland Assembly were held in June that year. The Assembly first assumed its powers in December 1999, although it was temporarily suspended between February and May 2000 (see p. 17). The responsibilities of the Executive Committee cover similar areas as those in Scotland. However, legislation on justice matters needs the consent of the Secretary of State for Northern Ireland.

The responsibilities of the UK Government over economic and monetary policy, employment, overseas affairs, defence and national security remain unchanged.

Human Rights

The Human Rights Act 1998 incorporates the European Convention on Human Rights into domestic law, enabling the British courts to deal with these issues and not just the European Court of Human Rights in Strasbourg (see chapter 14).

Principal Members of the Royal Family from the Reign of Queen Victoria to July 2000

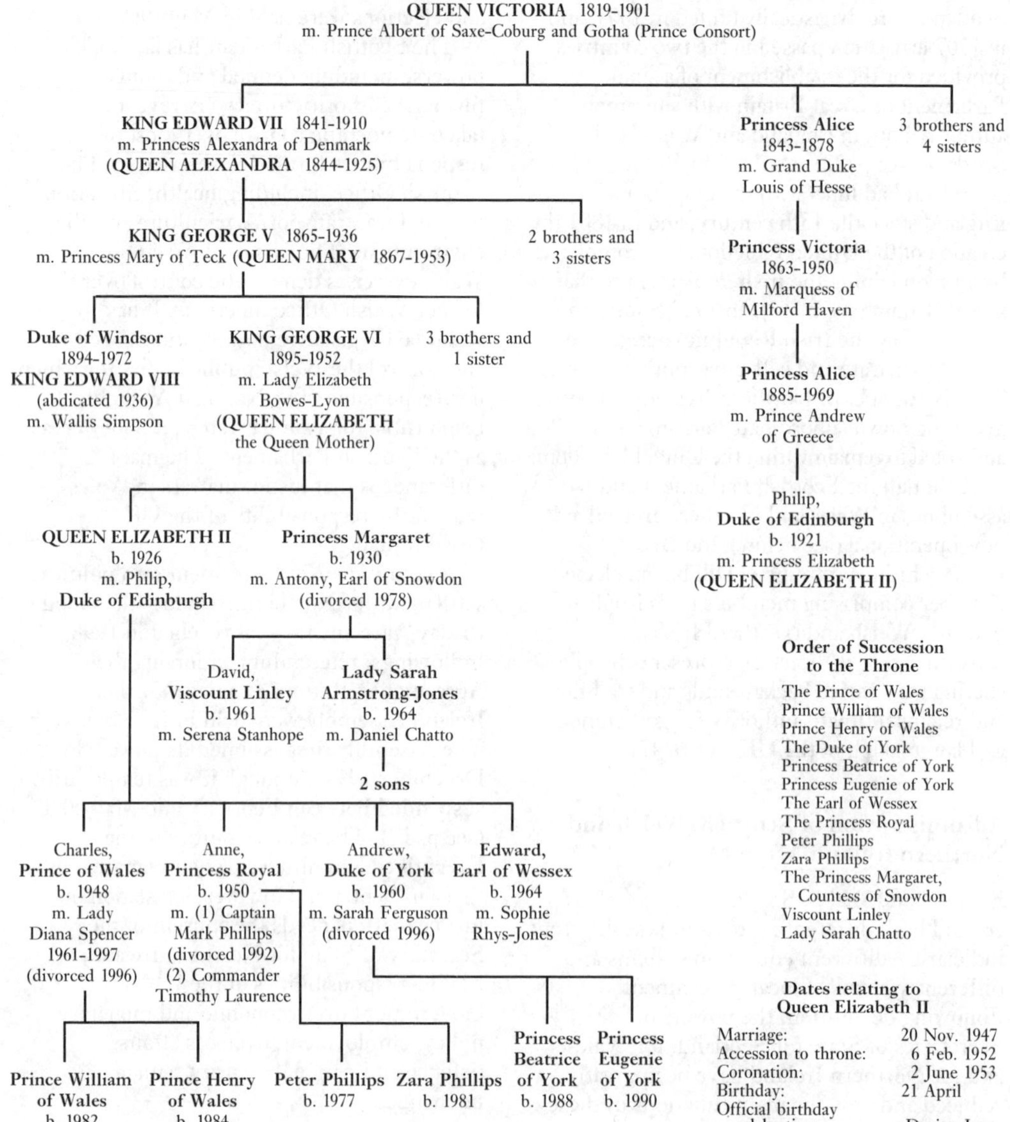

The Monarchy

The Monarchy is the oldest institution of government. Queen Elizabeth II is herself directly descended from King Egbert, who united England under his rule in 829. The only interruption in the history of the Monarchy was the republic, which lasted from 1649 to 1660.

The Queen's title in the UK is: 'Elizabeth the Second, by the Grace of God of the United Kingdom of Great Britain and

Northern Ireland and of Her other Realms and Territories Queen, Head of the Commonwealth, Defender of the Faith'.

In the Channel Islands and the Isle of Man the Queen is represented by a Lieutenant-Governor.

The Commonwealth

Although the seat of the Monarchy is in the UK, the Queen is also Sovereign of a number of Commonwealth countries.[2] In each of these the Queen is represented by a Governor-General, appointed by her on the advice of the ministers of the country concerned and completely independent of the British Government.

In UK Overseas Territories (see p. 75) the Queen is usually represented by governors, who are responsible to the British Government for the administration of the countries concerned.

Succession, Accession and Coronation

The title to the Crown is derived partly from statute and partly from common law rules of descent. Despite interruptions in the direct line of succession, the hereditary principle upon which it was founded has always been preserved. Sons of the Sovereign still have precedence over daughters in succeeding to the throne. When a daughter succeeds, she becomes Queen Regnant, and has the same powers as a king. The consort of a king takes her husband's rank and style, becoming Queen. The constitution does not give any special rank or privileges to the husband of a Queen Regnant.

Under the Act of Settlement of 1700, only Protestant descendants of Princess Sophia, the Electress of Hanover (a granddaughter of James I of England and VI of Scotland), are eligible to succeed. The order of succession can be altered only by common consent of the countries of the Commonwealth of which the Monarch is Sovereign.

The Sovereign succeeds to the throne as soon as his or her predecessor dies: there is no interregnum. He or she is at once proclaimed at an Accession Council, to which all members of the Privy Council (see p. 39) are summoned. Members of the House of Lords (see p. 41), the Lord Mayor and Aldermen and other leading citizens of the City of London are also invited.

The Sovereign's coronation follows the accession after a convenient interval. The ceremony takes place at Westminster Abbey in London, in the presence of representatives of the Houses of Parliament and of all the major public organisations in the UK. The Prime Ministers and leading members of the other Commonwealth nations and representatives of other countries also attend.

The Monarch's Role in Government

The Queen personifies the State. In law, she is head of the executive, an integral part of the legislature, head of the judiciary, the commander-in-chief of all the armed forces of the Crown and the 'supreme governor' of the established Church of England. As a result of a long process of evolution, during which the Monarchy's absolute power has been progressively reduced, the Queen acts on the advice of her government ministers. The UK is governed by Her Majesty's Government in the name of the Queen.

Within this framework the Queen still takes part in some important acts of government. These include summoning, proroguing (discontinuing until the next session without dissolution) and dissolving Parliament; and giving Royal Assent to Bills passed by Parliament. The Queen formally appoints important office holders, including the Prime Minister and other government ministers (see p. 53), judges, officers in the armed forces, governors, diplomats, bishops and some other senior clergy of the Church of England. She is also involved in pardoning people wrongly convicted of crimes; and in conferring peerages, knighthoods and other honours.[3] In

[2] The other Commonwealth states of which the Queen is Sovereign are: Antigua and Barbuda; Australia; The Bahamas; Barbados; Belize; Canada; Grenada; Jamaica; New Zealand; Papua New Guinea; St Kitts and Nevis; St Lucia; St Vincent and the Grenadines; Solomon Islands; and Tuvalu.

[3] Although most honours are conferred by the Queen on the advice of the Prime Minister, a few are granted by her personally—the Order of the Garter, the Order of the Thistle, the Order of Merit and the Royal Victorian Order.

international affairs the Queen, as Head of State, has the power to declare war and make peace, to recognise foreign states, to conclude treaties and to annex or cede territory.

With rare exceptions (such as appointing the Prime Minister), acts involving the use of 'royal prerogative' powers are now performed by government ministers, who are responsible to Parliament and can be questioned about particular policies. It is not necessary to have Parliament's authority to exercise these prerogative powers, although Parliament may restrict or abolish such rights.

The Queen holds Privy Council meetings (see p. 39), gives audiences to her ministers and officials in the UK and overseas, receives accounts of Cabinet decisions, reads dispatches and signs state papers. She is consulted on many aspects of national life, and must show complete impartiality.

The law provides for a regent to be appointed to perform the royal functions if the monarch is totally incapacitated. The regent would be the Queen's eldest son, the Prince of Wales, then those, in order of succession to the throne, aged 18 or over. In the event of her partial incapacity or absence abroad, the Queen may delegate certain royal functions to the Counsellors of State (her husband the Duke of Edinburgh, the four adults next in line of succession, and the Queen Mother). However, Counsellors of State may not dissolve Parliament (except on the Queen's instructions) or create peers.

Ceremonial and Royal Visits

Ceremony has always been associated with the British monarchy, and many traditional ceremonies continue to take place. Royal marriages and funerals are marked by public ceremony, and the Sovereign's birthday is officially celebrated in June by Trooping the Colour on Horse Guards Parade. State banquets take place when a foreign monarch or head of state visits the UK and investitures are held at Buckingham Palace, the Palace of Holyroodhouse in Scotland and Cardiff Castle in Wales to bestow honours.

Each year the Queen and other members of the Royal Family visit many parts of the UK. They are also closely involved in the work of many charities. For example, the Prince of Wales is actively involved in The Prince's Trust, set up to encourage small firms and self-employment in inner cities, while the Princess Royal is President of the Save the Children Fund. The Queen pays state visits to foreign governments, accompanied by the Duke of Edinburgh. She also tours the other countries of the Commonwealth.

Royal Income and Expenditure

The expenditure arising from the Queen's official duties is met by a payment from public funds known as the Civil List, and by government departments which meet the cost of, for example, royal travel (£16 million in 1999–2000) and the upkeep of the royal palaces and media and information services (£8.5 million in 1999–2000). In return, the Queen has surrendered the hereditary revenues to the Government (£133 million in 1999–2000).

In July 2000 a Royal Trustees' Report recommended that Civil List payments should remain at the 1991 level of £7.9 million a year for a further ten years from 2001. About three-quarters of the Queen's Civil List provision is required to meet the cost of staff. Under the Civil List, the Queen Mother and the Duke of Edinburgh receive annual parliamentary allowances (together amounting to £1 million) to enable them to carry out their public duties. The Prince of Wales does not receive a parliamentary annuity, since as Duke of Cornwall he is entitled to the annual net revenues of the estate of the Duchy of Cornwall.

The Queen's private expenditure as Sovereign is met from the Privy Purse, which is financed mainly from the revenues of the Duchy of Lancaster;[4] her expenditure as a private individual is met from her own personal resources.

Since 1993 the Queen has voluntarily paid income tax on all personal income and on that part of the Privy Purse income which is used

[4] The Duchy of Lancaster is a landed estate which has been held in trust for the Sovereign since 1399. It is kept quite apart from his or her other possessions and is separately administered by the Chancellor of the Duchy of Lancaster.

for private purposes. The Queen also pays tax on any realised capital gains on her private investments and on the private proportion of assets in the Privy Purse. In line with these changes, the Prince of Wales pays income tax on the income from the Duchy of Cornwall so far as it is used for private purposes.

The Privy Council

The Privy Council was formerly the chief source of executive power in the State; its origins can be traced back to the King's Court, which assisted the Norman monarchs in running the government. As the system of Cabinet government developed in the 18th century, however, much of the role of the Privy Council was assumed by the Cabinet (which is still, technically, a committee of Privy Counsellors), although the Council retained certain executive functions. Some government departments originated as committees of the Privy Council.

Nowadays the main function of the Privy Council is as a mechanism through which ministers advise the Queen on the approval of Orders in Council (which are made under prerogative powers, such as Orders approving the grant of Royal Charters of incorporation; and under statutory powers, which enact subordinate legislation). Responsibility for each Order, however, rests with the minister responsible for the policy concerned, regardless of whether he or she is present at the meeting where approval is given.

It is also through the Privy Council that ministers advise the Sovereign on the issue of royal proclamations, such as those summoning or dissolving Parliament. Ministers, as 'Lords of the Privy Council', also have their own statutory responsibilities, which are independent of the powers of the Sovereign in Council. These include supervising the registration authorities of the medical and allied professions.

There are about 500 Privy Counsellors at any one time since appointment as a Privy Counsellor is for life. Members consist of all members of the Cabinet, other senior politicians, senior judges and some appointments from the Commonwealth. It is only members of the government of the day, however, who play any part in its policy work. Membership is accorded by the Sovereign on recommendation of the Prime Minister; Privy Counsellors are entitled to be styled 'Right Honourable'.

Committees of the Privy Council

There are a number of Privy Council committees which normally comprise those ministers with the relevant policy interest. These include prerogative committees, such as those dealing with legislation from the Channel Islands and the Isle of Man, and with petitions for charters of incorporation. Committees may also be provided for by statute, such as those for the universities of Oxford and Cambridge and the Scottish universities. Except for the Judicial Committee, membership is confined to members of the current administration.

The Judicial Committee of the Privy Council is primarily the final court of appeal from courts in UK Overseas Territories and those Commonwealth countries which retained this avenue of appeal after independence. The Committee also hears appeals from the Channel Islands and the Isle of Man, and from the disciplinary and health committees of the medical and allied professions. It is also the Supreme Court for determining cases which bear on the powers and actions of the devolved administrations It has a limited jurisdiction to hear certain ecclesiastical appeals. The members of the Judicial Committee include the Lord Chancellor, the Lords of Appeal in Ordinary, other Privy Counsellors who hold or have held high judicial office and certain judges from the Commonwealth.

The secretariat of the Privy Council is the Privy Council Office, a government department of which the President of the Council, a Cabinet minister, is in charge.

Parliament

Origins of Parliament

The medieval kings were expected to meet all royal expenses, private and public, out of their own revenue. If extra resources were needed for an emergency, such as a war, the Sovereign would seek to persuade his barons in the Great Council—a gathering of leading men which met several times a year—to grant aid. During the 13th century several English kings found the private revenues and baronial aids insufficient to meet the expenses of government. They therefore summoned not only the great feudal magnates but also representatives of counties, cities and towns, primarily to get their assent to extraordinary taxation. In this way the Great Council came to include those who were summoned by name (those who, broadly speaking, were to form the House of Lords) and those who were representatives of communities—the Commons. The two parts, together with the Sovereign, became known as 'Parliament' (the term originally meant a meeting for *parley* or discussion).

Over the course of time the Commons began to realise the strength of its position. By the middle of the 14th century the formula had appeared which in substance was the same as that used nowadays in voting supplies to the Crown—that is, money to the Government—namely, 'by the Commons with the advice of the Lords Spiritual and Temporal'. In 1407 Henry IV pledged that henceforth all money grants should be approved by the House of Commons before being considered by the Lords.

A similar advance was made in the legislative field. Originally the King's legislation needed only the assent of his councillors. Starting with the right of individual commoners to present petitions, the Commons gained the right to submit collective petitions. During the 15th century they gained the right to participate in giving their requests—their 'Bills'—the form of law.

The subsequent development of the power of the House of Commons was built upon these foundations. The constitutional developments of the 17th century led to Parliament securing its position as the supreme legislative authority.

The Powers of Parliament

The three elements which make up Parliament—the Sovereign, the House of Lords and the elected House of Commons—are constituted on different principles. They meet together only on occasions of symbolic significance such as the State Opening of Parliament, when the Commons are summoned by the Sovereign to the House of Lords. The agreement of all three elements is normally required for legislation, but that of the Sovereign is given as a matter of course.

Parliament can legislate for the UK as a whole, and retains the powers to legislate for any parts of it separately. It has, however, undertaken not to legislate on devolved matters without the agreement of the devolved legislatures. Under devolution, it retains responsibility for 'reserved matters' in Scotland, Wales and Northern Ireland (see p. 35) under the Acts of Parliament which set up the administrations in these parts of the UK. In the Channel Islands and the Isle of Man, which are Crown dependencies and not part of the UK, legislation on domestic matters normally takes the form of laws enacted by Island legislatures, but UK laws are sometimes extended to the Islands, with their agreement, for example in areas such as immigration and broadcasting.

As there are no legal restraints imposed by a written constitution, Parliament may legislate as it pleases, subject to the UK's obligations as a member of the European Union (EU—see p. 69). It can make or change law, and overturn established conventions or turn them into law. It can even prolong its own life beyond the normal period without consulting the electorate.

In practice, however, Parliament does not assert its supremacy in this way. Its members bear in mind the common law and normally act in accordance with precedent. The House of Commons is directly responsible to the electorate, and during the 20th century the House of Lords increasingly recognised the supremacy of the elected chamber. The system of party government helps to ensure that Parliament legislates with its responsibility to the electorate in mind.

The Functions of Parliament

The main functions of Parliament are:

- to pass laws;

- to provide (by voting for taxation) the means of carrying on the work of government;
- to scrutinise government policy and administration, including proposals for expenditure; and
- to debate the major issues of the day.

In carrying out these functions Parliament helps to bring the relevant facts and issues before the electorate. By custom, Parliament is also informed before important international treaties and agreements are ratified. The making of treaties is, however, a royal prerogative exercised on the advice of the Government and is not subject to parliamentary approval.

The Meeting of Parliament

A Parliament has a maximum duration of five years, but in practice General Elections are usually held before the end of this term. The maximum life has been prolonged by legislation in rare circumstances such as the two world wars. Dissolution of Parliament and writs for a General Election are ordered by the Sovereign on the advice of the Prime Minister.

The life of a Westminster Parliament is divided into sessions. Each usually lasts for one year—normally beginning and ending in October or November. There are 'adjournments' at night, at weekends, at Christmas, Easter and the late Spring Bank Holiday, and during a long summer break usually starting in late July. The average number of 'sitting' days in a session is about 168 in the House of Commons and about 154 in the House of Lords.[5] At the start of each session the Sovereign's speech to Parliament outlines the Government's policies and proposed legislative programme. Each session is ended by prorogation. Parliament then 'stands prorogued' for a few days until the new session opens. Prorogation brings to an end nearly all parliamentary business: in particular, public Bills which have not been passed by the end of the session are lost, unless the Opposition has agreed they may be carried over to complete their passage the following session.

[5] Taken over the last seven sessions. This includes the 'short' session in the election year of 1997 (1996–97, 79 days) and the 'long' session in 1997–98, 228 days).

The House of Lords

Reform

The Government has begun a step-by-step reform of the House of Lords aimed at making the second chamber more representative of British society at the start of the 21st century. As a first step, the Government has:

- reduced the number of hereditary peers who have the right to sit and vote in the second chamber from over 750 to 92 (see p. 42); and
- reformed arrangements for the nomination of life peers, including setting up an independent Appointments Commission; this is an advisory non-departmental public body with two main functions: to make recommendations for non-party peers and to vet for propriety all nominations for peerages, including those from the political parties.

In January 2000 the Royal Commission on the Reform of the House of Lords (chaired by Lord Wakeham) published its report *A House for the Future*. The report rejected calls for a wholly elected upper chamber and recommended a reformed house of around 550 people with:

- a significant minority of regional members, chosen to reflect the views of regional electorates;
- representatives drawn from all sectors of society;
- a statutory minimum proportion (30 per cent) of women and of men;
- fair representation for members of ethnic minority groups; and
- a broader range of religious representation.

Current Composition

The House of Lords consists of the Lords Spiritual and the Lords Temporal. The Lords

Table 6.1: Transitional House of Lords Composition: by Party Strength, July 2000

Party	Lords Temporal		Lords Spiritual	Total
	Hereditary peers	*Life peers*		
Conservative	52	181		233
Labour	4	195		199
Liberal Democrat	5	58		63
Cross-bench	31	133		164
Other	—	10	26	36
Total	92	577	26	695

Source: House of Lords

Spiritual are the Archbishops of Canterbury and York, the Bishops of London, Durham and Winchester, and the 21 next most senior diocesan bishops of the Church of England. The present Lords Temporal consist of:

- 92 hereditary peers, who were selected to sit in the transitional chamber by ballot from among the membership of the former House of Lords;
- life peers created to assist the House in its judicial duties (Lords of Appeal or 'law lords');[6] and
- all other life peers.

In December 1999 there were 105 women peers, and 27 'law lords' (created under the Appellate Jurisdiction Act 1876).

Life peerages are created by the Sovereign on the advice of the Prime Minister. From autumn 2000, the interim Appointments Commission will have initial responsibility in respect of those people who offer useful advice but do not wish to be involved in party politics. Such peerages are usually granted in recognition of service in politics or other walks of public life or because one of the political parties wishes to have the recipient in the House of Lords.

Three main political parties are represented in the transitional House of Lords; the number of peers eligible to sit and declaring party allegiance at July 2000 is shown in Table 6.1.

Members of the House of Lords (the average daily attendance is about 386) receive no salary for their parliamentary work, but can claim for expenses incurred in attending the House (for which there are maximum daily rates) and certain travelling expenses.

Officers of the House of Lords

The House is presided over by the Lord Chancellor, who takes his place on the woolsack[7] as *ex-officio* Speaker of the House. In the Lord Chancellor's absence, his place is taken by a deputy.

As Clerk of the House of Lords, the Clerk of the Parliaments is responsible for the records of proceedings of the House of Lords and for the text of Acts of Parliament. The postholder is the accounting officer for the House, and is in charge of its administrative staff, known as the Parliament Office. The Gentleman Usher of the Black Rod, usually known simply as 'Black Rod', is responsible for security, accommodation and services in the House of Lords' part of the Palace of Westminster.

The House of Commons

The House of Commons is elected by universal adult suffrage (see p. 43) and consists of 659 Members of Parliament (MPs). In June 2000 there were 122 women MPs and nine MPs from ethnic minorities. Of the 659 seats, 529 are for England, 40 for Wales, 72 for

[6] The House of Lords is the final court of appeal for civil cases in the UK and for criminal cases in England, Wales and Northern Ireland.

[7] The woolsack is a seat in the form of a large cushion stuffed with wool from several Commonwealth countries; it is a tradition dating from the medieval period, when wool was the chief source of the country's wealth.

Scotland, and 18 for Northern Ireland. The number of Scottish seats is being reviewed in the light of the powers now devolved to the Scottish Parliament (see chapter 4).

General Elections are held after a Parliament has been dissolved and a new one summoned by the Sovereign. When an MP dies or resigns,[8] or is given a peerage, a by-election takes place. Members are paid an annual salary of £48,371 (from April 2000) and an office costs allowance (from April 2000) of up to £51,572. Other allowances include travel allowances, a supplement for London members and, for provincial members, subsistence allowances and allowances for second homes. (For ministers' salaries see p. 54.)

Officers of the House of Commons

The chief officer of the House of Commons is the Speaker, elected by MPs to preside over the House. Other officers include the Chairman of Ways and Means and two deputy chairmen, who act as Deputy Speakers. They are elected by the House on the nomination of the Government but are drawn from the Opposition as well as the government party. They, like the Speaker, neither speak nor vote other than in their official capacity (when deputising for the Speaker). Responsibility for the administration of the House rests with the House of Commons Commission, a statutory body chaired by the Speaker.

Permanent officers (who are not MPs) include the Clerk of the House of Commons, who is the principal adviser to the Speaker on the House's privileges and procedures. The Clerk's other responsibilities relate to the conduct of the business of the House and its committees. The Clerk is also accounting officer for the House. The Serjeant at Arms, who waits upon the Speaker, carries out certain orders of the House. The postholder is also the official housekeeper of the Commons' part of the building, and is responsible for security. Other officers serve the House in the Library, the Department of the Official Report (*Hansard*), the Finance and Administration Department, and the Refreshment Department.

[8] An MP who wishes to resign from the House can do so only by applying for an office under the Crown as Crown Steward or Bailiff of the Chiltern Hundreds, or Steward of the Manor of Northstead, thereby disqualifying him or herself from membership of the House of Commons.

Parliamentary Electoral System

For electoral purposes the UK is divided into constituencies, each of which returns one member to the House of Commons. To ensure that constituency electorates are kept roughly equal, four permanent Parliamentary Boundary Commissions, one each for England, Wales, Scotland and Northern Ireland, keep constituencies under review. They recommend any adjustment of seats that may seem necessary in the light of population movements or other changes. Reviews are conducted every eight to 12 years. The recommendations in the Commissions' last general reviews were approved by Parliament in 1995. The Parliamentary Boundary Commission for England has begun a general review and aims to produce its report at the end of 2005.

Voters

British citizens, together with citizens of other Commonwealth countries and citizens of the Irish Republic resident in the UK, may vote in parliamentary elections provided they are:

- aged 18 or over;
- included in the annual register of electors for the constituency; and
- not subject to any legal incapacity to vote.

People not entitled to vote include people under 18, members of the House of Lords, foreign nationals (other than Commonwealth citizens or citizens of the Irish Republic), some patients detained under mental health legislation, sentenced prisoners and people convicted within the previous five years of corrupt or illegal election practices. Members of the armed forces, Crown servants and staff of the British Council employed overseas (together with their wives or husbands if accompanying them) may be registered for an address in the constituency where they would live but for their service. British citizens living abroad may apply to register as electors for a period of up to 20 years after they have left the UK.

Voting Procedures

Each elector may cast one vote, normally in person at a polling station. Electors who cannot reasonably be expected to vote in person at their local polling station on polling day—for example, electors away on holiday—may apply for an absent vote at a particular election. Electors who are physically incapacitated or unable to vote in person because of the nature of their work or because they have moved to a new area may apply for an absent vote. People entitled to an absent vote may vote by post or by proxy, although postal ballot papers cannot be sent to addresses outside the UK.

Voting is not compulsory; 71.5 per cent of a total electorate of 44.2 million people voted in the General Election in May 1997. The simple majority system of voting is currently used. Candidates are elected if they have more votes than any of the other candidates (although not necessarily an absolute majority over all other candidates). The Government proposes to hold a referendum on the voting system for the House of Commons.

Candidates

British citizens and citizens of other Commonwealth countries, together with citizens of the Irish Republic, may stand for election as MPs provided they are aged 21 or over and are not disqualified. Those disqualified include undischarged bankrupts; people who have been sentenced to more than one year's imprisonment; clergy of the Church of England, Church of Scotland, Church of Ireland and Roman Catholic Church; peers; and holders of certain offices listed in the House of Commons Disqualification Act 1975.

A candidate's nomination for election must be proposed and seconded by two electors registered as voters in the constituency and signed by eight other electors. Candidates do not have to be backed by a political party. A candidate must also deposit £500, which is returned if he or she receives 5 per cent or more of the votes cast.

The maximum sum a candidate may spend on a general election campaign is £4,965 plus 4.2 pence for each elector in a borough constituency, or 5.6 pence for each elector in a county constituency. Higher limits have been set for by-elections in order to reflect the fact that they are often regarded as tests of national opinion in the period between General Elections. The maximum sum is £19,863 plus 16.9 pence for each elector in borough seats, and 22.2 pence for each elector in county seats. A candidate may post an election communication to each elector in the constituency free of charge. All election expenses, apart from the candidate's personal expenses, are subject to the statutory maximum.

The Political Party System

The party system, which has existed in one form or another since the 18th century, is an essential element in the working of the constitution. The present system depends upon the existence of organised political parties, each of which presents its policies to the electorate for approval; in practice most candidates in elections, and almost all winning candidates, belong to one of the main parties. A system of voluntary registration for political parties in the UK was introduced in 1998. Registration is necessary for the proportional representation electoral systems which involve 'lists' of candidates, used in elections to the Scottish Parliament, the National Assembly for Wales and, for the first time nationally in June 1999, for electing UK members to the European Parliament (see p. 69). Registration helps prevent the use of misleading descriptions on ballot papers at election, since only candidates representing a registered political party are permitted to have the name and emblem of the party printed on the ballot paper.

For the last 150 years a predominantly two-party system has existed in Britain. Since 1945 either the Conservative Party, whose origins go back to the 18th century, or the Labour

Party, which emerged in the last decade of the 19th century, has held power. The Liberal Democrats were formed in 1988 when the Liberal Party, which also traced its origins to the 18th century, merged with the Social Democratic Party, formed in 1981. Other parties include two national parties, Plaid Cymru (founded in Wales in 1925) and the Scottish National Party (founded in 1934). Northern Ireland has a number of parties. They include the Ulster Unionist Party, formed in the early part of the 20th century; the Democratic Unionist Party, founded in 1971 by a group which broke away from the Ulster Unionists; the Social Democratic and Labour Party, founded in 1970; and Sinn Féin.[9]

Since 1945 eight General Elections have been won by the Conservative Party and seven by the Labour Party; the great majority of members of the House of Commons have belonged to one of these two parties.

The party which wins most seats (although not necessarily the most votes) at a General Election, or which has the support of a majority of members in the House of Commons, usually forms the Government. By tradition, the leader of the majority party is asked by the Sovereign to form a government. About 100 of its members in the House of Commons and the House of Lords receive ministerial appointments (including appointment to the Cabinet—see p. 55) on the advice of the Prime Minister. The largest minority party becomes the official Opposition, with its own leader and 'shadow cabinet'.

Table 6.2: General Election Results by Party, 1997

	Number of MPs elected	*% share of vote*
Labour	418	43.2
Conservative	165	30.7
Liberal Democrat	46	16.8
Plaid Cymru	4	0.5
Scottish National	6	2.0
Northern Ireland parties	18	2.1
Others	1	0.5

The Party System in Parliament

Leaders of the Government and Opposition sit on the front benches of the Commons with their supporters ('the backbenchers') sitting behind them. Similar arrangements for the parties apply to the House of Lords; however, a significant number of Lords do not wish to be associated with any political party, and sit on the 'cross-benches'.

The effectiveness of the party system in Parliament rests largely on the relationship between the Government and the opposition parties. Depending on the relative strengths of the parties in the House of Commons, the Opposition may seek to overthrow the Government by defeating it in a vote on a 'matter of confidence'. In general, however, its aims are to contribute to the formulation of policy and legislation by constructive criticism; to oppose government proposals it considers objectionable; to seek amendments to Government Bills; and to put forward its own policies in order to improve its chances of winning the next General Election.

The detailed arrangements of government business are settled, under the direction of the Prime Minister and the Leaders of the two Houses, by the Government Chief Whips of each House in consultation with the Opposition Chief Whips. The Chief Whips together constitute the 'usual channels' often referred to when the question of finding time for a particular item of business is discussed. The Leaders of the two Houses are responsible for enabling the Houses to debate matters about which they are concerned.

Parliamentary party control is exercised by the Chief Whips and their assistants, who are chosen within the party (usually by the Leader). Their duties include keeping members informed of forthcoming parliamentary business, maintaining the party's voting strength by ensuring members attend important debates, and passing on to the party leadership the opinions of backbench members. Party discipline tends to be less strong in the Lords than in the Commons, since peers have less hope of high office and no need of party support in elections.

[9] Sinn Féin is the political wing of the IRA.

Financial Assistance to Parties

The Government plans to make party funding more open, control spending on elections and ensure the fair conduct of referendums. In December 1999, it introduced the Political Parties, Elections and Referendums Bill which contains provision for:

- a registration scheme to bring parties under specified funding controls;
- a requirement on parties to disclose the source and amount of donations above £5,000;
- a ban on the acceptance of donations made from outside the UK;
- national spending limits on parties determined by the number of constituencies and/or regions contested in an election—in a General Election, a party with candidates in all 659 seats could spend up to £19.77 million;
- a framework for the fair conduct of referendums; and
- a new Electoral Commission to supervise the financial restrictions on parties and oversee referendums—it would also take over the functions of the Boundary Commissions and the Local Government Commission for England, and have broad responsibility for electoral law, provide guidance on party political broadcasts and promote understanding of electoral and political matters.

Parliamentary Procedure

Parliamentary procedure is based on custom and precedent, partly codified by each House in its Standing Orders. The system of debate is similar in both Houses. Every subject starts off as a proposal or 'motion' by a member. After debate, in which each member (except the mover of the motion) may speak only once, the motion may be withdrawn: if it is not, the Speaker or Chairman 'puts the question' whether to agree with the motion or not. The question may be decided without voting, or by a simple majority vote. The main difference in procedure between the two Houses is that the Speaker or Chairman in the Lords has no powers of order; instead such matters are decided by the general feeling of the House, which is sometimes interpreted by the Leader of the House.

In the Commons the Speaker has full authority to enforce the rules of the House and must guard against the abuse of procedure and protect minority rights. The Speaker has discretion on whether to allow a motion to end discussion so that a matter may be put to the vote, and has powers to put a stop to irrelevance and repetition in debate. In cases of grave disorder the Speaker can adjourn or suspend the sitting. The Speaker may order members who have broken the rules of behaviour of the House to leave the Chamber or can initiate their suspension for a number of days.

The Speaker supervises voting in the Commons and announces the final result. In a tied vote the Speaker gives a casting vote (usually to maintain the *status quo*), without expressing an opinion on the merits of the question. Voting procedure in the House of Lords is broadly similar, although the Lord Chancellor may vote but does not have a casting vote.

Modernisation of the House of Commons

A Select Committee on Modernisation of the House of Commons, set up in 1997, made several recommendations for modernising the legislative process, most of which have now been implemented. Among them are:

- measures to improve the examination of proposed legislation, including a system for publishing Bills in draft and the setting up of *ad hoc* House of Commons or joint Committees to conduct pre-legislative scrutiny;
- the experimental use of another chamber—Westminster Hall, formally known as the Grand Committee Room—mainly for adjournment debates and debates on Green Papers and other consultative documents issued by the Government;
- reformed procedures for the scrutiny of European legislation;
- abolishing old-fashioned customs, such as giving preference to hearing Privy

Counsellors in debates and the rule preventing MPs from quoting from speeches made in the Lords;

- experimenting with the hours during which the House sits; and
- carrying over, in defined circumstances, public Bills from one session to the next.

Financial Interests

The Commons has a public register of MPs' financial (and some non-financial) interests. Members with a financial interest must declare it when speaking in the House or in Committee and must indicate it when giving notice of a question or motion. In other proceedings of the House or in dealings with other members, ministers or civil servants, MPs must also disclose any relevant financial interest. MPs cannot advocate matters in the House which are related to the source of any personal financial interest.

The House of Lords also has a Register of Interests, on lines similar to that for MPs. It, too, is open to public inspection.

Parliamentary Commissioner for Standards

The post of Parliamentary Commissioner for Standards was created in 1995, following recommendations of the Committee on Standards in Public Life (see p. 59). The Commissioner, who is independent of government, can advise MPs on matters of standards, and conduct a preliminary investigation into complaints about alleged breaches of the rules by Members. The Commissioner reports to the House of Commons Select Committee on Standards and Privileges.

Public Access to Parliamentary Proceedings

Proceedings of both Houses are normally public. The minutes and speeches (transcribed in *Hansard*, the Official Report) are published daily.

The records of the Lords from 1497 and of the Commons from 1547, together with the parliamentary and political papers of a number of former members of both Houses, are available to the public through the House of Lords Record Office. A wide range of information on all aspects of the workings of Parliament can be found on the Houses of Parliament website.

The proceedings of both Houses of Parliament may be broadcast on television and radio, either live or, more usually, in recorded or edited form. Complete coverage is available on cable and satellite television and the 'webcasting' of Parliament is currently being considered.

The Law-making Process

Statute law consists of Acts of Parliament and delegated legislation made by ministers and others under powers given to them by Act (see p. 49). While the interpretation of the law undergoes constant refinement in the courts (see p. 210), changes to statute law are made by Parliament.

Draft laws take the form of parliamentary Bills. Proposals for legislation affecting the powers of particular bodies (such as individual local authorities) or the rights of individuals (such as certain proposals relating to railways, roads and harbours) are known as Private Bills, and are subject to a special form of parliamentary procedure. Bills which change the general law and which constitute the more significant part of the parliamentary legislative process are Public Bills.

Public Bills can be introduced into either House, by a government minister or by an ordinary ('private' or 'backbench') member or peer. Most Public Bills that become Acts of Parliament are introduced by a government minister and are known as 'Government Bills'. Bills introduced by other MPs or Lords are known as 'Private Members' Bills'.

The main Bills which constitute the Government's legislative programme are announced in the Queen's Speech at the State Opening of Parliament, which usually takes place in November, and the Bills themselves are introduced into one or other of the Houses over the succeeding weeks.

Before a Government Bill is drafted, there may be consultation with professional bodies, voluntary organisations and other agencies interested in the subject, and with interest and pressure groups seeking to promote specific causes. 'White Papers', which are government statements of policy, often contain proposals for legislative changes; these may be debated in Parliament before a Bill is introduced. As part of the process of modernising procedures (see p. 46), some Bills are now published in draft for pre-legislative scrutiny before beginning their passage through Parliament. The Government may also publish consultation papers, sometimes called 'Green Papers', setting out proposals which are still taking shape and seeking comments from the public.

Passage of Public Bills

Public Bills must normally be passed by both Houses. Bills relating mainly to financial matters are almost invariably introduced in the Commons. Under the provisions of the Parliament Acts 1911 and 1949, the powers of the Lords in relation to 'money Bills' are very restricted. The Parliament Acts also provide for a Bill to be passed by the Commons without consent of the Lords in certain (very rare) circumstances.

The process of passing a Public Bill is similar in each House. On presentation the Bill is considered, without debate, to have been read for a first time and is printed. After an interval, which may be between one day and several weeks, a Government Bill will receive its second reading debate, during which the general principles of the Bill are discussed.

If it obtains a second reading in the Commons, a Bill will normally be submitted to a standing committee (see p. 50) for detailed examination and amendment. In the Lords, the committee stage usually takes place on the floor of the House, and this procedure may also be followed in the Commons if that House so decides (usually in cases where there is a need to pass the Bill quickly or where it raises matters of constitutional importance).

The committee stage is followed by the report stage ('consideration') on the floor of the House, during which further amendments may be made. In the Commons, the report stage is usually followed immediately by the third reading debate, when the Bill is reviewed in its final form. In the Lords, the third reading debate usually takes place on a different day; a Bill may be further amended at third reading.

After passing its third reading in one House, a Bill is sent to the other House, where it passes through all its stages once more and where it is, more often than not, further amended. Amendments made by the second House must be agreed by the first, or a compromise reached, before a Bill can go for Royal Assent.

In the Commons the House may vote to limit the time available for consideration of a Bill. This is done by passing a 'timetable' motion proposed by the Government, commonly referred to as a 'guillotine'. There are special procedures for Public Bills which consolidate existing legislation.

Royal Assent

When a Bill has passed through all its parliamentary stages, it is sent to the Queen for Royal Assent, after which it is part of the law of the land and becomes an Act of Parliament. The Royal Assent has not been refused since 1707. In the 1998–99 session 35 Public Bills were enacted.

Limitations on the Power of the Lords

Most Government Bills introduced and passed in the Lords go through the Commons without difficulty, but a Lords Bill which was unacceptable to the Commons would not become law. The Lords, on the other hand, do not generally prevent Bills insisted upon by the Commons from becoming law, though they will often amend them and return them to the Commons for further consideration.

By convention, the Lords pass Bills authorising taxation or national expenditure without amendment. A Bill that deals only with taxation or expenditure must become law within one month of being sent to the Lords, whether or not the Lords agree to it, unless the Commons directs otherwise. If no agreement is reached between the two Houses on a non-financial Commons Bill, the Lords can delay the Bill for a period which, in practice, amounts to at least 13 months. Following this the Bill may be submitted to the Queen for Royal Assent, provided it has been passed a second time by the Commons. There is one important exception: any Bill to lengthen the life of a Parliament requires the full assent of both Houses.

The limits to the power of the Lords are based on the belief that nowadays the main legislative function of the non-elected House is to act as a chamber of revision, complementing but not rivalling the elected House.

Private Members' Bills

Early in each session backbench members of the Commons ballot (draw lots) for the opportunity to introduce a Bill on one of the Fridays during the session when such Bills have precedence over government business. The first 20 members whose names are drawn win this privilege, but it does not guarantee that their Bills will pass into law. Members may also present a Bill on any day without debate, while on most Tuesdays and Wednesdays on which the Commons is sitting there is also an opportunity to seek leave to present a Bill under the 'ten minute rule'. This provides an opportunity for a brief speech by the member proposing the Bill (and by one who opposes it).

In most sessions some become law (eight in the 1998–99 session). Private Members' Bills do not often call for the expenditure of public money; but if they do they cannot proceed to committee stage unless the Government decides to provide the necessary money. Peers may introduce Private Members' Bills in the House of Lords at any time. A Private Member's Bill passed by one House will not proceed in the other unless taken up by a member of that House.

Private and Hybrid Bills

Private Bills are promoted by people or organisations outside Parliament (often local authorities) to give them special legal powers. They go through a similar procedure to Public Bills, but most of the work is done in committee, where procedures follow a semi-judicial pattern. Hybrid Bills are Public Bills which may affect private rights, for example, the Channel Tunnel Rail Link Bill, which was passed in 1996. As with Private Bills, the passage of Hybrid Bills through Parliament is governed by special procedures which allow those affected to put their case.

Delegated Legislation

In order to reduce unnecessary pressure on parliamentary time, primary legislation often gives ministers or other authorities the power to regulate administrative details by means of secondary or 'delegated' legislation (usually in the form of 'statutory instruments'). To minimise any risk that delegating powers to the executive might undermine the authority of Parliament or to the devolved legislatures, such powers are normally delegated only to authorities directly accountable to Parliament. Moreover, Acts of Parliament which delegate such powers usually provide for some measure of direct parliamentary control over proposed delegated legislation, by giving Parliament the opportunity to affirm or annul it. Certain Acts also require that organisations affected must be consulted before rules and orders can be made.

A joint committee of both Houses reports on the technical propriety of these 'statutory instruments'. In order to save time on the floor of the House, the Commons uses standing committees to debate the merits of instruments; actual decisions are taken by the House as a whole. In the Lords, debates on statutory instruments take place on the floor of the House. The House of Lords has appointed a delegated powers scrutiny committee which examines the appropriateness of the powers to make secondary legislation in Bills.

Parliamentary Committees

Committees of the Whole House

Either House may pass a resolution setting itself up as a Committee of the Whole House to consider Bills in detail after their second reading. This permits unrestricted discussion: the general rule that an MP or Peer may speak only once on each motion does not apply in committee.

Standing Committees

House of Commons standing committees debate and consider Public Bills at the committee stage. The committee considers the Bill clause by clause, and may amend it before reporting it back to the House. Ordinary standing committees do not have names but are referred to simply as Standing Committee A, B, C, and so on; a new set of members is appointed to them to consider each Bill. Each committee has between 16 and 50 members, with a party balance reflecting as far as possible that in the House as a whole. The standing committees currently still include two Scottish standing committees, and the Scottish, Welsh and Northern Ireland Grand Committees.

The Scottish Grand Committee comprises all 72 Scottish MPs (and may be convened anywhere in Scotland as well as at Westminster). It may consider the principle of any Scottish Bill at the second and third reading stages, where such a Bill has been referred to the Committee by the House for that purpose. It also debates other matters concerning Scotland. In addition, its business includes questions tabled for oral answer, ministerial statements and other debates, including those on statutory instruments referred to it.

The Welsh Grand Committee, consisting of all 40 Welsh MPs and up to five others who may be added from time to time, considers Bills referred to it at second reading stage, questions tabled for oral answer, ministerial statements, and other matters relating exclusively to Wales.

The Northern Ireland Grand Committee considers Bills at the second and third stages, takes oral questions and ministerial statements, and debates matters relating specifically to Northern Ireland. It includes all sitting Northern Ireland MPs and up to 25 others as nominated by the committee of selection. The Belfast Agreement envisages a continuing role for the Northern Ireland Grand and Select Committees to scrutinise the responsibilities of the Secretary of State.

There is a Standing Committee on Regional Affairs, consisting of all Members sitting for constituencies in England, plus up to five others. It was revived in April 2000.

There are also standing committees to debate proposed European legislation, and to scrutinise statutory instruments and draft statutory instruments brought forward by the Government.

In the Lords, various sorts of committees on Bills may be used instead of, or as well as, a Committee of the Whole House. Such committees include Public Bill Committees, Special Public Bill Committees, Grand Committees, Select Committees and Scottish Select Committees.

Select Committees

Select committees are appointed for a particular task, generally one of enquiry, investigation and scrutiny. They report their conclusions and recommendations to the House as a whole; in many cases their recommendations invite a response from the Government, which is also reported to the House. A select committee may be appointed for a Parliament, or for a session, or for as long as it takes to complete its task. To help Parliament with the control of the executive by examining aspects of public policy, expenditure and administration, 16 committees, established by the House of Commons, examine the work of the main government departments and their associated public bodies. The Foreign Affairs Select Committee, for example, 'shadows' the work of the Foreign & Commonwealth Office. The Environmental Audit Committee was set up in 1997 (see p. 306). The committees are constituted on a basis which is in approximate proportion to party strength in the House.

Other regular Commons select committees include those on Public Accounts, Standards and Privileges, and European Legislation. 'Domestic' select committees also cover the internal workings of Parliament.

Each House has a select committee to keep it informed of EU developments, and to enable it to scrutinise and debate EU policies and proposals, while three Commons standing committees debate specific European legislative proposals. Ministers also make regular statements about EU business.

In their examination of government policies, expenditure and administration, committees may question ministers, civil servants, and interested bodies and individuals. Through hearings and published reports, they bring before Parliament and the public an extensive body of fact and informed opinion on many issues, and build up considerable expertise in their subjects of inquiry.

In the House of Lords, besides the Appeal and Appellate Committees in which the bulk of the House's judicial work is transacted, there are two major select committees: on the European Community and on Science and Technology. *Ad hoc* committees may also be set up to consider particular issues (or, sometimes, a particular Bill), and 'domestic' committees—as in the Commons—cover the internal workings of the House.

Joint Committees

Joint committees, with a membership drawn from both Houses, are appointed in each session to deal with Consolidation Bills[10] and statutory instruments (see p. 49). The two Houses may also agree to set up joint select committees on other subjects.

Unofficial Party Committees

The Parliamentary Labour Party comprises all members of the party in both Houses. When the Labour Party is in office, a parliamentary committee, half of whose members are elected and half of whom are government representatives, acts as a channel of communication between the Government and its backbenchers in both Houses. When the party is in opposition, the Parliamentary Labour Party is organised under the direction of an elected parliamentary committee, which acts as the 'shadow cabinet'.

The Conservative and Unionist Members' Committee (the 1922 Committee) consists of the backbench membership of the party in the House of Commons. When the Conservative Party is in office, ministers attend its meetings by invitation and not by right. When the party is in opposition, the whole membership of the party may attend meetings. The leader appoints a consultative committee, which acts as the party's 'shadow cabinet'.

[10] A Consolidation Bill brings together several existing Acts into one, with the aim of simplifying the statutes.

Other Forms of Parliamentary Control

In addition to the system of scrutiny by select committees, both Houses offer a number of opportunities for the examination of government policy by both the Opposition and the Government's own backbenchers. In the House of Commons, the opportunities include:

- Question Time, when for 55 minutes on Monday, Tuesday, Wednesday and Thursday, ministers answer MPs' questions. The Prime Minister's Question Time takes place for half an hour every Wednesday when the House is sitting. Parliamentary Questions are one means of seeking information about the Government's intentions. They are also a way of raising grievances brought to MPs' notice by constituents. MPs may also put questions to ministers for written answer; the questions and answers are published in *Hansard*. There are about 60,000 questions every year.
- Adjournment debates, when MPs use motions for the adjournment of the House to raise constituency cases or matters of public concern. There is a half-hour adjournment period at the end of the business of the day, and opportunities for several adjournment debates on Wednesday mornings. Since November 1999, under experimental measures to modernise and reform parliamentary procedures, a second chamber, Westminster Hall, has also been widely used for adjournment debates. In addition, an MP wishing to discuss a 'specific and important matter that should have urgent consideration' may, at the end of Question Time, seek leave to move the adjournment of the House. On the very few occasions when leave is obtained, the matter is debated for three hours in what is known as an emergency debate, usually on the following day.

- Early day motions (EDMs) provide a further opportunity for backbench MPs to express their views on particular issues. A number of EDMs are tabled each sitting day; they are very rarely debated but can be useful in gauging the degree of support for the topic by the number of signatures of other MPs which the motion attracts.
- Opposition days (21 in the 1998–99 session) when the Opposition can choose subjects for debate. Of these days, 17 were at the disposal of the Leader of the Opposition and four at the disposal of the second largest opposition party.
- Debates on three days in each session on details of proposed government expenditure, chosen by the Liaison Committee (a select committee largely made up of select committee chairmen, which considers general matters relating to the work of select committees).

  Procedural opportunities for criticism of the Government also arise during the debate on the Queen's Speech at the beginning of each session; during debates on motions of censure for which the Government provides time; and during debates on the Government's legislative and other proposals.

Similar opportunities for criticism and examination of government policy are provided in the House of Lords at daily Question Time, during debates and by means of questions for written answer.

Control of Finances

The main responsibilities of Parliament, and more particularly of the House of Commons, in overseeing the revenue of the State and public expenditure, are to authorise the raising of taxes and duties, and the various objects of expenditure and the sum to be spent on each. Parliament also has to satisfy itself that the sums granted are spent only for the purposes which it intended. No payment out of the central government's public funds can be made, and no taxation or loans authorised, except by Act of Parliament. However, limited interim payments can be made from the Contingencies Fund.

The Finance Act is the most important of the annual statutes, and authorises the raising of revenue. The legislation is based on the Chancellor of the Exchequer's Budget statement (see p. 389). Scrutiny of public expenditure is carried out by House of Commons select committees (see p. 50).

Forcing the Government to Resign

The final control is the ability of the House of Commons to force the Government to resign by passing a resolution of 'no confidence'. The Government must also resign if the House rejects a proposal which the Government considers so vital to its policy that it has declared it a 'matter of confidence' or if the House refuses to vote the money required for the public service.

Parliamentary Commissioner for Administration

The Parliamentary Ombudsman—officially known as the Parliamentary Commissioner for Administration—investigates complaints from members of the public (referred through MPs) alleging that they have suffered injustice arising from maladministration. The Ombudsman is independent of government and reports to a select committee of the House of Commons. The Ombudsman's jurisdiction covers central government departments and agencies and a large number of non-departmental public bodies (NDPBs). He or she cannot investigate complaints about government policy, the content of legislation or relations with other countries.

In making investigations, the Commissioner has access to all departmental papers, and has powers to summon those from whom he wishes to take evidence. When an investigation is completed, he sends a report with his findings to the MP who referred the complaint (with a copy for the complainant). When a complaint is justified, the Ombudsman normally recommends that the department or other body provides redress (which can include a financial remedy for the complainant in appropriate cases). There is no appeal against the Ombudsman's decision. He submits an annual report to Parliament, and publishes selected cases twice a year.

The Ombudsman received 1,612 new complaints in 1999–2000 (an increase of 7 per cent over the previous year). He settled 1,601 complaints and completed 313 full investigations. Complaints against the Department of Social Security accounted for 47 per cent of the total received.

The Parliamentary Ombudsman also investigates complaints arising from breaches of the Code of Practice on Access to Government Information (see p. 58).

Separate arrangements for a Scottish Parliamentary Commissioner for Administration and a Welsh Administration Ombudsman have been set up to deal with complaints about the Scottish Executive, the National Assembly for Wales and devolved public bodies. Complaints to the Scottish Commissioner are referred through Members of the Scottish Parliament; complaints to the Welsh Administration Ombudsman can be made direct.

Parliamentary Privilege

Each House of Parliament has certain rights and immunities to protect it from obstruction in carrying out its duties. The rights apply collectively to each House and to its staff and individually to each member. They include freedom of speech; first call on the attendance of its members, who are therefore free from arrest in civil actions and exempt from serving on juries, or being compelled to attend court as witnesses; and the right of access to the Crown, which is a collective privilege of the House. Further privileges include the rights of the House to control its own proceedings (so that it is able, for instance, to exclude 'strangers'[11] if it wishes); to decide upon legal disqualifications for membership and to declare a seat vacant on such grounds; and to punish for breach of its privileges and for contempt. Parliament has the right to punish anybody, inside or outside the House, who commits a breach of privilege—that is, offends against the rights of the House.

The privileges of the House of Lords are broadly similar to those of the Commons. The law of privilege has been examined by a Joint Committee of both Houses of Parliament, which published its report in March 1999. The committee's main recommendation was to call for a Parliamentary Privileges Act codifying parliamentary privilege as a whole and explaining its relevance, both to MPs and to the electorate as a whole.

Her Majesty's Government

Her Majesty's Government is the body of ministers responsible for the conduct of national affairs. The Prime Minister is appointed by the Queen, and all other ministers are appointed by the Queen on the recommendation of the Prime Minister. Most ministers are members of the Commons, although the Government is also fully represented by ministers in the Lords. The Lord Chancellor is always a member of the House of Lords.

The composition of governments can vary both in the number of ministers and in the titles of some offices. New ministerial offices may be created, others may be abolished, and functions may be transferred from one minister to another.

Prime Minister

The Prime Minister is also, by tradition, First Lord of the Treasury and Minister for the Civil Service. The Prime Minister's unique position of authority derives from majority support in the House of Commons and from the power to appoint and dismiss ministers. By modern convention, the Prime Minister always sits in the Commons.

The Prime Minister presides over the Cabinet (see p. 55), is responsible for allocating functions among ministers and informs the Queen at regular meetings of the general business of the Government.

The Prime Minister's other responsibilities include recommending a number of appointments to the Queen. These include: Church of England archbishops, bishops and certain deans and some 200 other clergy in Crown 'livings'; senior judges, such as the

[11] All those who are not members or officials of either House.

Lord Chief Justice; Privy Counsellors; and Lord-Lieutenants. He or she also recommends certain civil appointments, such as Lord High Commissioner to the General Assembly of the Church of Scotland (after consultation with the First Minister), The Poet Laureate, The Constable of the Tower (of London), and some university posts; and appointments to various public boards and institutions, such as the BBC (British Broadcasting Corporation), as well as various royal and statutory commissions. Recommendations are likewise made for the award of many civil honours and distinctions and of Civil List pensions (pensions for people who have achieved eminence in the arts or science and are in financial need).

The Prime Minister's Office supports him in his role as head of government. This includes policy advice, tracking the delivery of government commitments and initiatives, and effective communications to Parliament, the media and the public.

Departmental Ministers

Ministers in charge of government departments are usually in the Cabinet; they are known as 'Secretary of State' or 'Minister', or may have a special title, as in the case of the Chancellor of the Exchequer.

Non-departmental Ministers

The holders of various traditional offices, namely the President of the Council, the Chancellor of the Duchy of Lancaster, the Lord Privy Seal, the Paymaster General and, from time to time, Ministers without Portfolio, may have few or no departmental duties. They are thus available to perform any duties the Prime Minister may wish to give them. In the present administration, for example, the President of the Council is Leader of the House of Commons, and the Chancellor of the Duchy of Lancaster is Minister for the Cabinet Office.

Lord Chancellor and Law Officers

The Lord Chancellor holds a special position, as both a minister with departmental functions and the head of the judiciary (see p. 211). The three Law Officers of the Crown advising the UK Government are the Attorney-General and the Solicitor-General (for England and Wales) and the Advocate-General for Scotland.

Other Ministers

Ministers of State are middle-ranking ministers. They normally have specific responsibilities, and are sometimes given titles which reflect these functions, for example, 'Minister for School Standards' and 'Minister for Small Business and E-Commerce'.

The most junior ministers are Parliamentary Under-Secretaries of State (or, where the senior minister is not a Secretary of State, simply Parliamentary Secretaries). They may be given responsibility, directly under the departmental minister, for specific aspects of the department's work.

Ministerial Salaries

The salaries of ministers in the House of Commons (from April 2000) range from £26,053 a year for junior ministers to £66,172 for Cabinet ministers. In the House of Lords salaries range from £57,244 for junior ministers to £85,983 for Cabinet ministers. The Prime Minister is entitled to a salary of £110,287.[12] The Lord Chancellor receives £167,760.

In addition to their ministerial salaries, ministers in the Commons, including the Prime Minister, receive a full parliamentary salary of £48,371 a year in recognition of their constituency responsibilities and can claim the other allowances which are paid to all MPs.

The Leader of the Opposition in the Commons receives a salary of £60,659 (and also the full parliamentary salary of £48,371); two Opposition whips in the Commons and the Opposition Leader and Chief Whip in the Lords also receive additional salaries.

[12] The present Prime Minister and his Cabinet colleagues have declined the full salary to which they are entitled; the Prime Minister draws instead a salary of £64,580, while Cabinet ministers in the Commons draw £48,516 and in the Lords £72,729.

The Cabinet

The Cabinet is composed of about 20 ministers (the number can vary) chosen by the Prime Minister and may include both departmental and non-departmental ministers. The Cabinet reconciles ministers' individual responsibilities with their collective responsibilities as members of the Government. It is the ultimate arbiter of all government policy.

Cabinet Meetings

The Cabinet meets in private and its proceedings are confidential, although after 30 years Cabinet papers may be made available for inspection in the Public Record Office at Kew, Surrey.

Normally the Cabinet meets weekly during parliamentary sittings, and less often when Parliament is not sitting. Cabinet Committees relieve the pressure on Cabinet itself by settling business in a smaller forum or at a lower level, when possible, or at least by clarifying issues and defining points of disagreement. Committees enable decisions to be fully considered by those ministers most closely concerned in a way that ensures that the Government as a whole can be expected to accept responsibility for them. They act by implied devolution of authority from the Cabinet and their decisions therefore have the same formal status as decisions by the full Cabinet.

There are Cabinet Committees dealing, for example, with defence and overseas policy, economic policy, home and social affairs, the environment, and local government. A new committee set up by the present Government, the Joint Consultative Committee, became the first to involve politicians from a party outside the Government—the Liberal Democrats. The Committee considers constitutional issues.

The membership and terms of reference of all ministerial Cabinet Committees are published. Where appropriate, the Secretary of the Cabinet and other senior Cabinet Office officials attend meetings of the Cabinet and its Committees.

The Cabinet Office

The Cabinet Office, together with HM Treasury and the Prime Minister's Office, is at the centre of the UK Government.

The Secretary of the Cabinet (a civil servant who reports directly to the Prime Minister) manages the Cabinet Secretariats, which serve ministers collectively in the conduct of Cabinet business and in the co-ordination of policy at the highest level. Since 1983, the Cabinet Secretary has had the additional role of Head of the Home Civil Service.

The current Chancellor of the Duchy of Lancaster is a Cabinet minister with the title Minister for the Cabinet Office and has ministerial responsibility for all parts of the Cabinet Office except the Cabinet Secretariats.

The Cabinet Office is responsible for current policies to:

- modernise and simplify government so that it works more effectively for the benefit of the people;
- implement a government programme to improve the accessibility and quality of public services; and
- provide the central strategic management of the Civil Service.

Ministerial Responsibility

'Ministerial responsibility' refers both to the collective responsibility for government policy and actions which ministers share, and to ministers' individual responsibility for their own departments' work.

The doctrine of collective responsibility means that all ministers unanimously support government policy once it has been settled. The policy of departmental ministers must be consistent with the policy of the Government as a whole. Once the Government's policy on a matter has been decided, each minister is expected to support it or resign. On rare occasions, ministers have been allowed free votes in Parliament on important issues of principle or conscience.

The individual responsibility of ministers for the work of their departments means that they have a duty to Parliament to account, and to be held to account, for the policies, decisions and actions of their departments and agencies.

Departmental ministers normally decide all matters within their responsibility. However, many issues cross departmental boundaries and require agreement between different ministers. Proposals require consideration by Cabinet or a Cabinet Committee where the issue is one that raises major policy concerns, is likely to lead to significant public comment or criticism, or where the departmental ministers concerned have been unable to agree.

On taking up office ministers must generally resign directorships in private and public companies, and must ensure that there is no conflict between their public duties and private interests. Detailed guidance on handling Ministers' financial interests is set out in the Ministerial Code.

Government Departments

Government departments and their agencies are the main instruments for implementing government policy and for advising ministers. They are staffed by politically impartial civil servants and generally receive their funds out of money provided by Parliament. They often work alongside local authorities, non-departmental public bodies, and other government-sponsored organisations.

The structure and functions of departments sometimes change to meet the needs of major changes in policy. A change of Government does not necessarily affect the functions of departments.

The work of some departments (for instance, the Ministry of Defence) covers the UK as a whole. Other departments, such as the Department of Social Security, cover England, Wales and Scotland, but not Northern Ireland. Others again, such as the Department of the Environment, Transport and the Regions (DETR), are mainly concerned with affairs in England. (For changes in responsibilities associated with devolution, see chapters 3, 4 and 5.)

The nine Government Offices for the Regions in England (see pp. 10–11) are responsible for administering some of the main programmes of the DETR, the Department of Trade and Industry, and the Department for Education and Employment. They also link these where appropriate to the programmes of other departments, some of which have seconded staff to the Government Offices. Some departments or agencies which have direct contact with the public throughout the country also have local offices.

Regional Development Agencies (RDAs) were formally launched in eight English regions in April 1999. The ninth, in London, followed in July 2000 when the new Greater London Authority took up its full powers and responsibilities. The RDAs are designed to provide co-ordinated regional economic development and regeneration, and help the English regions to improve their competitiveness relative to their European counterparts.

Voluntary regional chambers have been established in each region. The chambers provide a mechanism through which the RDAs can consult on their proposals and give an account of their activities.

Most departments are headed by ministers. However, some are non-ministerial departments headed by a permanent office holder and ministers with other duties are accountable for them to Parliament. For example, the Secretary of State for Education and Employment accounts to Parliament for the work of the Office for Standards in Education (OFSTED). OFSTED is headed by HM Chief Inspector of Schools in England, who is largely independent of the Secretary of State.

The functions of the main government departments and agencies are set out in Appendix 1, pp. 533–42.

Non-departmental Public Bodies

A non-departmental public body (NDPB or 'quango') is a national or regional public body, operating independently of ministers, but for which ministers are ultimately accountable.

There are two main categories of NDPB:

- **Executive NDPBs** are those with executive, administrative, commercial or regulatory functions. They are typically engaged in a wide variety of activities and are established in a number of different ways. Executive NDPBs carry out prescribed functions within a government framework but the degree of operational independence varies. Examples include the Arts Council of England, the Environment Agency and the Health and Safety Executive.

- **Advisory NDPBs** are those set up by ministers to advise them and their departments on particular matters. Examples include the Committee on Standards in Public Life and the Low Pay Commission. Some Royal Commissions are also classified as advisory NDPBs.

Other categories of NDPB include certain tribunals and boards of visitors to penal establishments.

There are currently over 1,000 NDPBs in the UK. A list of all NDPBs is held centrally by the Cabinet Office and is issued annually in the publication *Public Bodies*. An electronic directory of NDPBs is also maintained on the Cabinet Office website (www.cabinet-office.gov.uk/quango).

The Lobby

As press adviser to the Prime Minister, the Prime Minister's Official Spokesman and other staff in the Prime Minister's Press Office have direct contact with the parliamentary press through regular meetings with the Lobby correspondents. The Lobby correspondents are a group of political journalists with the special privilege of access to the Lobby of the House of Commons, where they can talk privately to government ministers and other members of the House. The Prime Minister's Official Spokesman is the accepted channel through which information about parliamentary business is passed to the media.

Modernising Government

The *Modernising Government* White Paper published in March 1999 set out key policies and principles underpinning the Government's long-term programme of reform to modernise public services based on five key commitments:

- developing policies to achieve lasting results rather than reacting to short-term pressures;
- delivering public services to meet the needs of citizens, rather than for the convenience of service providers;
- providing efficient, high-quality public services;
- 'information age' government using new technology to meet the needs of citizens and business; and
- valuing those who work in the public service.

New public service agreements (PSAs) with government departments (see p. 403) provide a way of measuring and monitoring the effective implementation of these commitments. The Government has implemented a number of measures which aim to improve public services. These include:

- the establishment of the Centre for Management and Policy Studies and the Central Government National Training Organisation which together are responsible for strengthening policy-making and Civil Service-wide training and development;
- electronic delivery of services—33 per cent of services are now available electronically and a 100 per cent target has been set for the year 2005; and
- a reform programme to create a more open, diverse and professional Civil Service.

Open Government

The Code of Practice on Access to Government Information commits government departments, agencies and executive public bodies within the jurisdiction of the Parliamentary Ombudsman to volunteer information, such as facts and analysis behind major policy decisions, and to answer requests for information.

National Statistics

A new independent national statistical service came into being in June 2000. National Statistics provides an accurate, up-to-date, comprehensive and meaningful picture of the UK economy and society to support the formulation and monitoring of economic and social policies by government at all levels. The Chancellor of the Exchequer is the Minister for National Statistics and is responsible for appointing the chairman and members of the new Statistics Commission, and the new post of National Statistician. The new Statistics Commission is an independent, non-executive advisory body, operating in a transparent and open way and producing an annual report to be laid before Parliament. Among its key responsibilities are:

- representing the views of users and suppliers in commenting on the National Statistics work programme;
- advising ministers of areas of widespread concern about the quality of official statistics;
- commenting on the application of a new Code of Practice (see below) and other procedures designed to promote statistical integrity; and
- reviewing the need for statistical legislation, reporting back to the Minister for National Statistics after two years.

The new National Statistician is the Head of National Statistics, Head of the Government Statistical Service, Director of the Office for National Statistics and the UK Government's chief professional adviser on statistical matters. The postholder has professional responsibility for the quality of the outputs comprising National Statistics and maintains and publishes a National Statistics Code of Practice to help achieve this.

One of the key changes under National Statistics is that all on-line data is now made available free of charge to non-profit-making end users.

The Parliamentary Ombudsman (see p. 52) offers an independent appeals mechanism for those seeking information under the Code who are dissatisfied with the response to their enquiry and with the results of any internal review of the original decision. Complaints to the Parliamentary Ombudsman must be referred through an MP.

Freedom of Information

As part of its commitment to greater openness in the public sector and involving people more in decisions which affect their lives, the Government, following wide consultation, introduced into Parliament a Freedom of Information Bill in November 1999.

The Bill is intended to supersede the non-statutory Code of Practice on Access to Government Information, creating a statutory right of access to recorded information held by public authorities. It also aims to weight the scales decisively in favour of openness and preserve confidentiality only where disclosure would be against the public interest.

The main provisions of the Bill are:

- a right of wide general access, subject to clearly defined exemptions and conditions;
- a requirement to consider discretionary disclosure in the public interest even when an exemption applies;
- a duty to publish information; and
- powers of enforcement through an independent information commissioner and Information Tribunal.

There would also be a requirement imposed on:

- police forces to give out information about the conduct of inquiries (provided it does not prejudice law enforcement);
- schools to explain how they apply their admissions criteria;
- health authorities to provide details of how they allocate resources between different treatments;
- the Prison Service to provide information on the performance of different prison regimes;

- hospitals and general practitioners to explain how they prioritise their waiting lists; and
- National Health Service (NHS) Trusts and health authorities to provide information on the administrative procedures that govern their private finance initiatives.

Service First

Launched in 1998 as part of the drive to modernise government, Service First defines the principles of good public service delivery, including: setting clear standards of service; consultation with users; a well-publicised and easy-to-use complaints procedure; and closer working with other providers to ensure better services which are simple to use and well co-ordinated.

Service First applies to all public services, at both national and local level, and to those privatised utilities retaining a monopoly element. In support of the programme, a range of guides has been produced covering issues such as drawing up a charter, consultation, and complaints handling. Other key elements of the programme include:

- the *Charter Mark Award Scheme*, which rewards excellence in delivering public services;
- *The People's Panel*, which consists of 5,000 members of the public randomly selected from across the UK, to provide views on public service delivery from a cross-section of the population; and
- *Better Government for Older People*, which aims to improve public services for older people by better meeting their needs, listening to their views, and recognising their contribution to society.

Committee on Standards in Public Life

This Committee was set up in 1994 against a background of increasing public concern about standards in many areas of public life. The Committee's standing terms of reference are 'to examine current concerns about standards of conduct of all holders of public office, including arrangements relating to financial and commercial activities, and make recommendations as to any changes in present arrangements which might be required to ensure the highest standards of propriety in public life'.

The Committee has published six reports. The first, in 1995, led to the appointment of a Parliamentary Commissioner for Standards (see p. 52) and a Commissioner for Public Appointments (see p. 60).

Reports in 1996 and 1997 examined standards of conduct in local public spending bodies and conduct in local government, and called for a radical change in the ethical framework within which local government operates. A proposal was made for a new criminal offence of misuse of public office.

In 1997 the Prime Minister gave the Committee additional terms of reference to review the funding of political parties. The Committee's report, published in 1998, called for a new regulatory regime, overseen by an independent Election Commission, for political party funding in the UK. Legislation to make party funding more transparent and to control spending on elections was introduced in December 1999 under the Political Parties, Elections and Referendums Bill which is still before Parliament (see p. 46).

In January 2000, the Committee published its latest report—*Reinforcing Standards*—which was the first major review of public sector ethics since the Committee produced its initial report in 1995. It concluded that, although the process of raising standards has been a success, more still needs to be done.

The recommendations of the new report called for changes to the rules covering:

- *Members of Parliament and disciplinary procedures*—by introducing proposed legislation on the criminal law of bribery to remove any uncertainty regarding the scope of this statutory offence and by holding disciplinary proceedings of the House of Commons in public (though not broadcasting them);
- *ministers*—by amending the Ministerial Code to make it clear that a minister, having had the advice of his or her Permanent Secretary on potential

conflicts of interest, must take full responsibility for any subsequent decision;

- *civil servants including special advisers*—by ensuring that training and induction of staff appointed on secondments or short-term contracts includes examination of ethical issues within the public sector and by limiting the total number of special advisers that can be appointed within Government;
- *lobbying of government by outside interests*—by strengthening current guidance on lobbying and self-regulation by lobbyists;
- *sponsorship*—by disclosing in departmental annual reports, and to the public on request, details, including the value received, of sponsorship of government activities by the private and voluntary sectors; and
- *government task forces*—by establishing an agreed definition of a task force which, among other things, should specify that it must operate within a time frame of not more than two years, otherwise it should be disbanded or reclassified as an advisory NDPB.

The rules relating to appointments to NDPBs and NHS bodies were also scrutinised. The Government responded to *Reinforcing Standards* in July 2000, accepting the majority of recommendations.

In April 2000 the Committee published a consultation paper on standards of conduct in the House of Lords. A report is expected to be published before the end of 2000.

Commissioner for Public Appointments

The Commissioner for Public Appointments is independent of government and is responsible for monitoring, regulating and auditing approximately 12,500 ministerial appointments to a range of public bodies including NDPBs, public corporations, nationalised industries, NHS Trusts and utility regulators. The Commissioner has issued a Code of Practice which encompasses the seven principles to be applied to these appointments—ministerial responsibility, merit, independent scrutiny, equal opportunities, probity, openness and transparency, and proportionality.

Civil Service Commissioners

The Civil Service Commissioners are responsible for upholding the fundamental principle, in the context of recruitment to the Civil Service, that selection should be on merit on the basis of fair and open competition. The Commissioners, who are independent of government, produce a mandatory Recruitment Code and audit the recruitment policies and practices of departments and agencies to ensure compliance. They are also responsible for approving appointments through external recruitment to the Senior Civil Service, and for hearing and determining appeals in cases of concern about propriety and conscience under the Civil Service Code.

The Civil Service

The constitutional and practical role of the Civil Service is to assist the duly constituted Government of the United Kingdom, the Scottish Executive or the National Assembly for Wales in formulating their policies, carrying out decisions and administering public services for which they are responsible.

Civil servants are servants of the Crown; in effect this means the Government of the United Kingdom, the Scottish Executive and the National Assembly for Wales. The executive powers of the Crown are generally exercised by ministers of the Crown, Scottish ministers and secretaries of the National Assembly for Wales, who are in turn answerable to the appropriate Parliament or Assembly. The Civil Service as such has no separate constitutional personality or responsibility. The duty of the individual civil servant is first and foremost to the minister or Assembly secretary in charge of the department in which he or she is serving. A change of minister, for whatever reason, does not involve a change of staff.

Cabinet ministers may appoint a maximum of two special advisers. All appointments are approved by the Prime Minister. (There are about 79 such advisers in the present administration.) The advisers are paid from public funds. Their appointments come to an end when the Government's term of office finishes, or when the appointing minister leaves the Government or moves to another appointment.

The Civil Service Code, introduced in 1996, is a concise statement of the role and responsibilities of civil servants. It was revised in May 1999 to take account of devolution. The Code includes an independent line of appeal to the Civil Service Commissioners on alleged breaches of the Code.

Civil servants constitute about 2 per cent of the working population in employment, and about 10 per cent of all public sector employees. The number of permanent civil servants fell from 751,000 in 1976 to 460,000 in April 1999 (a decrease of 39 per cent). These figures include the Senior Civil Service, which comprises around 3,000 of the most senior managers and policy advisers.

About half of all civil servants are engaged in providing services to the public. These include paying benefits and pensions, running employment services, staffing prisons, issuing driving licences, and providing services to industry and agriculture. A further quarter are employed in the Ministry of Defence and its agencies. The rest are divided between central administrative and policy duties; support services; and largely financially self-supporting services, for instance, those provided by the Royal Mint. Four-fifths of civil servants work outside London. Approximately 13,000 civil servants work in the Scottish Executive and 2,500 in the National Assembly for Wales.

Northern Ireland Civil Service

The Northern Ireland Civil Service (NICS) is modelled on its counterpart in Great Britain, and has its own Civil Service Commission. There were about 25,000 civil servants in the NICS in June 2000. There is a degree of mobility between the NICS and the Home Civil Service.

The Diplomatic Service

The Diplomatic Service, a separate service of some 3,000 people, provides staff for the Foreign & Commonwealth Office (FCO—see p. 92) in London and at British diplomatic missions abroad.

Terms and conditions of service are comparable, but take into account the special demands of the Service, particularly the requirement to serve abroad. Home civil servants, members of the armed forces and individuals from the private sector may also serve in the FCO and at overseas posts on loan or attachment.

Equality and Diversity

The Civil Service aims to create a culture in which the different skills, experience and expertise that individuals bring are valued and used. Its equal opportunities policy states that there must be no unfair discrimination on the basis of age, disability, gender, marital status, sexual orientation, race, colour, nationality, ethnic or national origin or (in Northern Ireland) community background. The Civil Service is committed to achieving greater diversity, particularly at senior levels, where women, people from ethnic minorities and those with disabilities are still under-represented.

In April 1999, the overall proportion of women in the Civil Service was 51 per cent; ethnic minority representation was 5.6 per cent, compared with 5.5 per cent in the economically active population; and at least 3.6 per cent of staff employed were disabled. Progress is monitored and reported on regularly by the Cabinet Office.

Central Management

Responsibility for central co-ordination and management of the Civil Service lies with the Prime Minister as Minister for the Civil Service, supported by the Cabinet Office led by the Head of the Home Civil Service through his chairmanship of the Civil Service Management Board. (The function of official Head of the Home Civil Service is combined with that of Secretary of the Cabinet.) The

Cabinet Office oversees the central framework for management of the Civil Service. Day-to-day responsibility for a wide range of terms and conditions has been delegated to departments and agencies, the Scottish Executive and the National Assembly for Wales.

Executive Agencies

Executive agencies were introduced to deliver government services more efficiently and effectively within available resources for the benefit of taxpayers, customers and staff. This involved setting up, as far as was practicable, separate units or agencies to perform the executive functions of government. Agencies remain part of the Civil Service, but under the terms of individual framework documents they enjoy greater delegation of financial, pay and personnel matters. Agencies are headed by chief executives who are normally directly accountable to ministers but are personally responsible for day-to-day operations. A chief executive's pay is normally performance-related.

No organisation carrying out a government function can become an agency until the 'prior options' of abolition, privatisation and contracting out have been considered and ruled out. These 'prior options' are reconsidered when agencies are reviewed, normally after five years of operation.

Local Government

Local Authorities' Powers

Local authorities can do only what they are empowered to do by Acts of Parliament, but their functions are far-reaching. Some are mandatory, which means that the authority must do what is required by law; others are discretionary, allowing an authority to provide services if it wishes. In certain cases, ministers have powers to secure a degree of uniformity in standards in order to safeguard public health or to protect the rights of individual citizens. Where local authorities exceed the statutory powers conferred on them, they are deemed to be acting outside the law and can be challenged in court.

The main link between local authorities and central government in England is the DETR. However, other departments, such as the Department for Education and Employment, the Department of Health and the Home Office, are also concerned with various local government functions. In Scotland, Wales and Northern Ireland local authorities now deal mainly with the devolved Parliament and Assemblies.

Reform of Local Government Structure

A major reform of local government took place in 1974 in England and Wales and in 1975 in Scotland. This created two main tiers of local authority throughout England and Wales: counties and the smaller districts. Local government in London had been reorganised along the same lines in 1965. In Scotland functions were allocated to regions and districts on the mainland; single-tier authorities were introduced for the three Islands areas. In Northern Ireland changes were made in 1973 which replaced the two-tier county council and urban/rural council system with a single-tier district council system.

The Local Government Act 1985 abolished the Greater London Council and the six metropolitan county councils in England. Most of their functions were transferred to the London boroughs and metropolitan district councils respectively in 1986 (see below).

Recent Changes

Further restructuring of local government later took place in non-metropolitan England and in Scotland and Wales. In 1992 the Local Government Commission was established to review the structure, boundaries and electoral arrangements of local government in England and to undertake periodic electoral reviews. In its structural reviews of local government in non-metropolitan England, the Commission considered whether the two-tier structure should be replaced by single-tier ('unitary') authorities in each area; for the most part it recommended the retention of two-tier government, but suggested unitary authorities for some areas, especially the larger cities.

Parliament approved reorganisation in 25 counties, creating a total of 46 new unitary councils (see map on p. 8). Implementation was completed in 1998.

In Scotland 29 new unitary councils replaced the previous system of nine regional and 53 district councils in 1996; the three Islands councils remained in being. In Wales 22 unitary authorities replaced the previous eight county councils and 37 district councils, again in 1996.

Principal Types of Local Authority

Greater London

Greater London is made up of the 32 London boroughs and the City of London, each with a council responsible for a number of key local services in its area. However, they work closely with the new Greater London Authority (GLA) on a range of London-wide issues, such as transport, economic development, strategic development and the environment.

English Metropolitan County Areas

The six metropolitan county areas—Tyne and Wear, West Midlands, Merseyside, Greater Manchester, West Yorkshire and South Yorkshire—have 36 district councils, but no county councils. The district councils are responsible for all services apart from those which require a statutory authority over areas wider than the individual boroughs and districts—namely, waste disposal (in certain areas); the fire services, including civil defence; and public transport. These are run by joint authorities composed of elected councillors nominated by the borough or district councils.

English Non-metropolitan Counties

Before the recent reforms, local government in England—outside Greater London and the metropolitan areas—was divided into counties and sub-divided into districts. All the counties and districts had locally elected councils with separate functions. County councils provided large-scale services, while district councils were

A Mayor and Assembly for London

In May 2000 Londoners voted for a directly elected Mayor and a separately elected Assembly for London. The resulting Greater London Authority took up its full powers and responsibilities in July 2000—the first time the capital city has had a strategic authority since the Greater London Council (GLC) was abolished in 1986. Future elections, again using a system of proportional representation, will take place every four years.

Fourteen new constituencies cover the whole of Greater London, each providing one member, and a further 11 'London-wide' members are allocated to ensure that the overall distribution of seats reflects the proportion of votes cast for each party.

The Mayor's primary role is to represent and promote London and, after consultation, to devise London-wide strategies for transport, planning, culture and the environment. He or she controls two new transport and economic bodies—Transport for London (TfL) and the London Development Agency (LDA)—and appoints their members. In addition, a new Metropolitan Police Authority (MPA) and London Fire and Emergency Planning Authority (LFEPA) have been established, to whose boards the Mayor appoints members of the Assembly. He or she sets a budget for all four new bodies and for the GLA.

The 25-member Assembly's prime duty is to hold the Mayor to account on London's behalf. It will scrutinise all of the Mayor's activities, the activities of the two new authorities (MPA and LFEPA) and the bodies responsible for transport and economic development (TfL and LDA). The Assembly has a key role in setting the GLA's budget, working closely with the Mayor on strategic priorities. The Mayor is obliged to consider its proposals and ultimately the Assembly may agree or amend the Mayor's budget.

responsible for the more local ones. These arrangements are broadly continuing in areas where two-tier local government remains.

County councils are responsible for transport, planning, highways, traffic regulation, education, consumer protection, refuse disposal, the fire service, libraries and the personal social services. District councils are responsible for environmental health, housing, decisions on most local planning applications, and refuse collection. Both tiers of local authority have powers to provide facilities such as museums, art galleries and parks; arrangements depend on local agreement. In areas where the new unitary authorities have been set up, county and district level functions have merged.

In addition to the two-tier local authority system in England, over 10,000 parish councils or meetings provide and manage local facilities such as allotments and village halls, and act as agents for other district council functions. They also provide a forum for discussion of local issues.

Scotland, Wales and Northern Ireland

In Scotland the 32 single-tier councils are responsible for the full range of local government services. In Wales the 22 single-tier councils have similar functions, except that fire services are provided by three combined fire authorities. In addition, about 750 community councils in Wales have functions similar to those of the parish councils in England (see above); in Scotland community councils exist to represent the views of their local communities to local authorities and other public bodies in the area. In Northern Ireland 26 district councils are responsible for delivering services to their local communities.

Fire Services in the UK

Every part of the UK is covered by a local authority fire service. Each of the 64 fire authorities must by law make provision for firefighting and maintain a brigade to meet efficiently all normal firefighting requirements. Each fire authority appoints a Chief Fire Officer (Firemaster in Scotland) who exercises day-to-day control from brigade headquarters. The fire services in England and Wales employ some 50,000 staff and spend around £1.5 billion each year. In 1999 local authority fire brigades attended about 935,000 fires or false alarms in the UK.

Election of Councils

Local councils consist of elected councillors. In England and Wales each council elects its presiding officer annually. Some districts have the ceremonial title of borough, or city, both granted by royal authority. In boroughs and cities the presiding officer is normally known as the Mayor. In the City of London and certain large cities, he or she is known as the Lord Mayor. In Scotland the presiding officer of the council of each of the four cities—Aberdeen, Dundee, Edinburgh and Glasgow—is called the Lord Provost.

Councillors are elected for four years. All county councils in England, borough councils in London, and about two-thirds of non-metropolitan district councils are elected in their entirety every four years. In the remaining districts (including all metropolitan districts) one-third of the councillors are elected in each of the three years when county council elections are not held. Unitary authorities in non-metropolitan districts and London boroughs have a pattern of elections similar to that in metropolitan districts.

In Scotland whole council elections are held every three years, with the next elections due in 2002. In Wales whole council elections are held every fourth year, with the next due in 2003.

County, district and unitary authority councillors are paid a basic allowance but may also be entitled to additional allowances and expenses for attending meetings or taking on special responsibilities.

Voters

Anyone may vote at a local government election in the UK provided he or she is:

- aged 18 years or over;
- a citizen of the UK or of another Commonwealth country, or of the Irish Republic, or a citizen of a member state of the EU;

- not subject to any legal incapacity to vote; and
- on the electoral register.

To qualify for registration a person must be resident in the council area on the qualifying date.

Candidates

Most candidates at local government elections stand as representatives of a national political party, although some stand as independents. Candidates must be British citizens, other Commonwealth citizens or citizens of a member state of the EU, and aged 21 or over. In addition, they must also either:

- be registered as local electors in the area of the relevant local authority; or
- have occupied (as owner or tenant) land or premises in that area during the whole of the preceding 12 months; or
- have had their main place of work in the area throughout this 12-month period.

No one may be elected to a council of which he or she is an employee. All candidates for district council elections in Northern Ireland are required to make a declaration against terrorism.

Electoral Areas and Procedure

Counties in England are divided into electoral divisions, each returning one councillor. Districts in England and Northern Ireland are divided into wards, returning one councillor or more. In Scotland the unitary councils are divided into wards and in Wales into electoral divisions; each returns one councillor or more. Parishes (in England) and communities (in Wales) may be divided into wards, returning at least one councillor.

The procedure for local government voting in Great Britain is broadly similar to that for parliamentary elections. In Northern Ireland district councils are elected by proportional representation on the grounds that it allows for the representation of sizeable minorities.

The electoral arrangements of local authorities in England are kept under review by the Local Government Commission (see p. 62), and in Wales and Scotland by the Local Government Boundary Commissions. Under legislation passed in 1997, electoral arrangements in England and Wales for parishes and communities can be reviewed by local councils.

Provision of Local Services

In recent years, there has been a move away from direct service provision, to a greater use of private contractors, and an increase in what is often called the 'enabling' role. Local authorities now carry out many functions in partnership with both public and private organisations.

The Government considers that councils should not be forced to put their services out to tender, but equally it sees no reason why a service should be delivered directly if more efficient means are available elsewhere. The Local Government Act 1999 therefore places a duty on local authorities to achieve best value.

The Best Value programme aims to encourage local accountability and involve local communities in deciding the quality, level and cost of local services. Local authorities are expected to set themselves challenging targets for the improvement of services following regular reviews of their performance. Local people may see how well their authority is performing through the publication of annual performance plans.

The Government of Wales Act requires the National Assembly to set up a Partnership Council to oversee relations between the Assembly and local government. A Commission to establish effective relations between local government and the new Scottish Parliament has been set up (see chapter 4).

Internal Organisation of Local Authorities

The Local Government Act 2000 requires local authorities to implement new decision-taking structures, including the option of a directly elected mayor. These arrangements will replace the traditional committee system of decision-taking for most council functions. In most authorities the arrangements will be based on one of three executive frameworks: a mayor and cabinet; a council leader and cabinet; or a mayor and council manager. Within these options local authorities will have considerable flexibility to adopt a constitution which reflects local circumstances. Small shire district councils with a population of fewer than 85,000 will, in addition to executive arrangements, have the option of reforming their existing committee system.

All new constitutions will be required to incorporate rigorous arrangements for review and scrutiny of councils' policies and decisions made.

Some decisions, such as the adoption of policies and the budget, will be reserved for the full council, but most of those relating to the implementation of policy will be for the executive. The executive will also be responsible for preparing the policies and budget to propose to the council.

Decisions may be taken by the executive collectively, individual members of the executive, committees of the executive or officers of the authority. The executive will also be able to delegate decision-making to area committees and to enter into partnership arrangements with other authorities.

The new arrangements will ensure that people know who in the council is responsible for taking decisions, how they can make their input into decision-making and how to hold decision-makers to account. In authorities where there is a directly elected mayor, he or she will have a strong mandate from local people to deliver a programme of policies.

Public Access

Under the Local Government Act 2000, the public (including the press) will be admitted to meetings of the executive where key decisions are being discussed. They will also have access to agendas, reports and minutes of meetings and certain background papers. Local authorities will also have to publish a Forward Plan setting out the decisions that will be taken over the coming months. Local authorities may exclude the public from meetings and withhold papers only in limited circumstances.

Employees

About 2 million people[13] are employed by local authorities in the UK. These include school teachers, police, firefighters and other non-manual and manual workers. Education is the largest service with 800,000 full-time equivalent jobs. Councils are individually responsible, within certain national legislative requirements, for deciding the structure of their workforces.

Senior staff appointments are usually made by the elected councillors. More junior appointments are made by heads of departments. Pay and conditions of school teachers are set by the Secretary of State for Education and Employment, after receiving recommendations from the School Teachers' Pay Review Body. Police pay is determined by a formula tied to median private sector non-manual pay settlements. Other pay and conditions of service are usually a matter for each council, although firefighters' pay increases are informed by a formula tied to the upper quartile of male manual workers' earnings. For other workers, most authorities follow the scales recommended as a result of national negotiation between authorities and trade unions.

Local Authority Finance

Local government expenditure accounts for about 25 per cent of public spending. In 1999–2000 expenditure by local authorities in the UK was about £81.2 billion. Current expenditure amounted to £72.9 billion; capital expenditure, net of capital receipts, was £5.3 billion; and debt interest £3.7 billion. Local government capital expenditure is financed primarily by borrowing within limits set by central government and from capital receipts from the disposal of land and buildings.

Local authorities in Great Britain raise revenue through the council tax (see chapter 24), which meets about 20 per cent of their revenue expenditure. Their spending is, however, financed primarily by grants from central government and by the redistribution

[13] Full-time equivalents.

Local Authority Expenditure and Funding in England, 2000–01

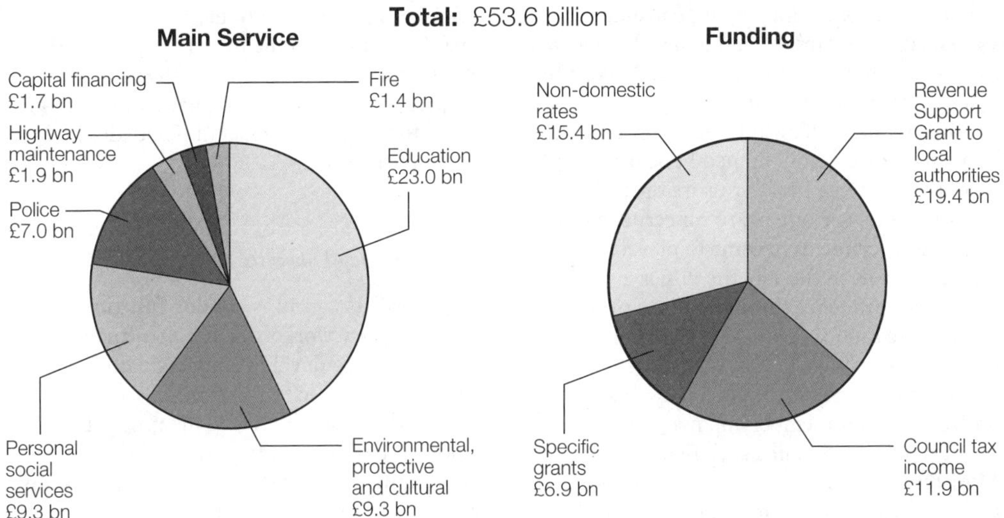

Source: Department of the Environment, Transport and the Regions

of revenue from the national non-domestic rate, a property tax levied on businesses and other non-domestic properties.

District councils in Northern Ireland continue to raise revenue through the levying of a domestic rate and business rates.

Financial Safeguards

Local councils' annual accounts must be audited by independent auditors appointed by the Audit Commission in England and Wales, or in Scotland by the Accounts Commission for Scotland. In Northern Ireland this role is exercised by the chief local government auditor. Local electors have a right to inspect the accounts to be audited. They may also ask questions and lodge objections with the auditor.

Local Government Complaints System

Local authorities are encouraged to resolve complaints through internal mechanisms, and members of the public will often ask their own councillor for help in this. Local authorities must also appoint a monitoring officer, whose duties include ensuring that the local authority acts lawfully in the conduct of its business.

Complaints of alleged local government maladministration leading to injustice may be investigated by independent Commissions for Local Administration, often known as 'the Local Ombudsman service'. There are three Local Government Ombudsmen in England, and one each in Wales and Scotland. A report is issued on each complaint fully investigated and, if injustice caused by maladministration is found, the Local Ombudsman normally proposes a remedy. The council must consider the report and reply to it. In 1999–2000 the Local Government Ombudsmen for England received 17,555 complaints, 11 per cent more than in 1998–99.

In Northern Ireland a Commissioner for Complaints deals with complaints alleging injustices suffered as a result of maladministration by district councils and certain other public bodies.

Pressure Groups

Pressure groups are informal organisations which aim to influence the decision-making of

Parliament and Government, to the benefit of their members and the causes they support. There is a huge range of groups, covering politics, business, employment, consumer affairs, ethnic minorities, aid to developing countries, foreign relations, education, culture, defence, religion, sport, transport, social welfare, animal welfare and the environment. Some have over a million members; others only a few dozen. Some exert pressure on a number of different issues; others are concerned with a single issue. Some have come to play a recognised role in the way the UK is governed; others seek influence through radical protest.

Pressure groups operating at a national level may influence how the UK is governed. Their actions may simply highlight a particular problem or their membership may indicate broad representation in a specific field. Ministers have a duty to give fair consideration and due weight to informed and impartial advice from civil servants, so pressure groups often seek to inform civil servants and thus influence the advice given to ministers.

Consultation to gain the consent and co-operation of as wide a range of organisations as possible and to ensure the smooth operation of laws and regulations is an important principle in the way government in the UK works.

In some instances a department is under a legal obligation to consult interested groups. The Government has a duty to consult organised interests, providing the pressure groups involved have a broad enough membership for them to represent a majority view, and that they observe confidentiality about their discussions with the department. Members of pressure groups often have direct expertise and an awareness of what is practicable, and so can offer useful advice to the Government in forming policy or drafting legislation. The contacts between civil servants and pressure group representatives may be relatively informal—by letter or telephone—or more formal, through involvement in working parties or by giving evidence to committees of inquiry.

Pressure Groups and Parliament

Lobbying—the practice of approaching MPs or peers, persuading them to act on behalf of a cause, and enabling them to do so by providing advice and information—has substantially increased in recent years. A common pressure group tactic is to ask members of the public to write to their MP about an issue—for example, the plight of political prisoners in particular countries—in order to raise awareness and persuade the MP to support the cause.

Parliamentary Lobbyists

Many pressure groups employ full-time parliamentary workers or liaison officers, whose job is to develop contacts with MPs and peers sympathetic to their cause, and to brief them when issues affecting the group are raised in Parliament. In July 1998 the Government issued guidance to civil servants who come into contact with groups and people outside the Government.

Public relations and political consultancy firms also specialise in lobbying Parliament and Government. Such firms are employed by pressure groups—as well as by British and overseas companies and organisations—to monitor parliamentary business, and to promote their clients' interests where they are affected by legislation and debate.

Raising Issues in Parliament

Other ways through which pressure groups may exert influence include:

- suggesting to MPs or peers subjects for Private Members' Bills (see p. 49); many pressure groups have ready-drafted bills waiting to be sponsored;
- approaching MPs or peers to ask Parliamentary Questions as a means of gaining information from the Government and of drawing public attention to an issue;
- suggesting to MPs subjects for Early Day Motions (see p. 52) and suggesting to peers subjects for debates; and
- orchestrating public petitions as a form of protest against government policy, or to call for action.

The UK in the European Union

As a member of the European Union, the UK is bound by the various types of European Community (EC) legislation and wider policies (for policies, see chapter 7). Almost all UK government departments are involved in EU-wide business, and European legislation is an increasingly important element of government.

The Community enacts legislation which is binding on the national governments of the 15 member states or, in certain circumstances, on individuals and companies within those states. British government ministers take part in the discussions and decision-making, and the final decision is taken collectively by all the member states.

The UK Representative Office (UKREP), based in Brussels, conducts most of the negotiations on behalf of the UK Government. The devolved administrations of Scotland and Wales are also represented by UKREP. In October 1999 a new office specifically aimed at helping to promote Scotland's interests within the EU opened in Brussels; an office fulfilling the same role for Wales opened in May 2000.

There are three legislative bodies:

The Council of the European Union is the main decision-making body. Member states are represented by the ministers appropriate to the subject under discussion. When, for instance, education matters are being discussed, the UK's Secretary of State for Education and Employment attends with his or her European counterparts. The Presidency of the Council changes at six-monthly intervals and rotates in turn among the 15 member states of the Union.

The *European Council*, which is not a legislative body and which usually meets twice a year, comprises the heads of State or Government accompanied by their foreign ministers and the President of the European Commission and one other Commissioner. The Council defines general political guidelines.

The European Commission is the executive body. It implements the Council's decisions, initiates legislation and ensures that member states put it into effect. Each of the 20 Commissioners, who are drawn from all member states (there are two from the UK), is responsible for a specific policy area, for example, education, transport or agriculture. The Commissioners are entirely independent of their countries, and serve the EU as a whole.

The European Parliament, which plays an increasingly important role in the legislative process, has 626 directly elected members (MEPs), including 87 from the UK. The Parliament is consulted about major decisions and has substantial shared power with the Council of the European Union over the EC budget. In areas of legislation, its role varies between *consultation*, where it can influence but does not have the final say in the content of legislation; the *co-operation and assent* procedures, where its influence is greater; and *co-decision* (introduced by the Maastricht Treaty and extended in the Amsterdam Treaty—see chapter 7), where a proposal requires the agreement of both the Council and the European Parliament.

Elections to the Parliament take place every five years, most recently in June 1999. In the UK, these were held under a proportional voting system,[14] bringing the country in line with the other member states.

The European Parliament meets in full session in Strasbourg for about one week every month, although its committee work normally takes place in Brussels.

EC legislation is issued in some areas jointly by the Council of the European Union and the European Parliament, by the Council in other areas, or by the Commission under delegated powers. It consists of Regulations, Directives and Decisions.

- *Regulations* are directly applicable in all member states, and have the force of law

[14] The regional list system is used for England, Scotland and Wales, under which an elector may cast his or her vote for a party list of candidates. England is divided into nine regions while Scotland and Wales each constitute one region. These 11 regions each return between four and 11 MEPs, depending on the size of the electorate of each region. Northern Ireland, which also constitutes one region, continues to use the single transferable vote system to return its three MEPs.

without the need for implementing further measures;

- *Directives* are equally binding as to the result to be achieved but allow each member state to choose the form and method of implementation; and
- *Decisions*, like Regulations, do not normally need national implementing legislation. They are binding on those to whom they are addressed.

European Parliament Elections, June 1999

UK Results by Party—MEPs elected

Conservative	36
Labour	29
Liberal Democrat	10
UK Independence Party	3
Green	2
Plaid Cymru	2
Scottish National Party	2
Democratic Unionist Party	1
Ulster Unionist Party	1
Social Democratic and Labour Party	1

Other EU Institutions

Each member state provides one of the judges to serve in the **European Court of Justice**, which is the final authority on all aspects of Community law. Its rulings must be applied by member states, and fines can be imposed on those failing to do so. The Court is assisted by a Court of First Instance, which handles certain cases brought by individuals and companies. The UK is also represented on the **Court of Auditors**, which examines Community revenue and expenditure, to see that it is legally received and spent.

Further Reading

The Royal Commission on the Reform of the House of Lords Report: *A House for the Future*. Cm 4534. The Stationery Office, 2000.

The Committee on Standards in Public Life's Sixth Report: *Reinforcing Standards*. Cm 4557. The Stationery Office, 2000.

The Funding of Political Parties in the United Kingdom. Cm 4413. The Stationery Office, 1999.

Modernising Government. Cm 4310. The Stationery Office, 1999.

Freedom of Information: Consultation on Draft Legislation. Cm 4355. The Stationery Office, 1999.

Websites

Central government: www.open.gov.uk and www.ukonline.gov.uk

Houses of Parliament: www.parliament.uk

British Monarchy: www.royal.gov.uk

National Statistics: www.statistics.gov.uk

7 Overseas Relations

As a democratic country with global foreign policy interests and an economy heavily dependent on international trade and investment, the United Kingdom supports the maintenance of an open and stable international order. Membership of the United Nations (UN), the European Union (EU), the Commonwealth, NATO, the Western European Union (WEU) and other major international organisations remains central to this objective.

INTERNATIONAL ORGANISATIONS

United Nations

The UK is a founder member of the UN and one of the five permanent members of the Security Council, along with China, France, Russia and the United States. It supports the purposes and principles of the UN Charter, including the maintenance of international peace and security, the development of friendly relations among nations, the achievement of international co-operation on economic, social, cultural and humanitarian issues, and the protection of human rights and fundamental freedoms. In 2000 the UK was the sixth largest contributor to the UN regular budget, the fifth largest contributor to peacekeeping operations (see p. 85), and one of the largest voluntary contributors to UN funds, programmes and agencies. In order to enhance the UN's effectiveness, the UK is continuing to press for modernisation of the organisation, including the implementation of management and budgetary proposals recommended by the UN Secretary General.

European Union

The UK is a member of the EU (see also pp. 69 and 77–82), which promotes social and economic progress, a common foreign and security policy, European citizenship and police and judicial co-operation in criminal matters. The other 14 EU member nations are Austria, Belgium, Denmark, Finland, France, Germany, Greece, the Irish Republic, Italy, Luxembourg, the Netherlands, Portugal, Spain and Sweden.

The Commonwealth

There are 54 members of the Commonwealth, including the UK. It is a voluntary association of independent states, nearly all of which were once British territories, and includes almost one in three people in the world. The members are Antigua and Barbuda, Australia, the Bahamas, Bangladesh, Barbados, Belize, Botswana, Brunei Darussalam, Cameroon, Canada, Cyprus, Dominica, Fiji,[1] The Gambia, Ghana, Grenada, Guyana, India, Jamaica, Kenya, Kiribati, Lesotho, Malawi, Malaysia, Maldives, Malta, Mauritius, Mozambique, Namibia, Nauru, New Zealand, Nigeria, Pakistan,[2] Papua New Guinea, St Kitts and Nevis, St Lucia, St Vincent and the Grenadines, Samoa, Seychelles, Sierra Leone, Singapore, Solomon Islands, South Africa, Sri Lanka, Swaziland, Tanzania, Tonga, Trinidad and Tobago, Tuvalu,[3] Uganda, United Kingdom, Vanuatu, Zambia and Zimbabwe.

The Queen is head of the Commonwealth and is head of state in the UK and 15 other member countries. The Commonwealth Secretariat, based in London, is the main agency for multilateral communication between member governments on matters relevant to the Commonwealth as a whole. The Secretariat promotes consultation and co-operation, disseminates information, and helps host governments to organise Heads of Government Meetings, ministerial meetings and other conferences. It administers assistance programmes agreed at these meetings, including the Commonwealth Fund for Technical Co-operation, which provides advisory services and training to Commonwealth developing countries.

Heads of Government Meetings are held biennially, most recently in Durban, South Africa, in November 1999. The next will take place in Brisbane, Australia, in 2001.

North Atlantic Treaty Organisation

Membership of NATO is central to UK defence policy (see p. 96). NATO's functions are to:

- help provide security and stability in the Euro-Atlantic area;
- provide a transatlantic forum for member states to consult on issues of common concern;
- deter and defend against any threat to the territory of any NATO member state;
- contribute to crisis management and conflict prevention on a case-by-case basis; and
- promote partnership, co-operation and dialogue with other countries in the Euro-Atlantic area.

Each of the 19 member states—Belgium, Canada, the Czech Republic, Denmark, France, Germany, Greece, Hungary, Iceland, Italy, Luxembourg, the Netherlands, Norway, Poland, Portugal, Spain, Turkey, the United Kingdom and the United States—has a permanent representative at NATO headquarters in Brussels. The Czech Republic, Hungary and Poland joined the Alliance as full members in 1999. The main decision-taking body is the North Atlantic Council. It meets at least twice a year at foreign minister level, and weekly at the level of permanent representatives. Defence ministers also meet at least twice a year.

Western European Union

The UK is a full member of the WEU, which provides a forum for co-operation and consultation on defence and security issues for European nations. The WEU's other full members are Belgium, France, Germany, Greece, Italy, Luxembourg, the Netherlands, Portugal and Spain. The Czech Republic, Hungary, Iceland, Norway, Poland and Turkey are associate members; Austria, Denmark, Finland, the Irish Republic and Sweden are observers. 'Associate partnership' has been extended to seven Central European and Baltic states.

EU heads of Government agreed at the Cologne European Council in June 1999 that the EU should itself be given responsibility for many of the military crisis management activities previously the remit of the WEU (see also p. 81).

---

[1] Fiji was suspended from the councils of the Commonwealth in June 2000 following a declaration of martial law by the Fiji military in response to an internal security crisis.

[2] Pakistan was suspended from the councils of the Commonwealth in October 1999 following a military coup.

[3] Tuvalu is a 'special' member, entitled to take part in all Commonwealth activities, with the exception of the biennial Commonwealth Heads of Government Meetings.

The Waterways Network in the UK
Orkney Islands
Shetland Islands
British Waterways
Managed by British Waterways
Managed by other authorities
Major restoration and construction projects planned or under active consideration
Waterways Ireland
Navigable waterway
Possible restoration or new extension
0 40 80 120 km
0 20 40 60 80 miles
SCOTLAND
Inverness
Fort William
Glasgow
Edinburgh
NORTHERN IRELAND
Coleraine
Londonderry
Lough Neagh
Lower Lough Erne
Upper Lough Erne
Enniskillen
Belfast
REPUBLIC OF IRELAND
Middlesbrough
Kendal
Lancaster
York
Blackpool
Leeds
Manchester
Liverpool
Sheffield
Lincoln
Chester
Derby
Nottingham
ENGLAND
Norwich
Birmingham
Worcester
Cambridge
WALES
Gloucester
Oxford
Harwich
Chepstow
London
Swansea
Bristol
Newbury
Reading
Cardiff
Bath
Taunton
Exeter
Exmouth
Map prepared from information supplied by Waterways Ireland and British Waterways

INLAND WATERWAYS

Built some 200 years ago to carry raw materials and finished goods for the rapidly expanding manufacturing industries, canals played a pivotal role in the Industrial Revolution and helped change the face of Britain. Today, this legacy of inland waterways provides the focus of a wide variety of leisure pursuits and regenerative developments.

The Caledonian Canal, Scotland.

The 80 km long Erne Waterway, located in the west of Northern Ireland, is formed of connected river, lake and canal sections. As one of Northern Ireland's premier natural assets, the waterway's leisure facilities are enjoyed by visitors both from within the UK and from overseas.

The horsedrawn barge *Kennet Valley* takes tourists on pleasure trips along the Kennet and Avon Canal in Berkshire during the summer months. The barge is one of the very few remaining in the country to be pulled solely by heavy horse.

Background picture: Fishing on the Stourbridge Canal, West Midlands.

Lock-keeper's cottage, Cullochy Lock Caledonian Canal.

Braunston Marina, Northamptonshire. One of the biggest and busiest marinas in England, with 250 permanent moorings.

Cruising on the Pontcysyllte Aqueduct, North Wales. Approximately 25,000 hire boat trips cruise the British Waterways network per year, representing a third of their overall traffic.

Background picture: Neptune's Staircase, on the Caledonian Canal, near Fort William.

One of the 50,000 rock bolts being driven into Standedge to stabilise the tunnel. Restoration work is expected to be completed by the summer of 2001.

The UK's longest canal tunnel (three and a quarter miles in length) is at Standedge on the Huddersfield Narrow Canal. Work to repair damage caused by roof falls and build up of silt and soot is under way as part of a scheme to re-open the canal to traffic.

Lockside improvements on the Llangollen Canal, which flows from North Wales into Shropshire, England. The canal environment is enhanced by laying paving slabs underneath the lock balance beams.

Crowds throng the towpath at Port Buchan in Broxburn, West Lothian, Scotland at the re-opening of the Broxburn to Ratho section of the Union Canal.

Spectators at Townhead Bridge in Kirkintilloch, East Dumbartonshire, Scotland on the re-opening of the Kirkintilloch to Bishopbriggs section of the Forth & Clyde Canal.

The European Union

The Commonwealth

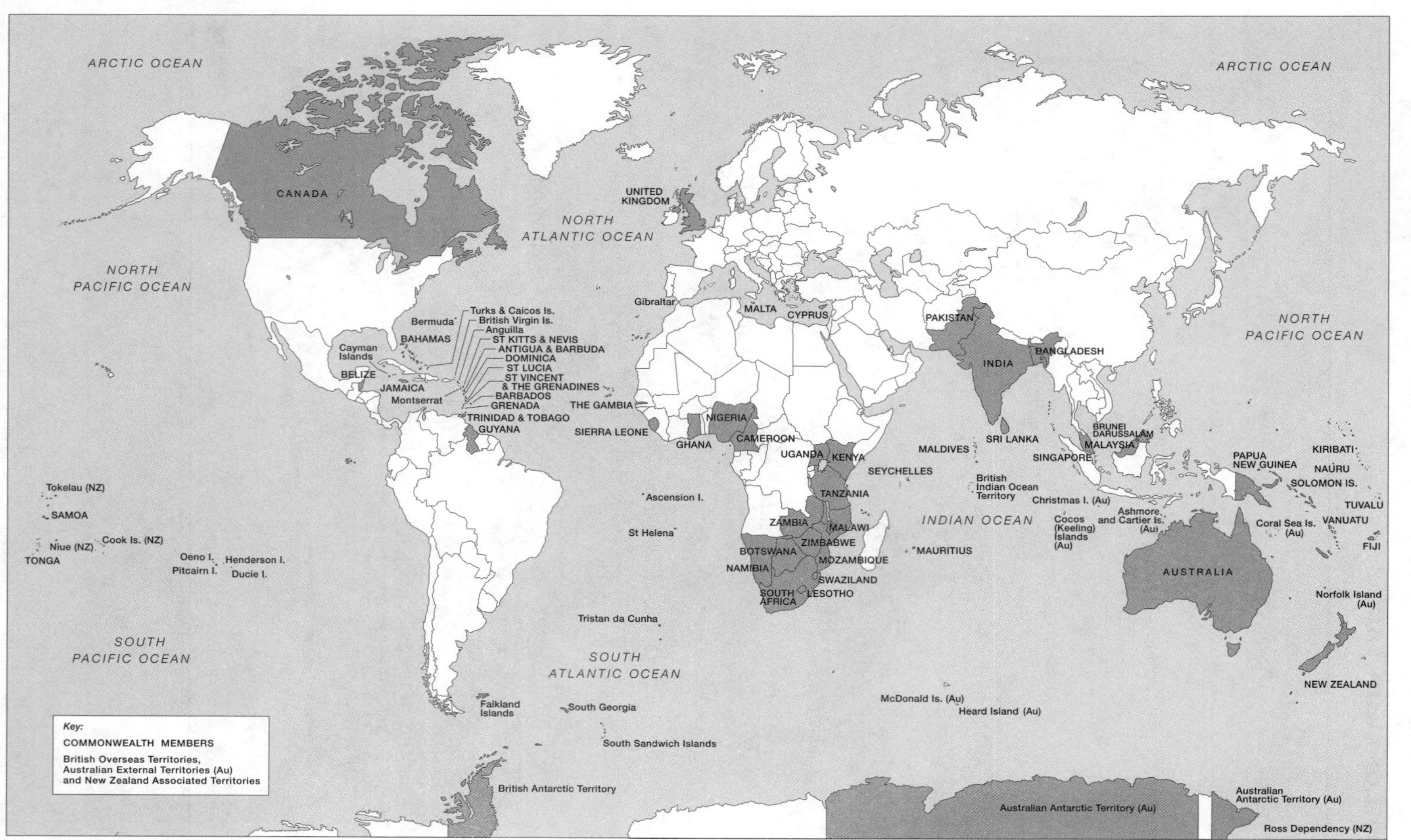

The Group of Eight

The UK is part of the Group of Eight (G8) leading industrialised countries. The other members are Canada, France, Germany, Italy, Japan, Russia (included as a full member from 1998, although the other countries continue to function as the G7 for some discussions) and the United States. The G8 is an informal group with no secretariat. Its Presidency rotates each year among the members, the key meeting being an annual summit of heads of government. Originally formed in 1975 (as the G7) to discuss economic issues, the G8 agenda now includes a wide range of foreign affairs and international issues such as terrorism, nuclear safety, the environment, UN reform and development assistance. Heads of state or government agree a communiqué issued at the end of summits which commits each country to co-ordinate individual action towards common goals.

The G8 summit meeting in July 2000, hosted by the Japanese Government in Okinawa, focused on development issues, including debt relief and health; information technology (IT); drugs and crime; and conflict prevention.

Organisation for Security and Co-operation in Europe

The UK participates in the Organisation for Security and Co-operation in Europe (OSCE), which is a pan-European organisation comprising 55 states. All states participate on an equal basis, and decisions are taken by consensus. The OSCE is based in Vienna, where the UK has a permanent delegation. The main areas of work are:

- early warning and prevention of potential conflicts through field missions and diplomacy and the work of the OSCE High Commissioner on National Minorities;
- observing elections and providing advice on human rights, democracy and law, and media;
- post-conflict rehabilitation, including civil society development; and
- promoting security through arms control and military confidence-building.

Council of Europe

The UK is a founding member of the Council of Europe, which is open to any European state accepting parliamentary democracy and the protection of fundamental human rights and the rule of law. There are 41 full member states. 'Special guest status' has been granted to Armenia, Azerbaijan, and Bosnia and Herzegovina. One of the Council's main achievements is its adoption of the European Convention on Human Rights in 1950 (see p. 211).

Other International Bodies

The UK belongs to many other international bodies, including: the International Monetary Fund (IMF), which regulates the international financial system and provides credit for member countries facing balance-of-payments difficulties; the World Bank, which provides loans to finance economic and social projects in developing countries; the Organisation for Economic Co-operation and Development (OECD), which promotes economic growth, support for less developed countries and worldwide trade expansion; and the World Trade Organisation (WTO—see p. 421). Other organisations to which Britain belongs or extends support include the regional development banks in Africa, the Caribbean, Latin America and Asia, and the European Bank for Reconstruction and Development.

OVERSEAS TERRITORIES

The UK's Overseas Territories have a combined population of nearly 180,000. The territories are listed on p. 76. Most have considerable self-government, with their own legislatures. Governors appointed by the Queen are responsible for external affairs, internal security and defence. Most domestic matters are delegated to locally elected governments and legislatures. Ultimate responsibility for government rests with the UK. The British Indian Ocean Territory, the British Antarctic Territory, and South Georgia and the South Sandwich Islands have non-resident Commissioners, not Governors. The UK aims to provide the Overseas

The Overseas Territories at a Glance

Anguilla (capital: The Valley)
Area: 96 sq km (37 sq miles) (Sombrero, 5 sq km).
Population: 10,700 (1996).
Economy: tourism, construction, offshore banking, fishing and farming.
History: British territory since 1650.

Bermuda (capital: Hamilton)
Area: 53.3 sq km (20.6 sq miles).
Population: 60,144 (1996).
Economy: financial services and tourism.
History: first British settlers in 1609–12. Government passed to Crown in 1684.

British Antarctic Territory
Area: 1.7 million sq km (660,000 sq miles).
Population: no permanent inhabitants. There are two permanent British Antarctic Survey stations staffed by 40 people in winter and 150 in summer. Scientists from other Antarctic Treaty nations have bases within the territory.
History: the Antarctic Peninsula was discovered in 1820. The British claim to the British Antarctic Territory dates back to 1908. The UK is one of 44 signatories to the 1961 Antarctic Treaty, which states that the Antarctic continent should be used for peaceful purposes only.

British Indian Ocean Territory
Area: 54,400 sq km (21,000 sq miles) of ocean.
Land area: the Chagos Archipelago with no permanent inhabitants.
Economy: territory used for defence purposes by the UK and United States; 1,500 military personnel plus 1,500 civilians.
History: archipelago ceded to Britain by France under 1814 Treaty of Paris.

British Virgin Islands (capital: Road Town)
Area: 153 sq km (59 sq miles).
Population: 19,100 (1997).
Economy: tourism and financial services.
History: discovered in 1493 by Columbus and annexed by Britain in 1672.

Cayman Islands (capital: George Town)
Area: 259 sq km (100 sq miles).
Population: 36,600 (1997).
Economy: tourism and financial services.
History: 1670 Treaty of Madrid recognised Britain's claim to islands.

Falkland Islands (capital: Stanley)
Area: 12,173 sq km (4,700 sq miles).
Population: 2,220 (1996), plus British garrison.
Economy: fishery management and sheep farming.
History: first known landing in 1690 by British Naval Captain, John Strong. Since 1833 they have been under continuous British occupation and administration.

Gibraltar
Area: 6.5 sq km (2.5 sq miles).
Population: 27,200 (1999).
Economy: financial services, tourism, port services.
History: ceded to Britain in 1713 under Treaty of Utrecht.

Montserrat (capital: Plymouth)
Area: 102 sq km (39 sq miles).
Population: 3,500 (1998).
Economy: agriculture and fishing.
History: colonised by English and Irish settlers in 1632.

Pitcairn, Ducie, Henderson and Oeno (capital: Adamstown)
Area: 35.5 sq km (13.7 sq miles).
Population: 54 (1998).
Economy: fishing, agriculture and postage stamp sales.
History: occupied by mutineers from the British ship *Bounty* in 1790; annexed as a British colony in 1838.

St Helena (capital: Jamestown)
Area: 122 sq km (47 sq miles).
Population: 5,000 (1998).
Economy: fishing and agriculture.
History: taken over in 1661 by British East India Company.

Ascension Island (St Helena Dependency)
Area: 88 sq km (34 sq miles).
Population: 1,123 (1998).
Economy: communications and military base.
History: British garrison dates from Napoleon's exile on St Helena after 1815.
Government: Governor of St Helena with local administration.

Tristan da Cunha (St Helena Dependency)
Area: 98 sq km (38 sq miles).
Population: 285 (1998).
Economy: fishing.
History: occupied by British garrison in 1816.
Government: Governor of St Helena with local administration and elected Island Council.

South Georgia and the South Sandwich Islands
No indigenous population. First landing by Captain Cook in 1775. Small British military detachment on South Georgia, plus British Antarctic Survey all-year research station on Bird Island.

Turks and Caicos Islands (capital: Cockburn Town)
Area: about 500 sq km (193 sq miles).
Population: 20,000 (1997).
Economy: tourism, financial services and fishing.
History: Europeans from Bermuda first occupied the islands from about 1678, then planters from southern states of America settled after the War of Independence in the late 18th century.

Territories with security and political stability, ensure efficient and honest government, and help them achieve economic and social advancement. None of the territories has expressed a desire for independence from the UK.

In 1999 the British Government published a White Paper, *Partnership for Progress and Prosperity*, which proposed offering British citizenship to all those residents of the Overseas Territories who do not already have it and who wish to take it up.[4] Preparation of the necessary parliamentary legislation is currently under consideration.

Offshore financial service industries are of major importance in several of the Territories. The UK Government's policy is to ensure that international standards of regulation are met in the Territories and that effective steps are taken to combat financial crime and regulatory abuse. The Territories are also required to abide by the same standards of human rights and good governance to which the UK subscribes.

A new Overseas Territories Department within the Foreign & Commonwealth Office (FCO) provides a single focus and direct point of contact with the UK Government, although Gibraltar, because of its EU status, is dealt with primarily by the FCO's European Departments. The Department for International Development (DFID—see p. 90) has also set up an Overseas Territories Unit, which administers aid to Anguilla, the British Virgin Islands, Montserrat, the Turks and Caicos Islands, St Helena (and its dependencies) and Pitcairn. A new Overseas Territories Consultative Council, comprising the Chief Minister or equivalent from each territory and British Ministers (and chaired by the relevant FCO minister), convened its first annual meeting in October 1999.

Falkland Islands

The Falkland Islands are the subject of a territorial claim by Argentina. The UK Government does not accept the Argentine claim and is committed to defending the Islanders' right to live under a government of their own choice. This right of self-determination is enshrined in the 1985 Falkland Islands Constitution.

The UK and Argentina, while sticking to their respective positions on sovereignty, maintain diplomatic relations and continue to discuss their common interests in the South Atlantic region, such as fisheries conservation and the exploitation of oil reserves.

Gibraltar

Spain ceded Gibraltar to Britain in perpetuity under the 1713 Treaty of Utrecht but has long sought its return. However, the UK is committed to the principle, set out in the preamble to the 1969 Gibraltar Constitution, that it will never enter into arrangements under which the people of Gibraltar would pass under the sovereignty of another state against their freely and democratically expressed wishes.

Gibraltar has an elected House of Assembly, and responsibility for a wide range of 'defined domestic matters' is devolved to elected local ministers. The territory is within the EU, as part of the United Kingdom member state, although it is outside the common customs system and does not participate in the Common Agricultural or Fisheries Policies or the EU's value added tax arrangements. The people of Gibraltar have been declared UK nationals for EU purposes.

In April 2000 the UK and Spain, with the support of the Government of Gibraltar, announced agreement on various issues concerning Gibraltar's participation in EU measures.

EUROPEAN UNION POLICY

In 1998 the British Prime Minister called for a 'step change' in the UK's relations with the rest of Europe, to form stronger links with the EU and applicant countries. The aims of this initiative are to maximise British influence in Europe by building bilateral alliances with EU member states and the applicants. Since then officials and ministers from all government

[4] The offer of right of abode is on a non-reciprocal basis, as the territories do not have the capacity to absorb uncontrolled numbers of new residents. The UK Government's decision on this follows the precedent set by Gibraltar and the Falkland Islands whose existing right of abode is also non-reciprocal.

departments have extended their contacts with their European counterparts and agreed a series of joint initiatives.

The Treaties

The Union had its origins in the post-Second World War resolve by Western European nations, particularly France and Germany, to prevent further conflict and establish lasting peace and stability.

Rome Treaty

The 1957 Rome Treaty, establishing the European Community, defined its aims as the harmonious development of economic activities, a continuous and balanced economic expansion and an accelerated rise in the standard of living. These objectives were to be achieved by the creation of a common internal market, including the elimination of customs duties between member states, free movement of goods, people, services and capital, and the elimination of distortions in competition within this market. These aims were reaffirmed by the 1986 Single European Act, which agreed measures to complete the single market (see p. 79). The UK joined the European Community in 1973.

Under the Rome Treaty, the European Commission speaks on behalf of the UK and the other member states in international trade negotiations. The Commission negotiates on a mandate agreed by the European Council. (For further information on overseas trade, see chapter 25.)

Maastricht Treaty

The 1992 Maastricht Treaty amended the Rome Treaty and made other new commitments, including moves towards economic and monetary union (see below). It established the EU, which comprises the European Community and intergovernmental arrangements for a Common Foreign and Security Policy (CFSP—see p. 81) and for increased co-operation on justice and home affairs policy issues (see p. 82). It also enshrined in the Treaty the principle of subsidiarity under which, in areas where the Community and member states share competence, action should be taken at European level only if its objectives cannot be achieved by member states acting alone and can be better achieved by the Community. In addition, the Treaty introduced the concept of EU citizenship as a supplement to national citizenship.

Amsterdam Treaty

In 1996 an intergovernmental conference was convened to consider further treaty amendments. This resulted in the Amsterdam Treaty, which entered into force in 1999, and provides for:

- the Council to take action to combat discrimination on the basis of gender, race, religion, sexual orientation, disability or age;
- more co-ordination by member states of measures designed to cut unemployment;
- integration of the social chapter (see p. 80) into the Treaty, following its adoption by the UK;
- new mechanisms to improve the co-ordination and effectiveness of the CFSP;
- an increase in the areas subject to co-decision between the Council of Ministers and European Parliament, and simplification of the co-decision procedure (see p. 69);
- a binding protocol on subsidiarity; and
- measures to enhance openness in the EU institutions.

Treaty Ratification

Any amendments to the Treaties must be agreed unanimously and must then be ratified by each member state according to its own constitutional procedures. In the UK, Treaty ratifications must be approved by Parliament before they can come into force.

Economic and Monetary Union

The Maastricht Treaty envisaged the achievement of economic and monetary union in preparatory stages, culminating with the adoption on 1 January 1999 of a single currency (the euro). In May 1998 a meeting of EU heads of state and government agreed that 11 of the 15 EU member states (excluding the UK, Denmark, Greece and Sweden) would take part in the single currency from its launch date. It also agreed the establishment of the European Central Bank (ECB) from June 1998.

On 1 January 1999 conversion rates between currencies of qualifying countries and the euro were legally fixed. The euro became the legal currency in those countries and the ECB assumed responsibility for formulating the monetary policy of the euro area. Since no euro banknotes or coins will be available until 1 January 2002, national currencies will continue to exist in parallel to the euro and national banknotes and coins will be used for all cash transactions.

The European Council meeting in Santa Maria da Feira (Portugal) in June 2000 confirmed Greece's entry into the euro zone from 1 January 2001. The UK Government's policy towards joining the single currency is described in chapter 23 (see p. 387).

Enlargement

Enlargement of the EU—to include those European nations sharing its democratic values and aims, which are functioning market economies, able to compete in the EU and to take on the obligations of membership—is a key policy objective for the Union. In 1998 an accession process with the applicant states was launched, and formal negotiations started with Poland, Hungary, Slovenia, Estonia, Cyprus and the Czech Republic. At the European Council meeting in Helsinki in December 1999, the EU agreed to invite six other countries—Bulgaria, Latvia, Lithuania, Malta, Romania and Slovakia—to open accession negotiations (which were launched in February 2000), and also recognised Turkey's candidature for membership.

The EU is preparing institutional changes to take account of enlargement. In March 1999 the Berlin European council agreed the EU's budgetary arrangements for the period 2000–06 (see below), including making financial provision for the first new member states to join the Union in that period. Following a decision at the Cologne European Council in June 1999, an intergovernmental conference to decide the institutional changes necessary for enlargement began in February 2000. These changes include the number of Commissioners in an enlarged Union, the weighting of votes in the Council and a review of the issues which might be decided by qualified majority voting. The intergovernmental conference should be concluded by December 2000.

European Community Budget

The Community's revenue consists of levies on agricultural imports from non-member countries, customs duties, the proceeds of value added tax receipts and contributions from member states based on gross national product (GNP).

In March 1999 the European Council agreed on budgetary amendments. The 'own resources' system for financing the EU maintains the current ceiling of 1.27 per cent of GNP; but, progressively from 2001, more revenue will be raised from contributions linked to GNP and less from VAT receipts and customs payments. It was also agreed that the UK's annual budget rebate (in place since 1984, and without which the British net contribution would be far greater than that justified by its share of Community GNP) would remain.

Single Market

The single market, providing for the free movement of people, goods, services and capital within the EU, came into effect in 1993 (see also p. 420). Largely complete in legislative terms, it covers, among other benefits, the removal of customs barriers, the liberalisation of capital movements, the opening of public procurement markets and the mutual recognition of professional qualifications.

Under the European Economic Area (EEA) Agreement, which came into force in 1994, most of the EU single market measures have been extended to Iceland, Norway and Liechtenstein. EEA member states comprise the world's largest trading bloc, accounting for 40 per cent of all global trade.

Agriculture, Fisheries and the Environment

The Common Agricultural Policy (CAP) was designed to secure food supplies and to stabilise markets. It also, however, created overproduction and unwanted food surpluses, placing a burden on the Community's budget. The Common Fisheries Policy is concerned with the conservation and management of fishery resources. See chapter 27 for further details of these policies, and of the UK's support for CAP reform (agreement on which was reached by EU member states in 1999).

Environmental considerations are integrated into all areas of EU policymaking. See chapter 20 for more information about EU environmental protection measures.

Regional and Infrastructure Development

The economic and social disparities within the EU are considerable, and will become more evident with further enlargement. To address the problem of regional imbalances there are a number of Structural Funds designed to promote economic development in underdeveloped regions and regenerate regions affected by industrial decline (see also p. 396)

Infrastructure projects and industrial investments are financed by the European Regional Development Fund. The European Social Fund supports training and employment measures for the unemployed and young people. The Guidance Section of the European Agricultural Guidance and Guarantee Fund supports agricultural restructuring and some rural development measures. The Financial Instrument of Fisheries Guidance promotes the modernisation of the fishing industry. A Cohesion Fund, set up under the Maastricht Treaty, provides financial help to reduce disparities between EU members' economies. Other initiatives promote new economic activities in regions affected by the restructuring of traditional industries, such as steel, coal and shipbuilding.

New funding levels for the Structural and Cohesion Funds in the period 2002–06 were agreed by the European Council in 1999.

The European Investment Bank, a non-profit-making institution, lends at competitive interest rates to public and private capital investment projects.

Employment and Social Affairs

The UK accepted the social chapter (a separate protocol to the Maastricht Treaty) in 1997 and agreed to implement the measures already adopted under it by the other 14 member states. Each year since 1997 EU member states have agreed guidelines to shape their national employment policies and published national action plans to show progress towards implementation. This process forms part of the European Employment Pact, approved by the European Council in June 1999. The pact involves three long-term interlinked processes aimed at:

- co-ordination of economic policy and improved interaction between wage developments and monetary, budget and fiscal policy, in order to preserve non-inflationary growth;
- greater efficiency of the labour markets by improving employability, entrepreneurship, adaptability of businesses and employees, and equal opportunities; and
- structural reform and modernisation to improve innovative capacity and efficiency of the labour market and the markets in goods, services and capital.

For details of EU education and youth programmes see chapter 10 (p. 140).

Research and Development

EU spending on research and development (R&D) plays an increasingly important role in enabling Europe to maintain the science and technology base necessary to remain competitive in world markets. Research collaboration among member states is promoted mainly through a series of framework programmes defining priorities and setting out the level of funding. The Government encourages UK companies and organisations to participate in collaborative R&D with European partners (see p. 438).

Common Foreign and Security Policy

The intergovernmental CFSP came into being in 1993 with the entry into force of the Maastricht Treaty. It provides for EU member states to agree unanimously common policies and/or joint actions on a wide range of international issues.

The Treaty of Amsterdam introduced several changes to make the policy more effective, including the appointment of a High Representative to help with the formulation, preparation and presentation of CFSP policy decisions, and the establishment of a Policy Planning and Early Warning Unit in the Council Secretariat to sharpen the preparation and focus of CFSP decisions. The Amsterdam Treaty preserves the principle that all policy should be decided by unanimity, but states that decisions implementing common strategies, which are themselves agreed by unanimity, will be by qualified majority voting. A member country may prevent a vote being taken by qualified majority voting for 'important and stated reasons of national policy'. Also, a member state may abstain and stand aside from an EU decision/action when its interests are not affected.

Common European Security and Defence Policy

In 1998 the UK launched an initiative to strengthen the EU's capacity to respond to crises, on the basis that, if the Union is to play a coherent and effective political role, this needs to be underpinned by a credible European military capability. The initiative envisaged that the EU should have the capacity for autonomous action, backed up by appropriate military forces, the means to decide to use them and a readiness to do so, in order to respond to international crises without prejudice to actions by NATO (which would remain the foundation of collective security). Hitherto the EU had looked to the WEU to carry out such military crisis management activity on its behalf.

This approach has been endorsed by the European Council which, at the summit in Helsinki in December 1999, agreed to set up a

Economic Reform

In March 2000 the Portuguese Presidency hosted a special European Council in Lisbon on Economic Reform, Employment and Social Inclusion. Member states agreed the UK's proposal that the EU should set itself the target of becoming, by 2010, the most competitive and dynamic knowledge-based economy in the world, capable of sustainable economic growth with more and better jobs and greater social cohesion. The objectives of the strategy include:

- expanding access to the Internet and e-commerce;
- improving the internal market in services, updating public procurement rules, and reducing state aids;
- improving co-ordination of national R&D programmes, and adopting by the end of 2001 a Community patent;
- removing barriers to small business growth;[5]
- promoting education, training and employability, giving higher priority to lifelong learning and basic IT skills;
- combating social exclusion and poverty through priority actions targeting specific groups (such as minorities or the disabled); and
- modernising social protection systems (in particular, pensions).

[5] A European Charter for Small Enterprises was endorsed at the European Council meeting in Santa Maria de Feira in June 2000.

rapid intervention force, numbering 50,000–60,000 personnel to deal with conflict prevention and the military and civilian aspects of crisis management, by 2003. The European Council in June 2000 agreed detailed arrangements for co-operation between the EU and NATO, in particular the basis for participation in European crisis management by the six members of NATO which are European countries but not EU members.

Justice and Home Affairs

The Maastricht Treaty established intergovernmental arrangements for increased co-operation among EU states on justice and home affairs issues. These issues include visa, asylum, immigration and other policies related to free movement of people, and police, customs and judicial co-operation in criminal matters (including co-operation through EUROPOL—see p. 90). This is a growing aspect of EU work and, since the entry into force of the Amsterdam Treaty, has both Community-based and intergovernmental-based areas of co-operation. A protocol annexed to the Amsterdam Treaty recognises the UK's right to exercise its own frontier controls.

REGIONAL RELATIONS

Central and Eastern Europe and Central Asia

European Security

The European security situation has been transformed over the last decade. In 1990 the UK and its NATO allies, together with former (Communist) Warsaw Pact states, set up the North Atlantic Co-operation Council to promote co-operation and understanding. In 1994 the Alliance invited the non-NATO states in Central and Eastern Europe and Central Asia to join a Partnership for Peace programme, a form of association which, among other things, enlists the Partners' assistance in peacekeeping operations. In 1997, the Euro-Atlantic Partnership Council was set up to develop closer political and military links between NATO countries and non-members.

The UK played a significant role in negotiations leading to:

- the 1997 Founding Act between NATO member states and Russia, introducing new mechanisms for a close and permanent relationship;[6]
- a NATO–Ukraine Charter for a Distinctive Partnership, also signed in 1997; and
- the accession to NATO, in March 1999, of the Czech Republic, Hungary and Poland.

Economic Help

The UK and other Western countries continue to help deal with the economic problems following the fall of Communism, and to promote the development of market economies. The IMF provides support for stabilisation programmes and the World Bank finance for structural reform to nearly all countries in the region. This is further bolstered by the European Bank for Reconstruction and Development's investments and its role in facilitating additional private investment. The EU's PHARE scheme[7] is primarily devoted to aiding Central European countries in the process of reform and development of their infrastructure. Countries of the former Soviet Union (excluding Estonia, Latvia and Lithuania) and Mongolia receive help through a parallel programme (TACIS),[8] which concentrates on democratisation, financial services, transport, energy (including nuclear safety) and public administration reform. The UK's Export Credits Guarantee Department (ECGD) provides insurance cover for exporters to a number of these countries.

---

[6] Relations between Russia and NATO were undermined in 1999 over Russia's opposition to the Alliance's military action against Serbia over developments in Kosovo (see p. 87). Steps to re-establish ties were agreed in February 2000.

[7] An aid programme for economic restructuring in Central Europe, which consists of many individual projects and operations to underpin the process of reform. It was initially applicable to Poland and Hungary, but has since been extended to other countries in Central Europe.

[8] An EU aid programme providing technical assistance to recipient countries.

Association and Co-operation Agreements

The EU has strengthened relations with Bulgaria, the Czech Republic, Estonia, Hungary, Latvia, Lithuania, Poland, Romania, Slovakia and Slovenia by signing Europe (Association) Agreements with them. The agreements provide an institutional framework to support the process of integration, and anticipate accession of these countries to the EU when they are able to assume the obligations of membership (see p. 79).

EU Partnership and Co-operation Agreements are in force with Russia, Ukraine, Moldova, Kazakhstan, Kyrgyzstan, Georgia, Armenia, Azerbaijan and Uzbekistan. A Trade and Co-operation Agreement with Albania and a Co-operation Agreement with Macedonia are in force. The purpose of these agreements is to reduce trade barriers, develop wide-ranging co-operation and increase political dialogue.

The EU plans to develop closer links through Stabilisation and Association Agreements with states in south-eastern Europe, providing that they meet the EU's conditions on democracy, electoral and media reform, and respect for human rights.

Middle East

Arab-Israeli Peace Process

The UK supported the breakthrough in the Middle East peace process in 1993, when Israel and the Palestine Liberation Organisation (PLO) agreed to mutual recognition and signed a Declaration of Principles on interim self-government for the Palestinians in Israeli-held territories occupied in 1967. The first stage of the Declaration was implemented in 1994, when the Palestinians adopted self-government in the Gaza Strip and the Jericho area. A peace treaty between Israel and Jordan was also signed in that year. The UK has continued to encourage peace negotiations between Israel, Syria and Lebanon.

In 1995 Israel and the PLO reached an agreement providing for a phased Israeli troop withdrawal from occupied Palestinian areas of the West Bank and for elections to a new Palestinian Council with legislative and executive powers. The UK took part in the international observation of the Palestinian elections in 1996 co-ordinated by the EU.

Progress in the process since then has been far from smooth, with frequent disruptions over political and security concerns. The UK has sought to complement the mediation efforts of the United States, based on the conviction that a lasting resolution must both protect Israel's security and provide a just exchange of land for peace; and, with its EU partners, it has reaffirmed the Palestinian right to self-determination including the option of statehood.

The Government expressed deep concern over the serious escalation of violence between Israelis and Palestinians which erupted from late September 2000.

Iraq

The UK condemned Iraq's invasion of Kuwait in 1990 and supported all UN Security Council resolutions designed to force Iraqi withdrawal and restore international legality. Because of Iraq's failure to withdraw, its forces were expelled in 1991 by an international coalition led by the United States, the UK, France and Saudi Arabia, acting under a UN mandate.

UN sanctions against Iraq, imposed at that time, still remain in force (although with substantial humanitarian exemptions), because Iraq has failed persistently to comply with the relevant Security Council resolutions, particularly relating to the supervision of the elimination of its weapons of mass destruction. In December 1999 the UK drafted and co-sponsored a further Security Council resolution creating the UN Monitoring, Verification and Inspection Commission (as the successor organisation to the former UN Special Commission on Iraq, or UNSCOM). The same resolution lifted the ceiling on Iraq's oil exports and expanded the humanitarian programme for Iraq.

UK and US warplanes continue to patrol 'no-fly' zones over southern and northern Iraq, established after the war in 1991 to protect the Shia minority in southern Iraq and the Kurdish population in the north against attacks by Iraqi regime forces.

Mediterranean

The UK and other EU member states are developing, on the basis of the Barcelona Declaration of 1995, closer links with 12 southern Mediterranean partners with the aim of promoting peace and prosperity in the region. Libya has also been invited to sign up to the Declaration. Association Agreements covering political dialogue, free trade and co-operation in a number of areas are already in force with several Mediterranean countries.

Asia-Pacific Region

The UK has well-established relations with Japan, China, the Republic of Korea, many South East Asian nations, Australia and New Zealand, and has defence links with some countries in the region. British commercial activity has developed through increased trade and investment and the setting up of business councils, joint commissions or industrial co-operation agreements. The UK is also taking advantage of increased opportunities for English language teaching, co-operation in science and technology, and educational exchanges.

The Asia-Europe Meeting (ASEM) process was inaugurated in 1996. ASEM is intended to foster closer economic and political ties between EU countries and Brunei, China, Indonesia, Japan, the Republic of Korea, Malaysia, Singapore, the Philippines, Thailand and Vietnam. The third ASEM conference was hosted in Seoul by the Government of the Republic of Korea in October 2000.

The UK and its EU and G8 partners continue to encourage India and Pakistan to join international nuclear non-proliferation regimes (see p. 87) and reduce bilateral tension over the disputed territory of Kashmir.

In 1998 Britain rejoined the South Pacific Commission, having withdrawn from membership in 1995. The Commission provides technical advice and assistance to its Pacific Island members, with which the UK has long-standing and Commonwealth ties.

Hong Kong

In 1997 the UK returned Hong Kong to Chinese sovereignty under the provisions of the 1984 Sino-British Joint Declaration, which guarantees that Hong Kong's way of life, including its rights and freedoms, will remain unchanged for 50 years from the handover. As set out in the Joint Declaration, Hong Kong is a Special Administrative Region (SAR) of China. The SAR Government enjoys a high degree of autonomy, except in foreign affairs and defence, which are the responsibility of the Chinese Government in Beijing.

The UK is represented in Hong Kong by one of the largest British diplomatic posts in the world. It continues to have responsibilities towards Hong Kong and the 3.5 million British passport holders living there. Hong Kong is the UK's second largest export market in Asia.

The Americas

The British Government considers that the close transatlantic links between the UK, the United States and Canada remain essential to guarantee the security and prosperity of Europe and North America.

The UK and the US co-operate very closely on nuclear, defence and intelligence matters. As founding members of NATO, Britain and the US are deeply involved in Western defence arrangements and, as permanent members of the UN Security Council, work closely together on major international issues. In addition, there are important economic links. The US is the UK's largest trading partner—UK exports of goods and services in 1999 amounted to £39.8 billion. Also, the UK and US are each other's biggest source of inward investment—in 1998 UK investment in the US represented 18.6 per cent of total foreign direct investment, while 16 per cent of total US overseas investment (41 per cent of US investment in Europe) was in the UK.

Strong political and economic links are maintained with Canada, with which the UK shares membership of the Commonwealth, NATO and other key international organisations. The UK is the fourth largest supplier of goods and services to Canada and the second largest source of inward investment (after the US).

Important British connections with Latin America date from the participation of British volunteers in the wars of independence in the early 19th century. Greater democracy and freer market economies in the region have enabled Britain to strengthen its relations with Latin America. The UK is now one of the largest investors in the region after the United States. The first summit of EU, Latin American and Caribbean heads of state and government (representing 48 countries) was held in Rio de Janeiro at the end of June 1999, with the aim of building a strategic partnership between the two regions based around a political, economic and cultural dialogue. Progress towards this end will be reviewed at the next summit in Spain in 2002.

The first UK/Caribbean Forum, held in 1998 in Nassau, Bahamas, marked the beginning of a new longer-term process of co-operation between the UK and the countries of the region. The second meeting, hosted by the British Government, in London in May 2000, agreed initiatives to encourage new investment in the Caribbean region, and to promote educational and judicial links.

Africa

The UK Government is giving political and practical support to efforts to prevent or end African conflicts; promoting trade, reducing debt and supporting development for lasting prosperity; and supporting African governments, organisations and individuals espousing the principles of democracy, accountability, the rule of law and human rights. The first EU-Africa summit was held in Cairo, Egypt, in April 2000.

Since the abolition of apartheid and the election of an African National Congress government in 1994, South Africa's relations with the UK have broadened into areas ranging from development assistance to military advice, and from sporting links to scientific co-operation. There has also been a steady flow of state and ministerial visits to and from South Africa. The UK is South Africa's largest single trading partner, and largest foreign investor. Both countries are committed to build on this relationship by promoting the further expansion of bilateral trade and investment. A trade, development and co-operation agreement between the EU and South Africa was signed in October 1999, providing for the creation of a free trade area and for further substantial development assistance from the EU.

PEACEKEEPING

The UN is the principal body responsible for the maintenance of international peace and security. In mid-2000 there were some 31,000 troops, military observers and police officers from 85 nations deployed to 18 peacekeeping operations around the world.

Britain and UN Peacekeeping

In 1999 the UK was the fifth largest contributor to the UN's peacekeeping costs, meeting 6 per cent of the £750 million total. The UK also provided manpower for UN-led or UN-authorised operations in Kosovo (troop numbers peaking at 11,000), Bosnia (some 2,400) and East Timor (250); plus 194 police officers on loan in those three areas, and 15 military observers in Sierra Leone (see p. 86); together with some 340 troops and military observers in Cyprus, the Democratic Republic of Congo, Kuwait and Georgia.

Cyprus

The UK has a contingent of 306 troops in the UN Force in Cyprus, established in 1964 to help prevent the recurrence of fighting between Greek and Turkish Cypriots. Since the hostilities of 1974, when Turkish forces occupied the northern part of the island, the Force has been responsible for monitoring the ceasefire and control of a buffer zone between the two communities.

Iraq/Kuwait

In 1991, UN Security Council Resolution 687 established a demilitarised zone extending 10 km into Iraq and 5 km into Kuwait to deter violations of the boundary and to observe hostile or potentially hostile actions. The UK, with the other permanent members of the

Sierra Leone
In May 2000 there was a serious deterioration in the security situation in war-torn Sierra Leone, as several hundred members of the UN peacekeeping mission there were taken hostage by rebel forces of the Revolutionary United Front. In response, the UK Government rapidly deployed to Sierra Leone around 600 British soldiers from the Parachute Regiment, supported by a Royal Navy amphibious group including 600 Royal Marines. Their objectives were to evacuate entitled personnel and to secure the main airport near the capital, Freetown, while the UN forces were built up. Having achieved these aims, the British force was withdrawn in June, although the UK Government announced that a UK-led international military advisory and training team would be sent to help create new, effective armed forces for Sierra Leone. In preparation for this, short-term British training teams were deployed from mid-June to provide intensive infantry training for new recruits. The UK has been the largest donor to the peace process in Sierra Leone, having committed about £70 million from the development budget.

At the end of August 2000, 11 British training team members were taken hostage by a rebel militia group. They were rescued on 10 September when British forces stormed the militia camp, killing around 25 and suffering one fatality of their own.

Security Council, contributes 11 personnel to the UN Iraq/Kuwait observer mission (UNIKOM).

Georgia

The UK contributes seven military personnel to the UN Observer Mission in Georgia, which was established in 1993. Its mandate includes monitoring a ceasefire between Georgian government troops and rebels in the Georgian region of Abkhazia.

Bosnia and Herzegovina

The UK supports the establishment of a peaceful, multi-ethnic and democratic Bosnia and Herzegovina, and is helping to implement the 1995 Dayton Peace Agreement. The Stabilisation Force (SFOR), around 21,000-strong in mid-2000, comprises troops from NATO nations and other contributing countries, including Russia and a number of other Partnership for Peace members (see p. 82). The UK contributes some 2,200 troops to SFOR. In addition, 80 UK police officers are with the UN International Police Task Force in Bosnia.

The main task of SFOR is to ensure continuing compliance with the military aspects of the Dayton Agreement, including monitoring the actions of the armed forces within the territory and inspecting weapon sites. It also provides broad support to the main organisations responsible for the civil aspects of the Agreement, including the Office of the High Representative, the International Police Task Force, the UN High Commissioner for Refugees, the OSCE and the UN Mission in Bosnia and Herzegovina. Although the Dayton military requirements have largely been met, many of the civil aspects have yet to be fully implemented.

The UK is assisting the International Criminal Tribunal in The Hague, which was set up to try those indicted for war crimes in the former Yugoslavia. With other SFOR contributors, British forces have detained several of those indicted. As well as contributing to the funding of the Tribunal, the UK provides staff, information and forensic science expertise.

The UK has committed to spend over £21 million in humanitarian and reconstruction aid in 1999–2002; it also contributes through the EU, OSCE and UN.

Kosovo

From early 1998 there was increasing international concern over the deteriorating situation in the province of Kosovo in the Federal Republic of Yugoslavia (FRY—comprising Serbia and Montenegro) and its implications for regional stability in south-eastern Europe. Excessive repression by Serbian security forces against the overwhelmingly ethnic Albanian population, and terrorism by Kosovo Albanian extremists, prompted widespread condemnation and calls for a peaceful solution based on the territorial integrity of the FRY and autonomy for Kosovo.

The situation worsened significantly at the beginning of 1999. The Rambouillet peace conference, held in Paris, broke up in mid-March with the refusal of the Yugoslav delegation to accept the settlement proposals. Later that month the UK and other NATO countries began intensive air operations against targets in the FRY in pursuit of a resolution to the Kosovo crisis.

In June 1999 the Yugoslav Parliament and Government accepted peace terms presented by special EU and Russian envoys. These entailed the withdrawal of Serbian security forces from Kosovo and deployment of an international security presence (with NATO participation at its core), enabling the return of displaced persons and refugees to their homes. With the subsequent authorisation of the UN, a multinational force (KFOR—including around 10,000 British troops) began deploying into Kosovo to begin the task of restoring peace to the province. About 3,500 British troops were still stationed in Kosovo in mid-2000, operating in co-operation with the UN-led civilian administration which is helping to establish self-government in the province.

As well as military support, the UK has contributed £68 million in humanitarian and emergency assistance since January 1999, and has pledged a further £22.5 million to alleviate the consequences of the Kosovo crisis.

ARMS CONTROL

Because of the global reach of modern weapons, the UK has a clear national interest in preventing proliferation of weapons of mass destruction and promoting international control.

Weapons of Mass Destruction

Nuclear Weapons

The main instrument for controlling nuclear weapons is the 1968 Treaty on the Non-Proliferation of Nuclear Weapons (NPT), to which the British Government is committed. The UK helped secure its indefinite extension in 1995, and participated in the sixth NPT review conference held in New York in April–May 2000.

The UK was also involved in the negotiations on the Comprehensive Test Ban Treaty (CTBT), which it signed in 1996 and ratified in 1998. The CTBT, with its permanent verification system, will come into force when it has been ratified by 44 named states. The British Government is pressing for negotiation of a treaty banning future production of fissile material for use in nuclear weapons.

While large nuclear arsenals and risks of proliferation remain, the Government considers that the UK's minimum nuclear deterrent (see p. 99) remains a necessary and continuing element of British security.

Biological Weapons

The 1972 Biological Weapons Convention provides for a worldwide ban on such weapons, but there are no effective compliance mechanisms. The UK and its EU partners are continuing to press in international negotiations to strengthen the Convention with a Protocol containing measures to improve compliance and transparency, including mandatory declarations of key facilities and challenge inspections.

Chemical Weapons

The 1993 Chemical Weapons Convention, which came into force in 1997, provides for a worldwide ban on chemical weapons. The Organisation for the Prohibition of Chemical Weapons is responsible for verification. During the negotiations the UK contributed to drawing up effective verification provisions. All the necessary British legislation is in place to license the production, possession and use of the most toxic chemicals and to implement the Convention's trade controls.

Conventional Armed Forces

The UK continues to work with its NATO partners and other European countries to develop and improve agreements to enhance stability in Europe in the light of the changed security environment. The main agreements reached are:

- the Conventional Armed Forces in Europe (CFE) Treaty (signed originally in 1990 and revised at an OSCE summit in November 1999),[9] which limits the numbers of heavy weapons in the countries of NATO and the former Warsaw Pact, and includes a verification regime. The CFE Treaty is widely regarded as a linchpin of European security;
- the Vienna Document, developed under the auspices of the OSCE, which is a politically binding agreement by 54 states on the promotion of stability and openness on military matters in Europe; it contains a wide range of confidence- and security-building measures, and verification arrangements; and
- the 1992 Open Skies Treaty, which provides for the overflight and photography of the entire territory of the 27 participating states to monitor their military capabilities and activities. The Treaty, which is being provisionally applied, requires ratification by Russia for entry into force.

The UN Register of Conventional Arms, which came into effect in 1992, is intended to allow greater transparency in international transfers of conventional arms and to help identify excessive arms build-ups in any one country or region.

Landmines

The UK signed the Ottawa Convention banning the use, production, trade, transfer and stockpiling of anti-personnel landmines in 1997. The Convention, which Britain ratified in 1998, entered into force on 1 March 1999. The UK destroyed its stockpile of anti-personnel mines by October 1999. It has a programme to support humanitarian demining activities, which is focused on helping affected countries develop the capacity to clear landmines and improving the co-ordination of international demining resources.

Export Controls

The UK participates in all of the international control regimes which govern the export of conventional arms, technology associated with weapons of mass destruction and 'dual-use' goods (those having a legitimate civil use as well as a potential military application).

In July 1997 the British Government issued new criteria for assessing licence applications for arms exports, one of which is that licences will not be granted if there is a clearly identifiable risk that weapons might be used for internal repression or international aggression. At the same time it banned the export of certain equipment for which there is clear evidence that it has been used for torture or other abuses; it also declared its commitment to preventing British companies from manufacturing, selling or procuring such equipment and to pressing for a global ban.

In 1998 EU member states agreed on a Code of Conduct on Arms Exports. It includes a mechanism whereby before any member state grants a licence which has been denied by another member state for an essentially identical transaction, it must first consult the member state which issued the denial.

HUMAN RIGHTS

The UK Government has stated its commitment to working for improvements in human rights standards across the world and, in July 2000, published its third annual human rights report describing the activities and initiatives pursued during the previous year. The £5 million Human Rights Project Fund, launched in 1998, provides flexible and direct financial assistance for grassroots human rights projects around the world. The UK has also supported the establishment of a strong International Criminal Court to try cases of genocide, crimes against humanity and war crimes. The Government signed the Court's

[9] In the light of Russia's breach of CFE limits through its military action against separatists in Chechnya, ratification of the 1999 revision by the UK and its NATO allies will depend on the level of all parties' compliance with the limits that have been agreed.

Statute in November 1998 and hopes to be among the first 60 states to ratify it.

International Conventions

United Nations

Universal respect for human rights is an obligation under the UN Charter. Expressions of concern about human rights do not, therefore, constitute interference in the internal affairs of another state.

The UK Government promotes the standards set out in the Universal Declaration of Human Rights, which was adopted by the UN General Assembly in 1948. Since this is not a legally binding document, the General Assembly adopted two international covenants on human rights in 1966, placing legal obligations on those states ratifying or acceding to them. The covenants came into force in 1976, the UK ratifying both in the same year. One covenant deals with economic, social and cultural rights and the other with civil and political rights. Other international instruments to which the UK is a party include those on:

- the elimination of racial discrimination;
- the elimination of all forms of discrimination against women;
- the rights of the child;
- torture and other cruel, inhuman or degrading treatment or punishment;
- the prevention of genocide;
- the abolition of slavery; and
- the status of refugees.

Council of Europe

The UK is also bound by the Council of Europe's Convention for the Protection of Human Rights and Fundamental Freedoms (ECHR), which covers areas such as:

- the right to life, liberty and a fair trial;
- the right to marry and have a family;
- freedom of thought, conscience and religion;
- freedom of expression, including freedom of the press;
- freedom of peaceful assembly and association;
- the right to have a sentence reviewed by a higher tribunal; and
- the prohibition of torture and inhuman or degrading treatment.

The rights and obligations of the ECHR are being enshrined in UK law upon the implementation of the Human Rights Act 1998 in October 2000 (see p. 211).

Organisation for Security and Co-operation in Europe

The OSCE's Office for Democratic Institutions and Human Rights (in Warsaw) promotes participating states' adherence to commitments on human rights, democracy and the rule of law, and takes a lead in monitoring elections within the OSCE area. The Office provides a forum for expert exchanges on the building of democratic institutions and the holding of elections in participating states. It also provides expertise and training on human rights, constitutional and legal matters, and promotes practical measures to strengthen civil administration.

CRIME AND TERRORISM

The UK supports international efforts to combat illegal drugs, working with producer and transit countries, especially those where drug production and trafficking represent a direct threat to the UK. Over 50 drug liaison officers are stationed in UK missions in key countries, in co-operation with the host authorities. Working with its EU partners, the UK is helping Latin American, Caribbean and Central Asian states to stem the transit of drugs across their territories. The UK is also involved in the United Nations drug control structure, and is one of the largest contributors to the UN International Drug Control Programme. It also participated in the negotiation of the EU drugs strategy for 2000–04, which was endorsed by the European Council in December 1999.

The UK contributes to international efforts to counter financial crime, for example through its membership of the Financial Action Task Force against money laundering, and its support for regional anti-money laundering groups.

Together with its EU partners, the UK is confronting serious and organised international crime through, for example, the establishment of the European Police Office (EUROPOL) to support investigations and operations conducted by national law enforcement agencies. EUROPOL powers and duties are set out in the EUROPOL Convention, which entered into force in 1998. EU member states also belong to the International Criminal Police Organisation (INTERPOL). UK liaison with INTERPOL is provided by the National Criminal Intelligence Service (see p. 217).

The British Government has stressed its condemnation of all terrorist acts, its opposition to concessions to terrorist demands and its commitment to ensuring that terrorists do not benefit from their acts. It works bilaterally with other like-minded governments, and multilaterally through the UN, EU and G8, to promote closer international co-ordination against terrorism. The UK is party to a series of international counter-terrorism conventions agreed since 1963. It signed the most recent—the International Convention for the Suppression of the Financing of Terrorism—in January 2000, and the British Government hopes to ratify it in 2001.

DEVELOPMENT CO-OPERATION

The UK Government's development policy is focused on achieving the international development targets agreed by the world's governments at UN conferences in the 1990s, particularly the goal of lifting 1 billion people out of 'abject' poverty by 2015. This involves action in key areas such as debt relief, sustained growth, and support for developing country governments committed to poverty reduction.

UK official development assistance will rise to 0.33 per cent of GNP in 2003–04. In line with this, the budget for the Department for International Development (DFID) will increase by 6.2 per cent to almost £3.6 billion in 2003–04, the highest ever level in real terms.

Promoting Sustainable Livelihoods

The UK is promoting broad-based economic growth in poorer countries, while also trying to ensure that poor people can participate in, and benefit from, such growth. The intention is to stimulate trade and private investment, both domestic and foreign.

The DFID also promotes regulation of utilities and financial markets to ensure fair competition and to prevent exploitation of market power. Well-regulated banks, credit co-operatives and stock markets boost domestic savings and promote private sector investment. Development assistance is provided at the national level in support of economic reform programmes, including the reform of public expenditure and taxation.

Poor people's access to land, resources and markets is particularly significant for growth, equity and poverty reduction. The DFID is encouraging land reform, including security of land tenure, in South Asia and Africa, and is supporting rural transport projects to improve access to markets in Mozambique, Nepal and Vietnam. It is also aiming to improve training in business and vocational skills, appropriate technologies and market information.

Debt Relief

The UK advocates action to address the debt burdens of the poorest, most indebted countries. Very high levels of unpayable debt constrain the ability of countries to tackle poverty effectively. In 1999 the British Government backed the revision of the Heavily Indebted Poor Countries (HIPC) debt initiative so that it provides wider and faster relief to countries committed to poverty reduction. Twenty HIPC countries are expected to receive relief by the end of 2000.

All aid debts owed to the UK by the poorest countries have already been cancelled. In December 1999 the Government announced that it would provide full debt relief on the remaining ECGD (see p. 425) debt for countries when they qualified for the HIPC initiative.

DFID Programme 1998–99: Bilateral Aid by Form of Aid

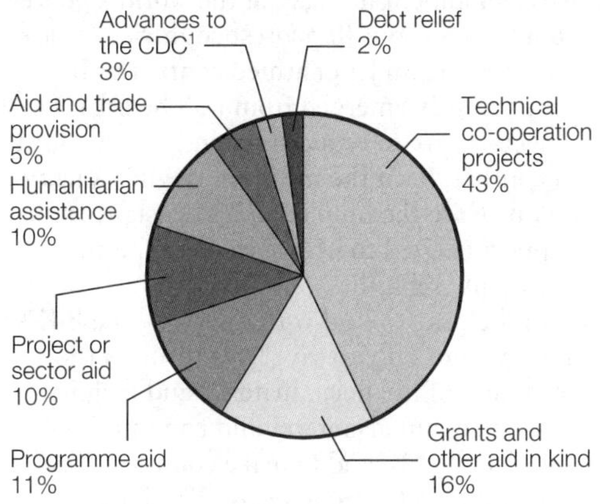

[1] Commonwealth Development Corporation–the UK's main instrument for stimulating investment in the poorer countries of the world.

Source: Department for International Development

DFID Programme 1998–99: Bilateral Aid by Region

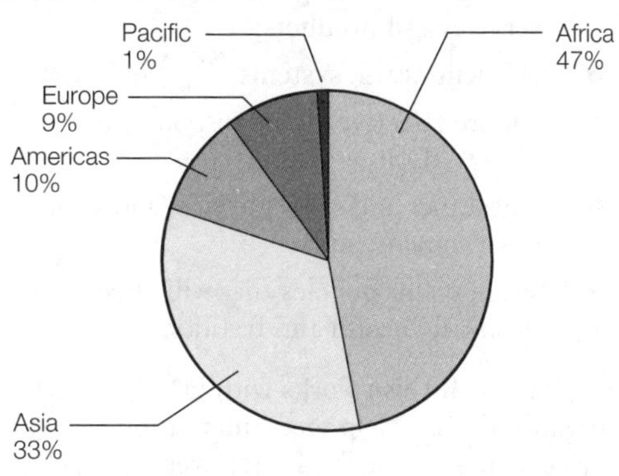

Source: Department for International Development

Good Governance and Human Rights

The DFID considers that effective governance is necessary for eliminating poverty, and is targeting issues such as democratic accountability (bringing poor people into the democratic process); fundamental freedoms (including rights to education, health and an adequate livelihood); the tackling of corruption; better revenue and public finance management; access to improved public services; and personal safety and security in the community with access to justice.

Women's Empowerment

An estimated 70 per cent of the world's poor are women and girls. Removing gender discrimination and supporting measures to improve women's equality are fundamental to reducing poverty. A priority in UK assistance is the promotion of women's basic education, together with policies aimed at breaking down inequalities between women and men in economic, political, social and cultural life. The proportion of DFID spending commitments aimed at gender equality doubled from 23 per cent in 1994–95 to 46 per cent in 1998–99.

Education

About 113 million children around the world do not go to school and many others drop out before attaining useful levels of basic education. Almost 900 million adults are illiterate, two-thirds of them being women. DFID resources are being focused on basic and primary education. Over three-quarters of UK current commitments to education—which exceed £800 million—are now in this area; two-thirds of these are concentrated in 11 of the poorest countries in sub-Saharan Africa and South Asia.

The UK is working with other governments to widen access to schools (particularly for girls), to improve the quality of education offered, and to keep children in school for the whole primary cycle. Another priority is the establishment of training in work-related skills. The DFID's Skills for Development Programmes are providing £25 million to this end.

Health

DFID aid is focusing on:

- tackling the priority diseases of the poorest, and strengthening access to care, services and products;
- efficient health systems;
- a more effective global response to HIV/AIDS;
- a healthier and safer physical and social environment; and
- social sector policies that will affect positively health and fertility.

The DFID also works with UN organisations to help meet international targets on issues such as safer pregnancy, child survival, contraception and other reproduction health services, and HIV/AIDS.

The Environment

The UK aims to support sustainable livelihoods of poor people through community-based approaches and national action promoting more secure access to natural resources and the better management of common property resources such as forests, land, fresh water and fisheries. It also aims to improve access by poor people to energy, water, transport, communications and shelter, through infrastructure development and the encouragement of private sector investment.

The UK is helping countries to set up their own national strategies for sustainable development and to meet their commitments under the multilateral environmental agreements for climate change, biodiversity, desertification and the depletion of the ozone layer.

The Global Environmental Facility (GEF) and the Multilateral Fund of the Montreal Protocol (MFMP) support developing countries and countries with economies in transition in Central and Eastern Europe and Central Asia to meet the additional costs of their commitments under the multilateral environmental agreements. Since their inception, the UK has committed £215 million to the GEF and US $95 million to the MFMP.

Conflict Reduction and Humanitarian Assistance

Violent conflict is one of the biggest barriers to development in many of the world's poorest countries. Of the 40 poorest countries, 24 are either in the midst of armed conflict or have only recently emerged from it. The DFID's objectives are to reduce the tensions that lead to conflict, limit the means of waging warfare, and provide the humanitarian assistance and support needed to help societies cope and eventually rebuild.

In helping to deal with disasters, the UK's aims are not only to save lives through the provision of financial, material and technical assistance, but also to rebuild communities and livelihoods, and to make countries less vulnerable to future hazards. The DFID provides humanitarian assistance through governments, UN agencies, the Red Cross, non-governmental organisations and, when necessary, through direct service delivery.

During 1999 and the first half of 2000 the UK responded to a number of natural disasters, including flooding in Mozambique and India, earthquakes in Turkey and droughts in Asia and Africa. Humanitarian responses have also been made to the effects of conflict in Kosovo, East Timor and Sierra Leone.

ADMINISTRATION OF FOREIGN POLICY

Foreign & Commonwealth Office

The Foreign & Commonwealth Office (FCO) is in charge of foreign policy. It is headed by the Foreign and Commonwealth Secretary, who is responsible for the work of the FCO and the Diplomatic Service (see p. 61). Diplomatic, consular and commercial relations are maintained with 184 countries (compared with 136 in 1968), and the UK has 223 diplomatic posts worldwide. British diplomatic missions also employ some 7,840 locally engaged staff. Staff overseas deal with political, commercial and economic work; entry clearance to the UK and consular work; aid administration; and information and other activities, such as culture, science and technology.

The FCO's executive agency, Wilton Park International Conference Centre in West Sussex, contributes to the solution of international problems by organising conferences in the UK, attended by politicians, business people, academics and other professionals from all over the world.

An important function of the FCO is to promote understanding of British foreign policies and to project an up-to-date image of the UK worldwide, beyond the reaches of government-to-government diplomacy. Key elements of FCO-funded public communication work include:

- publications, television and radio programmes, the FCO and Planet Britain websites (www.fco.gov.uk and www.planet-britain.org), and various other information initiatives;
- scholarship schemes for overseas students (see p. 141) and programmes for influential foreign visitors;
- the BBC World Service (see p. 270); and
- the British Council (see below).

The FCO is also developing a network of Internet-based information kiosks, placed in strategic locations around the world, to provide interactive access to British government services and information about the UK.

The London Radio Service and British Satellite News, both funded by the FCO, are used extensively by overseas radio and television broadcasters to supplement their news coverage.

Other Departments

Several other government departments are closely involved with foreign policy issues. The DFID administers the UK's development aid programmes. The Ministry of Defence maintains military liaison with the UK's NATO and other allies. The Department of Trade and Industry (DTI) has an important influence on international trade policy and commercial relations with other countries, including EU member states. The joint work of the FCO and DTI in support of British trade and investment overseas is co-ordinated through British Trade International (see p. 424). HM Treasury is involved in British international economic policy and is responsible for the UK's relations with the World Bank and other international financial institutions.

BRITISH COUNCIL

The British Council is the UK's principal agency for cultural relations overseas. Its purpose is to promote a wider knowledge of the UK and the English language and to encourage cultural, scientific, technological and educational co-operation between the UK and other countries. Its work also supports the FCO's objective of increasing respect and goodwill for the UK. The Council:

- helps people to study, train or make professional contacts in the UK;
- enables British specialists to teach, advise or establish joint projects abroad;
- teaches English and promotes its use;
- provides library and information services;
- supports legal reform overseas and works to enhance the protection of human rights;
- promotes scientific and technical training, research collaboration and exchanges; and
- encourages appreciation of British arts and literature.

The Council works in 243 towns and cities in 110 countries. It runs 222 libraries and information centres, which have about 370,000 members borrowing 8.9 million books, videos and tapes each year. Each year the Council co-funds around 700 science collaborations and administers over 625,000 British professional and academic examinations. In addition, it manages or supports 3,000 events each year with its international partners in the fields of the performing arts, film and television, visual arts, literature and design. The Council is financed partly by a grant from the FCO and partly by income from revenue-earning activities, such as English language teaching, the administration of examinations, and bilateral and international aid contract work. Some of the training and education programmes organised by the Council as part of the British aid programme receive funding from the DFID.

Educational Exchanges

The British Council recruits teachers for work overseas, organises short overseas visits by British experts, encourages cultural exchange visits, and organises academic interchange between British universities and colleges and those in other countries.

The British aid programme has helped fund certain Council programmes, such as:

- recruitment of staff for overseas universities;
- secondment of staff from British higher education establishments; and
- organisation of short-term teaching and advisory visits.

The British Council's Central Bureau for International Education and Training aims to raise standards in UK education and training through international partnership and exchange. This is achieved by the promotion of international mobility, vocational training and development, linking and exchange programmes, lifelong learning and multilateral partnerships. The Bureau is government-funded and is the UK national agency for many EU education and training programmes.

Further Reading

Foreign & Commonwealth Office Departmental Report 2000: The Government's Expenditure Plans 2000–2001 to 2001–2002. Cm 4609. The Stationery Office, 2000.

Department for International Development Departmental Report 2000. The Government's Expenditure Plans 2000–2001 to 2001–2002. Cm 4610. The Stationery Office, 2000.

Websites

Foreign & Commonwealth Office: www.fco.gov.uk

Department for International Development: www.dfid.gov.uk

British Council: www.britcoun.org

Commonwealth: www.thecommonwealth.org

8 Defence

The purpose of the UK's armed forces is to defend the country and its people, the Overseas Territories and British interests both at home and abroad. The UK is a member of NATO (the North Atlantic Treaty Organisation), and its armed forces assist in humanitarian and peacekeeping operations throughout the world.

UK SECURITY

Strategic Defence Review

In 1998 the Government published a comprehensive Strategic Defence Review, which reassessed the UK's security interests and defence needs, and considered how the roles, missions and capabilities of the armed forces should be adjusted to meet the new strategic realities. The Review concluded that there was no immediate or direct military threat to the UK or its Overseas Territories, but the end of the Cold War had introduced instability and uncertainty. There remained the potential threat of the proliferation of nuclear, chemical and biological weapons, organised crime and the break-up of existing states with attendant ethnic and religious conflict. In the new security environment, the Review concluded that Britain needs to have the capability to send highly trained and well-equipped forces very quickly around the world to prevent or contain crises; and that it should plan to be able to carry out either two medium-scale deployments (one of which could involve war-fighting) at the same time (similar to the size of the British contributions to NATO operations in Bosnia and Kosovo), or one large-scale deployment.

The planned changes outlined in the Review are also designed to reinforce the UK's contribution to international security through NATO, the European Union (EU) and the Western European Union (WEU—see p. 72), and through other international organisations such as the United Nations (UN—see p. 71) and the Organisation for Security and Co-operation in Europe (OSCE—see p. 75).

Defence Missions

The Review redefined the defence missions which underpin the UK's defence planning. These are:

- peacetime security;
- security of the Overseas Territories;
- defence diplomacy;
- support to wider British interests;

- peace support and humanitarian operations;
- responding to regional conflicts both inside and outside the NATO area; and
- responding to strategic attack on NATO.

Defence White Paper 1999

The Government published a Defence White Paper in December 1999 in which it examined whether the assumptions about the strategic context and the longer-term defence requirements set out in the Strategic Defence Review still held good. The Review had recognised that in the post-Cold War world the strategic environment would increasingly be altered by the arrival of new and often unexpected operational challenges. The Government believes that this judgment has been confirmed, with British armed forces conducting a range of operations across the world, some at short notice. Between May 1997 and August 2000, 39 operations were planned and co-ordinated.

NORTH ATLANTIC TREATY ORGANISATION

The UK is a founding member of NATO, membership of which is the cornerstone of British defence policy and most of the UK's forces are assigned to it. The Alliance embodies the transatlantic relationship that links North America and Europe in a unique defence and security partnership. The number of members was increased to 19 with the accession of the Czech Republic, Hungary and Poland in March 1999. The Alliance expects to invite other European states to join the organisation as and when the inclusion of these countries would serve the political strategic interests of the Alliance and also enhance security and stability in Europe.

Adaptation of NATO

NATO's initiatives are intended to adapt the organisation to the changed security environment in Europe. The Partnership for Peace programme, aimed at enhancing both political consultation and practical military co-operation between NATO and Partner states, and the Euro-Atlantic Partnership Council, which provides the framework for co-operation between NATO and its Partner countries (including former members of the Warsaw Pact), are key to the development of the new security relationship between NATO and other countries in Europe. The 1999 Washington summit approved new measures that will increase the ability of Partner countries to operate effectively in NATO-led crisis management operations. These include greater involvement of the 27 non-NATO states in the political consultation and decision-making process and in the operational planning and command arrangements. NATO is also committed to the sustained development of its relationship with Russia and Ukraine, following the historic agreements signed in 1997 that laid down unprecedented levels of consultation and co-operation.

NATO is also undergoing a period of internal adaptation, including the development of the European Security and Defence Identity (under which NATO assets and capabilities could be made available for EU- or WEU-led operations), a major review of the military command structure and the implementation of the Combined Joint Task Force concept. At the Washington summit the allies approved an updated strategic concept for NATO to reflect the changed political environment and the launch of an initiative to improve its defence capability to ensure the effectiveness of future multinational operations in all Alliance missions.

EUROPEAN DEFENCE

While NATO remains the foundation of Britain's security and defence policy, the Government believes that operations such as in Bosnia and Kosovo (see p. 86) have demonstrated that Europe needs to be able to make both a stronger and more coherent contribution to the Alliance and improve the collective capability to undertake EU-led crisis management operations where NATO as a whole is not engaged. At the Helsinki European Council in December 1999, on the basis of proposals developed by the UK, Italy and France (see also p. 81), EU member states committed themselves to modernising their armed forces such that by 2003 they would have a pool of deployed units from which a force up to corps levels (50,000 to 60,000 personnel, together with appropriate air and naval elements) could be assembled for a particular crisis management operation. This force would be sustainable for at least a year.

DEFENCE TASKS

The UK and its Overseas Territories

The armed forces are responsible for safeguarding Britain's territory, airspace and territorial waters. They also provide for the security and reinforcement of the Overseas Territories and support for the civil authorities in both the UK and the Overseas Territories.

Maritime Defence

The Royal Navy aims to ensure the integrity of the UK's territorial waters and the protection of its rights and interests in the surrounding seas, and of British interests around the world. The maintenance of a 24-hour, year-round presence in waters around the British Isles provides reassurance to merchant shipping, as well as security of the seas. The RAF also contributes to maritime requirements, for instance through the Nimrod force, which provides air surveillance of surface vessels and submarines.

Land Defence

The British Army aims to provide, through either the deployment of the whole or appropriate elements of its available forces, the capability to defend the UK and its Overseas Territories. In addition, the Army is committed to tasks such as providing military aid to support humanitarian operations, responding to regional conflict outside the NATO area and contributing forces to counter a strategic attack on NATO.

Air Defence

Air defence of the UK and the surrounding seas is maintained by a system of layered defences. Continuous radar cover is provided by the Air Surveillance and Control System (ASACS) supplemented by the NATO Airborne Early Warning Force, to which the RAF contributes six aircraft. The RAF also provides five squadrons of Tornado F3 air defence aircraft, supported by tanker aircraft and, in wartime, an additional F3 squadron. Royal Navy air defence destroyers can also be linked to the ASACS, providing radar and electronic warfare coverage and surface-to-air missiles. Ground-launched Rapier missiles defend the main RAF bases. Naval aircraft also contribute to British air defence.

Overseas Garrisons

The UK maintains garrisons in Gibraltar, the Sovereign Base Areas of Cyprus, the Falkland Islands and Brunei. Gibraltar provides headquarters and communications facilities for NATO in the western Mediterranean, while Cyprus provides strategic communications facilities as well as a base for operations in the eastern Mediterranean and beyond. The garrison on the Falkland Islands is a tangible demonstration of the Government's commitment to uphold the right of the islanders to determine their own future (see p. 77). The garrison in Brunei is maintained at the request of the Brunei Government. In addition, a jungle warfare training unit is maintained in Belize.

Northern Ireland

The armed forces provide support to the Royal Ulster Constabulary (RUC—see p. 216) in maintaining law and order and countering terrorism. The number of units deployed to the Province at any one time is dependent on the prevailing security situation. The Royal Navy patrols territorial waters around Northern Ireland and its inland waterways in order to deter and intercept the movement of terrorist weapons. The Royal Marines provide troops to meet Navy and Army commitments, while the RAF provides elements of the RAF Regiment and Chinook, Wessex and Puma helicopters.

Other Tasks

Other tasks include the provision of:

- military assistance to civil ministries, for example in maintaining the essentials of life in the community, providing fishery protection duties and helping in the fight against drugs;
- military aid to the civil community, including during emergencies; and
- military search and rescue.

Britain and its NATO Allies

Maritime Forces

Most Royal Navy ships are committed to NATO and are available for WEU and peacekeeping operations. Permanent contributions are made to NATO's Immediate Reaction and Rapid Reaction Forces in the Atlantic, the English Channel and the Mediterranean. The UK also contributes to NATO's Maritime Augmentation Forces, which are held at the lowest state of readiness and in peacetime comprise ships mainly in routine refit or maintenance.

The main components of the Fleet available to NATO are:

- three aircraft carriers operating Joint Force Harrier aircraft (see p. 99) and Sea King anti-submarine helicopters;
- 32 destroyers and frigates, and 22 mine counter-measure vessels;
- 12 nuclear-powered attack submarines; and
- amphibious forces, including a commando brigade, two assault ships and a helicopter carrier.

For information on Britain's independent nuclear deterrent see p. 99.

Land Forces

The multinational Allied Command Europe Rapid Reaction Corps (ARRC) is the key land component of NATO's Rapid Reaction Forces. Capable of deploying up to four NATO divisions, the ARRC is commanded by a British general, and some 55,000 British regular troops are assigned to it. Britain also provides two of the ten divisions available to the Corps—an armoured division of three armoured brigades stationed in Germany, and a division of three mechanised brigades based in Britain. An air-mobile brigade, assigned to one of the Corps' multinational divisions, is also sited in the UK.

Air Forces

The RAF contributes to NATO's Immediate and Rapid Reaction Forces. Around 100 aircraft and 40 helicopters are allocated to them. Tornado F3, Harrier and Jaguar aircraft, and Rapier surface-to-air missiles form part of the Supreme Allied Commander Europe's Immediate Reaction Force, while Harrier, Jaguar and Tornado GR1/4 aircraft provide offensive support and tactical reconnaissance for the Rapid Reaction Force. Chinook and Puma helicopters supply troop airlift facilities for the ARRC or other deployed land forces. The RAF provides Nimrod maritime patrol aircraft and search and rescue helicopters. The three Tornado GR1 squadrons stationed in Germany will be redeployed to the UK by 2002. Two Harrier offensive support squadrons were withdrawn from Germany to the UK in 1999.

Wider Security Interests

Military tasks to promote the UK's wider security interests may be undertaken by British forces unilaterally or multilaterally under UN, NATO, EU and WEU auspices. Contingents are deployed on UN operations in Cyprus, Georgia, East Timor, Bosnia, Sierra Leone, the Democratic Republic of Congo and on the Iraq/Kuwait border. Over Iraq (see p. 83), Tornado GR1/4s and Jaguars, supported by VC-10s, are policing the no-fly zones to ensure that Iraq does not resume repression of minorities and that it does not threaten its neighbours. The Royal Navy is deployed to the Gulf to enforce UN sanctions against Iraq. A substantial British contingent is deployed in Kosovo to help implement a peace agreement following the conclusion of air operations over the Federal Republic of Yugoslavia in 1999 (see p. 87).

The number of operations against trafficking in illicit drugs has increased in recent years, for example in the Caribbean, where a Royal Navy destroyer or frigate works closely with the authorities of the United States, the Overseas Territories and the Regional Security System to combat drug trafficking. Although primary responsibility for this task rests with the local law enforcement agencies or other government departments, the armed forces assist where they can do so without detriment to the performance of their other military tasks.

In the past three years, British troops have taken part in international evacuation or humanitarian relief operations in Rwanda, Somalia, Angola, Eritrea, the Democratic Republic of Congo, Sierra Leone, Mozambique, East Timor, the Caribbean and Central America.

NUCLEAR FORCES

Although the Trident submarine force is retained, the UK and other members of NATO have radically reduced their reliance on nuclear weapons. The UK is committed to pressing for progress in the negotiations towards mutual, balanced and verifiable reductions in nuclear weapons (see p. 87). When satisfied that verified progress has been made towards the goal of global elimination of nuclear weapons, the Government has said that it will ensure that the British nuclear weapons are included in the talks.

The Government undertook a fundamental re-examination of all aspects of Britain's nuclear posture in the Strategic Defence Review and concluded that fewer than 200 operationally available nuclear warheads were needed—a reduction of one-third. As a result, the UK now has only one Trident submarine on patrol at a time. It carries a reduced load of up to 48 warheads compared with the previous announced ceiling of 96. The submarine's missiles are not targeted and it is normally at several days' 'notice to fire'.

Defence diplomacy—the use of defence assets to build and promote stability and assist in the development of democratically accountable armed forces—is an established mission in UK defence planning. British service personnel and civilians working in defence are involved in a range of non-operational activities including;

- help in verifying arms control agreements (see p. 87);
- outreach programmes of bilateral assistance and co-operation with Russia and other countries in Central and Eastern Europe, Africa and Central Asia in areas such as English language training, advice on the management of defence training and short-term military training teams to assist in modernising and reforming armed forces; and
- training of some 4,000 military and civilian students from over 100 countries each year at UK defence establishments.

FORCE STRUCTURES AND CAPABILITIES

To achieve its policy objectives, the UK needs forces with a high degree of mobility, at sufficient readiness and with a clear sense of purpose, for combat operations, conflict prevention, crisis management and humanitarian activities. These forces must therefore be flexible and able to undertake the full range of military tasks.

Measures to increase a joint-service approach to defence, outlined in the strategic review, have led to the establishment of:

- Joint Rapid Reaction Forces, a pool of deployable forces (including 50 warships and support vessels, four army brigades and 100 combat aircraft), able to carry out a range of short-notice missions from war-fighting to peacekeeping operations, and to provide a first stage of a larger deployment;
- Joint Force Harrier, a joint command of Royal Navy and RAF Harrier aircraft able to operate from aircraft carriers or land bases;
- a new helicopter command of some 350 battlefield helicopters—Navy commando helicopters, Army helicopters (including

Apache attack helicopters when they enter service from 2001) and RAF support helicopters;

- a joint nuclear, biological and chemical defence regiment; and
- a joint doctrine and concepts centre for the development of defence doctrine.

These initiatives should aim to improve the Services' ability to work together efficiently and effectively and to project power to potential troublespots and crises. As well as addressing the equipment requirements for the Services (see p. 101), the Review sought to improve the way they are supported. Such measures include:

- a Defence Logistics Organisation, under a new post of Chief of Defence Logistics, covering all three Services;
- the establishment of two logistic lines of communication, each with a Joint Force Logistic Component Headquarters which will each be able to provide support to an operation of the type conducted in Bosnia and in Kosovo; and
- the restructuring of the management and organisation of the Defence Medical Services (including closer integration with the National Health Service) and a commitment to spend £140 million more on medical support to deployed forces in the period to March 2002.

Royal Navy

The focus for the Navy will continue to move from large-scale open-ocean warfare to force projection and offshore operations in conjunction with the other Services, based on:

- two new large aircraft carriers, capable of operating up to 50 aircraft and helicopters, which will enter service from 2012;
- a force of 32 destroyers and frigates, with the Type 42 destroyer being replaced by the Type 45 from 2008, and an increased number of mine counter-measure ships (22); and
- ten hunter-killer submarines, each able to fire Tomahawk land-attack missiles by 2008.

Army

Among measures aimed at improving mobility, firepower and the projection of forces are:

- an increase in the number of armoured or mechanised brigades from five to six through the conversion of the airborne brigade to a mechanised brigade;
- the creation of a new, powerful air assault brigade (combining two battalions of the Parachute Regiment), together with the new Westland Apache attack helicopter;
- the creation of an additional armoured reconnaissance regiment from an existing armoured regiment, which will be brought back from Germany;
- converting the tank regiments from eight units to six larger ones, with significantly more personnel and tanks; and
- increasing the operational utility of the Territorial Army (TA—see p. 102).

RAF

The emphasis of the new plans is on the ability to deploy appropriate types of aircraft rapidly to crises. Measures include:

- the procurement of new air-to-air, anti-armour and air-to-surface missiles for Tornado, Harrier and Eurofighter aircraft;
- improving the capability of the Nimrod reconnaissance aircraft to support both peacekeeping and war-fighting operations; and
- modernising the strategic airlift capability of the air transport fleet, in the short term by the leasing of four Boeing C-17 aircraft and, later in the decade, by the acquisition of a planned 25 Airbus A400M aircraft.

DEFENCE EQUIPMENT

Modern equipment is essential if one of the key aims of Britain's force restructuring programme is to be achieved, namely that of increasing the flexibility and mobility of the armed forces.

Improvements for the *Royal Navy* equipment programme include:

- the introduction of the fourth Trident submarine and the building of the Astute-class attack submarines;
- new aircraft, replacing the current Sea Harriers, for the two new aircraft carriers;
- a modernised destroyer and frigate fleet, including the introduction of the Type 45 destroyer which will deploy an anti-air missile system developed with France and Italy;
- new amphibious shipping to strengthen the amphibious force; and
- the Merlin anti-submarine helicopter.

The *Army* front line is being strengthened by:

- the introduction of the Challenger 2 main battle tank;
- Westland Apache attack helicopters equipped with new anti-tank missiles;
- improved Rapier and new Starstreak air defence missiles;
- new bridging equipment to increase mobility and flexibility; and
- a range of advanced surveillance, target acquisition and reconnaissance equipment.

Improvements for the *RAF* include:

- upgrading the Tornado GR1 fleet;
- upgrading the Jaguar aircraft until it is replaced, together with the Tornado F3 aircraft, by the Eurofighter;
- new Nimrod maritime patrol aircraft;
- orders for new air-launched missiles and guided bombs; and
- the introduction of EH101 and additional Chinook support helicopters and of improved Hercules aircraft.

Defence Procurement

Some £10 billion is spent each year on military equipment, including the procurement of spares and associated costs. When assessing options, consideration is given to the initial costs of a project and to those necessary to support it throughout its service life. Competition for contracts takes place wherever possible. Among the measures to improve the procuring of defence equipment, identified by the Strategic Defence Review's 'smart procurement' initiative, are the introduction of integrated teams, including representatives from industry, to control a project throughout its life. Equipment is to be acquired incrementally, with the basic equipment entering into service quickly and then being upgraded as technology improves. All defence projects are run on 'smart procurement' lines. The involvement of the private sector through the Public-Private Partnerships (see p. 405) is a major element of procurement strategy: under this policy, capital investment with a value of some £1 billion is being undertaken.

International Procurement Collaboration

The UK is a member of NATO's Conference of National Armaments Directors, which promotes equipment collaboration between NATO nations, and in the WEU's Western European Armaments Group, which is the main European forum for the discussion of armaments matters. The UK is also a founder member of OCCAR, an armament co-operation organisation formed with France, Germany and Italy for managing joint procurement activities. Current collaborative programmes in which the UK participates include:

- development of the Eurofighter (with Germany, Italy and Spain);
- a maritime anti-air missile system (France and Italy);
- a battlefield radar system (France and Germany);
- the EH101 helicopter (Italy);
- a multi-role armoured vehicle (France and Germany); and
- the large transport Airbus A400M aircraft (Belgium, France, Germany, Italy, Spain and Turkey).

THE ARMED FORCES

Table 8.1: Strength of Service and Civilian Personnel, April 2000

Royal Navy	42,800
Army	110,100
RAF	54,700
Regular reserves	59,600
Volunteer reserves	56,200
Civilians	115,100
UK-based	*100,300*
Locally based	*14,700*

Source: Defence Analytical Services Agency

Commissioned Ranks

Commissions in the armed services, either by promotion from the ranks or by direct entry based on educational and other qualifications, are granted for short, medium and long terms. All three Services have schemes for school, university and college sponsorships.

Commissioned ranks receive initial training at the Britannia Royal Naval College, Dartmouth; the Commando Training Centre, Lympstone; the Royal Military Academy, Sandhurst; or the Royal Air Force College, Cranwell. This is followed by specialist training, which may include degree courses at service establishments or universities. Courses of higher training for officers, emphasising the joint approach to the tactical and operational levels of conflict, are provided at the Joint Services Command and Staff College.

Non-commissioned Ranks

Engagements for non-commissioned ranks vary widely in length and terms of service. Subject to a minimum period, entrants may leave at any time, giving 18 months' notice (12 months for certain engagements). Discharge may also be granted on compassionate or medical grounds.

In addition to their basic training, non-commissioned personnel receive supplementary specialist training throughout their careers. Study for educational qualifications is encouraged and service trade and technical training leads to nationally recognised qualifications. New vocational training and educational initiatives to improve recruitment and retention were announced in the Strategic Defence Review. The Army Foundation College offers a 42-week course combining military training and the opportunity to acquire national qualifications. The course is intended to attract high-quality recruits who will go on to fill senior posts in front-line roles.

Reserve Forces

The reserve forces serve alongside the regular forces and are integral to the ability to expand the Services in times of crises. For example, under the current commitment, around 10 per cent of UK forces in Bosnia are reservists at any one time. In particular, reserves can provide skills and units not available or required in peacetime. The reserves include former members of the regular armed forces liable for service in an emergency (regular reserve) and volunteer reserves, recruited directly from the civilian community—the Royal Naval Reserve, the Royal Marines Reserve, the TA and the Royal Auxiliary Air Force.

The main contribution of reserves—both individuals and formed units—is to support regular forces in clearly identifiable and worthwhile roles. This requires their full integration into regular formations and ready availability for service, where necessary through selective compulsory call-out during situations short of a direct threat to the UK. Reserves should also be able to serve in peace support operations. A new Reserve Training Mobilisation Centre at Chilwell near Nottingham—another Strategic Review initiative—has been set up for this purpose. Under the Review, Royal Naval and RAF volunteer reserve numbers will increase, and, while the strength of the TA has been reduced from 56,000 to 41,200, it is more closely integrated with the Regular Army.

ADMINISTRATION

The Defence Budget

The defence budget for 2000–01 is £22.8 billion, rising to £23.4 billion in 2001–02,

£24 billion in 2002–03 and £24.8 billion in 2003–04. This represents the first planned increase in real terms in the defence budget since the mid-1980s. The Ministry of Defence believes that this will allow it to build on the measures outlined in the Strategic Review, while also taking into account the lessons learned from recent operations and other priorities such as the retention of personnel.

Defence Management

The Ministry of Defence is both a Department of State and the highest-level military headquarters. The Secretary of State for Defence is responsible for the formulation and conduct of defence policy and for providing the means by which it is conducted. Three junior ministers support the Secretary of State and have responsibilities for operational and policy issues for all armed services; defence equipment procurement, collaboration and research; and defence estate, environmental and public services respectively.

Ministers are in turn supported by two key officials: the Chief of the Defence Staff (CDS) and the Permanent Under Secretary (PUS) of State. The CDS is the professional head of the armed forces and the principal military adviser to the Secretary of State and the Government. The PUS is the Government's principal civilian adviser on defence and has primary responsibility for policy, finance and administration of the department. The PUS is also personally accountable to Parliament for the expenditure of all public money voted for defence purposes.

A number of senior-level committees underpin the management of defence:

- the Defence Council, the highest departmental committee with a range of powers vested in it. Chaired by the Secretary of State, it provides the formal legal basis for the conduct of defence;
- the Defence Management Board, which provides senior-level leadership and strategic management of defence and is chaired mainly by the PUS; and
- the Chiefs of Staff Committee, chaired by the CDS and the forum in which collective military advice is given to the Secretary of State and the Government.

An integrated civilian and military staff supports ministers, senior officials and top-level committees in the day-to-day management of defence. The department is divided into a number of budget areas responsible for the major functions of the ministry. These include the operational and personnel arms of each Service; the new Defence Logistics Organisation, which brought together the separate service logistic areas into a single integrated logistic organisation; and the Defence Procurement Agency, which is responsible for the acquisition and support of defence equipment. A large proportion of the Ministry of Defence's support activities are undertaken by defence agencies.

Further Reading

The Strategic Defence Review: Modern Forces for the Modern World. Cm 3999. Ministry of Defence. The Stationery Office, 1998.

Defence White Paper, 1999. Cm 4446. Ministry of Defence. The Stationery Office, 1999.

The Government's Expenditure Plans 2000/2001 to 2001/2002. Cm 4608. Ministry of Defence. The Stationery Office, 2000.

Kosovo. Lessons from the Crisis. Cm 4724. Ministry of Defence. The Stationery Office, 2000.

Websites

Ministry of Defence: www.mod.uk

NATO: www.nato.int

9 The Social Framework

The population of the United Kingdom is rising, partly due to increases in life expectancy and partly as a result of net inward migration. The number of older people has grown and is projected to continue to do so. The proportion of lone parent households with dependent children has increased considerably since the 1960s, as has the number of people living alone. Women have contributed heavily to the growth of the labour force and have increased their presence among those in power, politics and decision-making. Holidays abroad are now commonplace and communication has been accelerated globally by television, telephone and the Internet.

POPULATION PROFILE

The population of the UK in mid-1999 was estimated to be less than 59.5 million, the second largest in the European Union (EU). The majority of people (about 84 per cent) lived in England, with Northern Ireland having the smallest population of the four countries at 1.7 million (3 per cent). The population density in England is the highest, with about 381 inhabitants per square kilometre.

The population of the UK has increased by just over half since the beginning of the 20th century. Mid-1998-based projections suggest that it will rise to over 63.5 million by 2021. Longer-term projections suggest the population will peak around 2036 and then gradually start to fall.

Age and Gender

The UK has an ageing population. The proportion of the population aged 65 and over has increased from one person in 20 in 1901 to just over one in six in 1999. Projections suggest that the population will become gradually older with the median age expected to rise from just over 37 years in 1998 to nearly 42 years by 2021. In 1999 there were 1.4 million more children aged under 16 than people of pensionable age. Mid-1998-based projections suggest that by 2008 the population of pensionable age will exceed the number of children.

Although more boys are born each year than girls, in 1999 there were about 900,000 more women in the UK than men. Men outnumbered women in the younger age groups, until around the age of 50 the numbers of men and women were about equal. Above this age women increasingly outnumbered men, and there were nearly four times the number of women as men aged 90 and over. In 1999 there were around 8,000 centenarians in the UK, with more than eight women to every man. While the numbers are still very small, the rate of increase recently has been large—about 7 per cent a year—and the number has roughly doubled every decade since 1950. Population projections suggest that by 2036 there could be nearly 50,000 centenarians in the UK.

Births

In 1999 there were about 700,000 live births in the UK, representing 11.8 live births per 1,000 population. Almost 39 per cent of all births occurred outside marriage, around five times the level in 1966. Most of the increase in births outside marriage since the late 1980s has been in births registered jointly by both parents living at the same address, many of whom are cohabiting couples. In 1999 about eight in ten births outside marriage in England and Wales were jointly registered by both parents; three-quarters of these were to parents living at the same address.

Mortality

Life expectancy in the UK is increasing by around two years every decade for men and around one-and-a-half years for women. At birth the expectation of life is now approaching 75 years for males and 80 years for females.

There were about 629,000 deaths in the UK in 1999, a death rate of 10.6 per 1,000 population. There was a decline in mortality rates at most ages during the 20th century, particularly among children. Rising standards of living and developments in medical technology are among the factors that have contributed to improvements in mortality. The infant mortality rate (deaths of infants under one year old per 1,000 live births) was 6.3 for boys and 5.0 for girls in 1999. In general, in all age groups death rates are higher for men than women, and this helps to explain the gender imbalance among the older population.

Changes in the causes of death have accompanied this improvement in mortality. Sharp peaks in mortality occurred around the First World War, when deaths were mainly due to respiratory and infectious diseases. Such diseases now account for a relatively small proportion of all deaths. They have been overtaken by causes such as cancer and circulatory diseases which are much less responsive to modern preventive and curative medicine and whose incidence is concentrated at older ages.

HOUSEHOLDS AND FAMILIES

The number of households in Great Britain has risen, from 16.3 million in 1961 to 23.9 million in 1998, as the population has increased at the same time as average household size has fallen. These changes are linked to the rapid increase in the number of one-person households, which now comprise nearly one in three of all households, more than double the proportion in 1961. The proportion of lone parent households with dependent children has increased threefold since 1961, while over the same period there has been a decline in the proportion of households consisting of a couple with dependent children. In 1998–99 just over one in ten people in private households lived alone, while seven in ten people were in a household headed by a couple.

Marriage, Divorce and Cohabitation

In 1998 there were just under 305,000 marriages in the UK, one of the lowest numbers in the 20th century. The increasing prevalence of cohabitation helps to explain this decline. Of the marriages that took place in 1998, about 180,000 were first marriages for both partners, less than half the number in the peak year of 1970. A significant proportion of marriages—slightly over two in five—represent remarriages for one or both partners. The civil wedding ceremony was introduced in 1837. Since 1993 civil ceremonies have outnumbered religious ones, and by 1998 three in five weddings in Great Britain were conducted with civil ceremonies. More first marriages have a religious than a civil ceremony, while for second and subsequent marriages civil ceremonies outnumber religious ones by four to one. In addition, in recent years there has been a growing trend towards getting married abroad.

Although there has been a long-term rise in the number of divorces in the UK, in recent

Table 9.1: Households by Type of Household and Family, Great Britain *Per cent*

	1961	1981	1998–99
One person			
Under pensionable age	4	8	14
Over pensionable age	7	14	15
Two or more unrelated adults	5	5	2
One-family households[1]			
Couple			
No children	26	26	30
1–2 dependent children[2]	30	25	19
3 or more dependent children[2]	8	6	4
Non-dependent children only	10	8	6
Lone parent			
Dependent children[2]	2	5	7
Non-dependent children	4	4	3
Multi-family households	3	1	1
All households (=100%)(millions)	**16.3**	**20.2**	**23.9**[3]

[1] Other individuals who were not family members may also be included.
[2] May also include non-dependent children.
[3] Mid-year 1998.
Sources: Office for National Statistics, Department of the Environment, Transport and the Regions, National Assembly for Wales and Scottish Executive

years the increase appears to have levelled off, with the number granted in 1998—160,000—being below the peak of 1993. The divorce rate for both men and women in England and Wales fell to 12.9 per 1,000 married people in 1998, the lowest rate since 1989. The divorce rate in Scotland is lower than in England and Wales.

Cohabitation has become increasingly common in the last two decades. It is estimated that in 1996 there were nearly 1.6 million cohabiting couples in England and Wales. The proportion of all non-married women aged 18 to 49 who were cohabiting in Great Britain more than doubled in the 20 years to 1998–99, from 11 per cent to 29 per cent. The latest available, 1996-based, projections suggest that the trend towards increasing cohabitation will continue in the future, although the overall proportion of people living in couples is expected to fall.

Family Formation

In general, fertility rates for older women have increased since the early 1980s while those for younger women have declined. Women in their late twenties have the highest fertility rates—in 1999 there were 98 births per 1,000 women aged 25 to 29. The fertility rate for those aged 35 to 39 has risen fastest, nearly doubling between 1981 and 1999 to 39 births per 1,000 women in this age group, although it still remains lower than in 1961. This delay in childbearing may be related to increased female participation in education and the labour market.

The average completed family size has fallen from a recent peak of nearly 2.5 children per woman for women born in the mid-1930s and will inevitably fall below two children per woman for women born around 1960. Throughout the 1980s and 1990s fertility fell below the level needed for long-term natural replacement of the population. Average completed family size is expected to decline and level off at 1.8 children per woman for women born after 1970.

MIGRATION

Population movements occur within the UK as well as internationally. The most mobile

Marriages and Divorces, UK

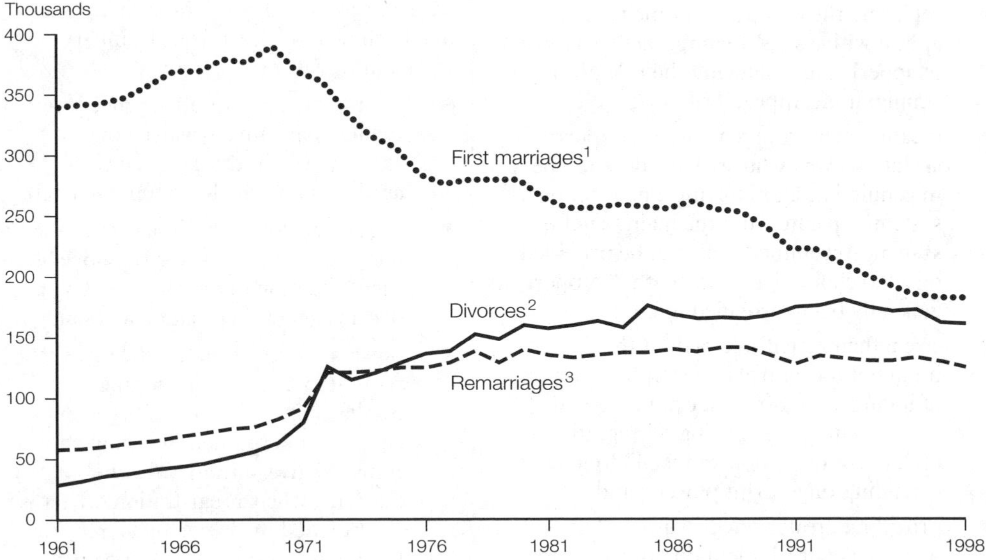

1 For both partners.
2 Includes annulments.
3 For one or both partners.

Sources: Office for National Statistics, General Register Office for Scotland and Northern Ireland Statistics and Research Agency

> The most popular names given to babies born in England and Wales in 1999 were Jack, followed by Thomas and James, for boys and Chloe, followed by Emily and Megan, for girls. Jack and Chloe were also the most popular names in Scotland, followed by Lewis and Ryan for boys and Rebecca and Lauren for girls.

age-group within the UK is young adults in their twenties, when many young people leave their parental home to study, work or set up their own home. During the second half of the 20th century there was a movement of population from the coal, shipbuilding and steel industry areas in the north of England and Wales to the south of England and the Midlands.

International Migration

In 1998 an estimated 178,000 more people migrated to the UK than from the UK. This was the highest on record and nearly double the figures for 1997 (92,000) and for 1996 (93,000). The net gain of foreign citizens in 1998 was a record 181,000 migrants and more of the net inflow was from the Old Commonwealth and the EU than in previous years.

Immigration into the UK is largely governed by the Immigration Act 1971 and the Immigration Rules made under it. The Rules set out the requirements to be met by those who are subject to immigration control and seek entry to, or leave to remain in, the UK. The 1971 Act has been amended by subsequent legislation, including the Immigration and Asylum Act 1999. The implementation of the 1999 Act has started and will continue throughout 2000–01. Its major provisions include:

- modernising the immigration control with the aim of helping it to deal with increasing passenger traffic and make enforcement of the control more effective;
- introducing measures to tackle clandestine entry, including a new civil penalty for drivers of lorries and other vehicles found to contain clandestine

entrants, and strengthening the carriers' liability regime;

- replacing the existing multiple rights of appeal with a single, comprehensive right of appeal, and enhancing the role of the Immigration Appeal Tribunal;
- creating new arrangements to support asylum seekers who are considered to be in genuine need, involving a new national system, separate from the main benefits system. Accommodation will be provided on a 'no choice' basis, with other support generally being provided in kind;
- strengthening enforcement of the immigration control by extending powers of immigration officers, extending and strengthening the existing immigration offences of deception and facilitation, and extending fingerprint powers; and
- providing greater safeguards for those who are detained, including putting the management and operation of detention centres on a statutory footing.

In implementing the Act, priority has been given to the provisions relating to the new asylum support arrangements, and to the civil penalty for carrying clandestine entrants. The phased implementation of both began in April 2000. The single, comprehensive right of appeal is due to be introduced in October 2000 to coincide with the implementation of the Human Rights Act 1998 (see p. 211).

The 1999 Act also places a duty on registration officers to report to the Home Office those marriages suspected of having been arranged for the purpose of evading immigration controls. The purpose of these measures is to prevent the abuse of the immigration system by those who are prepared to enter into marriage simply as a means to obtain settlement in the UK.

In 1999 some 97,000 people were accepted for settlement, 27,000 more than in 1998. When analysed by nationality there were substantial increases in acceptances from elsewhere in Europe and from Africa (see Table 9.2). Consequently, Africa, which accounted for nearly 30 per cent of total acceptances in 1999, replaced the Indian sub-continent as the leading region, followed by the rest of Asia and then Europe.

The 1999 Act also introduced changes to the Marriage Act 1949. These changes are due to come into effect from 1 January 2001 and consist of:

- a common 15-day notice procedure (which may only be waived in exceptional circumstances on application to the Registrar-General);
- a requirement for both parties to the marriage to personally give notice of their intention to marry, including a declaration of their nationality; and
- powers for registration officers to request evidence of name, age, marital status and nationality from couples underpinned by a power to refuse to give authority for the marriage when a registration officer is not satisfied that a person is free, legally, to contract the marriage.

Under the Immigration Rules, nationals of certain specified countries or territorial entities must obtain a visa before they can enter the UK. Other nationals subject to immigration control require entry clearance when coming to work or settle in the UK. Visas and other entry clearances are normally obtained from the nearest or other specified British diplomatic post in a person's home country.

Nationals of the European Economic Area (EEA)—EU member states plus Norway, Iceland and Liechtenstein—are not subject to substantive immigration control. They may work in the UK without restriction. Provided they are working or able to support themselves financially, EEA nationals have a right to reside in the UK.

Asylum

The UK has a tradition of granting protection to those in need, and is a signatory to the 1951 United Nations Convention, and Protocol, relating to the Status of Refugees. These provide that refugees lawfully resident should enjoy treatment at least as favourable as that accorded to the indigenous population. In the

Table 9.2: Acceptances for Settlement by Nationality

	1997	1998	1999
Europe	7,740	7,570	15,980
of which:			
European Economic Area	*110*	*270*	*n.a.*
Other Europe	*7,640*	*7,300*	*15,980*
Americas	7,790	10,780	8,520
Africa	13,200	16,090	27,020
Asia	25,610	30,120	40,090
of which:			
Indian subcontinent	*13,080*	*16,420*	*21,440*
Rest of Asia	*12,530*	*13,700*	*18,650*
Oceania	3,100	3,690	4,120
Other nationalities[1]	1,280	1,540	1,380
All nationalities	**58,720**	**69,790**	**97,120**

[1] Includes refugees from South-East Asia.
Source: Home Office

late 1980s the total started to rise dramatically from around 4,000 a year during 1985 to 1988 to 44,800 in 1991, and reached a record 71,000 in 1999, 54 per cent more than in 1998. The main nationalities applying for asylum in the UK in 1999 were people from the Federal Republic of Yugoslavia (16 per cent), Somalia (11 per cent), Sri Lanka (7 per cent), Afghanistan (6 per cent) and Turkey (4 per cent). In the first six months of 2000, applications for asylum averaged 6,145 a month. This was 22 per cent higher than in the same period a year earlier. An average of 570 applications a month were received from people from the Federal Republic of Yugoslavia between January and June 2000; an average of 500 applications a month were from Sri Lanka and 440 from China.

In the UK an estimated 32,300 asylum decisions were made in 1999, of which around 36 per cent were grants of asylum, double the proportion in 1998. Most failed asylum seekers continued to appeal against their refusal decision. Nearly 19,500 appeals were determined by independent adjudicators in 1999, and only 5,280 (27 per cent) were successful.

On 3 April 2000 the National Asylum Support Service took over responsibility for the provision of support for those asylum seekers who are destitute. The new arrangements apply to those seeking asylum on or after this date. Support will be provided until the asylum claim is finally decided. Those granted refugee status or who are allowed to remain exceptionally on humanitarian grounds are entitled to claim public funds.

Support under this new system is provided principally in kind, with vouchers issued to enable asylum seekers to obtain essential living needs. Where accommodation is provided this is on a no choice basis and dispersal will be throughout the UK.

NATIONAL AND ETHNIC GROUPS

Citizenship

Under the British Nationality Act 1981 there are three main forms of citizenship:

- British citizenship for people closely connected with the UK;
- British Dependent Territories citizenship for people connected with the dependent territories (now known as 'Overseas Territories'—see p. 75); and

- British Overseas citizenship for those citizens of the UK and Colonies who did not acquire either of the other citizenships when the 1981 Act came into force.

British citizenship is acquired automatically at birth by a child born in the UK if his or her mother or, if legitimate, father is a British citizen or is settled in the UK. A child adopted in the UK by a British citizen is also a British citizen. A child born abroad to a British citizen born, adopted, naturalised or registered in the UK is generally a British citizen by descent. The Act safeguards the citizenship of a child born abroad to a British citizen in Crown service, certain related services, or in service under an EU institution.

British citizenship may also be acquired:

- by registration for certain children, including those born in the UK who do not automatically acquire such citizenship at birth, or who have been born abroad to a parent who is a citizen by descent;
- by registration for British Dependent Territories citizens, British Overseas citizens, British subjects under the Act, British Nationals (Overseas) and British protected persons after five years' residence in the UK, except for people from Gibraltar who may be registered without residence;
- by registration for stateless people and those who have previously renounced British nationality;
- by registration for British Dependent Territories citizens connected with the Falkland Islands;
- by registration for certain women who are, or have previously been, married to men who served in the defence of Hong Kong during the Second World War;
- by registration for certain British nationals who are ordinarily resident in Hong Kong; and
- by naturalisation for all other adults aged 18 or over.

Naturalisation is at the Home Secretary's discretion. Requirements include five years' residence, or three years if the applicant's spouse is a British citizen. Those who are not married to a British citizen are also required to have a sufficient knowledge of English, Welsh or Scottish Gaelic; they must in addition intend to have their main home in the UK or be employed by the Crown, or by an international organisation of which the UK is a member, or by a company or association established in the UK.

In 1999 around 55,000 people were granted British citizenship in the UK; 4,000 applications were refused. A little over one in four of all successful applications were from citizens of Indian subcontinent countries, with Africa accounting for almost one in four and the rest of Asia representing about one in five.

Ethnic Groups

For centuries people from overseas have settled in the UK, either to escape political or religious persecution or in search of better economic opportunities. The Irish have long formed a large section of the population. Jewish refugees who came to the UK towards the end of the 19th century and in the 1930s were followed by other European refugees after 1945. Substantial immigration from the Caribbean and Indian subcontinent dates principally from the 1950s and 1960s, when the Government encouraged immigration as a means of addressing labour shortages, while many people of South Asian descent entered the UK as refugees from Kenya, Malawi or Uganda in the 1960s and 1970s.

Analysis of the Labour Force Survey by the Office for National Statistics has found that in 1999–2000, almost 4 million people in Great Britain described themselves as belonging to a non-White ethnic group, about one person in 15. In general, these groups tend to have a younger age profile than the White population, reflecting past immigration and fertility patterns. The Bangladeshi group has the youngest age structure: 41 per cent of Bangladeshis were under the age of 16 in 1999–2000, compared with 20 per cent of people in the White group.

The 1991 Census revealed that members of minority ethnic groups were heavily concentrated in the most populous areas of

England, with relatively small numbers in Scotland and Wales. Over half lived in the South East of England. The highest concentration was in the London borough of Brent, where nearly 45 per cent of the local population were from non-White groups.

Alleviating Racial Disadvantage

Although many members of the Black and Asian communities are concentrated in the inner cities, where there are problems of deprivation and social stress, progress has been made in some respects over the last 20 years in tackling racial disadvantage in the UK. For example, young people from some non-White ethnic groups are leading the way for participation in education. At the age of 16, young people from ethnic minority groups are more likely to be in full-time education than their White counterparts. For example, in 1998, 91 per cent of Indian, and 82 per cent of Black, 16 year olds were in full-time education, compared with 67 per cent of White people of the same age.

Furthermore, many individuals have achieved distinction in their careers and in public life, and the proportion of ethnic minority members occupying professional and managerial positions is increasing. In July 2000 there were nine Members of the House of Commons from ethnic minority groups.

The Home Office has overall responsibility within the Government for race equality policy and the legislation that is in place to help achieve that. Economic, environmental, educational and health programmes of central government and local authorities exist to combat disadvantage. There are also special allocations that channel extra resources into specific projects including, for example, the provision of specialist teachers for children needing English language tuition. The Government promotes equal opportunities through training programmes, including provision for unemployed people who need training in English as a second language.

Table 9.3: Resident Population by Ethnic Group, 1999–2000, Great Britain[1]

	Number of people (thousands)	Per cent
White	53,082	93.2
All non-White ethnic minority groups	3,832	6.7
of which:		
Black Caribbean	504	0.9
Black African	374	0.7
Black Other (non-mixed)	124	0.2
Black Mixed	184	0.3
Indian	942	1.7
Pakistani	671	1.2
Bangladeshi	257	0.5
Chinese	133	0.2
Other groups	644	1.1
All groups[2]	**56,927**	**100.0**

[1] Population in private households only.
[2] Includes those who did not state their ethnic group.
Source: Office for National Statistics (Labour Force Survey)

Race Relations Legislation

The Race Relations Act 1976, which applies to Great Britain, makes it unlawful for anybody to discriminate on racial grounds in relation to employment, training and education, the provision of goods, facilities and services, the provision of housing and certain other specified activities. It provides for individuals who have been discriminated against to bring proceedings and claim damages in employment tribunals (in employment and training cases) or designated county courts. Parallel legislation was introduced in Northern Ireland in 1997.

The Race Relations (Amendment) Bill, currently before Parliament, would, if enacted, outlaw discrimination in public authority functions not previously covered by the 1976 Act. This would mean that law enforcement, whether by the police, local authorities or tax inspectors, would for the first time be subject to race discrimination laws. Certain public appointments and the termination and terms and conditions of public appointments would also be subject for the first time to race discrimination laws, as would the implementation of government policies and services. The Bill would also place a general duty on public authorities to work towards the elimination of unlawful discrimination and promote equality of opportunity and good relations between people of different racial groups. The general duty would be supported by specific duties to be set out in regulations and they would be enforceable by the Commission for Racial Equality. The Commission would also be empowered to provide guidance in the form of statutory Codes of Practice.

It is a criminal offence to incite racial hatred under the provisions of the Public Order Act 1986. In order to protect ethnic minority communities from intimidation, the Crime and Disorder Act 1998 (see p. 214) created new offences of racial harassment and racially motivated violence. It also introduced court orders which prohibit named individuals from harassing the community, including racially motivated harassment. In addition, measures are being introduced as a result of the inquiry into the murder of Stephen Lawrence (see p. 219).

Commission for Racial Equality

The Commission for Racial Equality (CRE), established by the 1976 Act, is a publicly funded independent organisation working in Great Britain with both the public and private sectors to provide advice about the Race Relations Act, and how to tackle racial discrimination and promote racial equality. It also aims to help individuals with complaints about racial discrimination; in 1999–2000 about 11,000 people called the CRE for advice on such matters, and 1,563 applications were made for assistance with cases. It has power to investigate unlawful discriminatory practices and to issue non-discrimination notices requiring such practices to cease. It has an important campaigning and educational role, and has issued codes of practice on employment and housing. The CRE can also undertake or fund research. A Commission for Racial Equality for Northern Ireland was established in 1997, with similar powers. In October 1999 this was merged into the Equality Commission Northern Ireland, which also covers other grounds of unlawful discrimination.

The CRE supports the work of around 100 racial equality councils. These are autonomous voluntary bodies set up in most areas to promote equality of opportunity and good relations at the local level. The Commission helps to pay the salaries of officers employed by the racial equality councils, most of which also receive funds from their local authorities. It also gives grants to ethnic minority self-help groups and to other projects run by, or for the benefit of, ethnic minority communities.

Language

English is the main language spoken in the UK, and is also one of the most widely used in the world. Estimates suggest that 310 million people speak it as their first language, with a similar number speaking it as a second language. It is an official language in a large number of overseas countries, and is widely used internationally as the main language for purposes such as air traffic control, international maritime communications and academic gatherings.

Modern English derives primarily from one of the dialects of Old English (or Anglo-Saxon), itself made up of several Western Germanic dialects taken to Britain in the early 5th century. However, it has been very greatly influenced by other languages, particularly Latin and, following the Norman conquest, by French—the language of court, government and the nobility for many years after 1066. The re-emergence of English as the standard language of England was marked by events such as the Statute of Pleading in 1362, which laid down that English was to replace French as the language of law. The 14th century saw the first major English literature since Anglo-Saxon days, with works such as *Piers Plowman* by William Langland and the *Canterbury Tales* by Geoffrey Chaucer. However, there remained great regional variations in the language, and spellings were not always standardised.

Following the introduction of the printing press to England by William Caxton in the late 15th century, there was a considerable flowering of English literature in the 16th and early 17th centuries. William Shakespeare, Edmund Spenser and Christopher Marlowe produced work that is still famous today, while Cranmer's prayerbook and the Authorised ('King James') Version of the Bible also date from this period. About this time, too, translations of Latin, Italian and other European works into English vastly expanded the English language. The work of early lexicographers, of whom the most famous was Samuel Johnson (1709–84), led to greater standardisation in matters such as spelling.

ECONOMIC CHANGES

Marked improvements in the UK's standard of living took place during the 20th century. The average annual growth of the economy as measured by gross domestic product (GDP) in volume terms was 2.5 per cent between 1951 and 1999. Within the UK GDP per head varies. In 1998 it was highest in London, at over £16,200 per head, followed by the South East and East. Northern Ireland had the lowest regional GDP per head, at £9,400, followed by the North East and Wales. In 1998 GDP per head in London and the South East, relative to the UK average, each rose by about 2 percentage points, while it fell or remained about the same in all other regions.

Income and Wealth

Real household disposable income per head doubled between 1971 and 1999. At the same time the gap between those on high and low incomes grew, especially during the 1980s, although the gap stabilised in the 1990s. Lone parents tend to be over-represented among those on low incomes. In 1997-98, 43 per cent of lone parent families were in the bottom fifth of the income distribution.

Wages and salaries remain the main source of household income for most people, although the proportion they contribute has declined, from 52 per cent in 1987 to 49 per cent in 1999. Occupational pensions have become an increasingly important source of income for pensioners. Although average benefit income has grown in real terms, the proportion of income from benefits has fallen, particularly among those who have retired recently. The proportion of recently retired pensioners' income from occupational pensions was 28 per cent in 1997-98.

The tax and benefit system redistributes income from households on high incomes to those on lower incomes. Households make payments through direct and indirect taxes, and social security contributions, while benefits are received through both cash payments and provision of benefits in-kind, such as the National Health Service. Households with high incomes tend to pay more in taxes than they receive in income, while those on low incomes benefit more than they are taxed. The average original income of the top fifth of households—£51,000—is 17 times the average of the bottom fifth—£2,900. Benefits and, to a lesser extent, taxes reduce this inequality so that the ratio for final income is four to one. The types of household that tend to be net beneficiaries from the redistribution of taxes and benefits include lone parent families, families with three or more children, and retired households. Wealth continues to be much more unequally distributed than income, with the most wealthy 10 per cent of the population owning half the total marketable wealth of the household sector in 1996.

Social Exclusion

Social exclusion is the term given to what can happen when individuals or areas suffer from a combination of linked problems, such as unemployment, poor skills, low incomes, poor housing, bad health and family breakdown. A Social Exclusion Unit was set up in the Cabinet Office in 1997 to co-ordinate and improve government action to reduce social exclusion in England. There is close liaison with the Scottish, Welsh and Northern Ireland devolved administrations which have their own strategies for tackling social exclusion. So far the Unit has produced reports on truancy and school exclusion, rough sleeping, poor neighbourhoods, teenage pregnancy and 16 to 18 year olds not in employment, education or training. Actions are being implemented across all departments to deal with the problems identified in the reports.

SOCIAL TRENDS

Women and Men

Employment and Income

The economic and domestic lives of women changed considerably in the 20th century. Women took an increasingly important role in the labour market. In 1971, 91 per cent of men of working age, compared with 56 per cent of women, were economically active in the UK. By 2000 women's activity rates had increased to 73 per cent of women of working age, while men's activity rates slowly declined in the 1980s and 1990s to 85 per cent in 2000. The increase in the female labour force during the 20th century came mainly from a strong rise in the participation of married women. By spring 2000, 75 per cent of married or cohabiting women were economically active.

Despite the growth in female employment in recent years, women and men still tend to work in different occupations. Women employees outnumber men in clerical and secretarial occupations by nearly three to one while there are more than twice as many men as women managers and administrators. However, in recent years there has been some erosion of the traditional gender differences—the proportion of managers and administrators who were women increased from 30 per cent in spring 1991 to 33 per cent in spring 2000.

The average individual income of men was higher than that of women in all age bands in 1996–97, largely because of their higher levels of earnings, self-employment income and their longer hours of working. The gap between male and female earnings has been closing but the differential remains, with female full-time employees earning around four-fifths of the corresponding male hourly rate. The 'pay gap' increases with age. In addition, men are more likely than women to have certain investments such as pensions.

Public Policy

In March 2000 there were a record 122 women MPs in the Westminster Parliament, representing 19 per cent of the total number of seats, although this remains below the EU average of 25 per cent for lower houses. Women account for 37 per cent of the Members of the Scottish Parliament, 40 per cent of the Welsh Assembly and 13 per cent of the members of the Legislative Assembly in Northern Ireland. In September 2000 four women sat in the UK Cabinet, including the Leader of the House of Lords, who is also the Minister for Women. She chairs the Cabinet Sub-committee on Women's Issues. Support is provided by the Women's Unit in the Cabinet Office. In 1999 the Women's Unit carried out a consultation exercise, *Listening to Women*, to compile an audit of what matters to women in the UK. The Government is also seeking to improve communications with women's organisations. Following a government review in 1998, the Women's National Commission (an advisory body) was restructured with the aim of improving its representativeness, responsiveness and influence: some 200 women's organisations have registered as partners, including both small grassroots organisations and large national ones.

In Scotland, three out of 11 Cabinet ministers are women and the Scottish Executive has established an Equality Unit to take forward its work on equality.

The Government is working to ensure that the perspective of women is automatically taken into account in the development of government policies. It is also encouraging the development of 'family-friendly' employment policies and practices (see chapter 11). Measures include:

- the Working Families Tax Credit (see p. 176);
- introducing the national minimum wage to improve the pay of low paid workers, the majority of whom are women;
- extending maternity leave and improving maternity pay for low paid workers and the self-employed;
- facilitating a financial industry action group, within the Financial Services Authority, with the aim of improving financial services for women;
- increasing the availability, affordability and quality of childcare through the National Childcare Strategy and the

Childcare Tax Credit to help families on low incomes; and

- giving help through the New Deal programmes for lone parents, partners of the unemployed and the over 50s (see p. 152).

Equal Opportunities

The Sex Discrimination Act 1975 makes discrimination between men and women unlawful, with certain limited exceptions, in employment, education, training and the provision of housing, goods, facilities and services, and protects complainants and their supporters from victimisation. Discrimination against married people and discriminatory job recruitment advertisements are also unlawful. Under the Equal Pay Act 1970, women in Great Britain are entitled to equal pay with men when doing work that is the same or broadly similar, work which is rated as equivalent, or work which is of equal value. Parallel legislation on sex discrimination and equal pay applies in Northern Ireland.

The Equal Opportunities Commission (EOC), an independent statutory body, has the duties of working towards the elimination of sex discrimination; promoting equality of opportunity between women and men; promoting equality of opportunity in the fields of employment and vocational training for people who intend to undergo, are undergoing or who have undergone gender reassignment; and keeping under review the working of, and proposing amendments to, the Sex Discrimination Act and the Equal Pay Act. It provides advice to individuals and in some cases provides legal representation for individuals to bring sex discrimination and equal pay claims. The EOC runs an 'Equality Exchange', with around 700 members, which enables employers to exchange information on good practice. Further details of the Government's equal opportunities policies may be found in chapter 6, p. 61.

The Voluntary and Community Sector

Across the UK many thousands of voluntary and community organisations exist, ranging from national bodies to small local groups. Serving the community through volunteering is a long-established tradition in the UK. One in five adults interviewed in the 1998 survey of British Social Attitudes said that they had taken part in unpaid charitable work in the previous year and one in eight said they had done unpaid voluntary work for religious or church-related activities. Many volunteers are involved in work which improves the quality of life in their local communities, or give their time to help organise events or groups in areas as diverse as social welfare, education, sport, heritage, the environment and the arts.

The Government is keen to encourage productive partnerships between the statutory and voluntary sectors and also wants to see a greater public involvement in community life. An Active Community Unit has been established in the Home Office to encourage this, raise the profile of the voluntary and community sector within government and across society, and co-ordinate the work of government departments in this area.

In order to provide a general framework for enhanced relationships between government and the voluntary and community sector, 'Compacts' have been drawn up in all four countries of the UK in consultation with the sector, taking account of the distinct traditions of voluntary activity in each constituent nation. Monitoring the implementation and progress of the Compacts within government has been assigned to a ministerial group. Other public bodies and local government are being encouraged to adopt or adapt Compacts for use locally. As part of the Compact for England, in May 2000 two Codes of Good Practice were published: the Code on Funding which aims to improve the funding relationship between the Government and the voluntary and community sector and the Code on Consultation and Policy Appraisal which aims to improve the way in which the Government consults the sector. Further codes on volunteering, community groups, and Black and other minority ethnic voluntary and community organisations will follow.

Charities

The Charity Commission for England and Wales, a non-ministerial government

Table 9.4: Income and Expenditure of the Top[1] Fund-raising Charities, 1998–99

£ million

	Voluntary income	Total income	Total expenditure
Oxfam	106	170	155
National Trust	100	221	190
Imperial Cancer Research Fund	96	118	102
Cancer Research Campaign	80	89	88
Royal National Lifeboat Institution	79	94	60
British Heart Foundation	78	88	93
Salvation Army	66	83	79
Help the Aged	60	67	63
Diana Princess of Wales Memorial Fund[2]	59	97	20
Barnardo's	59	110	125

[1] Ranked by voluntary income.
[2] Accounts are for the period of 15 months.
Source: Charities Aid Foundation

department, is responsible for the registration, monitoring and support of organisations that are charitable in law. The Commission does not make grants. At the end of 1999 there were about 163,000 'main' charities registered with the Commission, that is excluding subsidiaries or branches of other charities. The charitable sector is a major part of the economy. The combined annual income of these 'main' charities registered with the Charity Commission for England and Wales in 1999 was just over £23 billion. The majority of these organisations had a recorded annual income of under £10,000; these represent nearly three-quarters of registered charities but less than 2 per cent of the total income. The financial wealth of registered charities, measured by annual income, is concentrated in a few very large charities. The Commission gives advice to trustees of charities on their administration, and has a statutory responsibility to ensure that charities make effective use of their resources. Recent legislation has strengthened the Commissioners' powers to investigate and supervise charities. These include new measures to protect charities and donors from bogus fund-raisers and a new framework for charity accounts and reports.

Funding

Voluntary organisations may receive income from several sources, including:

- central and local government grants;
- contributions from individuals, businesses and trusts;
- earnings from commercial activities and investments; and
- fees from central and local government for those services which are provided on a contractual basis.

The introduction of the National Lottery (see p. 117) has given charities and voluntary organisations the opportunity to secure substantial new funding for projects across a range of activities.

CAF (Charities Aid Foundation) is a registered charity that works to increase resources for the voluntary sector in the UK and overseas. As well as providing services that are both charitable and financial, CAF undertakes a comprehensive programme of research and publishing, and is established as a leading source of information on all aspects of the sector.

Another valuable source of revenue for charities is through tax relief and tax exemptions. The Gift Aid scheme provides tax relief on single cash donations, while under the Payroll Giving scheme, employees can make tax-free donations to charity from their earnings. In March 2000 the Budget included a number of measures to encourage donations to charity (see p. 407).

National Lottery

National lotteries have existed in Britain intermittently since 1569. Since the National Lottery was launched in 1994 most people in Britain have played it. It currently comprises a twice weekly draw, a weekly draw and scratchcard games.

Tickets or scratchcards are available from over 35,000 retail outlets. Camelot Group plc, a private sector consortium, has the franchise to run the Lottery until the end of September 2001. In the 1998–99 Family Expenditure Survey 56 per cent of households reported participating in the Saturday or Wednesday night lottery draws during the two-week diary-keeping period following interview. Those households that played spent an average of £3.80 a week on the Lottery in 1998–99.

Of every pound spent on the National Lottery, around 28 pence goes to good causes. By the beginning of April 2000 some £9.0 billion had been raised for good causes and over 57,000 awards for £7.7 billion had been made. By October 2001 the amount raised for good causes is expected to have reached at least £11.4 billion, around £2.4 billion more than originally forecast. Almost three-quarters of the awards have been for less than £50,000. Lottery money was originally shared equally among five good causes—sport, charities, the arts, heritage and projects to mark the year 2000 and the beginning of the third millennium. The National Lottery Act 1998 provided for a sixth good cause covering education, health and environment projects: the New Opportunities Fund. In the past grants have been awarded to several large prestigious projects but recently the number of awards going to small projects has doubled. The Awards for All scheme, run jointly by lottery distributors in England and Scotland, offers small grants of between £500 and £5,000 to small local groups to support arts, sport, heritage, charitable and other community activities. The scheme will continue until at least 2002.

A five-person National Lottery Commission regulates the Lottery. Its duties are to protect players' interests, to ensure the Lottery is run with propriety, and—subject to satisfying those two criteria—to maximise the amount raised for good causes. It will also select the next Lottery operator and is able to appoint a not-for-profit operator.

Leisure Trends

The most common leisure activities are home-based, or social, such as visiting relatives or friends. Television viewing is by far the most popular leisure pastime, with average viewing time for all people aged four and over being around 25 hours a week. Nearly all households have one television set or more, and almost nine in ten have a video recorder. In 1998–99, 13 per cent of households in the UK subscribed to satellite television while 9 per cent subscribed to cable television. Despite the increasing number of television channels in recent years, the proportion of people listening to the radio has remained fairly stable, with about nine in ten adults reporting listening in the four weeks prior to interview.

Listening to music is another popular activity. Purchases of compact discs (CDs) have risen very rapidly to 176 million in 1998 when they represented 84 per cent of all album sales. The proportion of households with a CD player grew from 15 per cent in 1989 to 68 per cent in 1998–99.

Other popular pursuits include reading, do-it-yourself home improvements, gardening and going out for a meal, for a drink or to the cinema. Eating out has increased in popularity. In 1999 British people spent, on average, £5.63 per person per week on food (excluding alcohol) eaten outside the home. This is reflected in the increase of 2,000 between 1996 and 1999 in the numbers of restaurants and takeaway shops operating in the UK. Nowadays 'fast food' outlets—selling, for example, hamburgers, pizza, chicken and the traditional fish and chips—are widespread in the UK's high streets. In restaurants one can eat food from many other countries—Chinese, Indian, Italian and French are among the most widely available cuisines. Sandwich bars and coffee shops are common, especially in towns and cities.

Car ownership increased steadily from three out of ten households in Great Britain in the early 1960s to seven out of ten households

Proportion of Adults who have accessed the Internet at some time: by Age, Great Britain, July 2000

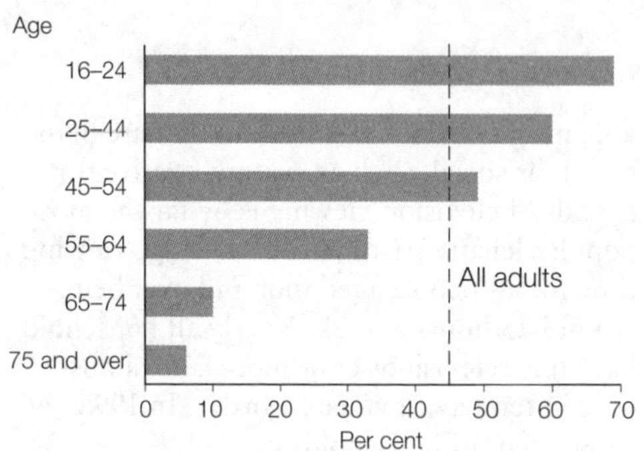

Source: Omnibus Survey, Office for National Statistics

in 1999. Whereas the proportion of households with one car changed little from the end of the 1960s, the proportion with two or more cars grew from 2 per cent in the early 1960s to 27 per cent in 1999.

Technological Change

People in Britain are continually expanding their access to, and use of, modern communication technology for both leisure and business purposes. Two items of technology that have become increasingly common for leisure and business use are mobile telephones (see p. 376) and computers. In 1998–99 a quarter of households in the UK owned at least one mobile telephone. The number of households owning home computers in the UK has also increased considerably, from just under one in six households in 1986 to a third in 1998–99. In the first quarter of 2000, 25 per cent of households had access at home to the Internet, compared with an average of 19 per cent in 1999–2000. By July 2000, 45 per cent of adults in Great Britain had accessed the Internet at some time, the equivalent of 20.4 million adults. Men were more likely to have ever used the Internet than women. The proportion steadily decreased with age—from 69 per cent of all 16 to 24 year olds to 6 per cent of those aged 75 and over. Although there

Households with Regular Use of a Car, Great Britain

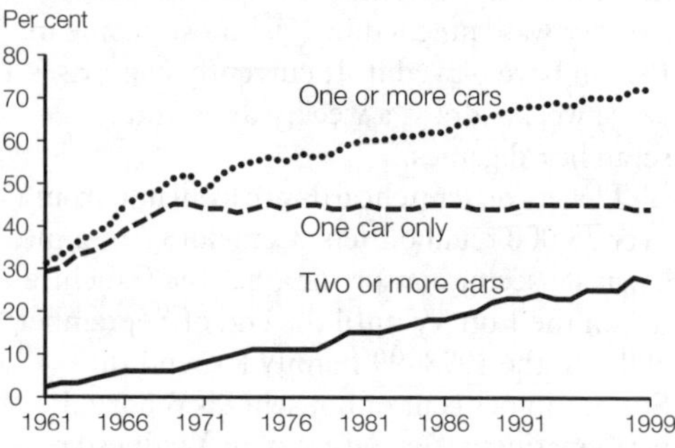

Source: Department of the Environment, Transport and the Regions

is a range of technology available, virtually all those—98 per cent—who used the Internet for personal use had done so mostly or exclusively using a computer. Among those who had accessed the Internet, seven in ten adults had done so from their own home.

Holidays

In 1998, 56 million holidays of four nights or more were taken by residents of Great Britain, 36 per cent more than in 1971. The number of holidays taken in Great Britain has been broadly stable over the last decade while the number taken abroad has grown. Spain remained the most popular holiday destination abroad in 1998, followed by France. The United States was the third most popular

Holidays[1] taken by Great Britain Residents: by Destination

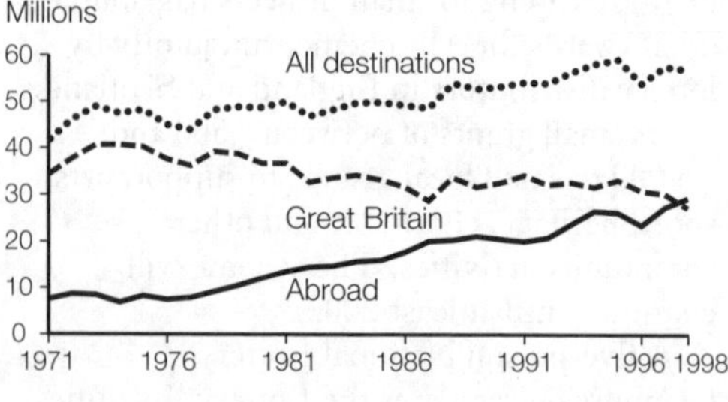

[1] Holidays of four nights or more.

Source: British National Travel Survey, British Tourist Authority

destination and the most popular non-European destination. Among adult residents of Great Britain who spent their holiday (of four nights or more) in Great Britain in 1998, the West Country was by far the most popular destination, accounting for over a quarter of such holidays. Scotland and southern England were the next most popular destinations.

Further Reading

Population Trends. Office for National Statistics. The Stationery Office.

Social Inequalities. Office for National Statistics. The Stationery Office, 2000.

Social Focus on Families. Office for National Statistics. The Stationery Office, 1997.

Social Focus on Older People. Office for National Statistics. The Stationery Office, 1999.

Social Focus on Young People. Office for National Statistics. The Stationery Office, 2000.

Social Focus on Women and Men. Office for National Statistics and Equal Opportunities Commission. The Stationery Office, 1998.

The 2001 Census of Population. Cm 4253. The Stationery Office, 1999.

Annual Reports

Annual Abstract of Statistics. Office for National Statistics. The Stationery Office.

British Social Attitudes. Ashgate Publishing.

Family Spending. Office for National Statistics. The Stationery Office.

International Migration. Office for National Statistics. The Stationery Office.

Living in Britain: Results from the General Household Survey. Office for National Statistics. The Stationery Office.

Social Trends. Office for National Statistics. The Stationery Office.

Travel Trends. Office for National Statistics. The Stationery Office.

Websites

Charity Commission: www.charity-commission.gov.uk

Commission for Racial Equality: www.cre.gov.uk

Home Office: www.homeoffice.gov.uk

Women's Unit: www.womens-unit.gov.uk

10 Education

All children in the United Kingdom are required by law to receive full-time education. After the age of 16, education is no longer compulsory and young people have a range of options. About 70 per cent of young people stay on in full-time education, either at school or at further education colleges. Around 10 per cent of 16 year old school leavers go into work and the remainder are guaranteed a place on government training programmes. In 1998–99 in England and Wales around 285,000 young people were in government work-based training. In Scotland, there were 38,400 young people in work-based training (including 13,900 Modern Apprenticeships) in 1999–2000. Nearly a third of all young people enter higher education.

In recent years, much emphasis has been placed on the concept of 'lifelong learning'. In England learning targets exist for 11 and 16 year olds, young people aged 19 and 21, as well as for adults. Statistics show that both young people and adults are becoming increasingly more qualified.

ADMINISTRATION

Government responsibility for education in the UK rests with the Department for Education and Employment (DfEE) in England, the National Assembly for Wales, the Department of Education and the Department of Higher and Further Education, Training and Employment in the Northern Ireland Executive, and in Scotland the Scottish Executive Education Department is responsible for primary and secondary education while the Scottish Executive Enterprise and Lifelong Learning Department has responsibility for lifelong learning and for further and higher education.

State schools in England and Wales are maintained by local government education authorities, or LEAs (the separate category of grant-maintained status having been ended from September 1999). Nearly all publicly maintained schools in Scotland are education authority schools, there being only two self-governing state schools. In Northern Ireland five education and library boards own, manage and run all controlled schools; they also fund most voluntary schools (see p. 125).

The education service in Great Britain is financed in the same way as other local government services (see chapter 6, p. 62), with education authorities providing funds to schools largely on the basis of pupil numbers. In Northern Ireland the costs of the education and library boards are met by the Northern Ireland Executive. There are also resources allocated to education authorities in England,

Wales and Scotland for specific purposes, such as training to improve school performance in literacy and numeracy or support for information technology.

Planned spending on education in the UK as a proportion of gross domestic product in 2000–01 is 4.8 per cent. In July 2000 the Government announced that total expenditure on education in the UK would rise by 6.6 per cent a year in real terms between 1999–2000 and 2003–04 to just under £58 billion.

SCHOOLS

Parents are required by law to see that their children receive full-time education, at school or elsewhere, between the ages of five and 16 in England, Scotland and Wales and four and 16 in Northern Ireland. About 93 per cent of pupils receive free education from public funds, while the others attend independent schools financed by fees paid by parents.

Pre-School Education

The expansion of education for children under the age of five is one of the more striking changes in education. In 1970–71 around 20 per cent of three and four year olds in the UK attended schools; by 1999–2000 this had risen to 64 per cent.

England and Wales

There has been a major expansion of pre-school education in recent years with a stated aim that all children should begin school with a basic foundation in literacy and numeracy. Targets have been set to:

- ensure that there are enough early education places, at least part-time, for all four year olds in England and Wales whose parents want one; and
- increase the percentage of three year olds with free nursery education places in England from 34 per cent in January 1997 to 100 per cent by 2004.

Children under Five[1] in Schools as a Percentage of Children aged Three and Four, UK

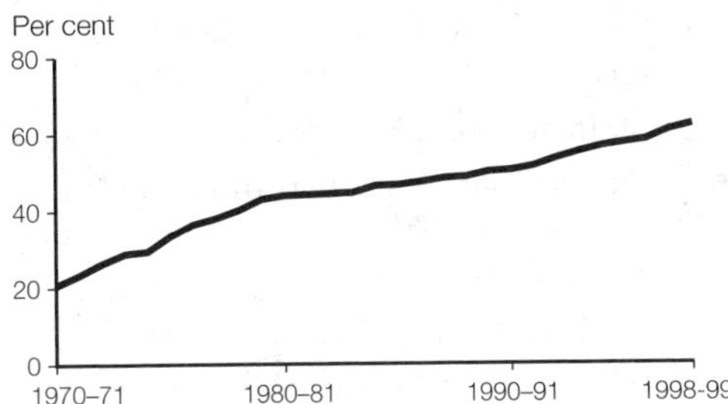

[1] Pupils aged three and four at 31 December each year. Data for 1998–99 for Wales and Scotland relate to 1997–98.

Sources: Department for Education and Employment, National Assembly for Wales, Scottish Executive and Northern Ireland Department of Education

Total spending on funding early education places has risen from £1 billion in 1996–97 to £1.6 billion in 2000–01. To realise universal provision for three year olds, it will rise to £2 billion in 2003–04.

The National Childcare Strategy was launched in 1998 with an aim to address the need for good quality affordable childcare for children up to the age of 14, and up to the age of 16 for children with special needs. By March 1999, 65,700 new childcare places had been created.

Sure Start

Sure Start is a programme which complements the National Childcare Strategy by supporting the development of local projects for children under four years of age and their families in many of the most disadvantaged areas in the country. It is intended that all families living in Sure Start areas should have access to a co-ordinated set of services which include: support for good quality play, learning and childcare experiences for children; primary and community healthcare and advice about childcare, health and development, and family health; and outreach and home visiting. By summer 2000 almost 100 programmes were providing help and support for children under four years of age.

Scotland

The Scottish Executive has set a number of targets, including:

- the provision of a nursery place for every three year old whose parents want it;
- the training of 5,000 new childcare workers;
- the expansion of support through family centres and mobile outreach services for at least 5,000 additional children;
- the provision (by 2003) of out-of-school care places for 100,000 children;
- support for 60 New Community Schools; and
- recruitment of 1,000 new teachers and 5,000 classroom assistants.

Northern Ireland

In Northern Ireland compulsory schooling begins at the age of four. Annual pre-school education development plans are drawn up for each education and library board area and annual childcare plans are drawn up for each health and social services board area. A phased expansion programme aims to increase the proportion of children in their final pre-school year who experience free pre-school education from 45 per cent in 1997–98 to 85 per cent by 2001–02 .

Primary Schools

England and Wales

Compulsory education starts in infant schools or primary school infant departments; at the age of seven, pupils transfer to separate junior schools or move to the primary school junior departments. In addition, there are some first schools which cater for ages from five to eight, nine or ten. They are the first stage of a three-tier (first, middle and secondary) school system. The usual age for transfer from primary to secondary school is 11.

Scotland

Primary education is defined by law in Scotland as education that is appropriate for children who have not attained the age of 12 years. Primary schools are organised by classes, by age, from primary 1 to primary 7. All primary school classes contain both boys and girls and cover the full range of abilities. There is no selection or streaming by ability and children are automatically moved by age from one class to the next.

Northern Ireland

All children are required to attend primary school, for seven years, from the beginning of the school year following their fourth birthday. At age 11 pupils have the option of sitting a transfer test prior to transfer from primary to secondary level education.

Class Sizes

There has been a recent trend to smaller primary class-sizes, particularly in infant classes. All LEAs and governing bodies in England and Wales are required by law to ensure all classes for five, six and seven year olds have 30 pupils or fewer by September 2001. In 1999–2000, 10 per cent of classes at Key Stage 1 in Great Britain had more than 30 pupils, compared with 31 per cent at Key Stage 2. Regional differences are evident: around 40 per cent of primary school Key Stage 2 classes in the South West, the North West and the East Midlands contained more than 30 pupils, compared with just 12 per cent in Northern Ireland and 15 per cent in Scotland.

Secondary Schools

England and Wales

Over 87 per cent of state secondary pupils in England and all state secondary pupils in Wales attend comprehensive schools. These largely take pupils without reference to ability or aptitude, providing a wide range of secondary education for all or most of the children in a district. Schools include those taking the 11 to 18 age-range, middle schools (8 to 14), and schools with an age-range of 11 or 12 to 16. The number of pupils attending non-maintained schools in England and Wales in 1998–99 was

587,000. Non-maintained schools are run by voluntary bodies, and include independent schools and non-maintained special schools.

Scotland

Scottish state secondary education is non-selective and nearly all secondary schools cover ages 12 to 18. Pupils are admitted without reference to ability or aptitude. In 1999–2000 around 314,000 pupils were in publicly funded secondary schools and a further 18,000 attended private schools.

Northern Ireland

In Northern Ireland secondary education is organised largely along selective lines, with grammar schools admitting pupils on the basis of tests in English, mathematics and science. In 1999–2000 around 62,000 pupils attended grammar schools (40 per cent of all secondary pupils), and over 92,000 attended non-grammar secondary schools of which over 7,000 pupils attended integrated schools. In 1999–2000 there were 16 integrated secondary schools, compared with nine in 1995–96.

City Technology Colleges and City Academies

There are 15 City Technology Colleges (CTCs) situated in English cities. These schools, which are state-funded independent schools run by private sponsors, operate outside the normal local government framework. They provide free education for 11 to 16 year olds in inner city areas with a curriculum which focuses on science, mathematics and technology.

From September 2001 the first City Academies will open. These will also be publicly funded independent schools involving sponsors from the private and voluntary sectors. They will be specialist schools which will replace either seriously failing schools or schools with poor GCSE[1] results, or will be established where there is an unmet demand for places.

[1] General Certificate of Secondary Education (see p. 127).

Specialist Schools

The specialist schools programme in England was launched in 1993. Specialist schools are state secondary schools specialising in technology, science and mathematics; modern foreign languages; sport; or the arts—in addition to providing the full National Curriculum (see p. 126). Any maintained secondary or special school catering for secondary age pupils in England can apply for designation.

By September 2000 there were over 530 specialist schools in 130 local education authorities across all parts of England, including 312 technology colleges, 99 language colleges, 67 sports colleges, and 57 arts colleges. Some specialist schools are located in Education Action Zones and some are also Beacon Schools (see p. 129). As part of this approach, schools work in partnership with local primary and other secondary schools and their wider communities to share the benefits of their additional resources and expertise.

Independent Schools

Independent schools providing full-time education for five or more pupils of compulsory school age must register by law with the appropriate government department and are subject to inspection. There are approximately 2,400 independent schools in the UK educating over 600,000 pupils.

Under the Music and Ballet Schools Scheme, the Government gives income-related help with fees to over 750 pupils (mainly boarding) at five specialist music schools, three ballet schools and for 80 choristers attending any of the 35 cathedral choir schools. Some 1,200 children attend the music and ballet schools. Choir schools educate over 14,000 pupils, 900 of them being choristers.

School Management

England and Wales

The School Standards and Framework Act 1998 established a new framework for school organisation which took effect from September 1999. There are three mainstream

Table 10.1: Number of Schools by Type in the UK, 1999–2000[1]

Type of school	Number
State nursery	2,825
State primary	23,052
State secondary	4,406
of which	
specialist schools	*535*
Independent schools	2,457
of which	
City Technology Colleges	*15*
Special schools[2]	1,523
Pupil referral units	322
All schools	**34,585**

[1] Includes 1998–99 data for Wales.
[2] Catering for children with special educational needs (see p. 130). The great majority of special schools are publicly maintained.
Sources: Department for Education and Employment, National Assembly for Wales, Scottish Executive and Northern Ireland Department of Education

categories—foundation, community and voluntary schools. There are 13,712 community schools, 7,059 voluntary schools and 854 foundation schools, giving a total of 21,625 maintained schools. Community schools consist of former county schools (owned and funded by LEAs); foundation schools include many of the former grant-maintained schools; and the voluntary category includes former voluntary schools, plus some former grant-maintained schools with a religious character. About 7,000 voluntary and foundation schools have a religious character. All state schools work in partnership with, and receive recurrent funding from, LEAs, managing their own budgets and staffing. Schools continue to be run by governing bodies, comprising parent, school staff, LEA and local community representation.

LEAs and school governing bodies responsible for admissions are expected to work with headteachers, the Churches and others in local forums to co-ordinate admission arrangements, taking account of statutory Codes of Practice issued in 1999. In England, disagreements on school organisation and school admissions are referred to an independent Adjudicator (although disputes about religious or denominational admission criteria are referred to the Secretary of State for Education and Employment for determination). In Wales, the National Assembly decides in all cases of disagreement. Admission authorities are no longer allowed to introduce selection by ability, unless it is for sixth form admission or is fair banding testing to ensure that pupils of all abilities are admitted, and that no one level of ability is over- or under-represented. Where existing partial selection by ability is challenged, the Adjudicator (in Wales the National Assembly) decides whether it should continue. In England, local parents are allowed to petition for a ballot and (if sufficient numbers locally wish it) to vote on whether to keep selective admission arrangements in the case of the 164 designated grammar schools which select pupils by high ability. One such ballot, which resulted in a vote for no change, has been held so far. The governing bodies of grammar schools may also publish statutory proposals to cease to be selective but none has done so to date.

Scotland

Nearly all schools in Scotland are education authority schools, which are financed by the authorities and central government. The headteacher of each school is responsible for decision-making on at least 83 per cent of school level expenditure. School Boards are currently established in around three-quarters of education authority schools. Boards consist of parents and teachers (both elected) and members co-opted from the local community. School Boards have a duty to promote contact between parents, the school and the community, and have certain specific responsibilities, such as involvement in the procedures for the appointment of senior staff and the community use of school premises. They may also take on further executive functions by delegation from their education authority.

A small number of grant-aided schools, mainly in the special sector, are run by boards of managers who also receive central government grants.

Northern Ireland

The main categories and numbers[2] of schools supported by public funds are:

- controlled schools—656 are managed by education and library boards through boards of governors;
- voluntary maintained schools—552 are managed by boards of governors consisting of members nominated by trustees (mainly Roman Catholic), along with representatives of parents, teachers and education and library boards;
- voluntary grammar schools—73 schools are managed by boards of governors; and
- grant-maintained/controlled integrated schools—43 schools, the former funded by the Department of Education but managed by boards of governors, while the latter are funded by education and library boards—the aim of these schools is to provide education for Roman Catholic and Protestant children together.

All publicly financed schools are managed by boards of governors, which include elected parents and teachers among their members. Virtually all schools have delegated budgets under which school governors decide spending priorities.

All schools must be open to pupils of all religions. However, most Roman Catholic pupils attend Catholic maintained schools or Catholic voluntary grammar schools, and most Protestant children are enrolled at controlled schools or non-denominational voluntary grammar schools. The Government has a statutory duty to encourage integrated education as a way of breaking down sectarian barriers. Existing controlled, grant-maintained and voluntary grammar schools can apply to become integrated following a majority vote by parents. In 1999–2000 there were 43 integrated schools: 16 post-primary integrated schools and 27 primary.

[2] The numbers include nursery schools, primary schools, post-primary schools, preparatory departments of grammar schools and special schools.

Table 10.2: Number of Pupils[1] by School Type in the UK, 1999–2000[2]

Type of school	Thousands
State nursery[3,4]	144
State primary[3,4]	5,338
State secondary[3]	3,857
Non-maintained schools[4]	618
Special schools[5]	114
Pupil referral units	9
All schools	**10,081**

[1] Head counts.
[2] Includes 1998–99 data for Wales.
[3] Excludes special schools.
[4] Nursery classes within primary schools are included in primary schools.
[5] Includes maintained and non-maintained sectors.
Sources: Department for Education and Employment, National Assembly for Wales, Scottish Executive and Northern Ireland Department of Education

Information for Parents and Parental Involvement

England and Wales

Parents have a statutory right to information about schools, to express a preference for a school for their child, and there is an appeal system if their choices are not met. Information includes:

- National performance tables, published annually, showing the latest public examination results, vocational qualification results and rates of absence on a school-by-school basis; and for primary schools, the National Curriculum assessment results at Key Stage 2 (see p. 126).
- Each maintained school must publish an annual prospectus for parents and prospective parents. This must include a summary of the school's National Curriculum assessment results, a summary of its public examination results and vocational qualification results (if applicable) and attendance rates.

Parents must be given a written annual report on their child's achievements containing details about progress in all subjects and activities; attendance record; results of National Curriculum assessments and public examinations including comparative results of pupils of the same age in the school and nationally; and arrangements for discussing pupils' reports with teachers.

Parents are entitled to see or be provided with a copy of their child's pupil record within 15 school days of making a written request. Unless there is a court order preventing it, all parents have a right to participate in decisions about their child's education.

Home/school agreements set out schools', pupils' and parents' responsibilities and are a statutory requirement for all maintained schools. Before adopting or revising an agreement, a school's governing body must consult all registered parents of pupils. Agreements should cover expectations about the standard of education that the school will provide, regular and punctual attendance, discipline and behaviour, homework and the information schools and parents will give to one another.

Scotland

Parents have a right of choice of school for their children, within certain limits. Information is published for parents on school costs, examination results, pupil attendance and absence, and the destinations of school leavers. Schools are required to provide parents with information about their children's attainment in each subject, teachers' comments on their progress, and details about steps to build on success or overcome difficulties.

Northern Ireland

The system of reporting to parents is broadly similar to that in England and Wales.

School Curriculum

England and Wales

The subjects taught to children between the ages of five and 16 in state schools are to a large extent determined by the National Curriculum, which has four Key Stages (see Table 10.3). At each of the stages the core subjects of English (and in Wales, Welsh), mathematics, science, technology, physical education, and religious education are taught. History, geography, art and music are also compulsory subjects in the earlier stages of the curriculum. A modern foreign language is added to the curriculum at Key Stages 3 and 4. For Key Stage 4 the study of history, geography, art and music becomes optional; in Wales a modern foreign language is optional at Key Stage 4. Other subjects, such as drama, dance, and classical languages, remain on the curriculum, but the teaching of them is optional, depending on the resources of individual schools.

The National Curriculum also contains general requirements for each subject and, for each Key Stage, programmes of study outlining what pupils should be taught, as well as attainment targets setting out expected standards of pupils' performance.

In England, revisions to the National Curriculum took effect in August 2000 and includes a new foundation subject 'citizenship' at Key Stages 3 and 4 from 2002.

In Wales, Welsh is a compulsory subject for pupils at all four Key Stages.

Religious education—all state schools must provide religious education, each LEA being responsible for producing a locally agreed syllabus. Syllabuses must reflect Christianity while taking account of the other main religions practised in the UK. Parents have the right to withdraw their children from religious education classes.

Sex education—state secondary schools are required to provide sex education for all pupils, including education about HIV/AIDS and

Table 10.3: Key Stages of the National Curriculum

	Pupil ages	Year groups
Key Stage 1	5–7	1–2
Key Stage 2	7–11	3–6
Key Stage 3	11–14	7–9
Key Stage 4	14–16	10–11

other sexually transmitted diseases. Parents are entitled to withdraw their children from sex education classes other than those required by the National Curriculum. All state schools must provide information to parents about the content of their sex education courses.

Literacy and numeracy—the Government has set targets to improve literacy and numeracy for 11 year olds in England with the aim of providing them with a satisfactory preparation for secondary education. The targets are for 80 per cent of 11 year olds to reach the standards for their age in literacy by 2002 and 75 per cent in numeracy. By autumn 1999, 71 per cent and 69 per cent of 11 year olds had reached the standards in literacy and numeracy respectively. Since September 1998 primary schools in England have devoted an hour to literacy during each teaching day, and since September 1999 pupils have also been taught a daily mathematics lesson. Literacy and numeracy summer schools are available to help those 11 year olds about to enter secondary education who have failed to meet the standards for English and mathematics. In 2000 approximately 32,490 pupils attended literacy summer schools, 19,590 attended numeracy summer schools and 14,400 have attended summer schools for more gifted and talented children.

The Government is also introducing a programme to raise standards at Key Stage 3. A pilot involving 17 LEAs and 204 schools is testing programmes designed to raise standards for all pupils across the whole curriculum in the early years of secondary education. There are new teaching and learning programmes for English, mathematics, science, and information and communications technology (ICT), including a programme of continuing professional development, as well as 'catch-up' programmes in English and mathematics for pupils who have not reached the required level for their age.

In Wales the National Assembly has adopted targets for attainment in the separate subjects of English, Welsh (first language), mathematics and science.

Assessment and testing—school pupils are formally assessed at three key stages before GCSE level—at the ages of seven, 11 and 14. The assessments at all three key stages cover the core subjects of English, mathematics and science (and Welsh in Welsh medium schools in Wales). The purpose of these assessments is to help inform teachers and parents about the progress of individual pupils and to give a measure of the performance of schools. There are two forms of assessment: tests and teacher assessment. Pupils' attainment is shown as a level on the National Curriculum scale. A typical seven year old is expected to achieve level two, a typical 11 year old level four, and a typical 14 year old between levels five and six.

In 2000 the proportion of boys reaching the required standard in English at all three key stages was considerably lower than that of girls. The widest gap was at Key Stage 3 where 55 per cent of boys compared with 72 per cent of girls reached or exceeded level five.

Qualifications—the General Certificate of Secondary Education (GCSE) is the main examination taken by pupils at the end of compulsory schooling at the age of 16. GCSE (Short Courses) are also available in a limited range of subjects; they occupy half the time of full GCSEs. In addition, the Part One General National Vocational Qualification (GNVQ)—a shortened version of the full GNVQ (see p. 134)—is available for 14 to 16 year olds. It covers seven vocational areas: art and design; business; engineering; health and social care; ICT; leisure and tourism; and manufacturing.

All GCSE and other qualifications offered to pupils in state schools must be approved by the Government. Associated syllabuses and assessment procedures must comply with national guidelines and be approved by the relevant qualification authority. The Qualifications and Curriculum Authority (QCA) and its Welsh counterpart are independent government agencies responsible for ensuring that the curriculum and qualifications available to young people and adults are of high quality, coherent and flexible.

The proportion of final year pupils achieving five or more GCSE grades A* to C in Great Britain has increased during the last decade for both boys and girls—from 46 per cent in 1992–93 to 55 per cent in 1998–99 for girls, compared with 37 per cent and 44 per cent for boys over the same period.

Scotland

Unlike England and Wales, there is no statutory national curriculum in Scotland. Pupils aged five to 14 study a broad curriculum based on national guidelines which set out the aims of study, the ground to be covered and the way the pupils' learning should be assessed and reported. Progression is measured by attainment of five levels based on the expectation of the performance of the majority of pupils at certain ages between five and 14. It is recognised that pupils learn at different rates and some will reach the various levels before others. The curricular areas are language, mathematics, environmental studies, expressive arts, and religious and moral education.

Knowledge and understanding of language and use of the skills of talking, reading and writing run throughout the curriculum, but they are the particular concern in the English Language element of the curriculum and in the pupils' study of a modern European language (which is currently being introduced into the curriculum for all pupils in the last two years of primary education). In Scotland there are 59 units in primary schools where education is offered through the medium of the Gaelic language. There are about 1,830 pupils attending these units. There are also a number of other schools where pupils are able to learn Gaelic as a second language.

Scottish education authorities must ensure that pupils are given religious instruction, although parents can withdraw their children if they wish. Government guidance on sex education is provided to education authorities and headteachers.

Pupils take the National Qualifications (NQ) at Standard Grade after four years of secondary education at the age of 16. NQ Standard Grade examinations are conducted by the Scottish Qualifications Authority (SQA). In 1998–99, 34 per cent of pupils in S4 (fourth year of lower secondary education) gained five or more Standard Grades at levels 1–2. The percentages achieving five or more Standard Grades at levels 1–4 and 1–6 were 76 and 91 per cent respectively.

Northern Ireland

The Northern Ireland curriculum, compulsory in all publicly financed schools, consists of religious education and six broad areas of study: English, mathematics, science and technology, the environment and society, creative and expressive studies and, in secondary schools and some primary schools, language studies. The main churches have approved a core syllabus for religious education and this must be taught in all grant-aided schools.

The curriculum also has cross-curricular educational themes, including cultural heritage, education for mutual understanding, health education and information technology. Secondary schools have two additional themes, namely, economic awareness and careers education.

Sex education is taught through the compulsory science programme of study and the health education cross-curricular theme.

Pupil assessment, which is statutory, is broadly in line with practice in England and Wales, taking place at eight, 11, 14 and 16. The GSCE examination is used to assess 16 year old pupils.

School Performance

England and Wales

All state schools in England and Wales are regularly inspected and inspection reports are published. The Office for Standards in Education (OFSTED) in England and the Office of Her Majesty's Chief Inspector in Wales (Estyn) aim to help improve the quality and standards of education through independent inspections and advice. Schools in England and Wales are normally inspected every six years, but more often where weaknesses are apparent, and schools must act on the inspectors' recommendations. Between inspections, school performance is regularly monitored by LEAs, which aim to ensure that schools' development plans meet national guidelines set out by the Government.

A statutory code of practice, issued under the School Standards and Framework Act 1998, governs relations between LEAs and schools. It states that the LEA needs to monitor data about all schools, and spread best practice among local schools and more widely. The LEA's resources should otherwise be focused on schools which monitoring information suggests need further improvement—that is, those in the categories of under-achieving, low performance, serious weakness or special measures.

Where a school found to be failing by inspectors does not make adequate progress, the DfEE or the National Assembly for Wales may either put the school under new management or require the LEA to close it, or a Fresh Start school can be opened. A Fresh Start school is one opened in place of a school in special measures which has closed. At the end of the summer term 2000, 1,141 schools had been found to be failing since the introduction of special measures in 1993. Of these schools, 611 had improved sufficiently to be removed from the special measures category and 132 had been closed, including 16 schools which have had Fresh Starts.

Excellence in Cities

Excellence in Cities was launched by the Government in 1999 with the aim of addressing educational problems of the major cities. It now covers secondary schools in all the major cities across nearly 60 local authority areas. There are six strands to the Excellence in Cities programme:

- Learning Mentors for all pupils who need them;
- Learning Support Units (units shared by schools where pupils with problems can be taught until they are ready to return to the classroom);
- a network of new City Learning Centres (school-based centres which share their latest ICT facilities with a network of other schools);
- more Beacon Schools and specialist schools (see below);
- small Education Action Zones; and
- extended opportunities for gifted and talented pupils.

Education Action Zones

The Education Action Zone (EAZ) initiative was introduced under the School Standards and Framework Act 1998 as an attempt to raise standards in disadvantaged urban and rural areas of England. An EAZ is typically made up of two or three secondary schools with their associated primary and special school provision working in partnership with parents, schools, businesses, the LEA, the local Training and Enterprise Council (TEC) and others. Each EAZ is run by an Action Forum made up of key partners of the zone including private sector representation.

By August 2000, 73 zones were in operation. Some 1,450 schools are participating in the zones, mostly in urban areas.

Beacon Schools

The Beacon School initiative is intended to raise standards through the spreading of good practice. Beacon Schools are those which have been identified as among the best performing in the country and represent examples of successful practices to be brought to the attention of the rest of the education service. They are expected to work in partnership with other schools to pass on their particular areas of expertise and so help others reach the same high standards as themselves. The initiative is open to all maintained schools in England in the nursery, primary, secondary and special sectors. By September 2000 there were 550 Beacon Schools in England. The network is set to expand to 1,000 schools from September 2001.

Scotland

HM Inspectors of Schools, a unit within the framework of the Scottish Executive Education Department, have the right to enter schools, including independent schools and certain other educational establishments, for the purpose of inspection. Reports are published on inspections and made available to the public. The findings and recommendations of these reports are followed up with the schools and with local authorities, governing bodies and other interested parties.

Northern Ireland

In Northern Ireland the purpose of inspection is to help to promote the highest possible standards of learning and teaching throughout the education system in Northern Ireland and to provide information to the Department of Education and others about the quality of education being offered.

Children with Special Educational Needs

A child is said to have special educational needs (SEN) if he or she has a learning difficulty which needs special provision. A child has learning difficulties if he or she has significantly greater difficulty in learning than most children of the same age or a disability which makes it difficult to use the normal educational facilities in the area. Every child has the right to receive a broad and balanced curriculum. For pupils with SEN, planning should take account of each pupil's particular learning and assessment requirements.

England and Wales

In January 2000, 1.71 million pupils were identified as having special educational needs, of whom some 252,600 had statements of SEN monitored by their local authority. Of those with statements, 60 per cent are educated in mainstream schools while most of the others are educated in special schools. State schools must try to provide for pupils with SEN and publish information about their SEN policy. LEAs must identify and assess the needs of those children with more severe or complex needs and involve parents in decisions about their children's education.

If an LEA believes that it should determine the education for the child, it must draw up a formal statement of the child's special needs and the action it intends to take to meet them. The LEA is required to comply with the parents' choice of school unless this is inappropriate for the child or incompatible with the efficient education of other children or with the efficient use of resources. Parents have a right of appeal to the Special Educational Needs Tribunal if they disagree with certain decisions by the LEA about their child. The Tribunal's verdict is final and binding on all parties.

In 1998 the Government published a programme of action setting out its strategy for raising standards for children with SEN in England. The main themes were:

- developing the knowledge and skills of all staff working with children with SEN;
- improving the SEN framework and developing a more inclusive education system;
- working in partnership with parents and carers; and
- promoting partnership in SEN provision locally, regionally and nationally.

Legislation is planned to take forward commitments made in the programme of action, as well as recommendations of the Disability Rights Task Force in respect of education. The disability provisions, which will cover England, Scotland and Wales, will place new duties on LEAs, schools (including independent schools and non-maintained special schools), further and higher education institutions, the youth service and adult education. For example, this will include a duty on education providers not to treat disabled pupils and students less favourably, without justification, than non-disabled pupils and students; and further and higher education institutions and LEAs (in respect of LEA-secured non-schools education) to make reasonable adjustments to enable disabled students to have full access to education services.

To support the implementation of the action programme in England, support for SEN in 1999–2000 was £35 million, with a further increase to £55 million for 2000–01. In addition, £30 million has been made available through the Schools Access Initiative in 2000–01 to make 1,900 mainstream schools more accessible to disabled pupils and those with sensory impairments.

Scotland

Education authorities must take special educational needs fully into account when making provision for pupils in their areas.

There are a small number of pupils (about 2 per cent of the school population) whose needs require the authority to open a record describing the special education necessary to meet them. This process incorporates a right of appeal.

Northern Ireland

Similar arrangements to those in England and Wales, including an appeal system, are in force.

Computer Technology in Schools

England and Wales

The rapid growth in information and communications technology (ICT) is having significant implications for teaching and learning in schools. In 2000, record numbers of young people took ICT examinations at age 16. In 2000, 86 per cent of primary schools and 98 per cent of secondary schools in England were connected to the Internet, compared with 17 per cent and 83 per cent respectively in 1998. All schools will be connected by 2002.

The National Grid for Learning (NGfL) was introduced in 1998 as the UK's national focal point for learning on the Internet, and a programme for connecting schools and other learning institutions. It is supported by a programme for training teachers in the use of ICT in the classroom and a rolling programme of independent evaluations of current and emerging educational technologies.

Scotland

The Scottish Consultative Council on the Curriculum was merged with the Scottish Council for Educational Technology in July 2000 and is now known as Learning & Teaching Scotland. It will have a new responsibility for advising on the use of ICT in education, which includes:

- keeping under review, and providing independent advice to Scottish ministers on, all matters relating to the school and pre-school curriculum, including the use of ICT to support delivery of the curriculum; and
- managing and supporting a programme of research and development work related to the school and pre-school curriculum and to the use of ICT in Scottish education.

Teachers

England and Wales

New teachers in maintained primary and secondary schools are required to be graduates. They must also hold Qualified Teacher Status (QTS). There are currently two main ways to become a teacher:

- the undergraduate route—taking a Bachelor of Education degree at a university or college of higher education. This route combines a degree with QTS and covers subject and professional studies with practical teaching experience in schools, where students teach a limited timetable under the supervision of an experienced teacher; or
- the postgraduate route—students need a degree (Bachelor of Arts or Science) or equivalent, that gives them the necessary foundation for the subject and age-range they want to teach. They then undertake a one-year Postgraduate Certificate in Education (PGCE) course leading to QTS. All postgraduate courses focus on professional preparation for teaching in a chosen subject and include the National Curriculum.

Teachers can also train on an employment-based route. This type of training leads to QTS and is available on the Graduate and Registered Teacher Programmes. These routes are for people at least 24 years old and offer the opportunity to earn a salary while following a training programme. They are particularly suitable for overseas-trained teachers who do not hold QTS, mature career changers, school support staff and people who have previous teaching experience. Trainees are expected to gain employment as an unqualified teacher in a school which is able to support their training programme.

The Graduate Teacher Programme (GTP) is for people already holding a degree. The normal duration of the course is one year. The Registered Teacher Programme (RTP) is for people who do not have a degree, but do have two years' higher education experience. This route takes up to two years and participants complete a degree while they train.

New arrangements for the development of the teaching profession in England are being implemented from September 2000. Key aspects include:

- requiring all trainee teachers, including those on employment-based routes, to meet the standards for the award of Qualified Teacher Status before they can qualify to teach;
- establishing an independent General Teaching Council for England;
- providing more training for headteachers;
- establishing the National College for School Leadership;
- introducing a new pay system for teachers;
- allocating to teacher training colleges resources to ensure that all teachers meet the required standards in numeracy, literacy and computer skills;
- requiring newly qualified teachers taking up their first teaching post to go through a further induction period, enabling them to consolidate their teaching skills;
- introducing a fast-track initiative to attract high quality graduates to the teaching profession and moving outstanding teachers quickly through the profession; and
- recruiting and training an extra 20,000 teaching assistants.

Similar reforms to the teaching profession are taking place in Wales, including the establishment of a General Teaching Council for Wales from September 2000.

Between 1986 and 1999, the number of full-time secondary school teachers in England and Wales decreased by 14 per cent, from about 221,000 to 191,000. In contrast, the number of full-time teachers in primary schools increased over the same period from 170,000 to 181,000, although the increase has fluctuated in intervening years.

Scotland

All teachers in education authority schools must be registered with the General Teaching Council (GTC) for Scotland. The GTC gives advice to the Minister for Children and Education on teacher supply and the professional suitability of teacher training courses. It is also responsible for disciplinary procedures under which teachers guilty of professional misconduct may be removed temporarily or permanently from the register.

Teacher qualification procedures are similar to England and Wales except the Scottish Executive must approve all pre-service teaching courses. They must also be validated by a higher education institution and accredited by the GTC as leading to registration. HM Inspectorate in Scotland has powers to inspect teacher education and training.

Revised national guidelines for teacher development and appraisal were issued in 1998, and a new qualification for headteachers—the Scottish Qualification for Headship—has now been introduced.

The Scottish Higher Education Funding Council is responsible for funding initial teacher education and setting intake levels to teacher education courses.

Northern Ireland

All new entrants to teaching in grant-aided schools are graduates and hold an approved teaching qualification. Arrangements have been developed under which initial teacher training is integrated with induction/early in-service training, the latter covering a period of three years. In addition, work continues on the development of a recognised qualification for headteachers, the Professional Qualification for Headship (NI), equivalent to the arrangements in England and Wales. A General Teaching Council will be established in Northern Ireland in the academic year 2000–01.

Teacher training is provided by the University of Ulster (at the Coleraine and Jordanstown campuses), Queen's University of Belfast and its two associated institutions,

Stranmillis University College and St Mary's University College. The principal courses are BEd Honours (four years) and the one-year Postgraduate Certificate of Education and around 700 new teachers qualify each year. The majority of the 23,000 teachers currently employed in Northern Ireland are graduates. Education and library boards have a statutory duty to provide curricular support services and in-service training.

Business and Community Links

England

From April 2001 the Learning and Skills Council (LSC—see p. 135) will have responsibility through local LSCs for ensuring the effective provision of education–business links.

Scotland

In Scotland the Education for Work and Enterprise agenda supports the transition of young people from education to the world of work. A very wide range of programmes is available; these are designed to introduce young people to patterns of employment, give them direct experience of the world of work, expose them to enterprise, or to re-engage disaffected young people in learning.

Careers

All young people in full-time education are entitled to careers information, advice and guidance. All schools are now required to provide a programme of careers education to pupils in years 9–11. This requirement applies to all registered pupils including those with special needs, at county, voluntary, grant-maintained and special schools.

In Northern Ireland careers education is one of the six compulsory education themes forming part of the secondary school curriculum (see p. 126).

All state secondary schools in England and Wales, and primary and secondary schools in Northern Ireland, provide leavers with a Record of Achievement setting out their school attainments, including public examination and National Curriculum assessment results. In Scotland the Record is not compulsory.

In England the current work of Careers Services with 13 to 19 year olds will be subsumed within the new Connexions Service which is being phased in from 2001. The Connexions Service will be a multi-agency support service, delivered by a network of personal advisers who will be based in a variety of settings including schools and colleges. It is intended to be particularly relevant to school-age pupils as they make Key Stage 4, post-16 or post-18 choices. The type of help currently provided by careers advisers will therefore be provided by personal advisers working within the Connexions Service.

The National Assembly for Wales is launching a careers guidance service, Careers Wales, in April 2001.

EDUCATION AND TRAINING AFTER 16

At age 16 young people are faced with the choice of whether to remain in education, go into training or seek employment. For those young people who do not seek full-time employment they have two routes that they can follow—one based on school and college education, and the other on work-based learning. In addition, under the Welfare-to-Work programme (see p. 151), all young unemployed people are guaranteed education and training opportunities, while those with poor basic skills have the option of participating in full-time study on an approved course.

About 70 per cent of 16 year old pupils choose to continue in full-time education in school sixth forms, sixth-form colleges (in England and Wales) and further education colleges. Broadly speaking, education after 16 outside schools is divided into further and higher education.

Education Maintenance Allowance

The Education Maintenance Allowance (EMA) is a weekly allowance for 16 to 19 year olds who continue in education beyond year 11. It was launched in September 1999 in 15 LEAs across England. Students can qualify for allowances of between £5 and £30 per week with additional bonuses paid termly if the young person meets certain attendance criteria and at the end of the course for achievement. EMAs are an experiment to test whether paying a weekly allowance increases post-16 participation, retention and achievement. Staying-on rates have improved by 5 per cent in EMA pilot areas compared to 2 per cent nationally.

Further Education

England, Wales and Northern Ireland

Having completed compulsory school education, students may continue to study for examinations that lead to higher education, professional training or vocational qualifications. These include the academic General Certificate of Education (GCE) Advanced (A) level and Advanced Subsidiary (AS) qualifications, General National Vocational Qualifications (GNVQs)/ Vocational A levels and job-specific National Vocational Qualifications (NVQs—see p. 135). The GCE A level is usually taken at age 18 after two years' full-time study. They are graded on a scale of A to E. A new Advanced Subsidiary (AS) qualification, representing the first year of a full A level and worth 50 per cent of the marks, was introduced in September 2000. The AS is designed to encourage the take-up of more subjects, particularly in the first year of post-16 study, provide better progression from GCSE into advanced level study and reduce the numbers who do not complete their studies.

In addition, new A level syllabuses, made up of six units, set at the same standard as the previous syllabuses and offering candidates the choice of linear (end of year) or modular (staged) assessment, to the same standard in each, were introduced.

There has been an increase in the proportion of young men and women in the United Kingdom achieving two or more A levels or equivalent. The proportion of young women who had achieved this has doubled since the mid-1970s, to 24 per cent in 1998–99. The increase in the proportion of young men has been by just under a half over the same period. In 1987–88 an equal proportion of young men and women achieved two or more A levels or equivalent (15 per cent) but since 1988–89 women have outperformed men at this level.

GNVQs, which are mainly undertaken by young people in full-time education between the ages of 16 and 19, provide a broad-based preparation for a range of occupations and higher education. There are three GNVQ levels—Vocational A levels (previously called Advanced GNVQs), Intermediate and Foundation. GNVQs/Vocational A levels may be taken in combination with other qualifications, such as GCE A levels or GCSEs.

Table 10.4: Students[1] in Further and Higher Education: by Type of Course and Gender, UK, 1998–99[2]

Thousands

	Males	Females
Further education[3]		
Full-time	539	528
Part-time	1,214	1,617
All further education	**1,754**	**2,145**
Higher education[4]		
Undergraduate		
Full-time	528	599
Part-time	229	304
Postgraduate		
Full-time	87	80
Part-time	130	124
All higher education	**974**	**1,107**

[1] Home and overseas students.

[2] Data for England and Wales are whole year counts.

[3] Data for England and Wales relate to 1997–98. Data for Scotland and Northern Ireland are snapshots taken around November. Excludes adult education centres.

[4] Data for Scotland and Northern Ireland are at December. Includes Open University.

Sources: Department for Education and Employment, National Assembly for Wales, Scottish Executive and Northern Ireland Department of Education

Achievement at GCE A Level or Equivalent:[1] by Gender, UK

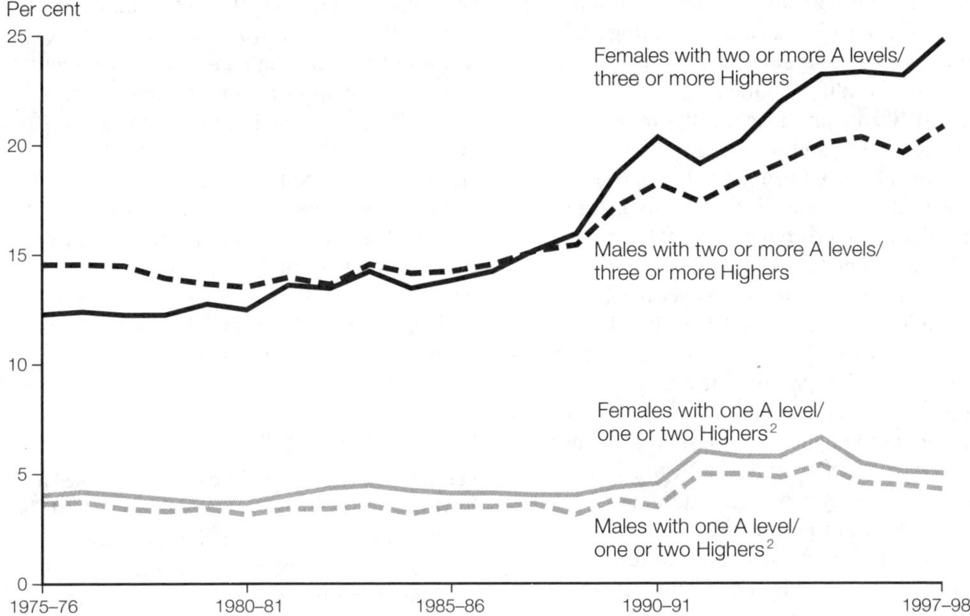

[1] Based on population aged 17 at the start of the academic year. Data to 1990–91 (1991–92 in Northern Ireland) relate to school leavers. From 1991–92 data relate to pupils of any age for Great Britain, while school performance data are used for Northern Ireland from 1992–93. Figures exclude sixth form colleges in England and Wales which were reclassified as further education colleges from 1 April 1993, and excludes GNVQ Advanced Qualifications.

[2] From 1996–97 figures only include two Highers.

Sources: Department for Education and Employment, National Assembly for Wales, Scottish Executive and Northern Ireland Department of Education

In 1998–99 there were around 23,000 advanced GNVQ entries by young people aged 17 in England, and of these just under 20,000 obtained a qualification.

A shortened version of the full GNVQ was made available in September 1999 to all schools and colleges. This Part One GNVQ is designed to broaden choices for young people. It is available in seven vocational subject areas: art and design, business, engineering, health and social care, information technology, leisure and tourism, and manufacturing. In England by the end of 1998/99 almost 10,000 15 year olds had obtained either an Intermediate or Foundation GNVQ Part One qualification. Almost 3,000 pupils obtained a GNVQ Part One qualification in Business, more than in any other subject.

England, Wales and Northern Ireland have a wide range of job-specific National Vocational Qualifications (NVQs), awards which recognise work-related skills and knowledge and provide a path for lifelong learning and achievement. Prepared by industry and commerce, including representatives from trade unions and professional bodies, NVQs are based on national standards of competence and can be achieved at levels 1 to 5.

The Qualifications and Curriculum Authority is responsible for supervising academic and vocational qualifications in England as well as the school curriculum. Corresponding bodies in Wales and Northern Ireland perform similar functions.

Learning and Skills Council

In June 1999 the Government published its White Paper *Learning to Succeed* which set out new proposals for restructuring post-16 education and training in England, including plans to establish a new Learning and Skills Council (LSC) to replace the Training and Enterprise Councils and the Further Education Funding Council.

The LSC became a legal entity on 1 September 2000, and will become fully operational from 1 April 2001. It will be a single, unitary organisation, and will operate at national level and through 47 local Learning and Skills Councils. The LSC will focus particularly on skills and employer needs at national, regional and local levels. It will have responsibility for planning, funding, monitoring and improving the quality of post-16 up to higher education level, and will have a wide remit ranging from basic skills to higher level skills in further education, work-based training for young people, and adult and community education. It will also take responsibility for school sixth form funding from 2002–03 onwards. The Council has a statutory duty to encourage participation in learning, and will work with employers and others to promote workforce development, and economic and community regeneration activity.

The national and local councils will each have a board of around 16 members, with experience of a wide variety of interests in post-16 education and training, including individual learners, employers, disadvantaged groups, education providers and the voluntary sector.

National Council for Education and Training for Wales

From April 2001 a new National Council for Education and Training for Wales will be responsible for strategic development and planning of all post-16 education and training (excluding higher education, but including community and adult learning and work-based training for young people). It will also be responsible for funding most post-16 learning, taking over the work of the Further Education Funding Council for Wales.

Scotland

In Scotland education for those aged 16 to 18 has been reformed. Traditional, fairly academically oriented 'Highers' (Higher Grade Scottish Certificate of Education) are being replaced by new 'Higher Still' courses and modules, which will offer students greater flexibility and, through a revised assessment system, more opportunities to demonstrate successful educational achievement. It is intended that the new system of Scottish Highers should be fully in place by 2003.

Higher National Certificates (HNCs) and Higher National Diplomas (HNDs) are a stepping stone to higher education or further training.

The Scottish Qualifications Authority is the national accreditation organisation.

Further Education Colleges

People over the age of 16 can take courses in further education colleges, where much of the study is work-related. Further education colleges also offer many government-sponsored training programmes. Many students on further education courses attend part-time (73 per cent in 1998–99), either by day release or block release from employment or during the evenings. The system has strong ties with commerce and industry.

Further education colleges in the UK are controlled by autonomous governing bodies, with representation from business and the local community. Public funding is allocated in England, Wales and Scotland through further education funding councils, although in England and Wales the new Learning and Skills Council and National Council for Education and Training for Wales will respectively be assuming this responsibility in April 2001. In Northern Ireland colleges are financed through the Northern Ireland Executive.

Independent inspectors assess the quality of the education provided by colleges. They publish reports containing quality assessments, and colleges are obliged to explain how they will put things right if there are major criticisms. Each college has to publish information about its examination results annually. Colleges in Scotland are inspected by the Schools Inspectorate and in Northern Ireland by the Education and Training Inspectorate. Further education

DV8 Physical Theatre was formed in 1986 and is based in London. The company was commissioned by the Sydney 2000 Olympic Arts Festival to perform *can we afford this*, a piece about how society measures individuals. DV8's diverse company of performers focuses on challenging preconceptions of what dance can, and should, address.

Cinemagic: Northern Ireland's Cinemagic Film Festival provides film-making opportunities for young people. Films from all over the world are shown at an international film festival held in Belfast each December, while an outreach programme held throughout the year gives young people access to film screenings and the chance to make their own films.

'Turning the Pages': this unique touch screen system has been developed by the British Library. A computer simulates the action of turning pages of a book, allowing the viewer to access electronic facsimiles from six of the outstanding treasures in the Library's collection, including the Lindisfarne Gospels. The Gospels, written on the island of Lindisfarne, Northumberland, are currently on display in the Laing Gallery, Newcastle upon Tyne as part of a temporary Millennium exhibition.

Redundant Technology Initiative: set up in 1997, this Sheffield-based arts group uses obsolete computers to create new artistic works. The group also campaigns for widespread low-cost access to information technology.

Autograph, the association of black photographers (UK), was founded in 1988 to promote and advocate photographers who explore issues relating to cultural diversity. The photograph was taken by Ingrid Pollard and is from the series 'Self Evident' 1995.

World Irish Dancing Championships: first held in Dublin in 1970, the event now attracts dancers from England, Scotland, Wales, New Zealand, Australia, Canada and the United States as well as Ireland. In 2000 the Championships were held in Belfast, the first time they had not taken place in the Irish Republic.

Notting Hill Carnival: from a small procession of Caribbean people in costume playing steel drums in the 1960s, the annual carnival through the streets of west London has evolved into a multicultural arts festival attended by up to 2 million people.

Edinburgh Military Tattoo: conceived and first performed in 1950 as the Army in Scotland's contribution to the Edinburgh International Festival, the event now attracts each year an audience of more than 200,000 from all over the world to experience music, ceremony, entertainment and theatre set against the backdrop of Edinburgh Castle.

colleges in Scotland also provide higher education level courses.

Higher Education

Around a third of young people in England and Wales, 40 per cent in Scotland and 45 per cent in Northern Ireland continue in education at a more advanced level beyond the age of 18. Higher education courses are taught in universities, further education colleges and the Open University (see below). They provide a variety of courses up to degree and postgraduate degree level, and increasingly cater for mature students.

Universities

Universities in the UK enjoy academic freedom, appoint their own staff, and decide which students to admit and award their own degrees. The universities of Oxford and Cambridge date from the 13th century, and the Scottish universities of St Andrews, Glasgow and Aberdeen from the 15th century. The University of Edinburgh was established in the 16th century. All the other universities were founded in the 19th and 20th centuries. There are 87 universities, and 64 institutions of higher education. The 1960s saw considerable expansion in new universities. There was also a substantial increase in 1992, when polytechnics and their Scottish equivalents were given their own degree-awarding powers and were allowed to take the university title. At the same time, similar provision was made for higher education colleges which met certain criteria. Higher education colleges have different backgrounds and missions. Some are very specialised, such as art and design or agriculture colleges, while others are multi-disciplinary. They vary in size from under 500 to more than 10,000 students. Some award their own degrees and qualifications, while in others students take degrees and qualifications validated by a university or national body. Applications for first-degree courses are usually made through the Universities and Colleges Admission Service (UCAS).

Students at university (in England, Wales and Northern Ireland) usually spend three years researching a subject in-depth and are awarded a Bachelor's degree (for example, Bachelor of Arts, BA; or Bachelor of Science, BSc) on the successful completion of their studies. There are some four-year courses, and medical and veterinary courses normally require five or six years. A full-time first degree in Scotland generally takes four years for Honours and three years for the broad-based Ordinary degree—a particular feature of the Scottish system. In 1998–99 just over 260,000 students gained a first degree in the UK, 24,000 more than in 1994–95. Of these 30,000 students graduated with a first degree in business and administrative studies, more graduates than any other subject.

A number of students go on to do postgraduate studies. These usually lead to an additional formally recognised qualification such as a Master's degree (for example, Master of Arts, MA; or Master of Science, MSc) or doctorate (PhD).

The Open University

The Open University is a non-residential university offering degree and other courses for adult students of all ages. Teaching is through a combination of specifically produced printed texts, corresponding tuition, television broadcasts, audio/video cassettes and, for some courses, computing and short residential schools. There is a network of tutorial centres for contact with part-time tutors, and with fellow students. Students do not need formal academic qualifications to register for most courses.

Its first degrees are the BA (Open) and the BSc (Open), which are general degrees awarded on a system of credits for each course completed. Either degree can be awarded with honours. The OU also offers honours degrees in selected subject areas. There is also an MMaths degree for students who have taken an approved combination of courses specialising in mathematics, and an MEng degree for those who have studied an approved combination of courses to achieve the highest professional status of Chartered Engineer. The OU offers a wide range of postgraduate courses.

Higher Education Funding Arrangements

Government finance for publicly funded higher education institutions (to help meet the costs of teaching, research and related activities) is distributed by higher education funding councils in England, Wales and Scotland, and in Northern Ireland, by the Department of Higher and Further Education, Training and Employment, following advice from the Northern Ireland Higher Education Council. The private University of Buckingham receives no public grants. Higher education institutions also receive publicly funded paid fee income on behalf of students who are below the assessment thresholds for the payment of full privately paid fees, and privately paid fee contributions.

As well as teaching students, institutions undertake paid training, research or consultancy for commercial firms. Many establishments have endowments or receive grants from foundations and benefactors.

Student Support

England and Wales—student support, depending on the type, is paid out by the Student Loans Company, local education authorities and the college or university. It includes:

- tuition fees—since 1998–99 full-time students have had a responsibility to make an income-assessed contribution towards their tuition fees. For 2000–01, the maximum fee contribution is £1,050, although most students are eligible for a grant towards their fees, depending on their own and their family's income;
- student loans—these are the main form of support for assistance with living costs. The maximum loan in 2000–01 for full-time students is £4,590. The amount of loan depends on where a student lives and studies, the length of the academic year, the course of study and the year of the course. The amount of loan paid also depends on the student's and his or her family's income. Loans are repaid on the basis of income after the student has left their course;
- dependant's allowance—these are grants for those students with family members who are financial dependants. The amount of grant depends on the student's and the dependant's income;
- access bursaries—paid to students aged 25 and over with dependants, according to need. The maximum is £1,000; and
- hardship funds—made at the discretion of the institution, the amount depending on the individual circumstances of the student.

There are also other types of grant for certain groups of student. These include a Disabled Students' Allowance, which helps with the costs incurred in attending a course as a direct result of a disability, and a Care Leavers' Grant which helps those who have been in care by providing a grant towards accommodation costs in the long, usually summer, vacation.

Scotland—the Scottish Executive is introducing a new student support scheme for full-time higher education:

- From the academic year 2000–01 tuition fees will no longer be payable by eligible full-time Scottish-domiciled students or EU students who are studying in Scotland. Student loan entitlement may be reduced, however, because any assessed parental or spouse contribution will now be set against the means-tested student loan entitlement rather than tuition fees.
- Young Student Bursaries of up to £2,000 a year will be available for those eligible students entering higher education in 2001–02 or later who need support while studying (for example, students from low-income groups).
- Mature students entering higher education for the first time in 2001–02 or later may be entitled to claim from the Mature Student Bursary Fund as well as their loan entitlement. Assistance through this scheme will be administered by the universities and colleges and is discretionary.
- Graduates (with some exemptions) will be expected to contribute £2,000 to the

Graduate Endowment in recognition of the benefits they gain from higher education and to provide similar opportunities for future generations.

Northern Ireland—student support arrangements in Northern Ireland operate on a parity basis with England and Wales. Students are expected to make a means-tested contribution to the cost of their tuition fees (£1,050 in 2000–01) and have access to student loans to cover their living costs.

A review of the student support system in Northern Ireland was announced in February 2000 and the outcome is to be announced before the end of 2000.

National Targets for Education and Training

The Government in 1998 launched the National Learning Targets for England for 2002 covering key stages of people's lives. Progress towards the targets is measured in autumn each year. Targets for England have been set which state that by 2002, 85 per cent of 19 year olds will be qualified to NVQ level 2 (equivalent to five GCSEs at grades A* to C) and 60 per cent of 21 year olds will be qualified to NVQ level 3 (to two A levels) or its equivalent. Steady progress has been made towards the targets. In 2000, 75 per cent of 19 year olds and 54 per cent of 21 year olds met these standards in England.

In addition to these targets for young people, a set of targets also exists for adults of working age. The first states that by the year 2002, 50 per cent of the workforce is to be qualified to NVQ level 3 (equivalent to two A levels), while the second states that 28 per cent of the workforce will have a professional, vocational, management or academic qualification at NVQ level 4 or above (equivalent to a first degree). By 2000, 47 per cent and 26 per cent of adults had achieved qualifications at levels 3 and 4 respectively.

Adult Education

Education for adults is provided by further education institutions, adult education centres and colleges run by LEAs, community organisations, and voluntary bodies such as the Workers' Educational Association. The duty to secure such education is currently shared by the further education funding councils (the Learning and Skills Council in England and the National Council for Education and Training for Wales from April 2001), LEAs, and the education and library boards in Northern Ireland. University departments of continuing education also provide courses for adults.

Other bodies concerned with the promotion of adult and community education include NIACE (the National Institute of Adult Continuing Education), Community Learning Scotland and the Basic Skills Agency (BSA—concerned with improving literacy and numeracy). NIACE and the BSA jointly manage the Adult and Community Learning Fund on behalf of the Department for Education and Employment. The fund supports innovative learning opportunities and aims to encourage people who have been reluctant to participate in learning in the past and who may be disadvantaged as a result.

General adult education courses available include languages, physical education/ sport/fitness and practical crafts/skills such as embroidery and woodwork. Nearly seven out of ten of all enrolments on adult education courses in England in November 1998 were for courses that did not lead to a formal qualification. In total, there were 1.1 million adults in England and Wales enrolled on adult education courses, and enrolment rates were higher for women than for men.

Lifelong Learning

In 1998 government policy on lifelong learning was outlined in a DfEE Green Paper, *The Learning Age: A Renaissance for a New Britain* (separate but parallel learning strategies for Wales, Scotland and Northern Ireland having also been published).

The strategy is intended to encourage the continuous development of people's skills, knowledge and understanding. The concept of developing lifelong learning underpins all areas of post-16 educational learning provision.

University for Industry (UfI)

The University for Industry (UfI), due to become fully operational during autumn 2000, will be a new national on-line and distributed learning network aimed at both individuals and business. UfI will operate in England, Wales and Northern Ireland.

UfI aims to play a key role in improving the nation's competitiveness by raising people's skill levels and employability. Its primary objective is to stimulate demand for lifelong learning among adults and small/medium enterprises by promoting the availability of, and improving access to, relevant high quality learning through the use of ICT.

By October 2000, over 700 *learndirect* development centres were in operation.

Individual Learning Accounts (ILAs)

Individual Learning Accounts are also a central part of the programme for lifelong learning. A learning account is a membership scheme with government helping people plan and pay towards for the cost of their learning.

The national framework of Individual Learning Accounts was launched in September 2000; £150 million of resources are being used to contribute £150 to the first million account holders to book eligible learning, providing the individual pays at least £25. Under the national framework, people will also be able to access 20 per cent and 80 per cent discounts on the cost of learning. The 20 per cent discount can be used on a wide range of learning while the 80 per cent discount will be narrowly focused to ICT literacy and basic mathematics. By mid-September 2000 almost 250,000 people had opened an Individual Learning Account.

Scotland

In 1998 the consultation paper *Opportunity Scotland* outlined a plan for lifelong learning in Scotland. Since devolution in 1999 the Scottish Executive has expanded on these plans in its *Programme for Government*, the aim being to offer greater and more equal access to a wider range of educational opportunities. To help achieve this aim, the following initiatives were introduced:

- The *Scottish University for Industry*, due to be launched in October 2000. Its services will be named *learndirect scotland* and aim to help people access learning opportunities and promote lifelong learning across all sectors of society. *Learndirect scotland* will offer information and advice on courses via its helpline, website or network of learning centres. It will also stimulate new ways of learning and commission ICT materials to meet any gaps in provision.
- *Individual Learning Accounts*, which will help people invest in their own learning with financial support from the Scottish Executive and, in some cases, from their employers with similar arrangements to those in England.

Northern Ireland

From September 2000, in Northern Ireland, Individual Learning Accounts will be available with an introductory incentive of £150 to the first 20,000 people opening accounts.

LINKS WITH OTHER COUNTRIES

Large numbers of people from other countries come to the UK to study, and many British people work and train overseas. The British aid programme (see chapter 7, p. 90) encourages links between educational institutions in the UK and developing countries.

European Union Schemes

Exchange of students is promoted by the EU's SOCRATES programme through the ERASMUS action which provides grants which enable university students from the EU, Norway, Iceland, Liechtenstein, Central and Eastern European and EU pre-accession countries (see p. 79) to study in other states. The programme covers all academic subjects, and the period of study normally lasts between three and 12 months. Between 1995 and 1999, 42,859 students participated in the programme. There are currently about 10,000 students from the UK participating in the scheme each year.

Other parts of the SOCRATES programme support partnerships between schools, language learning, study visits by senior educationalists and a range of multinational projects including open and distance learning and adult education. Competence in another European language is a feature and is supported in all activities.

The LEONARDO DA VINCI programme supports and complements vocational training policies and practices in participating countries, fostering transnational co-operation and innovation in training through pilot projects, placements and exchanges and research projects. Between 1995 and 1999 nearly 1,200 projects were supported in the UK. Of these 810 were placement-type projects through which over 13,000 young people undertook part of their vocational training in another member state. The other 372 projects were transnational pilot projects or research projects involving at least three countries co-operating to develop or disseminate innovative approaches to specific training problems and issues.

The Youth Programme supports youth exchange projects and volunteering activities in EU member states and related activities such as youth leader training. Between 1995 and 1999, 55,224 young people participated in the programme.

EU member states have created ten European schools, including one at Culham, Oxfordshire, for pupils aged between four and 19, to provide a multilingual education for the children of staff employed in EU institutions. Around 16,400 pupils attend these schools.

Overseas Students in the UK

About 275,000 overseas students are now studying in the UK at higher and further education institutions.

Most overseas students following courses of higher or further education pay fees covering the full cost of their courses. Nationals of other EU member states generally pay the lower level of fees applicable to British home students.

Government Scholarship Schemes

The Government makes provision for foreign students and trainees through its international development programme and other award and scholarship schemes. Around 2,400 receive awards from scholarship schemes, funded in part by the Foreign & Commonwealth Office (FCO) and the Department for International Development (DFID), were made in 1999–2000. The two main schemes funded by the FCO and DFID are:

- British Chevening awards, a worldwide programme offering outstanding graduate students and young professionals the opportunity to spend time studying at British universities and other academic institutions; and
- the Commonwealth Scholarship and Fellowship Plan, offering scholarships for study in other Commonwealth countries. Under the scheme in the UK scholarships are for postgraduate study or research for one to three years at British higher education institutions.

The FCO is also increasing the number of scholarships jointly funded with British or foreign commercial firms, and with academic and other institutions.

Other Schemes

Many other public and private scholarships and fellowships are available to students from overseas and to British students who want to study overseas. Among the best known are the British Council Fellowships, the Fulbright Scholarship Scheme, the British Marshall Scholarships, the Rhodes Scholarships, the Churchill Scholarships and the Confederation of British Industry Scholarships. The Overseas Research Students Awards Scheme, funded by the higher education funding councils, also provides help for overseas full-time postgraduate students with outstanding research potential. Most British universities and colleges offer bursaries and scholarships for which graduates of any nationality are eligible.

THE YOUTH SERVICE

The youth service—a partnership between local government and voluntary organisations—is concerned with the informal personal and social education of young people aged 11 to 25 (5 to 25 in Northern Ireland).

Local authorities maintain their own youth centres and clubs and provide most of the public support for local and regional voluntary organisations. In England, the service is estimated to reach around 3 million young people, with the voluntary organisations contributing a significant proportion of overall provision.

In England the DfEE supports the youth service through grants to the National Youth Agency, the National Council for Voluntary Youth Services and to the headquarters of some 80 National Voluntary Youth Organisations. Funded primarily by local government, the National Youth Agency provides support for those working with young people, and information and publishing services.

The National Assembly for Wales sponsors the Wales Youth Agency, which is the agent for payment of grant aid to national youth service bodies with headquarters in Wales; it is also responsible for the accreditation of training and staff development for youth workers.

In Scotland the youth service forms part of the community education provision made by local authorities. It is also promoted by Community Learning Scotland.

In Northern Ireland the education and library boards provide and fund youth clubs and outdoor activity centres. They assist with the running costs of registered voluntary youth units and provide advice and support to youth groups. Boards also help young people visiting the rest of Britain, Ireland and overseas. The Youth Council for Northern Ireland advises the education system on the development of the youth service. It promotes the provision of facilities, encourages cross-community activity and pays grants to the headquarters of voluntary bodies.

Voluntary Youth Organisations

National voluntary youth organisations work mainly through local groups, which raise most of their day-to-day expenses by their own efforts. Many receive financial and other help from local authorities, which also make available facilities in many areas. The voluntary organisations vary greatly in character and include the uniformed organisations, such as the Scouts and Girl Guides, church-based and other religious organisations, and particular interest groups. In Wales, Urdd Gobaith Cymru (the Welsh League of Youth) provides cultural, sporting and language-based activities for young Welsh speakers and learners.

Many voluntary youth organisations and local authorities provide services for the young unemployed, young people from ethnic minorities, young people in inner cities or rural areas and those in trouble or especially vulnerable. Many authorities have youth committees on which official and voluntary bodies are represented. They employ youth officers to co-ordinate youth work and to arrange in-service training.

Youth Workers

In England and Wales a two-year training course at certain universities and higher education colleges produces qualified youth and community workers; several undergraduate part-time and postgraduate courses are also available. In Scotland one-, two- and three-year courses are provided at teacher education institutions. Students from Northern Ireland attend courses run in universities and colleges in the UK and the Irish Republic.

In the English local authority sector there are a total of about 27,000 full- and part-time youth workers; 90 per cent of full-time youth workers and 33 per cent of part-timers are nationally qualified.

Other Organisations

Many grant-giving foundations and trusts provide finance for activities involving young people. The Prince's Trust and the Royal Jubilee Trust provide grants and practical help to individuals and organisations; areas of concern include urban deprivation, unemployment, homelessness and young offenders. Efforts are also made to assist ethnic minorities.

The Duke of Edinburgh's Award Scheme challenges young people from the UK and other Commonwealth countries to meet certain standards in activities such as community service, expeditions, social and practical skills, and physical recreation.

Further Reading

The Learning Age: a Renaissance for a new Britain. (Department for Education and Employment paper on lifelong learning). Cm 3790. The Stationery Office, 1998.

Education and Training Statistics for the United Kingdom. Department for Education and Employment, 1999.

Learning to Succeed: a new framework for post-16 learning. Department for Education and Employment. Cm 4392. The Stationery Office, 1999.

The Government's Expenditure Plans 2000–01 to 2001–02. Department for Education and Employment and Office for Standards in Education. Cm 4602. The Stationery Office, 2000.

Websites

Department for Education and Employment: www.dfee.gov.uk

Scottish Executive: www.scotland.gov.uk

National Assembly for Wales: www.wales.gov.uk

Northern Ireland Assembly: www.ni-assembly.gov.uk

11 The Labour Market

Over recent years, the labour market in the United Kingdom has undergone major change, with more women in the workforce, increased levels of part-time working and the continuing move towards employment in service industries, where over three-quarters of employees now work.

PATTERNS OF EMPLOYMENT

According to the Labour Force Survey (LFS), carried out by the Office for National Statistics (ONS), some 29.6 million people aged 16 and over were economically active[1] on a seasonally adjusted basis in the UK in April–June 2000. Of these, 15.4 million men and 12.5 million women were in employment, giving a total of 27.9 million (see Table 11.1), the highest level since the series began. The number of people aged 16 and over in employment rose by 338,000 in the year to April–June 2000.

One of the most significant long-term trends in the labour market has been the growth in the number of women in employment. In spring 2000 women accounted for around 45 per cent of all those in the labour force in the UK, and economic activity rates for women with children under five rose from 48 per cent to 58 per cent over the previous decade. In most service industries more than half of employees are women, while in manufacturing, construction, agriculture, and transport and communications women account for less than one-third of employees.

There are several reasons for the greater involvement of women in the workplace. Among these are that more women are putting off having children until their thirties and, when they do have children, they are far more likely to then return to work, making use of a growing number of childcare options, than were previous generations. In addition, many of the new jobs available in the service sector, particularly those involving computers and telephones, are in areas where women can compete for jobs with men on equal terms, whereas many of the more traditional jobs, which are declining in number, particularly those in the mining, construction and heavy engineering industries, require a degree of physical strength which puts women at a disadvantage.

More and more people are working part time, although women are more likely to do so than men. Part-time workers over the age of 16 now total 6.8 million. About 44 per cent of

[1] Defined as those who are either in employment (employee, self-employed, unpaid family worker or on a government-supported training programme) or unemployed and actively seeking work.

women in employment work part-time, compared with 9 per cent of men.

There has also been a gradual move away from manual to non-manual occupations, which are now held by around 61 per cent of those in employment.

The private sector share of employment rose from 71 per cent in 1981 to 82 per cent (22.9 million) in 1999. In 1999 jobs in the public sector increased for the first time since 1979 to 5 million, mainly reflecting higher employment in education and in NHS Trusts (see p. 188).

Around 1.2 million people had two or more jobs in April–June 2000, while roughly 1.7 million (7.1 per cent of employees) were engaged in temporary jobs (see Table 11.3). Around one in three people work in temporary jobs because they cannot find a permanent one. A similar proportion work in temporary jobs because they prefer to do so.

'Teleworking'—people working from home using information technology (IT)—is becoming more widespread. In spring 2000 some 312,000 people were classed as teleworkers whose main job was primarily in their own home; extending the definition to cover those working in different places using home as a base and those who spent at least one day a week working from home raised the number to 1.6 million.

In the period April–June 2000 around 3.2 million people were self-employed in the UK: 15 per cent of men and 7 per cent of women in employment are self-employed. Agriculture and fishing, and construction have the highest proportions of self-employed people, while relatively few of those engaged in manufacturing and public administration are self-employed.

Employment by Sector

The shift in jobs from manufacturing to service industries has continued in the past decade. In the year to March 2000 the number of workforce jobs, (a measure of the total number of *jobs*, rather than the number of *people* in employment) in service industries rose to nearly 21.1 million.

Transport and communications was one service sector to record a particularly large rise in workforce jobs in the year to March 2000, with the number of jobs up by over 4 per cent from the previous year to 1.7 million. A contributory factor was the growth in telephone call centres, which are provided by several companies, for example in banking, other financial services, retailing and transport. Call centres employ large numbers of people to deal with customer requests, and computer telephonists are one of the fastest growing occupational groups in the UK. The continuing growth in the number of mobile telephones in use in the UK (see p. 376) has also accounted for a large number of new jobs in this sector.

In the last ten years most other sectors have experienced falling levels of employment. Traditional manufacturing industries, such as steel and shipbuilding, have recorded

Table 11.1: Employment in the UK, April–June 2000

Thousands, seasonally adjusted

	Males	Females	Total
All aged 16 and over	22,762	23,831	46,593
Total economically active	16,381	13,171	29,552
of whom:			
In employment	15,395	12,535	27,930
ILO unemployed[1]	986	636	1,622
Economic activity rate (per cent)[2]	84.6	72.9	79.0
Employment rate (per cent)	67.6	52.6	59.9
ILO unemployment rate (per cent)	6.0	4.8	5.5

[1] International Labour Organisation definition of unemployment.
[2] For men aged 16 to 64 and women aged 16 to 59.
Source: Labour Force Survey, Office for National Statistics

Table 11.2: Regional Labour Market Structure, April–June 2000

Seasonally adjusted

	Economically active (thousands)[1]	Economic activity rate (per cent)[1]	ILO unemployment rate (per cent)
England	24,220	79.7	5.2
Wales	1,302	74.4	6.1
Scotland	2,476	78.3	7.2
Northern Ireland[2]	709	69.7	6.7
United Kingdom	**28,712**	**79.0**	**5.5**

[1] For men aged 16 to 64 and women aged 16 to 59.
[2] Figures for Northern Ireland are not seasonally adjusted.
Source: Labour Force Survey, Office for National Statistics

Table 11.3: Employment in the UK *Thousands, seasonally adjusted, April–June*

	1996	1997	1998	1999	2000
Employees	22,711	23,285	23,694	24,100	24,516
Self-employed	3,336	3,357	3,266	3,230	3,151
Unpaid family workers	122	116	100	100	111
Government-supported training and employment programmes	249	224	170	163	152
Employment	**26,417**	**26,982**	**27,230**	**27,592**	**27,930**
of whom:					
Full-time workers	*19,880*	*20,219*	*20,468*	*20,750*	*20,968*
Part-time workers	*6,538*	*6,716*	*6,762*	*6,843*	*6,962*
Workers with a second job	*1,289*	*1,256*	*1,191*	*1,315*	*1,180*
Temporary workers	*1,675*	*1,821*	*1,745*	*1,706*	*1,735*

Source: Labour Force Survey, Office for National Statistics

particularly large falls in employment. By March 2000 manufacturing accounted for 15 per cent of employee jobs, compared with 42 per cent in 1955.

Unemployment

Unemployment in the UK has fallen considerably since the peak at the end of 1992. In April–June 2000, 1.6 million people were unemployed, 5.5 per cent of those in the labour force, compared with 6.0 per cent in the same period of 1999, according to the International Labour Organisation (ILO) definition of unemployment. In April–June 2000 some 449,000 people had been unemployed for a year or more, of whom 254,000 had been out of work for two years or more. The UK unemployment rate is similar to that for the major G7 group of nations and substantially below the EU average. In April 2000 the ILO unemployment rate for those aged 15 and over was 5.9 per cent in the G7 and 8.5 per cent in the EU.

Unemployment among 16 to 24 year olds in the UK is running at double the overall rate. There are several reasons for the relatively high level of youth unemployment, including lack of skills, qualifications and experience. Unemployment rates tend to fall as the level of qualification increases. In spring 2000 the unemployment rate for those with no qualifications was around *four* times higher than for those with a higher educational qualification.

Among people with broadly similar educational qualifications, those from ethnic minorities tend to have higher unemployment rates than those from the White group.

Table 11.4: Workforce Jobs by Industry, UK, March 2000 *Seasonally adjusted*

	Workforce jobs (thousands)	Per cent of workforce jobs	Per cent change over previous year
Agriculture and fishing	538	1.9	2.9
Energy and water	217	0.8	–3.2
Manufacturing	4,285	15.3	–2.1
Construction	1,823	6.5	1.4
Services:	21,106	75.5	1.2
Distribution, hotels and restaurants	*6,144*	*22.0*	*0.7*
Transport and communication	*1,696*	*6.1*	*4.4*
Finance and business services	*5,151*	*18.4*	*0.6*
Public administration, education and health	*6,479*	*23.2*	*0.4*
Other services	*1,637*	*5.9*	*4.8*
All jobs	**27,968**	**100.0**	**0.7**

Source: Office for National Statistics

Unemployment:[1] by Gender, UK

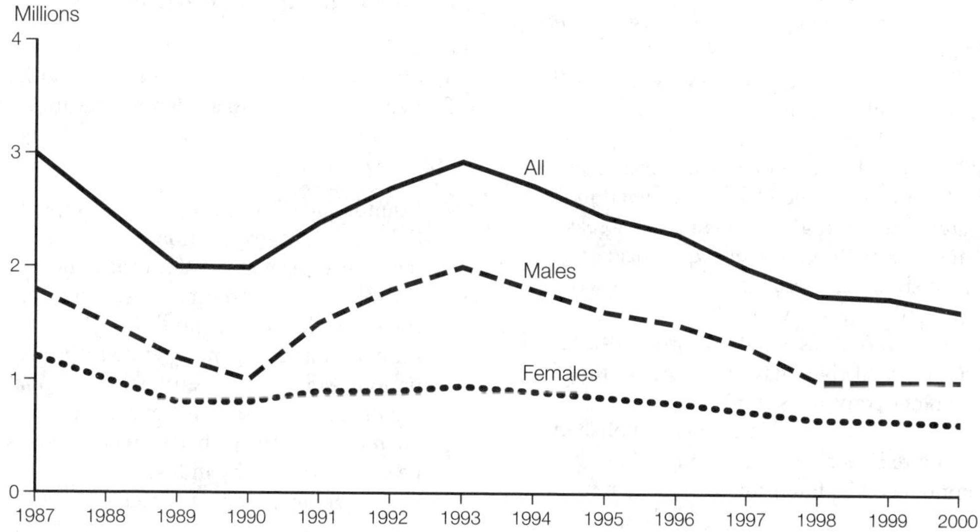

[1] At spring each year. Unemployment based on the ILO definition.

Source: Office for National Statistics

Unemployment rates are particularly high for young Black people; in spring 2000 the rate for those aged 16 to 24 was 33 per cent.

Areas that used to rely on heavy industries (such as steel, shipbuilding and coal mining) which have since declined are often among those with the highest rates of unemployment. Areas with the lowest levels of unemployment include the South East and East of England, with rates well below the UK average.

LABOUR MARKET POLICY

The Government's strategy aims to ensure employment opportunity for all who can work. It comprises the following key elements:

- helping people to move from welfare to work, through the New Deal and ONE—the Government's integrated, work-focused service providing benefits and employment advice (see p. 152);
- helping the transition into work, by aiming to remove barriers to work and ensure that people are not financially worse off when moving from welfare to work;
- making work pay, through reform of the tax and benefit system (see also chapters 12 and 24); and
- securing career progression in work, through lifelong learning.

TRAINING AND EDUCATION

Training and education are among the Government's top priorities (see also chapter 10) as it wishes to ensure that the UK workforce has the necessary skills to meet the challenges of a rapidly changing world economy. According to the LFS, in spring 2000, 3.6 million employees of working age (15.1 per cent) in the UK had received job-related training in the previous four weeks. Employees with higher level qualifications are almost six times more likely to have received training than those with no qualifications; younger employees are about two-and-a-half times more likely to have received training than older employees.

In June 1999 the Government published the White Paper *Learning to Succeed*, in which it announced its intention to create a new framework for the planning, funding and delivery of all post-16 education and training provision. The White Paper included measures affecting schools, colleges and work-based training, as well as a new focus for the Careers Service. In addition, under the Welfare-to-Work programme (see p. 151), all young unemployed people are guaranteed education and training opportunities, while those with poor basic skills have the option of participating in full-time study on an approved course. The Learning and Skills Act 2000, which covers England and Wales, provides for the implementation of these measures. The Act includes provision for:

- a new Learning and Skills Council for England, which will bring together for the first time into a single national body responsibility for planning and funding post-16 learning in England;
- a new Council for Education and Training in Wales;
- new arrangements for rigorous and independent external inspection of post-16 education and training;
- the Connexions Service to provide integrated support services for all 13 to 19 year olds; and
- powers to remove obstacles to collaboration between schools, education authorities and further education.

Training and Support Programmes

There are several programmes available to help increase workforce skills. These are either offered as alternatives to academic education for 16 to 19 year olds or as part of an existing employee's training:

- Foundation Modern Apprenticeships (FMAs—formerly National Traineeships) aim to offer broad and flexible learning programmes, including the key skills of communication, numeracy and IT, and operate to agreed national standards—National Vocational Qualification (NVQ) at Level 2 (see chapter 10) is the primary qualification to be achieved—set by industry and employers in 40 industry sectors.
- Advanced Modern Apprenticeships (AMAs—formerly Modern Apprenticeships) are designed to increase significantly the number of young people trained to technician, supervisory and equivalent levels. The primary achievement of an AMA is the NVQ at Level 3.
- The right to time off for study or training for 16 and 17 year olds came into effect in

Great Britain from September 1999 and came into operation in Northern Ireland in September 2000. Under this measure, young people are entitled to take paid time off to study or train towards a qualification, usually at NVQ Level 2.

- Individual Learning Accounts. Since April 1999 Training and Enterprise Councils (TECs—see below) have been providing starter accounts. For further information see chapter 10, p. 140.
- Career development loans are available to help people pay for vocational education or training in Great Britain. Loans of between £300 and £8,000 are provided through major banks, and interest payments on the loans during training and for one month after training are funded by the Department for Education and Employment (DfEE). The loans help to pay for courses lasting up to two years. By the end of January 2000, 125,000 people had received a career development loan, and £414 million had been lent.
- Small Firms Training Loans are deferred repayment bank loans. The programme helps firms with 50 or fewer employees to meet a range of vocational training-related expenses, including training consultancy. Loans of between £500 and £125,000 are available through major banks. Repayments can be deferred for between six and 12 months, according to the amount borrowed, and during this time interest payments on the loan are funded by the DfEE. By the end of June 2000 over £3.5 million had been lent to 523 small firms.
- The National Training Awards, an annual competition designed to promote good training practice, rewards those who have carried out exceptionally effective training. There were 787 entries in 1999 and 58 national winners.
- Work-Based Learning for Adults is open to those aged 25 and over who have been unemployed for six months or longer. The aim is to help adults without work move into sustained employment, including self-employment, through work-based learning.

In Scotland the government-funded training programme for young people is Skillseekers; all young people aged 16 and 17 are entitled to Skillseekers training. Its key elements are:

- training leading to a recognised qualification, up to Scottish Vocational Qualification (SVQ) Level 3;
- an individual training plan; and
- employer involvement.

Training Bodies

Learning and Skills Council

Under the Learning and Skills Act 2000, the national Learning and Skills Council for England (and the Council for Education and Training in Wales—see p. 136), will assume responsibility for government-funded training and workforce development from TECs with effect from April 2001. The Council, which will have 47 local arms across England, will have the aim of increasing the range of learning opportunities for businesses, communities and individuals. The two Councils will take over the roles of the 72 TECs/Chambers of Commerce Training and Enterprise (CCTEs) in England and Wales. These are independent companies with employer-led boards. Their objectives are to foster local economic development and stimulate employer investment in skills. Specifically, they are charged with developing the quality, effectiveness and relevance to the local labour market of government-funded training and business assistance programmes.

Local Enterprise Companies

A separate network of 22 Local Enterprise Companies (LECs) exists in Scotland. These have wider-ranging responsibilities than the TECs, covering both economic development and environmental improvement. LECs are also responsible for the delivery of the Scottish Executive's national training programmes. They run under contract to two non-departmental public bodies: Scottish Enterprise and Highlands and Islands

Enterprise (see p. 395). The enterprise networks are currently the subject of a review initiated by the Scottish Executive (see p. 395).

National Training Organisations

National Training Organisations (NTOs) are employer-led bodies which are responsible for the development of skills to meet the business needs of employment sectors throughout the UK. They have a primary role in encouraging employer involvement in the development and uptake of competence-based standards, education, training and qualifications to help businesses improve competitiveness in the UK and abroad. The NTOs Network was created in 1998, bringing together in a single network over 180 Industry Training Organisations (ITOs), Occupations Standards Councils and other interested bodies.

By August 2000, 76 NTOs had been officially recognised, covering 94 per cent of the workforce.

Targets and Standards

The National Learning Targets (see p. 139), launched in England in 1998, focus on the Government's priorities: a globally competitive economy, with successful firms operating in a fair and efficient labour market; and a society where everybody has an equal chance to realise their potential.

The Training Standards Council was established in 1998 to supervise a Training Inspectorate with the aim of raising standards of work-based training funded through TECs/CCTEs. Expenditure on training inspections through the Council and its Inspectorate is estimated at £6.9 million in 2000–01. From 1 April 2001, there will be new arrangements for the inspection of post-16 learning. The Office for Standards in Education (OFSTED) will have responsibility for inspecting provision for 16 to 19 year olds in schools and colleges (see chapter 10). The work of the Training Standards Council will be taken into the new Adult Learning Inspectorate, which will be responsible for the inspection of post-19 provision in colleges and for work-based learning for all post-16s. Further information on National Learning Targets can be found in chapter 10.

Investors in People

Investors in People is the National Standard which sets a level of good practice for improving an organisation's performance through its people. It is designed to improve business performance by linking the training and development of employees to an organisation's business objectives. Reported benefits include increased productivity, higher profits, lower rates of sickness and absenteeism, and improved morale. Over the past year Investors in People UK, which is responsible for the promotion, quality assurance and development of the Standard, has carried out an extensive review to simplify the Standard and make it more accessible, especially for small firms. At the end of September 2000, 19,579 organisations in the UK had been recognised as Investors in People, and a further 21,480 were committed to achieving the Standard. Over 8.6 million employees work in organisations involved in Investors in People, covering around 37 per cent of the UK workforce.

Northern Ireland

In Northern Ireland the Department for Higher and Further Education, Training and Employment (DHFETE) has responsibility for ensuring that the skills and labour needs of the local economy are met. The vocational training and employment activities of the Department are delivered through an executive agency, the Training and Employment Agency. The Agency has facilitated the development of sector training councils in each of the main industry private sectors to advise on training needs. A Skills Task Force has also been established.

Northern Ireland has its own range of training and employment programmes designed to raise skills levels and linked to NVQs. The main youth programme—Jobskills—serves the needs of 16 to 18 year olds and Modern Apprenticeships programmes are also delivered. In addition to New Deal, a Worktrack programme and a statutory organisation, Enterprise Ulster, provide a range of places for adults. A focused skills programme aimed at meeting immediate needs in the economy provides a range of skills opportunities, particularly in the high technology sector.

RECRUITMENT AND JOB-FINDING

Welfare-to-Work

The Government's Welfare-to-Work programme, covering the UK, is a series of measures designed with the aim of promoting an efficient labour market and tackling structural unemployment and inactivity, and social exclusion. The Government has introduced several key initiatives, including a number of New Deals, ONE (see p. 152) and Employment Zones (see p. 152). Common features of the measures for those seeking employment include:

- the assistance of personal advisers, providing a single point of contact and help;
- a 'gateway' period of concentrated diagnosis and support; and
- an emphasis on trying to obtain sustainable employment.

The Welfare-to-Work programme is currently funded by a windfall tax on the excess profits of the privatised utilities. Over £4 billion is being invested in the programme over the five years to 2001–02 in a number of New Deals including:

- £1.5 billion for young unemployed people;
- £600 million for the long-term unemployed;
- £220 million for lone parents;
- £210 million for sick and disabled people;
- £50 million for partners of the unemployed;
- £40 million for those aged over 50;
- £40 million for childcare; and
- £1.6 billion for schools.

A new Employment Opportunities Fund will be created to fund the New Deal, associated employment programmes, the ONE service and the establishment costs of the working age agency (see p. 153) after the windfall tax receipts have been spent.

Young Unemployed

The New Deal for the young unemployed is available to young people aged 18 to 24 who have been unemployed for more than six months. It begins with an intensive period of up to four months, of counselling, advice and guidance—the 'gateway'. If a young person has not left the 'gateway' after that time, he or she must choose one of four options:

- a job attracting a wage subsidy of £60 a week, payable to employers for up to six months;
- a work placement with a voluntary organisation;
- a six-month work placement with an Environment Task Force (see p. 309); and
- for those without basic qualifications, a place on a full-time education and training course, which might last for up to one year.

All these options include an element of education and training equivalent to one day a week. By the end of August 2000 there had been 532,200 starts on the New Deal since its launch in April 1998: 416,900 people had left, of whom 39 per cent had entered sustained unsubsidised jobs.

Long-term Unemployed

Under the New Deal for the long-term unemployed, which started in 1998, employers receive a subsidy of up to £75 a week for 26 weeks if they employ anyone who has been unemployed for two years or longer. From April 2001 the scheme will be extended as the New Deal 25 plus programme, with eligibility reduced to 18 months for those aged 25 and over. The programme will include:

- a 'gateway' period aimed at helping people into jobs, tackling barriers to work and providing people with communication skills, motivation and confidence-building;

- a period of full-time activity where individuals will be able to choose a mix, based on their needs, of subsidised employment, work-focused training, work experience, help with jobsearch or help with moving into self-employment;
- a period for those who do not find work through the full-time activity period involving intensive help to take advantage of their experience and move into work; and
- benefit penalties, if individuals do not take advantage of this assistance.

Other Groups

The New Deal for Lone Parents was launched in October 1998. It provides the opportunity for all lone parents on Income Support to meet a personal adviser and receive help and support to help improve their employment prospects. A package of improvements was introduced from May 2000 including more intensive support for lone parents about to move onto Jobseeker's Allowance as their children reach age 16, access to specialised resource centres to help with preparation for work and job search, and an extension of invitations to lone parents with children from the age of three.

From autumn 2000 in pathfinder areas, and nationally from April 2001, lone parents on Income Support with children over the age of five will be required to meet a specialist adviser to guide them through a series of choices, offered on a voluntary basis, including:

- work of 16 hours a week or more, to move lone parents onto the Working Families' Tax Credit (see p. 176);
- the opportunity to try some work under 16 hours a week; and
- the opportunity to undertake education and training.

There are also pilot schemes to help those who are disabled or on incapacity benefit who want training or work. The March 2000 Budget announced the first stage of the development of a nationwide service to help disabled people find work. The service will evaluate different approaches in order to develop the most effective policies for disabled people. A New Deal for partners of the unemployed, including the option of help needed to return to work, was established on a nationwide basis in April 1999.

New Deal 50 plus was introduced nationally from April 2000. This scheme enables people over 50 who return to full-time work after six months or more on benefits to claim a subsidy of £60 a week for their first year back in full-time employment.

Northern Ireland

In Northern Ireland there is a broadly similar system to Welfare-to-Work, although programmes such as ONE (see below) may be at a different stage of development. Responsibility for administration of programmes and services rests with the Northern Ireland DHFETE and the Department for Social Development and their executive agencies.

Employment Zones

Following a prototype scheme, Employment Zones began running in spring 2000 in 15 areas of Great Britain with concentrated, long-term unemployment. New approaches to tackle unemployment—including financial help for individual jobseekers through personal job accounts—are being adopted and are being provided by public, private and voluntary sector organisations selected to run the zones by open competition. About £112 million is available to support this initiative over the two years from spring 2000. The aim is to help around 50,000 long-term unemployed jobseekers aged 25 and over.

ONE

The ONE service was launched in four areas in June 1999 and extended to a further eight areas in November 1999. It is provided by the Employment Service, Benefits Agency and local authorities in partnership. It provides a single point of entry into the benefit system for people of working age who are unemployed or working less than 16 hours a week. Clients living within the 12 pilot areas meet a personal adviser at the outset of their claim and receive support and advice with the aim of identifying and overcoming barriers to work. For some people an immediate focus on work is not appropriate and in these cases the priority is to resolve their immediate financial needs by paying them the correct benefit and discussing the range of help which is available to them. Four pilots are testing call centre technology and four are being provided in partnership with the private and voluntary sectors. Since 3 April 2000 participation in a work-focused meeting has been a condition of receipt of benefits for new clients in all 12 areas.

Action Teams

In autumn 2000 Action Teams will be set up, initially for one year, in 40 communities in the UK with the lowest employment and highest unemployment, including the 15 Employment Zones. Funds of £45.5 million will be available for a period of a year from autumn 2000 for the Teams to work with jobless people in the most deprived areas, with the aim of removing barriers to employment and, by working with employers, identifying suitable vacancies in neighbouring areas and helping jobless people to fill them. Funding will be available for transport to enable people to access nearby vacancies. Action Teams will be led by the Employment Service in 25 areas and the Employment Zone contractors in the Employment Zone areas. The Teams will bring together secondees from the private and voluntary sectors.

Government Employment Services

The Government is planning to change the support for people of working age. The Employment Service and those parts of the Benefit Agency supporting people of working age are to be merged in 2001. The new agency will provide a single, integrated service to benefit claimants of working age and to employers.

Currently, the Government provides a range of services to jobseekers through the Employment Service, an executive agency of the DfEE. These include:

- a network of local offices, at which people can find details of job opportunities;
- advice and guidance so that people can find the best route back into employment, for example, by training; and
- a range of special programmes, including those for people with disabilities.

The Employment Service has a national network of over 1,000 Jobcentres and a budget in Great Britain of over £1,900 million for 2000–01, of which £838 million is connected with the New Deals. In 1999–2000 it placed over 1.3 million unemployed people into jobs and conducted nearly 4 million advisory interviews to help people find appropriate work or places on employment and training programmes. The Employment Service also has a key role in the delivery of the Government's Welfare-to-Work measures, particularly in relation to the New Deal programmes and ONE (see above).

Advisory Services

Through the main Jobcentre services, unemployed people have access to vacancies, employment advice and training opportunities. Employment Service advisers see all jobseekers when a claim is made for Jobseeker's Allowance (see p. 174) to assess their eligibility and to provide advice about jobs, training and self-employment opportunities. To receive the allowance, each unemployed person has to complete a Jobseeker's Agreement, which sets out his or her availability for work, the types of job for which he or she is looking, and the steps which, if taken, offer the best chance of securing work. Jobseekers are required to attend a job search review each fortnight and periodic intensive advisory interviews to assess their situation and see what additional help, if any, is needed and, if appropriate, to revise the Jobseeker's Agreement.

With the introduction of the New Deal programmes for the young and long-term unemployed, the range of Employment Service programmes was restructured and brought together into a new package of measures. Programme Centres have been introduced nationally and are gradually replacing traditional fixed-length job search courses with a modular approach that addresses the needs of individual jobseekers, and allows providers to take a flexible approach so that jobsearch help can be adapted for local delivery. Other programmes include Jobclubs (offering guidance on jobseeking, interview skills and other practical assistance), Jobplan workshops (a mandatory five-day programme of individual assessment) and work trial, where jobseekers spend up to a maximum of 15 days in an actual vacancy.

A new Learning and Work Bank, which will be set up later in 2000, will allow jobseekers to use the Internet to search for work, training or education at home, at call centres or kiosks, in shopping centres, bars or eventually via a mobile telephone. The Government is supporting the scheme with £68 million over the next two years. The scheme is being run in conjunction with a private sector firm, EDS, as part of the Private Finance Initiative.

Employment Agencies

There are many thousands of private employment agencies, including several large firms with significant branch networks. The law governing the conduct of employment agencies is less restrictive than in many other EU countries, but agencies must comply with legislation which establishes a framework of minimum standards designed to protect agency users, both workers and hirers. A review of the regulatory framework was launched by the Department of Trade and Industry (DTI) in 1999, and a revised series of regulations should be in force by early 2001.

PAY AND CONDITIONS

Earnings

Average gross weekly earnings of full-time employees on adult rates in Great Britain whose pay was unaffected by absence were £411 in April 2000, according to the ONS New Earnings Survey. Average earnings for men were £453 and for women £338. Earnings were higher for non-manual employees (£465) than for manual employees (£321), with managerial and professional groups the highest paid.

Minimum Wage

The National Minimum Wage Act 1998 set out the regulatory framework for the national minimum wage which was introduced on 1 April 1999. Minimum wage rates are:

- £3.70 an hour for those aged 22 or above (from 1 October 2000); and
- £3.20 an hour for workers aged 18 to 21, and for those aged 22 or over in the first six months of a new job with a new employer, and receiving accredited training.

Among those to whom the national minimum wage does not apply are:

- the self-employed;
- people under 18 years of age;
- apprentices and those on National Apprenticeship schemes under 19 years of age and those aged 19 to 25 in the first 12 months of their apprenticeship or Modern Apprenticeship—from 1 October 2000 this exemption will also apply to those on National Traineeships, Foundation Modern Apprenticeships or Advanced Modern Apprenticeships in England and Wales, Skillseekers in Scotland and Jobskills Traineeships in Northern Ireland;
- members of the armed forces; and
- people living in their employer's home and treated as part of the family (for example, au pairs).

Around 1.5 million low-paid workers are estimated to have become entitled to higher pay following the introduction of the national minimum wage, some two-thirds of whom are women and around 120,000 young people. Sectors most affected have been hospitality (hotels and catering), retailing, cleaning, hairdressing, social care, footwear and clothing manufacture, and private security.

Fringe Benefits

Fringe benefits are used by many employers to provide additional rewards to their employees. They include schemes to encourage financial participation by employees in their companies, pension schemes, private medical insurance, subsidised meals, company cars and childcare schemes. Company cars are provided for employees in a wide variety of circumstances. From April 2002, the tax charge for company cars will be linked to exhaust emissions. Around 1.7 million people in 1997–98 had a company car available for private use and about half of these received fuel for private motoring in their car.

By the end of March 2000, 3,790 profit-related pay schemes, which link part of pay to changes in a business's profits, were registered with the Inland Revenue, covering around 1.6 million people. Many companies have adopted employee share schemes, where employees receive free shares or options to buy shares at a discount from their employer without paying income tax. A new all-employee share ownership plan will be introduced later in 2000, allowing employees to buy shares from their pre-tax salary and to receive free shares, with tax incentives for longer-term shareholding.

Hours of Work

Most full-time employees have a basic working week of between 34 and 40 hours, and work a five-day week. When overtime is taken into account, average weekly hours worked by full-time workers in their main job in the UK in April–June 2000 were 38.0 hours: 39.9 hours for men and 34.2 hours for women. For part-time workers the average was 15.4 hours.

Both male and female full-time employees tend to work more hours than people in other EU countries. Hours worked tend to be longest in agriculture, construction, and transport and communications, and shortest in most service industries. Self-employed people work, on average, longer hours than full-time employees. A significant minority of employees have flexible working hours or are engaged in some sort of shift work.

Holiday entitlements have generally been determined by negotiation. In spring 2000 the average paid holiday entitlement for full-time workers was just under five weeks. However, some employees, such as part-time and temporary employees, may have much less holiday entitlement.

Two EC regulations, on working time and on young workers (in relation to hours of work of adolescents), came into force in the UK in 1998. They apply to full-time, part-time and temporary workers, although workers in certain sectors—including transport, sea fishing, other work at sea, and doctors in training—are currently exempt. They provide for:

- a maximum working week of 48 hours (on average), although individual workers can choose to work longer;
- a minimum of four weeks' annual paid leave;
- minimum daily and weekly rest periods; and
- a limit for night workers of an average eight hours' work in a 24-hour period.

There are specific provisions for adolescent workers in respect of these rights and entitlements.

INDUSTRIAL RELATIONS

Around a third of employees in Great Britain in 1999 were in workplaces covered by collective bargaining, which is generally more prevalent in large establishments and in the public sector. Collective bargaining mainly concerns pay and working conditions. In general, negotiations are now conducted more at a local level, although many large firms retain a degree of central control over the bargaining process. There are relatively few industry-wide agreements; where they do exist, they are often supplemented by local agreements in companies or factories (plant bargaining). The EC's European Works Councils Directive requires firms with 1,000 or more employees and which operate in two or more member states to establish European-level information and consultation procedures.

Regulations implementing the Directive in the UK took effect in January 2000. About 110 UK-based companies are affected by the Directive.

The results of the 1998 Workplace Employee Relations Survey were published in September 1999.[2] The Survey was sponsored by the DTI, the Advisory, Conciliation and Arbitration Service (ACAS) (see p. 159), the Economic and Social Research Council and the Policy Studies Institute. Among its key findings were:

- workplace flexibility has increased, with many more workplaces reporting greater use of contracting out, temporary agency workers, fixed-term employees and part-time workers;
- some workplaces have introduced management practices designed to foster employee commitment and improve performance, including procedures for dispute resolution, briefing meetings and performance appraisals;
- fewer workplaces are recognising trade unions—42 per cent, compared with 53 per cent in 1990;
- over half of employees expressed themselves as satisfied (46 per cent) or very satisfied (7 per cent) with their job—only 19 per cent being dissatisfied or very dissatisfied (the remaining 27 per cent were neither satisfied nor dissatisfied). Employees were more likely to be satisfied with their job when they could influence how they carried out their work, and when they thought management showed an understanding about balancing work and family responsibilities, encouraged skill development, involved employees and treated them fairly; and
- industrial action was reported in just 2 per cent of workplaces.

Individual Employment Rights

Employment protection legislation provides a number of safeguards for employees. For example, most employees have a right to a written statement setting out details of the main conditions, including pay, hours of work and holidays. Employees with at least two years of continuous employment with their employer are entitled to lump-sum redundancy payments if their jobs cease to exist and their employers cannot offer suitable alternative work.[3]

Minimum periods of notice are laid down for both employers and employees. Most employees who believe they have been unfairly dismissed have the right to complain to an employment tribunal (see p. 158), subject to the general qualifying period of one year's continuous service. If the complaint is upheld, the tribunal may make an order for re-employment or award compensation.

Legislation prohibits discrimination on grounds of sex or marital status (see p. 115) or disability or on grounds of race, nationality (including citizenship) or ethnic or national origin (see p. 111), in employment, training and related matters. In Northern Ireland discrimination in employment on grounds of religious belief or political opinion is unlawful. Under the Equal Pay Act 1970, women in Great Britain are entitled to equal pay with men when doing work that is the same or broadly similar, work which is rated as equivalent, or work which is of equal value. Despite this, there is a continuing pay gender gap. Among men and women working full-time the gap between their hourly earnings has narrowed since the mid-1970s. By 1999, in Britain, women's hourly earnings were 84 per cent of men's earnings.

Under the Disability Discrimination Act 1995, disabled people have the right not to be discriminated against in employment. Employers with 15 or more employees have a duty not to discriminate against disabled employees or applicants. The Disability Rights

[2] Published by Routledge in two volumes: *Britain at Work* by Mark Cully, Stephen Woodland, Andrew O'Reilly and Gill Dix, and the companion volume, *All Change at Work? British employment relations 1980–98; as portrayed by the Workplace Industrial Relations Survey series*, by Neil Millward, Alex Bryson and John Forth.

[3] The statutory redundancy payment is calculated according to a formula based on a person's age, the number of years of continuous service and his or her weekly pay. However, many employers pay more than the statutory amount.

Commission (see p. 165) began operating on 25 April 2000 to protect the rights of all disabled people, both those in work and out of work. It has powers to investigate cases of discrimination at work against people with disabilities, and to ensure employers comply with the appropriate legal regulations.

All pregnant employees have the right to statutory maternity leave with their non-wage contractual benefits maintained, and protection against dismissal because of pregnancy. Statutory maternity pay is payable by an employer for up to 18 weeks to women with at least six months' service with that employer.

New Rights

The Employment Relations Act 1999, and in Northern Ireland the Employment Relations (NI) Order 1999, introduced a package of family-oriented employment rights. Key elements are:

- a minimum of 18 weeks' maternity leave for all female employees (in line with statutory maternity pay;
- additional maternity leave for women after one year's service (reduced from the previous two years);
- 13 weeks' parental unpaid leave after one year's service for mothers and fathers after the birth of their baby or adopting a child on or after 15 December 1999;
- being able to return to the same job, or its equivalent, at the end of maternity and parental leave;
- clarification of the status of an employee's employment contract during periods of paternal or maternity leave;
- emergency time off unpaid to care for dependants; and
- protection against victimisation for exercising any of these rights.

The Government has launched a review looking at the issues surrounding maternity rights and paternity leave. The review will consider the steps needed to make sure that parents have choices to help them balance the needs of their work and their children so that they may contribute fully to the modern economy. In doing so, it will take into account:

- the impact of maternity pay and parental leave on business, particularly small and medium-sized enterprises (SMEs), and families, including whether it is possible to simplify the implementation of existing legislation;
- best practice in business and its impact, including the extent to which employers currently offer additional entitlements or flexible arrangements;
- factors affecting women's decisions to return to work after childbirth;
- factors affecting the take-up of parental and paternity leave; and
- the impact of returning to work part-time, working from home or on flexible hours.

Trade Union and Industrial Relations Law

Among the legal requirements governing industrial relations are:

- All individuals have the right not to be dismissed or refused employment (or the services of an employment agency) because of membership or non-membership of a trade union.
- Where a union is recognised by an employer for collective bargaining purposes, union officials are entitled to paid time off for undertaking certain trade union duties and training. The employer is also obliged to disclose information to the union for collective bargaining purposes.
- A trade union must elect every member of its governing body, its general secretary and its president. Elections must be held at least every five years and be carried out by a secret postal ballot under independent scrutiny.
- If a trade union wishes to set up a political fund, its members must first agree in a secret ballot a resolution adopting those political objectives as an aim of the union. The union must also

ballot its members every ten years to maintain the fund. Union members have a statutory right to opt out of contributing to the fund.

- For a union to have the benefit of statutory immunity when organising industrial action, the action must be wholly or mainly in contemplation or furtherance of a trade dispute between workers and their own employer. Industrial action must not involve workers who have no dispute with their own employer (so-called 'secondary' action) or involve unlawful forms of picketing. Before calling for industrial action, a trade union must obtain the support of its members in a secret postal ballot.

Recent Changes

Various changes to industrial relations legislation were introduced under the Employment Relations Act 1999 and in Northern Ireland the Employment Relations (NI) Order 1999. For example, new procedures concerning the recognition by employers of trade unions, which apply to organisations with over 20 workers, took effect in June 2000. Unions can be recognised, or derecognised, for collective bargaining purposes where this is the clear wish of the workers in the relevant bargaining units. Parties are encouraged to reach a voluntary agreement where possible, but if this proves impossible a strengthened Central Arbitration Committee (CAC) will decide the issues concerned. Other provisions include:

- an extended right for employees dismissed for taking part in lawfully organised official industrial action to complain of unfair dismissal to a tribunal;
- a legal right for employees to be accompanied by a fellow employee or trade union representative at a major hearing during disciplinary and grievance procedures;
- the establishment of powers to prohibit the blacklisting of trade unionists; and
- the establishment of a new Partnership Fund to contribute to the training of managers and employee representatives in order to assist and develop partnerships at work.

These provisions are being implemented, on a phased basis, between 1999 and 2001.

Employment Tribunals

Employment tribunals in Great Britain have jurisdiction over complaints covering a range of employment rights, including unfair dismissal, redundancy pay, equal pay, and sex and race discrimination. The Employment Rights (Dispute Resolution) Act 1998 streamlined tribunal procedures and encouraged voluntary settlement of disputes on employment rights. It also promoted a voluntary arbitration scheme, developed by ACAS (see p. 159), to settle unfair dismissal. These tribunals received 89,000 applications in 1999–2000. Northern Ireland has a separate tribunal system.

Labour Disputes

In the past 20 years there has been a substantial decline in working days lost through labour disputes. In 1999 there were 205 stoppages of work arising from labour disputes, and 242,000 working days were lost as a result. Stoppages over pay accounted for two-thirds of days lost. The United Kingdom has a good record in employment relations: in 1998 only 12 days were lost per 1,000 employees to labour disputes, compared with the EU average of 48.

Trade Unions

Trade unions have members in nearly all occupations. As well as negotiating pay and other terms and conditions of employment with employers, they provide benefits and services, such as educational facilities, financial services, legal advice and aid in work-related cases.

In autumn 1999 there were 7.1 million trade union members in Great Britain, according to the Labour Force Survey, almost

20 per cent fewer than in 1989.[4] The decline in membership was particularly noticeable where it has traditionally been high—among male employees, manual workers and those in production industries. Public administration has the highest density of union members, around 60 per cent of all employees (54 per cent among female employees). Sectors with relatively few union members include agriculture, forestry and fishing, hotels and restaurants, and wholesale and retail trade.

At the end of March 2000 there were 221 trade unions on the list maintained by the Certification Officer, who, among other duties, is responsible for certifying the independence of trade unions. To be eligible for entry on the list a trade union must show that it consists wholly or mainly of workers and that its principal purposes include the regulation of relations between workers and employers or between workers and employers' associations. A further 22 unions were known to the Certification Officer.

The national body of the trade union movement is the Trades Union Congress (TUC), founded in 1868. At the beginning of 1999 its affiliated membership comprised 74 trade unions, which together represented some 6.8 million people.

There are six TUC regional councils for England and a Wales Trades Union Council. The annual Congress meets in September to discuss matters of concern to trade unionists. A General Council represents the TUC between annual meetings.

In Scotland there is a separate national central body, the Scottish Trades Union Congress, to which UK unions usually affiliate their Scottish branches. Nearly all trade unions in Northern Ireland are represented by the Northern Ireland Committee of the Irish Congress of Trade Unions (ICTU). Most trade unionists in Northern Ireland are members of unions affiliated to the ICTU, while the majority also belong to unions based in Great Britain, which are affiliated to the TUC.

The TUC participates in international trade union activity, through its affiliation to the International Confederation of Free Trade Unions and the European Trade Union Confederation. It also nominates the British workers' delegation to the annual International Labour Conference.

The TUC initiated the TUC Partnership Institute in spring 2000 to provide an advisory and training service to help unions and employers establish partnerships at work.

Employers' Organisations

Many employers in the UK are members of employers' organisations, some of which are wholly concerned with labour matters, although others are also trade associations concerned with commercial matters in general. Employers' organisations are usually established on an industry basis rather than a product basis, for example, the Engineering Employers' Federation. A few are purely local in character or deal with a section of an industry or, for example, with small businesses; most are national and are concerned with the whole of an industry. At the end of March 2000, 101 listed employers' associations were known to the Certification Officer; a further 100 unlisted associations were in operation.

Most national organisations belong to the Confederation of British Industry (CBI—see p. 399), which represents directly or indirectly around 200,000 businesses.

ACAS

The Advisory, Conciliation and Arbitration Service (ACAS) is an independent statutory body with a general duty of promoting the improvement of industrial relations. ACAS aims to operate through the voluntary co-operation of employers, employees and, where appropriate, their representatives. Its main functions are collective conciliation; provision of arbitration and mediation; advisory mediation services for preventing

[4] There are two main sources of information on trade union membership: the ONS Labour Force Survey and data provided by trade unions to the Certification Office. Differences in coverage result in different estimates—for example, the Certification Office's figure for trade union membership in 1998 was 7.9 million, compared with 7.1 million obtained from the Labour Force Survey in autumn 1999.

disputes and improving industrial relations through the joint involvement of employers and employees; and the provision of a public enquiry service. ACAS also conciliates in disputes on individual employment rights, and in late 2000 plans to introduce a new voluntary system for resolving unfair dismissal claims.

In Northern Ireland the Labour Relations Agency, an independent statutory body, provides services similar to those provided by ACAS in Great Britain.

HEALTH AND SAFETY AT WORK

There has been a long-term decline in injuries to employees in the UK, partly reflecting a change in industrial structure away from the traditional heavy industries, which tend to have higher risks. In 1999–2000 the number of deaths of employees and the self-employed from injuries at work was 216, which represented a fatal injury rate of 0.8 per 100,000 workers. About 6.5 million working days were lost in 1997–98 as a result of work-related injuries.

The principal legislation is the Health and Safety at Work etc. Act 1974. It imposes general duties on everyone concerned with work activities, including employers, the self-employed, employees, and manufacturers and suppliers of materials for use at work. Associated Acts and regulations deal with particular hazards and types of work. Employers with five or more staff must prepare a written statement of their health and safety policy and bring it to the attention of their staff.

In June 2000 the Government announced new targets to cut workplace deaths, injuries and illness:

- to cut deaths and major injury accidents by 10 per cent by 2010;
- to reduce the rate of work-related ill-health by 20 per cent by 2010;
- to cut working days lost per 100,000 workers due to work-related injury and ill-health by 30 per cent by 2010; and
- to achieve half of the above improvements by 2004.

Health and Safety Commission

The Health and Safety Commission (HSC) has responsibility for developing policy on health and safety at work in Great Britain, including proposals for new or revised regulations and approved codes of practice. Recent work has concentrated on a simpler and more effective system of health and safety regulation.

The HSC has advisory committees covering subjects such as toxic substances, genetic modification and the safety of nuclear installations. There are also several industry advisory committees, each covering a specific sector of industry.

Health and Safety Executive

The Health and Safety Executive (HSE) is the primary instrument for carrying out the HSC's policies and has day-to-day responsibility for enforcing health and safety law, except where other bodies, such as local authorities, are responsible. Its field services and inspections are carried out by the Field Operations Directorate, which includes the Railway Inspectorate, the Safety Policy Directorate, the Health Directorate and the Hazardous Installations and Nuclear Safety Inspectorates.

The HSE's Technology Division provides technical advice on industrial health and safety matters. The Health and Safety Laboratory (HSL), an Agency of the HSE, supports HSE's mission to ensure that risks to health and safety from work activities are properly controlled. This involves HSL in two main areas of activity: operational support through incident investigations and studies of workplace situations; and longer-term work on analysis and resolution of occupational health and safety problems.

In premises such as offices, shops, warehouses, restaurants and hotels, health and safety legislation is enforced by inspectors appointed by local authorities, working under guidance from the HSE. Some other official bodies work under agency agreement with the HSE.

Northern Ireland

The general requirements of health and safety legislation in Northern Ireland are broadly similar to those for Great Britain and are enforced by the Health and Safety Executive for Northern Ireland (HSENI) and the district councils, with the latter having an enforcement role similar to that of local authorities in Great Britain. The HSENI, established in April 1999 and funded by the Department of Enterprise, Trade and Investment, took over the functions previously discharged by the Health and Safety Agency, the Employment Medical Advisory Service and the Health and Safety Division of the then Department of Economic Development.

Further Reading

Fairness at Work. Cm 3968. Department of Trade and Industry. The Stationery Office, 1998.

The Government's Expenditure Plans 2000–01 to 2001–02. Department for Education and Employment and Office for Standards in Education. Cm 4602. The Stationery Office, 2000.

Labour Market Trends. Office for National Statistics. Monthly.

Learning to Succeed: a new framework for post-16 learning. Department for Education and Employment. Cm 4392. The Stationery Office, 1999.

Social Focus on the Unemployed. Office for National Statistics. The Stationery Office, 1998.

Annual Reports

Advisory, Conciliation and Arbitration Service. ACAS.

Certification Officer. Certification Office for Trade Unions and Employers' Associations.

Health and Safety Commission. HSC.

Websites

Department for Education and Employment: www.dfee.gov.uk

Department of Trade and Industry: www.dti.gov.uk

12 Social Protection

The responsibility for delivering social care support to older people, people with physical disabilities, learning disabilities or people with mental health problems, and children in need of care falls to local authorities and voluntary organisations, who work within a policy framework set out by central government.

Provisions in the Care Standards Act 2000 aim to improve standards in care services, set new checks on private healthcare and reform regulation of early years childcare and education. The Children (Leaving Care) Bill currently before Parliament is intended to improve the prospects of young people living in, and leaving, local authority care. Additional measures contained in the Welfare Reform and Pensions Act 1999 and the Child Support, Pensions and Social Security Bill are meant to promote incentives to work, reduce poverty and welfare dependency, and strengthen community and family life.

Personal Social Services

Personal social services help older people, people with disabilities, children and young people, those with mental health problems or learning disabilities, their families and carers. Major services include residential and day care, and domiciliary services—provided for people needing support to live in their own homes. In certain circumstances direct cash payments may be made to enable individuals to secure for themselves the relevant services which they have been assessed as needing. Services are administered by local authorities, but central government is responsible for establishing national policies, issuing guidance and overseeing standards.

Much of the care given to older people and disabled people comes from families and self-help groups. One in eight adults gives informal care and one in six homes has a carer. Many of these carers are elderly themselves. There are around 6 million informal carers in the UK, about 58 per cent of whom are women. The Carers and Disabled Children Act 2000 ensures for the first time that support is directed at carers themselves, bringing their needs in line with those of the person they are looking after.

Caring for Vulnerable People

The Care Standards Act 2000 aims to raise the standards in care services, monitor private healthcare provision and reform the regulation of care for young people.

The Care Standards Act will:

- set up a National Care Standards Commission—an independent, non-departmental public body to regulate private hospitals and clinics, children's homes and care homes for older people and disabled people. It will regulate other care services for the first time, including care to people at home and fostering agencies. It will also have powers to close down services if they are not up to standard;
- set up a General Social Care Council (GSCC) to raise professional and training standards for the social care workforce of 1 million, 80 per cent of whom hold no relevant qualifications and only 40,000 are professional social workers. The GSCC will take over from the Central Council for Education and Training in Social Work (CCETSW) the statutory duty to regulate training for professional social work and offer an increased level of protection to users of social care services;
- reform the regulation system for childminders and day care services and transfer the responsibility to a new Early Years Directorate within the Office for Standards in Education (OFSTED—see p. 128); and
- establish a new list of people judged unsuitable to work with vulnerable adults in the care sector. It will work in the same way as the existing Protection of Children list, and will be a means of ensuring that people who have abused or mistreated vulnerable adults in their care do not find their way back into such positions again.

Older People

Older people represent the fastest growing section of the community. The proportion of the population in the United Kingdom aged 75 and over rose from 4 per cent in 1961 to 7 per cent in 1999. However, the number of older people in the population is expected to grow less quickly in the next decade than it has in the previous one.

Services for older people are designed to help them live at home whenever possible. These services may include advice and help given by social workers, domestic help, the provision of meals in the home, sitters-in, night attendants and laundry services, as well as direct payments, day centres, lunch clubs and recreational facilities. Adaptations to the home can overcome a person's difficulties in moving about, and a range of equipment is available for people with poor hearing or eyesight or people with physical disabilities. Alarm systems help older people obtain assistance in an emergency. In some areas 'good neighbour' and visiting services are arranged by the local authority or a voluntary organisation. Older people who live in residential care homes or nursing homes are subject to means-test charging. Local authorities contribute to care costs for those who cannot pay the full charge.

The most marked trend in residential care provision over recent years has been the continuing increase in the number of places provided in the private and voluntary sectors and the corresponding fall in the number provided in local authorities' own homes (see chart on p. 164).

As part of their responsibility for social housing, local authorities provide homes designed for older people ('sheltered accommodation'); some of these developments have resident wardens. Housing associations and private builders also build such accommodation. Many local authorities provide free or subsidised travel for older people within their areas.

A Royal Commission on the funding of long-term care for older people in the UK was set up in 1997. The Commission's report—*With Respect to Old Age: Long-term Care—Rights and Responsibilities*—was published in March 1999 and made two main recommendations:

- personal care, which includes nursing care and some social care tasks such as help with bathing, should be funded by general taxation, subject to an assessment of need; and
- a National Care Commission should be established to take a strategic overview of long-term care and represent the

Places in Residential Care Homes for Elderly People:[1] by Type of Care Home

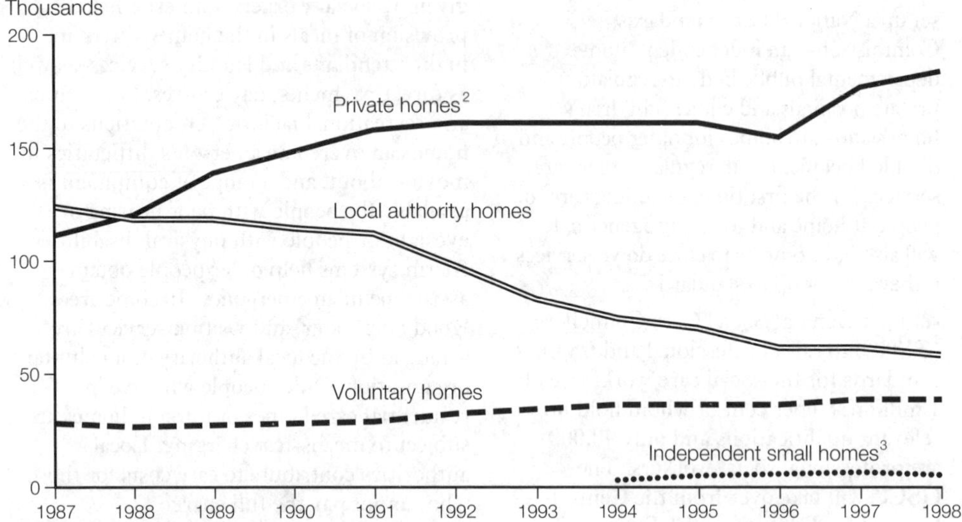

[1] Covers England, Wales and Northern Ireland. Data are not available for Wales in 1996. From 1 April 1988 data for Northern Ireland are for financial years and therefore the information for 1998 does not include Northern Ireland.

[2] Independent homes in Wales.

[3] England only.

Sources: Department of Health, National Assembly for Wales and Department of Health, Social Services and Public Safety, Northern Ireland

interests of older people. (The Scottish Executive has indicated that it intends to put legislation through the Scottish Parliament to set up a similar Commission for Scotland.)

The Government's response to the Royal Commission on Long-term Care was set out in the NHS Plan in July 2000 (see p. 184). This announced a package of proposals designed to make the funding of long-term care clearer and fairer, together with wide-ranging improvements to health and social care services for all older people. Changes (to be implemented as soon as parliamentary approval allows) include making NHS nursing care free in all settings and disregarding the value of a person's home from the means test for the first three months after admission to a care home. A National Care Standards Commission has been established through the Care Standards Act 2000, which will take up many of the roles proposed by the Royal Commission.

Long-term Care Charter

The Government published its long-term care charter—*Better Care, Higher Standards*—in December 1999. The charter sets out the values on which people can expect their local housing, health or social services to be based (such as treating users and carers with courtesy, honesty and respecting their dignity) and requires local authorities and health services to agree and make public local standards in the following six key areas:

- helping users and carers to find out about services;
- understanding and responding to the needs of users and carers;
- finding a suitable place to live;
- helping people to stay independent;
- getting the right health care; and
- helping carers to care.

The NHS Plan announced the piloting of Care Direct as a new, single point of access to information about social care, health and housing services, and social security benefits. In addition to the £150 million invested for intermediate care and related services in 2000, the NHS Plan announced major new investment, rising to around £900 million annually by 2004.

Disabled People

Over the past ten years there has been increasing emphasis on rehabilitation and the provision of day, domiciliary and respite support services to enable disabled people to live independently in the community wherever possible.

Local authority social services departments help with social rehabilitation and adjustment to disability. They are required to identify the number of disabled people in their area and publicise services. About 413,000 people with physical disabilities or frailty in England receive community-based services. These may include advice on personal and social problems arising from disability, as well as on occupational, educational, social and recreational facilities, either at day centres or elsewhere. Other services provided may include adaptations to homes (such as ramps for wheelchairs, stairlifts and ground-floor toilets), the delivery of cooked meals, support with personal care at home and direct payments with which disabled people can purchase support to meet their assessed need. Local authorities and voluntary organisations may provide severely disabled people with residential accommodation or temporary facilities to allow their carers relief from their duties. Special housing may be available for those able to look after themselves. Some authorities provide free or subsidised travel for disabled people on public transport, and they are encouraged to provide special means of access to public buildings.

In 1997 responsibility for disability issues was transferred from the Department of Social Security to the Department for Education and Employment as a signal that disabled people's willingness and ability to take advantage of education, training and employment opportunities was valued by society. The New Deal for Disabled People, part of the Government's Welfare-to-Work programme (see p. 151), aims to help disabled people find and keep work.

Disability Rights Commission

A Disability Rights Commission (DRC) was established in April 2000. Its main aims are to:

- work towards the elimination of discrimination against disabled people;
- promote equal opportunities for disabled people;
- encourage good practice; and
- advise the Government on the operation of the Disability Discrimination Act 1995 and the Disability Rights Commission Act 1999.

The Equality Commission (see p. 19) has a similar role in Northern Ireland.

People with Learning Disabilities

The Government encourages the development of local services for people with learning disabilities and their families through co-operation between health authorities, local authorities, education and training services, voluntary and other organisations.

Local authority social services departments are the leading statutory agencies for planning and arranging such services. They provide or arrange short-term care, support for families in their own homes, residential accommodation and support for various types of activity outside the home. People with learning disabilities may also be able to receive direct payments. The main aims are to ensure that, as far as possible, people with learning disabilities can lead full lives in their communities. People with learning disabilities form the largest group for local authority-funded day centre places and the second largest group in residential care. A new national learning disability strategy, designed to eliminate inconsistencies in service delivery, is due to be published by the end of 2000.

The National Health Service (NHS) provides specialist services when the ordinary primary care services cannot meet healthcare needs. Residential care is provided for those with severe or profound disabilities whose needs can effectively be met only by the NHS.

In May 2000, the Scottish Executive published *The Same As You?*, its review of services for people with a learning disability. By focusing on inclusion, it aims to improve the lives of people with learning disabilities and their families.

People with a Mental Health Problem

Government policy aims to ensure that people with mental health problems should have access to all the services they need as locally as possible. A cornerstone of community care policy for people with mental health problems is the Care Programme Approach. Under this, each patient should receive an assessment and a care plan, have a key worker appointed to keep in touch with him or her, and be given regular reviews. The Care Programme Approach is subject to audit, enabling health authorities (health boards in Scotland) to identify any problems with the quality of its implementation. The separate Welsh Mental Health Strategy employs many of the same broad principles in delivering services in Wales. In Scotland, each health board works with its local authority care partners, users of mental health services and their carers to develop joint strategies to provide local and comprehensive mental health services.

While the total number of places for people with mental health problems in the large hospitals has continued to fall, the provision of alternative places has increased in smaller NHS hospitals, local authority accommodation and private and voluntary sector homes. At 31 March 1999 there were 29,000 registered beds in private nursing homes (including mental nursing homes) and private hospitals and clinics in England intended for people with mental health problems and 38,000 places in residential care homes. In 1998–99 the average daily number of available NHS hospital beds for people with mental health problems in England was 36,000 with a further 1,400 residential beds.

Arrangements made by social services authorities for providing care for mentally ill people in the community include direct payments, day centres, social centres and residential care. Social workers help patients and their families with problems caused by mental illness. In some cases they can apply for a mentally disordered person to be compulsorily admitted to and detained in hospital. Special bodies provide important safeguards for patients to ensure that the law is used appropriately.

Supervision registers for discharged patients most at risk are maintained by the providers of services for mentally ill people and allow hospital staff to keep track of them.

There are many voluntary organisations concerned with those suffering from mental illness (such as MIND, SANE and the Scottish Association for Mental Health), or learning disabilities (such as MENCAP or its Scottish equivalent ENABLE), and they play an important role in providing services for these groups of people. Central Government provides funding to many similar voluntary bodies.

Help to Families

Local authorities must safeguard the welfare of any child in need, and promote the upbringing of such children by their families, by providing an appropriate range and level of services for them. These services can include advice, guidance, counselling, help in the home, or family centres, and can be provided for the family of the child in need or any member of the family, if this will safeguard the child's welfare. Local authorities can provide these services directly or arrange for them through, for example, a voluntary organisation. They are also required to publicise the help available to families in need. Many local authorities or specialist voluntary organisations run refuges for women, often with young children, whose home conditions have become intolerable, because of, for example, domestic violence. The refuges provide short-term accommodation and support while attempts are made to relieve the women's problems.

Day Care for Children

Day care facilities are provided for young children by childminders, voluntary agencies, private nurseries and local authorities. In 1999 in England and Wales, there were 351,000 childminder places for children under eight; 258,000 day nursery places; 119,000 after school clubs; and 373,000 playgroup places.

In allocating places, where local authorities have their own provision, priority is given to children with special social, learning or health needs. From September 2001 the newly formed Early Years Directorate of OFSTED will take over responsibility from local authorities for the regulation of day care providers for children aged under eight.

Child Protection

Child protection is the joint concern of a number of different agencies and professions. Area child protection committees determine how the different agencies should co-operate to help protect children from abuse and neglect in their area.

Children in Care

Local government authorities must provide accommodation for children who have no parent or guardian, who have been abandoned, or whose parents are unable to provide for them.

In England and Wales a child may be brought before a family proceedings court if he or she is neglected or ill-treated, exposed to moral danger, beyond the control of parents, or not attending school. The court can commit children to the care of a local authority under a care order. Certain pre-conditions have to be satisfied to justify an order. These are that the children are suffering or are likely to suffer significant harm because of a lack of reasonable parental care or because they are beyond parental control. However, an order is made only if the court is also satisfied that this will positively contribute to the children's well-being and be in their best interests. In court proceedings children are entitled to separate legal representation. All courts have to treat the welfare of children as the paramount consideration when reaching any decision about their upbringing. There is a general principle that, wherever possible, children should remain at home with their families.

In Scotland children who have committed offences or are in need of care and protection may be brought before a Children's Hearing, which can impose a supervision requirement on a child if it thinks that compulsory measures are appropriate. Under these requirements most children are allowed to remain at home under the supervision of a social worker, but some may live with foster parents or in a residential establishment while under supervision. Supervision requirements are reviewed at least once a year until ended by a Children's Hearing.

The Government has set up the Quality Protects programme in England to improve the management and delivery of children's social services; it is a key part of the Government's wider strategy for tackling social exclusion. Starting in 2000, a special grant of £375 million over three years will support this strategy, subject to the preparation and achievement of satisfactory action plans by each local authority. In Wales the National Assembly's Children First programme has similar objectives.

Fostering and Children's Homes

Local authorities have a duty to ensure that the welfare of children being looked after away from home is properly safeguarded as regards their health, education, contact with their families and way of life. When appropriate, children in care are placed with foster parents, who receive payments to cover the child's living costs. Alternatively, the child may be placed in residential care. Children's homes may be provided by local authorities, voluntary organisations or private companies or individuals. Voluntary children's homes, which are registered by the Department of Health, are inspected by the Social Services Inspectorate, while local authorities' social services departments inspect the children's homes which they are responsible for registering.

Under the Care Standards Act (see pp. 162–3), all children's homes will be required to register with the National Care Standards Commission. The Commission will also take on the role of inspecting all children's homes, including small private children's homes accommodating three or fewer children, which are not currently subject to any inspection process.

Local authorities are as far as possible expected to work in partnership with the parents of children who are in their care. They are required to produce a plan for the future of each child in their care and to prepare a child for leaving that care. Local authorities are also expected to have a complaints procedure for considering representations about children's services. The Children Act 1989 requires the involvement of an independent person at each stage of consideration of a representation or complaint.

The number of children looked after by local authorities in England, Wales and Northern Ireland increased from 55,000 in 1994 to 59,000 in 1998. The number of children placed in foster homes increased by around 12 per cent over the same period and the number placed in children's homes declined by 17 per cent. Scotland has a different definition of children in care which means data are not comparable with the rest of the United Kingdom. At 31 March 1999, 31,900 children in England and Wales were on child protection registers.

Young People Leaving Local Authority Care

Improving the life chances of young people living in and leaving local authority care is the principal aim of the Children (Leaving Care) Bill which was introduced into the House of Lords in November 1999. The basis of the Bill is to impose new and stronger duties upon local authorities to support care leavers until they are at least 21.

Subject to parliamentary approval, the Bill would:

- impose a new duty on local authorities to assess and meet the needs of eligible young people aged 16 and 17, both those whom they continue to look after and those who have left care;
- require local authorities to keep in touch with young people formerly in their care until they are 21, or 24 if they are still receiving local authority help with higher education or training;
- oblige local authorities to provide all eligible young people with an adviser offering them support and guidance for their future and working with them on an action plan to help them live independently;
- specify that the local authority which last looked after a young person would continue to have responsibility regardless of where that individual moved in the country; and
- simplify the financial regime so that young people were better informed in how to use the social security benefits system and claim what they were entitled to.

Adoption

Local authority social services departments are required by law to provide an adoption service, either directly or by arrangement with approved voluntary adoption societies. Adoption is one way children in care are able to leave—around a third of all children adopted are looked after by a local authority prior to their adoption. In 1999, 3,000 children were placed for adoption in England and Wales. Under adoption law it is illegal to receive an unrelated child for adoption through an unapproved third party. The Registrars-General of England and Wales, and of Scotland keep confidential registers of adopted children.

Adopted people may be given details of their original birth record on reaching the age of 18 (or 16 if adopted in Scotland), and counselling is provided to help them understand the circumstances of their adoption. An Adoption Contact Register enables adopted adults and their birth parents to be given a safe and confidential way of making contact if that is the wish of both parties. A person's details are entered only if they wish to be contacted. In Scotland a similar service is provided through BirthLink.

Finance

In 1997–98, gross expenditure in England on personal social services was £10 billion. Local authorities' expenditure on services for older

Local Authority Personal Social Services Gross Expenditure by Client Group, England, 1997–98

Total: £10 billion

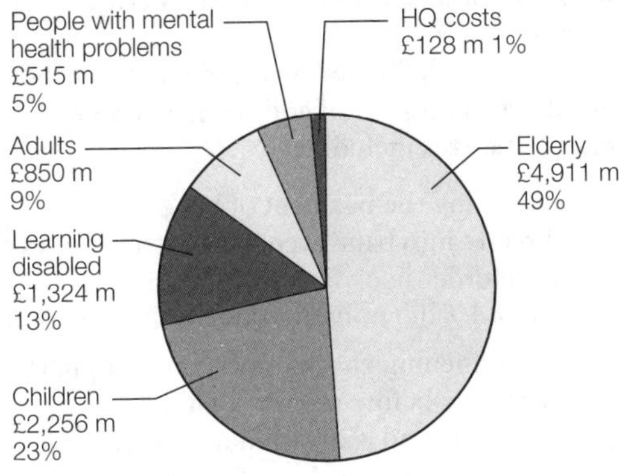

Source: *Department of Health. The Government's Expenditure Plans 2000–2001*

people and children accounted for nearly three-quarters of this (see pie chart above).

Social Security

The social security system is designed to secure a basic standard of living for people in financial need. It provides income during periods of inability to earn (including periods of unemployment), help for families and assistance with costs arising from disablement.

Table 12.1: Planned Benefit Expenditure by Departmental Objective, 2000–01

	£ million
Support for people of working age	17,550
Support for families and children	8,533
Support for disabled people	25,355
Support for people over working age	49,962
Total planned benefit expenditure	**101,400**

Source: *The Government's Expenditure Plans 2000/01–2001/02*: Social Security Departmental Report

Social security is the largest single area of government spending. In each year from 1994–95 to 1999–2000 spending on social security benefits in Great Britain represented about 30 per cent of total government expenditure. At 1999–2000 prices, spending grew from £98.1 billion to £99.3 billion over this five-year period, representing a growth rate of about 0.25 per cent a year on average.

MODERNISING THE SYSTEM

Welfare Reform

The Government's central aim for welfare reform is to promote an ethic of work and savings. After wide consultation in 1998, the Welfare Reform and Pensions Act received Royal Assent in November 1999.

The main measures in the Act are:

- the introduction of new stakeholder pension schemes (see below);
- pension sharing for divorced couples;
- revisions to benefits for widows and widowers;
- a single gateway to the benefit system for those of working age (the ONE service—see p. 152); and
- a new benefits structure for people with disabilities or long-term illness.

Through the Act's provisions, the Government aims to support and strengthen the framework for occupational pensions. The new stakeholder pensions—for those people who do not have access to an employer's occupational pension scheme and for whom a personal pension may not be suitable—will be introduced in April 2001.

Stakeholder pensions, which will be provided by private sector companies, must satisfy a number of minimum government standards to ensure that they offer value for money and flexibility. These standards include:

- not charging more than 1 per cent a year on the value of each member's funds;
- enabling members to transfer into or out of a stakeholder pension, or stopping payment for a time, without facing any charge;

- accepting contributions of £20 or more, though some may accept lower payments; and
- being run in the interest of their members by either trustees or scheme managers.

Another long-term government objective is to ensure that everyone has the opportunity to build up an adequate pension to guarantee security in retirement. The Government plans to introduce a new State Second Pension to replace SERPS (see p. 172) from 2002.

The statutory framework necessary to establish State Second Pensions is contained in the Child Support, Pensions and Social Security Bill 1999 currently before Parliament. For the first time, carers, others with domestic responsibilities who were unable to contribute to a second pension in their own right, and people suffering a long-term illness or disability with broken work records would benefit from additional pension provision. The Government expects that about 11 million people nationwide will be better off when they retire as a result.

Other measures in the Bill would strengthen arrangements for child maintenance (see p. 176). These include:

- giving the Child Support Agency (CSA) far-reaching powers to enforce maintenance payments;
- introducing fines of up to £1,000 for absent parents who deliberately try to evade the CSA; and
- requiring absent parents to pay 15 per cent of their wages for a single child, rising to 20 per cent for two children and 25 per cent for three children or more.

Fighting Fraud

The Government recognises the difficulties of measuring a covert activity such as fraud, but around £2 billion is lost each year in Great Britain through confirmed fraud and a further £3 billion in cases where fraud has probably taken place but no claimant has been proved guilty.

To combat this, the Benefits Fraud Inspectorate was set up in 1997 to examine and report on standards of performance in the administration of all social security benefits, in particular anti-fraud work, within the Department of Social Security's agencies and local authorities. It also carries out work for the Social Security Agency in Northern Ireland.

In January 2000 the Government introduced a number of additional counter-fraud initiatives including:

- extending the payment of benefits directly into bank accounts, cutting losses from order book fraud which costs around £200 million a year;
- strengthening checks on Income Support claimants before money is paid out, saving around £200 million a year;
- cross-checking Department of Social Security (DSS) and local council records, saving £20 million in bogus claims;
- a new scheme stopping benefit cheques being mailed on to fraudsters using false addresses; and
- faster data transfer between the Benefits Agency and local councils.

ADMINISTRATION

In April 1999 the Contributions Agency merged with the Inland Revenue (see p. 406) to provide customers with a single point of contact for tax and National Insurance (NI) matters. Major changes in the way the work of the DSS is managed and organised came into effect in April 2000. The aim is to:

- improve the Department's ability to deliver the Government's modernisation agenda; and
- streamline internal services so that resources are more clearly focused on supporting the front-line delivery of services to the public.

The main parts of the new organisation are:

- three Client Directorates, each responsible for designing and developing the full range of services to children, people of working age and pensioners respectively;

- a Corporate Services Directorate, in charge of corporate strategy, finance, planning, personnel and procurement across the Department;
- a Communication Directorate, looking after internal and external communications;
- the Benefits Agency (BA), administering and paying the majority of benefits;
- the Child Support Agency, assessing and collecting maintenance payments for children (see p. 176);
- the War Pensions Agency, delivering welfare support to war disablement pensioners and war widows;
- The Appeals Service (TAS), providing an impartial re-examination of decisions under appeal; and
- independent statutory bodies, carrying out a range of functions on behalf of the Department.

Advice about Benefits

The DSS produces a range of information material in English and other languages as well as in different formats (audio or videotapes, braille and large print). There is also a website providing general information on entitlement and liability, while telephone helplines provide information on a number of benefits.

CONTRIBUTIONS

Entitlement to National Insurance benefits such as Retirement Pension, Incapacity Benefit, contributory Jobseeker's Allowance, Maternity Allowance and Widow's Benefit, is dependent upon the payment of contributions. The amount an employee can earn before employer NI contributions are charged is aligned with the personal allowance for income tax (see p. 409). There are five classes of contributions. *The rates given below are effective from April 2000 to April 2001:*

- Class 1—paid by employees and their employers. Employees earning between £67 and £75 a week earn a National Insurance credit and do not pay contributions. Contributions on earnings at or above £76 a week in non-contracted-out employment are at the rate of 10 per cent up to the upper earnings limit of £535 a week. Employers' contributions are at the rate of 12.2 per cent and are charged on everything earned at or above £84 per week. There is no upper earnings limit for employers' contributions.
- Class 1A—paid by employers who provide their employees with fuel and/or a car for private use. A Class 1A contribution is payable on the cash equivalent of the benefit provided.
- Class 2—paid by self-employed people. Class 2 contributions are at a flat rate of £2 a week. The self-employed may claim exemption from Class 2 contributions if their net earnings are expected to be below £3,825 for the 2000–01 tax year. Self-employed people are not eligible for unemployment and industrial injuries benefits.
- Class 3—paid voluntarily to safeguard rights to some benefits. Contributions are at a flat rate of £6.55 a week.
- Class 4—paid by the self-employed on their taxable profits over a set lower limit (£4,385 a year), and up to a set upper limit (£27,820 a year) in addition to their Class 2 contribution. Class 4 contributions are payable at the rate of 7 per cent.

Employees who work after pensionable age (60 for women and 65 for men) do not pay contributions but the employer continues to be liable. Self-employed people over pensionable age do not pay contributions.

BENEFITS

Social security benefits can be grouped into three types:

- **means-tested**, available to people whose income and savings are below certain levels;
- **contributory**, paid to people who have made the required contributions to the

Social Security Benefit Expenditure, Great Britain, 2000–01: by Broad Groups of Beneficiaries

Total: £101.4 billion

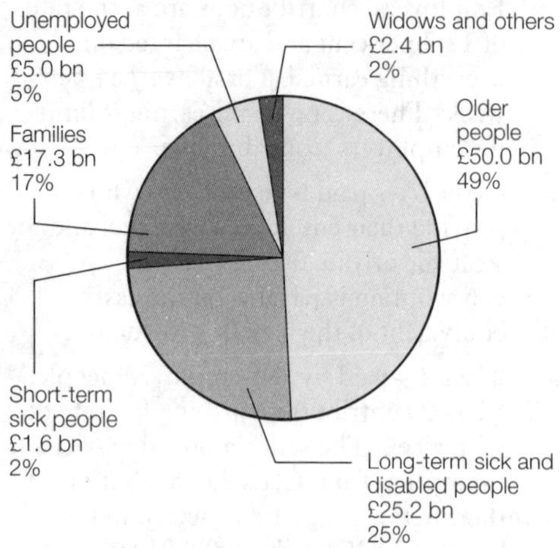

Source: *Social Security Departmental Report: The Government's Expenditure Plans 2000/01–2001/02*

National Insurance Fund,[1] from which benefits are paid; and

- **benefits which are neither means-tested nor contributory** (mainly paid to cover extra costs, for example of disability, or paid universally, for example Child Benefit).

General taxation provides over half the income for the social security programme, employers' NI contributions around a quarter and employees' NI contributions about a fifth. From April 2000, responsibility for deciding appeals across the whole range of DSS business has been taken on by a new executive agency, The Appeals Service.

For most contributory benefits there are two conditions. First, before benefit can be paid at all, a certain number of contributions must have been made. Second, the full rate of benefit cannot be paid unless contributions have been made or credited to a specific level over a set period. A reduced rate of benefit is payable dependent on the level of contributions made or credited. For example, a great many of those receiving retirement pensions and widows' benefits receive a percentage-based rate of benefit. Benefits are increased annually in line with percentage increases in retail prices. The main benefits (payable weekly) are summarised on pp. 172–80. *Rates given are those effective from April 2000 until April 2001.*

[1] The National Insurance Fund is a statutory fund into which all NI contributions payable by employers, employees and self-employed people are deposited, and from which contributory benefits and their administration costs are paid.

Retirement

A state **Retirement Pension** is a taxable weekly benefit payable, if the contribution conditions have been met, to women from the age of 60 and men from the age of 65. Legislation was introduced in 1995 to equalise the state pension age for men and women at 65. The change will be phased in over ten years, starting from April 2010. Women born before 6 April 1950 will not be affected; their pension age will remain at 60. The new pension age of 65 will apply to women born on or after 6 April 1955. Pension age for women born between these dates will move up gradually from 60 to 65.

The state pension scheme consists of a basic weekly pension of £67.50 for a single person and £107.90 for a married couple, together with an additional earnings-related pension (sometimes called 'SERPS'—state earnings-related pension). Pensioners may have unlimited earnings without affecting their pensions. Those who have put off their retirement during the five years after state pension age may earn extra pension.

A *non-contributory retirement pension* of £40.40 a week is payable to people aged 80 or over who have lived in Britain for at least ten years since reaching the age of 60, and who have not qualified for a contributory pension. People whose pensions do not give them enough to live on may be entitled to Income Support (see p. 174).

Rights to basic pensions are safeguarded for people whose opportunities to work are limited while they are looking after a child or a sick or disabled person. Men and women may receive the same basic pension, provided they have paid full-rate NI contributions when working. The earnings-related pension scheme will eventually be calculated as 20 per cent rather than 25 per cent of earnings, and is being phased in over ten years starting in

Table 12.2: Estimated Numbers Receiving Benefits in Great Britain 2000–01 (forecast)[1]

Benefit	*Contributory (C) or non-contributory (NC)*	*Thousands*
Retirement Pension	C	10,947
Widow's Benefit	C	257
Jobseeker's Allowance		
contribution-based	C	196
income-based	NC	899
Incapacity Benefit	C	
short-term (lower rate)		96
short-term (higher rate) and long-term		1,490
Maternity Allowance	C	17
Non-contributory Retirement Pension	NC	24
War Pension	NC	286
Attendance Allowance	NC	1,284
Disability Living Allowance	NC	2,171
Invalid Care Allowance	NC	382
Severe Disablement Allowance	NC	400
Industrial Injuries Disablement Benefit[2]	NC	322
Reduced Earnings Allowance[2]	NC	165
Industrial Death Benefit	NC	15
Income Support	NC	3,892
Child Benefit	NC	
number of children		12,763
number of families		7,072
One parent benefit/ Child Benefit (Lone Parent)	NC	842
Housing Benefit	NC	
rent rebate		2,356
rent allowance		1,836
Council Tax Benefit	NC	5,090

1 Figures are for beneficiaries at any one time.
2 Figures refer to the number of pensions being paid, and not to the number of recipients.
Source: *The Government's Expenditure Plans 2000/01–2001/02*: Social Security Departmental Report

1999. However, the pensions of people who retired in the 20th century will be unaffected.

As part of its plan to improve the income of women in retirement, from April 2000 provisions in the Welfare Reform and Pensions Act 1999 have enabled the courts to divide pension rights equally between divorcing couples.

Occupational and Personal Pensions

Employers may 'contract out' their employees from the state earnings related pension scheme (SERPS) and provide their own occupational pension instead. Contracted-out salary-related schemes must meet a statutory test of overall quality and offer benefits that are broadly the same as, or better than, SERPS. They receive a flat-rate refund of National Insurance contributions and an age-related top-up based on a percentage of earnings between the lower and upper earnings limit on which National Insurance contributions are based. Membership of an employer's contracted-out scheme is voluntary; the State remains responsible for the basic pension.

Occupational pension schemes currently have over 10.3 million members accruing pension rights. The occupational pension rights of those who change jobs before pensionable age, who are unable or do not want to transfer their contracted-out salary-related pension rights, are now offered some protection against inflation. Most workers leaving a scheme at least a year before its pension age and with two years' pensionable service have the right to a fair transfer value. The trustees or managers of pension schemes have to provide full information about their schemes. Occupational schemes must provide equal treatment between male and female members.

As an alternative to their employer's scheme or SERPS, people are entitled to choose a personal pension available from a bank, building society, insurance company or other financial institution.

Employees can also contract out of SERPS using a personal pension plan rather than an occupational scheme. A personal pension used this way is called an appropriate personal pension and it also receives National Insurance rebates which are age-related.

The Pensions Ombudsman deals with complaints of maladministration against occupational and personal pension schemes and adjudicates on disputes of fact or law. A pensions registry helps people trace lost benefits.

Unemployment

Jobseeker's Allowance

Jobseeker's Allowance (JSA) is a benefit for people needing financial support because of unemployment. Claimants must be capable of, and available for, work, and actively seeking it. They must normally be aged at least 18 years and under pension age. JSA can be either contribution-based or income-based:

- *Contribution-based JSA*: those who have paid enough NI contributions are entitled to a personal JSA for up to six months (£52.20 a week for a person aged 25 or over), regardless of any savings or partner's income.
- *Income-based JSA*: those on a low income are entitled to an income-based JSA, payable for as long as the jobseeker requires support and continues to satisfy the qualifying conditions. The amount a claimant receives comprises an age-related personal allowance (£52.20 a week for a person aged 25 or over), allowances for dependent children and premium payments for those with extra expenses, for example, disabled children.

Benefit is paid at rates determined by family circumstances on a basis similar to Income Support (see below).

Back to Work Bonus

Recipients of JSA (see above) and people aged under 60 who receive Income Support can benefit from a Back to Work Bonus. This is intended to increase incentives to take up or keep part-time work, and encourage people to move off benefit and into employment. Those who have been unemployed for three months or more and are working part-time may keep the first £5 of their earnings (£10 for couples; £15 for lone parents, disabled people and some people in special occupations) in any week in which they work while still receiving benefit. An amount equal to half of any earnings above that level counts towards the build-up of a bonus amount. When the unemployed person moves off JSA because of an increase in earnings or hours of work, he or she will be able to claim a tax-free lump sum of up to £1,000. The part-time (up to 24 hours a week) earnings of a partner can also contribute towards building up a Back to Work Bonus, which can be paid if the couple leave benefit as a result of an increase in the partner's earnings or hours of work.

Income Support

Income Support is payable to certain people aged 16 or over who are not required to be available for work, and whose income and savings are below certain set levels. They include lone parents, pensioners, carers and long-term sick and disabled people. Income Support is made up of: a personal allowance based on age and on whether the claimant is single, a lone parent or has a partner; age-related allowances for dependent children and additional sums known as premiums; and housing costs. From this total amount other income, including some other social security benefits, is deducted.

Income Support is not payable if savings exceed £8,000. Savings between £3,000 and £8,000 will reduce the amount received. For people living permanently in residential care or a nursing home, the allowance is not payable if savings exceed £16,000; and savings between £10,000 and £16,000 will affect the amount received.

Families

Most pregnant working women receive **Statutory Maternity Pay** directly from their employer. It is paid for a maximum of 18 weeks to any woman who has been working for the same employer for 26 weeks and who earns on average at least £67 a week. She will receive 90 per cent of her average weekly earnings for the first six weeks and a rate of £60.20 a week for the remaining 12 weeks.

Women who are not eligible for Statutory Maternity Pay because, for example, they are self-employed, or have recently changed jobs or left their job, may qualify for a weekly **Maternity Allowance**, which is payable for up to 18 weeks and is based on average earnings. If average weekly earnings are equal to or more than the lower earnings limit, this amounts to £60.20 a week. If average weekly earnings are at least £30 a week but less than the lower earnings limit, the sum paid is 90 per cent of average earnings. All pregnant employees have the right to take 14 weeks' maternity leave.

A **Sure Start Maternity Grant** of up to £200 may be made if the mother or her partner receive Income Support, income-based Jobseeker's Allowance, Working Families' Tax Credit or Disabled Person's Tax Credit and have savings under £500 (£1,000 for people aged 60 and over). It is also available if a baby is adopted.

The main social security benefit for children is **Child Benefit**. This is a tax-free, non-contributory payment of £15 a week for the eldest qualifying child of a couple, and £10 for each other child. Child Benefit is payable for children up to the age of 16, and for those up to 19 who continue in full-time non-advanced education. It is generally not payable to people whose entry into the UK is subject to immigration control.

People claiming Child Benefit for an orphaned child they have taken into their family may be entitled to **Guardian's Allowance**. This is a tax-free non-contributory benefit of £9.85 a week for the eldest child and £11.35 for each other child who qualifies. In certain circumstances

Table 12.3: Recipients of Benefits for Families, Great Britain

	1994–95	*Thousands* 1999–2000
Child Benefit		
Children	12,640	12,695
Families	6,950	7,030
Lone parent families		
One parent benefit only	548	620
One parent benefit and Income Support[1]	373	311
Income Support only[1]	676	608
Other benefits		
Maternity Allowance	11	12
Statutory Maternity Pay[2]	95	100
Family Credit[3]	575	757

[1] Income Support data includes some income-based Jobseeker's Allowance claimants. Income-based JSA replaced Income Support for the unemployed from October 1996.
[2] Estimated average weekly number of recipients, rounded to the nearest 5,000.
[3] New claims for Family Credit ceased after the introduction of the Working Families' Tax Credit in October 1999.
Source: Department of Social Security

Guardian's Allowance can be paid even if one parent is still alive.

Child Support Agency (CSA)

An estimated 1 million lone parents in the UK bring up 1.7 million children in households where no one is working. The CSA and its counterpart in Northern Ireland are responsible for assessing child maintenance and, where requested by either parent, collecting and enforcing child maintenance payments from, and for tracing, absent parents.

If any person is living with and caring for a child, and one, or both, of the child's parents are living elsewhere in the UK, he or she may apply to have child support maintenance assessed and collected by the CSA (or its Northern Ireland counterpart). If that person or their present partner claims Income Support or income-based Jobseeker's Allowance, they may be required to apply for child support maintenance if asked to do so by the CSA (or its Northern Ireland counterpart).

Assessments for child support maintenance are made using a formula which takes into account each parent's income and makes allowance for essential outgoings. (A system of departures from the formula allows the amount of maintenance payable to be varied in a small number of cases.) A child maintenance bonus worth up to £1,000 may be payable to parents living with and caring for a child who have been in receipt of Income Support or income-based Jobseeker's Allowance and in receipt of child maintenance when they leave benefit for work.

Working Families' Tax Credit

Working Families' Tax Credit (WFTC) replaced Family Credit in October 1999. It is an Inland Revenue administered tax credit paid, since April 2000, through workers' pay packets. Families (couples or lone parents) are eligible if they:

- have one or more children;
- work at least 16 hours a week;
- are resident and entitled to work in the UK; and
- have savings of £8,000 or less.

There are four components to WFTC:

- basic credit—£53.15;
- credit for working over 30 hours per week—£11.25;
- tax credit for each child
  —£25.60 (aged up to 15 years)
  —£26.35 (aged 16 to 18); and
- childcare tax credit—up to 70 per cent of eligible costs up to a maximum of £100 for one child and £150 for two or more children.

The WFTC award, which normally lasts for 26 weeks, is calculated by adding the credits together. If the family income (after tax and national insurance contributions) is above £91.45 per week, this is reduced by 55 pence for each £1 above £91.45.

By introducing a higher income threshold before the new WFTC is withdrawn and withdrawing it at a rate of 55 per cent, WFTC is designed to improve work incentives and to encourage people to move into and remain in employment. It is central to the Government's major programme of tax and benefit reform, representing a step towards greater integration of the tax and benefits systems.

Social Fund

Payments, in the form of loans or grants, may be available to people on low incomes to help with expenses which are difficult to pay for out of regular income. There are two kinds. *Discretionary* payments are:

- budgeting loans for important intermittent expenses;
- community care grants to help, for example, people resettle into the community from care, or to remain in the community, to ease exceptional pressure on families, to set up home as part of a planned resettlement programme and to meet certain travel expenses; and
- crisis loans to help people in an emergency or as a result of a disaster where there is serious risk to health or safety. People do not have to be receiving any form of benefit to qualify for this loan.

The Social Fund also provides *regulated* payments (payments that are not cash-limited) to help people awarded certain income-related benefits with the costs of maternity or funerals, or with heating during very cold weather and winter fuel payments.

Widows

Widow's Payment. Widows under the age of 60—or those over 60 whose husbands were not entitled to a state retirement pension when they died—receive a tax-free single payment of £1,000 following the death of their husbands, provided that their husbands have paid a minimum number of NI contributions. Women whose husbands have died of an industrial injury or prescribed disease may also qualify, regardless of whether their husbands have paid NI contributions.

Widowed Mother's Allowance, a taxable benefit of £67.50 a week, is payable to a widowed mother with at least one child for whom she is getting Child Benefit. Additional tax-free amounts of £9.85 for a child for whom the higher rate of Child Benefit is payable, and £11.35 for each subsequent child, are available.

Widow's Pension. A taxable, weekly benefit of £67.50 is payable to a widow who is 55 years or over when her husband dies or when her entitlement to Widowed Mother's Allowance ends. A percentage of the full rate is payable to widows who are aged between 45 and 54 when their husbands die or when their entitlement to Widowed Mother's Allowance ends. Special rules apply for widows whose husbands died before 11 April 1988. Entitlement continues until the widow remarries or begins drawing retirement pension. Payment ends if she lives with a man as his wife.

A man whose wife dies when both are over pension age inherits his wife's pension rights just as a widow inherits her husband's rights.

Sickness and Disablement

A variety of benefits are available for people unable to work because of sickness or disablement. Employers are responsible for paying **Statutory Sick Pay** to employees from the fourth day of sickness for up to a maximum of 28 weeks. There is a single rate of Statutory Sick Pay for all qualifying employees provided their average gross weekly earnings are at least £67.00 a week. The weekly rate is £60.20.

Incapacity Benefit is also for people who become incapable of work. Entitlement to Incapacity Benefit begins when entitlement to Statutory Sick Pay ends or, for those who do not qualify for Statutory Sick Pay, from the fourth day of sickness. There are three types:

- short-term benefit for people under pension age: a lower rate of £50.90 a week for the first 28 weeks; and a higher rate of £60.20 a week between the 29th and 52nd week;
- short-term benefit for people over pension age: lower rate of £64.75; higher rate of £67.50; and
- long-term benefit rate of £67.50 a week (after 52 weeks of incapacity).

Extra benefits may be paid for dependent adults and children. Incapacity Benefit is taxable from the 29th week of incapacity.

The medical test of incapacity for work usually applies after 28 weeks' sickness. It assesses ability to perform a range of work-related activities rather than the ability to perform a specific job.

Severe Disablement Allowance is a tax-free benefit for people who have not been able to work for at least 28 weeks because of illness or disability but who cannot get Incapacity Benefit because they have not paid enough NI contributions. The benefit is £40.80 a week, plus additions of up to £14.20 depending on the person's age when they became incapable of work. Additions for adult dependants and for children may also be paid. Claims may be made by people aged between 16 and 65. Once a person has qualified for the allowance, there is no upper age limit for receipt. New claimants must satisfy the same incapacity test as that used in Incapacity Benefit (see above).

People who become incapable of work after their 20th birthday must also be medically assessed as at least 80 per cent disabled for a minimum of 28 weeks. People already in receipt of certain benefits, such as the higher rate of the Disability Living Allowance care component (see below), will automatically be accepted as 80 per cent disabled.

From April 2001, Severe Disablement Allowance will be abolished for new claims. People under 20, or 25 if they were in education or training before reaching 20, may be able to receive Incapacity Benefit without having to satisfy the contributions conditions.

Other Benefits

Disability Living Allowance is a non-contributory tax-free benefit to help severely disabled people aged under 65 with extra costs incurred as a result of disability. Entitlement is measured in terms of personal care and/or mobility needs. There are two components: a care component which has three weekly rates—£53.55, £35.80 and £14.20; and a mobility component which has two weekly rates—£37.40 and £14.20, payable from age five or older.

Attendance Allowance is a non-contributory tax-free benefit to provide financial help to severely disabled people aged 65 or older with extra costs incurred as a result of disability. It is measured in terms of personal care needs by day and/or night. The two rates are £53.55 and £35.80.

A non-contributory **Invalid Care Allowance** of £40.40 weekly may be payable to people between 16 and 65 who have given up the opportunity of a full-time paid job because they are providing regular and substantial care of at least 35 hours a week, to a severely disabled person in receipt of either Attendance Allowance or the higher or middle care component of Disability Living Allowance. An additional carer's premium may be paid if the recipient is also receiving Income Support, income-related Jobseeker's Allowance, Housing Benefit or Council Tax Benefit.

Disabled Person's Tax Credit (DPTC) replaced Disability Working Allowance in October 1999. It is payable under the same rules as those for the new Working Families' Tax Credit (see p. 176).

Industrial Injuries Disablement Benefit

Various benefits are payable for disablement caused by an accident at work or a prescribed disease caused by a particular type of employment. The main benefit is the tax-free **Industrial Injuries Disablement Benefit**: up to £109.30 a week is usually paid after a qualifying period of 15 weeks if a person is at least 14 per cent or more physically or mentally disabled as a result of an industrial accident or a prescribed disease.

Basic Disablement Benefit can be paid in addition to other NI benefits, such as Incapacity Benefit. It can be paid whether or not the person returns to work and does not depend on earnings. The degree of disablement is assessed by an independent adjudicating medical authority and the amount paid depends on the extent of the disablement and on how long it is expected to last. Except for certain progressive respiratory diseases, disablement of less than 14 per cent does not attract Disablement Benefit. In certain circumstances additional allowances may be payable.

Housing and Council Tax Benefits

Housing Benefit is an income-related, tax-free benefit which helps people on low incomes meet the cost of rented accommodation. The amount paid depends on personal circumstances, income, savings, rent and other people sharing the home. It also normally depends on the general level of rents for properties with the same number of rooms in the locality.

Most single people under 25 years old who are not lone parents and who are renting privately have their Housing Benefit limited to the average cost of a single non-self-contained room (that is, shared use of kitchen and toilet facilities) in the locality.

Council Tax Benefit helps people to meet their council tax payments (the tax set by local councils to help pay for services—see p. 412). The scheme offers help to those claiming Income Support and income-based Jobseeker's Allowance and others with low incomes. It is subject to rules broadly similar to those governing the provision of Housing Benefit (see above). A person who is solely liable for the council tax may also claim benefit for a second adult who is not liable to pay the council tax and who is living in the home on a non-commercial basis. In Northern Ireland, where council tax does not apply, people on low incomes may get help to pay for their domestic 'rates' from a means-tested housing benefits scheme. For owner occupiers, this can be claimed from the Rates Collection Agency, while those renting property can claim their benefit from the Housing Executive.

War Pensions and Related Services

Pensions are payable for disablement as a result of service in the armed forces or for certain injuries received in the merchant navy or civil defence during wartime, or to civilians injured by enemy action. The amount paid depends on the degree of disablement: the pension for 100 per cent disablement for an officer is £6,053 a year; for other ranks it is £116 a week.

There are a number of extra allowances. The main ones are for unemployability, restricted mobility, the need for care and attendance, the provision of extra comforts, and as maintenance for a lowered standard of occupation. An age allowance of between £7.75 and £23.90 is payable weekly to war pensioners aged 65 or over whose disablement is assessed at 40 per cent or more.

Pensions are also paid to war widows and other dependants. (The standard rate of pension for a private soldier's widow is £87.55 a week.) War Widow's Pension is also payable to a former war widow who has remarried and then become widowed again, divorced or legally separated.

The War Pensioners' Welfare Service helps and advises war pensioners, war widows and other dependants. It works closely with ex-Service organisations and other voluntary bodies which give financial help and personal support to those disabled or bereaved as a result of war.

Concessions

Other benefits for which unemployed people and those on low incomes may be eligible include exemption from health service charges (see p. 190), grants towards the cost of spectacles (see p. 191), legal aid (see p. 232) and free school meals for their children. People on low incomes, as well as all pensioners, widows and long-term sick people on Incapacity Benefit, receive extra help to meet the cost of VAT (value added tax) on their fuel bills.

Reduced charges are often made to unemployed people, for example, for adult education and exhibitions, and pensioners are usually entitled to reduced transport fares. From November 2000, pensioners aged 75 and over will no longer be required to pay for their television licence (see p. 268).

Table 12.4: Tax Liability of Social Security Benefits

Not taxable	*Taxable*
Attendance Allowance	Incapacity Benefit (long-term or short-term higher rate)
Child Benefit	Industrial Death Benefit Pensions
Child's Special Allowance	Invalid Care Allowance
Council Tax Benefit	Jobseeker's Allowance[1]
Disability Living Allowance	Retirement Pension
Guardian's Allowance	Statutory Maternity Pay
Housing Benefit	Statutory Sick Pay
Incapacity Benefit (short-term lower rate)	Widowed Mother's Allowance
Income Support	Widow's Pension
Industrial Injuries Disablement Benefit/Reduced Earnings Allowance	
Maternity Allowance	
Severe Disablement Allowance	
War Disablement Pension	
War Widow's Pension	

[1] That part of the Jobseeker's Allowance equivalent to the individual or couple rate of personal allowance, as appropriate.
Source: Inland Revenue

Taxation

The general rule is that benefits which replace lost earnings are subject to tax, while those intended to meet a specific need are not (see Table 12.4). Various income tax reliefs and exemptions are allowed on account of age or a need to support dependants.

Benefit Controls on People from Abroad

Residence Test

All claimants must be habitually resident in the Common Travel Area (that is, the UK, the Irish Republic, the Channel Isles or the Isle of Man) before a claim for Income Support, income-based Jobseeker's Allowance, Housing Benefit or Council Tax Benefit can be paid. This is in line with most other European countries, which also limit access to their benefit systems to those who have lived in the country for some time.

Asylum Seekers

Generally only people who claim refugee status *as soon as* they arrive in the UK can claim income-based Jobseeker's Allowance, Income Support, Housing Benefit and Council Tax Benefit. Their eligibility to receive this will stop if their asylum claim is refused by the Home Office. The Immigration and Asylum Act 1999 (see p. 107), among other things, replaces cash benefits for asylum seekers with a voucher system.

ARRANGEMENTS AND COMPARISONS WITH OTHER COUNTRIES

As part of the European Union's efforts to promote the free movement of labour, regulations provide for equality of treatment and the protection of benefit rights for employed and self-employed people who move between member states. The regulations also cover retirement pensioners and other beneficiaries who have been employed, or self-employed, as well as dependants. Benefits covered include Child Benefit and those for sickness and maternity, unemployment, retirement, invalidity, accidents at work and occupational diseases.

The UK has reciprocal social security agreements with a number of other countries which also provide cover for some NI benefits and family benefits.

A comparison of the expenditure on social protection benefits per head for the 12 EU countries for which data are available (Austria, Denmark, Finland, France, Germany, the Irish Republic, Italy, the Netherlands, Portugal, Spain, Sweden and the UK) indicates that, in general, spending is much higher in the more northerly countries than in the south. Denmark spent the most per head in 1996; at just under £5,000 this was three times the amount spent by Portugal, the country which spent the least. The UK spent around £3,000 per head of population, just below the average for the EU.

Further Reading

With Respect to Old Age: Long-term Care—Rights and Responsibilities. Cm 4192; vols I-II. Royal Commission on Long-term Care. The Stationery Office, 1999.

Caring about Carers: A National Strategy for Carers. Department of Health, 1999.

The Government's Expenditure Plans 2000/01–2001/02. Social Security Departmental Report. Cm 4614. The Stationery Office, 2000.

The Government's Expenditure Plans 2000–2001. Department of Health Departmental Report. Cm 4603. The Stationery Office, 2000.

Websites

Department of Health: www.doh.gov.uk

Department of Social Security: www.dss.gov.uk

13 Health Services

In July 2000 the Government issued a National Health Service Plan in England. A new system of integrated care is envisaged, based on making all parts of the health and social care system work better together, and improving both clinical performance and health service productivity. In addition, plans are being developed which aim to improve patient care, tackle inequalities in healthcare provision, and tackle the causes of avoidable ill-health. Across the UK, spending is planned to grow by an average of 6.1 per cent a year in real terms over the four years from 1999–2000, reaching nearly £69 billion in 2003–04.

The National Health Service (NHS) provides a full range of medical services, available to all residents, regardless of their income. This basic principle was endorsed by the NHS Plan. Central government is directly responsible for the NHS, which is administered by health authorities and health boards throughout the UK. The Department of Health (DH) is responsible for national strategic planning in England and, within that department, the NHS Executive, with eight regional offices, is responsible for developing and implementing policies for the provision of health services. The Scottish Executive Health Department, the National Assembly for Wales and the Department of Health, Social Services and Public Safety in Northern Ireland have similar responsibilities. Policies and initiatives for health in Scotland, Wales and Northern Ireland are similar to those for England, but may feature distinctive approaches which reflect the health variations in the different parts of the UK.

The National Assembly for Wales is considering how best to take forward the issues raised in the NHS Plan for England, and will be publishing the NHS Wales Strategy around the end of 2000 or the start of 2001. In Northern Ireland the Executive's *Programme for Government*, published in October 2000, includes a section on working for a healthier population.

Public Health

During the 20th century life expectancy at birth in the UK increased substantially, from 45.0 years for males and 48.7 for females in 1901 to 74.9 and 79.8 years respectively in 1997 to 1999. Both life expectancy and healthy life expectancy rose in Great Britain between 1981 and 1997, but healthy life expectancy did not increase by as much as life expectancy. Both males and females born in 1997 could therefore expect to spend more years in poor health or with a limiting long-standing illness than those born in 1981. Life expectancy and healthy life expectancy are higher for women than for men, but women can also expect to live a larger number and a greater proportion of their remaining years in poor health or with a limiting long-standing illness than men.

Mortality rates are lower in England than in the rest of the UK. Within England mortality rates are higher in northern regions than in the south. Local authorities in the UK with the highest levels of mortality tend to be located in urban and industrial areas, particularly areas classified as coalfields, manufacturing centres or ports and industry, characterised by high unemployment, a high proportion of terraced housing and a high proportion of social housing. Over the period 1991 to 1997, East Dorset had the lowest mortality rate in the UK and Glasgow the highest.

Over the 20th century there were significant changes in the types of disease that people suffered from. The incidence of childhood diseases are now at their lowest ever levels and some diseases have been virtually eliminated through the use of vaccines. Other widespread illnesses, such as cancer and heart disease, have become more prominent. Advances in surgical techniques and intensive care have helped to reduce deaths arising from accidents or premature birth. In 1999, 39 per cent of deaths in England and Wales were from circulatory disease such as heart attacks and strokes, 24 per cent from cancer and 17 per cent from respiratory disease. Less than 1 per cent of deaths resulted from infectious diseases.

Health Strategies

In July 1999 the Government published a White Paper, *Saving Lives: Our Healthier Nation (OHN)*, setting out its health strategy for England. Similar strategies have been published for Wales, Scotland and Northern Ireland. The two main aims are to improve the health of the population as a whole and to reduce inequalities, particularly by improving the health of the least well off.

The White Paper set out action to combat the four major causes of premature death and avoidable ill-health: cancer, coronary heart disease and stroke, accidental injury and mental illness. Targets have been set for 2010 in each priority area, compared with figures for the three years 1995 to 1997:

- *cancer*—to reduce the death rate in people under 75 by at least a fifth;
- *coronary heart disease and stroke*—to reduce the death rate in people under 75 by at least two-fifths;
- *accidents*—to reduce the death rate by at least a fifth and the serious injury rate by one-tenth; and
- *mental health*—to reduce the death rate from suicide and undetermined injury by at least one-fifth.

Towards a Healthier Scotland was published in February 1999 and subsequently endorsed by the Scottish Parliament.

The Government has a range of policies across departments which aim to tackle the underlying causes of ill-health and health inequality, such as poverty, unemployment, poor housing and pollution. Policies like Sure Start (see p. 121), Welfare-to-Work (see p. 151) and the New Deal for Communities (see p. 352) all aim to improve health. There are also strategies for other important public health issues, such as HIV/AIDS and sexual health (including teenage conceptions), drugs, alcohol, food safety, water fluoridation and communicable diseases.

Cancer Care

Cancer is one of the main *OHN* target areas. It causes 156,000 deaths a year in the UK. Cancer services are organised at three levels:

- *primary care* for initial care;
- *cancer units* in many local hospitals of sufficient size to support a multidisciplinary team with the expertise and facilities to treat more common cancers; and
- *cancer centres* situated in larger hospitals to treat less common cancers and to support smaller cancer units by

providing services not available in all local hospitals.

Cancer networks are being developed as a key element in the structure for cancer treatment. These bring together NHS providers (cancer units and centres), health authorities, Primary Care Groups and the voluntary sector.

The NHS Cancer Plan, published in September 2000, includes a new target to reduce the smoking rate among manual groups from 32 per cent in 1994 to 26 per cent by 2010, extra funding, a new standard for waiting times, and expansion of 'on-the-spot' booking systems by 2002 (see box). Also announced in the Cancer Plan were an increase in the number of cancer specialists, additional resources for hospices and specialist palliative care, and an increase in government funding for cancer research.

Nine cancer networks across England have introduced 'on-the-spot' booking systems, which are intended to improve patient care by:

- providing rapid urgent appointments with specialists;
- introducing 'one-stop clinics' where all diagnostic tests can be carried out in one visit, with results available that day;
- enabling patients to pre-book appointments; and
- co-ordinating surgery with follow-up therapy.

Additional resources for cancer services are being provided, including:

- extra investment in breast, colorectal, lung and outpatient cancer services with the aim of improving the speed of access and quality of care;
- £80 million from the Modernisation Fund over two years from 2000 to cut waiting times, support improvements to gynaecological cancer services and modernise cancer services;
- funding from the New Opportunities Fund of £93 million to purchase over 300 items of equipment for the NHS Breast Screening Programme and £23 million for a palliative care and information initiative, concentrating on projects targeted at ethnic minorities and socially disadvantaged groups; and
- investment in cancer equipment, including 200 CT scanners, 50 magnetic resonance imaging scanners, and 80 liquid cytology units to improve cervical cancer screening, if pilot studies are successful.

Cancer Screening

Cancer screening programmes are in operation for breast cancer and cervical cancer. About one in ten women in the UK develop breast cancer, which results in some 14,000 deaths each year. The UK was the first country in the European Union (EU) to introduce a nationwide breast screening programme, under which women aged between 50 and 64 are invited for mammography (breast X-ray) every three years by computerised call and recall systems. Women aged 65 and over are entitled to request screening. Under the NHS Plan, the screening programme will be extended to women aged 65 to 70 by 2004. In 1998–99 in England:

- 76 per cent of women aged 50 to 64 invited for screening were screened;
- 1.2 million women of all ages were screened within the programme; and
- 7,561 cases of cancer were diagnosed among women screened.

The nationwide cervical screening programme aims to reduce death from cancer of the cervix by inviting women aged between 20 and 64 (20 and 60 in Scotland) to take a smear test at least once every five years. Cervical screening is not a test for cancer but for abnormalities which if left untreated may develop into cancer. As at March 1999, in England 84 per cent of women invited to attend had been screened over the previous five years and in Wales 82 per cent. In 1998–99 in Scotland 87 per cent of women invited to attend had been screened over the last 5½ years. Deaths from cervical cancer in England and Wales have fallen since the programme began, from 1,942 in 1988 to 1,106 in 1999, and in Scotland from 191 in 1988 to 122 in 1999.

Other screening programmes will be introduced if and when they are proved to be effective. Pilot studies are under way for colorectal screening. Other possibilities for future screening programmes are prostate, lung and ovarian cancers.

Coronary Heart Disease

The UK has one of the highest premature death rates from circulatory disease (including heart disease and stroke) in Europe. Coronary heart disease kills more than 110,000 people a year in England and Wales. In Scotland about 13,000 people died from the disease in 1998. Although this was some 6,000 fewer than in 1975, coronary heart disease rates in Scotland are 15 per cent above the UK average. UK death rates from coronary heart disease for both males and females under 65 have fallen steadily for the last 20 years, from 151 to 59 per 100,000 males and from 39 to 16 per 100,000 females between 1979 and 1999.

The Coronary Heart Disease National Service Framework (NSF), published in 2000, set out a ten-year programme to improve prevention and treatment in England. An extra £230 million a year is planned to be invested in heart disease services by 2003–04. By April 2001 the first 139 rapid access chest pain clinics, designed to assess within two weeks all patients with new onset of chest pain that could be due to angina, are expected to be in place. By 2003 the national network is expected to be completed, enabling 200,000 patients a year to be diagnosed early.

In Scotland a Coronary Heart Disease Task Force was established in 1998. Recognising that many cases are preventable, the Task Force is considering a needs assessment of interventions needed for treatment, how to prioritise those waiting for cardiac surgery, and improving access to cardiac services.

Mental Health

Mental health problems are a major cause of ill-health, disability and mortality. In 1999–2000 there were nearly 2.1 million attendances at NHS facilities for psychiatric specialities in England, of which 282,000 were new attendances.

The Mental Health Services NSF sets out a ten-year programme designed to raise standards of mental health care. The NHS Plan involves extra annual investment, of over £300 million by 2003–04, including the provision of:

- 1,000 new mental health care workers helping GPs, and 500 additional community mental health staff;
- 50 teams to be established over the next three years to help reduce the period of untreated psychosis in young people;
- over 300 'crisis resolution' teams to help deal quickly with people with acute mental illness experiencing a crisis and who would otherwise need to be admitted to hospital;
- 230 teams to deal with the small number of high users of services, many of whom also have a problem with substance misuse;
- women-only day centres in every health authority by 2004; and
- more staff to increase respite care.

In Scotland, mental health continues as a priority with forward planning and responsive services based on the 1997 *Framework for Mental Health Services in Scotland.*

The National Health Service

The NHS is based on the principle that there should be a full range of publicly funded services designed to help the individual stay healthy. The services are intended to provide effective and appropriate treatment and care where necessary while making the best use of available resources. All taxpayers, employers and employees contribute to the cost so that those members of the community who do not require healthcare help to pay for those who do. Most forms of treatment, such as hospital care, are generally provided free, although some may incur a charge.

NHS PLAN

The Government published *The NHS Plan* for England in July 2000. This followed earlier changes to the NHS announced in the 1997 White Paper *The new NHS: modern, dependable* and implemented under the Health Act 1999 (see p. 187). These changes have removed the internal market, with the intention of improving access to, and services provided by, the health services. Similar plans are to be published for Wales, Scotland and Northern Ireland, which will differ in some details from those in England but will be designed to achieve similar aims. The National Assembly for Wales shares many of the priorities and objectives in the NHS Plan. In conjunction with the NHS, the National Assembly is developing a strategy for health services in Wales, setting out longer-term developments to meet local circumstances.

The NHS Plan sets out how the NHS will be modernised to meet the changing needs of the people in the 21st century. Its aims are for:

- people to be more involved in managing their own care, through NHS Direct (see p. 189) and other new services;
- more emphasis on screening and occupational health to prevent ill-health;
- more GPs to book hospital appointments by e-mail and call up computerised medical records;
- hospital appointments to be on time;
- reduced delays with special one-stop test and treatment centres developed to speed up surgery for common complaints;
- the provision of new modern hospitals with smaller and more intimate wards; and
- the development of intermediate care to prevent people having to be admitted to hospital in the first place and to allow them to recuperate at home.

A Modernisation Board is to be set up to advise the Secretary of State for Health on, and help oversee implementation of, the NHS Plan. Membership will include health professionals, patient representatives and NHS managers.

Standards

The Department of Health will set national standards for England, in three forms:

- National Service Frameworks (NSFs) for key conditions and diseases (see p. 188);
- guidance on treatments and interventions from the National Institute for Clinical Excellence (see p. 189); and
- a limited number of national targets, including shorter waiting times, and quality of care and facilities for people in hospital.

Performance Assessment Frameworks, currently covering a variety of matters in England, including health improvement, access to services, and delivery of healthcare, apply to health authorities. From April 2001 a new version will apply to NHS Trusts and Primary Care Trusts providing community services. Results will be published by the independent Commission for Health Improvement (CHI). In Wales, a new Performance Management Framework for the NHS was launched in April 2000.

The CHI will inspect all local health bodies, including NHS hospital care and community and primary care services. With the support of the Audit Commission, it will inspect every NHS organisation every four years, or every two years for organisations that fail to meet a number of the main targets. It expects to complete 25 inspections during 2000 and 100 a year thereafter. It will be asked to look into any Trusts where there are serious concerns about clinical practice or safety.

Local NHS organisations that perform well will be given more freedom to run their own affairs. They will also have automatic access to a new National Health Performance Fund, to be established in April 2001, which will be able to distribute £500 million a year by 2003–04. However, organisations that fail to perform well will be required to produce a detailed recovery plan, and will receive intensive support from the Modernisation Agency and NHS regional offices. Persistent failure by a Primary Care Group or Trust could result in the transfer of responsibility to a neighbouring Group or Trust.

Investment and Planned Service Improvements

Some £7 billion of new capital investment is planned in the NHS in the period to 2010 through an expanded role for the Private Finance Initiative (PFI). Major investment will include over 100 new hospital schemes between 2000 and 2010; the modernisation or substantial refurbishment of up to 3,000 GP premises by 2004; new equipment, particularly for cancer, renal and heart disease services (see p. 182); and new information technology (IT) systems in hospitals and surgeries. The NHS Plan indicates an increase in the number of NHS hospital beds (see p. 196), from the 1999–2000 level of an average 186,000 overnight beds available in England. A further 7,000 NHS beds are expected to be available by 2004, of which some 2,100 will be in general and acute wards and the rest in intermediate care. In partnership with the private sector, 20 new diagnostic and treatment centres are planned by 2004 to increase the number of operations that can be treated in a single day or with a short stay.

A new Modernisation Agency will be set up to help local clinicians and managers redesign services around the needs of patients, spreading best practice and stimulating change.

Improvements are planned in the treatment of cancer, heart disease and mental health services (see pp. 183–4). This includes expanding cancer screening, providing rapid access chest pain clinics across England by 2003, shorter waiting times for heart operations, and increasing the number of immediate response mental health teams.

For older people, nursing care in nursing homes will be free. New intermediate care services will be introduced with the aim of helping people to recover and resume independent living more quickly, so speeding up discharge from hospital when patients are ready to leave. Elderly people and their carers will have personal care plans.

To try to reduce inequalities, primary care in deprived areas will be improved, more help will be available for people to give up smoking and, to improve the diet of young children, fruit will be made freely available in schools for 4 to 6 year olds.

Additional resources are planned to increase the number of NHS staff from the current level (see Table 13.1, p. 192), with the recruitment of 7,500 more consultants, 2,000 more GPs, 20,000 extra nurses and 6,500 more therapists, and the provision of 1,000 more medical school places.

Targets

The NHS Plan includes a number of targets set by the Government for the NHS. Among the targets which the NHS is expected to meet by 2004 are that:

- patients will be able to see a GP within 48 hours;
- hospital consultants, currently working only in hospitals, will deliver approximately 4 million outpatient consultations a year in primary care and community settings;
- GPs will be able to refer patients to up to 1,000 specialist GPs, for example in ophthalmology, orthopaedics, dermatology and ear, nose and throat surgery, instead of referring them to hospital; and
- average waiting time in accident and emergency departments in hospitals will fall to 1 hour 15 minutes, with a maximum waiting time of 4 hours.

Targets to be met by the NHS by the end of 2005 include:

- the replacement of waiting lists for appointments and admission by booking systems (see p. 197);
- a reduction in the maximum waiting time for a routine outpatient appointment from six to three months; and
- a reduction in the maximum waiting time for inpatient treatment from 18 to six months.

Patient Involvement

The Plan is designed to increase patients' involvement in how the NHS works. Letters about patients will be copied to them, and 'smart' cards will be introduced allowing patients easier access to health records. If an operation is cancelled, the patient may choose a new date within 28 days of the original date or the hospital will pay for it to be carried out at another hospital of the patient's choice.

Relations with the Private Sector

The Government has announced its intention to negotiate an agreement with private healthcare providers (see p. 198) to enable the NHS to make better use of facilities in private hospitals, although NHS care will remain free at the point of delivery. Among the areas envisaged for co-operative working are:

- NHS doctors and nurses using operating theatres and facilities in private hospitals or the purchase of services by the NHS;
- the transfer of patients between the NHS and the private sector when appropriate for clinical reasons; and
- the development and provision by the private and voluntary sectors of intermediate care facilities to support the Government's strategy for improving preventive and rehabilitation services.

ADMINISTRATION

The Health and Personal Social Services Programmes consist of:

- NHS Hospital and Community Health Services (HCHS), providing all hospital care and a range of community services;
- NHS Family Health Services (FHS), providing general medical, dental, pharmaceutical and some ophthalmic services, and covering the cost of medicines prescribed by GPs;
- Central Health and Miscellaneous Services (CHMS)—in Scotland, Other Health Services (OHS);
- provision of social care by local authorities, supported by the DH and the Department of the Environment, Transport and the Regions' programmes in England, and the Scottish Executive in Scotland; and
- the administration of the DH.

The Health Act 1999 provided for:

- the replacement of the internal NHS market, including the abolition of the GP fundholding scheme and its replacement by Primary Care Groups;
- the establishment of free-standing Primary Care Trusts;
- a new duty of quality requiring NHS Trusts, Primary Care Trusts and health authorities to assure and improve their quality of care;
- the establishment of the Commission for Health Improvement, to provide independent advice and expertise to the NHS on developing and improving the quality of NHS services;
- a new duty of partnership between the NHS and local authorities, with strengthened arrangements for joint working;
- a duty for health authorities to prepare Health Improvement Programmes; and
- better provision for the regulation of healthcare professionals.

Health Authorities

There are 99 health authorities in England and five in Wales, 15 health boards in Scotland and four health and social services boards in Northern Ireland, all of which are responsible for identifying the healthcare needs of the people living in their area. They secure hospital and community health services and arrange for the provision of services by family doctors, dentists, pharmacists and opticians, as well as administering their contracts. The latter is undertaken by Primary Care Trusts/Island Health Boards in Scotland. The health authorities and boards co-operate closely with local authorities responsible for social work, environmental health, education and other services. There are community health councils (local health councils in Scotland and area health and social services councils in Northern Ireland) covering all parts of the country, representing local opinion on the services provided.

Health authorities have two main roles: to ensure that *service improvements* for local people are coherently planned and delivered; and to provide strategic leadership for *improving health and tackling health inequalities*. They are responsible for preparing a Health Improvement Programme in partnership with local Primary Care Groups, Primary Care Trusts, NHS Trusts, local authorities, local people and voluntary groups, and ensuring that the Programme meets the needs of the local population.

Primary Care Groups and Trusts

GP fundholding was abolished in October 1999 (except in Northern Ireland where the fundholding scheme is due to end in March 2001 and future arrangements in primary care are under consideration). Primary Care Groups were introduced in each area in April 1999. They give responsibility for determining services for patients to GPs, community nurses, other health professionals, managers, social services, health authorities, NHS Trusts and the public. The Groups, which control two-thirds of local NHS budgets, are accountable to the local health authority and are responsible for commissioning services for their local communities. Typically Groups may each serve about 100,000 patients. They have a single unified budget, which allows GPs to choose how best to meet patients' needs. All Primary Care Groups are expected to work closely with social services to provide properly integrated care.

The first 17 Primary Care Trusts became operational on 1 April 2000. They are larger, more independent statutory bodies than the Primary Care Groups, involving groups of doctors, nurses and social care professionals—as well as other organisations and agencies—working in partnership to shape local health and social care services. They carry out many functions formerly performed by health authorities and are also able to provide a range of community health services directly. Under the NHS Plan, they will identify and maintain registers of those at the greatest risk from serious illness, so that people can be offered preventive treatment.

In Scotland primary care became a Primary Care Trust function in April 1999, to establish a single organisation with responsibility for delivering primary, community and long–stay health services.

NHS Trusts

NHS Trusts remain responsible for treatment and care, but are also party to the local Health Improvement Programmes. Short-term contracts under the internal market have ended and NHS Trusts are agreeing long-term service agreements with Primary Care Groups and Primary Care Trusts. These agreements are generally organised around care groups (such as children) or disease areas (such as heart disease). NHS Trusts are now required to meet quality standards, to co-operate with other parts of the NHS, and to take part (alongside Primary Care Groups, Primary Care Trusts and local authorities) in developing the local Health Improvement Programme (see above). NHS Trusts publish details of their performance, including the costs of treatments and services.

Each NHS Trust (Health and Social Services Trust in Northern Ireland) is run by a board of executive and non-executive directors/trustees, subject to provisions in the Health Act 1999. Trusts are free to employ their own staff and set their own rates of pay, and can carry out research and provide facilities for medical education and other forms of training. All Trust board meetings are now open to the public. Measures have been taken to make boards more reflective of the local communities.

Standards

National Service Frameworks (NSFs) set national quality and efficiency standards and describe service models for a defined service or care group. They put in place programmes to support implementation and establish performance measures against which progress within an agreed timescale can be measured. Following existing frameworks for cancer and paediatric intensive care, NSFs for coronary heart disease and mental health have been published (see p. 184); an NSF for older people is planned in autumn 2000 and one for diabetes in 2001. The first comprehensive

NHS Cancer Plan was published in September 2000 (see p. 183). The standards contained in NSFs also apply to Wales, but separate implementation arrangements are being developed.

The *National Institute for Clinical Excellence (NICE)* was established in April 1999 to develop national standards for best practice in clinical care within the NHS. This includes drawing up new guidelines based on clinical and cost effectiveness and ensuring that they apply to all parts of the NHS. The Institute's membership is drawn from the health professions, the NHS, academics, health economists and patients. It appraises drugs and technologies and produces clinical guidelines. Areas covered in NICE's work programme include breast and ovarian cancer, coronary heart disease, cervical screening, multiple sclerosis, hepatitis C, colorectal cancer, and Alzheimer's disease. By September 2000 NICE had carried out nine appraisals and its first guideline is expected to be announced in winter 2000. NICE had also completed 11 GP referral protocols.

Health Education and Development

In England, Scotland and Northern Ireland responsibility for health education lies with separate NHS authorities working alongside the national health departments. In England the former Health Education Authority was succeeded in April 2000 by two new bodies: the Health Development Agency (HDA) and Health Promotion England. The HDA aims to improve the health of people in England—in particular, to reduce inequalities in health between those who are well off and those on low incomes or reliant on state benefits. Its three major roles are research, setting standards, and training and resources. Health Promotion England promotes campaigns on a number of subjects, including childhood immunisation, drugs, alcohol and sexual health.

In Wales a health promotion division has been established in the National Assembly for Wales, with responsibility for health promotion policy and strategy, and the development and delivery of national programmes and initiatives to promote health and wellbeing. In Scotland the authority is the Health Education Board and in Northern Ireland the Health Promotion Agency.

Almost all NHS health authorities/health boards have their own health education service, which works closely with health professionals, health visitors, community groups, local employers and others to determine the most suitable local programmes.

NHS Direct

NHS Direct is a 24-hour helpline, where the initial contact is with a nurse, giving immediate healthcare advice and support over the telephone, so that people are better able to care for themselves and their families. Since December 1999, 65 per cent of the population in England have had access to the service. It will be extended to cover the whole of England by the end of October 2000. Over 1 million calls have been made to NHS Direct. Discussions are under way about the introduction of the NHS Direct concept in Scotland.

NHS Direct On-line, a complementary extension to the telephone-based services, was launched in December 1999 using the Internet and is linked to other health-related websites. The service now receives about 1 million 'hits' every day. It includes an electronic version of the NHS Direct Healthcare Guide, which takes the top 20 symptoms about which people seek advice from NHS Direct. Users answer a series of 'yes' or 'no' questions which prompt advice on how serious a health worry might be. While not a diagnostic tool, NHS Direct

The first of 36 pilot *Walk-In Centres* opened in Soho in central London in January 2000. They are designed to provide quick and convenient access to basic primary care services without the need for an appointment. They are nurse-led, treat minor injuries and illnesses, and give health advice and information on other local services, complementing the more traditional GP service. Eight centres will be in supermarkets or shop fronts and six alongside hospital accident and emergency departments.

On-line provides advice and directs users to a course of action depending on their answers. The website address is www.nhsdirect.nhs.uk.

Under the NHS Plan, the Government's intention is that by 2002 all NHS Direct sites will be able to refer people to local pharmacies and by 2004 NHS Direct will provide health information via digital television, and be able to act as a gateway to out-of-hours healthcare, including GP co-operative or deputising services.

Health Action Zones

Twenty-six 'Health Action Zones' have been set up in deprived areas of England. The zones involve local partnerships between the health service, local councils, voluntary groups and local businesses, and receive government funding. Their aim is to make measurable improvements in the health of local people and in the quality of treatment and care. Working closely with the DH, the participants co-operate to tackle inequalities and deliver better services and healthcare. They focus on areas such as smoking cessation programmes, children's and young people's health, mental health, older people's health, and the health of ethnic minorities.

Two Health Action Zones were established in Northern Ireland in April 1999 and an initiative to encourage local healthcare partnerships has been launched in Scotland.

NHSnet

NHSnet is the short name for a range of voice and data services used by the NHS, covering radio, telephone and computer-based communications. All health authorities and most Trusts are connected to NHSnet, as are a number of major NHS suppliers. All GPs in Scotland are connected to NHSnet. Under the GPnet programme, by 2002 every GP practice in England will be connected to NHSnet and will be able to receive hospital pathology test results. NHSnet will also support the longer-term goal of introducing electronic health records to replace the paper-based records. This will make possible, for example, secure access by doctors to a patient's records in an emergency when patients are away from home. An equivalent scheme, HPSSnet, has been set up in Northern Ireland by Northern Ireland Health and Personal Social Services (HPSS).

Finance

The NHS is financed mainly through general taxation with an element of National Insurance contributions (see chapter 12), paid by employed people, their employers and self-employed people. In 1999–2000 an estimated 79 per cent of the NHS was financed through general taxation, with 13 per cent from National Insurance contributions and 8 per cent from charges and other receipts.

The Government's Spending Review (see p. 401), published in July 2000, gave details of extra funding for the NHS. Expenditure on the NHS, net of receipts, is forecast to rise from £54.2 billion in 2000–01 to £68.7 billion in 2003–04. This represents an increase in funding in real terms of an average 6.1 per cent a year. Extra resources have also become available following the Government's decision, announced in November 1999, that revenue raised from higher duties on cigarettes and tobacco in real terms would be spent on improved healthcare.

Health authorities may raise funds from other, non-government, sources. For example, some hospitals increase revenue by taking private patients, who pay the full cost of their accommodation and treatment. They also use private finance for NHS capital projects, under the Private Finance Initiative (see p. 405).

In addition, reforms to the National Lottery have set up a new good cause, the New Opportunities Fund, which provides complementary funding for health, education and the environment. The Fund has provided £300 million in the UK to support a series of targeted initiatives. One of the first is to establish a network of healthy living centres which offer people fitness checks, fitness routines, and advice on diet and healthy lifestyles.

Charges

Around 530 million prescription items, worth around £5.3 billion, were dispensed in England

NHS Gross Expenditure, England, 1999–2000

Total: £43.4 billion

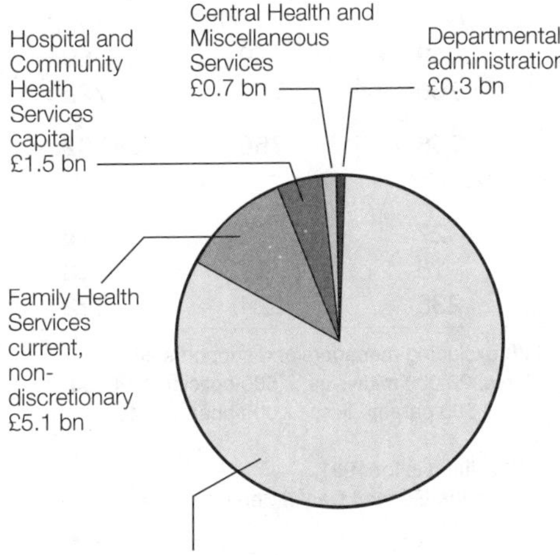

Source: *Department of Health. The Government's Expenditure Plans 2000–2001*

in 1999, an increase of 35 per cent in real terms since 1994. The proportion of items provided free of charge increased from 83 per cent in 1994 to 85 per cent in 1999. The following groups are exempted from prescription charges: people aged 60 and over; children under 16 and young people aged 16, 17 or 18 in full-time education; women who are pregnant or have given birth in the previous 12 months; and people with certain medical conditions. In addition, people who receive (or whose partners receive) certain social security benefits (see chapter 12), or who otherwise qualify on low income grounds, do not pay prescription charges. In 1999, 52 per cent of all prescription items dispensed by community pharmacies and appliance contractors in England were for elderly people, an increase from around 44 per cent in 1994.

There are charges for most types of NHS dental treatment, including examinations, based on a proportion of the fee paid to the dentist. However, the following people are entitled to free treatment: women who begin a course of treatment while pregnant or within 12 months of having a baby; children under 18; full-time students under 19; and adults on low incomes or receiving the same benefits or tax credits as for free prescriptions.

Free NHS sight tests are available for people aged 60 and over, children, full-time students under the age of 19, adults on low incomes or receiving the same benefits or tax credits as for free prescriptions, and people who have, or are at particular risk of, eye disease. Just over 10 million sight tests were paid for by health authorities in England and Wales in the year to 31 March 2000.

NHS Workforce

The NHS is one of the largest employers in the world, with a workforce of nearly 1 million people.

Of the 968,000 employees in NHS hospital and community health services in England in September 1999 (equivalent to 782,000 whole-time staff), 430,000 were nursing, midwifery and health visiting staff. The Government has taken steps to address current shortages of nurses and midwives through the launch of the first national recruitment campaign in February 1999 and an increase in training places for nurses, midwives and health visitors.

For the most part, family practitioners (GPs, dentists, optometrists and community pharmacists) are either self-employed or (in the case of pharmacists and optometrists) are employed by independent businesses. They, or their companies, agree to provide services on the NHS's behalf, and are paid by health authorities for doing so.

Doctors and Dentists

Only people on the medical or dentists' registers may practise as doctors or dentists in the NHS. University medical and dental schools are responsible for undergraduate teaching; the NHS provides hospital and community facilities for training. Full registration as a doctor requires five or six years' training in a medical school and hospital and the community, with a further year's experience in a hospital. For a dentist, five years' training at a dental school is required plus satisfactory completion of one year's mandatory vocational training before working

Table 13.1: Health and Personal Social Services Staff, England, 1989–99[1]

Whole-time equivalents (thousands)

	1989	1994	1998	1999
Directly employed NHS staff:				
Medical and dental	44	49	59	60
Non-medical and dental	744	706	707	722
All health service staff	**788**	**756**	**766**	**782**
General medical practitioners (excluding GP retainers)[2]	27	27	28	28
General dental practitioners[3]	15	16	17	18
Personal social services	239	238	224	222

[1] On a typical day in the NHS in England in 1999 the number of staff (excluding managers and support staff) included 90,000 doctors, 395,500 nurses, 25,500 healthcare assistants, 23,000 midwives, 7,500 opticians, 14,000 radiographers, 15,000 occupational therapists, 13,000 health visitors, 6,500 paramedics, 11,000 pharmacists, 19,000 physiotherapists and 105,000 practice staff in GP surgeries.
[2] Whole-time equivalent figures are estimated. The figure in the 1989 column is for 1991.
[3] Headcount. Principals, assistants and vocational dental practitioners in the General Dental Service.
Source: Department of Health

as a principal in the General Dental Services of the NHS is permitted. Most GPs are paid by a system of fees and allowances designed to reflect responsibilities, workload and practice expenses. All general dental practitioners are paid by a combination of capitation fees for children registered with the practice, continuing care payments for adults registered, and a prescribed scale of fees for individual treatments.

The regulating body for the medical profession is the General Medical Council (GMC) and, for dentists, the General Dental Council. The main professional associations are the British Medical Association and the British Dental Association.

Nurses, Midwives and Health Visitors

Nursing students undertake the pre-registration Diploma in Higher Education (Project 2000) programme, which emphasises health promotion as well as care of the sick and enables students to work either in hospitals or in the community. The programme lasts three years and consists of periods of college study combined with practical experience in hospital and in the community.

Midwifery education programmes for registered general/adult nurses take 18 months, but the direct entry programme lasts

Measures are being taken by the Government to improve clinical governance, following a number of criminal cases involving doctors, notably the case of Harold Shipman (who was convicted in January 2000 of murdering 15 elderly women patients)—a public inquiry is to be held into the issues surrounding this particular case. The measures include:

- a review by the Commission for Health Improvement of local clinical governance arrangements;
- a report by the Chief Medical Officer—*Supporting Doctors, Protecting Patients*—setting out plans to ensure any problems in a doctor's performance are picked up at an early stage; and
- a decision that all doctors will be appraised annually from 2001, supporting GMC plans to revalidate doctors regularly to ensure that they keep their professional practice up to date. A National Clinical Assessment Authority will be established from April 2001 to provide a rapid objective assessment of an individual doctor's performance where necessary.

three years. Health visitors are registered adult nurses who have a further specialist qualification in health visiting. District nurses are registered adult nurses who have a further specialist qualification in district nursing and care for clients in the community.

The United Kingdom Central Council for Nursing, Midwifery and Health Visiting is responsible for regulating and registering these professions. Four National Boards—for England, Wales, Scotland and Northern Ireland—are responsible for ensuring that training courses meet Central Council requirements as to their type, content and standard. The Government intends to replace these with a single regulatory body, the Nursing and Midwifery Council.

Pharmacists

Only people on the register of pharmaceutical chemists may practise as pharmacists. Registration requires four years' training in a school of pharmacy, followed by one year's practical experience in a community or hospital pharmacy approved for training by regulatory bodies for the profession—the Royal Pharmaceutical Society of Great Britain or the Pharmaceutical Society of Northern Ireland. Community pharmacists are paid professional fees for dispensing NHS prescriptions, as well as being reimbursed for the cost of the drugs and appliances concerned.

Optometrists (Ophthalmic Opticians)

The General Optical Council regulates the professions of ophthalmic optician and dispensing optician. Only registered ophthalmic opticians (or registered ophthalmic medical practitioners) may test sight; training for the former takes four years, including a year of practical experience under supervision. Dispensing opticians take a two-year full-time course with a year's practical experience, or follow a part-time day-release course while employed with an optician. Ophthalmic medical practitioners and optometrists providing general ophthalmic services for the NHS receive approved fees for each sight test carried out.

Other Health Professions

The Council for Professions Supplementary to Medicine (CPSM) and its 12 professional boards regulate the initial training and subsequent practice of health professions: chiropodists; radiographers; orthoptists; physiotherapists; occupational therapists; dietitians; medical laboratory scientific officers; prosthetists and orthotists; arts therapists (art, drama and music therapists); speech and language therapists; clinical scientists; and paramedics. The boards are responsible for promoting high standards of professional education and conduct among members, approving training institutions, qualifications and courses, and maintaining registers of those who have qualified for state registration—state registration in these professions is mandatory for employment in health authorities, Trusts and local authority social services.

The Government intends to replace the CPSM by a Health Professions Council (HPC), which will have scope to regulate any new professions. The HPC will also be represented on the Council of Health Regulators.

Dental therapists and dental hygienists are almost exclusively recruited from certified dental nurses who have taken at least one year's training. Dental therapists then take a two-to-three-year training course and dental hygienists take a course lasting two years; both carry out specified dental work under the supervision of a registered dentist.

Openness in the NHS

The Code of Practice on Openness in the NHS is designed to make NHS organisations (including GPs, dentists and pharmacists) more accountable and provide greater public access to information. It sets out the information that health authorities/boards and NHS Trusts should publish or otherwise make available. This includes information about services provided, the targets and standards set and results achieved, and the costs and effectiveness of services, details of important proposals on health policies or proposed changes in the way the services are delivered, and information for people on how to access their health records.

NHS Complaints System

Under the current NHS complaints system, complaints should be resolved speedily at local level, but if the complainant remains dissatisfied with the local response he or she can request an independent review of the complaint. Where an independent review panel investigation takes place, a report setting out suggestions and recommendations will be produced. Complainants who remain dissatisfied, or whose request for a panel investigation is turned down, can refer their complaint to the Health Service Commissioner.

In 1998–99 some 86,000 written complaints were made about hospital and community health services in England, and nearly 38,900 complaints were made about family health services. In Scotland, 7,257 written complaints were made about hospital and community health services and 2,710 written complaints were made about family health services.

The NHS intends to set up before the end of 2000 a new national mandatory reporting system for England for logging all failures, mistakes and errors.

The new Patient Advocacy and Liaison Service (PALS) will be established in every NHS Trust in England by 2002. Patient advocates will be able to handle patient and family concerns and have direct access to a Trust's chief executive. They will be able to steer patients towards the complaints process where necessary.

Health Service Commissioners

Health Service Commissioners (one each for England, Scotland and Wales) are responsible for investigating complaints directly from members of the public about health service bodies. The three posts are at present held by one person (with a staff of about 250), who is also Parliamentary Commissioner for Administration (Ombudsman—see p. 52). As Health Service Commissioner, he reports annually to Parliament. In Scotland he reports to the Scottish Parliament and in Wales to the National Assembly. In Northern Ireland complaints about health and social services bodies are investigated by the Commissioner for Complaints (the Ombudsman).

The Health Service Commissioner can investigate complaints that a person has suffered hardship or injustice as a result of:

- a failure in a service provided by a health service body;
- a failure to provide a service which the patient was entitled to receive or maladministration by an NHS authority; or
- action by health professionals arising from the exercise of clinical judgment.

Complaints must be sent to the Commissioner in writing, and the health service body concerned should first have been given a reasonable opportunity to respond.

In 1999–2000 a total of 2,526 written complaints were received in England regarding both hospital and community health services and family health services.

NHS Charters

Patient's Charters originally set out national standards of service that the NHS aims to achieve. A new NHS Charter will replace the Patient's Charter in England by 2001. The Charter in England will be entitled 'Your Guide to the NHS' and will provide information on how patients can access appropriate services to meet their healthcare needs, set out a series of standards for each stage in the patient's care, and include improvements patients can expect in the future. In Wales, a Health and Social Care Charter will be launched in 2001, backed up with local charters at local health group level. In Northern Ireland consideration is being given to issuing a revised HPSS Charter for Patients and Clients in 2001. In Scotland discussions continue about the future of the Patient's Charter.

FAMILY HEALTH SERVICES

The Family Health Services are those provided to patients by doctors (GPs), dentists, opticians and pharmacists. In England there were 251 million consultations with GPs in 1998–99.

GPs provide the first diagnosis in the case of illness, give advice and may prescribe a suitable course of treatment or refer a patient to the more specialised services and hospital consultants. Primary healthcare teams also include health visitors and district nurses, midwives, and sometimes social workers and other professional staff employed by the health authorities. Most GPs in Great Britain and about half in Northern Ireland work in health centres. As well as providing medical and nursing services, health centres may have facilities for health education, family planning, speech therapy, chiropody, assessment of hearing, physiotherapy and remedial exercises. Dental, pharmaceutical and ophthalmic services, hospital out-patient and supporting social work services may also be provided.

There have been increases in primary healthcare staff in recent years. For example, between 1989 and 1999 the number of general medical practitioners (excluding retainers) in England rose by 0.8 per cent a year on average to 29,987. Similarly, the number of general dental practitioners continues to grow, rising to 17,715 in October 1999, 2.7 per cent more than in 1998.

Initiatives in Primary Care

The NHS Plan envisages that by 2004 patients will be able to see a primary care professional within 24 hours and a GP within 48 hours. More services will also be available in primary care centres, with some 4 million consultant outpatient appointments a year in primary care and community settings, and up to 1,000 specialist GPs being able to take referrals from other GPs.

A major target of the NHS Plan is reducing inequality in access to services. To improve the equitable distribution of GPs across the NHS, a new Medical Education Standards Board will monitor the number and distribution of doctors in primary care, and by 2004, 200 new Personal Medical Services schemes are planned, mainly in disadvantaged areas.

In 1997 the Government launched its Investing in Dentistry scheme in England, to help improve dental care in areas of poor availability and poor oral health. Similar schemes are in operation in Scotland and Wales. The dental strategy for England aims to ensure that by the end of 2001 everyone who wants to will be able to be treated by an NHS dentist. Pilot dental services are being set up to encourage innovation to meet differences in local dental needs, and Dental Access Centres are being set up in a number of locations to relieve the most acute access problems—for example, high streets, clinics and some of the new primary care Walk-In Centres (see p. 189). By the end of 2000 there will be around 40 Dental Access Centres, providing both routine and emergency dental care.

In 1999 the Review of Prescribing, Supply and Administration of Medicines recommended extending the authority to prescribe to other health professionals. By 2001, around 23,000 district nurses, health visitors and GP practice nurses who also have a health visiting or district nursing qualification will be trained to prescribe a limited range of medicines. From 2004 both the range of medicines and the number of nurses is to be extended. The Government has also announced its intention to introduce legislation to allow supplementary prescribing by other health professionals, such as pharmacists, physiotherapists and chiropodists, as soon as parliamentary time permits.

Midwives, Health Visitors and District Nurses

Midwives provide care and support to women throughout pregnancy (see p. 199), birth and the postnatal period (up to 28 days after the baby is born). They work in both hospital and community settings. Health visitors are responsible for the preventive care and health promotion of families, particularly those with young children. They identify local health needs and work closely with GPs, district nurses and other professions. District nurses give skilled nursing care to people at home or elsewhere outside hospital; they also play an important role in health promotion and education. Practice nurses are based in GP surgeries. They carry out treatments and give advice on health promotion, working closely with GPs and with other community nurses.

HOSPITAL AND SPECIALIST SERVICES

District general hospitals offer a broad spectrum of clinical specialities, supported by a range of other services, such as anaesthetics, pathology and radiology. Almost all have facilities for the admission of emergency patients, either through accident and emergency departments or as direct referrals from GPs. Treatments are provided for in-patients, day cases, out-patients and patients who attend wards for treatment such as dialysis. Some hospitals also provide specialist services covering more than one region or district, for example, for heart and liver transplants, craniofacial services, and rare eye and bone cancers. There are also specialist hospitals such as the world-famous Hospital for Sick Children at Great Ormond Street, Moorfields Eye Hospital, and the National Hospital for Neurology and Neurosurgery, all in London. These hospitals combine specialist treatment facilities with the training of medical and other students, and international research.

The NHS Plan envisages that around three-quarters of operations in England will be carried out on a day care basis, with no overnight stay required.

Less than a third of hospitals now pre-date the formation of the NHS in 1948. While much has been done to improve existing hospital buildings, the largest building programme in the history of the NHS is currently in progress, including several major Private Finance Initiative schemes (see p. 197). Altogether over 100 new hospital schemes are planned between 2000 and 2010.

The main contribution of NHS Trusts (see p. 188) remains the provision of hospital and community services to patients. The services they provide are subject to quality standards set by the NICE (see p. 189) and to the new 'earned autonomy' system to be established under the NHS Plan (see p. 185).

National Beds Inquiry

The National Beds Inquiry was set up because of concerns that reductions in hospital beds had gone too far. The Inquiry, which reported in February 2000, found that the long-term trend of reducing the number of hospital beds could no longer meet changing needs. Instead, it said that acute and community beds and services needed to expand to meet expected future patient needs. It put forward three possible models for debate and consultation:

- maintaining the balance of service objectives and settings broadly as at present;
- more investment in hospitals and a significant increase in hospital acute beds; and
- expanding intermediate care services to treat older people in the community rather than in hospital, so releasing some of the beds currently occupied by elderly patients.

Respondents to the National Beds Inquiry Consultation with the public and health professionals (published in February 2000) envisaged a service providing care in the right place to meet patients' needs with no discernible divide between the different elements of the health and social care system. In particular, there was support for:

- developing care closer to home;
- at least maintaining adequate acute beds;
- greater integration of NHS care with social services, focused on the patient; and
- disease prevention and early intervention in the community.

Intermediate care would be central to the new approach, concentrating on maintaining and restoring independence and on rehabilitation. It would include:

- 'drop-in' facilities;
- fast access to diagnostics and pathology;
- multi-disciplinary teams with a mixture of nurse, therapist, consultant and GP-led services;
- fast access to acute services and in-patient settings where necessary; and
- timely discharge into appropriate settings.

The private and voluntary sectors would have important roles to play. The new environment would be supported by electronic patient records and more use of new technology.

Waiting Lists

Half of all admissions to hospital are immediate. The other half are placed on a waiting list before the admission takes place. Of patients admitted from waiting lists, half are admitted within six weeks, and around two-thirds within three months.

A major government target is to reduce waiting lists in England to 100,000 below (and in Scotland to 10,000 below) the level in May 1997, by the end of the present Parliament. At the end of July 2000 just over 1 million patients were waiting for NHS treatment. The Government made £320 million available to reduce waiting lists and times in England in 1999–2000 and will invest a further £300 million in 2000–01 from the Modernisation Fund. It is developing a new *National Booked Admissions Programme*, under which patients are able to pre-book their appointments for a convenient time. Almost all the first 24 pilot sites have improved non-attendance rates and a further 60 pilots are under way. An extra £40 million has been made available by the National Assembly for Wales to reduce waiting lists by 15,000 during 2000–01.

Private Finance Initiative

The Private Finance Initiative (PFI) was launched in 1992 to promote partnership between the public and private sectors on a commercial basis (see chapter 24). In the health service it involves new facilities being designed, built, maintained and owned by the private sector, which then leases the completed facilities back to the NHS. Clinical services continue to be provided by NHS staff, and the NHS remains in control of key planning and clinical decisions. The Government introduced legislation in 1997 to clarify the powers of NHS Trusts to sign PFI agreements, and, following a review of PFI hospital building schemes in England, announced a major new hospital building programme.

Organ Transplants

United Kingdom Transplant (a special health authority of the NHS) provides a 24-hour support service to all transplant units in the UK for the matching and allocation of organs for transplant. In many cases transplants are multi-organ. During 1999, 1,621 kidney transplants were performed, and at the end of 1999 there were 5,904 patients waiting for kidney transplants.

There are seven designated thoracic transplant centres in England, and one in Scotland. In 1999, 230 heart, 110 lung, and 50 heart/lung transplants were performed. There are six designated liver transplant units in England and one in Scotland. In 1999, 691 liver transplants were performed.

A similar service exists for corneas and, in 1999, 2,275 were transplanted in the UK.

A voluntary organ donor card system enables people to indicate their willingness to become organ donors in the event of their death. The NHS Organ Donor Register is a computer database of those willing to be organ donors. At December 1999 it contained 8.5 million names. Commercial dealing in organs for transplant is illegal in the UK.

Blood Services

Blood services are run by the Blood Services in England and North Wales, the Scottish National Blood Transfusion Service, the Welsh Blood Service and the Northern Ireland Blood Transfusion Agency. The UK is self-sufficient in blood components.

In the UK over 3 million donations are given each year by voluntary unpaid donors. These are made into many different life-saving products for patients. Red cells, platelets and other components with a limited 'shelf life' are prepared at blood centres, whereas the production of plasma products is undertaken at the Bio Products Laboratory in Elstree (Hertfordshire) and the Protein Fractionation Centre in Edinburgh.

Donors are normally aged between 17 and 70. Blood centres are responsible for blood collection, screening, processing and supplying hospital blood banks. They also provide laboratory, clinical, research, teaching and specialist advisory services and facilities. These blood centres are subject to nationally co-ordinated quality audit programmes, through the Medicines Control Agency.

Ambulance and Patient Transport Services

NHS emergency ambulances are available free to the public through the 999 telephone call system for cases of sudden illness or collapse and for accidents. They are also available for doctors' urgent calls. Rapid response services, in which paramedics use cars and motorcycles to reach emergency cases, have been introduced in a number of areas, particularly London and other major cities with areas of high traffic density. Helicopter ambulances, provided through local charities, serve many parts of the country and an integrated NHS-funded air ambulance service is available throughout Scotland. Between 1998–99 and 1999–2000 the number of emergency calls to the NHS rose by 7 per cent to 4.1 million and the number of emergency patient journeys grew by 5 per cent to 2.9 million.

Non-emergency patient transport services are free to NHS patients considered by their doctor (or dentist or midwife) to be medically unfit to travel by other means. In many areas the ambulance service organises volunteer drivers to provide a hospital car service for non-urgent patients. Patients on low incomes may be eligible for reimbursement of costs of travelling to hospital.

Rehabilitation

NHS and social services undertake rehabilitation work for large numbers of people of all ages to restore and maintain their independence and social participation. Rehabilitation plays an important role in improving the quality of life of people, enabling them to return to, or remain in, employment or education and preventing inappropriate admissions to hospital or long-term care.

Health and social services are encouraged to develop a range of rehabilitative options and to be flexible in meeting people's needs. A new Partnership Grant, announced in the *Modernising Social Services* White Paper and totalling nearly £650 million over three years, has a particular emphasis on improving rehabilitation services and avoiding unnecessary admissions to hospital and other institutional care.

Hospices

Hospice or palliative care is a special type of care for people whose illness may no longer be curable; it enables them to achieve the best possible quality of life during the final stages. The care may be provided in a variety of settings: at home (with support from specially trained staff), in a hospice or palliative care unit, in hospital or at a hospice day centre.

Hospice or palliative care focuses on controlling pain and other distressing symptoms and providing psychological support to patients, their families and friends, both during the patient's illness and into bereavement.

Palliative care was first developed in the UK in 1967 by the voluntary hospices and continues to be provided by them in many areas, but is now also provided within NHS palliative care units, hospitals and community services.

Hospices and palliative care services mostly help people with cancer, although patients with other life-threatening illnesses, such as AIDS, are also cared for. Several hospices provide respite care for children from birth to 16 years of age.

The National Council for Hospices and Specialist Palliative Care Services is an organisation which brings together both voluntary and health service providers in England, Wales and Northern Ireland, in order to provide a co-ordinated view of the service. Its Scottish counterpart is the Scottish Partnership Agency for Palliative and Cancer Care.

Private Medical Treatment

Some NHS hospitals share expensive equipment with private hospitals, and NHS patients are sometimes treated (at public expense) in the private sector when it represents value for money. The scale of private practice in relation to the NHS is, however, relatively small. According to the ONS Family Expenditure Survey, the proportion of UK households covered by private health insurance increased from 6 per cent in 1985 to 9 per cent in 1998–99.

Many overseas patients come to the UK for treatment in private hospitals and clinics.

Harley Street in London is an internationally recognised centre for medical consultancy.

Complementary Medicine

Complementary medicine (or complementary therapies) can cover a range of therapies and practices, the best known being osteopathy, chiropractic, homoeopathy, acupuncture and herbalism. With the exception of homoeopathy, complementary medicine is usually available only outside the NHS. There is a wide variety of regulatory and professional arrangements ranging from statutory regulation to little or no regulation. The Government is providing funding to encourage professional self-regulation.

Parents and Children

Special preventive services are provided under the NHS to safeguard the health of pregnant women and of mothers with young children. Services include free dental treatment; health education; and vaccination and immunisation of children against certain infectious diseases (see p. 204). Under the NHS Plan, further screening programmes are planned by 2004, including a new national linked antenatal and neonatal screening programme for haemoglobinopathy and sickle cell disease.

Nearly all births take place in hospital, although there was an increase during the 1990s in the popularity of home births: these accounted for 2.2 per cent of births in England and Wales in 1999, compared with around 1 per cent during the 1980s. Home births in Scotland remain relatively constant at under 1 per cent. A woman is entitled to care throughout her pregnancy, the birth and the postnatal period. Care may be provided by a midwife, a community-based GP, a hospital-based obstetrician, or a combination of these. The birth may take place in a hospital maternity unit, a midwife/GP-led unit, or at home. After the birth, a midwife will visit until the baby is at least ten days old and after that a health visitor's services are available. Throughout her pregnancy and for the first year of her baby's life, a woman is entitled to free prescriptions and dental care.

Prescriptions for children, including older children (up to the age of 19 when in full-time education), are free of charge.

A comprehensive programme of health surveillance, provided for pre-school children (under five years of age), is run by community health trusts and GPs who receive an annual payment for every child registered on the programme. (In Scotland this is carried out by the Community Paediatric Service which may be based in the primary care or acute services trust.) This enables doctors, dentists and health visitors to oversee the health and development of pre-school children so that any health problems are picked up and appropriate intervention arranged as early and as quickly as possible. Health Promotion England (see p. 189) produces *Birth to Five*, a guide to the early stages of development, nutrition, weaning and common childhood ailments; it is made available to all first-time mothers free of charge. The Scottish equivalent is *Ready Steady Baby!* by the Health Education Board for Scotland.

There is a welfare food scheme for mothers on low income, where distribution of formula feed and vitamins is free of charge. This is often undertaken at the child health clinic. The NHS Plan envisages that the scheme will be reformed by 2004 to improve access to a healthy diet for children in poverty. Increased support for breastfeeding will continue in England through the Infant Feeding Initiative on tackling health inequalities in this area. The Scottish Executive funds the Scottish Breastfeeding Group and the National Breastfeeding Adviser, who actively promote breastfeeding in Scotland.

New mothers also receive a Personal Child Health Record for their child. It enables and prompts parents to keep a record of immunisation (see p. 204), tests, birth details and health checks. This is not done in Scotland although the concept is being piloted. Children of school age attending a state-maintained school have access to the school health service, as well as usually being registered with a GP and local dentist. In addition to providing health advice to children and young people, the school health service assists teachers with pupils having medical needs.

Child guidance and child psychiatric services provide help and advice to families and children with psychological or emotional problems. In recent years special efforts have been made to improve co-operation between the community-based child health services and local authority education and social services for children. This is particularly important in the prevention of child abuse and for the health and welfare of children in care (see p. 167).

Human Fertilisation and Embryology

The world's first 'test-tube baby' was born in the UK in 1978, as a result of the technique of *in vitro* fertilisation. This opened up new horizons for helping with problems of infertility and for the science of embryology. The social, ethical and legal implications were examined by a committee of inquiry and led eventually to the passage of the Human Fertilisation and Embryology Act 1990, one of the most comprehensive pieces of legislation on assisted reproduction and embryo research in the world.

The Human Fertilisation and Embryology Authority (HFEA) licenses and controls centres providing certain infertility treatments, undertaking human embryo research or storing gametes or embryos. The HFEA maintains a code of practice giving guidance to licensed centres and reports annually to Parliament.

Sexual Health

The Government's public health strategy aims to ensure the provision of effective sexual health services. Free contraceptive advice and treatment are available from GPs, family planning clinics and tailored services for young people. Clinics are able to provide condoms and other contraceptives free of charge.

The DH is developing a national sexual health and HIV strategy to bring together current initiatives in sexual health and HIV, including work on chlamydia. The Scottish Executive is also developing plans for a sexual health strategy for Scotland. In addition, it is funding £3 million in a demonstration project which aims to foster responsible sexual behaviour on the part of young people, with emphasis on the avoidance of unwanted teenage pregnancies and sexually transmitted diseases.

Teenage Pregnancies

Live birth rates to women under 20 in England and Wales are the highest in Western Europe. In 1998 the conception rate for women under the age of 18 was 47 per thousand in England and Wales, and 9 per thousand for those under the age of 16. Just over 40 per cent of pregnancies in under 18s, and about half in under 16s, result in an abortion.

The Social Exclusion Unit report on Teenage Pregnancy, issued in June 1999, set two goals: to halve by 2010 the rate of conceptions in England among those aged under 18; and to lessen the risks of social exclusion by getting more teenage parents back into education, training or employment. A cross-departmental Teenage Pregnancy Unit, located within DH, has been set up to oversee implementation of this strategy. A £60 million package of measures includes:

- a national publicity campaign to reinforce the report's key messages;
- improved access to contraceptive and sexual health services for teenagers;
- new guidance on sex and relationships education in school; and
- special action targeted on prevention for the most vulnerable groups, including children looked after by a local authority, those excluded from school and young offenders.

Abortion

Under the Abortion Act 1967, as amended, a time limit of 24 weeks applies to the largest category of abortion—risk to the physical or mental health of the pregnant woman—and also to abortion because of a similar risk to any existing children of her family. There are three categories in which no time limit applies: to prevent grave permanent injury to the physical or mental health of the woman; where there is a substantial risk of serious foetal handicap; or where continuing the pregnancy would involve a risk to the life of the pregnant woman greater

Today Britain is a modern industrialised nation, but around the country there are people who pursue activities which maintain strong links to the past. Knowledge is passed down from generation to generation to ensure that crafts and skills practised in a simpler age continue into the 21st century.

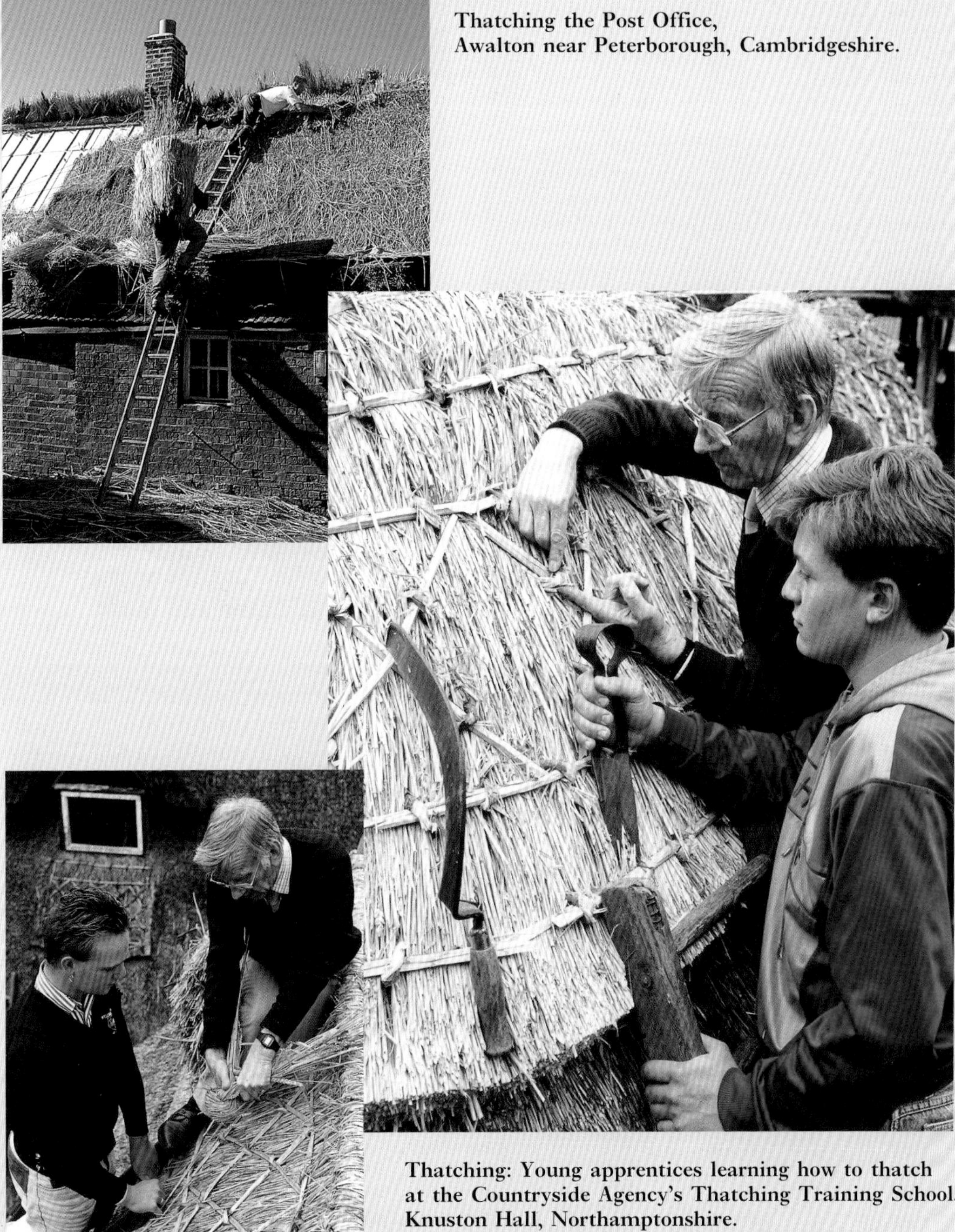

Thatching the Post Office, Awalton near Peterborough, Cambridgeshire.

Thatching: Young apprentices learning how to thatch at the Countryside Agency's Thatching Training School, Knuston Hall, Northamptonshire.

Charcoal Burning: Production of charcoal in Lincolnshire and Sussex.

Slate Splitting: Slate is still cut and prepared as roofing material at Blaenau Ffestiniog, Gwynedd.

Forging: In rural areas throughout Britain there is still a need for local blacksmiths shoeing horses, working with the farming community, as well as producing decorative iron work.

Dry Stone Walling: Work being carried out on a dry stone wall, Stanbury Moor, Upper Worth Valley, West Yorkshire.

Turf Cutting: Peat being cut in County Armagh, Northern Ireland.

Hedge Laying: Craftsmen lay new hedges at Hydebridge Nature Reserve, Pencombe, Hereford.

Sustainable regeneration of woodland scheme at the National Botanic Garden of Wales.

Cheese Making: Cheeses are made all round Britain and each has its own distinctive character.

Rennet added to coagulate the milk and produce firm curd.

Freshly milled curd being put into the mould.

Llangloffan Farmhouse Cheese maturing room, Pembrokeshire.

Adult Cigarette Smoking[1] in Great Britain by Gender

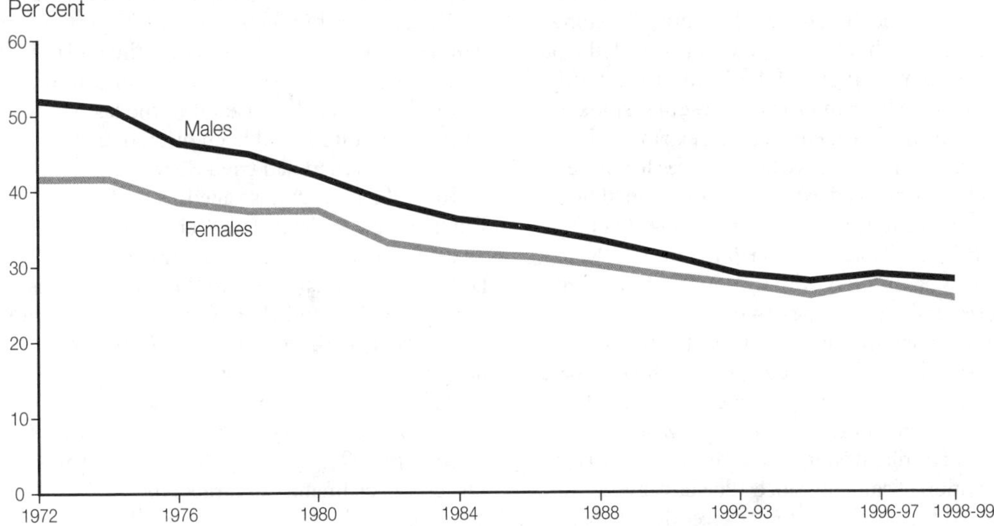

[1] By people aged 16 and over, except for 1972 which included those aged 15. Data are collected every two years.

Source: General Household Survey, Office for National Statistics

than if the pregnancy were terminated. The Act does not apply in Northern Ireland.

Between 1998 and 1999 the number of legal abortions on women resident in England and Wales fell by 2.3 per cent to 173,701, and the overall rate fell slightly from 13.9 to 13.6 for every 1,000 women aged between 14 and 49.

Substance Misuse

Tobacco Control

Cigarette smoking is the single greatest cause of preventable illness and death in the UK. It is associated with around 120,000 premature deaths a year (mainly from cancer and heart and respiratory diseases)—nearly one-fifth of all deaths.

Action to reduce smoking, especially among children and young people, is a government priority. A White Paper—*Smoking Kills*—published in December 1998, set out a number of targets for the UK including:

- to reduce smoking among children from 13 per cent to 9 per cent or less by 2010, with a fall to 11 per cent by 2005;
- to reduce adult smoking so that the overall rate falls from 28 per cent to 24 per cent or less by 2010, with a fall to 26 per cent by 2005; and
- to reduce the percentage of women who smoke during pregnancy from 23 per cent to 15 per cent by 2010, with a fall to 18 per cent by 2005.

The NHS Cancer Plan, launched in September 2000 (see p. 183), introduced a further target, to reduce smoking rates among manual groups from 32 per cent in 1998 to 26 per cent by 2010.

In September 1999, the Government produced a Public Places Charter which committed signatories to improve the facilities for customers who do not smoke in public houses, bars and restaurants. According to the DH, it is anticipated that half of licensed hospitality venues will be signed up to the Charter by 2002.

Smoking peaked in the 1950s and 1960s and fell steadily in the 1970s and 1980s (see chart above). Smoking rates, which used to be higher for men than for women, have fallen more among men than among women, narrowing the difference to 28 per cent for men in Great Britain and 26 per cent for women in 1998–99.

The proportion of regular smokers among secondary school pupils aged 11 to 15 fell from 13 per cent in 1996 to 9 per cent in 1999. Boys are less likely than girls to be regular smokers.

The NHS Plan envisages an expansion in specialist smoking cessation services for those smokers who need extra help to give up. The services include nicotine replacement therapy (NRT), available on prescription from GPs, providing the body with nicotine in decreasing doses until the craving can be coped with, to complement the newly available treatment, buproprion. Of the 14,600 people who set a date to quit smoking through these services in Health Action Zones in England in 1999–2000, 39 per cent had still given up a month later. Increased cessation of smoking since 1965 has almost halved the number of lung cancer deaths that would otherwise have been expected in the UK.

Advertising

The Government is preparing primary legislation to ban tobacco advertising as soon as parliamentary time permits. In December 1999 the Government launched an advertising campaign against smoking, costing up to £50 million over three years and initially targeted at adult smokers. Campaigns aimed at teenagers, pregnant women, ethnic minorities and other target groups will follow.

Drug Misuse

The misuse of drugs, such as heroin, cocaine and amphetamines, is a serious social and health problem. In England, during the six months to September 1999, the number of users reported as presenting to drug misuse agencies (30,545) had risen 7 per cent from the previous six months. Around half were in their twenties and one in seven under 20, while about three-quarters were male. Heroin was the most widely used drug among this group, being taken by 59 per cent of users.

A survey of secondary school children aged 11 to 15 in 1999 found that 7 per cent of 11 to 15 year olds in England had used drugs in the month before the survey, and the proportion who had used drugs at some time in their lives was 15 per cent. The pattern varies with age: only 1 per cent of 11 year olds had used drugs in the last year, but 30 per cent of 15 year olds had done so. Cannabis was by far the most likely drug to have been used (11 per cent of 11 to 15 year olds had used it in the last year). Many more pupils had been offered drugs (35 per cent) than had tried them.

In 1998, among those aged 16 to 24 in England and Wales, 29 per cent had used drugs in the last year and 19 per cent in the last month, similar levels to those in previous surveys in 1994 and 1996. Cannabis was again the most likely drug to be used (27 per cent had used it in the last year).

The Government published its ten-year drugs strategy, *Tackling Drugs to Build a Better Britain*, in 1998. In May 1999 the UK Anti-Drugs Co-ordinator set targets to:

- substantially reduce the proportion of people under 25 reporting use of illegal drugs in the last month and previous year, and to reduce the proportion of young people using heroin and cocaine, which cause the greatest harm, by 25 per cent by 2005 and 50 per cent by 2008; and
- increase the participation of problem drug misusers, including prisoners, in drug treatment programmes, by 66 per cent by 2005 and 100 per cent by 2008.

Over the period 1999–2000 to 2001–02 some £70.5 million from the NHS and Personal Social Services Modernisation Fund is targeted to drugs misuse.

A new long-term strategy for tackling substance misuse in Wales was launched in May 2000. *Tackling Substance Misuse in Wales: A Partnership Approach* covers the full range of substances that are misused in Wales including illegal drugs, alcohol, prescription-only medicines, over-the-counter medicines and volatile substances. The new Welsh strategy embraces the key aims of the UK anti-drugs strategy.

Prevention

As part of the Government's anti-drugs strategy, a new Drugs Prevention Advisory Service was set up in 1999 (see p. 215). It works with Drug Action Teams in England to encourage good drug prevention practice and to assist in developing appropriate demonstration programmes. In Wales a Strategic Prevention Action Plan on Drugs and Alcohol has been published.

The Government makes funds available through local education authorities in England and Wales to provide in-service training for teachers involved in drug prevention work in schools. As part of the National Curriculum in England and Wales (see chapter 10), children in primary and secondary schools receive education on the dangers of drug misuse. In Scotland, education authorities are encouraged to address health education, including drug education, within a comprehensive programme of personal and social education.

Drug Prevention Projects targeted at young people at particular risk of drug misuse have been commissioned in Health Action Zones (see p. 190) with funding of £4 million for 1998–99 and 1999–2000 and a second round of funding of £1.8 million in 2000–01. The projects are intended to address the needs of vulnerable young people, including truants and those excluded from school, young people in public care, young offenders, young homeless people and children of drug misusing parents.

UK National Drugs Helpline

The National Drugs Helpline gives advice and information to anyone in the UK concerned about drugs. In 1999–2000 it received 0.4 million calls. The telephone number is 0800 77 66 00.

Solvent Misuse

Government policy aims to prevent solvent misuse through educating young people, parents and health professionals about the dangers and signs of misuse, and, where practicable, restricting the sales of solvent-based liquefied gas and aerosol products to young people.

In England, Wales and Northern Ireland it is an offence to supply such substances to children under 18 if the supplier knows or has reason to believe they are to be used to induce intoxication. In Scotland proceedings can be taken under the common law. Since October 1999 it has been an offence in the UK to sell butane lighter refills to people under 18; these refills are implicated in more than 50 per cent of deaths from solvent abuse.

The DH funds a hospital-based unit in London to collect and publish annual mortality statistics associated with volatile substance misuse. There were 70 deaths in 1998 in the UK. Of these, 34 were aged 15 to 19, accounting for one in 45 deaths in this age group. The drug use survey among 11 to 15 year olds in England found that about 2 per cent had used glue and a similar proportion butane gas in 1999.

Alcohol Misuse

Alcohol is consumed by over 90 per cent of the adult population. While the vast majority drink sensibly and safely, alcohol misuse does cause preventable illness and social problems, and is a factor in many accidents. The latest Department of Health guidelines are that consistently drinking four or more units a day for men or three or more units for women is not advised, because of the progressive health risks. In 1998–99, 38 per cent of adult males and 21 per cent of adult females in Great Britain consumed more than the advised number of units of alcohol a day.

Part of the funds allocated to Health Promotion England (see p. 189) is for promoting sensible drinking in England, and equivalent bodies are similarly funded in other parts of Britain. 'Drinkline' provides confidential telephone advice about alcohol problems and services in England and Wales.

Treatment and rehabilitation within the NHS includes in-patient and out-patient services in general and psychiatric hospitals and some specialised alcohol treatment units. Primary care teams and voluntary organisations providing treatment and rehabilitation in hostels, day centres and advisory services also play an important role.

There is close co-operation between statutory and voluntary organisations. In

England, Alcohol Concern plays a prominent role in improving services for problem drinkers and their families; increasing public awareness of alcohol misuse; and improving training for professional and voluntary workers. The Scottish Council on Alcohol has a similar role in Scotland.

The Government is preparing a new strategy to tackle alcohol misuse in England, for publication later in 2000. Its broad aims are:

- to encourage people to drink sensibly in line with guidance, so as to avoid alcohol-related problems;
- to protect individuals and communities from anti-social and criminal behaviour related to alcohol misuse; and
- to provide services that enable people to overcome their alcohol misuse problems.

In Scotland, developing a new strategy will be the responsibility of the Scottish Advisory Committee on Alcohol Misuse. A report, *Reducing Alcohol Related Harm in Northern Ireland*, was published in June 1999 and the resulting strategy for the Province was published in September 2000.

Communicable Diseases

Health authorities/health boards have a key responsibility for prevention and control of infectious disease, liaising closely with colleagues in environmental health departments of local authorities. They are assisted by the Public Health Laboratory Service, which aims to protect the population from infection through the detection, diagnosis, surveillance, prevention and control of communicable diseases in England and Wales. Similar facilities are provided in Scotland by the Scottish Centre for Infection and Environmental Health and, in Northern Ireland, by the Communicable Disease Surveillance Centre, the Northern Ireland Public Health Laboratory and other hospital microbiology laboratories.

Immunisation

Health authorities/health boards carry out programmes of immunisation against diphtheria, measles, mumps, rubella, poliomyelitis, tetanus, tuberculosis, whooping cough (pertussis) and haemophilus influenzae type B infection ('Hib'). The UK is the first country in the world to use a new vaccine to protect against meningitis Group C. This vaccine was introduced into the immunisation programme from November 1999, and the programme is on schedule to immunise all children under age 18 by the end of 2000. By autumn 2000 the incidence of disease in the age groups so far vaccinated had fallen by up to 85 per cent.

Immunisation is not compulsory. Parents are provided with information about the safety and efficacy of vaccines and are encouraged to have their children immunised. Immunisations are mainly given by GPs and their practice nurses. Annual immunisation rates for the UK were 96 per cent for tetanus in 1998–99, 95 per cent for diphtheria and polio, and 94 per cent for whooping cough. The incidence of such diseases in childhood is at its lowest ever level. Since the introduction of the Hib vaccine in 1992, Hib meningitis has been almost completely eliminated in young children.

Vaccination against influenza is recommended for certain groups at increased risk of serious illness from influenza. The groups were extended in 1998–99 to include all people aged 75 or over, and from 2000–01 to include everyone aged 65 or over.

HIV/AIDS

Although the UK has a relatively low prevalence of HIV/AIDS as a result of sustained public education and health campaigns, about 3,000 new infections are reported each year. The use of combination drug therapy is delaying disease progression, and mortality has fallen substantially. HIV-related deaths are estimated to have fallen by about two-thirds from over 1,500 in 1994 to around 500 in 1999. As a consequence, the number of individuals within the population infected with HIV is increasing. During 1999 over 19,000 individuals were reported to have received HIV-related treatment and care from statutory health services. Anonymous surveillance data give an estimated prevalence of HIV infection at just under 30,000 at the end of 1998.

HIV is more prevalent in London than elsewhere in the UK, reflecting a higher concentration of 'at risk' groups. Within Scotland prevalence is higher in Edinburgh than elsewhere. Those most vulnerable to HIV infection are homosexual/bisexual men, injecting drug users and people from high prevalence regions, for example sub-Saharan Africa. Although the UK has not seen a substantial spread of HIV to the heterosexual population, the HIV prevalence in pregnant women giving birth in London is relatively high at one in 450 in 1998 (compared with one in 6,550 in the rest of the UK).

The Government has introduced a range of initiatives to encourage pregnant women to have an HIV test as an integral part of their antenatal care. Most HIV-infected pregnant women accept measures to decrease the risk of passing the infection to their babies. Health authorities have a national objective to reduce the number of children who acquire HIV from their mothers by 80 per cent by 2002.

Government strategies to reduce HIV transmission include:

- HIV/AIDS health promotion aimed at both the general population and groups at risk;
- information on antenatal HIV testing to help pregnant women to reach informed decisions, for example about ways of reducing the risk of transmission to babies; and
- the National AIDS Helpline, which provides confidential information and advice on all aspects of HIV and AIDS.

Tuberculosis

The UK has an excellent record of tuberculosis (TB) control. Notifications of TB in the UK have reached the relatively low levels of around 6,500 cases a year, compared with nearly 50,000 in 1950. This compares with a low of 5,745 cases in 1987 but is still well below the 1980 level of over 9,000. These lower levels have been achieved and maintained through an immunisation programme, treatment of identified cases and screening of their close contacts, screening and treatment for immigrants from countries with a high prevalence of TB and active surveillance of TB. This success is against a worldwide resurgence in TB that is having a small but important impact on trends in the UK. The Government has a two-pronged approach to prevention and control of TB in new immigrants to the UK: first to screen those at highest risk at ports of entry, and then to offer more detailed screening, including skin testing, locally when they arrive at their destination.

Eating Habits and Nutrition

Since the early 1970s there have been marked changes in the British diet. One feature has been the long-term rise in consumption of poultry, while that of red meat (such as beef and veal) has fallen. Consumption of fresh fruit has increased since 1970, while consumption of fresh green vegetables, including cabbages, peas and beans, was lower in 1999 than in 1970. In addition, the use of convenience food—both frozen and ready meals—has increased. Despite these changes, the British diet is still noticeably different to that in other countries such as those in the Mediterranean, being relatively low in fruit, vegetables and fish. However, there have been important changes within these broad types of food, so that mushrooms and salad vegetables have superseded traditional vegetables, such as swedes and parsnips. Health considerations appear to have been influencing some aspects of diet in recent years, for example, in the long-term fall in red meat sales, and the growth in low-fat spread consumption.

Features of the pattern of consumption in 1999 compared with 1998 included:

- household consumption of carcass beef and veal was virtually the same as in both 1997 and 1998—lower than in 1995 but above the long-term trend evident at that time;
- consumption of poultry, pork, and mutton and lamb all fell slightly in 1999, while frozen convenience meat and meat products (including frozen ready meals) rose by 8 per cent;
- a 2 per cent rise in consumption of fresh vegetables in the home, the third annual

Changing Patterns in Consumption of Foods at Home, Great Britain

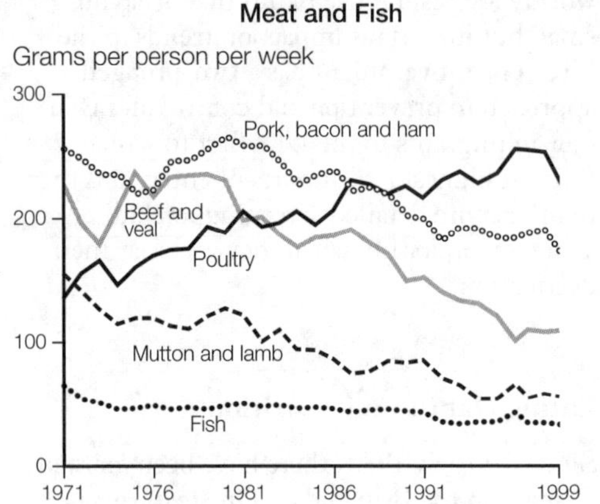

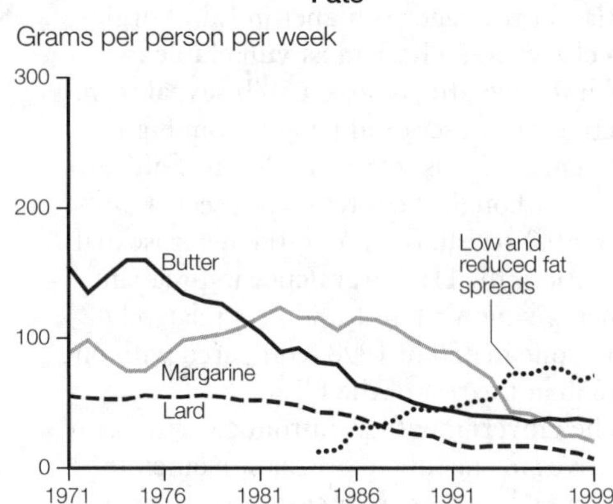

Source: National Food Survey, Ministry of Agriculture, Fisheries and Food

rise in the four years following its low point in 1995;

- annual household consumption of fresh potatoes declined by 6 per cent and there were falls in consumption of oranges (20 per cent) and apples (7 per cent) with rises in grapes (13 per cent) and bananas (2 per cent);
- margarine consumption declined by 23 per cent in 1999 and was only a fifth of that recorded ten years ago, while consumption of reduced fat spreads has doubled over the last ten years, and increased by 7 per cent in 1999;
- consumption of tea in the home fell by 9 per cent in 1999, the fourth year in succession that tea consumption has fallen; and
- consumption of beer and lager in the home fell by 3 per cent and 5 per cent respectively while wine consumption in the home remained close to its 1998 level.

Energy intakes from food continued to decline—to an average of 1,690 kilocalories (kcal) in 1999, compared with 1,740 kcal in 1998. The percentage of food energy derived from fat continued its long-term decline in 1999 and the proportion of food energy derived from saturated fatty acids also fell.

The proportion of adults who are obese or overweight has increased—in 1998, 21 per cent of women and 17 per cent of men aged 16 and over in England were classified as obese, compared with 8 per cent and 6 per cent respectively in 1980 in Great Britain. The likelihood of being overweight increases up to the age of 65 and then declines at older ages.

The Committee on the Medical Aspects of Food and Nutrition Policy published its report *Nutritional Aspects of the Development of Cancer* in 1998. It noted that research suggests that diet might contribute to about one-third of all cancers. Its main recommendations are consistent with the Government's healthy eating advice to the effect that a healthy and balanced diet is one which is varied and rich in fruit and vegetables and dietary fibre. The report also underlined the importance of maintaining a healthy body weight throughout adult life.

The major supermarket groups and most food manufacturers have introduced voluntary labelling schemes indicating the energy, fat, protein and carbohydrate content of food. Nutrition labelling is compulsory on products for which a nutritional claim is made.

The Department of Health is piloting 'five a day' projects testing the feasibility of changing fruit and vegetable consumption. The results of these studies will form the foundations of a general guidance pack

A survey on diet and nutrition among young people aged 4 to 18, carried out in 1997, was published in June 2000. It is part of the National Diet and Nutrition Survey programme, run jointly by the Food Standards Agency and the Department of Health. Among some of the findings:

- boys ate significantly larger average amounts than girls, the most marked differences being for pizza, white bread, breakfast cereals, semi-skimmed milk, bacon and ham, sausages, baked beans and potato chips. In contrast, girls consumed significantly larger amounts of 'other' raw and salad vegetables, raw tomatoes, and apples and pears;
- during the seven-day recording period in the survey no citrus fruit had been eaten by 76 per cent of boys and 72 per cent of girls, while 61 per cent of boys and 56 per cent of girls had not eaten any leafy green vegetables;
- 1 per cent of boys and 5 per cent of girls reported that they were vegetarian or vegan, although this was 10 per cent for girls aged 15 to 18;
- 2 per cent of boys and 6 per cent of girls reported that they were dieting to lose weight, rising to 16 per cent of girls aged 15 to 18: and
- young people, particularly boys, in households of lower socio-economic status reported lower intakes than average of energy, fat and most vitamins and minerals.

intended for publication in 2002. By 2004 every child in nursery school and those aged four to six in infant schools will be entitled to a free piece of fruit each school day.

The Scottish Diet Action Plan 'Eating for Health' provides the framework for wide-ranging action to tackle Scotland's poor health, with a particular focus on children and young people. The most recent initiatives in this area include fruit for infants, breakfast clubs, and school fruit and salad bars.

ENVIRONMENTAL HEALTH

Environmental health provides public health protection through control of the physical environment—atmospheric pollution and noise; contaminated land, food and water; waste management; housing; occupational health and safety; communicable diseases; and statutory nuisances. In the UK no single government department is responsible for environmental health as a whole, although the DH advises other government departments on the health implications of their policies. Local authorities provide environmental health services and employ professionally trained environmental health officers, concerned with inspection, health promotion and regulation.

The Institute for Environment and Health, established by the Medical Research Council (see p. 441), is concerned mainly with research and management of research into the hazards to which people may be exposed through the environment. In Scotland the Scottish Centre for Infection and Environmental Health provides surveillance and advisory services on environmental health matters.

DH, the National Assembly for Wales, the Scottish Executive and the Northern Ireland Department of Health, Social Services and Public Safety have established the National Focus, a unit based in Cardiff, to co-ordinate work on responses to chemical incidents and surveillance of health effects of environmental chemicals.

Accidents

In 1999 there were 235,000 road accidents involving personal injury in Great Britain, and there were over 3,400 deaths and nearly 317,000 injuries (see p. 363).

The Department of Trade and Industry records home and leisure accidents needing hospital treatment. Data for 1998 show that every 6 hours one older person dies from an accidental fall in the home. Altogether 1.1 million people in the UK go to a hospital casualty department each year as a result of a fall in the home. Around 33,000 people experience falls from ladders each year, and burns from barbecues are thought to affect 625 people.

Food Safety

Under the Food Safety Act 1990, it is illegal to sell or supply food that is unfit for human consumption or falsely or misleadingly labelled. The Act covers a broad range of commercial activities related to food production, to the sources from which it is derived, such as crops and animals, and to articles which come into contact with food. There are also more detailed regulations, which apply to all types of food and drink and their ingredients. Local authorities are responsible for enforcing food law in two main areas: trading standards officers deal with the labelling of food, its composition and most cases of chemical contamination; and environmental health officers deal with hygiene, with cases of microbiological contamination of foods, and with food which is found to be unfit for human consumption.

The UK Food Standards Agency, which began operating in April 2000, is responsible for all aspects of food safety and standards. The Agency will contribute to the targets to reduce coronary heart disease and stroke, and identify new ways to help disadvantaged consumers to improve their diets. It also sets and audits standards for the enforcement of food law by local authorities. An example of this is the statutory scheme for licensing butchers' shops throughout the UK, which will come into force in autumn 2000.

CJD and Public Health

CJD (Creutzfeldt-Jakob disease) is a rare transmissible spongiform encephalopathy in humans. In 1996 the Government announced that the National CJD Surveillance Unit in Edinburgh had identified a previously unrecognised form of the disease, variant CJD (vCJD).[1] The Spongiform Encephalopathy Advisory Committee (SEAC) concluded that the most likely explanation, in the absence of any credible alternative, was that these cases were linked to exposure to BSE (see p. 455) before the introduction of the specified bovine offal ban in 1989. In 1997 SEAC concluded that the agent causing BSE is the same as that causing vCJD. However, these results did not provide information about the route of infection. In light of the increased number of cases of vCJD, the Committee has concluded that vCJD is an acquired prion disease caused by exposure to a BSE-like agent. Cases of vCJD are increasing—there were 84 probable and definite cases in 2000 up to 28 September, compared with 83 in the whole of 1999.

To safeguard public health the Government is providing additional funding for research into CJD and BSE, including the work carried out at the National CJD Surveillance Unit which monitors the incidence of the disease.

An independent public inquiry set up to establish and review the history of the emergence and identification of BSE and vCJD in the UK reported in October 2000. (See chapter 27 for details of government measures to control the spread of BSE.)

Safety of Medicines

Only medicines that have been granted a marketing authorisation issued by the European Medicines Evaluation Agency or the Medicines Control Agency may be sold or supplied to the public. Marketing authorisations are issued following scientific assessment on the basis of safety, quality and efficacy.

HEALTH ARRANGEMENTS WITH OTHER COUNTRIES

The member states of the European Economic Area (EEA—see p. 79) have special health arrangements under which EEA nationals resident in a member state are entitled to receive emergency treatment, either free or at a reduced cost, during visits to other EEA countries. Treatment is provided, in most cases, on production of a valid Form E111 which, in the UK, people normally obtain from a post office before travelling. There are also arrangements for people who go to

[1] Sometimes referred to as new variant CJD (nvCJD)

another EEA country specifically for medical care, or who require continuing treatment for a pre-existing condition. Unless falling into an exempt category (for example, foreign students) or covered by an appropriate EC form, visitors to the UK are generally expected to pay for routine, non-emergency treatment, or if the purpose of their visit is to seek specific medical treatment. The UK also has a number of separate bilateral agreements with certain other countries, including Australia and New Zealand.

Further Reading

The NHS Plan: A plan for investment, a plan for reform. Cm 4818. The Stationery Office, 2000.

Department of Health Annual Report 2000. The Government's Expenditure Plans 2000–2001. Cm 4603. The Stationery Office, 2000.

Better Health Better Wales. Cm 3922. The Stationery Office, 1998.

Designed to Care: Renewing the National Health Service in Scotland. Cm 3811. The Stationery Office, 1998.

Fit for the Future (consultation paper on the future of the Health and Personal Social Services in Northern Ireland). The Stationery Office, 1998.

The New NHS: Modern, Dependable. Cm 3807. The Stationery Office, 1997.

NHS Wales—Putting Patients First. Cm 3841. The Stationery Office, 1998.

Our Healthier Nation: A Contract for Health. Cm 3852. The Stationery Office, 1998.

Reducing Health Inequalities: an Action Report. The Stationery Office, 1998.

Report of the Independent Inquiry into Inequalities in Health. The Stationery Office, 1998.

Saving Lives: Our Healthier Nation. Cm 4386. The Stationery Office, 1999.

Teenage Pregnancy. Cm 4342. The Stationery Office, 1999.

Towards a Healthier Scotland. Cm 4269. The Stationery Office, 1999.

Working Together for a Healthier Scotland. Cm 3584. The Stationery Office, 1998.

Annuals

Health and Personal Social Services Statistics for England. The Stationery Office.

Health in Scotland Annual Report. Scottish Executive.

Health Statistics Wales. National Assembly for Wales.

On the State of the Public Health. The Annual Report of the Chief Medical Officer of the Department of Health. The Stationery Office.

Scottish Health Statistics. Information and Statistics Division, National Health Service in Scotland.

Welsh Health: Annual Report of the Chief Medical Officer. National Assembly for Wales.

Website

Department of Health: www.doh.gov.uk

14 Criminal and Civil Justice

The United Kingdom does not have a single legal system. Instead, England and Wales, Scotland and Northern Ireland have their own systems, with considerable differences in law, judicial procedure and court structure. There is, however, substantial similarity on many points and a large volume of modern legislation, including EC legislation, applies throughout the UK. In all three systems there is a common distinction between criminal law and civil law.

Introduction

Criminal and Civil Law

Criminal law deals with wrongs affecting the community for which a prosecution may be brought in the criminal courts. Civil law is about deciding disputes between two or more parties—individuals, companies or other organisations—and for providing a means of legal scrutiny of the actions of public bodies. The purpose of civil proceedings is not to punish, but to obtain compensation or some other appropriate remedy, although in England and Wales the payment of damages may sometimes have a punitive element.

The distinction between civil and criminal matters is not precise. Courts may be classified as criminal courts and civil courts, but in England and Wales, and Northern Ireland, magistrates' courts have both a civil and a criminal jurisdiction as have the sheriff courts in Scotland. Conduct may amount to both a civil and a criminal wrong. However, the court of trial and the rules of procedure and evidence will usually differ in civil and criminal cases.

Sources of Law

Statutes passed by Parliament are the ultimate source of law. There are no legal limits on what may be done by Act of Parliament, although a legal duty exists to comply with European Community (EC) law. A statute may also confer power on a minister, local authority or other executive body to make delegated legislation (see p. 49).

An Order made by a minister of the Crown is the usual means of bringing a modern statute into effect. The Order allows provisions to become effective when practical. Pilot schemes can be set up to test the operation of statutory provisions. Changing policies or circumstances may sometimes mean that provisions are not brought into effect, and may be repealed.

Many key areas of law have, over the centuries, developed through the decisions of the courts. This is known as *common law*. The doctrine of binding precedent means that decisions of higher courts bind those courts lower down in the court hierarchy. This ensures consistency of judicial approach. Judges give reasons for their decisions, and principles of law are stated, developed and modified. When the legality of government action is being tested, a court will try to ensure that it is not overstepping its proper role; it should avoid examining the merits of the particular action or policy being challenged.

European Sources

EC law, which applies in the UK as a member of the European Union (see p. 71), derives from the EC treaties, from the Community legislation adopted under them, and from the decisions of the European Court of Justice. That court has the ultimate authority, under the Treaty of Rome, to decide points of EC law. Where a point arises before a British court, it may refer the point of law to the Court of Justice for it to decide. Sometimes a court is obliged to make a reference to the European Court.

The decisions of the Court of Justice do not directly bind British courts, but the UK is under treaty obligations to uphold EC law. Consequently, British courts are obliged to apply EC law, even at the expense of not applying the provision of an Act of Parliament. If a rule of statute or common law is incompatible with Community law, it is Community law that will be applied by a British court.

European Convention on Human Rights

The European Convention on Human Rights is an international treaty containing a statement of some basic human rights, such as right to life, prohibition of torture, right to a fair trial, right to respect for family and private life, freedom of expression and freedom of assembly. Most Convention rights can be limited by public authorities under certain circumstances. Individual rights sometimes have to be balanced against one another or the wider public interest.

The Convention was ratified by the UK in 1951, but not incorporated into UK domestic law. However, the judgments of the European Court of Human Rights have been binding in international law on the UK, and successive governments have responded to adverse findings by amending domestic law or practice where necessary.

The Human Rights Act 1998, taking full effect on 2 October 2000, requires all public authorities, including courts of law, to act in accordance with the Convention rights (unless an Act of Parliament leaves no choice). It enables individuals to rely on those rights in any legal proceedings and to bring a claim against a public authority which has acted incompatibly with those rights. The Act requires a court to give effect to legislation, as far as possible, in a way that is compatible with Convention rights. A court cannot declare invalid an Act of Parliament which is incompatible with the Convention, but the higher courts may make a declaration of incompatibility. It will be up to Parliament to decide what action to take, if any, following such a declaration.

The Convention is already in force in Scotland in respect of all Acts of the Scottish Parliament.

Personnel of the Law

The law is enforced by judicial officers, ranging from judges in the House of Lords and the superior courts to stipendiary and lay justices who, together with juries in certain cases, are responsible for deciding disputed cases. The law also depends on officers of the court who have general or specialised functions of an administrative, and sometimes of a judicial, nature in the courts to which they are attached.

Judges are legally qualified, being appointed from the ranks of practising barristers and advocates or solicitors. They have independence of office, and can be removed only in rare and limited circumstances involving misconduct or incapacity. They are not subject to ministerial control or direction.

Lay magistrates in England and Wales, and justices of the peace in Scotland, are trained in order to give them sufficient knowledge of the law, including the rules of evidence, and of the nature and purpose of sentencing. There are over 30,000 lay magistrates and 90 stipendiary—legally qualified and salaried—magistrates in England and Wales, and 4,000 justices of the peace in Scotland. In Northern Ireland there are 17 resident magistrates (drawn from practising solicitors or barristers, with powers similar to those of stipendiary magistrates) and 21 deputy (part-time) magistrates. Although people are free to conduct their own cases if they so wish, barristers (in Scotland, advocates) and solicitors, or other authorised litigators, generally represent the interests of parties to a dispute. There are over 10,000 practising barristers in England and Wales and around 80,000 practising solicitors. Scotland has over 400 practising advocates and some 8,250 solicitors; in Northern Ireland there are about 450 barristers. Barristers practise as individuals, but join a group of other barristers, in Chambers. Advocates in Scotland practise as individuals; they do not operate from Chambers and work independently of each other. Solicitors usually operate in partnership with other solicitors, unless employed. Large firms of solicitors will comprise not only qualified staff, but also legal executives and support staff. Certain legal functions may be performed by non-lawyers—licensed conveyancers (qualified conveyancers in Scotland) can act in conveyancing matters (the transfer of interests in land).

Traditionally, rights of audience in the higher courts—the Judicial Committee of the Privy Council, House of Lords, Court of Appeal, High Court and Crown Court, High Court of Justiciary (Scotland) and Court of Session (Scotland)—have mostly been limited to barristers and advocates, who are regarded as specialist court pleaders. However, legislation in 1990 opened the door for other professional bodies to apply to become authorised to grant their members rights of audience in the higher courts. In 1993 it became possible for solicitors in private practice to obtain the same rights of audience as barristers and advocates. In 1999 the Institute of Legal Executives and the Chartered Institute of Patent Agents were authorised to grant rights of audience to their members. The Access to Justice Act 1999 (not applicable in Scotland) established the principle that all barristers and solicitors should acquire full rights of audience on call to the Bar or admission to the Roll. It also extended the ability for employed barristers and solicitors to acquire rights of audience in the higher courts, to which they had previously been excluded.

The two branches of the profession have separate professional bodies: the Bar Council for barristers (in Scotland, the Faculty of Advocates); and the Law Society of England and Wales, Law Society of Scotland and Law Society of Northern Ireland for solicitors. The profession is self-regulating, with the professional bodies exercising disciplinary control over their members.

The Legal Services Ombudsman for England and Wales oversees the way in which relevant professional bodies handle complaints about barristers, solicitors, legal executives, licensed conveyancers and patent agents. The Scottish Legal Services Ombudsman performs a similar task. In Northern Ireland there is a Lay Observer with somewhat lesser powers.

Crime in the UK

Crime Statistics

There are two main measures of the scale of crime in the UK: the recording of crimes by the police, and periodic surveys which ask representative samples of the population about their experiences of crime.

Recorded Crime

In the year ended March 2000 in England and Wales:

- overall recorded crime totalled 5.3 million offences, representing an increase of 3.8 per cent over the previous 12 months (see Table 14.1);
- the overall clear-up rate was 25 per cent;
- about 83 per cent of offences recorded by the police were against property, while 13 per cent involved violence; and

Table 14.1: Notifiable Crimes Recorded by the Police in England and Wales for the Year ended March 2000 *Thousands*

Offence group	**1999–2000**
Violence against the person	581.0
Sexual offences	37.8
Burglary	906.5
Robbery	84.3
Theft and handling stolen goods	2,223.6
Fraud and forgery	334.8
Criminal damage	945.7
Drug offences	121.9
Other	65.7
Total	**5,301.2**

Source: Home Office

- theft of, or from, vehicles accounted for about 20 per cent of all recorded crimes.

Notifiable offences recorded by the police broadly cover the more serious offences. In 1998 the Government amended the way notifiable offences are recorded in England and Wales, changing the counting rules so that the number of crimes corresponds more closely to the number of victims. In 1999 there was a change in the way clear-ups are counted, with some circumstances no longer qualifying as clear-ups.

In Scotland there were 436,000 crimes recorded by the police in 1999, an increase of 1 per cent compared with 1998. The overall crime clear-up rate was 43 per cent.

Recorded crime in Northern Ireland in 1999–2000 totalled 119,000 offences. About 71 per cent of recorded offences were against property. The overall clear-up rate was 30 per cent.

Principal Crime Surveys

The British Crime Survey (BCS) is a large household survey first conducted in 1982, which has a sample representative of people aged 16 and over in private households in England and Wales. The BCS asks respondents whether they have experienced certain personal and household crimes in the preceding year, regardless of whether or not they reported the incident to the police. The survey therefore provides a measure of those crimes not reported to, or recorded by, the police. The latest BCS, published in October 2000, estimated that there were 14.7 million crimes in 1999, 10 per cent lower than in 1997. Burglary was down 21 per cent from 1997 (to its lowest level since 1991) and theft of vehicles decreased by 11 per cent from its 1997 level. The number of violent crimes fell by 4 per cent. The proportion of people who were victims of some type of crime once or more during 1999 fell from 34 to 30 per cent.

The 1996 Scottish Crime Survey estimated that just under 1 million crimes were committed against individuals and private households in Scotland during 1995. This was 8 per cent fewer than the number estimated in the 1993 survey.

Crime Reduction

Within the Home Office, the Crime Reduction Unit aims to encourage and develop strategies and tactics to reduce crime. The Unit supports the police crime reduction effort through its Crime Prevention College (in North Yorkshire), which is the national centre for training police officers in prevention skills. Since April 2000 every police authority and crime and disorder reduction partnership (see p. 214) has been asked to set five-year targets for the reduction of two key offences—vehicle crime and domestic burglary—and five metropolitan forces have been set the additional target of reducing street robberies.

Crime reduction initiatives include:

- a £250 million Crime Reduction Programme, announced in 1998, which focuses on reducing burglary and promoting targeted policing;
- a £150 million investment in closed-circuit television (CCTV) surveillance systems in public areas such as housing estates, shopping centres, railway stations and car parks;
- Neighbourhood Watch schemes, in which residents look out for suspicious activity in their area and inform the police;

- crime reduction action teams, which meet regularly to examine crime problems in their area and to suggest practical solutions;
- youth action groups, encouraging young people to tackle problems relevant to them—for example bullying, vandalism or drug misuse; and
- partnerships set up under the Crime and Disorder Act 1998, which bring together the police, local authorities and other relevant agencies to develop strategies for dealing with local crime problems.

The Scottish Crime Prevention Council has been disbanded and will be replaced by the Scottish Community Safety Forum. In Northern Ireland, there is a Crime Prevention Panel.

Crime and Disorder Act 1998

The Crime and Disorder Act 1998 has created a framework that aims to keep individuals, particularly young offenders, out of the criminal justice system, and to ensure timely action to prevent reoffending. Particular emphasis is placed on preventing offending behaviour by persons under 18 (see p. 223).

The Act requires police services and local authorities in England and Wales to develop statutory partnerships for crime prevention and the promotion of community safety. The partnerships must examine local levels of crime and disorder, consult local people and then set targets for tackling the problems that have been identified. The statutory provisions do not, however, apply to Scotland, where police forces and local authorities already enter into such partnerships.

Prohibitive anti-social behaviour orders (ASBOs) may be applied to individuals or groups whose threatening and disruptive conduct harasses the local community. Anyone in breach of such an order is guilty of a criminal offence. The Act also empowers the courts to grant an order against convicted sex offenders, prohibiting behaviour which causes concern for public safety (for example, loitering near schools). Anti-social behaviour orders and sex offender orders are applicable throughout the UK. By September 2000, around 50 ASBOs had been issued.

Helping Victims and Witnesses

In England and Wales a government-funded organisation, Victim Support, provides practical help and emotional support to victims of crime with the help of 16,000 volunteers. It also runs the Witness Service, which advises victims and other witnesses attending Crown Court centres (and is developing similar services in magistrates' courts). Victim Support Scotland provides a volunteer-based service similar to that provided by Victim Support in England and Wales. A separate scheme operates in Northern Ireland.

In 1998 the Government published a report—*Speaking up for Justice*—on improving the treatment of witnesses (including children) who become involved in the criminal justice system in England and Wales. Twenty-six of the report's recommendations required statutory force and were included in the Youth Justice and Criminal Evidence Act 1999. The implementation plan includes:

- pagers for intimidated witnesses so that they do not have to wait at court buildings in the same room as the defendant (introduced at the end of 1999);
- a ban on the cross-examination of victims of rape and serious sexual assault by unrepresented defendants, and greater restrictions on questioning a rape victim about their sexual history (introduced in April 2000);
- video-recorded evidence, live CCTV links, screens and communication aids for adult and child witnesses likely to be distressed by facing the defendant in court (to be introduced by the end of 2000 in the Crown Court); and
- new measures to help child and adult witnesses including video-recorded pre-trial cross-examination, and intermediaries to help them give evidence and understand questioning.

Blameless victims of violent crime in England, Wales and Scotland may be eligible for compensation from public funds under the Criminal Injuries Compensation Scheme. In Northern Ireland there are separate statutory arrangements for compensation for criminal injuries, and for malicious damage to property.

Drug Misuse

In 1998 there were around 140,000 seizures of illegal drugs in the UK, and a similar number of drug-related offences. The Government's UK Anti-Drugs Co-ordinator was appointed in that year to co-ordinate the fight against illegal drugs and draw up a national strategy (*Tackling Drugs to Build a Better Britain*). This cross-government strategy—focusing mainly on England, but reflecting the UK and international dimension of the problem—has four main elements:

- helping young people resist drug misuse in order to achieve their full potential in society;
- protecting communities from drug-related anti-social and criminal behaviour;
- enabling people to overcome drug problems through treatment; and
- stifling the availability of illegal drugs on the streets.

The Crime and Disorder Act 1998 introduced drug treatment and testing orders, targeted at persistent offenders (aged 16 and over) with drug problems who show a willingness to co-operate with treatment. The orders are coming into effect across England and Wales from October 2000.

The Drugs Prevention Advisory Service (DPAS) was launched in April 1999 to promote community-based drugs prevention at local, regional and national level in line with the objectives of the Government's national strategy. In particular, the DPAS provides information, advice and support to local Drug Action Teams (the bodies charged with local implementation of the national strategy) to encourage good drugs prevention practice based on available and emerging evidence, and promotes consistent and coherent prevention policy across Government. DPAS teams have been established in each of the nine Government Regions in England.

In an effort to reduce the availability of drugs in Scotland and to target organised drug crime, the Scottish Drug Enforcement Agency was launched in June 2000.

Countering Terrorism

In the light of serious terrorist attacks that have taken place in the UK, it has been the Government's view that the ordinary criminal law is not sufficient to deal with terrorism effectively. The law has been supplemented by the Prevention of Terrorism (Temporary Provisions) Act 1989 (PTA) and successive Northern Ireland (Emergency Provisions) Acts (EPA), and more recently amended and reinforced by the Criminal Justice (Terrorism and Conspiracy) Act 1998 (see below).

The PTA has a UK-wide application while the EPA applies only in Northern Ireland. Both Acts are temporary and must be renewed by Parliament each year. They are intended to strike a balance between providing powers that are necessary to protect the public and safeguarding the rights of individuals. They give the security forces wider powers to question and arrest people suspected of involvement in terrorism and to search property, including vehicles.

The Criminal Justice (Terrorism and Conspiracy) Act 1998 aimed to underpin the Good Friday Agreement in Northern Ireland (see p. 16) by making it easier to secure the conviction of members of proscribed organisations which are not observing a complete and unequivocal ceasefire. It also made it an offence to conspire in the UK to commit terrorist or other serious offences in another country.

With the aim of rationalising these arrangements, the Terrorism Act 2000 is introducing permanent UK-wide counter-terrorism legislation, providing for:

- the adoption of a new definition of terrorism (including ideological and religious motivation for terrorist acts) which would extend to domestic as well as Irish and international terrorism;
- a new offence of inciting terrorist acts abroad from within the UK;
- stronger powers for dealing with terrorist fund-raising;

- a new judicial authority to consider applications for extensions of detention of terrorist suspects; and
- a review of the provisions of the Criminal Justice (Terrorism and Conspiracy) Act 1998.

Exclusion order powers under the current legislation are not carried forward into the new legislation.

The Regulation of Investigatory Powers Act 2000 provides for the closer regulation of telephone tapping, surveillance and encryption (decoding e-mail messages) activities carried out by law enforcement agencies. One of the aims of the Act is to ensure that law enforcement operations are consistent with the duties imposed on public authorities by the European Convention on Human Rights and the Human Rights Act 1998.

Police Service

Government ministers, together with police authorities and chief constables, are responsible for providing an effective and efficient police service in the UK.

Organisation

There are 52 police forces organised on a local basis—43 in England and Wales, eight in Scotland and one (the Royal Ulster Constabulary—RUC) in Northern Ireland. The Metropolitan Police Service and the City of London force are responsible for policing London.

Police strength in England and Wales is about 124,400 (of which the Metropolitan Police numbers around 25,500). There are some 14,700 officers in Scotland and 8,400 (plus 3,800 reserves) in the RUC. Each force in Great Britain has volunteer special constables who perform police duties in their spare time, without pay, acting in support of regular officers. They number about 20,000 in all.

Policing in Northern Ireland is undergoing considerable change as a result of a report by the independent Patten Commission. This was set up under the terms of the Good Friday Agreement of April 1998. The Patten Commission reported in September 1999 and, in accepting the report, the Government brought forward a Police Bill to implement changes which will require a change in law (see p. 20). Other non-statutory administrative and structural changes to policing are already under way.

Police forces are maintained in England and Wales by local police authorities. In the 41 police areas outside London, they normally have 17 members—nine locally elected councillors, three magistrates and five independent members. In July 2000 the Home Secretary's duties as the police authority for the Metropolitan Police District were assumed by a new Metropolitan Police Authority (MPA), the majority of whose 23 members are elected representatives from the London Assembly. For the City of London Police Area, the authority is the Common Council of the Corporation of London. Police authorities, in consultation with the chief constables and local community, set local policing objectives, while the Government sets key objectives for the police as a whole. The police authorities in Scotland are composed of elected councillors. In Northern Ireland the Secretary of State appoints the Police Authority (although a new Policing Board is due to replace the Authority in 2001 as part of the Patten reforms).

Police forces are headed by chief constables (in London the Commissioner of the City of London Police, and the Commissioner of the Metropolitan Police), appointed by their police authorities with government approval. They are responsible for the direction and control of their forces and for the appointment, promotion and discipline of all ranks below assistant chief constable. On matters of efficiency they are generally answerable to their police authorities.

Independent inspectors of constabulary report on the efficiency and effectiveness of police forces.

National Crime Bodies

The National Criminal Intelligence Service (NCIS), which was put on an independent statutory footing in 1998, has the leading role in collecting and analysing criminal intelligence for use by police forces and other law enforcement agencies in the UK. It has a headquarters and south-east regional office in London, five other regional offices in England and offices in Scotland and Northern Ireland. NCIS co-ordinates the activities of the Security Services in support of the law enforcement agencies against organised crime, and liaises with the International Criminal Police Organisation (INTERPOL), which promotes international co-operation between police forces. It also provides the channel for communication between the UK and EUROPOL (see p. 90).

In 1998 a National Crime Squad, with 1,400 officers, replaced six regional crime squads in England and Wales. Its role is to prevent and detect organised and serious crime across police force and national boundaries and to support provincial forces in their investigation of serious crime. The Scottish Crime Squad performs the same function in Scotland.

Forensic Science Service (FSS)

The FSS, a Home Office executive agency, provides scientific support in the investigation of crime to police forces in England and Wales through six regional laboratories. It also operates the national DNA database, which provides intelligence information to police forces by matching DNA profiles taken from suspects to profiles from samples left at the scenes of crime. In Scotland forensic science services are provided by forces' own laboratories. Northern Ireland has its own laboratory.

Powers and Procedures

England and Wales

Police powers and procedures are defined by legislation and accompanying codes of practice. Evidence obtained in breach of the codes may be ruled inadmissible in court. The codes must be accessible in all police stations.

- *Stop and search*—Police officers can stop and search people and vehicles if they reasonably suspect that they will find stolen goods, offensive weapons or implements that could be used for burglary and other offences. An officer must record the grounds for the search, and anything found, and the person stopped is entitled to a copy of the officer's report.
- *Arrest*—The police may arrest a suspect on a warrant issued by a court, but can arrest without warrant for *arrestable* offences (for which the sentence is fixed by law or for which the term of imprisonment is five years or more). This category includes *serious arrestable* offences such as murder and rape. There is a general power of arrest for all other offences if it is inappropriate to proceed by way of a court summons, or if an officer believes a suspect may injure someone else or damage property.
- *Detention and questioning*—Suspects must be cautioned before the police can ask any questions about an offence. They must be told that they do not have to say anything, but that anything they do say may be given in evidence in court, and that it may be harmful to their defence if they fail to mention something during questioning which they later rely on in court. For *arrestable* offences, a suspect can be detained in police custody without charge for up to 24 hours. Someone suspected of a *serious arrestable* offence can be held for up to 96 hours, but not beyond 36 hours unless a warrant is obtained from a magistrates' court.

  If someone thinks that his or her detention is unlawful, he or she may apply to the High Court for a writ of *habeas corpus* against the person responsible, requiring them to appear before the court to justify the detention. *Habeas corpus* proceedings take precedence over others.
- *Charging*—Once there is sufficient evidence, the police have to decide whether a detained person should be charged with an offence. If the police institute criminal proceedings against a

suspect, the CPS (see p. 220) then takes control of the case.

Scotland and Northern Ireland

The police in Scotland can arrest someone without a warrant, under wide common law powers, if suspects are seen or reported as committing a crime or are a danger to themselves or others. They also have specific statutory powers of arrest for some offences. In other cases they may apply to a justice of the peace for a warrant. As in England and Wales, Scottish police have powers to enter a building without a warrant if they are pursuing someone who has committed, or attempted to commit, a serious crime. A court can grant the police a warrant to search premises for stated items in connection with a crime, again as in England and Wales. The police may search anyone suspected of carrying an offensive weapon. Someone suspected of an imprisonable offence may be held for police questioning without being arrested, but for no more than six hours without being charged. If arrested, suspects must be charged and cautioned. The case is then referred to the procurator fiscal (see p. 227).

The law in Northern Ireland relating to police powers in the investigation of crime and to evidence in criminal proceedings is similar to that in force in England and Wales.

Firearms

The policy in Great Britain is that the police should not generally be armed but that there should be specialist firearms officers, deployed on the authority of a senior officer where an operational need arises. In 1998–99 there were over 11,000 operations in Great Britain where firearms were issued to the police. Most forces operate armed response vehicles to contain firearms incidents. In Northern Ireland police officers are issued with firearms for their personal protection.

Police Discipline

An officer may be prosecuted if suspected of a criminal offence. Officers are also subject to a code of conduct. If found guilty of breaching the code, an officer can be dismissed.

Revised conduct and efficiency arrangements for England and Wales came into effect in April 1999. The main changes include introducing the civil standard of proof at disciplinary hearings; a fast-track procedure to deal with officers caught committing serious criminal offences; and separate formal procedures (for the first time) for dealing with unsatisfactory performance.

Complaints

Members of the public can make complaints against the police if they feel that they have been treated unfairly or improperly. In England and Wales the investigation of such complaints by the force concerned is overseen, or in more serious cases supervised, by the Police Complaints Authority. In 1998–99 over 30,000 complaints were handled by the Authority, less than 3 per cent of which were substantiated. In Scotland complaints of misconduct against police officers are overseen by chief constables. Police authorities have statutory responsibility for dealing with complaints against chief officers. Allegations of criminal misconduct are referred to the procurator fiscal for investigation. HM Inspectorate of Constabulary for Scotland also considers representations from complainants dissatisfied with the way the police have handled their complaints. In Northern Ireland the Independent Commission for Police Complaints has been superseded by a Police Ombudsman.

Community Relations

Within every police authority there are police/community liaison consultative arrangements, involving representatives from the police, local government and community groups. Home Office and police service initiatives have sought to ensure that racist crime is treated as a police priority.

The need to recruit more members of the ethnic minorities to the police service, and retain them, has been recognised. In England and Wales there are about 2,570 officers from ethnic minorities (2 per cent of police numbers in England and Wales). The corresponding figure for Scotland is about 50 (less than 1 per cent of police numbers). In April 1999 the Government set new targets for the number of ethnic minority officers in England and Wales (with the basic aim of achieving a similar proportion of ethnic minority officers to that of the population in a particular police force area).

Dealing with Racism

In March 1999 the Government announced an action plan to take forward the recommendations of the Stephen Lawrence inquiry[1] to restore confidence in policing and counter racism in England and Wales. By mid-2000 measures being introduced to that end included:

- an extension of the race relations legislation—through the Race Relations (Amendment) Bill, currently before Parliament—which would make direct and indirect discrimination in all public authorities unlawful, and place a duty on public authorities to promote race equality;
- citizenship classes in schools, to be introduced into the National Curriculum (see p. 126) in 2002, to ensure that pupils are taught about the cultural diversity of Britain;
- the setting of targets for the recruitment and retention of ethnic minorities in the Civil Service and other public bodies;
- the introduction of specific criminal offences of racially aggravated violence, harassment and criminal damage; and
- a programme of research into the use by the police of their powers to stop and search people (with the aim of ensuring these powers are used fairly).

[1] In 1993 a young black student, Stephen Lawrence, was murdered in a racist attack in south-east London. Concerns about inadequacies in the investigation of the case by the Metropolitan Police Service led ultimately to an official inquiry, which reported in February 1999. The report was critical, with some exceptions, of police conduct, claiming there was a combination of professional incompetence, institutional racism and a failure of leadership by senior officers.

In July 1999 the Scottish Executive published a separate action plan to implement the recommendations of the inquiry in Scotland.

Legal System of England and Wales

Responsibility for the administration and management of the English legal system is divided between various government departments and agencies.

The *Lord Chancellor* is the head of the judiciary and sits as a member of the judicial committee of the House of Lords. He also presides over the House of Lords in its legislative capacity, and is a senior Cabinet minister heading a government department. The Lord Chancellor's Department has overall responsibility (exercised through the Court Service) for the court system, including the Supreme Court (comprising the Court of Appeal, High Court and Crown Court) and the county courts in England and Wales. The Lord Chancellor advises the Crown on the appointment of most members of the higher judiciary, and appoints most magistrates. In addition, he has responsibility for the civil justice process, for promoting general reforms of the civil law and for the legal aid arrangements.

The *Home Secretary* has overall responsibility for criminal law, the police service, the prison system, the probation service, and for advising the Crown on the exercise of the royal prerogative of mercy.

The *Attorney-General* and the *Solicitor-General* are the Government's principal legal advisers, providing advice on a range of legal matters, including proposed legislation. They may represent the Crown in appropriate domestic and international cases of difficulty or public importance, although do not always do so. As well as exercising various civil law functions, the Attorney-General has final responsibility for enforcing the criminal law. The Solicitor-General is the Attorney-General's deputy.

The Crown Prosecution Service is headed by the *Director of Public Prosecutions (DPP)*, who is accountable to the Attorney-General.

Structure of the Courts in England and Wales

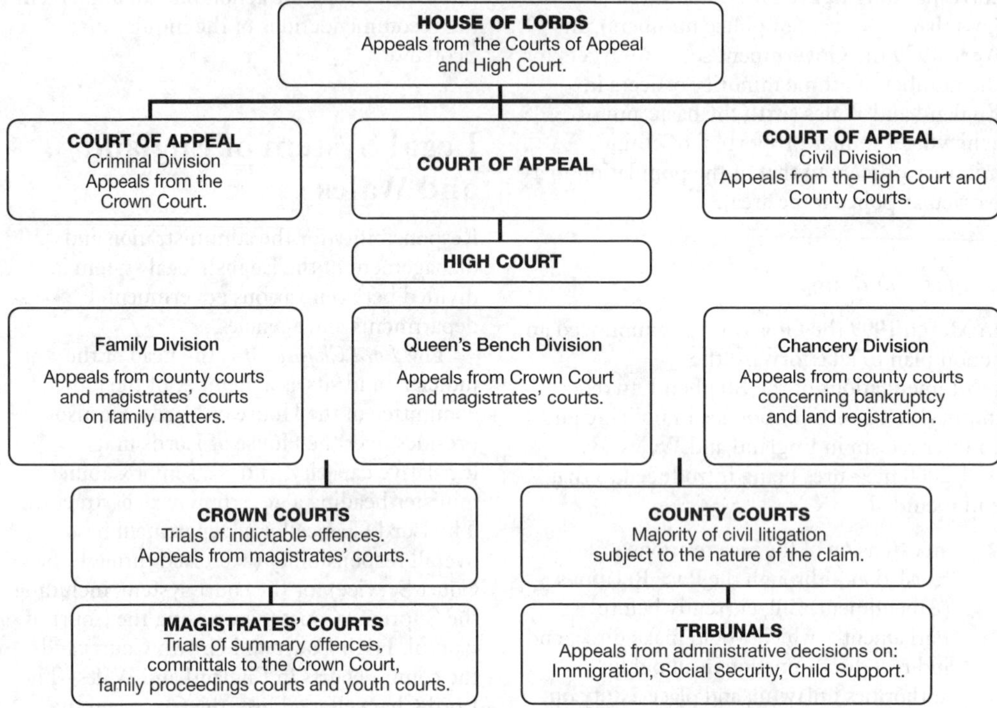

Other prosecuting authorities include the Serious Fraud Office, which answers to the Attorney-General, and bodies such as the Inland Revenue, Customs and Excise Commissioners, local authorities and trading standards departments which prosecute cases within their own sphere of activity. Private prosecutions by individuals are permitted in respect of most crimes, but some require the consent of the Attorney-General and they may be taken over by the DPP.

Some administrative functions are performed by senior members of the judiciary: the Lord Chief Justice,[2] for example, has some responsibilities for the organisation and work of the criminal courts. Other functions are performed by statutory committees. The Civil Procedure Rules Committee, created by the Civil Procedure Act 1997, is responsible for making rules that govern the civil justice process, and comprises members of the judiciary, members of the legal profession and lay representatives.

Responsibility for the management of functions often lies with executive bodies or agencies. Examples include the Prison Service, the Forensic Science Service, and the Youth Justice Board.

The Government is advised by a range of bodies of a statutory and non-statutory nature. These include the police inspectorates, the magistrates' courts service, the probation service, the Audit Commission, the Criminal Justice Consultative Committee, law reform bodies such as the Law Commission and *ad hoc* Royal Commissions and departmental committees.

PROSECUTION AND THE CRIMINAL COURTS

Prosecution Arrangements

Crown Prosecution Service

The CPS is the government department responsible for prosecuting people in England

[2] The Lord Chief Justice is head of the Queen's Bench Division of the High Court, and ranks second only to the Lord Chancellor in the judicial hierarchy.

and Wales who have been charged with a criminal offence. It works closely with the police, but is an independent body. With headquarters in London and York, the service operates under a structure (introduced in April 1999) of 42 geographical Areas in England and Wales. The Areas correspond to the 43 police forces in England and Wales, with the CPS London Area covering the operational boundaries of both City of London and Metropolitan Police Forces. Each Area is headed by a Chief Crown Prosecutor (CCP), who is responsible for prosecutions within the Area, supported by an Area Business Manager. The CPS:

- advises the police on possible prosecutions;
- reviews prosecutions started by the police to ensure that the right defendants are prosecuted on the right charges before the appropriate court;
- prepares cases for court; and
- prosecutes cases at magistrates' courts and instructs counsel to prosecute cases in the Crown Court and higher courts.[3]

The decision by the CPS on whether or not to go ahead with a case is based on two criteria. Crown Prosecutors must be satisfied that there is enough evidence to provide a realistic prospect of conviction against each defendant on each charge. If there is enough evidence, prosecutors must then decide whether a prosecution is in the public interest. A prosecution will usually take place unless there are public interest factors against it clearly outweighing those in favour.

Serious Fraud Office

Cases of serious or complex fraud are prosecuted by the Serious Fraud Office. Investigations are conducted by teams of lawyers, accountants, police officers and other specialists. The Office has wide powers that go beyond those normally available to the police and prosecuting authorities.

[3] Under a change in legal rules, a number of CPS lawyers are now qualified to appear in some cases in the Crown Court and other higher courts.

Initial Stages

For minor offences, the police may decide to caution the offender rather than prosecute. A caution does not amount to a conviction, and will not take place unless the person admits the offence. Under the Crime and Disorder Act 1998, cautioning for young offenders is being replaced with the final warning scheme (see p. 224).

If the police decide to charge a person, that person may be released on bail to attend a magistrates' court. If not granted police bail, the defendant must be brought before a magistrates' court (or, if under 18, a youth court) as soon as possible. There is a general right to bail, but magistrates may withhold bail if there are grounds for believing that an accused person would abscond, commit an offence, or otherwise obstruct justice. If bail is refused, an accused has the right to apply again, subject to certain limitations, to the Crown Court or to a High Court judge. In certain circumstances, the prosecution may appeal to a Crown Court judge against the granting of bail by magistrates.

Once a person has been charged, it is for the CPS to decide whether the case should proceed.

Criminal Courts

Criminal offences are divided into: *summary* offences, which are the least serious and are triable only in a magistrates' court; and *indictable* ones, which are subdivided into 'indictable-only' offences (such as murder, manslaughter or robbery) which must be tried on indictment[4] at the Crown Court by judge and jury, and *either-way* offences, which may be tried either summarily or on indictment. Either-way offences, such as theft and burglary, can vary greatly in seriousness. A magistrates' court decides whether an either-way case is serious enough to warrant trial in the Crown Court, but if the magistrates decide in favour of summary trial, the accused person can elect to have trial by jury in the Crown Court (although this right would be abolished under legislation currently before Parliament—see p. 222).

[4] An indictment is a written accusation against a person, charging him or her with serious crime triable by jury.

Where a case is to be tried on indictment, the magistrates' court must be satisfied that there is a case to answer. In most cases this is accepted by the defence and the magistrates do not need to consider the evidence. If the defence challenges the case, the magistrates consider the documentary evidence: no witnesses are called to give evidence. If there is a case to be answered, the accused is committed for trial.

A magistrates' court usually comprises three lay magistrates, known as justices of the peace (JPs), who sit with a court clerk to advise them on law and procedure. In some areas a stipendiary (paid professional) magistrate sits instead of the JPs. Stipendiary magistrates are becoming increasingly common, although most cases are still dealt with by lay magistrates.

Responsibility for running the magistrates' courts service locally rests with magistrates' courts committees (MCCs), made up of lay magistrates selected by their colleagues. The number of MCCs is being reduced, and their areas increased, to improve efficiency and to bring their boundaries into closer alignment with those of other criminal justice agencies, such as the police and CPS.

Youth courts are specialist magistrates' courts, which sit separately from those dealing with adults. They deal with all but the most serious charges against people aged at least ten (the age of criminal responsibility) and under 18. JPs who have been specially trained sit in youth courts. Proceedings are held in private.

The Crown Court sits at about 90 venues, in six regional areas called circuits, and is presided over by High Court judges, circuit judges and part-time recorders. The type of judge who will preside over a case, with a jury of 12 members of the public, will depend on which Crown Court the case is being heard in: not all Crown Courts deal with cases of the same level of seriousness.

An independent review of the practices and procedures of, and the rules of evidence applied by, the criminal courts in England and Wales was announced by the Lord Chancellor in December 1999. The review is expected to report around the end of 2000.

> In 1998 nearly 2 million defendants were dealt with at magistrates' courts, while 100,000 were dealt with in the Crown Court. The Government is proposing to transfer the decision on mode of trial in either-way offences from the defendant to the court. The Criminal Justice (Mode of Trial) Bill sought to provide that the decision where either-way cases are heard should rest with the courts, and that the defendant's right to elect Crown Court trial should be removed. In September 2000 this Bill was rejected by the House of Lords.

Trial

Criminal trials have two parties: the prosecution and the defence. The law presumes the innocence of an accused person until guilt has been proved beyond reasonable doubt by the prosecution. Accused people have a right at all stages to remain silent; however, an adverse inference may be drawn from their failure to mention facts when questioned which they later rely upon in their defence. There are rules governing the pre-trial disclosure of material by both the prosecution and the defence. A judge may, in a case to be tried on indictment, hold a preliminary hearing, where pleas of guilty or not guilty are taken. If the defendant pleads guilty the judge will proceed to sentence. In contested cases, the prosecution and defence are expected to help the judge in identifying key issues, and to provide any additional information required for the proper and efficient trial of the case.

Criminal trials normally take place in open court. The burden of proof is on the prosecution, and strict rules of evidence govern how matters may be proved. Certain types of evidence may be excluded because of their prejudicial effect, or because of their unreliability. Documentary statements by witnesses are allowed with the consent of the other party or in limited circumstances at the discretion of the court. Otherwise evidence is taken from witnesses testifying orally on oath. Child witnesses may testify without taking the oath and their evidence must be received by the court unless the child is incapable of giving intelligible testimony. A child in some circumstances can testify through a live TV link, and the court may consider a video-recorded interview as the evidence of the child, subject to the defence having the right to question the child in cross-examination. Further measures to help both child witnesses and adult vulnerable or intimidated witnesses to give their best evidence in court are being introduced under the Youth Justice and Criminal Evidence Act 1999 (see p. 225).

The Jury

In jury trials the judge decides questions of law, sums up the case to the jury, and discharges or sentences the accused. The jury is responsible for deciding questions of fact. The jury verdict may be 'guilty' or 'not guilty', the latter resulting in acquittal. Juries may, subject to certain conditions, reach a verdict by a majority of at least 10–2.

If an accused person is acquitted, there is no right of prosecution appeal, and the accused cannot be tried again for that same offence. However, an acquittal may be set aside and a retrial ordered if the acquittal has been tainted by a conviction for interfering with or intimidating a juror.

A jury is independent of the judiciary and any attempt to interfere with its members is a criminal offence. People aged between 18 and 70 whose names appear on the electoral register are, with certain exceptions, liable for jury service; they are chosen at random.

Sentencing

The court will sentence the offender after considering all the relevant information, which may include a pre-sentence report and any other necessary specialist report, and a plea in mitigation by a defence advocate. The powers of the magistrates' court in respect of sentence are limited to a maximum period of six months' imprisonment. The offender may be sent to the Crown Court for sentence if the magistrates feel their powers of sentence are insufficient.

A custodial sentence can be imposed only where the offence is so serious that a custodial sentence alone is justified. In 1998, 7 per cent of males and 3 per cent of females found guilty of all offences received a custodial sentence. A term of up to two years' imprisonment may be suspended. Courts are required to impose minimum three-year sentences on offenders convicted of a third offence of domestic burglary. A second serious violent or sexual offence requires a court to impose a life sentence unless there are exceptional circumstances. Life imprisonment is the mandatory sentence for murder, and is available for certain other serious offences.

Community sentences may include probation orders (involving supervision in the community—see p. 231); community service orders (unpaid work within the community); combination orders (elements of both probation supervision and community service work); curfew orders (requiring the offender to remain at a specified place for specified periods, usually monitored by electronic tagging); and drug treatment and testing orders. Punishment for breach of community orders is under review.

A fine is the most common punishment, with most offenders fined for summary offences. A court may also impose compensation orders, which require the offender to pay compensation for personal injury, loss or damage resulting from an offence; or impose a conditional discharge, whereby the offender may be resentenced for the original offence if the discharge is broken by reoffending.

In May 2000 the Government announced a review of the legal framework for sentencing and its impact on reducing reoffending. The review will explore the possibility of introducing more flexible sentencing options which link up custodial and community penalties.

Young Offenders

Offenders aged ten to 17 years come within the jurisdiction of youth courts, but may also be tried in an adult magistrates' court or in a Crown Court, depending on the nature of the offence.

Custodial sentences are available to the courts where no alternative is considered appropriate. The main custodial sentence for those aged 15 and over is currently detention in a young offender institution. Remission of

Table 14.2 Offenders sentenced for Indictable Offences, England and Wales: by Type of Offence and Type of Sentence, 1998–99

Offence group	Discharge	Fine	Community sentence	Immediate custody	Other	All sentenced
Theft and handling stolen goods	31,023	31,261	38,592	21,818	1,998	125,247
Drug offences	7,354	23,455	8,622	8,458	452	48,783
Violence against the person	5,752	4,866	13,800	11,077	1,013	37,119
Burglary	2,515	1,285	12,264	14,547	313	31,087
Fraud and forgery	3,800	3,457	7,573	4,130	272	19,645
Criminal damage	2,963	1,960	3,877	1,176	686	10,722
Motoring	513	5,036	1,812	1,554	51	9,016
Robbery	143	23	1,356	3,962	62	5,562
Sexual offences	249	291	1,176	2,687	76	4,590
Other offences	6,160	22,958	7,957	7,903	3,940	49,331
All indictable offences	**60,472**	**94,592**	**97,029**	**77,312**	**8,863**	**341,102**

Source: Home Office

part of the sentence for good behaviour, release on parole and supervision on release are available. A secure training order may be given to those persistent offenders aged 12 to 14 who fulfil certain strict criteria.

Non-custodial penalties include: conditional discharge; fines and compensation orders (where the parents of offenders may be ordered to pay); supervision orders (where the offender would have to comply with certain requirements, which might include a stay in local authority accommodation); and attendance centre orders. Those aged 16 or 17 may also be given the same probation, community service, combination and curfew orders as older offenders.

A number of measures taken under the Crime and Disorder Act 1998 aim to prevent offending and reoffending by young people. Local authorities are required to produce annual youth justice plans detailing how youth justice services in their areas are provided and funded. They must also establish one or more youth offending teams, with membership drawn from the police, social services, the probation service, health and education authorities and, if considered appropriate locally, the voluntary sector. As well as supervising existing community sentences, these teams provide and supervise a range of new orders and powers under the Act (see below).

The 1998 legislation provides for a statutory final warning scheme to replace the practice of repeat cautioning by the police; this began in June 2000. The scheme is intended to provide a swift response to early incidences of criminal behaviour, and a final warning will also trigger referral to a youth offending team to draw up a rehabilitation programme to address the factors which led the young person into offending.

New orders include: a *reparation order*, which requires young offenders to make non-financial reparation to the victim(s) of their offence or to the community which they have harmed; and an *action plan order*, which requires them to comply with an individually tailored action plan intended to address their offending behaviour. These new orders took effect nationally from June 2000. In addition, a *detention and training order*, combining custody and community supervision, came into force in April 2000.

The new criminal orders are complemented by a range of other powers. These include *parenting orders*, which require a parent or guardian to attend counselling and guidance sessions, and may direct them to comply with specified requirements; and *child safety orders*, which place a child under ten who is at risk of becoming involved in crime or is behaving in an anti-social manner under the supervision of a specified, responsible officer. Both orders also took effect in June 2000.

Furthermore, under the provisions of the Youth Justice and Criminal Evidence Act 1999, young offenders convicted in court for the first time and pleading guilty, in specified pilot areas, can be sentenced to referral to a panel of expert youth workers and local community representatives (unless the crime is serious enough to warrant custody). The referral orders will last between three and 12 months, with the panel establishing a programme of corrective reparation in order to tackle the offending behaviour and prevent reoffending.

The Youth Justice Board for England and Wales, which began operation in 1998, monitors the youth justice system, promotes good practice and advises the Home Secretary on the operation of the system and the setting of national standards.

Appeals

A person convicted by a magistrates' court may appeal to the High Court, on points of law, and to the Crown Court, by way of re-hearing. Appeals from the Crown Court go to the Court of Appeal (Criminal Division). A further appeal can be made to the House of Lords on points of law of public importance. A prosecutor cannot appeal against an acquittal, but mechanisms exist to review over-lenient sentences and rulings of law. Alleged miscarriages of justice in England, Wales and Northern Ireland are reviewed by the Criminal Cases Review Commission, which is independent of both government and the courts. Referral of a case requires some new argument or evidence not previously raised at the trial or on appeal.

Coroners' Courts

The coroner (usually a senior lawyer or doctor) must hold an inquest if the deceased died violently, unnaturally, suddenly, of unknown causes, while in prison or in other specified circumstances. The coroner's court establishes how, when and where the deceased died. A coroner may sit alone or, in certain circumstances, with a jury.

CIVIL JUSTICE SYSTEM

Jurisdiction in civil matters is split between the High Court and the county courts. Some 90 per cent of all cases are dealt with by the county courts, but most civil disputes do not go to court at all. Many are dealt with through statutory or voluntary complaints mechanisms, or through mediation and negotiation. Arbitration is a common form of adjudication in commercial and building disputes. Ombudsmen have the power to determine complaints in the public sector, and, on a voluntary basis, in some private sector activities (for example, banking, insurance and pensions).

A large number of tribunals exist to determine disputes. About 80 different types of tribunal are supervised by a statutory supervisory body, the Council on Tribunals, and deal with disputes such as liability for tax (Commissioners for Income Tax), eligibility for social benefit (Social Security Appeals Tribunals) and the compulsory treatment of an individual for mental health problems (Mental Health Review Tribunals).

Courts

The High Court is divided into three Divisions (see chart on p. 220).

- The Queen's Bench Division deals with disputes relating to contracts, general commercial matters (in a specialist Commercial Court), and liability in tort (general civil wrongs, such as accidents caused by negligence, or defamation of character). A Queen's Bench Divisional Court has special responsibility for dealing with applications for judicial review of the actions of public bodies, and has the power to declare the action of a public individual, department or body unlawful.

- The Chancery Division deals with disputes relating to land, wills, companies and insolvency.
- The Family Division deals with matters relating to divorce and the welfare of children.

About 270 county courts deal with claims in contract and in tort, with family matters (including divorce and the welfare of children) and a wide range of statutory matters. Magistrates' courts have limited civil jurisdiction, in family matters (when they sit as a Family Proceedings Court) and in miscellaneous civil orders.

Appeals in civil cases in the county courts or High Court generally go to the Court of Appeal (Civil Division). Appeals from magistrates' courts in civil matters go to the High Court, on matters of law, or to the Crown Court, if the case is to be reheard. A further appeal on points of law of public importance goes to the House of Lords. The Access to Justice Act 1999 is reforming the jurisdiction of the courts to hear appeals in civil and family cases, and the constitution of the Civil Division of the Court of Appeal (see below).

Reform of the Civil Justice System

Amendments to the civil justice system were implemented in 1999, introducing:

- a unified code of procedural rules, replacing separate sets of High Court and county court rules, the objective being to enable the courts to deal with cases more appropriately. This includes the court taking a more active case management role than before, so that cases are dealt with in a way which is proportionate to their value, complexity and importance;
- pre-action protocols (for clinical negligence and personal injury cases), setting standards and timetables for the conduct of cases before court proceedings are started. This requires more exchange of information and fuller investigation of claims at an earlier stage. People should therefore be in a better position to make a realistic assessment of the merits of a case far earlier than before, encouraging them to settle disputes without recourse to litigation. If litigation is unavoidable, cases coming to court should be better prepared than before; and
- a system of three tracks to which disputed claims are assigned by a judge according to the value and complexity of the case. These are the:
  - — small claims track, which deals with cases worth less than £5,000 at an informal hearing by a district judge;
  - — fast track, which deals with cases worth from £5,000 to £15,000, setting a fixed timetable from allocation to trial; and
  - — multi-track, for cases over £15,000, or of unusual complexity, which is supervised by a judge and given timetables tailored to each case.

Judges have a key role in ensuring that the procedures deliver the objectives of reducing cost, delay and complexity, by managing cases to ensure that litigants and their representatives keep to the timetable, and undertake only necessary work.

The Access to Justice Act 1999 is reforming the workings of the appeals system according to the principles of proportionality and efficiency, by:

- diverting from the Court of Appeal those cases which, by their nature, do not require the attention of the most senior judges in the country; and
- making various changes to the working methods and constitution of the Court, which will enable it to deploy its resources more effectively.

The Civil Justice Council has been established to oversee the working of the civil justice system, and to make proposals for its improvement.

Legal System of Scotland

Scots law belongs to a small group of 'mixed' legal systems which have legal principles, rules and concepts modelled on both Roman and English law. The main sources of Scots law are judge-made law, certain legal treatises having 'institutional' authority, legislation, and EC law. The first two sources are sometimes referred to as the common law of Scotland. Legislation, as in the rest of the UK, consists of statutes (Acts of Parliament) or subordinate legislation authorised by Parliament.

PROSECUTION AND THE CRIMINAL COURTS

Awaiting Trial

When arrested, an accused person may be released by the police to await summons, on an undertaking to appear at court at a specified time, or be held in custody to appear at court on the next working day. Following that appearance, the accused may be remanded in custody until trial or released by the court on bail. If released on bail, he or she must undertake to appear at trial when required, not to commit an offence while on bail, and not to interfere with witnesses or obstruct justice. There is a right of appeal to the High Court against the refusal of bail, or by the prosecutor against the granting of bail, or against the conditions imposed.

Prosecution Arrangements

The Crown Office and Procurator Fiscal Service provides Scotland's independent public prosecution and deaths investigation service. The Department is headed by the Lord Advocate, assisted by the Solicitor-General for Scotland (who are the Scottish Law Officers and members of the Scottish Executive). The Crown Agent, a senior civil servant, is responsible for the running of the Department.

Prosecutions in the High Court are prepared by procurators fiscal and Crown Office officials, and are conducted by the Lord Advocate and the Solicitor-General for Scotland; they in turn delegate the bulk of their work to advocates depute, collectively known as Crown Counsel, of whom there are 13. In all other criminal courts the decision to prosecute is made, and prosecution carried out, by procurators fiscal, who are the Lord Advocate's local representatives (one for each sheriff court). They are lawyers and full-time civil servants subject to the direction of the Department.

The police report gives details of alleged crimes to the local procurator fiscal who has discretion whether or not to prosecute. He or she may receive instructions from the Crown Counsel on behalf of the Lord Advocate.

The office of coroner does not exist in Scotland. Instead the local procurator fiscal inquires into sudden or suspicious deaths. When appropriate, a fatal accident inquiry may be held before the sheriff; this is mandatory in cases of death resulting from industrial accidents and deaths in custody.

Criminal Courts

There are three criminal courts in Scotland: the High Court of Justiciary, the sheriff court and the district court. Cases are heard under one of two types of criminal procedure.

- In *solemn procedure* in both the High Court of Justiciary and the sheriff court, an accused person's trial takes place before a judge sitting with a jury of 15 lay people. As in England and Wales, the alleged offence is set out in a document called an indictment. The judge decides questions of law and the jury decides questions of fact and may reach a decision by a simple majority. They may decide to find the accused 'guilty', 'not guilty' or 'not proven'; the last two are acquittals and have the effect that the accused cannot be tried again for the same offence.
- In *summary procedure* in sheriff and district courts, the judge sits without a jury and decides questions of both fact and law. The offence charged is set out in a document called a summary complaint.

Pre-trial hearings (diets) in summary and solemn cases are intended to establish the state of readiness of both the defence and the prosecution.

The *High Court of Justiciary* is the supreme criminal court in Scotland, sitting in Edinburgh, Glasgow and other major urban centres. It tries the most serious crimes and has exclusive jurisdiction in cases involving murder, treason and rape.

The 49 *sheriff courts* deal mainly with less serious offences committed within their area of jurisdiction. These courts are organised in six sheriffdoms; at the head of each is a sheriff principal. There are over 100 permanent sheriffs, most of whom are appointed to particular courts. The sheriff has jurisdiction in both summary and solemn criminal cases. In the summary court, the sheriff may impose prison sentences of up to three months (although more in some cases) or a fine of £5,000. Under solemn procedure, the sheriff may impose imprisonment for up to three years and unlimited financial penalties, and has an additional power of remit to the High Court of Justiciary if he or she thinks a heavier sentence should be imposed. The sheriff also has available a range of non-custodial sentences, principally community service and probation.

District courts, which deal with minor offences, are the administrative responsibility of the local authority. The longest prison sentence which can be imposed is generally 60 days and the maximum fine is £2,500. The bench of a district court will usually be made up of one or more lay Justices of the Peace. A local authority may also appoint a stipendiary magistrate, who must be a professional lawyer of at least five years' standing, and who has the same summary criminal jurisdiction and powers as a sheriff. At present, only Glasgow has stipendiary magistrates sitting in the district court. A government review of the operation of the district courts was announced in May 2000.

Sentencing

In Scotland a court must obtain a social enquiry report before imposing a custodial sentence if the accused is aged under 21 or has not previously served a custodial sentence. A report is also required before making a probation or community service order, or in cases involving people already subject to supervision.

Non-custodial sentences available to the courts include fines, probation orders, community service orders, restriction of liberty orders (monitored by electronic tagging) and supervised attendance orders (which provide an alternative to imprisonment for fine default, and incorporate aspects of work and training).

Children

Criminal proceedings may be brought against any child aged eight years or over, but the instructions of the Lord Advocate are necessary before anyone under 16 years of age is prosecuted. Most children under 16 who have committed an offence or are considered to be in need of care and protection may be brought before a Children's Hearing. The hearing, consisting of three lay people, determines whether compulsory measures of care are required and, if so, the form they should take.

Young people aged between 16 and 21 serve custodial sentences in young offender institutions. Remission of part of the sentence for good behaviour, release on parole and supervision on release are available.

Appeals

The High Court of Justiciary sits as the Scottish Court of Criminal Appeal. In both solemn and summary procedure, a convicted person may appeal against conviction, or sentence, or both. The Court may authorise a retrial if it sets aside a conviction. There is no appeal from this court in criminal cases. The Scottish Criminal Cases Review Commission has responsibility for considering alleged miscarriages of justice and referring cases meeting the relevant criteria to the Court of Appeal for review.

CIVIL COURTS

The main civil courts are the Court of Session (the supreme court, subject to appeal only to the House of Lords in London) and the sheriff court (the principal local court).

The *Court of Session* sits in Edinburgh, and may hear cases at first instance as well as those transferred to it and appealed from sheriff courts and from tribunals. A leading principle of the court is that cases originating in it are both prepared for decision, and decided, by judges sitting alone whose decisions are subject to review by several judges. The total number of judges is 32, of whom 24, called Lords Ordinary, mainly decide cases in the first instance. This branch of the court is called the Outer House. The other eight judges are divided into two divisions of four judges each, forming the Inner House. The First Division is presided over by the Lord President of the Court of Session and the Second Division by the Lord Justice-Clerk. The main business of each division is to review the decisions of the Lords Ordinary or inferior courts which have been appealed to it.

In addition to its criminal jurisdiction, the *sheriff court* deals with most civil litigation in Scotland. The value of the subject matter with which the court can deal has, with very few exceptions, no upper limit, and a broad range of remedies can be granted. Cases dealt with may include debts, contracts, reparation, rent restrictions, actions affecting the use of property, leases and tenancies, child protection issues and family actions. There is a right of appeal in some cases from the sheriff to the sheriff principal and then, in some cases, to the Court of Session.

Civil Proceedings

The formal proceedings in the Court of Session are started by serving the defender with a summons or, in sheriff court cases in ordinary actions, an initial writ. A defender who intends to contest the action must inform the court; if he or she fails to do so, the court normally grants a decree in absence in favour of the pursuer. Where a case is contested, both parties must prepare written pleadings, after which a hearing will normally be arranged.

In summary actions involving sums between £750 and £1,500 in the sheriff court, a statement of claim is incorporated in a summons. The procedure is designed to enable most actions to be settled without the parties having to appear in court. Normally, they, or their representatives, need appear only when an action is defended.

In cases below £750 a special small claim procedure enables those who do not have legal advice to raise claims themselves. The procedures are similar to, but less formal than, the summary procedure. In addition to the courts, there is a wide range of tribunals which administer justice in special types of case. Many of these are common to the rest of Great Britain; others, such as the Land Court, the Lands Tribunal and the Children's Hearings, are peculiar to Scotland.

ADMINISTRATION OF THE SCOTTISH LEGAL SYSTEM

The Scottish Executive Justice Department, under the Minister for Justice, is responsible for civil law and criminal justice, including criminal justice social work services, police, prisons, courts administration, legal aid, and liaison with the legal profession in Scotland. The Scottish Court Service, an executive agency, deals with the work of the Supreme Courts and the sheriff courts.

The Lord Advocate and the Solicitor-General for Scotland provide the Scottish Executive with advice on legal matters and represent its interests in the courts. Since devolution, advice to the UK Government on Scots law is provided by the Advocate-General for Scotland.

The role of the Scottish Parliament is to make laws in relation to devolved matters in Scotland. In these areas, it is able to amend or repeal existing Acts of the UK Parliament and to pass new legislation of its own in relation to devolved matters. It is also able to consider and pass private legislation, promoted by individuals or bodies (for example, local authorities) in relation to devolved matters. Examples of laws passed in the first year of the Parliament include the abolition of the feudal system of land tenure, and the introduction of a new system to manage the welfare and finances of adults with incapacity.

The Court of Session and the High Court of Justiciary enact the rules regulating their own procedure and the procedures of the sheriff courts and the lay summary courts. The Court of Session and Criminal Courts Rules Councils, and the Sheriffs Courts Rules Council, consisting of judges and legal practitioners, advise the courts about amending the rules.

Legal System of Northern Ireland

Northern Ireland's legal system is similar to that of England and Wales. Jury trials have the same place in the system, except in the case of offences involving acts of terrorism (see p. 230). In addition, the course of litigation is the same and the legal profession has the same two branches.

Superior Courts

The Supreme Court of Judicature comprises the Court of Appeal, the High Court and the Crown Court. All matters relating to these courts are under the jurisdiction of the UK Parliament. Judges are appointed by the Crown.

The *Court of Appeal* comprises the Lord Chief Justice (as President) and two Lords Justices of Appeal. The High Court comprises the Lord Chief Justice and five other judges. The practice and procedure of the Court of Appeal and the High Court are virtually the same as in the corresponding courts in England and Wales. Both courts sit in the Royal Courts of Justice in Belfast.

The Court of Appeal has power to review the civil law decisions of the High Court and the criminal law decisions of the Crown Court, and may in certain cases review the decisions of county courts and magistrates' courts. Subject to certain restrictions, an appeal from a judgment of the Court of Appeal can go to the House of Lords.

The *High Court* is divided into a Queen's Bench Division, dealing with most civil law matters; a Chancery Division, dealing with, for instance, trusts and estates, title to land, mortgages and charges, wills and company matters; and a Family Division, dealing principally with matrimonial cases, adoption, wardship, patients' affairs and undisputed probate matters.

The *Crown Court* deals with all serious criminal cases.

Inferior Courts

The inferior courts are the county courts and the magistrates' courts, both of which differ in a number of ways from their counterparts in England and Wales.

County courts are primarily civil law courts. They are presided over by one of 14 county court judges, two of whom—in Belfast and Londonderry—have the title of recorder. Appeals go from the county courts to the High Court. The county courts also deal with appeals from the magistrates' courts in both criminal and civil matters. In civil matters, the county courts handle most actions in which the amount or the value of specific articles claimed is below a certain level. The courts also deal with actions involving title to, or the recovery of, land; equity matters such as trusts and estates; mortgages; and the sale of land and partnerships.

The day-to-day work of dealing summarily with minor local criminal cases is carried out in *magistrates' courts* presided over by a full-time, legally qualified resident magistrate. The magistrates' courts also exercise jurisdiction in certain family law cases and have a very limited jurisdiction in other civil cases.

Terrorist Offences

People accused of offences specified under emergency legislation (see p. 215) are tried in the Crown Court without jury. The onus remains on the prosecution to prove guilt beyond reasonable doubt and the defendant has the right to be represented by a lawyer of his or her choice. The judge must set out in a written statement the reasons for conviction and there is an automatic right of appeal to the Court of Appeal against conviction and/or sentence on points of fact as well as of law.

Administration of the Law

Court administration is the responsibility of the Lord Chancellor, while the Northern Ireland Office, under the Secretary of State, deals with policy and legislation concerning criminal law, the police and the penal system. The Lord Chancellor has general responsibility for legal aid, advice and assistance.

The Director of Public Prosecutions for Northern Ireland, who is responsible to the Attorney-General, prosecutes all offences tried on indictment, and may do so in other (summary) cases. Most summary offences are prosecuted by the police.

Prison Service

The Prison Service in England and Wales, the Scottish Prison Service and the Northern Ireland Prison Service are all executive agencies. There are currently 137 prison establishments in England and Wales (eight of which are run by private contractors), 17 Scottish establishments and four in Northern Ireland.

Prison accommodation ranges from open prisons to high-security establishments. Sentenced prisoners are classified into different risk-level groups for security purposes. Women prisoners are held in separate prisons or in separate accommodation in mixed prisons. There are no open prisons in Northern Ireland.

In recent years the prison population as a whole has been growing steadily in Great Britain. For example, the average daily prison population in England and Wales rose from 44,566 in 1993 to 64,771 in 1999. In Scotland the figure rose from 5,637 in 1993 to 6,030 in 1999.

Independent Oversight of the Prison System

Every prison establishment in England, Wales and Northern Ireland has a board of visitors, comprising volunteers drawn from the local community appointed by the Home Secretary or Secretary of State for Northern Ireland. Boards, which are independent, monitor complaints by prisoners and concerns of staff, and report as necessary to ministers. In Scotland, visiting committees to prisons are appointed by local authorities.

Independent Prisons Inspectorates report on the treatment of prisoners and prison conditions, and submit annual reports to Parliament. Each prison establishment is visited about once every three years.

In England and Wales prisoners who fail to get satisfaction from the Prison Service's internal request and complaints system may complain to the independent Prisons Ombudsman. In Scotland, prisoners who exhaust the internal grievance procedure may apply to the independent Scottish Prisons Complaints Commission.

Privileges and Discipline

Prisoners in the UK may write and receive letters, be visited by relatives and friends, and make telephone calls. Privileges include a personal radio; books, magazines and newspapers; and watching television. Offences against prison discipline are dealt with by prison governors, who act as adjudicators. In England, Wales and Scotland measures to counter drug misuse in prisons include mandatory drug testing. Voluntary testing has been piloted in Northern Ireland, but there is no mandatory programme. People awaiting trial in custody have certain rights and privileges not granted to convicted prisoners.

Early Release of Prisoners

There are statutory arrangements governing the early release of prisoners. Offenders serving shorter terms (less than four years) may be automatically released at specific points in their sentences, while those detained for longer require Parole Board approval or the consent of a government minister.

Probation

The Probation Service in England and Wales supervises offenders in the community under direct court orders and after release from custody. It also advises offenders in custody. All young offenders and all prisoners in England and Wales sentenced to 12 months' imprisonment and over are supervised on release by the Probation Service, or, in the case of certain young offenders, by local authority social services departments or youth justice teams.

A court probation order requires offenders to maintain regular contact with their probation officer, who is expected to supervise them. The purpose of supervision under a probation order is to secure the rehabilitation of the offender, to protect the public and to prevent the offender from committing further offences. A probation order can last from six months to three years; an offender who fails to comply without good reason with any of the requirements can be brought before the court again. The Probation Service also supervises those subject to community service orders, combination orders and those released from prison on parole. The probation service in

England and Wales dealt with around 120,000 new offenders in 1999. Just under half this total were commencing probation orders; a similar number were commencing community service orders

HM Inspectorate of Probation has both an inspection and an advisory role, and also monitors any work that the Probation Service carries out in conjunction with the voluntary and private sectors.

> The Criminal Justice and Court Service Bill, currently before Parliament, would provide for a new National Probation Service of England and Wales. The proposed new structure would bring the existing 54 probation services into a national, unified service comprising a national headquarters and 42 area boards.

In Scotland local authority social work departments supervise offenders on probation, community service and other community disposals, and offenders subject to supervision on release from custody. With effect from September 2001, responsibility for delivery of community disposals will pass to 11 mainland groupings of local authorities

In Northern Ireland the probation service is administered by the government-funded Probation Board, whose membership is representative of the community.

Legal Aid

Someone who needs legal assistance or representation may be able to get help with legal costs from publicly funded schemes. People who qualify for help may have all their legal costs paid for, or may be asked to make a contribution, depending on their means and, in civil cases, the outcome of the case.

England and Wales

Legal aid funding arrangements have been reformed (under the provisions of the Access to Justice Act 1999), replacing the Legal Aid Board with the Legal Services Commission (LSC). The LSC administers two separate schemes for funding services:

- the Community Legal Service (CLS), which was launched in April 2000. The CLS replaced civil legal aid with a CLS Fund, through which funding is targeted on quality-assured services in priority areas of need; and
- the Criminal Defence Service for funding criminal cases (being launched in April 2001), which will aim to achieve quality assurance and improve value for money in publicly funded defence services.

Legal help and representation is provided from the Community Legal Service Fund if applicants qualify for it—which depends on their financial circumstances and the nature of their case. The CLS Fund supports eligible people in paying for help with legal problems, including divorce and other family issues, welfare benefits, credit and debt problems, housing and property disputes, immigration and nationality issues, clinical negligence cases, challenges to decisions by government departments and other public bodies, and actions against the police. The CLS Fund is not available for most personal injury cases (except clinical negligence cases), as the Government believes that such cases are best conducted by way of conditional fee ('no win, no fee') arrangements between solicitors and clients.

In criminal proceedings the LSC makes arrangements for duty solicitors to assist unrepresented defendants in the magistrates' courts. Solicitors are also available, on a 24-hour basis, to give advice and assistance to people being questioned by the police. These services are not means-tested and are free. Criminal legal aid may be granted by the court if it appears to be in the interests of justice and if a defendant is considered to require financial assistance. A contribution towards the costs may be payable.

Scotland

The Scottish Legal Aid Board is responsible for managing legal aid in Scotland. Its main tasks are to grant or refuse applications for legal aid; to pay solicitors or advocates for the legal work that they do; and to advise Scottish ministers on legal aid matters. Where legal aid is granted to the accused in criminal proceedings, he or she is not required to pay any contribution towards expenses.

Northern Ireland

Civil legal aid in the Province is administered by the Law Society for Northern Ireland. Where legal aid is granted for criminal cases it is free.

Other Legal Advice

The CLS will provide the framework for local networks of legal advice services throughout England and Wales. The networks will include solicitors' firms, Citizens Advice Bureaux, law centres, local authority services and other independent advice centres.

Further Reading

The Lord Chancellor's Departments: Departmental Report 2000. The Government's Expenditure Plans 2000–2001 to 2001–2002. Cm 4606. The Stationery Office, 2000.

Home Office Annual Report 1999–2000. The Government's Expenditure Plans 2000–2001 to 2001–2002. Cm 4605. The Stationery Office, 2000.

Websites

Lord Chancellor's Department: www.open.gov.uk/lcd

Home Office: www.homeoffice.gov.uk

Scottish Executive: www.scotland.gov.uk

15 Religion

Britain in the 21st century is a multicultural, multi-faith society. Everyone in the United Kingdom has the right to religious freedom. Religious organisations and groups may conduct their rites and ceremonies, promote their beliefs within the limits of the law, own property and run schools.

INTRODUCTION

Historically, Christianity has been the most influential and important religion in Britain, and it remains the declared faith of the majority of the people. The influence of Christianity has been widespread, extending beyond the spheres of prayer and worship. Churches and cathedrals make a significant contribution to the architectural landscape of the nation's cities and towns. The church is actively involved in voluntary work and the provision of social services—many schools and hospitals were founded by men and women who were strongly influenced by Christian motives. Easter and Christmas, the two most important events in the Christian calendar, are still recognised as public holidays.

In addition to Christians, there are large communities of Muslims, Hindus, Jews and Sikhs, and smaller communities of practising Baha'is, Buddhists, Jains and Zoroastrians. Most of these religious communities are also involved in voluntary work and show practical concern for the less privileged. Although members within a community share many beliefs and practices, there may be significant differences, within each community, of tradition, organisation, language and ethnicity.

As well as the 7.9 million active members of religions, the UK also has a large proportion of people who may involve themselves in formal religious ceremonies only at times of crisis or significant events such as birth, marriage and death. Organisations such as the British Humanist Association and the National Secular Society offer the opportunity for members to debate and explore moral and philosophical issues in a non-religious setting.

There has been a significant development of other forms of religious expression, with the growth of a range of independent churches and also of other groups sometimes referred to as 'cults' or 'sects' which have now become known collectively as new religious movements. These tend to be smaller and less formal than longer established churches, and rely more on the inspiration of their leader or founder.

A distinction is often drawn between community size figures and active membership figures, with the former representing a broader form of identification with religion and the latter a closer association. Current community size estimates suggest 40 million people in Britain identify themselves as Christians; on the same basis there are over 1 million Muslims; around half a million

Table 15.1: Active Faith Membership[1] in the United Kingdom, 1970–98

Thousands

Group	1970	1980	1990	1998
Christian: Trinitarian[2]	9,272	7,529	6,624	6,012
of whom:				
Anglican	*2,987*	*2,180*	*1,728*	*1,650*
Roman Catholic	*2,746*	*2,455*	*2,198*	*1,833*
Free Churches	*3,539*	*2,894*	*2,698*	*2,529*
Christian: Non-Trinitarian	276	349	455	537
Hindu	80	120	140	161
Jewish	120	111	101	94
Muslim	130	306	495	637
Sikh	100	150	250	380
Others	26	52	86	107
Total membership	**10,004**	**8,617**	**8,151**	**7,928**

[1] Active adult members.

[2] Trinitarian means acceptance of the historic formulary of the Godhead as three eternal persons.

Source: Christian Research

Hindus, half a million Sikhs; and around a third of a million Jews.

Relations with the State

Two churches have a special status with regard to the State. In England, the Anglican *Church of England* is legally recognised as the official, or established, Church and is subject to Parliament. A similar situation applied in Scotland until the early 20th century regarding the Presbyterian *Church of Scotland.* Since then the Church continues to be recognised as the national Church, but it is completely self-governing. There is no longer an established Church in Wales or Northern Ireland. No church is financially supported by the State, although many ministers of religion work as army chaplains, and in schools and hospitals, and will consequently draw a salary from the State for that work, and the churches may also receive funds for their social and educational work.

Religious Education

In England and Wales all state schools must provide religious education, each local education authority being responsible for producing a locally agreed syllabus. Syllabuses must reflect Christianity, while taking account of the teaching and practices of the other principal religions represented in the UK. State schools must provide a daily act of collective worship. Parents may withdraw their children from religious education.

In Scotland, education authorities must ensure that schools provide religious education and regular opportunities for religious observance. The law does not specify the form of religious education, but it is recommended that pupils should be provided with a broad-based curriculum, through which they can develop a knowledge and understanding of Christianity and other world religions, and develop their own beliefs, attitudes and moral values and practices.

In Northern Ireland a core syllabus for religious education has been approved by the main churches and this must be taught in all state schools. Integrated education is encouraged and all schools must be open to pupils of all religions, although in practice most Catholic pupils attend Catholic maintained or Catholic voluntary grammar schools, and most Protestant children are enrolled at controlled schools or non-denominational voluntary grammar schools. However, the number of inter-denominational

As well as non-denominational state schools, there are in England and Wales around 4,000 voluntary schools receiving the bulk of their funding from the State. Most of these schools still seek to maintain a particular religious tradition. Until 1997, mainly for historical reasons, virtually all such schools were Anglican or Roman Catholic. Since then, as part of a wider government initiative to increase parental choice, state-funded schools representing other religions have been established. Two Muslim state primary schools have been approved in Birmingham and London, as well as two Sikh schools, a Seventh-day Adventist school, and five Jewish primary schools. Further plans include proposals for state schools representing the Greek Orthodox Church and Hindu religions. In Scotland the State fully funds denominational schools, almost all of which are Roman Catholic.

schools is increasing. In 1998–99, over 12,000 primary and secondary school pupils received their education at 'integrated' schools not attached to any particular religion.

Church Maintenance

The State does not contribute to the general expenses of church maintenance, although some state aid does help repair historic churches. In 1998–99 the joint scheme of English Heritage and the Heritage Lottery Fund offered grants to churches totalling £26 million. Assistance is also given to meet some of the costs of repairing cathedrals, with £3 million available from English Heritage in 2000–01.

The Churches Conservation Trust (formerly the Redundant Churches Fund), funded jointly by the Government and the Church of England, preserves Anglican churches of particular cultural and historical importance that are no longer used as regular places of worship. At present over 300 churches are maintained in this way.

The Historic Chapels Trust was established to take into ownership redundant chapels and other places of worship in England of outstanding architectural and historic interest (other than those which are eligible for vesting in the Churches Conservation Trust). Buildings of all denominations and faiths can be taken into care. These have included Nonconformist chapels, Roman Catholic churches, private Anglican chapels and synagogues.

Social Involvement

The Church of England's Church Urban Fund is an independent charity which raises money to enable those living in the most disadvantaged urban areas to set up local projects to help alleviate the effects of poverty. These projects help support a wide range of community-based programmes concerned with issues such as education, employment, young people and poverty. Although rooted in the Christian faith, the Fund does not restrict its grants on the basis of religious belief. By 2000 it had made grants totalling £37 million to nearly 2,900 different projects.

The General Assembly of the Church of Scotland debates annual reports from its Committee on Church and Nation, on social, economic and political matters; and, through its Board of Social Responsibility, it is the largest voluntary social work agency in Scotland. The Board currently runs more than 80 projects offering care and support to over 4,000 people every day. Churches in Wales and Northern Ireland, and other faith communities also have a concern for social issues.

In England, the Inner Cities Religious Council, based in the Department of the Environment, Transport and the Regions, provides a forum in which the Government and the faith communities work together on issues relating to urban regeneration. Chaired by a government minister, the Council comprises senior leaders of the Christian, Hindu, Jewish, Muslim and Sikh faiths.

The Census and Religious Affiliation

Religion is to be included as a topic in the 2001 Census throughout the United Kingdom. Questions have not normally been asked about religious beliefs in censuses or for other official purposes, except in Northern Ireland. The Scottish Parliament had approved similar legislation in March 2000. Unlike other Census questions, however, there is no legal penalty for failing to answer the question about religion, reflecting the sensitivity that some people feel about disclosing such information.

THE CHRISTIAN COMMUNITY

Church of England

The Church of England became the established church during the Reformation in the 16th century. Conflicts between Church and State culminated in the Act of Supremacy in 1534, which repudiated papal supremacy and declared Henry VIII to be the Supreme Head of the Church of England. The title was altered to 'Supreme Governor' by Elizabeth I when she acceded to the throne in 1558. The Church of England's form of worship was set out in successive versions of the Book of Common Prayer from 1549 onwards.

The Church of England plans to publish in November 2000 *Common Worship*, containing its new services. *Common Worship* replaces the Alternative Service Book and will be used alongside the traditional Book of Common Prayer. *Common Worship* contains modern language and forms of service side by side with traditional versions. As well as being published in book form, it will be available as a CD-Rom and can be accessed over the Internet.

There have been various attempts to sever all links between church and state, among them the 'disestablishmentarian' campaign of the 19th century. Recent constitutional reforms (outlined in chapter 6) have not altered the link.

The Monarch is the 'Supreme Governor' of the Church of England and must always be a member of the Church, and promise to uphold it. The Church can regulate its own worship. Church of England archbishops, bishops and deans of a number of cathedrals are appointed by the Monarch on the advice of the Prime Minister, although the Crown Appointments Commission, which includes lay and clergy representatives, plays a key role in the selection of archbishops and diocesan bishops. Clergy of the Church, together with those of the Church of Scotland, the Church of Ireland and the Roman Catholic Church, may not sit in the House of Commons. The two archbishops (of Canterbury and York), the bishops of London, Durham and Winchester, and 21 other senior bishops sit in the House of Lords.

The Church of England is divided into two provinces: Canterbury, comprising 30 dioceses, including the Diocese in Europe; and York, with 14 dioceses. The dioceses are divided into archdeaconries and deaneries, which are in turn divided into about 13,000 parishes, although in practice many of these are grouped together. Altogether, there are about 13,000 Church of England clergy, excluding those in mainland Europe. In 1998, 177,000 people were baptised in the Church in the two provinces, excluding the Diocese in Europe; of these, 129,000 were under one year old, representing 21 per cent of live births. In the same year there were 40,000 confirmations. In 1998 nearly 66,000 marriages were solemnised in the Church of England. These accounted for 67 per cent of marriages with religious ceremonies, and 26 per cent of marriages in England.

In 1998 the General Synod, the central governing and legislative body, approved proposals to overhaul the central organisation and structure of the Church. The number of Church Commissioners (see below) was reduced by two-thirds and some of their powers transferred to an Archbishops' Council which became the Church's central co-ordinating body. The Council is the centre of an administrative system dealing with inter-church relations, inter-faith relations, social questions, recruitment and training for the ministry, and missionary work.

The Church Commissioners are responsible for a large part of the Church of England's invested assets. The Crown appoints a Member of Parliament from the backbenches of the governing party to the unpaid post of Second Church Estates Commissioner, to represent the Commissioners in Parliament. The Church

Commissioners provide a fifth of the Church's total annual income, with most of the remainder provided by local voluntary donations. The average annual stipend of a Church of England priest is about £16,480; additional benefits include free housing (valued in 1999 at £8,270) and a non-contributory pension.

The Church of England reported an increase in the ordination of new clergy between 1998 and 1999 (from 468 to 481), and in the number of people in training for ordination. There are at present over 1,450 people in training.

The first women priests were ordained in 1994 and by 1999 they numbered 2,100. Women priests cannot, however, be appointed bishop or archbishop.

Other Anglican Churches

The Church of England is part of a worldwide Communion of Anglican churches. These are similar in organisation and worship to the Church of England and originated from it. There are four distinct Anglican Churches in the United Kingdom: the Church of England, the Church in Wales, the Episcopal Church in Scotland, and the Church of Ireland (which also operates in the Irish Republic). Each is governed separately by its own institutions.

The Anglican Communion comprises 38 autonomous Churches in the UK and abroad, and three regional councils overseas, with a total membership of about 70 million. Links between the components of the Anglican Communion are maintained by the Lambeth Conference of Anglican bishops, which is held in Canterbury every ten years, the last conference having taken place in 1998. Presided over by the Archbishop of Canterbury, the Conference has no executive authority, but enjoys considerable influence as an opinion-forming group.

The Anglican Consultative Council, an assembly of lay people and clergy as well as bishops, meets every two or three years to allow consultation within the Anglican Communion. Since 1979 the Primates (the senior archbishop or presiding bishop) of the Churches of the Anglican Communion have met regularly to discuss theological, social and international issues.

Church of Scotland

The Church of Scotland became the national church following the Scottish Reformation in the late 16th century and legislation enacted by the Scottish Parliament. The Church's status was then consolidated in the Treaty of Union of 1707 and by the Church of Scotland Act 1921, the latter confirming its complete freedom in all spiritual matters. The Church appoints its own office bearers, and its affairs are not subject to any civil authority.

The adult communicant membership is over 600,000 and there are around 1,200 ministers serving in parishes. Both men and women may join the ministry. The Church of Scotland has a Presbyterian form of government, that is government by church courts or councils, composed of ministers, elders, and deacons. The 1,600 congregations are governed locally by courts known as Kirk Sessions, consisting of ministers and elders. The next court is the Presbytery, responsible for a geographical area made up of a number of parishes; and finally there is the General Assembly, the supreme court, consisting of elected ministers, elders and deacons. The General Assembly meets annually under the chairmanship of an elected moderator, who serves for one year. The Monarch is normally represented by the Lord High Commissioner at the General Assembly.

There are also a number of independent Scottish Presbyterian churches, largely descended from groups which broke away from the Church of Scotland. They are very active in the Highlands and Islands.

Free Churches

The term 'Free Churches' is often used to describe those Protestant churches in the UK which, unlike the Church of England and the Church of Scotland, are not established churches. Free Churches have existed in various forms since the Reformation, developing their own traditions over the years. Their members have also been known as dissenters or nonconformists because of their more informal ecclesiastical structures and patterns of worship. Although this historical experience has given these churches a certain sense of shared identity, they otherwise vary greatly in doctrine, worship and church government. All the major Free Churches—Methodist, Baptist, Presbyterian, United Reformed and Salvation Army—have ministers of both sexes.

The Methodist Church, the largest of the Free Churches, originated in the 18th century following the Evangelical Revival under John Wesley (1703–91). It has 353,000 adult full members and a community of more than 1.2 million. The present Church is based on the 1932 union of most of the separate Methodist Churches. It has 3,727 ministers and student ministers and 6,452 places of worship.

The Baptists first achieved an organised form in Britain in the 17th century. Today they are mainly organised in groups of churches, most of which belong to the Baptist Union of Great Britain (re-formed in 1812) with about 145,000 members, 1,780 ministers and 2,100 places of worship. There are also separate Baptist Unions for Scotland, Wales and Ireland, and other independent Baptist Churches.

The third largest of the Free Churches is the United Reformed Church, with some 96,500 members, 1,090 serving ministers and 1,775 places of worship. It was formed in 1972 upon the union of the Congregational Church in England and Wales (the oldest Protestant minority in the UK, whose origins can be traced back to the Puritans of the 16th century) with the Presbyterian Church of England (a church closely related in doctrine and worship to the Church of Scotland). Further unions have taken place: in 1981 with the Reformed Association of the Churches of Christ and in 2000 with the Congregational Union of Scotland.

The Salvation Army was founded in the East End of London in 1865 by William Booth (1829–1912). Within the UK it is the largest, most diverse provider of social services after the Government. The Salvation Army also has a strong musical tradition. It is one of the biggest providers of hostel accommodation, offering over 3,000 beds every night. Other services include work with alcoholics, prison chaplaincy and a family tracing service which receives 5,000 enquiries each year. The Salvation Army in the UK is served by 1,600 officers (ordained ministers) and runs over 800 local church and community centres.

The Religious Society of Friends (Quakers), with about 17,000 adult members and 9,500 attenders in the UK and 490 places of worship, was founded in the middle of the 17th century under the leadership of George Fox (1624–91). It has no ordained ministers and no formal liturgy or sacraments. Silent worship is central to its life as a religious organisation and emphasis is also placed on social concern—Quakers have a long tradition of carrying out voluntary work in prisons—and peacemaking.

Among the other Free Churches are: the Presbyterian Church in Ireland, the largest Protestant church in Northern Ireland, where it has around 300,000 members; the Presbyterian (or Calvinistic Methodist) Church of Wales, with 49,750 members and the largest of the Free Churches in Wales; and the Union of Welsh Independents with 40,750 members.

Pentecostal Organisations and Charismatic Groupings

A recent development has been the rise of Pentecostalism and the charismatic movement. A number of Pentecostal bodies were formed in the UK at the turn of the 20th century. The two main Pentecostal organisations in the UK today are the Assemblies of God, with approximately 54,000 members, over 900 ministers and over 650 places of worship; and the Elim Pentecostal Church, with around 62,000 members. Since the Second World War immigration from the Caribbean has led to a significant number of Black Majority Pentecostal churches, and these are a growing presence in British (and especially English) Church life.

In the early 1960s a Pentecostal charismatic movement began to influence some followers in the Church of England, the Roman Catholic Church and the historic Free Churches. The Christian 'house church' movement (or 'new churches') began in the 1970s when some of the charismatics began to establish their own congregations. Services were originally held in private houses although many congregations have now acquired their own buildings. The movement, whose growth within the UK has been most marked in England, is characterised by lay leadership and is organised into a number of loose fellowships.

Roman Catholic Church

The formal structure of the Roman Catholic Church in England and Wales, which was suppressed after the Reformation, was restored in 1850, and that of the Scottish Roman Catholic Church, suppressed in the early 17th century, in 1878. There are now seven Roman Catholic provinces in Great Britain—five in England and Wales and two in Scotland. There are 30 dioceses in Great Britain—22 in England and Wales and eight in Scotland. Each province is under an archbishop; each diocese is under a bishop. There are separate Bishops' Conferences for England and Wales and for Scotland. There are 2,843 parish churches in England and Wales and 828 other churches and chapels open to the public. Scotland has 463 parish churches.

The Roman Catholic Church in Ireland is organised as a unit covering the whole island. There are 1,329 parishes, and 2,646 churches. Northern Ireland is covered by seven dioceses, some of which also have territory in the Irish Republic.

There are approximately 12,000 members of religious orders in England, Scotland and Wales. These orders undertake teaching and chaplaincy, and social work such as nursing, childcare and running homes for the elderly.

Other Churches

Other Protestant Churches include the Unitarians and Free Christians, whose origins go back to the Reformation. The Christian Brethren are a Protestant body organised by J.N. Darby (1800–82). There are two branches: the Open Brethren and the Closed or Exclusive Brethren.

Many Christian communities founded by migrant communities, including the Orthodox, Lutheran and Reformed Churches of various European countries, the Coptic Orthodox Church and the Armenian Church, have established their own centres of worship, particularly in London. All these churches operate in a variety of languages. The largest is probably the Greek Orthodox Church, many of whose members are of Cypriot origin.

There are also several other religious groups in the UK which were founded in the United States in the 20th century. These include the Church of Jesus Christ of the Latter-Day Saints (the Mormon Church, with about 180,000 members), the Jehovah's Witnesses (146,000 members), the Christadelphians, the Christian Scientists, and the Seventh-day Adventists. The Spiritualists have about 36,000 members, over 500 churches and nearly 300 ministers.

Co-operation among the Churches

Churches Together in Britain and Ireland is the main co-ordinating body for the Christian churches in the UK. The Council co-ordinates the work of its 32 member churches and associations of churches, in the areas of social responsibility, international affairs, church life, world mission, racial justice and inter-faith relations. The Council's member churches are also grouped in separate ecumenical bodies, according to country: Churches Together in England, Action of Churches Together in Scotland, Churches Together in Wales (Cytûn), and the Irish Council of Churches.

The Free Churches' Council, with 19 member denominations, includes most of the Free Churches of England and Wales. It promotes co-operation among the Free Churches (especially in hospital chaplaincy and in education matters).

The Evangelical Alliance, with a membership of individuals, churches or societies drawn from 20 denominations, represents over 1 million evangelical Christians.

Inter-church discussions about the search for Christian unity take place internationally, as well as within the UK, and the main participants are the Anglican, Baptist, Lutheran, Methodist, Orthodox, Reformed and Roman Catholic Churches. In 1999 the Church of England and the Methodist Church began formal discussions on a move towards unity. The Baptist Union, the Moravian Church, the Roman Catholic Church and the United Reformed Church had participating observers at the discussions. Informal trilateral contact between the Church of England, the Methodist Church and the United Reformed Church also began in 1999.

Alpha, a course that offers a practical introduction to the Christian faith, originated from an Anglican West London church in 1980. It is now being used as a form of evangelism by every major denomination. By 1999, an estimated 7,000 courses were being run each year in churches and institutions (including prisons and educational establishments) across the UK, attended by approximately 250,000 people.

OTHER FAITH COMMUNITIES

The Buddhist Community

The Buddhist community in the UK has followers both of British or Western origin, and of South Asian and Asian background. In 1907, a Buddhist Society of Great Britain and Ireland was formed but did not become firmly established. In 1924, Christmas Humphreys (1901–83) founded the Buddhist Centre of the Theosophical Society from what remained of the earlier society. This became the Buddhist Lodge of the Theosophical Society in 1926, and was constituted as a new and independent organisation—the Buddhist Society—in 1943. The Society promotes the principles, but does not adhere to any particular school, of Buddhism. The Network of Buddhist Organisations links many of the various Buddhist educational, cultural, charitable and teaching organisations.

Although religious buildings are not as central to Buddhist life as to that of some other religious traditions, there are over 500 Buddhist groups and centres, including some 50 monasteries and temples in the UK.

The Hindu Community

The Hindu community in the UK originates largely from India, although others have come from countries to which earlier generations had previously migrated, such as Kenya, Tanzania, Uganda, Zambia and Malawi. Migrants have also come from Fiji and from Trinidad and other Caribbean islands. The number of members is around 400,000 to 550,000, although some community representatives suggest a considerably higher figure (of close to 1 million). They are predominantly Gujaratis (between 65 per cent and 70 per cent) and Punjabis (between 15 per cent and 20 per cent). Most of the remainder have their ancestral roots in other parts of India, such as Uttar Pradesh, West Bengal, and the Southern states, as well as other countries such as Sri Lanka.

The first Hindu temple, or mandir, was opened in London in the 1950s and there are now over 120 mandirs in the UK; many are affiliated to the National Council of Hindu Temples (UK). Other national bodies serving the Hindu community include the Hindu Council (UK) and Vishwa Hindu Parishad.

The Swaminarayan Hindu Temple, in north London, is the first purpose-built Hindu temple in Europe, having a large cultural complex with provision for conferences, exhibitions, marriages, sports and health clinics.

The Jewish Community

Jews first settled in England at the time of the Norman Conquest. They were banished by royal decree in 1290, but readmitted following the English Civil War (1642–51). Sephardi Jews, who originally came from Spain and Portugal, have been present in the UK since the mid-17th century. The majority of Jews in the UK today are Ashkenazi Jews, of Central and East European origin, who fled persecution in the Russian Empire between 1881 and 1914, and Nazi persecution in Germany and other European countries from 1933 onwards.

The Jewish community in the UK numbers about 283,000, around 30 per cent of whom are affiliated to synagogues. Of the total number of synagogue-affiliated households, most Ashkenazi Jews (60 per cent) acknowledge the authority of the Chief Rabbi, while the more strictly observant (7 per cent) have their own spiritual leaders, as do the Sephardim. The Reform movement (founded in 1840), the Liberal and Progressive movement (founded in 1901) and the recently established Masorti movement account for most of the remaining synagogue-affiliated community membership.

Jewish congregations in the UK number about 365. The Board of Deputies of British Jews is the officially recognised representative body for these groups. Founded in 1760, it is elected mainly by synagogues, but a growing number of communal organisations are also represented. The Board serves as the voice of the community to both government and the wider non-Jewish community.

The Muslim Community

A significant Muslim community has existed in the UK since Muslim seamen and traders, from the Middle East and the Indian subcontinent, settled around the major ports in the early 19th century. There was further settlement from those demobilised from military service in the British army after the First World War, and of workers seeking, or recruited for, employment in the mills and factories in the 1950s and 1960s because of a shortage of labour following the Second World War. The 1970s saw the arrival of significant numbers of Muslims of Asian origin from Kenya and Uganda. There are also well-established Turkish Cypriot and Iranian Muslim communities, while more recently Muslims from Somalia, Iraq, Bosnia and Kosovo have sought refuge in the UK. There are between 1.5 million and 2 million Muslims in the UK and estimates from within the community suggest that the proportion of young people is significantly higher than the national average.

There are over 1,000 mosques and numerous community Muslim centres throughout the UK. Mosques are not only places of worship; they also offer instruction in the Muslim way of life and facilities for education and welfare. The first mosque in the UK was established at Woking, Surrey, in 1890. Mosques now range from converted buildings in many towns to the Central Mosque in Regent's Park, London, and its associated Islamic Cultural Centre, one of the most important Muslim institutions in the western world. The Central Mosque has the largest congregation of practically every minority ethnic community in the UK, and during festivals it may number over 30,000. The main conurbations in the Midlands, North West and North East of England, and in Scotland also have their own central mosques with a range of community facilities.

Sunni and Shi'a are the two principal traditions within Islam and both are represented among the Muslim community in the UK. Sufism, the mystical aspect of Islam, can be found in both traditions, and members of some of the major Sufi traditions have also developed branches in British cities.

The Muslim Council of Britain, founded in 1997, is a recent example of a representative body of established national and regional Muslim bodies as well as local mosques, organisations and specialist institutions. The Council aims to promote co-operation, consensus and unity on Muslim affairs in the UK. A number of other representative bodies such as the Union of Muslim Organisations has been set up to co-ordinate the social, cultural, economic and functional aspects of Muslim life in Britain.

The Sikh Community

Most of the Sikh community in the UK are of Punjabi ethnic origin. A significant minority came from East Africa and other former British colonies to which members of their family had migrated, but the vast majority have come to the UK directly from the Punjab. There are between 400,000 and 500,000 members, making it the largest Sikh community outside the Indian subcontinent.

The first gurdwara, or temple, in the UK was opened in Shepherd's Bush, London, in 1911. The largest is situated in Southall, Middlesex. Gurdwaras cater for the religious, educational, social welfare and cultural needs of their community. A granthi is usually employed to take care of the building and to conduct prayers. There are over 200 gurdwaras in the UK, the vast majority being in England and Wales.

Other Faiths

Jainism is an ancient religion brought to the UK by immigrants mainly from the Gujarat and Rajasthan areas of India. It is estimated that there are between 25,000 and 30,000 members in the UK. The Zoroastrian religion, or Mazdaism, is mainly represented in the UK by the Parsi community. Founders of the UK community originally settled in the 19th century and it is estimated that there are between 5,000 and 10,000 members. The Baha'i movement originated in Persia in the 19th century. The UK community has around 6,000 members connected to 200 local groups and 180 local spiritual assemblies. Rastafarianism, with its roots in the return-to-Africa movement, emerged in the West Indies early in the 20th century. It arrived in the UK with immigration from Jamaica in the 1950s.

New Religious Movements

A number of new religious movements, established since the Second World War and often with overseas origins, are active in the UK. Examples include the Church of Scientology, the Transcendental Meditation movement, the Unification Church and various New Age groups. INFORM (Information Network Focus on Religious Movements), which is supported by the main Churches, carries out research and seeks to provide information about new religious movements.

CO-OPERATION BETWEEN FAITHS

The Inter Faith Network for the United Kingdom links a wide range of organisations with an interest in inter-faith relations, including the representative bodies of the Baha'i, Buddhist, Christian, Hindu, Jain, Jewish, Muslim, Sikh and Zoroastrian communities. The Network promotes good relations between faiths in the UK, and runs a public advice and information service on inter-faith issues. The Council of Christians and Jews works for better understanding among members of the two religions and deals with educational and social issues. Churches Together in Britain and Ireland (see p. 240) has a Commission on Inter Faith Relations. There are now many organisations in the UK dealing wholly, or in part, with inter-faith issues. Many towns and cities now have inter-faith councils or groups whose focus is working for good inter-faith relations locally.

Faith and the Year 2000

In the UK many national and civic millennium celebrations had a specifically Christian framework. For example, during the first weekend of the new millennium celebrations there were national Millennium church services held in Belfast, Cardiff, Edinburgh and London. However, the Government was keen to ensure that the celebrations were relevant and accessible to people of all faiths. The church services were therefore complemented by a 'Shared Act of Reflection and Commitment' by the faith communities of the UK hosted by the Government in the Houses of Parliament and organised on their behalf by the Inter Faith Network.

Among the Christian celebrations were a passion play with a cast of 1,000 held in Greenwich Park over the Easter holiday period; and Jesus Day 2000, a global street celebration of Christ's millennium in cities throughout the UK. Additionally, promoting the Christian significance of the year 2000 are 'TimeLord', a poster originating as a colour supplement feature, updated and reprinted because of its relevance to the millennium; and the Jesus Video Project, issued with an accompanying magazine version of Luke's Gospel entitled 'The Man Behind the Millennium'.

Further Reading

UK Christian Handbook 2000/2001, ed. Peter Brierley and Heather Wraight. Harper Collins.

UK Christian Handbook—Religious Trends No. 1, 1998–99, ed. Peter Brierley. Paternoster Publishing.

Religions in the UK : A Multi-Faith Directory, ed. Paul Weller, University of Derby and The Inter Faith Network for the United Kingdom, 1997.

16 Culture

The arts and cultural sectors make important contributions to the wider economy in the UK. Consumer spending on the performing arts alone in 1999 is estimated at about £850 million. Arts and culture are a major influence on business location and decisions affecting tourism. The arts are seen by Government as having a role in helping to lift personal and community self-esteem, and developing skills and confidence that open up wider economic and social opportunities. New space, new work and new talent have a role in the regeneration of some of Britain's inner cities. The performing and visual arts, as well as the fine arts market, make important contributions to the balance of payments.

Among developments during 1999–2000 have been the launches of significant new museums and arts complexes—among them Tate Modern and Somerset House in London and The Lowry in Salford Quays; the flourishing of British arts festivals; and a record amount given in arts sponsorship.

Government Policy

The Department for Culture, Media and Sport (DCMS) implements government policy and administers expenditure on national museums and art galleries in England, the Arts Council of England (see p. 245), the British Library and other national arts and heritage bodies. Other responsibilities include the regulation of the film and music industries, broadcasting and the press, the National Lottery and the export licensing of antiques.

DCMS's stated aim is to improve the quality of life for all through cultural activities and to strengthen the creative industries.

Among its targets are:

- to promote competitiveness, at home and abroad, in the creative industries and improve the collection of statistical data so that meaningful comparisons can be regularly made;
- to implement a jointly funded strategy for the British film industry;
- to increase visitor numbers to the major national museums in line with the removal of all entry charges (see p. 258), if trustees decide to remove charges while maintaining the quality of exhibitions;

Table 16.1: Attendance[1] at Cultural Events, Great Britain *Per cent*

	1987–88	1991–92	1995–96	1996–97	1997–98
Cinema	34	44	51	54	54
Plays	24	23	23	24	23
Art galleries/exhibitions	21	21	22	22	22
Classical music	12	12	12	12	12
Ballet	6	6	7	7	6
Opera	5	6	6	7	6
Contemporary dance	4	3	4	4	4

[1] Per cent of resident population aged 15 and over attending 'these days'.
Source: Target Group Index, BRMB International

- to attract new audiences for the performing arts—with the help of the New Audiences Fund;
- to raise standards of care of collections and public access through the Challenge Fund;
- to double the number of public library Internet connections; and
- to establish a new funding council for the performing and visual arts and for film, and new arrangements for supporting the crafts.

The National Assembly for Wales, the Scottish Parliament and the Northern Ireland Assembly have responsibility for the arts in their countries, including museums, galleries and libraries, and their respective Arts Councils (see below). The Scottish Executive published a National Cultural Strategy in August 2000.

Government funds are distributed to arts organisations indirectly, through bodies such as the Arts Councils, the Film Council and Scottish Screen.

The Creative Industries Task Force, set up in 1998 to identify issues vital to the economic health of the creative industries, organised a work programme which included skills development, ensuring access to capital, stressing the importance of intellectual property, export promotion, regional activity, and Britain's image overseas.

The Quality, Efficiency and Standards Team (QUEST) monitors financial management across DCMS sectors.

Arts Councils

The independent Arts Councils of England, Scotland, Wales and Northern Ireland are the main channels for the distribution of government grants and Lottery funding to the visual, performing and community arts and to literature. The Arts Councils give financial assistance and advice not only to the major performing arts organisations, but also to small touring theatre companies, experimental performance groups and literary organisations. They provide funds for training arts administrators and help to develop sponsorship and local authority support. In addition to promoting education and public access to, and participation in, performing and visual arts and literature, the Arts Councils commission research into the effects of the arts and develop forward strategies.

The Arts Council of England (ACE) is the strategic authority for the arts in England and acts as their 'champion'. It rewards quality through its annual award allocations and through its stabilisation programme, which helps arts organisations manage long-term change. ACE's Recovery Programme is designed to provide rapid, shorter-term help to arts groups with pressing financial difficulties.

ACE funds the major national arts producing organisations, including the Royal Opera, the Royal Ballet, the Birmingham Royal Ballet, English National Opera (ENO), the Royal Shakespeare Company (RSC), the Royal National Theatre (RNT) and the South Bank Centre; and the main touring companies, such as Opera North and English National Ballet, while delegating decisions for regional and local activities to the ten English Regional Arts Boards (RABs). Other sources of money for the RABs are the British Film Institute and local authorities.

Finance

In England planned central government expenditure through the DCMS in 2000–01 amounts to £226.3 million for museums and galleries; £237.6 million for the visual and performing arts; £103.7 million for broadcasting and the media (including film); and £107.7 million for libraries and archives. ACE has a grant of £237.2 million in 2000–01 (an increase of £10 million on 1999–2000). In addition, the National Lottery arts proceeds distributed by the Arts Councils amount to about £186 million in 2000–01 (£150 million for the ACE).

Planned 2000–01 expenditure by the Arts Councils for Scotland, Wales and Northern Ireland is respectively £29.5 million, £15.4 million and £7.5 million, between 4 and 9 per cent up on 1999–2000. The Scottish Executive is also providing £40 million for Scotland's National Galleries and Museums, National Library and film industry, while the National Assembly for Wales is giving some £38.8 million for Wales's National Museum, National Library and other arts. Planned spending by the Department of Culture, Arts and Leisure for Northern Ireland on the National Museums (see p. 261), arts and libraries amounts to just over £40 million in 2000–01.

National Lottery

By December 1999, Lottery awards of over £1.4 billion had been announced by the Arts Councils for arts projects. Grants for the acquisition of works of art from the Heritage Lottery Fund (HLF—see p. 322) to museums, galleries and other organisations between June 1995 and April 2000 amounted to £60.8 million. The Lottery's New Opportunities Fund has £120 million to help develop a network of community centres, linked to libraries and the National Grid for Learning (see p. 131), to open up access to information. Millennium Festival Awards for All, allowing community organisations to apply for grants of up to £5,000, have been available throughout Great Britain since April 1999. Larger one-off Lottery awards support millennium arts projects. The Millennium Theatre in Londonderry, which has received £2.5 million, will open at the end of 2000.

NESTA

The National Endowment for Science, Technology and the Arts has initial finance of £200 million from the National Lottery. It aims to help talented individuals or groups to develop their full potential; to turn creativity into products and services that are effectively exploited with rights effectively protected; and to contribute to public knowledge and appreciation of science, technology and the arts. It grants fellowships worth up to £75,000 over three years.

Local Authorities

Local authorities maintain about 1,000 local museums and art galleries, and a network of public libraries (see p. 263). They also provide grant aid for professional and amateur orchestras, theatres, and opera and dance companies. In England total expenditure on museums, galleries and libraries for 1999–2000 was £937 million. Fourteen authorities are piloting Local Cultural Strategies, a DCMS scheme to bring cultural issues into the heart of local government planning.

The Corporation of London, the local authority for the City of London, is one of the largest sponsors of the arts in the UK, with a budget of £49 million in 1999–2000 from various resources. The Corporation owns, funds and manages the Barbican Centre (Europe's largest multi-arts and conference centre), which has the London Symphony Orchestra and RSC as residents; owns, funds and manages the Guildhall School of Music and Drama; jointly funds and manages the Museum of London with the DCMS; and funds various other cultural activities.

Business and Other Sponsorship

Total UK business investment in the arts rose by 22 per cent in 1998–99, to over £140 million. London attracted most of the investment—£64.5 million—followed by Scotland and the West Midlands. Museums and galleries received £31.7 million each; theatre received £17 million; music £12.3 million; and opera £13 million. The year saw a large rise in sponsorship of capital projects, and smaller rises in corporate donations and sponsorship. As one example, HSBC, the UK's largest bank, is giving £1.5 million over three years to the National Youth Theatre, the National Youth Orchestra, the National Youth Ballet and the National Opera Studio.

Among sponsorship from charitable trusts, the Jerwood Foundation gives about £3.5 million a year in capital and revenue grants, with emphasis on encouraging young performers. In 1999 the opening of the new Jerwood Library at Trinity Hall in Cambridge took place and in January 2000 the Foundation pledged £500,000 over five years to the Young Singers Programme at ENO. In addition to its £3 million towards the renewal of the Royal Court Theatre in London (with two auditoriums—the Jerwood Theatre Downstairs and the Jerwood Theatre Upstairs), it plans to continue with revenue funding for the theatre of up to £100,000 a year, provided it comes up with new plays by young writers. The first grants in the Artworks programme (to introduce children to the visual arts) of the Vivien Duffield Foundation were also announced. To celebrate National Children's Art Day on 5 May 2000, £20,000 was made available to create special events in museums and galleries throughout the UK.

Arts & Business exists to promote and encourage partnerships between business and the arts. It has over 350 business members and manages the Arts & Business New Partners Programme on behalf of ACE and the DCMS. Under the programme, investments can be made in arts/business partnerships, which bring benefits to both parties. Arts & Business New Partners was launched in April 2000, replacing the former Pairing Scheme, which raised £10 million from business and contributed over £160 million (including £52 million from the Government) to the arts over 16 years. Arts & Business also runs the Arthur Andersen Skills Bank and the NatWest Board Bank, which enable 3,000 volunteers from companies to loan their skills, in computing, accountancy, marketing or personnel, to local arts groups on a part-time basis.

Some £4 million from the Foundation for Sport and the Arts, run by the Pools Promoters Association, was used to help the arts in 1999 in the form of awards. Many arts organisations also benefit from the fund-raising activities of Friends groups and from private individuals' financial support.

Cultural Diversity

The Arts Councils promote cultural diversity in the arts. The Scottish Arts Council (SAC), for example, while supporting Gaelic culture, is also funding the Indian Mahila Cultural Committee in Glasgow and the African and Caribbean Resource Centre in Scotland. CADMAD, funded by the Arts Council of Wales (ACW), runs a cultural diversity training programme for artists and arts organisations. Measures to foster cultural diversity in Northern Ireland include funding for arts in both the Irish language and Ulster Scots. The Councils encourage the growth of Caribbean carnival across the UK, of which the most famous is the annual Notting Hill Carnival, the largest street festival in Europe. In recent years the Belfast Carnival has attracted an international audience. With financial support from ACE's Regional Black Theatre Initiative, Kuumba, an arts centre in Bristol, takes part in youth projects with the Bristol Old Vic, while the work of black writers in Britain has been promoted through Listening Posts. This included CDs of authors reading their own work, distributed through festivals, libraries and the media.

Arts and Disability

The National Disability Arts Forum and other similar national agencies are funded by ACE, as are creative organisations, such as Candoco Dance Company, composed of disabled and non-disabled dancers, and Graeae, a theatre company promoting performers with disabilities. ACE also supports an apprenticeship scheme for disabled people in arts organisations, such as the RSC, which is part of an initiative aimed at increasing employment opportunities for disabled people in the arts; and projects involving disabled artists in schools. The SAC supports ArtLink and Project Ability, which promote the development of disabled people's creativity.

Provision of access, in the widest sense, for disabled people in arts buildings is a major criterion for capital grants made from the National Lottery (see p. 117).

Arts Centres

Over 200 arts centres in the UK give people the chance of seeing a range of specialist art and of taking part in activities, especially educational projects. Nearly all the centres are professionally managed, while using the services of volunteers. They are assisted mainly by the Arts Councils, RABs and local authorities, while ACE currently funds two national centres in London, the South Bank Centre and the Institute of Contemporary Arts, popular for its art films and avant-garde exhibitions. Pier Arts Centre at Stromness (Orkney) and Dundee Contemporary Arts, the latter with two galleries, two cinemas, a print studio and activity rooms, are two of the centres supported by the SAC. The ACW funds Chapter Arts Centre in Cardiff, which helps to promote international artists and collaborations.

The British Council

The British Council (see p. 93) is the UK's international organisation for educational and cultural relations. It works in 243 cities in 110 countries to promote international understanding of British creativity in the arts, literature and design, as well as education, good governance and science. It aims to represent a modern and culturally diverse picture of the UK. In 1999 it supported some 3,000 cultural events overseas. The Visiting Arts Office of Great Britain and Northern Ireland is a joint venture of the British Council with the Foreign & Commonwealth Office, the Arts Councils and the Crafts Council. It encourages the inward flow to the UK of arts from other countries.

Broadcasting

Arts programmes broadcast by BBC radio and television and the independent companies (see chapter 17) have won many international awards, such as at the Prix Italia and Montreux International Television Festivals. Independent television companies also give grants for arts promotion in their regions. Broadcasting has created its own art forms—nothing like the arts documentary or drama series exists in any other medium.

Among British successes in the 1999 51st international Emmy awards, which honour the best television shows, Helen Mirren and Peter O'Toole won the awards for Best Actress and Best Actor in a mini-series or movie (*The Passion of Ayn Rand* and *Joan of Arc* respectively); *Horatio Hornblower*, a joint British-American production, won the award for Best Mini-Series; while Tracey Ullman won Best Guest Actress for her part in *Ally McBeal*. For the second year running the 88-year-old Thora Hird won the BAFTA television award for Best Actress (ITV's *Lost for Words*). Other BAFTA awards went to Michael Gambon for Best Actor in *Wives and Daughters* (BBC ONE) and to Channel 4's 'This is Modern Art' for Best Arts Programme. Honor Blackman, Diana Rigg, Linda Thorson and Joanna Lumley won special awards for their contribution to *The Avengers/New Avengers*.

The BBC has five orchestras, which employ many of Britain's full-time professional musicians. Each week it broadcasts about 100 hours of classical and other music (both live and recorded) on Radio 3 (see p. 269). BBC Radio 1 broadcasts rock and pop music, and much of the output of BBC Radio 2 is popular and light music. BBC Music Live in May 2000 featured more than 6,000 events, for all tastes, throughout the UK. In the drumming relay, a beat travelled from Londonderry across Great Britain to the Channel Islands. Of the two national commercial radio stations which broadcast music, Classic FM offers mainly classical and Virgin Radio plays rock. Much of the output of the UK's local radio stations is popular and light music.

Attendance at the 1999 Promenade Concerts (the 'Proms'), the world's largest music festival, was 88 per cent of capacity. For the 2000 season the BBC commissioned seven works from British composers, including Robin Holloway's First Symphony and a religious work by Jonathan Harvey (*Mothers shall not cry*). A Millennium Youth Day, in which some 800 young musicians filled the Albert Hall, premièred four compositions and joined in a performance of Walton's *Belshazzar's Feast*. Star international symphony orchestras, such as the Berlin, Dallas, San Francisco and Rotterdam orchestras, contrasted with a late-night prom that featured the Cuban band Los Van Van and Vocal Sampling, a group which creates a 20-strong salsa band with their voices.

Festivals

Some 500 professional arts festivals take place in the UK each year. In 1999 they attracted some £10 million in sponsorship from business. Their appeal has broadened, with what had been mainly classical music festivals now offering jazz, contemporary, world and early music. There are many more literature and film festivals, such as Brief Encounters in Bristol for short films, 60 or so festivals concentrating on poetry, and visual arts festivals, such as the Liverpool Biennial.

The 2000 Edinburgh International Festival featured some 180 performances of music, theatre, opera and dance, as well as lectures and discussions. Its home-grown element included the Scottish Chamber Orchestra with Christian Zacharias performing a cycle of Mozart's piano concertos; a series of concerts celebrating Scottish song; and Scottish Opera performing *Das Rheingold*. The Abbey Theatre, Dublin performed Valle-Inclán's *Barbaric Comedies* and the New York City Ballet made its first visit to Britain for 11 years. The Edinburgh Festival Fringe, with programmes (including street events) to suit all tastes, takes place alongside the main events. In 2000 there were over 17,000 performances by over 600 different companies. Other annual Edinburgh events include the International Film Festival and the Book Festival.

At the 2000 53rd Aldeburgh Festival its artistic director, Thomas Adès, conducted the first performance of his choral work *America* and Britten's *Peter Grimes* was given in concert. The St Magnus festival in Orkney included two premières by the festival's founder, Peter Maxwell Davies.

For a calendar of the main arts events in the UK in 2000, see Appendix 5, p. 551.

DRAMA

Among unusual theatrical events in 1999, the RSC at Stratford-upon-Avon performed Shakespeare's *Edward III*, the first professional group to do so after the play was officially restored to the canon in 1998 and computer analyses of the language had satisfied scholars that it was Shakespeare's work. Fanny Burney's comedy *A Busy Day* (c. 1800), lost until the 1980s, had its first West End staging in 2000. An ACE Lottery grant of £6 million has contributed most of the cost of building the Theatre by the Lake at Keswick (Cumbria) on the banks of Derwentwater. The ten-strong repertory company celebrated its opening with an early 19th-century musical play, *The Lakers* by James Plumptre, a skit on early tourism in the Lake District.

A full-size reconstruction in London of the Elizabethan Rose Theatre (on the site of Collins Music Hall), using the set (oak, with a thatched roof) made famous in the film *Shakespeare in Love*, is being planned, as part of a £27 million development.

ACE and the RABs are spending more than £50 million to support drama, including regional theatre, in 2000–01—21 per cent of ACE's total grant. In Scotland, Dundee Repertory Theatre received a further £286,000 SAC Lottery grant in early 2000 to create Scotland's only full-time ensemble company, in addition to the £2.4 million granted in 1999 for building improvements to expand its range of work. The ACW has established Clwyd Theatr Cymru as a Wales National Performing Arts Company, supported major building work at the Grand Theatre in Swansea, and funded new equipment at the Sherman in Cardiff.

In 1999 the London West End theatres were credited with bringing £1 billion into the London economy, when additional expenditure on travel, accommodation and

In February 2000 London's Royal Court Theatre re-opened after a four-year restoration, costing £28 million, under retiring artistic director Stephen Daldry. The opening play, under new artistic director Ian Rickson, was *Dublin Carol* by Conor McPherson.

London's Donmar Warehouse, of which Sam Mendes is artistic director, gained a £270,000 annual grant from ACE, to help assure its future.

The RNT topped the winners at the 2000 Olivier Awards for achievement in the West End theatre: Trevor Nunn for Best Director (Nick Dear's adaptation of Gorky's *Summerfolk*; *Troilus and Cressida*; *The Merchant of Venice*); *Honk! The Ugly Duckling* by George Stiles and Anthony Drewe, and directed by Julia McKenzie, for Best New Musical; and Bernstein's *Candide* for Outstanding Musical Production. Henry Goodman won Best Actor for his Shylock in *The Merchant of Venice* and Roger Allam and Patricia Hodge were Best Supporting Actor and Actress, in Edward Bulwer-Lytton's *Money* (1840). Simon Russell Beale won Best Actor in a Musical (*Candide*). Away from the RNT, Janie Dee took Best Actress award (having already won the *Evening Standard* and Critics' Circle awards) for her performance in Alan Ayckbourn's *Comic Potential*, and Barbara Dickson was Best Actress in a Musical (*Spend, Spend, Spend*). Peter O'Toole won an award for Outstanding Achievement. The BBC award for Best New Play went to *Goodnight Children Everywhere* (RSC at the Pit) by Richard Nelson.

British candidates won eight out of 21 Tony awards in New York: Jennifer Ehle for Best Actress and Stephen Dillane for Best Actor (in Tom Stoppard's *The Real Thing*); Michael Blakemore for Best Director twice (in Michael Frayn's *Copenhagen*—which also won Best Play—and in his revival of *Kiss Me Kate*); Roy Dotrice for Best Featured Actor; Elton John and Tim Rice for Best Musical Score (*Aida*); and Bob Crowley for Best Scenic Design. In January 2000 Kenneth Branagh received the John Gielgud Golden Quill award, given by the Shakespeare Guild of the United States to an outstanding interpreter of the Bard.

meals has been added to the cost of a ticket. As well as popular musicals, such as *Cats* and *The Phantom of the Opera* (which has taken £2 billion worldwide), more serious plays, such as Conor McPherson's *The Weir*, have enjoyed long runs. Famous film actors returning to the London stage have contributed to the revival of theatre-going.

The RNT's director, Trevor Nunn, has in 1999–2000 run a repertory system with a permanent ensemble, handling works from Shakespeare to musicals, on all three stages. The RNT's See a Play programme encourages young people aged between 15 and 26 to sign up for a series of plays for £5 a ticket. Critics praised the Shoreditch Shakespeare project (at the old Gainsborough studios) in 2000, conceived by the Almeida Theatre's artistic directors, Jonathan Kent and Ian McDiarmid, which gave Ralph Fiennes in Shakespeare's *Richard II* and *Coriolanus*. In 2000–01 the RSC at Stratford is giving all eight of Shakespeare's history plays ('This England—The Histories') from *Richard II* (with Samuel West) to *Richard III*. One of the events of 2000 was Kathleen Turner at the Gielgud as Mrs Robinson in Neil Simon's *The Graduate*, adapted and directed by Terry Johnson. At the autumn 1999 Belfast Festival an Irish cast's version of Beckett's *Waiting for Godot* was noted for its 'minute care and power'.

In 1999 the SAC launched the three-year Scotland Onstage initiative to stimulate the best in Scottish theatre. Eighteen winners were announced at Christmas 1999, with awards totalling £480,000. Successes have included Noël Coward's *Cavalcade* at Glasgow Citizens Theatre and the children's play *The Happy Prince*, a collaboration between the MacRobert in Stirling and the Lemon Tree in Aberdeen.

Some of the UK's 300 professional theatres are privately owned, but most belong to local authorities or to non-profit-making organisations. In January 2000 Andrew

Lloyd-Webber's Really Useful Group (with NatWest Equity Partners) bought control for £87.5 million of ten London theatres, including the Apollo, Theatre Royal (Drury Lane), Her Majesty's, Cambridge and the Gielgud.

London

London's 100 or so theatres include:

- the RNT, which stages modern and classical plays in its three auditoriums on the South Bank;
- the Barbican Centre, with two auditoriums, and home for half the year to the RSC, with a varied drama programme for the other half, including the Barbican International Theatre Event; and
- the Royal Court Theatre in Sloane Square, home to the English Stage Company, which specialises in new work.

Since its opening in 1996, Shakespeare's Globe on London's South Bank has attracted an attendance of 250,000 a year, with about 90 per cent capacity, brings in £2.4 million at the box office and runs at a profit. With its exhibition centre, it cost £30 million to build, with a grant of £12.4 million from ACE lottery funds. It has established itself as a centre for Shakespearean studies and is contributing to the regeneration of the neighbourhood.

In 1999 West End attendances increased slightly on 1998. Total West End box office takings were £266.6 million compared with £257.9 million in 1998.

Table 16.2: West End Theatres, 1989 and 1999

	1989	1999
Attendances	10.9 m	11.9 m
Increase/decrease on previous year	+0.4%	+0.1%
Average number of theatres open during year	42	44
Number of performances	16,436	17,089
Number of productions	237	265

Note: The 51 theatres which are represented in membership of the Society include both grant-aided and commercial managements.
Source: *The Society of London Theatre Box Office Data Report 1999*

Theatre for Young People

The RNT's Education Programme encourages access to drama on a national level through youth theatre projects, touring productions, workshops, rehearsed readings, work in schools and a nationwide membership scheme. The year 1999 saw the culmination of the third cycle of BT's National Connections youth programme, a partnership between 150 youth theatre companies and ten theatres across the UK. The National Youth Theatre in London, the touring National Youth Theatre of Wales and the Scottish Youth Theatre in Glasgow offer early acting opportunities to the young. ACE supports several national touring companies that produce plays for children, including Pop-Up, Quicksilver and Theatre Centre.

Training

The DCMS and the Department for Education and Employment (DfEE) disburse £19 million a year in grants for drama and dance students for tuition and maintenance. Over 800 students a year cover their tuition fees on the same basis as other higher and further education pupils. All training must be at accredited institutions and towards recognised qualifications, with annual evaluation by the DCMS and DfEE to ensure that standards are maintained. Among drama schools which train actors, directors, technicians and stage managers are the Royal Academy of Dramatic Art (RADA), the Central School of Speech and Drama, the London Academy of Music and Dramatic Art (LAMDA), and the Drama Centre (all in London); the Bristol Old Vic School, the Royal Scottish Academy of Music and Drama (Glasgow) and the Welsh College of Music and Drama (Cardiff). Competition to enter the School of Performing Arts at Stratford-upon-Avon College is keen.

MUSIC

In the UK more people attend live music performances than football matches. In 1999, 200.3 million music albums and 75.7 million singles were sold in the UK, while turnover increased by 1.1 per cent on the previous year to £1,133.4 million. Gross overseas earnings by the UK music industry were some £1.3 billion, of which more than half came from the sales of recordings, and the net surplus on overseas trade was about £500 million. The industry is worth about £4 billion a year (with domestic consumers spending about £3.3 billion a year on pop, classical music and opera) and employs about 130,500 people. The Government's Music Industry Forum advises the DCMS on how best it can promote the use of digital technologies, stimulate exports and see to the health of the industry's creative base.

Orchestral and Choral Music

London leads the world for the wide range of music available throughout the year. In classical music alone, there are four symphony orchestras with public subsidy, two more at the BBC, one at ENO and one at Covent Garden. The London Symphony (LSO—which gave 85 concerts in 1999–2000), with an ACE grant of £1.3 million in 1999–2000, gets matching funding from the Corporation of London, and, from its residence at the Barbican Centre in the City, has attracted sponsorship from banks and City firms. In 2000 the LSO marked the 75th birthday of Pierre Boulez with a project to trace the development of orchestral music through the 20th century, with performances all over the world. Every year it gives a series of concerts in New York.

National Orchestra Week in March 2000 celebrated orchestras and orchestral music throughout the UK and was partly funded by ACE's New Audiences Programme. Open days enabled the public to take part in workshops and discussions, to attend rehearsals and to meet the players. Concerts by English orchestras at the Royal Festival Hall from January to July were given by the Philharmonia, the London Philharmonic (under Bernard Haitink), the BBC Symphony (under Andrew Davis), and the City of Birmingham Symphony (under Simon Rattle). The smaller Queen Elizabeth Hall featured the Orchestra of the Age of Enlightenment and chamber groups: the London Mozart Players, the Academy of St Martin-in-the-Fields and the English Chamber Orchestra. The Bournemouth Symphony, Manchester's Hallé Orchestra and the Royal Liverpool Philharmonic are well-known orchestras outside London. The Royal Scottish National Orchestra and the Scottish Chamber Orchestra each give over 100 performances a year and attract over £2 million and £1.3 million respectively in SAC funding and sponsorship. In December 1999 the acclaimed BT Scottish Ensemble made a special tour (*Tabula Rasa*) of Scotland, its programme including Vivaldi and Arvo Pärt.

Among Britain's famous choral groupings is the Sixteen (16 singers specialising in early English polyphony and Renaissance music, under their conductor Harry Christophers), with an international reputation and 70 CDs to their name, who embarked on a tour during 2000 of 14 of England's cathedrals. At the Covent Garden festival in London in May, they gave Handel's oratorio *Israel in Egypt*, the choir and small orchestra (playing period instruments) forming an oval surrounded by the audience. English and Welsh choral societies have done much to foster the oratorio tradition at the leading music festivals. English ecclesiastical choral singing is exemplified by the choirs of cathedrals and by those of the colleges at Cambridge and Oxford. The choir at Westminster Cathedral is known for its more astringent tone (based on that of the Sistine Chapel at Rome) and has inspired works from modern English composers.

Two celebrated events in the musical calendar are the Leeds International Pianoforte Competition for young pianists and the biennial Cardiff Singer of the World Competition, which attracts outstanding young singers, and distinguished adjudicators, from all countries. The BBC Young Musicians contest in 2000 was won by the 18-year-old cellist Guy Johnston (playing Shostakovich's Cello Concerto).

Pop and Rock Music

In 1999–2000 the Welsh contribution to British pop, with the Stereophonics, Manic Street Preachers, Catatonia and Super Furry Animals as leading groups, and the veteran Tom Jones, was again marked. Super Furry Animals issued their fourth album, 'Mwng', entirely in Welsh. Home-grown black talent is also significant. Music of black origin accounted for 40 per cent of all singles and 21 per cent of all album sales in the UK in 1998. Black Voices, an *a capella* group from Birmingham, have intrigued audiences. In 1999 the Technics Mercury Music Prize (worth £25,000) went to Talvin Singh, whose music is a fusion of Indian classical melodies with present-day British dance music. Lynden David Hall's album *The Other Side* earned him approval as one of Britain's best soul singers. At the international Grammy Awards in Los Angeles the British singer Sting won two awards, for Best Pop Album (*Brand New Day*) and Best Male Pop Vocalist. Phil Collins won for the soundtrack of the film *Tarzan* and Elton John received the 'legend' award. Club music also continued to be influential and scored successes in the United States. In 2000 Robbie Williams became the most honoured artist yet at the Brit Awards by winning two more, for Best British Single and Best British Video (*She's the One*). Best British Female Solo Artist was Beth Orton and Best British Male Solo Artist was Tom Jones. The Scottish group Travis won two awards, for Best British Group and Best British Album (*The Man Who*). Its success underscored a renewed interest in guitar music. The Spice Girls won a special award for Outstanding Contribution. At the *Q* Awards in 1999, Keith Richards of the Rolling Stones received the *Q* Lifetime Achievement award.

At the 2000 Ivor Novello Awards for popular songwriters, Paul McCartney was given a fellowship of the British Academy of Composers and Songwriters; the Pet Shop Boys won an Outstanding Contribution to British Music award; Fran Healy of Travis was Songwriter of the Year (*Why does it always rain on me?*); and Elton John and Tim Rice won for International Achievement in Musical Theatre, for their musical *The Lion King*, which opened in London in 1999.

Folk Music

Folk and traditional music has always been strong in all parts of the UK. In Northern Ireland, bands perform in pubs and clubs, playing fiddles and other customary instruments. Irish acoustic groups are also in the Celtic tradition. Scottish and Welsh festivals honour Gaelic and Celtic music and song. The SAC highlights the diversity of Scottish traditional music: its sampler CD, *Seriously Scottish*, places traditional music alongside other contemporary forms. The sisters Jennifer and Hazel Wrigley have recorded guitar and fiddle duets (*Mither o'the Sea*) which show the strength of the Orkney tradition. English folk groups since the early 1970s, such as Steeleye Span, have blended the traditional and rock, and even used Gregorian chant, when arranging material of their own. Jazz and blues have influenced the songs of Maddy Prior, whose voice has helped increase the popularity of English folk music over 30 years. Kate Rusby sings in a Yorkshire dialect, and has been praised for her 'wit, character and invigorating freshness'. In February 2000 the BBC launched the Folk Awards.

Jazz and Blues

The Brecon, Cheltenham and London Oris jazz festivals, Edinburgh International Jazz and Blues Festival, and venues such as Ronnie Scott's in London's Soho, have helped win new audiences for jazz in the UK and showed how it can evolve when exposed to other musical influences, such as pop and Latin American, and how its rhythms can change. With John Rae's Celtic Feet, an Edinburgh group, folk has met modern jazz. In spring 2000 the keyboard and flugelhorn player Django Bates demonstrated the meeting of jazz and classical music when, with his jazz quartet, Human Chain, he joined the Britten Sinfonia for a series of concerts. The 2000 Bishopstock Blues Festival, held in Devon in May, featured Jools Holland and Steve Earle.

Training

Professional training in music is given at universities and conservatoires. The leading

London conservatoires are the Royal Academy of Music, the Royal College of Music, the Guildhall School of Music and Drama, and Trinity College of Music. Outside London are the Royal Scottish Academy of Music and Drama (RSAMD), including the Alexander Gibson School in Glasgow, the Royal Northern College of Music in Manchester, the Welsh College of Music and Drama in Cardiff, and the Birmingham Conservatoire.

Other Educational Schemes

The National Foundation for Youth Music, set up in 1999, aims to improve opportunities for young people to get involved in music-making, with £10 million a year from ACE Lottery funds and donations from other sources, including British Phonographic Industry. In addition, some £150 million from the DfEE's standards fund will be used over three years to help buy musical instruments for schools, restore free tuition and provide extra training for teachers. The LSO's educational outreach programme, Discovery, will have use of St Luke's, a disused Hawksmoor church in east London, in restoration for classes and rehearsals. UBS, the international financial services organisation, has guaranteed the project with £3.5 million, to attract support from ACE and the Jerwood Foundation.

Nearly a third of the players in the European Community Youth Orchestra come from the UK. There is also a National Youth Jazz Orchestra and a network of other youth jazz orchestras and wind bands.

OPERA

London's Royal Opera House (ROH) at Covent Garden reopened in December 1999 after a £214 million restoration and redevelopment. Verdi's *Falstaff* (under Haitink) relaunched the building with Bryn Terfel in the title role. The ROH's ACE grant has increased by £4 million to £20 million for 2000–01 and it has cut prices for seats with restricted views. The auditorium (2,100 seats), the rake of the stalls, the Vílar Floral Hall, restored as a meeting place and bar, the covered terrace overlooking Covent Garden piazza, and Linbury studio won wide admiration.

ENO won a 2000 Olivier award for Outstanding Achievement in Opera (for its high standard of production and championing of the works of Handel). David McVicar's 1999 staging of Handel's *Alcina* (1735) brought praise for conductor Charles Mackerras for his mastery of Handelian splendour and for principal mezzo Sarah Connolly as 'a star of our baroque firmament'. ENO's world première of British composer Mark-Anthony Turnage's new opera *The Silver Tassie* won high praise.

Welsh National Opera's (WNO) production of Humperdinck's *Hansel and Gretel* in 1999 at Sadler's Wells in London also won an Olivier award, for Best New Opera Production. Among WNO's other successes was John Crowley's staging of Britten's *The Turn of the Screw*, under Carlo Rizzi, with sopranos Janice Watson and Mary Lloyd-Davies singled out for their 'standards of expressiveness and dramatic power'. Critics warmed to Opera North's spring 2000 production of Ponchielli's *La Gioconda* and to Scottish Opera's rendition of Verdi's *Macbeth*, also performed at the Vienna Festival in May 2000.

Glyndebourne Opera (East Sussex), which relies on private patrons for its summer season, through its education department staged *Zoë*, an opera performed by and aimed at senior teenagers. One of its main season offerings in 2000 was Janáček's *Jenufa* (with Amanda Roocroft and Anja Silja) which won acclaim from audiences and critics alike. Castleward Opera in Co. Down revived Flotow's *Martha*, to widespread enthusiasm. Other country house opera ventures included Garsington (Oxfordshire), where the stage is a garden terrace, and Longborough (Gloucestershire), where a Wagner 'mini-*Ring*' was performed in a converted Cotswolds barn.

DANCE

The Royal Ballet is to have an enhanced status and more performances at the ROH. In the 2000 season it gave retrospective performances in honour of its two most important choreographers, Frederick Ashton and

Kenneth MacMillan; its celebration of contemporary International Choreography ended with ballets by Siobhan Davies and Ashley Page; and a quadruple bill focused on the legacy of Diaghilev and the Ballets Russes. English National Ballet was at the Coliseum at Christmas and the New Year with *Nutcracker* (directed by Derek Deane) and *Coppélia* (choreographer Ronald Hynd). Birmingham Royal Ballet brought David Bintley's *Arthur—Part One* and *Giselle* to the ROH in early summer 2000 and Northern Ballet Theatre presented *Carmen* at Sadler's Wells in March. Scottish Ballet embarked on a new era of classical and contemporary dance with the appointment of Robert North as artistic director. Rambert Dance Company, Britain's oldest ballet troupe, has become known for its forward-looking creativity. At Sadler's Wells in 2000 it initiated a series of promenade performances.

Spring Loaded, a showcase of Britain's dance and performance artists during March–June 2000, began and ended with works by Yolande Snaith. The Richard Alston Dance Company's acclaimed new programme (including 'The Signal of a Shake') came to London in March.

Training

Professional training for dancers and choreographers is provided mainly by specialist schools, which include the Royal Ballet School, the Central School of Ballet, the Northern School of Contemporary Dance (Leeds) and the London Contemporary Dance School.

All government-funded dance companies provide dance workshops and education activities. Phoenix Dance Company and English National Ballet, for example, have won awards for their projects. Ludus Dance Company, in Lancaster, works mainly with young people. The National Youth Dance Company gives a chance for young people to work with professionals.

FILMS

More than 500 new screens have been built in the UK since 1996. There are 186 multiplexes (five or more screens) with 1,727 screens. The number of feature films made with some UK investment and production involvement in 1999 rose to 103, compared with 91 in 1998. Of these, 97 UK-producer films included 71 wholly UK productions, of which 66 were made mainly or entirely in the UK. The number of international co-productions involving UK producers increased from 15 in 1998 to 26 in 1999. The number of foreign-producer films shot in the UK fell from 11 to six. Total investment in these titles was £570.1 million, compared with £487.2 million in 1998. Major US studios played a significant role in 1999, investing in 19 UK films with a combined budget of £303.6 million. The biggest wholly UK production in 1999 was the James Bond movie *The World is not Enough* (director Michael Apted), with a budget of £50 million; next came *The Beach* (director Danny Boyle), filmed almost entirely outside Britain, with a budget of £23.5 million, and *The End of the Affair* (with Julianne Moore and Ralph Fiennes; director Neil Jordan), on £20 million. Of the 97 UK-producer films, 37 received public funding, 17 of these benefiting from ACE, SAC and ACW National Lottery grants.

In 1999, UK cinemas took £583 million at the box office, from 360 films on release, compared with £539 million in 1998, from 356 films. Wholly UK films took a 16.5 per cent market share in 1999, earning £96 million between them and increasing their share sixfold. (The 190 US films released in 1999 earned £470 million between them—80.5 per cent of all takings, compared with 83.9 per cent in 1998.) Admissions to cinemas which take advertising rose from 135.2 million in 1998 to 139.1 million in 1999. (Admissions to the National Film Theatre—NFT—and regional film theatres numbered 360,000.) Britain excels in the digital technologies of film-making, which gives it importance as a centre in the final stages of production.

Film Council

The Film Council (FC), which came into being in April 2000, channels the majority of public funding for film production in the UK; it will be responsible for distributing £150

In 1999 the average European film took 78 per cent of European admissions in its home market; 42 of Europe's top 50 releases (which included nine from the UK) in 1999 saw at least half of their ticket sales come from the home market. An exception was *Notting Hill* (with Julia Roberts and Hugh Grant; director Roger Michell). While it topped the list of most successful European films in Europe, only 27 per cent (7.4 million out of 27.4 million) of its admissions came from the UK. Of the top films at the UK box office in 1999, *Notting Hill* (second) took £30.3 million; *The World is not Enough* (fifth) £20.6 million and *Shakespeare in Love* (sixth) £20.3 million. In March 2000 British successes at the Academy Awards were Sam Mendes as Best Director (*American Beauty*, which also won the award for Best Film); Michael Caine as Best Supporting Actor (*The Cider House Rules*); Christine Blundell and Trefor Proud, and Lindy Hemming, for Best Make-up and Best Costume Design respectively (Mike Leigh's *Topsy-Turvy*); Phil Collins for Best Original Song (*You'll be in my heart* in *Tarzan*); and Kevin MacDonald for Best Documentary Feature (*One Day in September*). Mendes and Collins had previously won Golden Globe awards, judged by the Hollywood Foreign Press Association. Janet McTeer also won a Golden Globe for Best Actress (*Tumbleweeds*). At the BAFTA awards in April *American Beauty* was judged Best Film. Maggie Smith won Best Supporting Actress (*Tea with Mussolini*) and Jude Law Best Supporting Actor (*The Talented Mr Ripley*). Lynne Ramsay won the Carl Foreman award for Newcomer in British Film (*Ratcatcher*). Best Adapted Screenplay went to Neil Jordan for his version of Graham Greene's *The End of the Affair*. The Alexander Korda award for Outstanding British Film went to *East is East*, produced by Leslee Udwin and directed by Damien O'Donnell, on a budget of £2.5 million and which had taken £14 million at the box office before opening in the United States. The Orange Audience award went to *Notting Hill*, to mark its popularity.

Sam Mendes also won the £12,000 Hamburg Shakespeare prize in 2000 for his contribution to the arts.

million of Lottery and government grant to the UK film industry during 2000–03. It has a wide remit, with cultural and industry objectives: to create a coherent structure for the UK film industry and to develop film culture in the UK.

New film production funds and initiatives, totalling £22 million, have been announced. The FC's New Cinema Fund will make £5 million available to radical and innovative film-makers looking to use the latest digital technology. Its £10 million Premiere Production Fund is geared towards the making of popular mainstream films and the £5 million Film Development Fund will be targeted at developing projects more intensively before going into production. The FC has absorbed the British Film Commission, which aims to attract foreign film-making and production investment into the UK, and British Screen Finance, a private sector company which previously provided funding to British productions and co-productions. The FC has earmarked 20 per cent of its production funds towards encouraging European co-productions. It also funds the British Film Institute (*bfi*; see p. 257) to deliver its cultural and educational objectives and has fully absorbed *bfi* Production.

The FC also helps to fund the British Film Office in Los Angeles, which promotes both British exports and the advantages of British studios to US film-makers.

Animation

Two prizes at the British Animation Awards in 2000 went to Tim Hope's *The Wolfman*, a six-minute film made on a home computer in a bedroom, manipulating hand-drawn characters into 3-D imagery. Richard Goleszowski's *Robbie the Reindeer: Hooves of Fire*, shown by the BBC at Christmas 1999, also won an award. In addition, the FC contributes £50,000 a year to a scheme for experimental animation, in conjunction with Channel 4.

Government Support

Government help for the film industry allows a 100 per cent tax write-off on the production and acquisition costs for British movies with budgets of up to £15 million. The Government supports a number of organisations that promote the film industry, headed by the FC. In addition, the Government provides grants to *Scottish Screen*, which promotes film-making in Scotland and receives 13 per cent of SAC Lottery funding on the arts, and to the *Northern Ireland Film Commission* (NIFC), which has a similar remit in the Province.

The Government has clarified the definition criteria for British films, making it more straightforward for internationally financed productions to be classified as British and in the process benefit from a UK film tax credit. This new definition is already benefiting international productions wanting to shoot in the UK, such as the Steven Spielberg/Tom Hanks 11-hour TV series, *Band of Brothers*, which started filming in spring 2000.

British Film Institute

The development of the moving image as an art form is promoted by the *bfi*, and by Scottish Screen and the NIFC.

The *bfi* maintains the J. Paul Getty Conservation Centre, which contains over 275,000 films and 200,000 television programmes, together with extensive collections of stills, posters and designs. The *bfi* National Library forms the world's largest collection of film-related books, periodicals, scripts and other written materials.

On the South Bank *bfi* activities include running the NFT, which screens over 2,000 films and television programmes each year, and the *bfi* London IMAX cinema, with Britain's largest screen. The *bfi* also runs the annual London Film Festival, the 44th in 2000, and supports newer festivals in the UK, such as the Leeds Children's Film Festival and the Brief Encounters short film festival in Bristol. A new UK cinema exhibition strategy also brings non-mainstream films into high street multiplexes, and a network of independent cinemas across the UK also receives *bfi* support. Its educational activities include courses, conferences and other events, and helping to formulate national film education policy.

Training in Film Production

The National Film and Television School is financed jointly by the Government and by the film, video and television industries (£5.5 million in 1999–2000). It offers postgraduate and short course training for directors, editors, camera operators, animators and other specialists. The School enrols 50–60 full-time students a year and about 850 on short course programmes. The London International Film School, the Royal College of Art and some universities and other institutions of higher education also offer courses in production. The Skills Investment Fund, worth £1.5 million and run by Skillset, the National Training Organisation for the industry, aims to boost UK film production training. The FC makes £5 million available for the Film Training Fund, for screenwriters to gain expertise in producing commercially attractive screenplays; and a further £1 million to First Movies, to enable children to make a first film using low-cost digital technology.

Cinema Licensing and Film Classification

Public cinemas must be licensed by local authorities, which have a legal duty to prohibit the admission of children to unsuitable films, and may prevent the showing of any picture. In assessing films the authorities normally rely on the judgment of an independent non-statutory body, the British Board of Film Classification (BBFC), to which all items must be submitted. It does not use any written code of censorship, but can require cuts to be made before granting a certificate; on rare occasions, it refuses a certificate.

Films passed by the BBFC are put into one of the following categories:

- U (universal), suitable for all;
- PG (parental guidance), in which some scenes may be unsuitable for young children;
- 12, 15 and 18, for people of not less than those ages; and
- Restricted 18, for restricted showing only at premises to which no one under 18 is admitted, for example, licensed cinema clubs.

Videos

The BBFC is also legally responsible for classifying videos under a system similar to that for films. It is an offence to supply commercially a video which has not been classified or to supply it in contravention of its designation.

MUSEUMS, GALLERIES AND THE VISUAL ARTS

About 80 million visits a year are made to the UK's 2,500 or so museums and galleries open to the public (in contrast to the 800 museums in 1980), which include the major national collections, about 1,000 independent museums, and 800 receiving support from local authorities. About a third of international visitors come to the UK because of its museums. Some 40,000 staff are employed in this sector. The Government's 24-Hour Museum website (www.24hourmuseum.org. uk), which provides a gazetteer of all UK museums and galleries, a magazine, search facilities and educational resources, receives about 300,000 'hits' a month. The £15 million Designated Challenge Fund made its first awards (£2.7 million) in 1999 to 49 institutions in England, to encourage them to raise their standards of collection care and access.

Museums and galleries in the UK receive about £620 million a year in public expenditure. National museums are financed chiefly from government funds; some charge for entry to their permanent collections and special exhibitions; all children (since 1999) and pensioners (since April 2000) have free access to those sponsored by the DCMS, and visits by children have gone up by 22 per cent. In addition, the Government has asked that from April 2001 the main national museums in England that charge for admission should reduce their entry fee to £1. The DCMS has set aside £7 million in direct funding (in addition to the £30 million set aside in 1998 to make free admissions possible) if the museums accept this offer. In Scotland admission to the National Galleries of Scotland is free of charge, and the Scottish Executive is making an additional £2 million a year available to enable the National Museums of Scotland to abolish admission charges from 1 April 2001.

Museums and galleries maintained by local authorities, universities and independent or privately funded bodies may receive help in building up their collections through grants via the Area Museum Councils, which are funded by Resource: the Council of Museums, Archives and Libraries, which replaced the Museums and Galleries Commission in April 2000, and the Area Museum Councils throughout the UK. Support to national and regional public and independent museums and galleries is also given by the Arts Councils and by trusts, voluntary bodies, the Heritage Lottery Fund and the National Art Collections Fund.

Resource is the strategic agency working with and on behalf of museums, archives and libraries across the UK. It also provides funds to the seven English Area Museum Councils, which supply services and their own small grants to individual museums, and to the Cultural Heritage National Training Organisation and the Museum Documentation Association.

Resource advises ministers on the Acceptance in Lieu scheme, whereby pre-eminent works of art may be accepted by the Government in settlement of tax and allocated to public galleries. Items accepted in 1999–2000 include Van Dyck's portrait of Abbé Scaglia (National Gallery) and the Powis archive (Shropshire Records and Research Centre).

By August 2000 UK museums were estimated to have benefited from £598.5 million of National Lottery money, as well as some £100 million from the Millennium Fund. Recent Arts Lottery grants have included nearly £16 million to the New Art Gallery, Walsall, and £1.2 million to the new

Milton Keynes Art Gallery. Heritage Lottery grants included £15 million to the development of Manchester's City Art Gallery and £15.9 million to the new wing of the National Portrait Gallery.

Among noted exhibitions in 1999–2000, Liverpool staged *Trace*, the UK's first Biennial of Contemporary Art, featuring 61 artists from 24 countries. The Tate St Ives featured the work of Wilhelmina Barns-Graham, since 1940 at the heart of the St Ives School of modern British painting. For its *Encounters* exhibition in 2000, the National Gallery in London persuaded 24 of the world's leading artists—including Auerbach (Constable), Caulfield (Zurbarán), Freud (Chardin) and Hockney (Ingres)—to create new works in response to past masters in the Gallery. Tate Britain has launched a scheme, backed by a £375,000 Lottery grant, to distribute some 175 of its greatest artworks to galleries around England. A British surrealist, Eileen Agar (d. 1991), had a retrospective at the Scottish National Gallery of Modern Art and at Leeds City Art Gallery. 'Sonic Boom—the Art of Sound' at the Hayward Gallery in London explored sound with cacophony and visual effects. The London Science Museum's Wellcome wing, costing £50 million, of which £23 million was financed through a Lottery grant, was unveiled in 2000. The Wallace Collection has created extra space (launched to celebrate its centenary in June 2000) in its mansion (1777) in London's Manchester Square, at a cost of £10.5 million.

The Jerwood Prize (worth £30,000) is awarded annually and reserved solely for painters. It was won in 1999 by the British abstract painter Prunella Clough, who has since died. Film and video artist Steve McQueen won the Tate's 1999 Turner Prize. The 1999 NatWest Art Prize (worth £26,000) went to the photorealist Jason Brooks, while the National Portrait Gallery's £10,000 BP Portrait Award in 2000 went to Victoria Russell for her 'Two Women in White'.

The former Tate Gallery in London was relaunched in 2000 in two parts: the old Gallery on Millbank, restored at a cost of £32.3 million (of which £18.75 million came from the Heritage Lottery Fund), became Tate Britain. Housed in two-thirds of the transformed Bankside power station, Tate Modern is London's first specialist gallery of 20th-century art, with works by Picasso, Mondrian, Pollock, Bacon, Warhol and others (including an unrivalled collection of late 20th-century minimalist and conceptual art). The project cost £134 million, with £50 million from government funding. An extra £5 million a year of government funding will keep admission free.

The collector Sir Denis Mahon has arranged to leave 58 Baroque paintings, done in Italy (among them works by Guercino, Guido Reni, Domenichino and Luca Giordano), to the National Art Collections Fund, to be allocated to institutions that do not charge for admission.

The 'British Art Show', organised by the Hayward Gallery, spotlighting contemporary visual art and held every five years, in 2000 displayed works by 57 artists, such as Paula Rego, Martin Creed and David Shrigley; it began in Edinburgh and then toured to Southampton, Cardiff and Birmingham. The Hayward also organised 30 touring exhibitions to 120 places in the UK, reaching an audience of 1.4 million. These shows included pieces from ACE's national loan collection of 7,000 works by modern British artists. The Arnolfini (Bristol), MOMA (Oxford) and Whitechapel Art Gallery (London) also launch touring shows of modern and contemporary art.

National Collections

The national museums and art galleries contain some of the world's most comprehensive exhibits of objects of artistic, archaeological, scientific, historical and general interest. The English national museums are:

- British Museum;
- Natural History Museum;
- Victoria and Albert Museum (fine and decorative arts);

Table 16.3: Visits to National Museums and Galleries in England, 1999–2000

	Number of visits million	% increase/decrease over 1998–99
British Museum[1]	5.0	–9
Imperial War Museum	1.4	0
National Gallery[1]	4.8	+10
National Maritime Museum	0.7	–7
National Museums & Galleries on Merseyside	0.8	–5
National Portrait Gallery[1]	1.0	0
Natural History Museum	1.7	–10
National Museum of Science & Industry	2.7	+23
Royal Armouries	2.8	–2
Tate Gallery[1]	2.6	–13
Victoria and Albert Museum (V&A)	1.3	–13
Wallace Collection	0.2	0

[1] Free admission.

Source: DCMS

- National Museum of Science & Industry, including the Science Museum and its two regional institutes, the National Railway Museum (York) and the National Museum of Photography, Film and Television (Bradford);
- National Gallery (Western painting from about 1260 to 1900);
- Tate Britain, devoted to British art since the 15th century, with collections in Liverpool and St Ives, Cornwall (St Ives School and modern art);
- Tate Modern (20th-century international art);
- National Portrait Gallery;
- Imperial War Museum, which has three sites in London and one at Duxford (which includes the American Air Museum) in Cambridgeshire;
- Royal Armouries, Britain's oldest museum, which has exhibits in the Tower of London (relating to the Tower's history), Leeds (arms and armour) and Fort Nelson, near Portsmouth (artillery);
- National Army Museum;
- Royal Air Force Museum;
- National Maritime Museum;
- Wallace Collection (paintings, furniture, arms and armour, and *objets d'art*); and
- National Museums & Galleries on Merseyside.

In Scotland the national collections are held by the National Museums of Scotland and the National Galleries of Scotland. The former include the Royal Museum, the Museum of Scotland, the Scottish National War Museum and the Scottish Agricultural Museum, in Edinburgh; the Museum of Flight, near North Berwick; and the Museum of Costume at Shambellie House near Dumfries. The new Museum of Scotland, built at a cost of £52 million and devoted to the history of Scotland, has won instant fame for its imaginative displays and distinctive architecture.

The National Galleries of Scotland comprise the National Gallery of Scotland, the Scottish National Portrait Gallery, the Scottish National Gallery of Modern Art, and the Dean Gallery, housing the Paolozzi gift of sculpture and graphic art, and renowned Dada and Surrealist collections. The National Galleries also have deposits at Paxton House near Berwick upon Tweed and Duff House in Banff. In 1999–2000 the National Museums of Scotland attracted some 800,000 visitors, and the National Galleries of Scotland 960,000.

The National Museum of Wales in Cardiff has a number of branches, including the Museum of Welsh Life at St Fagans, the Slate Museum at Llanberis and the Industrial and Maritime Museum in the Cardiff Bay development.

The National Museums and Galleries of Northern Ireland comprise the Ulster Museum in Belfast, the Ulster Folk and Transport Museum in County Down, and the Ulster-American Folk Park in County Tyrone.

Other Collections

The highly praised New Art Gallery, Walsall, built at a cost of £21 million, houses a collection of European Art bequeathed by Kathleen Garman (widow of the sculptor Jacob Epstein) and Sally Ryan, while The Lowry at Salford Quays, which cost £96 million (£64 million of which came from ACE Lottery funds), has galleries dedicated to the works of L. S. Lowry. In London the Dulwich Picture Gallery has benefited from an extensive, and warmly received, makeover (by Rick Mather) costing £8 million, while a £48 million (including a £20.75 million Lottery grant) development of Somerset House provided space for the Gilbert Collection of 800 pieces of English and European decorative art.

Other important collections in London include the Museum of London; the Courtauld Institute Galleries (containing masterpieces of 14th–20th-century European painting); and the London Transport Museum.

Museums outside London include those associated with universities, such as the Ashmolean in Oxford, the Fitzwilliam at Cambridge and the Hunterian in Glasgow. The Burrell Collection, also in Glasgow, has an unrivalled display of tapestries, paintings and *objets d'art*.

Among a number of national art exhibiting institutions is the Royal Academy of Arts, at Burlington House in London, which holds an annual Summer Exhibition (232nd in 2000), the world's largest open present-day art display, and other important ones during the year. Anyone claiming the status of an artist of 'distinguished merit' and seeking 'reputation and encouragement' may submit works to the Summer Exhibition. In 2000, 1,516 were chosen, representing 628 artists, from an entry of over 13,000. The Royal Scottish Academy holds annual exhibitions in Edinburgh. There are also children's shows, including the National Exhibition of Children's Art.

Open-air museums depict the life of an area or preserve early industrial remains, such as the Weald and Downland Museum in West Sussex, the Ironbridge Gorge Museum in Shropshire and the North of England Open Air Museum at Beamish in County Durham. Skills of the past are revived in a number of 'living' museums, such as the Gladstone Pottery Museum near Stoke-on-Trent and the Quarry Bank Mill at Styal in Cheshire.

Training in Art and Design

Most practical education in art and design is provided in the art colleges and fine and applied art departments of universities (these include the Slade School of Art and Goldsmiths' College of Art, London), which have absorbed the former independent art schools, and in further education colleges and private art schools. Some of these institutions award degrees at postgraduate level. The Royal College of Art in London is the only postgraduate school of art and design in the world. Art is also taught at an advanced level at the four Scottish art schools.

University courses concentrate largely on academic disciplines, such as the history of art. The Courtauld and Warburg Institutes of the University of London and the Department of Classical Art and Archaeology at University College London are leading institutions. Art is a foundation subject in the National Curriculum in England (see p. 126). The Society for Education through Art, among other activities, encourages schools to buy original works by organising an annual 'Pictures for Schools' exhibition.

Export Control of Works of Art

The UK market is second only to that of the United States. The UK's art and antiques trade handles about 70 per cent of European art sales, employs about 50,000 people, brought in about £470,000 in foreign currency in 1999–2000 and has an annual turnover of £2.5 billion. Auctions of works of art take place in the main auction houses (two of the longest established being Sotheby's and Christie's), and through private dealers.

A licence is required before certain items can be exported, and if a DCMS Expert Adviser objects to the granting of a licence, the matter is referred to the Reviewing Committee on the Export of Works of Art. If the Committee considers a work to be of national importance, it can recommend to the Government that a decision be deferred on the licence application for a specified time to give a chance for an offer to be made to buy it at or above the recommended fair market price.

The UK has resisted an EU proposal to impose artists' resale rights, whereby the price of any work of art sold during an artist's lifetime, or for 70 years after his or her death, would include a tax payable to the artist or heirs. It has, however, agreed an EU compromise—a 15-year transitional period (from 2000) to phase in the measure and a maximum payment on any work at £7,650, with a minimum value of a work of £4,000.

LITERATURE AND LIBRARIES

Over 200 literary prizes are awarded yearly in the UK, ranging in value from £30 to £30,000, and for many different categories of work. The winner of the 1999 Booker Prize for Fiction (worth £20,000; UK and Commonwealth citizens eligible) was the South African writer J. M. Coetzee, for *Disgrace*, while the Whitbread awards (valued at £2,000 each with £21,000 extra for Book of the Year; for British subjects), announced in January 2000, were distributed as follows:

- Poetry award and Whitbread Book of the Year: Seamus Heaney, for his translation of the Anglo-Saxon epic *Beowulf*;
- Novel award: Rose Tremain, *Music and Silence*;
- First Novel award: Tim Lott, *White City Blue*;
- Biography award: David Cairns, *Berlioz*; and
- Children's Book of the Year (£10,000): J. K. Rowling, *Harry Potter and the Prisoner of Azkaban*.

Billy's Rain, a collection of poems by Hugo Williams, won the 1999 T. S. Eliot Prize (worth £5,000). J. K. Rowling was named Author of the Year by more than 100 members of the British book industry at the British Book Awards in February 2000. The Orange Prize for Fiction (£30,000) in 2000, open to any woman writing in English, went to the British author Linda Grant for *When I Lived in Modern Times*.

Authors' Copyright and Performers' Protection

Original literary, dramatic, musical or artistic works (including computer programs and databases), films, sound recordings, cable programmes, broadcasts and the typographical arrangement of published editions, are automatically protected by copyright in the UK if they meet the legal requirements for protection. In general terms, copyright protection may also be given to works first published in (or, in the case of a broadcast or a cable programme, made in or sent from) EU member states, or from countries party to international copyright conventions, the World Trade Organisation or reciprocal agreements. The copyright owner has rights against unauthorised reproduction, public performance, broadcasting, rental and lending, issue to the public and adaptation of his or her work; and against importing, possessing, dealing with or providing means for making unauthorised copies. In most cases the author is the first owner of the copyright, and the term of copyright in literary, dramatic, musical and artistic works is generally the life of the author and a period of 70 years from the end of the year in which he or she dies. For films the term is 70 years from the end of the calendar year in which the death occurs of the last to die of the following: principal director, authors of the screenplay and dialogue, or composer of music specifically created for and used in the film. Sound recordings are protected for 50 years from the end of the year of making or release, and broadcasts for 50 years from the end of the year of broadcast.

Subject to qualifying requirements, performers are also given automatic protection against unauthorised broadcast or inclusion in a cable television programme, or recording, of live performances, reproduction of recordings, and issue to the public or rental or lending of copies of a recording. These rights in performances last for 50 years from the year of performance or release of a recording of it. Performers also have a right to equitable remuneration for the playing in public, or inclusion in a broadcast or cable programme service, of a commercially published sound recording of their performance. There is also a right against extraction and re-utilisation of the contents of a database ('*sui generis* database rights'), where there has been substantial investment in obtaining, verifying or presenting the contents of the database.

Literary and Philological Societies

Societies to promote literature include the English Association, the Royal Society of Literature and the Welsh Academy (Yr Academi Gymreig). The leading society for studies in the humanities is the British Academy for the Promotion of Historical, Philosophical and Philological Studies (the British Academy).

Other specialist societies are the Early English Text Society, the Bibliographical Society and several devoted to particular authors, such as Jane Austen and Charles Dickens. The Poetry Society sponsors poetry readings and recitals. London's South Bank Centre and the British Library run programmes of literary events.

Public Libraries

Local authorities in Great Britain and education and library boards in Northern Ireland have a duty to provide a free lending and reference library service. There are almost 5,000 public libraries in the UK. In Great Britain more than 34 million people (58 per cent of the population) are members of their local library and about half of these borrow at least once a month. About 480 million books and 37 million audio-visual items were borrowed from UK public libraries in 1999–2000. Adult fiction accounted for 50 per cent, adult non-fiction for 25 per cent and children's books for 23 per cent.

Many libraries have collections of CDs, records, audio- and video-cassettes, and musical scores for loan to the public, while a number also lend from collections of works of art, which may be originals or reproductions. Most libraries hold documents on local history, and all provide services for children, while reference and information sections, and art, music, commercial and technical departments, meet a growing demand. The information role is important for all libraries: nearly all have personal computers for public use and, in November 1999, 41 per cent had Internet connections. A government initiative under the New Opportunities Fund (see p. 117) is providing £20 million for information and communications technology training of library staff and £50 million for enabling library material to be stored and accessed in digitised form.

The Government is advised (since April 2000) by Resource. It is committed to networking all public libraries and connecting them to the National Grid for Learning by 2002. The DCMS/Wolfson Public Libraries Challenge Fund has mounted a £3 million campaign to persuade people, especially the young, of the joys of reading as a leisure pursuit.

Public Lending Right Scheme

The Public Lending Right Scheme gives registered authors royalties from a central fund (totalling just over £5 million in 1999–2000) for the loans made of their books from public libraries in the UK. Payment is made according to the number of times an author's books are lent out. The maximum yearly payment an author can receive is £6,000.

The Library Association

The Library Association is the principal professional organisation for those engaged in library and information management. Founded in 1877, the Association has some 25,000 members. It maintains a Register of Chartered Members and is the designated authority for the recognition of qualifications gained in other EU member states.

The British Library and National Libraries

The British Library (BL), the national library of the UK, is custodian of the most important research collection in the world (150 million items spanning 3,000 years). It is also the largest UK publicly funded building constructed in the 20th century. The total floor space is approximately 100,000 sq metres. The basements, the deepest in London, have 300 km of shelving for 12 million books. There are 11 reading areas, three exhibition galleries and a conference centre with a 255-seat auditorium. British publishers are legally obliged to deposit a copy of their publications at the BL. The National Libraries of Scotland and Wales, the Bodleian at Oxford and the Cambridge University Library (and the Library of Trinity College, Dublin) can also claim copies of all new British publications under legal deposit.

Some 447,000 reader visits are made to the BL each year. The reading rooms are open to those who need to see material (for example, manuscripts, newspapers, journals, stamps and maps, as well as books) not readily available elsewhere or whose work or studies require the facilities of the national library. During March–October 2000 the BL exhibition 'Chapter and Verse' celebrated 1,000 years of English literature, with readings by distinguished actors and authors.

The BL's Document Supply Centre at Boston Spa (West Yorkshire) is the national centre for inter-library lending within the UK and between the UK and other countries. It dispatches over 4 million documents a year.

Other Libraries

As well as public and national libraries there are nearly 700 more in higher and further education, about 5,600 in schools and 2,220 specialised libraries within other public and private sector organisations (such as commercial companies, research councils and government departments).

The university book collections of Oxford and Cambridge number over 7 million and more than 6 million items respectively. The combined stores of the colleges and institutions of the University of London total 9 million volumes, the John Rylands University Library of Manchester contains 3.5 million volumes, Edinburgh 2.5 million, Leeds 2.3 million, and Durham, Glasgow, Liverpool and Aberdeen each have over 1 million volumes. Many universities have vital research collections in special subjects—the Barnes Medical Library at Birmingham and the British Library of Political and Economic Science at the London School of Economics, for example.

Besides a number of private collections, such as that of the London Library (for private subscribers), there are the collections of such learned societies as the Royal Institute of International Affairs, the Royal Geographical Society and the Royal Academy of Music. The Poetry Library in the South Bank Centre, owned by ACE, is a collection of 20th-century poetry written in or translated into English; it has about 60,000 volumes.

The Public Record Office (PRO) in London and in Kew (Surrey) houses the records of the superior courts of law of England and Wales and of most government departments, as well as millions of historical documents, such as *Domesday Book* (1086) and autograph letters and documents of the sovereigns of England. Public records, with a few exceptions, are available for inspection by everyone 30 years after the end of the year in which they were created. The Scottish Record Office in Edinburgh and the PRO of Northern Ireland in Belfast serve the same purpose.

> In 2000 the BL relaunched an 'adopt a book' scheme (www.bl.uk/adoptabook), to provide funds in addition to its preservation budget (£6.76 million in 2000–01) to prevent thousands of volumes from deteriorating. Depending on the size of the donation, a donor's name appears alone, or with others, on a permanent bookplate.

Books

In 1999 about 123 million books were sold in the UK. British publishers issued over 110,000

Tate Modern

The total cost of transforming the former Bankside Power Station, London, to a building housing the national collection of international and British 20th century art was £134 million, of which £56.2 million was raised through the National Lottery. Tate Modern is on three levels with an internal floor area of 34,000 square metres, 14,000 square metres of which are display space.

Dulwich Picture Gallery

Refurbishment of Sir John Soane's 19th century gallery in south-east London and the creation of a new building adjoining it has been made possible with assistance of a £5 million award from the Heritage Lottery Fund.

The Lowry Project

In the heart of the re-developed Salford Quays, Greater Manchester, The Lowry arts complex has received £68.9 million in National Lottery funding. It is a new centre for creativity, bringing together a wide variety of performing and visual arts under one roof, and takes its name from L. S. Lowry, one of the most popular British artists of the 20th century.

The British Museum Great Court Project

The Great Court scheme, supported by funds from the National Lottery, will transform the two-acre inner courtyard of the British Museum, London, making it the largest covered public square in Europe. It will house an education centre, exhibition galleries and new visitor services. The restored reading room will contain a new public reference library devoted to the study of world cultures.

The Science Museum

Two new projects totalling a £50 million development—the Wellcome Wing and the Making of the Modern World Gallery at the Science Museum, London, received a £23 million contribution from the Heritage Lottery Fund. The new exhibits are designed to tell the story of the Industrial Revolution as well as science past, present and future.

Dynamic Earth by night.

Restless earth: the display recreates the eruption of a volcano with lava, smoke and sulphurous smell effects.

Tropical rainforest: in a humid atmosphere visitors can experience rainstorms and a display of changing jungle animals.

Dynamic Earth

One of the biggest Millennium Commission projects in Scotland, Dynamic Earth, Edinburgh, received an award of £15 million from the National Lottery. The project recounts the evolution of the planet through a journey going back 4,500 million years using 11 state-of-the-art earthscapes.

The National Botanic Garden of Wales

The first national botanic garden to be created in the United Kingdom for more than 200 years, the National Botanic Garden of Wales, Llanarthne, Carmarthenshire, received £21.6 million funding from the Millennium Commission.

The Broadwalk links the entrance with the Great Glasshouse.

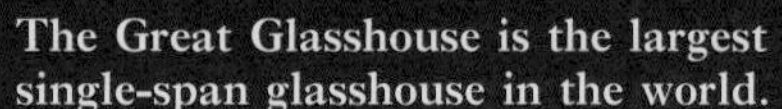

The Great Glasshouse is the largest single-span glasshouse in the world.

The Eden Project

With the help of a £40 million grant from the Millennium Commission, the Eden Project is transforming a disused clay pit in Cornwall into a global garden. Geodesic domes are being created to house plants from three of the world's climactic zones. The Eden Project focuses on the relationship between plants, people and resources, and aims to promote their responsible and sustainable management.

Children look out of the visitor centre at work in progress.

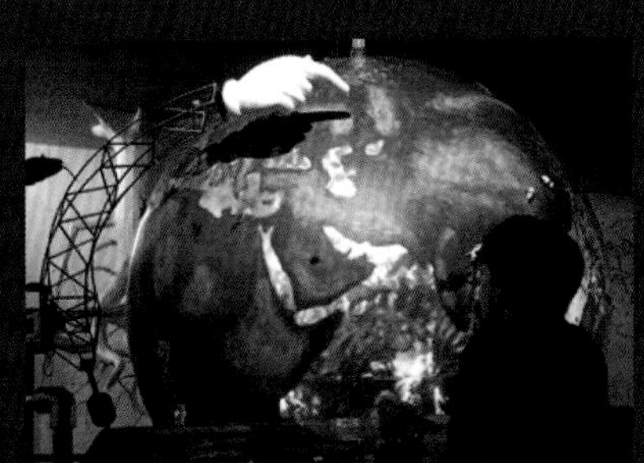

Humid Tropics dome under construction.

'The Globe', one of the visitor centre's automata.

Odyssey Project

Regeneration of Laganside, Belfast, transforming the east bank of the River Lagan from a derelict dockland to a thriving industrial and commercial zone has been helped by a £45 million grant from the Millennium Fund. When completed, the site will provide a range of leisure and recreational facilities for Northern Ireland's capital city.

Millennium Festival Awards

The National Lottery provides funding for grants up to £5,000 for small projects under the Millennium Festival Awards for All programme in England and Scotland and a similar scheme in Wales.

Forge Community Partnership, Barnsley, South Yorkshire. A grant has helped fund social and economic regeneration projects in the local community.

Newport Somali Association, Newport, South Wales. A pilot advocacy scheme now operates to support the Somali community.

Visually Impaired People's Club, Welshpool. The group's social activities have been increased under the awards scheme.

Valley Teen Club, Ammanford, Carmarthenshire. New information technology equipment has been provided for a group of young people.

separate titles (including new editions). The UK book industry exported books worth £890 million in 1999, 8.3 per cent up on 1998. J. K. Rowling's Harry Potter books were successful both in the UK and overseas (18.5 million copies of the first three were printed; the fourth was published in 2000).

Among the leading trade organisations are the Publishers Association (PA), which has 200 members; and the Booksellers Association, with about 3,300 members. The PA, through its International Division, promotes the export of British books. The Welsh Book Council and the Gaelic Books Council support the publication of books in Welsh and in Gaelic. The Book Trust encourages reading and the promotion of books through an information service and a children's library.

Historical Manuscripts

The Royal Commission on Historical Manuscripts locates, reports on, and gives information and advice about historical papers outside the public records. It also advises private owners, grant-awarding bodies, record offices, local authorities and the Government on the acquisition and maintenance of manuscripts. The Commission maintains the National Register of Archives (the central collecting point for information about British historical manuscripts) and the Manorial Documents Register, which are available to researchers.

CRAFTS

The crafts in the UK have an annual turnover estimated at £400 million. Government aid amounted to £2.5 million in 1999–2000. Policy and funding for the crafts in England are the responsibility of ACE, which is required to allocate at least £3.4 million, £3.6 million and £3.8 million for crafts for the years 1999–2000, 2000–01 and 2001–02 respectively, with a further £750,000 for development. The Crafts Council runs the National Centre for Crafts in London, organises the annual Chelsea Crafts Fair (which generated sales of £2.6 million for the trade in 1999), and co-ordinates British groups at international fairs. Five Crafts Council exhibitions took place at its London gallery in 1999 (nearly 42,000 visitors) before going on tour. Craft Forum Wales has a membership of 640 craft business groups in Wales; they had a turnover of £27.5 million in 1999. Craftworks, an independent company, is the development agency for Northern Ireland. The ACNI also funds crafts promotion, while the SAC has a Crafts Department, which promotes crafts and helps craftworkers in Scotland.

Further Reading

Department for Culture, Media and Sport: Annual report 2000. Cm 4613. The Stationery Office, 2000.

Website

Department for Culture, Media and Sport: www.culture.gov.uk

17 The Media

Digital terrestrial and satellite television services in the UK were launched in 1998. Cable and commercial digital radio services got under way in 1999. Newspapers throughout the UK—despite a gradual decline in hard-copy circulation for some titles—continue to serve a wide readership. Increasingly the Internet is providing an additional medium for information, entertainment and communication.

Television and Radio

Three public authorities oversee television and radio services. They are accountable to Parliament, but are otherwise independent in their day-to-day running of business. The authorities are:

- the BBC (British Broadcasting Corporation), which broadcasts television and radio programmes;
- the ITC (Independent Television Commission), which licenses and regulates commercial television services including cable, satellite and independent teletext services; and
- the Radio Authority, which licenses and regulates commercial radio services, including cable and satellite.

The Department for Culture, Media and Sport is responsible for government policy towards broadcasting.

There are five terrestrial analogue television channels, offering a mixture of drama, light entertainment, films, sport, educational, children's and religious programmes, news and current affairs, and documentaries. These comprise two national BBC networks, financed almost wholly by a licence fee, and the commercial ITV (Channel 3), Channel 4 and Channel 5 services, which are funded by advertising and sponsorship. In Wales, S4C—Sianel Pedwar Cymru—broadcasts programmes on the fourth channel.

Satellite television and cable services are mainly funded by subscription income. The largest satellite programmer is BSkyB (British Sky Broadcasting), which dominates subscription-based television in the UK.

The UK's first digital satellite and terrestrial television services (see pp. 271 and 273) were launched in 1998, providing the existing analogue programmes in a digital format, together with free-to-air and

Television Audience Share Figures, UK, April 1999–March 2000

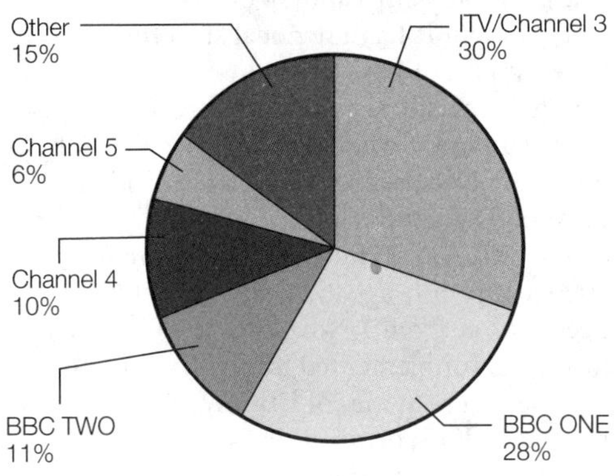

Source: Independent Television Commission

subscription and pay-per-view[1] services. Digital cable services began in 1999.

> A government-commissioned report on UK television exports, published in November 1999, found that 13 per cent of exported television programmes shown at prime time anywhere in the world come from Britain. This figure, although substantially behind that of the United States (68 per cent), is six times greater than Australia, France, Germany and Italy, each with 2 per cent.

The BBC has five national radio networks, which together transmit all types of music, news, current affairs, drama, education, sport and a range of features programmes. There are also 39 BBC local radio stations serving England and the Channel Islands, and national radio services in Scotland, Wales and Northern Ireland, including Welsh and Gaelic language stations. BBC national and local radio services currently attract just over 50 per cent of listeners (with local radio accounting for nearly 11 per cent of that figure).

[1] Pay-per-view allows subscribers to pay for a specific programme, such as a film, sporting event or concert.

There are three national commercial radio stations. About 240 independent local radio (ILR) services are also in operation, supplying local news and information, sport, music and other entertainment, education and consumer advice. The first commercial digital radio services started in 1999.

DIGITAL BROADCASTING

The transition from analogue to digital transmission technology has the potential to expand broadcasting capacity enormously. Digital broadcasting is a more effective way of transmitting services. It allows much more information than before to be transmitted, and can offer many more channels, extra services, interactivity, and higher quality picture and sound to viewers and listeners with new receiving equipment.

Digital television services can be received through an existing television aerial, a cable connection or a satellite dish. Viewers who choose to receive them by any of these means need either a special set-top box decoder, enabling reception of digital broadcasts through an analogue television set, or an integrated digital television set. Radio listeners also need to invest in new sets to hear digital radio.

Legislation was passed in 1996 setting out a regulatory framework for the introduction of digital terrestrial broadcasting (and paving the way for more broadly based competitive media groups—see p. 280). The Broadcasting Act 1996 provided for:

- the licensing of six digital terrestrial television (DTT) 'multiplexes',[2] and the providers of the programmes or other services on them; and
- the licensing of digital radio services on two national multiplexes, with a multiplex for local services in most parts of the UK.

The existing public service broadcasters have guaranteed capacity on the multiplexes. Licences to operate commercial DTT

[2] Through the process known as multiplexing, the signals of several broadcasters are combined into a single stream on a single-frequency channel. There is therefore no longer a direct one-to-one relationship between a television service and a frequency.

multiplexes were awarded by the ITC in 1997, and all DTT multiplexes started broadcasting in 1998. The Radio Authority awarded the national commercial radio multiplex licence in 1998 (with services beginning in November 1999), and is concentrating on advertising local commercial multiplex licences in most of the main population centres across the UK.

Many of the new services on digital television are available on a subscription or pay-per-view basis. Any broadcaster wishing to offer pay-television needs to use a 'conditional access' system (covering encryption, scrambling and subscription management services) to ensure that only those who have paid for a particular service receive it.

Existing analogue transmissions will continue for some time, but the Government wants to announce a switch-off date for analogue services as soon as is practicable. In 1999 it said that the switch-over to digital broadcasting could start to happen as early as 2006 and be completed by 2010, provided that all viewers who can receive the current free-to-air analogue services can receive them digitally. By April 2000 about 2.5 million households in the UK had switched to digital television.

THE BBC

The BBC is the UK's main public service broadcaster. A Royal Charter and Agreement govern its constitution, finances and obligations. Its Board of Governors appoints the Director-General, who heads the bodies in charge of the daily running of the Corporation. It has a regional structure throughout the UK.

The Government is reviewing the future regulation of broadcasting and telecommunications, taking account of the implications of the increasing convergence between the two sectors. Following on from the report *Regulating Communications: the Way Ahead*, published in 1999, the Government proposes to issue a White Paper later in 2000. The aim is to promote the global competitiveness of the UK's media and communications industries, as well as protect the interests of the consumer. The White Paper will include proposals for changing existing broadcasting and telecommunications legislation, encompassing both infrastructure and content issues.

The domestic services of the BBC are financed almost wholly by a licence fee. All households or premises with a television set must buy an annual licence (costing £104 for colour and £34.50 for black and white in 2000–01; people aged 75 and over get their licences free from 1 November 2000). Licence income is supplemented by profits from the commercial activities of BBC Worldwide (see p. 269). BBC World Service's radio broadcasting operations (see p. 270) are financed by a grant from the Foreign & Commonwealth Office.

In response to the report of an independent review panel (published in August 1999) on the future financing of the BBC, the Government announced new funding plans in February 2000 for the Corporation over the period to 2006–07. These provide for additional annual support through the licence fee, aimed at ensuring the Corporation's continuing ability to meet its public service obligations and its effective operation in a competitive market. The plans also include new efficiency targets and arrangements to increase accountability, with independent scrutiny of the BBC's fair trading policies and financial reporting.

BBC Television

The BBC broadcasts 22,000 hours of television each year on its two domestic channels to national and regional audiences. BBC ONE is the channel of broad appeal (including documentaries and current affairs, features, drama and light entertainment, sport, religion and children's programmes), while BBC TWO aims for more innovation and originality in its programming.

Network programmes are made at, or acquired through, Television Centre in London and six bases throughout the UK (Glasgow in Scotland, Cardiff in Wales, Belfast in Northern Ireland, and Birmingham,

Bristol and Manchester in England); or they are commissioned from independent producers—the BBC must ensure that at least 25 per cent of its original programming comes from the independent sector.

The Corporation provides a range of digital channels available free-to-air, including:

- an extended BBC ONE and BBC TWO in widescreen;
- BBC News 24 (a 24-hour news channel);
- BBC Choice, a supplementary service to complement and enhance the network schedules;
- BBC Parliament (coverage of proceedings in the House of Commons, House of Lords, the new Parliament in Scotland and the new assemblies in Wales and Northern Ireland—see p. 274); and
- BBC Knowledge (the UK's first fully integrated public service multimedia learning service).

The BBC's Online channel on the Internet provides constantly updated news, sport, finance, travel and other information.

Education is a central component of the Corporation's public service commitment on its domestic channels. A wide range of educational programmes is broadcast for primary and secondary schools (over 90 per cent of which use BBC schools television), further education colleges and the Open University (see p. 137), while programmes for adults cover numeracy, literacy, language learning, health, work and vocational training. Books, pamphlets, computer software, and audio and video cassettes are produced to supplement the programmes.

BBC Network Radio

BBC Network Radio, broadcasting to the whole of the UK, transmits 43,000 hours of programmes each year on its five networks (broadcasting 24 hours a day):

- Radio 1 is a contemporary music station, serving a young target audience (with almost 11 per cent of the overall radio audience share during October–December 1999);
- Radio 2 offers a broad range of music, light entertainment, documentaries, public service broadcasting and popular culture (nearly 13 per cent of audience share);
- Radio 3 covers classical and jazz music, drama, documentaries and discussion (over 1 per cent share);
- Radio 4 offers news and current affairs coverage, complemented by drama, science, the arts, religion, natural history, medicine, finance and gardening features; it also carries parliamentary coverage and cricket in season on Long Wave, and BBC World Service overnight (11 per cent share);
- Radio 5 Live broadcasts news, current affairs and extensive sports coverage (over 4 per cent share).

BBC Worldwide

With responsibility for the BBC's commercial activity, BBC Worldwide is a major international broadcaster and a leading distributor and co-producer of BBC programmes.

BBC Worldwide is developing premium channels to compete in the international market-place. Its core service is BBC World, an advertiser-funded, 24-hour international news and information channel. The channel provides news bulletins, in-depth analysis and reports, and is available to about 168 million homes around the world. BBC Prime, an entertainment and drama channel for Europe and Africa, has nearly 9 million subscribers.

In its first commercial broadcasting venture in the UK, the BBC began themed subscription services in 1997, in partnership with Flextech plc, under the brand name UKTV. These services are not funded by the licence fee.

In 1998 BBC Worldwide signed an agreement with a US media company, Discovery Communications Inc., creating a BBC-branded network (BBC America) in the United States and jointly developing quality channels for pay-television around the world.

BBC Worldwide is the third largest publishing house in the UK. Its operations cover magazines, books, videos, audio sales, CD-ROMs and a commercial on-line service.

BBC World Service

BBC World Service broadcasts by radio in English and 42 other languages worldwide. It has an estimated global weekly audience of about 150 million listeners. This excludes any estimate for listeners in countries where it is difficult to survey audiences. The core programming of news, current affairs, business and sports reports is complemented by cultural programmes, including drama, literature and music.

While maintaining short wave broadcasts for mass audiences, BBC World Service is making programmes more widely available on FM frequencies and delivering services in major languages through digital broadcasting and on the Internet.

BBC World Service programmes in English and many other languages are made available by satellite for rebroadcasting by agreement with local or national radio stations, networks and cable operators. BBC World Service Radio International sells recorded programmes to other broadcasters in 110 countries.

BBC Monitoring, the international media monitoring arm of BBC World Service, provides transcripts of radio and television broadcasts from over 140 countries. As well as providing a vital source of information to the BBC, this service is used by other media organisations, government departments, the commercial sector and academic institutions.

INDEPENDENT BROADCASTING

Independent Television Commission

The ITC is responsible for licensing and regulating commercial television services (including BBC commercial services) operating in, or from, the UK. It does not make, broadcast or transmit programmes.

The ITC must ensure that a wide range of commercial television services is available throughout the UK and that they are of a high quality and appeal to a variety of tastes and interests. It must also ensure fair and effective competition in the provision of these services, and adherence to the rules on media ownership.

The Commission regulates the various television services through licence conditions, codes and guidelines. The codes cover programme content, advertising, sponsorship and technical standards. If a licensee does not comply with the conditions of its licence or the codes, the ITC can impose penalties. These range from a formal warning or a requirement to broadcast an apology or correction, to a fine. In extreme circumstances, a company's licence may be shortened or revoked.

ITV (Channel 3)

ITV is made up of 15 regionally based television companies, which are licensed to supply programmes in the 14 independent television geographical regions. There are two licences for London, one for weekdays and the other for the weekend. An additional ITC licensee provides a national breakfast-time service, transmitted on the ITV network.

The ITV licences for Channel 3 are awarded for a ten-year period by competitive tender to the highest bidder (who has to have passed a quality threshold). Licensees must provide a diverse programme service designed to appeal to a wide range of viewers' tastes and interests. They have a statutory duty to present programmes made in, and about, their region.

Each company plans the content of the programmes to be broadcast in its area. These are produced by the company itself, by other programme companies, or are bought from elsewhere. As with the BBC, at least 25 per cent of original programming must come from the independent sector. About one-third of the output is made up of informative programmes—news, documentaries, and coverage of current affairs, education and religion—while the remainder covers drama, entertainment, sport, arts and children's programmes. Programmes are broadcast 24 hours a day throughout the country. A common national and international news service is provided by Independent Television News (ITN).

ITV (Channel 3) companies are obliged to operate a national programme network. The ITV Network Centre, which is owned by the companies, independently commissions and schedules programmes.

Operating on a commercial basis, licensees derive most of their income from selling advertising time. Their financial resources and programme production vary considerably, depending largely on the population of the areas in which they operate. Newspaper groups can acquire a controlling interest in ITV companies, although measures are in force to deter any undue concentrations of media ownership (see p. 280).

Granada Media and Carlton, the two largest regional ITV (Channel 3) television companies, jointly own ONdigital, which occupies three of the six multiplexes licensed for digital terrestrial television. ONdigital services were launched in 1998 and had attracted 673,000 subscribers by the end of March 2000.

Channel 4 and S4C

Channel 4 provides a national 24-hour television service, although Wales has its own corresponding service—S4C (Sianel Pedwar Cymru). Channel 4 is a statutory corporation, licensed and regulated by the ITC, and funded by selling its own advertising time.

Channel 4's remit is to provide programmes with a distinctive character and to appeal to tastes and interests not generally catered for by ITV (Channel 3). It must present a suitable proportion of educational programmes and encourage innovation and experiment. Channel 4 commissions programmes from the ITV companies and independent producers, and buys programmes from overseas.

The fourth analogue channel in Wales is allocated to S4C, which is regulated by the Welsh Fourth Channel Authority. Members of the Welsh Authority are appointed by the Government. S4C must ensure that a significant proportion of programming—and the majority between 18.30 and 22.00 hours—is in the Welsh language. At other times it transmits Channel 4 programmes. In 1998 S4C launched a new digital service incorporating current analogue Welsh programmes and additional material. Roughly 15 per cent of S4C's income comes from advertising, programme sales, publicity and merchandising; the remainder comes from a government grant, the level of which is fixed by statute.

Channel 5

The UK's newest national terrestrial channel went on air in 1997, its ten-year licence having been awarded by competitive tender to Channel 5 Broadcasting Limited. Channel 5 serves about 70 per cent of the population and is supported by advertising revenue.

Like ITV (Channel 3), the new service is subject to positive programming requirements. It must show programmes of quality and diversity, with a wide range of original productions and commissions from independent producers.

Gaelic Broadcasting

The Gaelic Broadcasting Committee is an independent body committed to ensuring that a wide range of quality television and radio programmes is broadcast in Gaelic for reception in Scotland. Its members are appointed by the ITC, in consultation with the Radio Authority. The Committee distributes government money to programme makers through the Gaelic Broadcasting Fund.

The Radio Authority

The Radio Authority's licensing and regulatory remit covers all independent radio services, including national, local, cable and satellite services. Its three main tasks are to plan frequencies, appoint licensees with a view to broadening listener choice, and regulate programming and advertising.

The Radio Authority has to make sure that licensed services are of a high quality, and offer programmes which will appeal to many different tastes and interests. It has published codes covering engineering, programmes, news and current affairs, and advertising and sponsorship, to which licensees must adhere.

Independent National Radio

There are currently three independent national radio services, whose licences were awarded by the Radio Authority through competitive tender, and which broadcast 24 hours a day:

- Classic FM, which broadcasts mainly classical music, together with news and information;
- Virgin 1215, which plays broad-based rock music (and is supplemented by a separate Virgin station which operates under a local London licence); and
- Talk Sport, a speech-based service.

Independent Local Radio

Independent local radio (ILR) stations broadcast a wide variety of programmes and news of local interest, as well as music and entertainment, traffic reports and advertising. There are also stations serving ethnic minority communities. The Radio Authority awards independent local licences, although not by competitive tender; the success of licence applications is in part determined by the extent to which applicants widen choice and meet the needs and interests of the people living in the area and in part by whether they have the necessary financial resources to sustain programme plans for the eight-year licence period. Local radio stations do not have guaranteed slots on digital local radio multiplexes.

The Radio Authority also issues restricted service licences (RSLs)—short-term RSLs, generally for periods of up to 28 days, for special events or trial services, and long-term RSLs, primarily for student and hospital stations, to broadcast to specific establishments.

TELETEXT, CABLE AND SATELLITE SERVICES

Teletext Services

Teletext is written copy broadcast on television sets. There are several teletext services; one is operated by the BBC and others by independent television. They offer constantly updated information on a variety of subjects, including news, sport, travel, weather conditions and entertainment. The teletext system allows the television signal to carry additional information which can be selected and displayed as 'pages' of text and graphics on receivers equipped with the necessary decoders. About 16 million homes have sets with teletext decoders. The BBC and Channels 3, 4 and 5 increasingly provide subtitling for people with hearing difficulties. The ITC awards teletext licences for the capacity on Channels 3, 4, and 5 by competitive tender for a period of ten years.

Cable Services

Cable services are delivered to consumers through underground cables and are paid for by subscription. The franchising of cable systems and the regulation of cable television services are carried out by the ITC, while the Radio Authority issues cable radio licences. ITC licences are required for systems capable of serving more than 1,000 homes. Systems extending beyond a single building and up to 1,000 homes require only an individual licence regulated by OFTEL (see p. 376).

'Broadband cable' systems can carry between 30 and 65 television channels using analogue technology (including terrestrial broadcasts, satellite television and channels delivered to cable operators by landline or videotape), as well as a full range of telecommunications services. Digital technology is being introduced which will support up to 500 television channels. The major cable operators (NTL and Telewest) started converting their networks to digital transmission during 1999.

There are no specific quality controls on cable services. However, if cable operators also provide their own programme content as opposed to just conveying services, they require a programme services licence from the ITC, which includes consumer protection requirements.

There are currently around 140 operating cable franchises, covering areas which include over 80 per cent of all homes and nearly all urban areas in the UK. By April 2000 there were over 12.6 million homes able to receive broadband cable services; of these 3.3 million subscribed to television services.

Cable also has the capacity for computer-based interactive services such as video-on-demand,[3] home shopping, home banking, security and alarm services, electronic mail and high-speed Internet access (see p. 377). It can additionally supply television services tailored for, and directed at, local communities. Local and community television services operate under location-specific restricted service licences (making use of spare frequencies as and when they are available). The first such services began in late 1998 in the Isle of Wight, followed by services in Oxford, Leicester, Lanarkshire, Londonderry and Edinburgh. Over 100 other cities and towns have asked the ITC to identify spare analogue frequencies for their own local stations.

Satellite Services

Direct broadcasting by satellite, by which television is transmitted directly by satellite into people's homes, has been available throughout the UK since 1989. The signals from satellite broadcasting are received through specially designed aerials or 'dishes'. Most services are paid for by subscription. Some offer general entertainment, while others concentrate on specific areas of interest, such as sport, music, children's programmes and feature films.

All satellite television services provided by broadcasters established in the UK are licensed and regulated by the ITC. Around 250 satellite television service licences, and about 20 digital programme service licences, were in force in April 2000. Many of these are foreign language services, some of them designed for ethnic minorities within the UK and others aimed primarily at audiences in other countries. Viewers in the UK may also receive a variety of television services from other European countries. Satellite services must comply with the ITC's programmes, advertising and sponsorship codes, but they are not subject to any positive programming obligations.

BSkyB is the UK's largest satellite programmer, with about 7.8 million subscribers at the end of 1999. Of these almost 4 million were 'direct to home' subscribers (over 2 million of which were subscribers to digital services). BSkyB's digital satellite service, SkyDigital (carrying more than 140 channels), was launched in 1998, and new interactive services started in October 1999.

Satellite radio services must be licensed by the Radio Authority if they are transmitted from the UK for general reception within the country, or if they are transmitted from outside the UK but are managed editorially from within it.

OTHER ASPECTS

Advertising and Sponsorship

The BBC may not raise revenue from broadcasting advertisements or from commercial sponsorship of programmes on its public service channels. Its policy is to avoid giving publicity to any firm or organised interest except when this is necessary in providing effective and informative programmes. It does, however, cover sponsored sporting and artistic events. Advertising and sponsorship are allowed on commercial television and radio services, subject to controls. The ITC and the Radio Authority operate codes governing advertising standards and programme sponsorship, and can impose penalties on broadcasters failing to comply with them.

Advertisements on independent television and radio are broadcast in breaks during programmes as well as between programmes. Advertisers are not allowed to influence programme content. Advertisements must be distinct and separate from programmes. Advertising on terrestrial television is limited to an average of seven minutes an hour during the day and seven-and-a-half minutes in the peak evening viewing period. Advertising is prohibited in broadcasts of religious services and in broadcasts to schools. Political advertising and advertisements for betting (other than the National Lottery, the football pools and bingo) are prohibited. All tobacco advertising is banned on television and cigarette advertisements are banned on radio. Religious advertisements may be broadcast on commercial radio and television, provided

[3] Video-on-demand enables viewers to dial into a video library, via a cable or telephone network, and call up a programme or film of their choice, which is then transmitted to that household alone.

they comply with the guidelines issued by the ITC and the Radio Authority.

Sponsorship in Independent Broadcasting

In return for their financial contribution, sponsors receive a credit associating them with a particular programme. The ITC's Code of Programme Sponsorship and the Radio Authority's Advertising and Sponsorship Code aim to ensure that sponsors do not exert influence on the editorial content of programmes and that sponsorships are made clear to viewers and listeners. News and current affairs programmes may not be sponsored. Potential sponsors for other categories of programme may be debarred if their involvement could constrain the editorial independence of the programme maker in any way. References to sponsors or their products must be confined to the beginning and end of a programme and around commercial breaks; on television they must not appear in the programme itself. All commercial radio programmes other than news bulletins may be sponsored.

Since 1998 the ITC has permitted masthead programming (programmes with the same title as a magazine and made or funded by its publishers) on all UK commercial television services (Channels 3, 4, and 5 having previously been excluded).

Broadcasting Standards

The independence enjoyed by the broadcasting authorities carries with it certain obligations over programme content. Broadcasters must display, as far as possible, a proper balance and wide range of subject matter, impartiality in matters of controversy and accuracy in news coverage, and must not offend against good taste. Broadcasters must also comply with legislation relating to obscenity and incitement to racial hatred.

The BBC, the ITC and the Radio Authority apply codes providing rules on impartiality, the portrayal of violence, and standards of taste and decency in programmes, particularly during hours when children are likely to be viewing or listening. Television programmes broadcast before 21.00 hours (or 20.00 hours on certain cable and satellite services) are required to be suitable for a general audience, including children.

Broadcasting Standards Commission (BSC)

The BSC acts as a forum for public concern about fairness and taste and decency on television and radio. It decides on complaints received from the public about taste and decency, and adjudicates on claims of unfair or unjust treatment in broadcast programmes and of unwarranted infringement of privacy in programmes or in their preparation. It also undertakes and commissions research and the monitoring of public attitudes, and has drawn up a code of practice on both broadcasting standards and fairness which the broadcasters and regulators are required to reflect in their own programme guidelines. In 1999–2000 the Commission received 126 fairness complaints which were within its remit; 76 fairness adjudications were completed, of which 28 per cent were upheld in full or in part. It also received 5,138 complaints about standards; of those adjudicated upon, 25 per cent were upheld in full or in part.

Parliamentary Broadcasting

The proceedings of both Houses of Parliament may be broadcast on television and radio, either live or, more usually, in recorded and edited form on news and current affairs programmes. The BBC has a specific obligation to transmit on radio an impartial account day by day of the proceedings in both Houses of Parliament. In 1998 the Corporation took over a dedicated parliamentary channel (initially launched in 1992 by a group of cable operators) which is now known as BBC Parliament, transmitting continuous coverage of daily proceedings. The proceedings of the Scottish Parliament and the assemblies for Wales and Northern Ireland are also broadcast live on occasions and in recorded and edited form on a regular basis by the BBC.

Party Political Broadcasts

In the absence of paid political advertising in the UK, there is a long-standing practice that broadcasters make time available for party political and election broadcasts on television and radio. Recent reforms to the system have been introduced by broadcasters to reflect the increased number of elections in the UK following devolution and to refocus broadcasts between elections at key times in the political calendar (for example, the Budget, the Queen's Speech and party conferences). The content of these broadcasts is the responsibility of the parties, although they have to comply with ground rules laid down by the broadcasters. In addition, the Government may make ministerial broadcasts on radio and television, with opposition parties also being allotted broadcast time.

Audience Research

Both the BBC and the commercial sector are required to keep themselves informed on the state of public opinion about the programmes and advertising that they broadcast. This is done through the continuous measurement of the size and composition of audiences and their opinions of programmes. For television, this work is undertaken through BARB (the Broadcasters' Audience Research Board). Joint research is undertaken for BBC radio and for commercial radio by RAJAR (Radio Joint Audience Research).

The BBC, the commercial sector and the BSC conduct regular surveys of audience opinion on television and radio services. Public opinion is further assessed by the BBC and ITC through the work of their advisory committees and councils.

European Agreements

The UK has implemented two European agreements on cross-border broadcasting—the European Community Broadcasting Directive and the Council of Europe Convention on Transfrontier Television. These aim to ensure the free flow of television programmes and services throughout participating countries, setting minimum standards on advertising, sponsorship, taste and decency, and the portrayal of sex and violence. If a broadcast meets these standards then no participating country may prevent reception in its territory.

The Press

On an average weekday it is estimated that well over half of people aged 15 and over in the UK read a national morning newspaper (59 per cent of men and 50 per cent of women in 1999–2000). Nearly nine out of ten adults read a regional or local newspaper every week. National papers have an average (but declining) total circulation of some 13.5 million on weekdays and about 14.8 million on Sundays. There are more than 1,300 regional and local newspaper titles.

While newspapers are almost always financially independent of any political party, they often express obvious political leanings in their editorial coverage, which may derive from proprietorial and other non-party influences. Ownership of the national press lies in the hands of a number of large corporations (see Table 17.1), most of which are involved in the whole field of publishing and communications. There are around 120 regional press publishers—ranging from those owning just one title (about half of them) to a few controlling more than 100 each.

In addition to sales revenue, newspapers and periodicals earn considerable amounts from advertising. Indeed, the press is the largest advertising medium in the UK. The British press receives no subsidies from the state.

NATIONAL AND REGIONAL TITLES

The National Press

The national press consists of ten morning daily papers and ten Sunday papers (see Table 17.1). At one time London's Fleet Street area was the centre of the industry, but now all the national papers have moved their editorial and printing facilities to other parts of London or away from the capital altogether. Editions of several papers, such as the *Financial Times*, *Guardian* and *Daily Mirror*, are also printed in other countries.

National newspapers are often described as 'quality', 'mid-market' or 'popular' papers on the basis of differences in style and content. Five dailies and four Sundays are usually described as 'quality' newspapers, which are directed at readers who want full information

Table 17.1: National Newspapers

Title and foundation date	Controlled by	Circulation average (January–June) 1970	1980	1990	2000
Dailies					
Populars					
Daily Mirror (1903)	Trinity Mirror	4,570,000	3,604,000	3,106,000	2,263,000
Daily Star (1978)	United News & Media	n.a.	1,034,000	916,000	613,000
Sun (1964)	News International	1,616,000	3,770,000	3,896,000	3,569,000
Mid-market					
Daily Mail (1896)	Daily Mail & General Trust	1,865,000	1,966,000	1,689,000	2,387,000
Express (1900)	United News & Media	3,563,000	2,260,000	1,574,000	1,062,000
Qualities					
Financial Times (1888)	Pearson	170,000	197,000	291,000	459,000
Daily Telegraph (1855)	Telegraph Group	1,409,000	1,450,000	1,081,000	1,031,000
Guardian (1821)	Guardian Media Group	304,000	366,000	427,000	395,000
Independent (1986)	Independent Newspapers	n.a	n.a.	413,000	224,000
Times (1785)	News International	388,000	297,000	426,000	722,000
Sundays					
Populars					
News of the World (1843)	News International	6,229,000	4,294,000	5,046,000	4,023,000
Sunday Mirror (1963)	Trinity Mirror	4,841,000	3,793,000	2,902,000	1,927,000
People (1881)	Trinity Mirror	5,140,000	3,820,000	2,577,000	1,523,000
Mid-market					
Mail on Sunday (1982)	Daily Mail & General Trust	n.a.	n.a.	1,896,000	2,298,000
Sunday Express (1918)	United News & Media	4,263,000	3,045,000	1,696,000	974,000
Qualities					
Sunday Telegraph (1961)	Telegraph Group	764,000	1,017,000	590,000	808,000
Independent on Sunday (1990)	Independent Newspapers	n.a.	n.a.	n.a.	247,000
Observer (1791)	Guardian Media Group	822,000	973,000	559,000	417,000
Sunday Times (1822)	News International	1,439,000	1,424,000	1,176,000	1,360,000
Sunday Business (1998)	European Press	n.a.	n.a.	n.a.	67,000

n.a. = not applicable.
Source: Newspaper Publishers Association

on a wide range of public matters. Popular newspapers tend to appeal to those who want to read shorter, entertaining stories with more human interest. 'Mid-market' publications cater for the intermediate readership. Quality papers are normally broadsheet in format, while mid-market and popular papers are tabloid.

Many newspapers are printed in colour and most produce extensive supplements as part of the Saturday or Sunday edition, with articles on personal finance, travel, home improvement, food and wine, fashion and other leisure topics.

Increasing competition from other media in the delivery of news, information and entertainment has had its effects on the national press over the last few decades, with a gradual decline in circulation discernible for many titles.

Regional Newspapers

Most towns and cities throughout the UK have their own regional or local newspaper. These range from morning and evening dailies to Sunday papers and others which are published just once a week. They mainly include stories of regional or local attraction, but the dailies also cover national and international news, often looked at from a local viewpoint. In addition, they provide a valuable medium for local advertising. The regional and local press has, overall, been experiencing falling sales, but this decline has slowed considerably in recent years, from 2.3 per cent in 1995 to 1.2 per cent in 1999.

London has one paid-for evening paper, the *Evening Standard*. Its publisher (Associated Newspapers) also produces a free newspaper, *London Metro*, launched in 1999. There are also local weekly papers for every district in Greater London; these are often different local editions of one centrally published paper.

Of the Scottish papers, the *Daily Record* has the highest circulation. The press in Wales includes Welsh-language and bilingual papers (and Welsh community newspapers receive an annual grant as part of the Government's wider financial support for the Welsh language). Newspapers from the Irish Republic, as well as the British national press, are widely read in Northern Ireland.

Around 700 free distribution newspapers, mostly weekly and financed by advertising, are published in the UK.

Table 17.2 lists the average net circulations of the leading paid-for regional daily, Sunday and weekly newspapers across the UK.

Table 17.2: Top Regional Newspaper Circulations, (July–December 1999 average)

	Circulation
Regional daily newspapers	
Daily Record (Scotland)	637,353
Evening Standard (London)	437,447
Express & Star (West Midlands)	183,759
Manchester Evening News	173,179
Liverpool Echo	155,920
Belfast Telegraph	117,207
Glasgow Evening Times	108,838
Evening Chronicle (Newcastle upon Tyne)	107,511
Leicester Mercury	102,640
Herald (Scotland)	100,603
Regional Sunday newspapers	
Sunday Mail (Glasgow)	759,567
Sunday Post (Dundee)	684,749
Scotland on Sunday (Edinburgh)	109,273
Sunday Sun (Newcastle upon Tyne)	106,342
Sunday Life (Belfast)	94,768
Sunday World (Northern Ireland edition)	71,847
Wales on Sunday (Cardiff)	66,239
Sunday Herald (Glasgow)	54,316
Sunday Independent (Plymouth)	34,705
Regional weekly newspapers	
West Briton (Cornwall)	50,616
Essex Chronicle	49,705
Kent Messenger	47,949
Surrey Advertiser	45,615[1]
Chester Chronicle	44,178
Western Gazette (Somerset)	43,165
Derbyshire Times	41,939
Hereford Times	41,164
Kent & Sussex Courier	40,464

[1] January–December 1999.

Source: Audit Bureau of Circulations/Newspaper Society

Ethnic Minority Publications

Many newpapers and magazines in the UK are produced by ethnic minority communities. Most are published weekly, fortnightly or monthly. A Chinese newspaper, *Sing Tao*, the Urdu *Daily Jang* and the Arabic *Al-Arab*, however, are dailies.

Afro-Caribbean newspapers include *The Gleaner*, *The Voice* and *Caribbean Times*, which are all weeklies. The *Asian Times* is an English language weekly for people of Asian descent. Ethnic language publications appear in Bengali, Gujarati, Hindi and Punjabi. The fortnightly *Asian Trader* and *Asian Business* are both successful ethnic business publications, while *Cineblitz International* targets those interested in the Asian film industry.

THE PERIODICAL PRESS

There are almost 9,000 separate periodical publications, which carry advertising. They are generally defined as either 'consumer' titles, offering readers leisure-time information and entertainment, or 'business and professional' titles, which provide people with material of relevance to their working lives. Within the former category, there are general consumer titles, which have a wide appeal, and consumer specialist titles, aimed specifically at groups of people with particular interests, such as motoring, sport or music. A range of literary and political journals, appearing monthly or quarterly, caters for a more academic readership. There are also many in-house and customer magazines produced by businesses or public services for their employees and/or clients.

The periodical industry has experienced rapid growth—over the last ten years the number of consumer titles rose from about 2,200 to 3,170, and business titles from around 4,200 to 5,700. More than 80 per cent of adults (84 per cent of women) read a consumer magazine. About 95 per cent of business and professional people read a publication relevant to their market (with the highest concentrations in medicine, business management, sciences, architecture and building, social sciences, and computers).

The two top-selling weekly consumer magazines, *What's on TV* and *Radio Times*, carry full details of the forthcoming week's television and radio programmes and have sales in the region of 1.5 million. *Reader's Digest*, which covers a very broad range of topics, has the highest sales (over 1.1 million) among monthly magazines.

Women's magazines traditionally enjoy large readerships, while several men's general interest titles reached high levels of circulation during the 1990s (see Table 17.3).

Children have an array of comics and papers, while magazines like *Smash Hits* and *It's Bliss*, with their coverage of pop music and features of interest to young people, are very popular with teenagers.

Leading journals of opinion include the *Economist*, an independent commentator on national and international affairs, finance and business, and science and technology; *New Statesman*, which reviews social issues, politics, literature and the arts from an independent socialist point of view; and the *Spectator*, which covers similar subjects from a more conservative standpoint. A rather more irreverent approach to public affairs is taken by *Private Eye*, a satirical fortnightly.

Weekly listings' magazines like *Time Out* provide details of cultural and other events in London and other large cities.

Table 17.3: Top Women's and Men's Titles

	Average net circulation (January–June 1999)
Women's titles	
Take a Break	1,230,758
Woman	670,241
Bella	572,151
Woman's Own	569,019
Woman's Weekly	547,953
Men's general interest titles	
FHM	702,514
Loaded	371,548
Maxim	315,102
Men's Health	233,653

Source: Audit Bureau of Circulations/Periodical Publishers Association

PRESS INSTITUTIONS

Trade associations include the Newspaper Publishers Association, whose members publish national newspapers, and the Newspaper Society, which represents British regional and local newspapers (and is believed to be the oldest publishers' association in the world). The Scottish Daily Newspaper Society represents the interests of daily and Sunday newspapers in Scotland; the Scottish Newspaper Publishers Association acts on behalf of the owners of weekly newspapers in Scotland; and Associated Northern Ireland Newspapers is made up of proprietors of weekly newspapers in Northern Ireland. The membership of the Periodical Publishers Association includes most publishers of business, professional and consumer magazines.

The Society of Editors is the officially recognised professional body for newspaper editors and their equivalents in radio and television. It exists to defend press freedom and to promote high editorial standards. There is also a British Society of Magazine Editors. Organisations representing journalists are the National Union of Journalists, Chartered Institute of Journalists and British Association of Journalists. The main printing union is the Graphical, Paper and Media Union. The Foreign Press Association helps the correspondents of overseas newspapers in their professional work.

The Press Association is the national news agency of the UK and Irish Republic, delivering comprehensive news and sports coverage, photographs, weather reports and listings to the national and regional print, broadcast and electronic media. A number of other British and foreign agencies and news services have offices in London, and there are smaller agencies based in other British cities. Most regional agencies are members of the National Association of Press Agencies.

PRESS CONDUCT AND LAW

Press Complaints Commission

In a free society, there is a delicate and sometimes difficult balance in the relationship between the responsibilities of the press and the rights of the public. A policy of press self-regulation, rather than statutory control or a law of privacy, operates in the UK. The Press Complaints Commission, a non-statutory body whose 16 members are drawn from both the public and the industry, deals with complaints about the content and conduct of newspapers and magazines, and operates a Code of Practice agreed by editors covering inaccuracy, invasion of privacy, harassment and misrepresentation by the press. The Commission's jurisdiction also extends to publications on the Internet placed there by publishers who already subscribe to the Code. In 1999 the Commission dealt with 2,500 complaints, resolving about 90 per cent of cases pursued under the Code.

The Press and the Law

There is no state control or censorship of the newspaper and periodical press, and newspaper proprietors, editors and journalists are subject to the law in the same way as any other citizen. However, certain statutes include sections which apply to the press. There are laws governing the extent of newspaper ownership in television and radio companies (see p. 280), the transfer of newspaper assets, and the right of press representatives to be supplied with agendas and reports of meetings of local authorities.

There is a legal requirement to reproduce the printer's imprint (the printer's name and address) on all publications, including newspapers. Publishers are legally obliged to deposit copies of newspapers and other publications at the British Library (see p. 264).

Publication of advertisements is governed by wide-ranging legislation, including public health, copyright, financial services and fraud legislation. Legal restrictions are imposed on certain types of prize competition.

Laws on contempt of court, official secrets and defamation are also relevant to the press. A newspaper may not publish comments on the conduct of judicial proceedings which are likely to prejudice the reputation of the courts for fairness before or during the actual proceedings; nor may it publish before or during a trial anything which might influence the result. The unauthorised acquisition and publication of official information in such areas as defence and international relations, where such unauthorised disclosure would be harmful, are offences under the Official Secrets Acts 1911 to 1989. These are restrictions on publication generally, not just through the printed press.

Most legal proceedings against the press are libel actions brought by private individuals.

Advertising Practice

Advertising in all non-broadcast media, such as newspapers, magazines, posters, sales promotions, cinema, direct mail, and electronic media (such as CD-ROM and the Internet) is regulated by the Advertising Standards Authority (ASA). The ASA is an independent body whose role is to ensure that advertisers conform to the British Codes of Advertising and Sales Promotion. These require that advertisements and promotions are legal, decent, honest and truthful; are prepared with a sense of responsibility to the consumer and society; and respect the principles of fair competition generally accepted in business.

The ASA monitors compliance with the Codes and investigates complaints received. Pre-publication advice is available to publishers, agencies and advertisers from the Committee of Advertising Practice. If an advertisement is found to be misleading or offensive, the ASA can ask the advertiser to change or remove it. Failure to do so can result in damaging adverse publicity in the ASA's monthly report of its judgments, the refusal of advertising space by publishers, and the loss of trading privileges. Advertisers found guilty of placing irresponsible or offensive posters can face a two-year period of mandatory pre-vetting. The ASA can also refer misleading advertisements to the Director General of Fair Trading (see p. 396), who has the power to seek an injunction to prevent their publication.

Media Ownership

Legislation in 1990 laid down rules enabling the ITC and Radio Authority to keep ownership of the broadcasting media widely spread and to prevent undue concentrations of single and cross-media ownership, in the wider public interest. The Broadcasting Act 1996 relaxed those rules, both within and across different media sectors, to reflect the needs and aspirations of the industry against the background of accelerating technological change:

- allowing for greater cross-ownership between newspaper groups, television companies and radio stations, at both national and regional levels; and
- introducing 'public interest' criteria by which the regulatory authorities can assess and approve (or disallow) mergers or acquisitions between newspapers and television and radio companies.

The 1996 Act overturned the rule that no one company could own more than two of the ITV (Channel 3) licences; instead, a new limit was set whereby no company could control franchises covering more than 15 per cent of the total television audience. Local newspapers with more than a 50 per cent share of their market may own a local radio station, providing at least one other independent local radio station is operating in that area. An additional regulation is the Office of Fair Trading's limit of 25 per cent on any company's share of television advertising revenue.

The Media and the Internet

The Internet plays an increasingly important role in the provision and distribution of information and entertainment. Broadly, it is a loose collection of computer networks around the world—it links thousands of academic, government and public computer systems, giving millions of people access to a wealth of stored information and other resources. No one owns it—there is no centralised controlling or regulating body. Access to the system usually requires a computer with the necessary software, a telephone and a modem (allowing computers to communicate with each other over a telephone line). However, it is now possible to receive television-based services, and the Internet is increasingly likely in the future to be accessed through interactive digital television and mobile telephones. Among the most common uses of the Internet are the sending and receiving of e-mail (text that can be sent directly to another computer linked to the system), the publication of information and, increasingly, commercial transactions.

The system dates from the 1960s, when it began life in the military and academic communities in the United States, but it has only assumed widespread significance in commercial and consumer terms during the 1990s. It is the World Wide Web (WWW or the web) which has given the Internet its user appeal and accessibility. The web consists of many thousands of 'sites' on the Internet, which can be viewed by a browser (software that provides a window in a computer screen on which the pages are displayed). Users can move from page to page in search of whatever information or service they are after.

Most national newspaper groups, press institutions and prominent magazine publishers in the UK have set up their own websites. These offer a range of editorial, directory and advertising services. It is estimated that more than 75 per cent of the local and regional press also operate a website. Broadcasters and regulators, including the BBC, the ITV companies, Channel 4, Channel 5, Sky, the ITC and the Radio Authority, are similarly represented on the web.

Further Reading

Department for Culture, Media and Sport Annual Report 2000: The Government's Expenditure Plans 2000–01 to 2001–02. Cm 4613. The Stationery Office, 2000.

Regulating Communications: the Way Ahead. Department for Culture, Media and Sport and Department of Trade and Industry, 1999.

Websites

Department for Culture, Media and Sport: www.culture.gov.uk

British Broadcasting Corporation (BBC): www.bbc.co.uk

Independent Television Commission (ITC): www.itc.org.uk

18 Sport and Active Recreation

Sport is one of the UK's most popular leisure activities, with nearly half of all adults taking part each week in one or more sporting activities. UK sportsmen and sportswomen hold over 50 world titles in a variety of sports, such as professional boxing, rowing, snooker, squash and motorcycle sports. In the 2000 Olympics in Sydney the Great Britain team won 28 medals: 11 gold (the most since the Olympic Games of 1920), ten silver and seven bronze.

In 1996–97 (the latest period for which information is available), 71 per cent of men and 57 per cent of women took part in at least one sporting activity in the four-week period before they were interviewed for the General Household Survey in Great Britain and the Continuous Household Survey in Northern Ireland. Walking (including rambling and hiking) was by far the most popular form of active recreation in the UK (see Table 18.1).

Many important sporting events are held each year in the UK, including the Wimbledon Lawn Tennis Championships, the FA Cup Final, the Open Golf championship and the Grand National steeplechase. In 1999 the UK hosted both the cricket and rugby union world cups, with the finals being held respectively at Lord's and the Millennium Stadium in Cardiff. Most of the matches in the Rugby League World Cup will be staged in the UK in October and November 2000, with the final taking place at Old Trafford (Manchester), and the World Track Cycling Championships will be held in Manchester in October 2000. The Commonwealth Games will take place in Manchester in 2002. Two major athletics events—the 2003 world indoor championships and the 2005 world outdoor championships—will be staged in the UK.

SPORTS POLICY

A 'Sports Cabinet', established in 1998, is involved in identifying strategic priorities for sport. It is headed by the Secretary of State for Culture, Media and Sport and includes the ministers responsible for sport in England, Wales, Scotland and Northern Ireland.

In April 2000 the Government published *A Sporting Future for All*, its new sports strategy for England designed to increase participation in sport and encourage greater success for the top sportsmen and sportswomen.

Participation

The Government wishes to ensure that sporting opportunities are widely available to the entire community, irrespective of age,

Table 18.1: Trends in Participation in the Most Popular Sports and Physical Activities in Great Britain, 1987–96

% participation by those aged 16 and over in the previous four weeks

	1987	1990	1993	1996
Men				
Walking	41	44	45	49
Snooker/pool/billiards	27	24	21	20
Cycling	10	12	14	15
Indoor swimming	10	11	12	11
Soccer	10	10	9	10
Women				
Walking	35	38	37	41
Keep fit/yoga	12	16	17	17
Indoor swimming	11	13	14	15
Cycling	7	7	7	8
Snooker/pool/billiards	5	5	5	4

Source: *General Household Survey: Trends in Adult Participation in Sport in Great Britain 1987–96* (Sport England/UK Sport)

Table 18.2: British Olympic Medallists[1] at the Sydney Olympics, September–October 2000

Gold medals

Athletics: Jonathan Edwards—triple jump
Athletics: Denise Lewis—heptathlon
Boxing: Audley Harrison—super-heavyweight
Cycling: Jason Queally—1 km time trial
Modern pentathlon: Stephanie Cook
Rowing: men's coxless four
Rowing: men's eight
Sailing: Ben Ainslie—Laser class
Sailing: Iain Percy—Finn class
Sailing: Shirley Robertson—Europe class
Shooting: Richard Faulds—men's double trap

Silver medals

Athletics: Steve Backley—javelin
Athletics: Darren Campbell—200 metres
Canoeing: Paul Ratcliffe—K1 slalom
Cycling: men's sprint
Equestrianism: three-day event team
Judo: Kate Howey—middleweight
Rowing: women's quad sculls
Sailing: Ian Barker and Simon Hiscocks—49er class
Sailing: Ian Walker and Mark Covell—Star class
Shooting: Ian Peel—men's trap

Bronze medals

Athletics: Kelly Holmes—800 metres
Athletics: Katharine Merry—400 metres
Badminton: Simon Archer and Joanne Goode—mixed doubles
Canoeing: Tim Brabants—K1 1,000 metre sprint
Cycling: Yvonne McGregor—3,000 metre pursuit
Cycling: men's team pursuit
Modern pentathlon: Kate Allenby

[1] Names of members of teams are given in the appropriate entry in the section on Popular Sports (see pp. 293–304).

Table 18.3: Selected Domestic Sporting Champions 1999–2000

Basketball
Dairylea Dunkers Championship—Manchester Giants

Cricket
PPP Healthcare County Championship—Surrey
NatWest Trophy—Gloucestershire
Benson & Hedges Cup—Gloucestershire
Norwich Union National Cricket League—Gloucestershire

Football
FA Carling Premiership—Manchester United
AXA-sponsored FA Cup—Chelsea
Worthington Cup—Leicester City
Bank of Scotland Premier League—Glasgow Rangers
Tennents Scottish Cup—Glasgow Rangers

Hockey
Premier Division (Men)—Cannock
Premier Division (Women)—Hightown

Ice Hockey
Sekonda Superleague—Bracknell Bees
Sekonda Superleague play-off final—London Knights
Benson & Hedges Cup (1999)—Manchester Storm

Rugby League
Super League Grand Final—St Helens
Silk Cut Challenge Cup—Bradford Bulls

Rugby Union
Six Nations Championship—England
Allied Dunbar Premiership—Leicester
Tetley's Bitter Cup—Wasps
Welsh/Scottish League—Cardiff
WRU Cup—Llanelli

Tennis (1999)
National Champion (men)—Jamie Delgado
National Champion (women)—Hannah Collin

Note: This table gives a list of champions from selected sports. For details of major international sporting achievements, see Table 18.2 and the section on Popular Sports, pp. 293–304.

gender, social background, location or ability. For young people its strategy includes a series of measures to reverse the decline of physical education (PE) and sport in schools, and raise standards:

- a new fund—Space for Sport and Arts—which will provide up to £150 million of new funds over two years (of which £75 million will be from the Government and up to £75 million from the National Lottery) for primary schools in England to provide new multi-purpose sports and arts facilities for pupils and the wider community;
- the creation by 2003 of 110 Specialist Sports Colleges (of which 67 had been designated by mid-2000);
- encouraging schools to provide a range of after-school activities (including PE and sport) for all pupils, irrespective of age or ability;
- establishing up to 600 school sports co-ordinators to develop more inter-school competitive games; and
- ensuring that the most talented 14 to 18 year olds have access to appropriate coaching and support.

Specialist Sports Colleges have a particular focus on PE and sport, and provide high-quality facilities and training to support the most talented and promising pupils. Working with the national governing bodies of sport, those Sports Colleges that are best placed to develop particular sports specialisms to the highest levels will be identified so that the most gifted 14 to 19 year olds can be given top coaching and support. Some Sports Colleges are already experimenting with a more flexible timetable which allows talented pupils to focus on developing their sporting careers, including undertaking the necessary additional training and receiving the required coaching, but still provides the pupils with a full education programme. At a Sports College talented pupils can receive specialist coaching, flexible study arrangements and individual tutorial support to ensure that they realise both their sporting and academic potential. The Government envisages that Sports Colleges will play an important part in reaching new talent from groups who are traditionally under-represented in sport, including ethnic minorities and those from deprived backgrounds. Where appropriate, Sports Colleges will be linked to the network centres of the United Kingdom Sports Institute (see p. 289), so that pupils can have access to their sports science, sports medicine and coaching facilities, and can receive support on leaving school if they embark on a sporting career.

The strategy also includes measures to raise participation more widely in the community. Previously the Government had announced expenditure of £125 million from the Lottery's New Opportunities Fund (see p. 117) to help communities to create new areas of open space, or enhance existing open spaces, and introduced tighter planning controls to minimise the loss of playing fields to development. It now envisages investing between £1.5 billion and £2 billion in community sports facilities in England in the next ten years. Local authorities will conduct an audit of sports facilities in England to determine where the need for new or improved facilities is greatest. Sport England (see p. 287) and the Local Government Association will then compile a comprehensive national database of sports facilities, which will form the basis of strategic planning for sports development.

Sport England, the Youth Justice Board for England and Wales and the UK Anti-Drugs Co-ordination Unit have established a new sports-based initiative to promote regular participation in sport by young people, citizenship and to reduce drug misuse by promoting a healthy lifestyle—24 'Positive Futures' projects have been set up in England to work with young people aged 10 to 16.

> The Government's view is that sport is an important component of regeneration, and can have a beneficial effect in helping the development of run-down areas. In January 2000 Sport England announced the first 12 Sport Action Zones. The zones are areas of high economic and social deprivation where basic sports provision falls below an acceptable standard. Eventually up to 30 zones will be established. Sport England will target these areas for improving sporting provision.

Sporting Excellence

As well as the Specialist Sports Colleges, two main schemes are designed to promote sporting excellence:

- *The World Class Performance Programme* provides support to the UK's most talented athletes to enable them to improve their performance and win medals in major international competitions. Since April 1997 grants totalling £79 million have been committed to more than 35 sports in the Programme, and around 1,700 athletes have received support.
- *The World Class Events Programme* aims to ensure that major international events can be attracted to, and staged successfully in, the UK. About £1.6 million a year is currently available to support funding of up to 35 per cent of the cost of bidding for and staging events. By June 2000, over £8 million had been awarded to assist with staging 59 international events and bids for a further ten events.

The national sports strategy envisages some changes to strengthen the programmes, including establishing targets for assessing performance. The level of success in achieving targets set by the national governing bodies will be a key factor in decisions on future levels of funding.

The Government wishes to see improvements in coaching, and a review of coaching and coach education will be undertaken by the end of 2000. The Sports

Councils, the National Coaching Foundation (see p. 291) and sporting governing bodies will work together to develop a 'fast track' system for top-class performers to become coaches.

Relations with Governing Bodies of Sport

The Government is encouraging sporting governing bodies to develop strategic plans for their sports, which would widen participation and develop sporting talent. Governing bodies receiving funding from the Sports Councils are already required to produce development plans, from the grass roots to the highest competitive levels, and, in order to have access to Lottery funds, for their top athletes, they need to prepare 'world-class performance' plans with specific performance targets. The new plans would include high-quality youth sport programmes and coaching education systems, a talent development framework and targets for the development of their sport. For governing bodies that adopt new strategic plans, the Government intends that they should have greater control of the distribution of funding from the Sports Councils and the National Lottery. Under these proposals, all major sports bodies receiving significant revenues from broadcasting would be required to set aside at least 5 per cent of these revenues for investment in grass roots facilities in their sports.

> Football receives substantial revenues from broadcasting rights. The Government, together with the Football Association (FA) and the FA Premier League, established in 2000 a Football Foundation, which will channel at least 5 per cent of television revenues from professional football into grass roots development. The Foundation's priorities will be improving the provision and maintenance of football pitches, and coaching at a local level. The Government hopes that the new body will prove a model for other professional sports to follow.

Sport on Television and Radio

Major sporting events (such as the Olympic Games) receive extensive television and radio coverage and are watched or heard by millions of people. Football matches attract very high ratings, especially when the UK's national teams are involved in the final stages of international tournaments, most recently for England's matches against Portugal, Germany and Romania in the final stage of Euro 2000 (the European Championship). Several other sports, including rugby, horse racing, cricket and athletics, also achieve high ratings figures.

For several years, many satellite and cable channels have concentrated on sport. Live coverage of a number of major events and competitions is now shown exclusively by subscription broadcasters. In the Government's view, there are a small number of sporting occasions to which everyone should have access. These events are included on a protected list ('Group A') and cannot be shown on subscription channels unless they have first been offered to the UK's universally available free-to-air broadcasters (the BBC, the ITV network and Channel 4). Live coverage of events on the 'Group B' list may be shown by satellite and cable channels on the condition that an acceptable level of secondary coverage is made available to the universally available free-to-air channels. The current list is as follows:

Group A Events (with full live coverage protected)
Olympic Games
FIFA World Cup football finals tournament
European Football Championship finals tournament
FA Cup Final
Scottish FA Cup Final (in Scotland)
the Grand National
the Derby
Wimbledon Tennis Championships finals
Rugby League Challenge Cup Final
Rugby World Cup Final

Group B Events (with secondary coverage protected)
Cricket Test matches played in England
Wimbledon Tennis Championships (other than the finals)
Rugby World Cup Finals tournament (other than the Final)

Six Nations Rugby Union matches involving home countries
Commonwealth Games
World Athletics Championship
Cricket World Cup—Final, semi-finals and matches involving home nations' teams
Ryder Cup
Open Golf Championship

Crowd Safety and Control

The Football Trust has provided grant aid to help football clubs to complete the safety work required by the Government in response to the Taylor Report following the Hillsborough stadium disaster in 1989, when 96 spectators died. Since May 2000 the Football Trust's work has been continued by the Football Foundation. In England and Wales, licences issued by the Football Licensing Authority (FLA) require all clubs in the Premier League and those in the First Division of the Football League to have all-seater grounds, and clubs in the second and third divisions of the Football League have to ensure that any terracing retained complies with the highest safety standards, as outlined in guidance from the FLA. The FLA will be succeeded by a new Sports Ground Safety Authority (SGSA), which will have a wider role in advising other sports on outdoor ground safety; the SGSA is expected to be in operation by April 2001.

In Scotland the all-seating policy is being implemented through a voluntary agreement under the direction of the Scottish football authorities.

The Government tries to work closely with the police, football authorities and the governments of other European countries to implement crowd control measures. For example, prior to Euro 2000 there was close co-operation with the authorities of Belgium and the Netherlands (the co-hosts of the tournament) and also with the French authorities to try to ensure that as far as possible anyone previously involved in football hooliganism was unable to gain entry to those countries at the time of the tournament. In addition, the Football (Offences and Disorder) Act 1999 imposed a duty on the courts to make a banning order whenever someone is convicted of a football-related offence if a ban would help prevent violence or disorder connected with football matches. The Act also provided for the imposition of passport conditions on anyone subject to an international football banning order. However, serious disturbances, involving violent and disruptive behaviour, did occur in Belgium. The Government has announced that, following discussions with the FA and the Premier League, any supporter convicted of hooliganism, or against whom there was good evidence of hooliganism, would be banned for life from attending football matches in England. Anyone subject to a domestic or international ban would have to surrender his or her passport when major international games involving England were in progress.

ORGANISATION AND ADMINISTRATION

Sports Councils

Government responsibilities and funding for sport and recreation are largely channelled through five Sports Councils:

- the United Kingdom Sports Council, operating as UK Sport;
- the English Sports Council, operating as Sport England;
- the Sports Council for Wales;
- the Scottish Sports Council, operating as sportscotland; and
- the Sports Council for Northern Ireland.

UK Sport takes the lead on all aspects of sport and physical recreation which require strategic planning, administration, co-ordination or representation for the UK as a whole. Its main functions include:

- co-ordinating support to sports in which the UK competes internationally (as opposed to the four home countries separately);
- tackling drug misuse;
- co-ordinating policy for bringing major international sports events to the UK; and

- representing British sporting interests overseas and increasing influence at international level.

All the Sports Councils distribute Exchequer and Lottery funds. UK Sport focuses on elite athletes, while the home country Sports Councils are more concerned with the development of sport at the community level by promoting participation by all sections of the population, giving support and guidance to facility providers, and supporting the development of talented sportsmen and women, including people with disabilities. They also manage the National Sports Centres (see pp. 290–1).

Sports Governing Bodies

Individual sports are run by over 410 independent governing bodies. Some have a UK or Great Britain structure, while others are constituted on a home country basis. Their functions include drawing up rules, holding events, regulating membership, selecting and training national teams, and producing plans for their sports (see p. 286). There are also organisations representing people who take part in more informal physical recreation, such as walking. Most sports clubs in the UK belong to, or are affiliated to, an appropriate governing body.

Other Sports Organisations

The main sports associations in the UK include:

- the Central Council of Physical Recreation (CCPR), the largest sport and recreation federation in the world, which comprises 202 UK bodies and 66 English associations, most of which are governing bodies of sport. The British Sports Trust is a charity set up by the CCPR to run a volunteer sports leadership programme, and in 1999 it enrolled an estimated 48,000 people. The Scottish Sports Association, the Welsh Sports Association and the Northern Ireland Sports Forum are equivalent associations to the CCPR. Their primary aim is to represent the interests of their members to the appropriate national and local authorities, including the Sports Councils, from which they may receive some funding;
- the British Olympic Association (BOA), comprising representatives of the 35 national governing bodies of Olympic sports, which organises the participation of British teams in the Olympic Games, sets standards for selection and raises funds. It organised a team of over 300 competitors to represent the UK in the Sydney Olympics in September 2000 and the team won a total of 28 medals (see p. 283); pictures of some of the medallists are in the section between pp. 296 and 297. The BOA is supported by sponsorship and by donations from the private sector and the general public, and works closely with UK Sport. It makes important contributions to the preparation of competitors in the period between Games, such as arranging training camps, and for the Sydney Olympics had a holding camp on the Gold Coast in Queensland for all team members. The BOA also works through its steering groups to deliver programmes to national governing bodies and their athletes in areas such as acclimatisation, psychology and physiology. Its British Olympic Medical Centre at Northwick Park Hospital in Harrow provides medical services for competitors before and during the Olympics; and
- the Women's Sports Foundation, which promotes the interests of women and girls in sport and active recreation. It encourages the establishment of women's sports groups throughout the UK and organises events and activities. It runs both the Sportswomen of the Year Awards and an annual nationwide awards scheme for girls and young women between the ages of 11 and 19.

Sport for Disabled People

Sport for disabled people is organised by a wide range of agencies in the UK. Single-disability, multi-sport organisations co-ordinate disability-specific recreation and development opportunities and events. These agencies are the British Amputee and Les Autre Sports Association, British Blind Sport, British Wheelchair Sports Foundation, Cerebral Palsy Sport and the United Kingdom Sports Association for People with Learning Disability. The British Deaf Sports Council organises sporting opportunities for hearing-impaired people and co-ordinates British interests at the World Deaf Games.

Multi-disability, multi-sport organisations are responsible for the co-ordination and development of sport on a pan-disability basis within each home country and, where possible, endorse integration into mainstream sport activities. These agencies are the English Federation of Disability Sport, Disability Sport Cymru, Scottish Disability Sport and Disability Sport Northern Ireland. In addition, Disability Sport England runs some training courses and regional or national events in England.

The remit of the British Paralympic Association (BPA) is to ratify selection, and fund and manage the Great Britain Paralympic Team in the winter and summer Paralympic Games. The BPA is the British member of the International Paralympic Committee. A team of over 200 competitors will represent the UK in the Paralympics in Sydney in October 2000.

UK Sport is reviewing disability sport, with a key objective being the organisational inclusion/integration of able-bodied and disabled sport across a range of sports, particularly at the high-performance level. Nine sports already have a degree of integration: athletics, swimming, cycling, sailing, judo, equestrianism, powerlifting/weightlifting, wheelchair tennis/tennis and archery. The Commonwealth Games in Manchester in 2002 will be the first to include an integrated programme of events for people with disabilities. All distributing bodies of Lottery funding are required to ensure that applicants incorporate access and availability for people with disabilities.

SPORTS FACILITIES

The UK has a range of world-class sporting facilities including 13 National Sports Centres, operated by the home country Sports Councils. Several of the major facilities have seen considerable improvements in recent years, including many football grounds, Aintree and Cheltenham racecourses, and the Wimbledon tennis complex. The Millennium Stadium in Cardiff has been rebuilt and now has a capacity of 72,500; it is the world's biggest stadium with a retractable roof. It hosted the final of the Rugby World Cup in November 1999.

Further improvements in major sports facilities are in hand, or planned, including:

- in Manchester, where modern facilities are being provided for the Commonwealth Games to be held in 2002, including a new 50,000-seat sports stadium costing £90 million, and an Olympic-sized swimming complex—the Games are expected to attract over 5,000 athletes from the Commonwealth nations;
- the redevelopment of Wembley Stadium in London, creating a new 90,000 capacity all-seater national stadium for football and rugby league, which is due to open in 2003; and
- a new purpose-built athletics stadium, able to accommodate 50,000 spectators, which is to be built at Picketts Lock, Edmonton (London), and will stage the 2005 World Athletics Championship.

United Kingdom Sports Institute

The United Kingdom Sports Institute (UKSI) is being set up under the strategic direction of UK Sport and in partnership with the home country Sports Councils, and will be fully operational by summer 2002. It will provide facilities and integrated support services to potential and elite athletes and teams. Its Athlete Career and Education programme, designed to enhance athletes' personal development and sporting performance, and the High Performance Coaching Programme were launched in 1999.

All sports have access to the UKSI's services, although it concentrates on Olympic sports and those minority sports lacking a commercial element. The UKSI central services team is part of UK Sport and based in London. It co-ordinates a network of regional centres in England, Scotland, Wales and Northern Ireland. The UKSI's funds come mainly from the National Lottery.

UKSI Regional Network

England

In England the UKSI network is managed by the English Institute of Sport (part of Sport England). It is based around a number of key centres, of which four are based around National Sports Centres:

- Crystal Palace in London, which is a leading competition venue for a wide range of sports and a major training centre, and has Olympic-size swimming and diving pools, and a sports injury centre;
- Bisham Abbey in Berkshire, which caters for a number of sports, including tennis, football, hockey, weightlifting, squash, rugby union and golf;
- Lilleshall National Sports Centre in Shropshire, which is used by a variety of national teams and has extensive playing fields for football and hockey, together with facilities for archery and gymnastics; and
- the National Water Sports Centre at Holme Pierrepont in Nottinghamshire, one of the most comprehensive water sports centres in the world, with facilities for rowing (including a 2,000-metre regatta course), canoeing, water-skiing, powerboating, ski-racing, angling and sailing—the East Midlands Network Centre is jointly based here and around the extensive facilities planned at Loughborough University.

The other network centres are based around the Don Valley Stadium in Sheffield, Gateshead International Stadium, Manchester Sports City, the University of Bath and Norwich Sportspark.

Wales

The centre of the UKSI network in Wales is the Welsh Institute of Sport in Cardiff, run by the Sports Council for Wales, which is the premier venue in Wales for top-level training and for competition in many sports. The Institute has close links with other specialist facilities, including the National Watersports Centre at Plas Menai in north Wales, which is a centre of excellence for sailing and canoeing; the national indoor athletics centre at University of Wales Institute, Cardiff; and the cricketing school of excellence at Sophia Gardens, Cardiff. In May 1999 the Sports Council for Wales launched a new strategy: *A Strategy for Welsh Sport—Young People First.*

Plas y Brenin National Mountain Centre, in Snowdonia National Park in north Wales, is run by Sport England. It offers courses in rock climbing, mountaineering, canoeing, orienteering, skiing and most other mountain-based activities, and is the UK's leading training institution for mountain instructors.

Scotland

The Scottish Institute of Sport, set up by sportscotland in 1998, is initially catering for seven sports: athletics, badminton, curling, football, hockey, rugby and swimming. Its network will include its headquarters in Stirling, six area institutes and the three National Sports Centres run by sportscotland:

- Glenmore Lodge near Aviemore, which caters for a range of activities, including hill walking, rock climbing, mountaineering, skiing, kayaking and canoeing;
- Inverclyde in Largs, which has many indoor and outdoor facilities, including a gymnastics hall, golf training, and sports medicine and sports science facilities of an international standard; and
- the Scottish National Water Sports Centre—Cumbrae—on the island of Great Cumbrae in the Firth of Clyde.

Northern Ireland

The Sports Council for Northern Ireland has announced a partnership with the University of Ulster for the development of a Northern Ireland network centre of the UKSI. This will involve creating high-quality training facilities and support services, primarily at the University's Jordanstown campus, with the establishment of links with nearby facilities. It is envisaged that the centre will include the development of an indoor training centre, athletics training track, sports medicine facilities, a 50-metre training pool and outdoor pitches, with support services such as sports science and coaching.

The Tollymore Mountain Centre in County Down, run by the Sports Council for Northern Ireland, offers courses in mountaineering, rock climbing, canoeing and outdoor adventure. Leadership and instructor courses leading to nationally recognised qualifications are also available.

The Council's Youth Sport programme has pioneered innovative ways of involving young people in sport.

Local Facilities

Local authorities are the main providers of basic sport and recreation facilities for the local community. In England they manage over 1,500 indoor sports centres. Other facilities include parks, lakes, playing fields, playgrounds, tennis courts, artificial pitches, golf courses and swimming/leisure pools. The national sports strategy envisages that new investment in grass roots facilities should be concentrated on schools, for use by pupils during the school hours and by the wider community at other times.

Over 150,000 voluntary sports clubs are affiliated to the national governing bodies of sport. Some local clubs cater for indoor recreation, but more common are those which provide sports grounds, particularly for cricket, football, rugby, hockey, tennis and golf. Many clubs linked to businesses and other employers cater for sporting activities. Commercial facilities include fitness centres, tenpin bowling centres, ice and roller-skating rinks, squash courts, golf courses and driving ranges, riding stables and marinas.

SUPPORT SERVICES

Sports Medicine

The National Sports Medicine Institute (NSMI), funded by UK Sport and Sport England, is responsible for the co-ordination of sports medicine services. Based at the medical college of St Bartholomew's Hospital, London, its facilities include a physiology laboratory, library and information centre.

In Scotland a network of 29 accredited sports medicine centres provides specialist help with sports injuries. Wales has 11 sports medicine centres, accredited by the NSMI, which are linked closely with the UKSI network in Wales. The Northern Ireland Sports Medicine Centre is a partnership between the Sports Council for Northern Ireland and a local healthcare trust.

Sports Science

The development of sports science support services for the national governing bodies of sport is being promoted by the Sports Councils, in collaboration with the British Olympic Association and the National Coaching Foundation, in an effort to raise the standards of performance of national squads. The type of support provided may cover biomechanical (human movement), physiological or psychological factors.

Coaching

The National Coaching Foundation (NCF) works closely with sports governing bodies, local authorities, and higher and further education institutions. Supported by the Sports Councils, it provides a comprehensive range of services for coaches in all sports. In 1999, 30,000 coaches and 20,000 schoolteachers participated in NCF programmes.

DRUG MISUSE

UK Sport aims to prevent doping and achieve a commitment to drug-free sport and ethical sporting practices. Its Ethics and Anti-Doping Directorate co-ordinates a drugs-testing programme and conducts a comprehensive education programme aimed at changing attitudes to drug misuse. Samples are analysed at a laboratory accredited by the International Olympic Committee, at King's College, University of London; UK Sport is responsible for reporting the results to the appropriate governing body. In 1999–2000 the drugs-testing programme involved 50 national governing bodies and 20 international sporting federations from 44 sports. A total of 6,141 tests were conducted—5,050 in competition and 1,091 out of competition—and 98.1 per cent were negative. UK Sport provides a Drug Information Line to allow athletes to check whether a licensed medication is permitted or banned under their governing body's regulations, and issues a comprehensive guide on drugs and sport for competitors and officials. The UK is working closely with international colleagues in the newly established World Anti-Doping Agency.

SPONSORSHIP AND OTHER FUNDING

Sport is a major industry in the UK, and a joint Department of Trade and Industry/Sports Industries Federation competitiveness analysis, published in July 1999, found that it is worth almost £5 billion a year. Consumer expenditure on sport is estimated at £13 billion a year, and the industry employs about 440,000 people. The private sector makes a substantial investment in sport, with more than 2,000 UK companies involved. The sports sponsorship market was estimated to be worth £376.5 million in 1999.

Sponsorship may take the form of financing specific events or championships, such as horse races or cricket leagues, or grants to sports organisations or individual performers. Motor sport and football receive the largest amounts of private sponsorship. Two recent examples of major sport sponsorship are the signature in February 2000 by Manchester United of a new four-year sponsorship agreement worth £30 million with Vodafone (the biggest sponsorship deal in European football) and an eight-year agreement under which the Squash Rackets Association sold the commercial rights to the British Open Championships to Fablon Investments/Eye Group for £2 million.

Sponsorship is encouraged by a number of bodies, including the Institute of Sports Sponsorship (ISS), which comprises some 100 UK companies involved in sponsoring sport; and the Sports Sponsorship Advisory Service, administered jointly by the CCPR (see p. 288) and the ISS, and funded by Sport England, and similar advisory services of sportscotland and the Sports Council for Wales.

Under the EC's Tobacco Advertising Directive, the Government intends to ban tobacco sponsorship of sport from 2003 in most cases and from 2006 for certain exceptional global events. It has set up a task force of business and sponsorship experts to help the sports affected. Seven sports have sought assistance to make the transition—rugby league, clay pigeon shooting, billiards and snooker, pool, darts, ice hockey and angling.

Sport is one of the main recipients of funds raised by the National Lottery, and 62 sports have received Lottery funding. By July 2000 awards totalling £1.1 billion had been made to over 3,100 projects in the UK.

Sportsmatch

Sportsmatch aims to increase the amount of business sponsorship going into grass roots sport and physical recreation. It offers matching funding for new sponsorships and for the extension of existing ones. Priority is given to projects involving disabled people, the young and ethnic minorities and to projects in deprived areas.

In England the ISS runs the scheme on behalf of Sport England. Since 1992 Sportsmatch has approved 3,113 awards in England, totalling £22 million and covering about 70 different sports. Football, rugby union, cricket, tennis and basketball have received most awards. In Scotland and Wales the scheme is managed by the appropriate Sports Council's Sponsorship Advisory Service.

SportsAid

SportsAid (the Sports Aid Foundation) raises funds to help talented young British sportspeople meet their training and competition expenses. The criteria for

SportsAid grants are talent and the need for financial help. Youngsters must normally be aged between 12 and 18, but there is no age limit for disabled people. SportsAid relies on fund-raising, commercial sponsorship and donations from the corporate and public sectors. The Scottish SportsAid Foundation, SportsAid Cymru/Wales and the Ulster Sports and Recreation Trust have similar functions.

Foundation for Sport and the Arts

The Foundation for Sport and the Arts, set up by the football pools promoters in 1991, funds small-scale projects in sport and the arts. This initiative followed the 1991 Budget, in which pools betting duty was reduced by 2.5 per cent, provided that the money forgone by the Government was paid into the new Foundation; a further cut in duty announced in the 1999 Budget will ensure that funding continues until at least 2002. The Foundation has made awards to schemes benefiting over 100 sports.

Betting and Gaming

Gross expenditure on all forms of gambling, including the National Lottery, is estimated at approximately £40 billion a year. In February 2000 the Government set up an independent gambling review to examine the law on gambling. The review has a wide remit and will examine the ways in which gambling might change in the next ten years (for example, in the light of economic pressures, the growth of e-commerce, technological developments and leisure trends), the social impact of gambling, and regulatory issues.

A new survey, published in June 2000, found that 72 per cent of adults in Great Britain gamble at least once a year. The survey was carried out by the National Centre for Social Research for a consortium representing the gambling industry, the Home Office and other regulatory authorities, and GamCare (the national centre addressing the social impact of gambling). It found that the National Lottery was by far the most popular gambling activity in the UK. Some 65 per cent of the adult population had bought Lottery tickets in the year leading up to the survey, and half the adult population participated in the Lottery each week. For one in four people the purchase of National Lottery tickets was their only form of gambling. According to the survey, other forms of gambling in which people had participated over the past year included:

- scratchcards (22 per cent);
- fruit machines (14 per cent);
- horse racing (13 per cent);
- private bets with friends or workmates (11 per cent);
- football pools (9 per cent);
- bingo (7 per cent); and
- casino gambling (3 per cent).

New types of gambling, including spread betting and gambling on the Internet, were played by only a small number of people (around 1 per cent). The survey found that less than 1 per cent of adults would be classed as problem gamblers.

POPULAR SPORTS[1]

Some of the major sports in the UK, many of which were invented by the British, are described below.

Angling

Angling is one of the most popular sports, with an estimated 3 million anglers in the UK. In England and Wales the most widely practised form of angling is for coarse fish (freshwater fish other than salmon or trout). The rivers and lochs of Scotland and in Wales are the main areas for salmon and trout

[1] Statistics for participation in particular sports in this section are usually provided by the relevant governing body.

fishing. Separate organisations represent game, coarse and sea fishing clubs in England, Wales, Scotland and Northern Ireland, and there are separate competitions in each of the three angling disciplines.

The UK has several world champion anglers. In 1999 Bob Nudd became the first angler to be world champion for the fourth time when winning the world freshwater fishing championships, and England retained the men's team title. England also won the team gold in the 2000 European freshwater fishing championships held in Nottingham.

Athletics

In the UK athletics incorporates many activities, including track and field events, cross country and road running, race walking, and fell and hill running. Mass participation events, notably marathons and half marathons, are popular. The largest UK marathon is the London Marathon each April, with over 31,500 runners completing the 2000 event. The Great North Run, a half marathon, takes place between Newcastle upon Tyne and South Shields each October. In these and other similar events, many runners are sponsored, raising considerable amounts for charities and other good causes. The governing body for the sport is UK Athletics. It has made successful bids to host the world indoor and outdoor championships in 2003 and 2005 respectively (see p. 282).

At the Sydney Olympics in September 2000 Jonathan Edwards and Denise Lewis won gold medals in the triple jump and the heptathlon respectively. Four other athletes won medals: two silver, for Steve Backley in the javelin and Darren Campbell in the 200 metres, and two bronze, for Kelly Holmes and Katharine Merry in the 800 metres and 400 metres respectively. British athletes held world records in two events in September 2000: Jonathan Edwards in the triple jump, achieved in 1995 when he became the first man to jump beyond 18 metres; and Colin Jackson in the 110 metre hurdles (achieved in 1991).

Badminton

Badminton takes its name from the Duke of Beaufort's country home, Badminton House, where the sport was first played in the 19th century. The game is organised by the Badminton Association of England and the Scottish, Welsh and Irish (Ulster branch) Badminton Unions. Around 2 million people play badminton regularly. The Badminton Association of England has a coach education system to develop coaches for players of all levels and a development department with a network of part-time county development officers.

The All England Badminton Championships, staged at the National Indoor Arena in Birmingham, is one of the world's leading tournaments. At the Olympic Games in September 2000, Simon Archer and Joanne Goode won the bronze medal in the mixed doubles, the first Olympic medal ever won by British badminton competitors in the Olympics. At the 2000 European Championships Joanne Goode and Donna Kellogg won the ladies doubles.

Basketball

Over 3 million people participate in basketball in the UK. The English Basketball Association is the governing body in England, with similar associations in Wales, Scotland and Ireland (Ulster Branch). All the associations are represented in the British and Irish Basketball Federation, which acts as the co-ordinating body for the UK and the Irish Republic.

The leading clubs play in the National Basketball Leagues, which cover six divisions for men and two for women, while there are also leagues for younger players. Mini-basketball has been developed for players under the age of 12. Wheelchair basketball is played under the same rules, with a few basic adaptations, and on the same court as the running game.

The English Basketball Association runs various development schemes for young people which aim to increase participation and improve the quality of basketball. With support from National Lottery funds, some

10,000 outdoor basketball goals have been installed in parks and play areas in England.

Bowls

The two main forms of bowls are lawn (flat green and crown green) and indoor bowls. About 6,000 flat green lawn bowling clubs are affiliated to the English, Scottish, Welsh and Irish Bowling Associations, which, together with Women's Bowling Associations for the four countries, play to the laws of the World Bowls Board. Crown green bowls and indoor bowls have their own separate associations. The World Bowls Tour now organises bowls at the professional level. Proposals for a single world governing body are under discussion.

British bowlers have achieved considerable success in international championships. Scotland (represented by Alex Marshall and George Sneddon) won the pairs event at the world outdoor championships in April 2000 in Johannesburg. The Scottish pairing of Margaret Letham and Joyce Lindores won the women's world pairs title in Australia in March 2000 and England won the overall team title. At the 2000 world indoor championships, held in Hopton-on-Sea (Norfolk), Robert Weale won the singles event, while David Gourlay and Alex Marshall won the pairs title.

Boxing

Boxing in its modern form is based on the rules established by the Marquess of Queensberry in 1865. In the UK boxing is both amateur and professional, and in both strict medical regulations are observed.

All amateur boxing in England is controlled by the Amateur Boxing Association of England. There are separate associations in Scotland and Wales, and boxing in Northern Ireland is controlled by the Irish Amateur Boxing Association. The associations organise amateur boxing championships as well as training courses for referees and coaches. Headguards must be used in all UK amateur competitions.

Professional boxing in the UK is controlled by the British Boxing Board of Control. The Board appoints referees, timekeepers, inspectors, medical officers and representatives to ensure that regulations are observed, and that contests take place under carefully regulated conditions. Medical controls and safety measures must be in place at all licensed tournaments, to minimise the risk to boxers. The Board nominates challengers for British championships and represents the interests of British licensed boxers in the international championship bodies of which it is a member.

> Lennox Lewis became the first undisputed world heavyweight champion since 1992, and the UK's first undisputed world heavyweight champion since 1897, when beating Evander Holyfield in Las Vegas in November 1999 to add two other versions of the title to his existing World Boxing Council (WBC) title. In August 2000 the UK had four other world champions (as recognised by organisations of which the British Boxing Board of Control is a member): Naseem Hamed, who holds the World Boxing Organisation (WBO) featherweight title and Paul Ingle (who holds the International Boxing Federation version); Joe Calzaghe (WBO super-middleweight); and Johnny Nelson (WBO cruiserweight).
>
> Audley Harrison was the first British gold medallist in boxing at the Olympic Games since 1968 when winning the super-heavyweight division at the Sydney Olympics.

Chess

There are local chess clubs and leagues throughout the UK, and chess is also played widely in schools and other educational establishments. Domestic competitions include the British Championships, the National Club Championships and the County Championships. The Hastings Chess Congress, which started in 1895, is the world's longest running annual international chess tournament. A number of UK chess players feature among the world's best, including Michael Adams and Nigel Short.

The governing bodies are the British Chess Federation (responsible for England and for co-ordinating activity among the home nations), the Scottish Chess Association and the Welsh and Ulster Chess Unions. Chess is not currently recognised as a sport, but the Government has announced plans to make it so by introducing legislation in Parliament.

Cricket

The rules of cricket became the responsibility, in the 18th century, of the Marylebone Cricket Club (MCC), based at Lord's cricket ground in north London, and it still frames the laws today. The England and Wales Cricket Board (ECB) administers men's and women's cricket in England and Wales. The Scottish Cricket Union administers cricket in Scotland.

Cricket is played in schools, colleges and universities, and amateur teams play weekly games in cities, towns and villages. There is a network of First Class cricket, minor county cricket and club games with a variety of leagues. A number of changes have been made to the main professional cricket competitions. A two-division structure was introduced in 2000 for the PPP Healthcare County Championship, which is played by 18 county teams in four-day matches. Promotion and relegation are also a feature of the two-division one-day Norwich Union National Cricket League. Two other main one-day competitions are held: the NatWest Trophy and the Benson & Hedges Cup.

Each summer two visiting teams play Test cricket against England in two-match and five-match series of five-day Test matches; a ten-match one-day triangular competition, the NatWest Series, is also contested. In 2000 the visiting teams were the West Indies and Zimbabwe. England also play Test cricket against Australia, India, New Zealand, Pakistan, South Africa and Sri Lanka. A team representing England usually tours one or more of these countries in the UK winter. The ECB has recently introduced a system of contracts for elite cricketers, under which they are under contract to the Board rather than to their counties.

Cycling

Cycling includes road and track racing, time-trialling, mountain biking (downhill, cross-country and dual slalom), cyclo-cross (cross-country racing), touring and BMX (bicycle moto-cross). Mountain bikes are increasingly popular and make up the majority of the sales of bicycles.

The British Cycling Federation (BCF) has 14,000 members and 1,200 affiliated clubs. It is the internationally recognised governing body for British cycle sport. The Road Time Trials Council controls road time trials and has around 1,030 member clubs. In 1999 nearly 97,000 rides were completed in open time trials in England and Wales. The CTC (Cyclists' Touring Club), with 70,000 members and affiliates, is the governing body for recreational (including off-road) and urban cycling, and hosts the CTC rally each year in York. CTC Scotland and the Scottish Cyclists' Union represent cyclists in Scotland. Wales and Northern Ireland have separate federations affiliated to the BCF.

The World Track Cycling Championships will be held at the Manchester Velodrome in October 2000.

The British cycling team won four medals in the Olympic Games in Sydney in September 2000. Jason Queally won a gold medal in the 1 km time trial, in an Olympic record time, and then, along with Craig MacLean and Chris Hoy, won a silver medal in the men's sprint. Bronze medals were won by Yvonne McGregor in the 3,000 m pursuit and by the team of Bryan Steel, Paul Manning, Bradley Wiggins and Chris Newton in the men's team pursuit; Rob Hayles and Jonny Clay were also awarded bronze medals—they were part of the squad but were not involved in the final.

Equestrianism

Leading equestrian events are held at a number of locations throughout the year. The Badminton Horse Trials, sponsored by Mitsubishi Motors, is one of the UK's largest

BRITISH OLYMPIC SUCCESS

At the Olympic Games in Sydney, British athletes won 28 medals. his included 11 gold medals, the best British performance since the Olympics of 192

A list of medal winners is given on page 283.

GOLD MEDALS WON BY STEVE REDGRAVE

1984 (Los Angeles): coxed four
1988 (Seoul): coxless pair
1992 (Barcelona): coxless pair
1996 (Atlanta): coxless pair
2000 (Sydney): coxless four

Steve Redgrave displaying his gold med

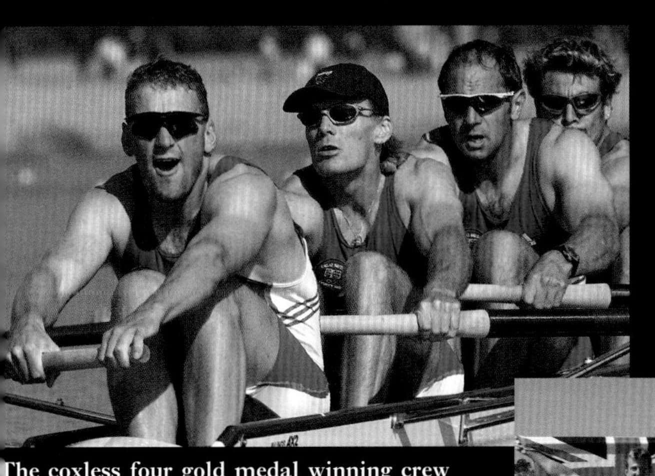

The men's eight, celebrating with their cox, after securin a gold medal on the Olymp rowing course.

he coxless four gold medal winning crew f Matthew Pinsent, Tim Foster, Steve edgrave and James Cracknell. For Steve edgrave it was a fifth consecutive lympic gold medal, while for Matthew insent it was his third gold.

Stephanie Cook, winning the final event, the 3,000 metres. She had started the race in eighth place, but made up a deficit of 49 seconds on the original leader to take the gold medal.

Stephanie Cook (right), celebrating with Kate Allenby, after winning the gold and bronze medals respectively in the first Olympic women's modern pentathlon.

Denise Lewis won the heptathlon gold medal in the Sydney Olympics, having been the bronze medallist in Atlanta in 1996. She has also twice been a silver medallist in the World Athletics Championships, in 1997 and 1999.

Paul Ratcliffe won silver in the K1 slalom, one of two British medallists in canoeing.

Jason Queally won two medals in cycling: an individual gold in the 1 km time trial and a team silver in the Olympic pursuit, with fellow Britons Chris Hoy and Craig MacLean.

Britain was the most successful nation in sailing/yachting at the Olympics.

Left: Ben Ainslie (a silver medallist four years ago) on his way to gold in the Laser class.

Right: Britain's sailing medallists display their medals: three gold and two silver.

Audley Harrison outboxed his opponent from Kazakhstan in the super-heavyweight final, achieving the first British gold medal in boxing since 1968.

Steve Backley won a silver medal in the javelin for the second successive Olympics; he also took the bronze in the 1992 Games.

World record holder Jonathan Edwards achieved a season's best of 17.71 metres in clinching gold in the triple jump.

Richard Faulds, gold medallist in the double trap shooting.

sporting events, attracting around 250,000 spectators. The major show jumping events include the Horse of the Year Show at Wembley in London and the Hickstead Derby in West Sussex.

The British Equestrian Federation (BEF) acts as the international secretariat on behalf of its members, which include the British Show Jumping Association, the British Horse Trials Association, British Dressage, British Horse Driving Trials Association, British Endurance Riding Association and British Equestrian Vaulting. These associations act as the governing bodies of the different sporting disciplines in the UK and oversee the organisation of the major national and international events. The British Horse Society, which includes British Riding Clubs, is responsible for promoting training, road safety, rights of way and the welfare of horses, while the Pony Club provides training for children.

In September 1999 the British three-day event team—consisting of Jeanette Brakewell, Pippa Funnell, Tina Gifford and Ian Stark—won the European Championships at Luhmuhlen (Germany), and Pippa Funnell won the individual title. At the Olympic Games a year later, the team of Jeanette Brakewell, Pippa Funnell, Leslie Law and Ian Stark won the silver medal.

Exercise and Fitness

Exercise and fitness is a term covering a variety of activities—such as exercise to music, aqua exercise, weight training and circuit training—which aim to improve health and fitness. The Keep Fit Association (KFA), which has 900 teachers and a membership of 8,500, promotes fitness through movement, exercise and dance for people of all ages and abilities. Its national certificated training scheme for KFA teachers is recognised by local education authorities throughout the UK. Autonomous associations serve Scotland, Wales and Northern Ireland.

Field Sports

Field sports in the UK include hunting, shooting, stalking and hare coursing. There are over 300 recognised packs of quarry hounds in the UK, of which more than 180 are foxhound packs recognised by the Masters of Fox Hounds Association. Most hunts organise 'point-to-point' race meetings (see p. 299). The Countryside Alliance promotes the interests of field sports.

In June 2000 the report of the Committee of Inquiry into Hunting with Dogs in England and Wales was published. The Committee looked at the contribution of hunting to the rural economy, animal welfare issues, the consequences of a ban on hunting, pest control, and the social and cultural impact. It found that between 6,000 and 8,000 full-time equivalent jobs depend on hunting, but up to 70 per cent more jobs might be affected by a ban, although most employment effects could be offset in the long term. However, the effects on some communities would be more serious in the short term. It said that a ban on hunting with dogs would not have any significant impact on the population of foxes in lowland areas, but could lead to an increase in numbers in upland areas where the fox population causes more damage. Although hunting caused concern on animal welfare grounds, alternatives such as shooting and snares also had adverse effects.

In response to the report, the Government has announced that it will introduce a Government Bill in the next parliamentary session containing a series of legislative options. The main interest groups will be consulted before the Bill is produced, and Members of Parliament will have a free vote on the options.

Football

Association football is controlled by separate football associations in England, Wales, Scotland and Northern Ireland. In England 320 clubs are affiliated to the Football Association (FA) and more than 42,000 clubs to regional or district associations. The FA, founded in 1863, and the Football League, founded in 1888, were both the first of their kind in the world. In Scotland there are 78 full and associate clubs and nearly 6,000 registered clubs under the jurisdiction of the Scottish Football Association.

In England the FA Premier League comprises 20 clubs. A further 72 full-time professional clubs play in three main divisions run by the Football League. Over 2,000 English League matches are played during the season, from August to May. New centres of excellence for coaching and developing young players are being set up, with a contribution of £20 million from the FA Premier League being matched by £20 million from Sport England's Lottery Fund.

Three Welsh clubs play in the Football League, while the National League of Wales contains 20 semi-professional clubs. In Scotland 12 clubs play in the Scottish Premier League, while a further 30 clubs play in the Scottish Football League, equally divided into three divisions. In Northern Ireland, 16 semi-professional clubs play in the Irish Football League.

The major annual knock-out competitions are the FA Cup (sponsored by AXA) and the Worthington Cup in England, the Tennents Scottish Cup and the CIS Insurance Cup in Scotland, the Irish Cup and the Welsh FA Cup.

Football has seen an influx of money, particularly into the top British clubs (such as Arsenal, Chelsea, Liverpool, Manchester United, Tottenham Hotspur, Rangers and Celtic), and many leading footballers from other countries have been attracted to the leading UK clubs. Turnover of the FA Premier League reached £670 million in 1998–99, and the League is the wealthiest in Europe.

In 1999 Manchester United won the European Cup (the final of the European Champions League), and the Toyota Cup in Japan (an annual event between the two top teams of Europe and Latin America), and in January 2000 participated in the first FIFA World Club Championship in Brazil.

Gaelic Games

Gaelic Games, increasingly popular in Northern Ireland, cover the sports of Gaelic football, ladies' Gaelic football, handball, hurling, camogie (women's hurling) and rounders. There are over 700 clubs (incorporating more than 2,550 teams) in Northern Ireland affiliated to the Gaelic Athletic Association, the Ladies Gaelic Football Association and the Camogie Association, the official governing bodies responsible for Gaelic Games.

Golf

Golf originated in Scotland and since 1897 the rules have been administered worldwide (excluding the United States) by the Royal and Ancient Golf Club (R & A), which is situated at St Andrews. The Golfing Union of Ireland and parallel unions in Wales, Scotland and England are the national governing bodies for men's amateur golf. These bodies are affiliated to the R & A and are represented on the Council of National Golf Unions, which is the UK co-ordinating body responsible for handicapping and organising home international matches. Women's amateur golf in Great Britain is governed by the Ladies' Golf Union. Club professional golf is governed by the Professional Golfers' Association (PGA) and tournament golf by the European PGA Tour and the European Ladies Professional Golfers' Association. Women's golf in the home countries is governed by the English Ladies Golf Association, the Welsh Ladies Golf Union, Scottish Ladies Golf Association and the Irish Ladies Golf Union.

The main tournament of the British golfing year is the Open Championship, one of the world's four 'major' events. Other important competitions include the World Matchplay Championship at Wentworth; the Walker Cup and Curtis Cup matches for amateurs, played between Great Britain and Ireland and the United States; and the Ryder Cup and Solheim Cup matches for men and women professionals respectively, played every two years between Europe and the United States.

There are over 2,000 golf courses in the UK. Some of the most famous include St Andrews (which staged the 2000 Open Championship), Royal Lytham and St Anne's, Royal Birkdale, and Carnoustie.

Paul Lawrie won the 1999 Open Championship. Colin Montgomerie was top of the European list of money winners in 1999 for the seventh year running. Laura Davies headed the women's European list for the fifth time and in May 2000 she recorded her 60th tournament victory. In June 2000 the veteran golfer Neil Coles became the first golfer to win a professional event in six different decades when he won an event on the European Senior Tour; he is also the oldest man to win a tournament on this tour.

Greyhound Racing

Greyhound racing is one of the UK's most popular spectator sports, with about 4 million spectators a year. The rules for the sport are drawn up by the National Greyhound Racing Club (NGRC), the sport's judicial and administrative body. The representative body is the British Greyhound Racing Board.

Meetings are usually held three times a week at each track, with at least ten races a meeting. The main event of the year is the Greyhound Derby, run in June at Wimbledon Stadium, London. Tracks are licensed by local authorities. There are 32 major tracks that operate under the rules of the NGRC and around 30 smaller independent tracks.

Gymnastics

Gymnastics is divided into seven main disciplines: artistic (or Olympic) gymnastics, rhythmic gymnastics, sports acrobatics, general gymnastics, sports aerobics, trampolining, and gymnastics and movement for people with disabilities.

The governing body for the sport is British Gymnastics, to which 925 clubs are affiliated. It is estimated that between 3 million and 4 million schoolchildren take part in some form of gymnastics every day.

Highland Games

Scottish Highland Games cover a wide range of athletic competitions, including running, cycling and dancing. The heavyweight events are the most popular and include throwing the hammer, tossing the caber and putting the shot. Over 70 events of various kinds take place throughout Scotland, the most famous being the annual Braemar Gathering.

The Scottish Games Association is the official governing body responsible for athletic sports and games at Highland and Border events in Scotland.

Hockey

The modern game of hockey was founded in England in 1886. A single association—English Hockey—now governs men's and women's hockey in England; there are similar single associations in Scotland and Wales. Cup competitions and leagues exist at national, divisional or district, club and school levels, both indoors (six-a-side) and outdoors, and there are regular international matches and tournaments. The National Hockey Stadium in Milton Keynes is the venue for all major hockey matches played in England.

Horse Racing

Horse racing takes two main forms—flat racing and National Hunt (steeplechasing and hurdle) racing. The turf flat race season lasts from late March to early November, but all-weather flat racing and National Hunt racing take place throughout the year. Great Britain has 59 racecourses and about 13,000 horses currently in training. Point-to-point racing, restricted to amateur riders on horses which are qualified by going hunting, takes place between January and June, and is growing in popularity.

The Derby, run at Epsom, is the outstanding event for three-year-old horses in the flat racing calendar. Other classic races are: the 2,000 Guineas and the 1,000 Guineas, both held at Newmarket; the Oaks (Epsom); and the St Leger (Doncaster). The meeting at Royal Ascot in June is another significant flat racing event. The most important National Hunt meeting is the National Hunt Festival held at Cheltenham in March, which features the Gold Cup and the Champion Hurdle. The Grand National, run at Aintree, near Liverpool, since the 1830s, is the world's most famous steeplechase; the race is televised around the world, with an estimated total audience of approximately 515 million in 84 countries in 2000.

As the governing authority for racing, the British Horseracing Board (BHB) is responsible for strategic and financial planning, the fixture list, race programmes, relations with the Government and the betting industry, and central marketing. The Jockey Club, as the regulatory authority, is responsible for licensing, discipline and security.

In March 2000 the Government announced that the Horserace Totalisator Board (the Tote), which provides pool betting facilities on racecourses and in off-course betting offices as well as offering telephone and Internet betting, would be sold to the racing industry. Legislation is planned both to effect this transfer and to abolish the Horserace Betting Levy Board and the annual levy under which a proportion of horserace betting turnover by bookmakers and the Tote is returned to the racing industry. The Government's view is that these functions do not need to be in the public sector, and that arrangements under which racing receives income from bookmaking should be decided on a commercial basis. The BHB is preparing a plan as to how racing would be funded following abolition of the levy.

Ice Hockey

Ice hockey is a significant indoor spectator sport, with over 2 million spectators each season. Eight teams contest the British Superleague, and 16 the Benson & Hedges Cup. A further ten teams take part in the British National League, run by the British Ice Hockey Association, while there is also the English Premier League; a new English National League, in two sections (north and south) has recently been established. There are around 7,500 players in the UK.

Ice Skating

Ice skating has four main disciplines: ice figure (single and pairs), ice dance, speed skating and synchronised skating. Participation in ice skating is concentrated among the under-25s, and is one of the few sports that attracts more female than male participants. The governing body is the National Ice Skating Association of UK Ltd, to which 75 clubs are affiliated. There are over 70 rinks in the UK. A new ice skating arena has recently opened in Nottingham, with a second ice pad due to open in June 2001. Construction of a twin ice pad facility is in progress in Sheffield. Both of the facilities in Nottingham and Sheffield have received funding from the Sport England National Lottery Sports Fund.

Judo

Judo is popular not only as a competitive sport and self-defence technique, but also as a means of general fitness training. An internationally recognised grading system is in operation through the sport's governing body, the British Judo Association.

At the world championships in Birmingham in October 1999 Graeme Randall won the light-middleweight title, while Kate Howey and Karen Roberts won bronze medals in the middleweight and light-middleweight divisions respectively. In May 2000 Karina Bryant won her second European heavyweight title at the European Championships in Wroclaw (Poland). At the Olympic Games in September 2000 Kate Howey won the silver medal in the middleweight event.

Martial Arts

Various martial arts, mainly derived from the Far East, are practised in the UK. There are recognised governing bodies for karate, ju-jitsu, aikido, Chinese martial arts, kendo, taekwondo and tang soo do. The most popular martial art is karate, with over 100,000 participants. For the first time, taekwondo was a full Olympic sport at the Sydney Olympics, and two people represented the UK. In January 2000 the two main governing bodies came together under the aegis of a reconstituted British Taekwondo Council.

Motor-car Sports

Four-wheeled motor sports include motor racing, autocross, rallycross, rallying and karting. In motor racing the Formula 1 Grand Prix World Championship is the pinnacle of the sport. The British Grand Prix is currently held at Silverstone (Northamptonshire), but the next race, in July 2001, is expected to be the last British Grand Prix at the track. From 2002 it is due to be transferred to Brands Hatch (Kent).

The governing body for four-wheeled motor sport in the UK is The Royal Automobile Club Motor Sports Association, which issues licences for competitors and events. It also organises the Rally of Great Britain, an event in the World Rally Championship, and the British Grand Prix.

The UK has had more Formula 1 world champions than any other country, the most recent being the 1996 champion Damon Hill. David Coulthard finished in third place in the 2000 World Championship, following Grand Prix victories at Silverstone (for the second successive year), Monaco and the French Grand Prix.

UK car constructors, including McLaren and Williams, have enjoyed outstanding success in Grand Prix and many other forms of racing. Most of the cars in Formula 1 have been designed, developed and built in the UK. The UK also provides a large proportion of the cars used in the US Indy Car Championships. The UK motor sport industry is estimated to generate an annual turnover of over £1.3 billion (of which exports account for 60 per cent) and to employ more than 50,000 people.

Motorcycle Sports

Motorcycle sports include road racing, moto-cross, grass track, speedway, trials, drag racing, enduro (endurance off-road racing) and sprint. There are between 40,000 and 50,000 competitive motorcyclists in the UK.

The governing bodies of the sport are the Auto-Cycle Union, for Great Britain, and the Motor Cycle Union of Ireland (in Northern Ireland). The major events of the year include the Isle of Man TT races, the British Road Race Grand Prix and the British Superbike series. The Auto-Cycle Union also provides off-road training by approved instructors for riders of all ages.

Carl Fogarty is by far the most successful rider in the World Superbike Championships since they began in 1988, winning the world title on four occasions, most recently in 1999, and winning 59 races. However, in September 2000 he announced his retirement following an injury earlier in the season.

In September 2000 Mark Loram won the world speedway title, the first British winner of the event since 1992. In 1999 Lee Richardson won the world under-21 individual championship.

Mountaineering

The representative body is the British Mountaineering Council (BMC), which works closely with the Mountaineering Councils of Scotland and Ireland. The main areas of work include access and conservation. The BMC estimates that the number of active climbers is around 150,000, while there are also many hill walkers. There are over 300 mountaineering and climbing clubs in the UK, and three National Centres for mountaineering activities run by the Sports Councils (see pp. 290–1).

UK mountaineers have been prominent among the explorers of the world's great mountain ranges. The best-known is Sir Chris Bonington, who has climbed Everest and led many other expeditions.

Netball

More than 60,000 adults play netball regularly in England and a further 1 million young people play in schools. The sport is played almost exclusively by women and girls, although male participation has increased in recent years.

The All England Netball Association is the governing body in England, with Scotland, Wales and Northern Ireland having their own separate organisations. National competitions are staged annually for all age-groups, and England plays a series of international matches against other countries, both in England and overseas.

Rowing

Rowing takes place in many schools, universities and rowing clubs throughout the

UK. The main types of boats are single, pairs and double sculls, fours and eights. The governing body in England is the Amateur Rowing Association (ARA); similar bodies regulate the sport in Scotland, Wales and Ireland (Ulster Branch). The ARA is also the governing body for representative international teams for Great Britain, in World and Olympic competition.

The University Boat Race, between eight-oared crews from Oxford and Cambridge, has been rowed on the Thames almost every spring since 1836. The Head of the River Race, also on the Thames, is the largest assembly of racing craft in the world, with more than 420 eights racing in procession. At the Henley Regatta in Oxfordshire crews from all over the world compete each July in various kinds of race over a straight course of 1 mile 550 yards (about 2.1 km).

The British rowing team won two gold medals and a silver medal in the Olympic Games in Sydney in September 2000, its best result since 1948. Steve Redgrave became the first competitor in Olympic history to win a gold medal in an endurance sport in five consecutive Olympics when taking gold in the coxless fours, together with Matthew Pinsent (with whom he had won the coxless pairs in the 1992 and 1996 Olympics), James Cracknell and Tim Foster. The men's eight of Louis Attrill, Simon Dennis, Luka Grubor, Ben Hunt-Davis, Andrew Lindsay, Fred Scarlett, Steve Trapmore and Kieran West, together with cox Rowley Douglas, also won gold. In winning silver, the women's quad sculls of Guin Batten, Miriam Batten, Katherine Grainger and Gillian Lindsay achieved Britain's first women's Olympic medal in rowing.

Rugby League

Rugby league (a 13-a-side game) originated in 1895 following the breakaway from rugby union (see below) of 22 clubs in the north of England, where the sport is still concentrated. In the UK there are 30 professional clubs, with about 1,500 professional players, and some 400 amateur clubs with a total of around 40,000 players.

The governing body of the professional game is the Rugby Football League, while the amateur game is governed by the British Amateur Rugby League Association. The major domestic club match of the season is the Silk Cut Challenge Cup Final.

The two main leagues take place in the summer. The Tetley's Bitter Super League consists of 12 clubs—11 from the north of England and one from London—while 18 clubs play in the Northern Ford Premiership.

Sixteen nations will contest the Lincoln Financial Group World Cup in October and November 2000. It will be staged in England, Wales, Scotland, Ireland and France, with the final at Old Trafford (Manchester).

Rugby Union

Rugby union football (a 15-a-side game) originated at Rugby School in the first half of the 19th century. The sport is played under the auspices of the Rugby Football Union in England (the International Rugby Board internationally) and parallel bodies in Wales, Scotland and Ireland. Each of the four countries has separate national league and knock-out competitions for its domestic clubs; however, the two premier sides in Scotland play in a league with Welsh clubs. Northampton became European club champions in May 2000 when winning the Heineken Cup, beating Munster in the final.

The first Six Nations Championship, contested by England, Scotland, Wales, Ireland (a team from the Irish Republic and Northern Ireland), France and Italy, was held in 2000; previously this had been the Five Nations Championship involving the home countries and France. Overseas tours are undertaken by the national sides and by the British and Irish Lions, a team representing Great Britain and Ireland. Tours to the UK are made by teams representing the major rugby-playing nations.

The 1999 Rugby World Cup took place in Wales, England, Scotland, Ireland and France, with the final in the Millennium Stadium in Cardiff.

Sailing

Sailing comprises yacht and dinghy racing and cruising, powerboat racing, motor cruising, jet skiing and windsurfing on inland and offshore waters. The Royal Yachting Association (RYA) is the national governing body for boating in the UK and aims to make boating in all its forms as accessible as possible; it also includes RYA Sailability, the charity for disabled sailors. It administers the Yachtmaster yachting qualification. According to the British Marine Industries Federation, about 7.8 million people participate in the sport. Among well-known yachting events in the UK are the Admiral's Cup, Cowes Week and the Fastnet Race.

In January 1999 Ben Ainslie won the Laser class world Championship in Melbourne, and in June 2000 he won the Laser class European championship for the fourth time. Jerry Peachment won the World Formula II powerboating title in 2000.

> In the Olympic Games in September 2000 the British team was the most successful nation in sailing, winning five medals. Gold medals were won by Ben Ainslie (in the Laser class), Iain Percy (Finn class) and Shirley Robertson (Europe class), while silver medals were won by Ian Barker and Simon Hiscocks in the 49er event and by Ian Walker and Mark Covell in the Star class.

Skiing and Other Winter Sports

Skiing takes place in Scotland from December to May and also at several English locations when there is sufficient snow. The five established winter sports areas in Scotland are Cairngorm, Glencoe, Glenshee, the Lecht and Nevis Range. All have a full range of ski-lifts, prepared ski-runs and professional instructors.

There are over 115 artificial or dry ski-slopes throughout the UK, and 1.5 million people take part in the sport. The British Ski and Snowboard Federation is the representative body for international competitive skiing and snowboarding. The four home country ski councils are responsible for the development of the sport, mainly through coaching, race training and arranging competitions.

The four-man bobsleigh team of Sean Olsson, Dean Ward, Paul Attwood and Courtney Rumbolt won a bronze medal at the 1998 Winter Olympics in Nagano in Japan.

Snooker and Billiards

Snooker was invented by the British in India in 1875 and is played by approximately 7 million people in the UK. British players have dominated the major professional championships. The main tournament is the annual Embassy World Professional Championship, held at the Crucible Theatre in Sheffield. In May 2000 Mark Williams won a closely contested final when defeating Matthew Stevens by 18 frames to 16.

The controlling body for the non-professional game in England is the English Association for Snooker and Billiards. Scotland, Wales and Northern Ireland have separate associations. The World Professional Billiards and Snooker Association organises all world-ranking professional events and holds the copyright for the rules. The representative body for women is the World Ladies' Billiards and Snooker Association.

Squash

Squash derives from the game of rackets, which was invented at Harrow School in the 1850s. The governing body for squash in England is the Squash Rackets Association; there are separate governing bodies in Wales, Scotland and Northern Ireland. The British Open Championships is one of the major world events in the sport.

The number of players in the UK is estimated at over 1.5 million, of whom more than 500,000 compete regularly in inter-club league competitions. There are nearly 9,000 squash courts in England, provided mainly by squash clubs, commercial organisations and local authorities.

For the first time the UK has two individual world squash champions. In September 1999 Peter Nicol won the men's

World Championships in Cairo, regaining the position of world number one, while in October 1999 Cassie Campion took the women's title when winning the final of the World Open Championships in Seattle. In mid-2000 the UK had ten men and nine women in the respective top 20 world rankings.

Swimming

Swimming is a popular sport (see Table 18.1) and form of exercise for people from all age-groups. Competitive swimming is governed by the Amateur Swimming Association (ASA) in England and by similar associations in Scotland and Wales. Together these three associations form the Amateur Swimming Federation of Great Britain, which co-ordinates the selection of Great Britain teams and organises international competitions. Instruction and coaching are provided by qualified teachers and coaches who hold certificates awarded mainly by the ASA.

Table Tennis

Table tennis originated in England in the 1880s. Today it is played by all age-groups, and in a variety of venues, ranging from small halls to specialist, multi-table centres. It is also a major recreational and competitive activity for people with disabilities. The governing body in England is the English Table Tennis Association. There is also an English Schools Association and separate associations in Scotland, Wales and Ireland (where the association covers both Northern Ireland and the Irish Republic).

Tennis

The modern game of tennis originated in England in 1873 and the first championships were played at Wimbledon in 1877. The governing body for tennis in Great Britain is the Lawn Tennis Association (LTA), to which Tennis Wales and the Scottish LTA are affiliated. Tennis in Northern Ireland is governed by Tennis Ireland (Ulster Branch).

The Wimbledon Championships, held within the grounds of the All England Club, are one of the four tennis 'Grand Slam' tournaments. They attracted 457,000 spectators in 1999 and generated a surplus of £30.2 million which was invested in British tennis. Prize money totalled £8.1 million in 2000. Tim Henman reached the semi-finals in the 1998 and 1999 Wimbledon Championships. Lee Childs and James Nelson won the boys' doubles at the US Open in September 2000.

About 5 million people play tennis in the UK. There are national and county championships, while national competitions are organised for schools. Short tennis has been introduced for children aged five and over.

The LTA has a five-year plan for developing tennis in Great Britain, with the aim of expanding participation, encouraging regular competition and producing more world-class tennis players. Tennis facilities are being improved, with more indoor tennis centres, clay courts and floodlit courts. The LTA's Play Tennis 2000 initiative is designed to attract more people to play tennis.

Further Reading

A Sporting Future for All. Department for Culture, Media and Sport, 2000.

Websites

Department for Culture, Media and Sport: www.culture.gov.uk

UK Sport: www.uksport.gov.uk

Sport England: www.english.sports.gov.uk

19 Sustainable Development

The term 'sustainable development' was first introduced in 1987, in the Brundtland Report *Our Common Future*: the report of the World Commission on Environment and Development. A widely used international definition is 'development that meets the needs of the present without compromising the ability of future generations to meet their own needs'. The UK Government has adopted a strategy for sustainable development which includes 15 'headline indicators' against which progress will be monitored. A Sustainable Development Commission was set up in 2000 to help monitor progress.

Introduction

Following the Rio de Janeiro 'Earth Summit' in 1992 (the United Nations Conference on Environment and Development), the UK's first strategy on sustainable development was published in 1994. In May 1999 the Government published a revised strategy—*A better quality of life: A strategy for sustainable development for the United Kingdom*. This builds on its predecessor by emphasising social progress which recognises the needs of everyone as well as effective protection of the environment, prudent use of natural resources, and maintenance of high and stable levels of economic growth and employment. A further report was published in December 1999 entitled *Quality of life counts: Indicators for a strategy for sustainable development for the United Kingdom*, which provides a baseline assessment of the sustainable development indicators (see p. 306).

The establishment of the Scottish Parliament, the National Assembly for Wales and the Northern Ireland Assembly means that, where matters are devolved, the new administrations decide how to proceed in the light of their country's particular circumstances. Accordingly, while some of the policies described in this strategy apply to the UK as a whole, others are exclusive to England.

Sustainable development requires international co-operation. For the UK, the European Union (EU) is especially influential. Changes to the Treaty of Rome, agreed in the Treaty of Amsterdam (see p. 78), give sustainable development a much greater prominence in Europe by making it a requirement for environmental protection concerns to be integrated into EU policies.

Indicators of Sustainable Development

The most widely used measure of the economic progress of the nation is gross domestic product (GDP, see p. 381) and, in the context of sustainable development, this has been complemented by two further initiatives: the use of a range of economic, social and environmental indicators of sustainable development and the incorporation of environmental data into the National Accounts.

In 1996, the Office for National Statistics produced a first set of Environmental Accounts for the UK—integrating environmental statistics with the economic indicators in the National Accounts. The most recent results were published in the Office for National Statistics compendium, *The Blue Book*, in August 2000.

Also in 1996, the UK published a set of approximately 120 indicators of sustainable development, and in the revised sustainable development strategy, published in May 1999, these were expanded to just under 150 indicators. The new set will be at the core of future reports on progress. The most recent report, *Quality of life counts*, gives more detail illustrating past and recent trends and providing a baseline assessment against which future progress can be measured. This report includes a subset of 15 key headline indicators, which are intended to give a broad overview and to focus attention on what development means. Progress will be reported annually and will inform future decision-making.

The 15 headline indicators, covering economic, social and environmental concerns, are:

- total output of the economy (GDP);
- total and social investment (investment in education, healthcare, roads, railways, buses, water and sewage) as a percentage of GDP;
- the proportion of people of working age who are in work;
- indicators of success in tackling poverty and social exclusion;
- qualifications at age 19;
- expected years of healthy life;
- homes judged unfit to live in;
- the level of recorded crime;
- emissions of greenhouse gases;
- days when air pollution is moderate or high;
- road traffic;
- rivers of good or fair quality;
- populations of wild birds;
- new homes built on previously developed land; and
- waste arisings and management.

In addition, a core series of 29 local indicators, linked to some of the national ones, have been developed specifically for English local authorities to use.

The Scottish Executive is currently looking at adopting a similar set of sustainable development indicators relevant to Scotland.

Government Role

The Government is committed, as part of its strategy for sustainable development, to integrating environmental considerations into its decision-making at all levels, and in every sphere of its activities. To ensure that this happens, a number of committees and panels have been set up.

Each main central government department has appointed a *Green Minister*. Individually, they are responsible for sustainable development within their own departments, their associated agencies and non-departmental public bodies (NDPBs). Collectively, they promote the integration of sustainable development across government and the wider public sector, encourage the use of environmental appraisals as part of policy-making and continue to ensure departments better manage their operational environmental impacts. In July 1999 they produced their first annual report which set out their achievements and future work programme. A second report is expected to be published in November 2000.

Green Ministers report to the *Cabinet Committee on the Environment*, which has responsibility, at the strategic level, for ensuring that environmental considerations are fully integrated into all areas of policy, to help achieve sustainable development. The Committee is chaired by the Deputy Prime Minister. In addition, the parliamentary *Environmental Audit Committee* (EAC) looks at the effects of policies and programmes on sustainable development and the environment across all departments and monitors the work of *Green Ministers* through an annual inquiry.

Days when Air Pollution is Moderate or Higher, UK

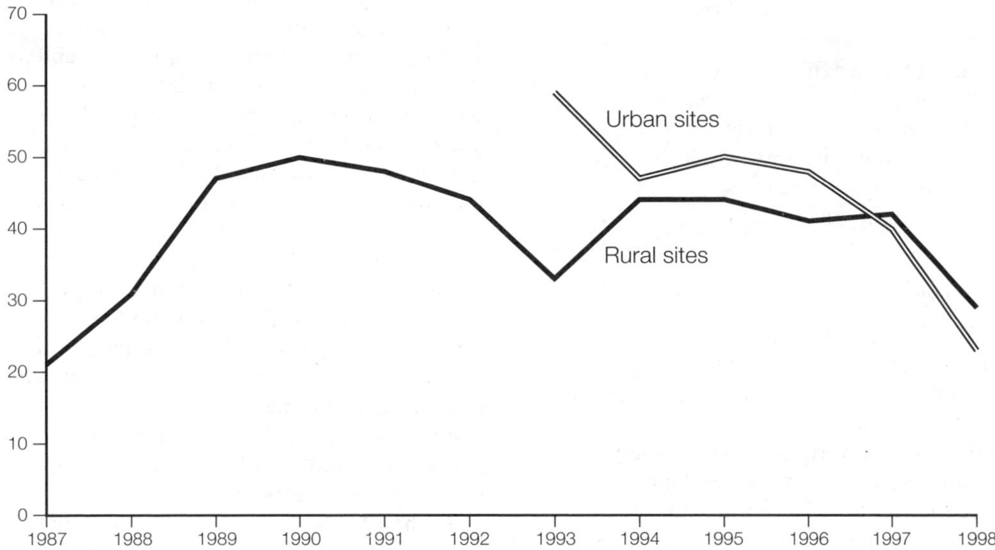

Source: Department of the Environment, Transport and the Regions

A *Sustainable Development Unit* was set up within the Department of the Environment, Transport and the Regions (DETR) in 1997 as a focal point for policy, strategy and planning on sustainable development. It works closely with other departments and is able to offer advice on the best way in which sustainable development can be taken into account in managing policy and operations. The Unit promotes freedom of access to information on the environment, public participation in decisions that affect the environment and access to legal recourse in environmental matters. The Unit also oversees UK ratification of the United Nations Economic Commission for Europe (UNECE) Aarhus Convention.

In 2000 the *Sustainable Development Commission* was established. Its main role is to encourage sustainable development in the UK, review progress and build consensus on the actions needed if further progress is to be achieved.

The Commission supersedes *The British Government Panel on Sustainable Development*—an independent body, which advised government on issues of major strategic importance to sustainable development. In 2000 it published its sixth and final report covering five major topics: sequestration of carbon dioxide (disposal by storage); world trade, investment and sustainable development; noise nuisance; ethical aspects of biotechnology and genetically modified organisms; and fisheries.

The Commission also supersedes *The UK Round Table on Sustainable Development*, which was established in 1995 to bring together members from all parts of the UK and from a wide variety of backgrounds. Its main purpose was to identify ways of achieving development in a sustainable manner. In 2000 it published four reports: *Planning for Sustainable Development in the 21st Century; Indicators of Sustainable Development; Not too difficult! Economic instruments to promote Sustainable Development within a modernised economy*; and *Delivering Sustainable Development in the English Regions*. Other organisations set up to help formulate or implement policy in this area are the *Advisory Committee on Business and the Environment* (ACBE) (see p. 310), the *Trades Union and Sustainable Development Advisory Committee* (TUSDAC) (see p. 310) and *Going for Green*, which seeks to persuade individuals and groups to commit themselves to sustainable development (in Scotland, this role is taken by *Forward Scotland*).

> One of the current projects of *Going for Green* is the *Don't Choke Britain Initiative*, which aims to persuade people to adopt a healthier lifestyle, for example, by encouraging them to consider walking and cycling rather than driving.

Local and Regional Sustainable Development

At the Rio de Janeiro 'Earth Summit' in 1992 an 'Agenda for the 21st Century' (Agenda 21) was adopted by the international community. It set out a framework of objectives and activities for governments, civil society and businesses, on sustainable development necessary for the 21st century. In 1997 the UK Government announced that all UK local authorities should adopt Local Agenda 21 (LA21) strategies by the end of 2000. From autumn 2000, local authorities will have a statutory duty to promote and improve the economic, social and environmental well-being of their areas, building on the achievements of LA21.

The sustainable development strategy, *A better quality of life*, encouraged the Government Offices for the Regions in England to develop regional sustainable development frameworks by the end of 2000. Frameworks should set sustainable development objectives for the region as a point of reference for other regional activity and be backed up by indicators and targets which support the national indicators. By July 2000, frameworks had been published in the North West and the West Midlands. Twenty-six of Scotland's local authorities expect to have adopted their LA21 strategies by the end of 2000.

Taxes

'Green taxes' are one tool available to government in its efforts to promote sustainable development. One example of this is the introduction of reductions of up to £500 in Vehicle Excise Duty for lorries and buses with clean exhausts.

Other measures include the 'climate change levy' (see p. 490) which will be applied to sales of electricity, coal, natural gas and liquefied petroleum gas (LPG) to the non-domestic sector (business, commerce, agriculture and the public sector) from April 2001. Its aims will be to encourage business energy efficiency and help meet the UK's target for reducing greenhouse gas emissions by 12.5 per cent, set under the Kyoto Protocol. Beyond that, it will help the UK to move towards the Government's goal of a 20 per cent cut in CO_2 emissions in the UK. The levy package is expected to save at least 5 million tonnes of carbon a year by 2010. The levy should raise around £1 billion in 2001–02, all of which will be returned to business through a cut in employers' National Insurance contributions and £150 million of additional support for energy efficiency measures.

In the 1999 Budget, a staged increase in landfill tax to encourage the diversion of waste from landfill was announced, bringing the standard rate of tax to £15 per tonne by 2004, with a review thereafter (for waste disposal—see p. 325). The landfill tax credit scheme enables landfill site operators to channel up to 20 per cent of their landfill tax liability into environmental bodies for approved projects, which include reclamation of polluted land, research and education activities to promote re-use and recycling, provision of public parks and amenities, and restoration of historic buildings.

In the 2000 Budget, the Government announced an aggregate levy for virgin sand, gravel and crushed rock, due to be introduced from April 2002.

Education and Training

In 1998 the Government set up an expert panel (for England) to consider the provision of education for sustainable development in schools, youth services, further and higher education, at work and at home. The panel has commissioned a number of studies to develop its strategy, including: a survey of sustainable development learning by school leavers; a good practice guide for the further education sector and a survey of best practice in business; research into appropriate languages

Waste Arisings and Management, UK, 1998

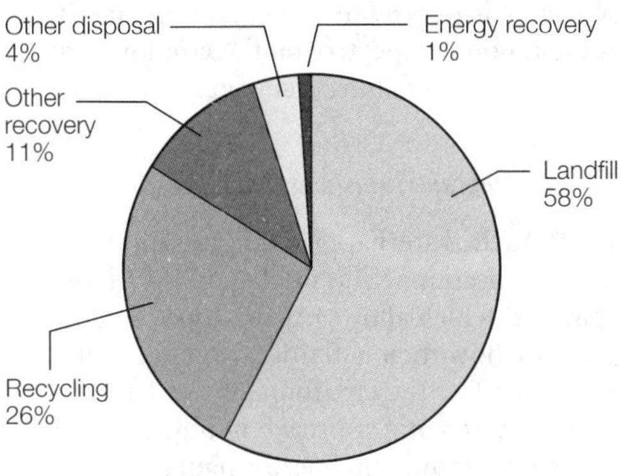

Source: *Quality of life counts*, DETR

for sustainable development education; a study into sources of funding for education for sustainable development work and the feasibility of an *Investors in Sustainable Development* award or accreditation for industry.

In Scotland, education for sustainable development has been led by a group of experts, associated with the *Advisory Group on Sustainable Development* since 1995, and is now integrated into the Scottish curriculum. A Ministerial Group on Sustainable Scotland has been set up to promote sustainable development issues with its priorities being waste, energy and travel. The Sustainable Action Fund is giving over £1 million in grants for 2000–01 to organisations promoting sustainable development.

The Environmental Education Council for Wales has developed a Welsh educational strategy, and launched the first phase of its Environment Network Centres in 1998.

The Environment Task Force (ETF), one of four options available to 18–24 year olds under the New Deal for Young People (see p. 151), was launched in 1998. The ETF aims to improve long-term employment prospects through a combination of high-quality work experience and training through sustainable development projects.

Business and the Consumer

A number of initiatives have been introduced to help both business and consumers to become more environmentally aware. For example, households are being encouraged not only to recycle their waste, but also to buy products that contain recycled material.

The Government is encouraging trade associations and other representative bodies to develop and implement strategies within at least six business sectors by the end of 2000, building on existing initiatives and best practice.

The Environmental Technology Best Practice Programme (ETBPP), launched in 1994, is a 13-year programme that promotes the use of better environmental practices that reduce business costs for industry and commerce. It provides information and advice on environmental technologies and techniques by means of publications, events, and a freephone UK helpline. By March 2000 the ETBPP had stimulated savings for businesses of £100 million a year as a result of their adopting better environmental practices and cleaner technology. The ETBPP works in partnership with the Energy Efficiency Best Practice Programme (EEBPP, see p. 492) which supports energy efficiency measures. In April 1999 the Government launched the *Sustainable Technologies Initiative* (STI), to build on the ETBPP and the EEBPP. The STI is providing £7.8 million of support over the next three years for the development of new technologies that will help businesses to be more efficient in their use of resources, and produce less waste and pollution.

The Queen's Awards for Environmental Achievement are presented in recognition of products, technology or processes developed by British industry which offer major environmental benefits. Awards are granted only for products, technology or processes which have achieved commercial success. In 2000 there were seven awards, for:

- Crossfield Limited of Warrington for MACROSORB systems for treating and recycling textile waste waters;
- the Paxton Division of McKechnie Components Limited of Walsall, West Midlands, for its 'Maxi-Nest' reusable transport packaging system;
- the Renewable Energy Company of Stroud (Gloucestershire) for 'Ecotricity';

- Strattons Hotel of Swaffham, Norfolk;
- TSL Group PLC of Wallsend, North Tyneside, for its pollution-free Spectrosil synthetic silica;
- Tesco Distribution Ltd of Hatfield (Hertfordshire) for its 'Maxi-Nest' reusable transport packaging system; and
- D.W.Windsor Ltd of Hoddesdon (Hertfordshire) for its Diamond Optic light control system.

A similar scheme is the *European Environmental Awards* sponsored by the European Commission and the United Nations Environmental Programme. This award scheme (which runs every two years) recognises and rewards companies that are making significant contributions to economic and social development without detriment to the environment. In 2000, 12 UK companies were nominated for the award and the judging is due to take place in autumn 2000.

The Advisory Committee on Business and the Environment (ACBE) consists of business leaders appointed by the Government and serving in a personal capacity. It enables government and business to discuss environmental issues and aims to help the business community to demonstrate good environmental practice and management.

ACBE has produced eight progress reports on its work to date. ACBE's 1998 report, *Climate Change: A Strategic Issue for Business*, was influential in the development of the climate change levy. A recent business initiative on carbon emissions trading has been led by an ACBE/Confederation of British Industry Emissions Trading Group. ACBE issued a report in October 1999 on carbon trusts and low carbon technologies and a report in May 2000 on how business can contribute to the development of the flexible mechanisms outlined in the Kyoto Protocol (see pp. 331–2).

Many leading companies now address environmental issues in their annual reports and over 90 publish separate environmental performance reports. To further encourage the top 350 UK businesses to report publicly on their major environmental impacts, the Government has produced guidance to help companies measure and report on greenhouse gas emissions and waste. Guidance on water use is due to be published in autumn 2000. The TUSDAC was set up in 1998. Its key objective is to provide the Government with a trade union perspective on the employment consequences of climate change.

Environmental Management Systems

In 1996, the International Organisation for Standardisation (ISO) published ISO 14001, a standard which allows organisations to evaluate how their activities, products and services affect the environment, and gives them a systematic approach to improving their overall environmental performance. Certification is achieved only after an audit of the organisation's environmental management system by an independent body, such as the British Standards Institution (see p. 394). Accreditation of certification bodies in the UK is carried out by the United Kingdom Accreditation Service (UKAS).

The Eco-Management and Audit Scheme (EMAS) is a voluntary European Commission scheme to register sites which have established an environmental management system such as ISO 14001 and which have additionally produced an independently verified public statement about the site's environmental performance. Although EMAS was introduced primarily for industry, participation has been piloted in the UK to include local government. By May 2000, 73 industrial sites in the UK and seven local authorities had registered under the scheme.

Environmental Labelling

Consumers often need assistance to make environmental choices in the goods they buy and often rely on the information given on product labels. To help them, the Government encourages accurate and relevant environmental labelling, as part of an integrated approach to reducing the environmental impact of consumer products. In 1998 the Government launched a voluntary Green Claims Code which sets out guidance for businesses making environmental claims about their products. In June 2000 the code was revised in line with ISO 14021—the international standard on environmental labelling (which was adopted in 1999).

The Government's Market Transformation Programme encourages the take-up of more energy-efficient domestic appliances. The mandatory EU energy labelling scheme provides graded information on product performance, and EU measures have also resulted in the removal of inefficient appliances from the market. The Government has wound up the UK Ecolabelling Board and has taken over the function of the competent body for the voluntary EU Ecolabelling scheme in the UK. The *Advisory Committee on Consumer Products and the Environment* assists the development of a comprehensive approach to consumer product policy and strategic environmental labelling issues.

Biodiversity

The Convention on Biological Diversity was another major initiative stemming from the 'Earth Summit' in Rio de Janeiro in 1992. The UK is one of 177 parties to the Convention. The parties have agreed to develop national strategies and programmes for the conservation and sustainable use of biological diversity, and in particular to protect the world's growing number of endangered species. In 1994, the UK published a Biodiversity Action Plan, which combines new and existing nature conservation initiatives with its emphasis on a partnership approach. It contains objectives for conserving and enhancing plants, animals and habitats, promoting public awareness and contributing to international conservation efforts. The UK Biodiversity Group advises the Government on implementation, representing a partnership of statutory, voluntary and private sectors.

By the start of 2000 action plans for 391 species and 45 habitats had been established in the UK and over 30 local biodiversity action plans were at various stages of implementation. Current work involves analysing the reports from lead partners (a range of statutory and voluntary conservation groups) on progress towards species and habitat targets. A millennium biodiversity report, accounting for the progress made so far towards the implementation of the action plans, is due for publication at the beginning of 2001.

All government departments have agreed to incorporate biodiversity concerns into their policies and programmes and into the management of their own estates.

Since the 1992 'Earth Summit' the UK has committed about £280 million to projects that focus on, or contribute to, policy objectives on biodiversity in 53 developing countries. In light of the internationally agreed development targets to halve the proportion of people living in extreme poverty by 2015, and associated targets for the creation of sustainable livelihoods for people in poverty and the protection of the environment, projects funded in the last few years have focused on the relationship between biodiversity and poverty. Some examples of these include improving people's livelihoods through sustainable use and conservation for biodiversity, and the protection of those livelihoods by preventing biodiversity loss. It has also committed £215 million to the Global Environment Facility, which supports the Biodiversity Convention.

The UK continues to participate in international efforts to implement the Convention. In January 2000 at a meeting of the Conference of the Parties, negotiations on the Biosafety Protocol were concluded. This Protocol—the first one to the Biodiversity Convention—will give countries the chance to make informed decisions (based on a risk assessment) on the transboundary movement of genetically modified organisms.

Further Reading

The Brundtland Report: *Our Common Future*. Organisation for Economic Co-operation and Development, 1987.

A better quality of life: A strategy for sustainable development for the United Kingdom. DETR. The Stationery Office, 1999.

Quality of life counts: Indicators for a strategy for sustainable development for the United Kingdom: a baseline assessment. DETR. The Stationery Office, 1999.

Government Panel on Sustainable Development, *Sixth Annual Report*. DETR, 2000.

UK Round Table on Sustainable Development, *Planning for Sustainable Development in the 21st Century*. DETR, 2000.

UK Round Table on Sustainable Development, *Indicators of Sustainable Development*. DETR, 2000.

UK Round Table on Sustainable Development, *Not too difficult! Economic instruments to promote Sustainable Development within a modernised economy*. DETR, 2000.

UK Round Table on Sustainable Development, *Delivering Sustainable Development in the English Regions*. DETR, 2000.

Advisory Committee on Business and the Environment, *Climate Change: A strategic issue for business*, 1998.

Sustainable Scotland: Priorities and Progress. Scottish Executive, 2000.

Down to Earth: A Scottish Perspective on Sustainable Development. Scottish Executive, 1999.

Biodiversity: The UK Action Plan. DETR. The Stationery Office, 1994.

Action for Scotland's Biodiversity. Scottish Executive, 2000.

Websites

Department of the Environment, Transport and the Regions: www.environment.detr.gov.uk

UK Biodiversity Group: www.jncc.gov.uk/ukbg

Scottish Biodiversity Group: www.scotland.gov.uk/biodiversity

Advisory Committee on Business and the Environment: www.environment.detr.gov.uk/acbe/index.htm

20 Environmental Protection

During 2000 several new strategies were developed: waste strategies for England and Wales and for Northern Ireland (following the adoption of a similar strategy for Scotland); the Climate Change Draft UK programme; and the UK-wide Air Quality Strategy. Rural issues have also been on the agenda, with the introduction into Parliament of the Countryside and Rights of Way Bill for England and Wales, the National Parks (Scotland) Act, and with rural White Papers planned for both England and Scotland.

Government funding for countryside and wildlife programmes in England and Wales will rise from £161 million in 2001–02 to £207 million in 2002–03. For Scotland funding will increase from £51.1 million to £52.6 million and for Northern Ireland it will increase from £1.58 million to £1.62 million.

Conservation

The Department of the Environment, Transport and the Regions (DETR) is responsible for countryside policy and environmental protection in England. It works closely with the Ministry of Agriculture, Fisheries and Food (MAFF) to ensure that objectives for the countryside are integrated with agricultural policies. The Environment Group of the Scottish Executive Rural Affairs Department, the National Assembly for Wales (NAfW) and the Northern Ireland Executive have broadly equivalent responsibilities for other parts of the UK. The four bodies are responsible for implementing the Biodiversity Action Plan, the overarching framework for conservation work in the UK. Many of the conservation functions are delegated to agencies, which are described below. In addition, local authorities and many voluntary organisations are actively involved in environmental conservation and protection.

The Countryside and Wildlife

Countryside and Wildlife Agencies

The Wildlife and Countryside Directorate (WACD), the DETR directorate responsible for policy on wildlife and countryside, sponsors four non-departmental public bodies:

- the Countryside Agency;
- English Nature;
- the Joint Nature Conservation Committee; and
- the National Forest Company.

The Countryside Agency is the statutory body whose stated aims are to conserve and enhance the countryside; promote social equality and economic opportunity for the people who live there; and help everyone, wherever they live, to enjoy this natural asset. It was created in April 1999 by the merger of the Countryside Commission and part of the Rural Development Commission, and has a budget of nearly £50 million for 2000–01. In May 2000 the Countryside Agency published *The state of the countryside 2000*, a compendium of information about the countryside, for example, how land is used for business and for enjoyment and what it is like to live in or visit the countryside. The Countryside Agency is expected to have a key role in implementing the measures that arise out of the forthcoming Rural White Paper for England. It will be assisted by a National Countryside Access Forum, where representatives of the main interest groups will advise on the way the legislation is implemented.

The Countryside Agency launched a survey of all rural parishes in September 2000 to gather information about key services in rural England. The findings will be used to identify rural needs and help the Countryside Agency to develop policies to counteract rural social exclusion and deprivation. The summary results will be available from April 2001 to all county councils and rural community councils for use in planning for development and service provision.

The purpose of English Nature is to promote the conservation of England's wildlife and natural features and provide advice to the Government on nature conservation. Its budget for 2000–01 is £49.6 million. In Scotland the Countryside and Natural Heritage Unit of the Environment Group sponsors Scottish Natural Heritage (SNH), a body with both the nature conservation duties and powers of English Nature, and the countryside and landscape powers of the Countryside Agency. English Nature works closely with SNH and the Countryside Council for Wales (CCW), which has responsibility in Wales for landscape and nature conservation and countryside recreation. The budgets for these two organisations for 2000–01 are £42.4 million and £33.5 million respectively. In Northern Ireland, the Environment and Heritage Service (EHS), an Agency within the Department of Environment (DOE), protects and manages landscapes, habitats and species and also has an environmental protection role. Its budget for 2000–01 is £26.2 million.

English Nature, the CCW and SNH are also responsible for providing advice and disseminating information to the Government and the public on nature conservation, for notifying land of special interest due to its wildlife, geological and natural features and for establishing National Nature Reserves.

The Joint Nature Conservation Committee (JNCC) is the statutory committee through which English Nature, the CCW and the SNH exercise their joint functions. It is responsible for advice and research on international and national nature conservation matters and for setting common standards for monitoring, research and the analyses of resultant information. Among other initiatives, the JNCC has worked with a consortium of agencies and bodies concerned with the environment, including the Natural Environment Research Council (NERC), the Environment Agency, the Natural History Museum, the Royal Society for the Protection of Birds (RSPB) and several others, to establish a National Biodiversity Network. The system (which is accessed via the Internet) delivers information about the management of biodiversities, nationally and locally. At the international level, the JNCC is working on implementing the Convention on Biological Diversity (see p. 311).

The Rural Development Plan for England for 2000 to 2006—jointly developed by MAFF with the DETR and other organisations—is the central programme for implementing the new statutory rural development regulation in England. This was introduced as part of the Agenda 2000 reforms of the EU's Common Agricultural Policy (CAP) and sets the framework for bringing agricultural and rural policy closer together. The Plan marks a change in approach by the Government to rural areas by introducing a gradual reduction in direct production subsidies and a gradual increase in support for sustainable farming, forestry, rural enterprises and communities.

The Countryside and Rights of Way Bill, currently before Parliament, is being introduced by the Government with the aim of giving people greater freedom to explore open countryside in England and Wales. Proposals in the Bill cover:

- access to over 1.6 million hectares (4 million acres) of mountain, moor, heath, down and registered common land, of England and Wales, much of which will be opened up to the public for the first time;
- new powers to enable public and private landowners to create additional permanent access rights through their woodlands and other land;
- a new duty for local authorities to prepare improvement plans for rights of way in their area; and
- new measures for the strategic planning and management of rights of way networks.

Nevertheless, the 'right to roam' will not be unrestricted. It will be limited in scope to avoid activities which cause harm or damage, provide for closure of access land and other restrictions to take account of the need for conservation and of land management, defence and national security.

National Parks, Areas of Outstanding Natural Beauty and National Scenic Areas

National Park status recognises the national importance of the area concerned, in terms of landscape, biodiversity and as a recreational resource. However, the name National Park does not signify national ownership and most of the land in National Parks is owned by farmers and other private landowners. There are seven National Parks in England and three in Wales. While there are currently no National Parks in Northern Ireland or Scotland, the Scottish Parliament passed the National Parks (Scotland) Act in July 2000, paving the way to establish Scotland's first National Park—Loch Lomond and the Trossachs—by the summer of 2002, with the second in the Cairngorms a few months later.

In England and Wales each Park is administered by an independent National Park Authority. The Countryside Agency and the CCW designate National Parks and Areas of Outstanding Natural Beauty (AONBs), subject to confirmation by the Secretary of State for the Environment, Transport and the Regions or NAfW respectively. In October 1999 the Countryside Agency began the designation process of the New Forest as a National Park and in April 2000 the designation process began in the South Downs.

There are 37 AONBs in England, five in Wales and nine in Northern Ireland. Designation started in 1956 with the Gower in Wales and the most recent addition was the Tamar Valley in Cornwall in 1995. Two more—Erne Lakeland and Fermanagh Caveland—have been proposed for designation. In Northern Ireland the Council for Nature Conservation and the Countryside advises the Government on natural landscapes and the designation of AONBs.

The primary objective of the AONB designation is the conservation and enhancement of the natural beauty of the landscape, although many of them also fulfil a greater recreational purpose. In June 2000 the Government announced its intention to introduce amendments to the Countryside and Rights of Way Bill (see box), which would give a stronger role to local authorities and communities in improving the conservation of AONBs.

The budget for the management of AONBs in England grew from £2.1 million in 1998–99 to £5.9 million in 2000–01.

Table 20.1: National Parks and Other Designated Areas, 1999

	National Parks area (sq km)[1]	% of total area	Areas of Outstanding Natural Beauty (sq km)[2]	% of total area
England	9,936[3]	8[3]	20,510	16
Wales[4]	4,129	20	727	4
Scotland	—	—	10,018	13
Northern Ireland	—	—	2,849	20

[1] 1 square kilometre = just over a third of a square mile.
[2] National Scenic Areas in Scotland.
[3] Including the Norfolk Broads.
[4] AONB includes an extra 326 sq km of a cross-border area covering England and Wales.
Sources: Countryside Agency, Countryside Council for Wales, Scottish Natural Heritage, Environment and Heritage Service (NI)

In Scotland there are four regional parks and 40 National Scenic Areas (NSAs), together covering 11,000 sq km (4,250 sq miles). In NSAs certain developments are subject to consultation with SNH and, in the event of a disagreement, with the Scottish Executive.

Forest and Country Parks

There are 17 forest parks in Great Britain, covering nearly 3,000 sq km (1,150 sq miles), which are administered by the Forestry Commission (see p. 466). The Countryside Agency recognises over 200 country parks and more than 250 picnic sites in England. A further 35 country parks in Wales are recognised by the CCW, and there are also 36 country parks in Scotland. Northern Ireland has eight Forest Parks, three Forest Drives and over 40 minor forest sites. All are administered by the Forest Service Agency, an agency of the Department of Agriculture and Rural Development.

The National Forest Company is responsible for creating a new forest between Burton-on-Trent and Leicester, and so far has planted 2,600 hectares. The Heart of the National Forest Visitor Centre, the first phase of a £17 million Millennium Discovery Centre complex in north-west Leicestershire, opened in 1999 and attracted 55,000 visitors in its first five months. It will be fully open by early 2001.

Public Rights of Way and Open Country

County, metropolitan and unitary councils in England and Wales (see chapter 6) are responsible for keeping public rights of way signposted and free from obstruction. Public paths are usually maintained by these 'highway authorities', which also supervise landowners' duties to repair stiles and gates. In Scotland planning authorities are responsible for asserting and protecting rights of way. Subject to public consultation, and, if necessary, a public inquiry, local authorities in Great Britain can create paths, close paths no longer needed for public use, and divert paths to meet the needs of either the public or landowners. Farmers in England and Wales are required by law to restore any cross-field public paths damaged or erased by agricultural operations. England has about 169,000 km (106,000 miles) of rights of way: 132,000 km of footpaths, 29,000 km of bridleways, 3,000 km of byways open to all traffic and 5,000 km of roads used as public paths. There are also 13 long-distance routes in England and Wales, designated as National Trails. Ten of the National Trails have been fully developed and three are in the process of being completed.

Horseriding and cycling in the countryside are also encouraged. The Pennine

Disabled people are expected to be able to access more of the UK countryside as a result of an initiative by the Field Fare Trust. The BT Millennium Miles Project will identify and record at least 2,000 miles of pathways for access by people with disability.

Bridleway—currently under construction—will be the first long-distance trail designed specifically for horseriders and cyclists. About a quarter of the rights of way in England may be lawfully used by horseriders and cyclists.

Common land in England and Wales totals more than 550,000 hectares and the open character of commons has made them popular for informal recreation. While four-fifths of common land is privately owned, people other than the owner may have rights over it, for example, as pasture land. The DETR estimates that 65 per cent of common land has no remaining rights over it and only one-fifth of common land has a right of public access. Commons are largely unimproved, therefore, have high amenity and wildlife value and are protected by law and by nature conservation designations. For example, 45 per cent of the common land in England is found within National Parks, and 33 per cent is designated as SSSIs (see p. 318). Ministerial consent is usually required to undertake works on them or to enclose areas by fencing. In February 2000, the Government launched a public consultation exercise aimed at finding ways to improve the protection and management of common land in England and Wales.

The Countryside Agency has established at least 250 new Millennium Greens in and on the edge of cities, towns, villages and hamlets across England to mark the year 2000, with the aid of a £10 million Lottery grant from the Millennium Commission. By the start of 2000, over 250 communities had received grants to help them prepare their plans, acquire their land and begin to create their local Millennium Green. Examples include the Earlham Marsh Millennium Green in Norfolk, Winston Millennium Green in Co. Durham and Aberfeldy Millennium Green in Tower Hamlets, London. The Agency is also looking for new opportunities and funding to continue with work to provide new open spaces for local people.

There is currently no automatic right of public access to open country in England and Wales, where local authorities can secure access by means of agreements with landowners. If agreements cannot be reached, authorities may acquire land or make orders for public access.

A similar situation prevails in Northern Ireland, where the primary responsibility lies with district councils. In Scotland, there is a tradition of freedom to roam. The Scottish Executive plans to formalise a right of responsible access as part of the legislation on land reform.

The Coast

Local planning authorities are responsible for planning land use at the coast; they also aim to safeguard and enhance the coast's natural attractions and preserve areas of scientific interest. The policy for the protection of the coastline against erosion and flooding is administered by MAFF, NAfW, the Scottish Executive and the Department of Agriculture and Rural Development for Northern Ireland. Operational responsibility lies with local authorities and the Environment Agency.

Certain stretches of undeveloped coast of particular beauty in England and Wales are defined as Heritage Coast. There are 45 Heritage Coasts, protecting 1,540 km (960 miles), about 35 per cent of the total length of coastline.

The National Trust (see p. 323), through its Neptune Coastline Campaign, raises funds to acquire and protect stretches of coastline of great natural beauty and recreational value. Around £34 million has been raised since 1965 and the Trust now protects around 940 km (600 miles) of coastline in England, Wales and Northern Ireland. The National Trust for Scotland owns large parts of the Scottish coastline and protects others through conservation agreements.

Table 20.2: Areas in the UK Protected for their Wildlife, March 2000

Type of site[1]	Number of sites	Area (sq km) [2]
National Nature Reserves	383	2,198
Local Nature Reserves	718	435
Sites of Special Scientific Interest (SSSIs)(Great Britain only)	6,545	22,682
Areas of Special Scientific Interest (ASSIs)(Northern Ireland)	177	866
Statutory Marine Nature Reserves	3	194
Areas protected by international agreements		
Candidate Special Areas of Conservation (SACs)[3]	340	17,659
Special Protection Areas (SPAs)[3]	216	9,748
Ramsar sites[3]	147	6,702

[1] Some sites may be included in more than one category.
[2] One square kilometre = 100 hectares (247 acres), or just over a third of a square mile.
[3] See p. 320.
Source: Joint Nature Conservation Committee

English Nature has supported 13 groups in developing and managing a variety of marine conservation initiatives. So far, 36 estuary management plans have been completed or are in preparation, covering 39 estuaries or 85 per cent of England's total estuaries by area (the Dee and Severn estuary plans were jointly funded with the CCW). There are also 29 informal marine consultation areas in Scotland. In addition, SNH has established the Focus on Firths initiative to co-ordinate management of the main Scottish estuaries. In Wales the CCW provides grants to the Arfordir (or Coastal) Group, which is concerned with the sustainable management of the whole coast of Wales. Altogether there are 163 estuaries in the UK, representing about 30 per cent of the North Sea and Atlantic seaboard of Western Europe. The UK also has about 75 per cent of the European chalk coast.

Wildlife Protection

The protection of wildlife is an essential part of the UK Government's sustainable development agenda. The UK has over 100,000 separate species, out of a global total estimated by the JNCC as being between 5 million and 15 million. The primary conservation legislation in Great Britain is the Wildlife and Countryside Act 1981, which provides for a range of measures to protect plants and animals from damage and destruction, including: affording protection to wild birds and threatened wild plants and animals, and enabling the effective conservation of SSSIs (see below). The list of protected species is reviewed by the three statutory nature conservation agencies, acting jointly through the JNCC, every five years, when recommended changes can be submitted to the Government. In 1998 a further 28 species of flora and fauna were added to the list of protected species.

Sites of Special Scientific Interest and Areas of Special Scientific Interest

Habitat protection is mainly achieved through the networks of Sites of Special Scientific Interest (SSSIs) in Great Britain, and Areas of Special Scientific Interest (ASSIs) in Northern Ireland. By the end of March 2000, 6,545 SSSIs had been notified in Great Britain and 177 ASSIs in Northern Ireland, for their plants, animals or geological or physiographical features. Some SSSIs and ASSIs are of international importance and have been designated for protection under the EC Wild Birds and Habitats Directives or the Ramsar Convention (see p. 320). Most SSSIs and ASSIs are privately owned, but about 40 per cent are owned or managed by public bodies such as the Forestry Commission, Ministry of Defence and the Crown Estate.

English Nature, the CCW and SNH have powers to enter into land management agreements with owners and occupiers of SSSI land, where this is necessary to safeguard sites from damaging operations and to support the management of their natural features. The Council for Nature Conservation and the Countryside advises the Government in Northern Ireland on nature conservation matters, including the establishment and management of land and marine nature reserves and the declaration of ASSIs.

The Countryside and Rights of Way Bill (see p. 315) seeks to improve the protection and management of SSSIs in England and Wales, including enhanced powers for the conservation agencies and powers to refuse consent for damaging activities. Penalties for deliberate damage to SSSIs will be increased to a maximum of £20,000 in the magistrates' court, with unlimited fines in the crown court.

Wildlife Trusts (based on conurbations, counties or regions), RSPB and the Scottish Wildlife Trust play an important part in protecting wildlife throughout the UK. The RSPB owns 161 reserves in the UK covering 111,542 hectares of land. During 1999–2000 it acquired 2,075 hectares of land, including two new reserves and a farm. The RSPB is the largest voluntary wildlife conservation body in Europe, with over 1 million members.

An important role in combating wildlife crime is played by the Partnership for Action Against Wildlife Crime, with representatives from the organisations involved in wildlife law enforcement in the UK. It provides a strategic overview of wildlife law enforcement issues and promotes increased awareness of wildlife crime and the damage done to certain threatened species. Wildlife crime takes many forms and has been increasing in recent years: for example, theft of eggs from birds of prey, illegal shooting, trapping, poisoning, digging up of wild plants, and the illicit trade in endangered species. DNA testing is playing an increasing role in combating crime of this kind, and there are now specialist wildlife officers in almost every police force in the UK. Two of the most recent initiatives to be developed include a National Wildlife Crime Unit to tackle organised wildlife crime and tougher penalties for persistent wildlife criminals.

The Countryside and Rights of Way Bill proposes to strengthen the species enforcement provision of the Wildlife and Countryside Act in England and Wales. Its measures will include the option of custodial sentences for wildlife offences and provide police officers and DETR wildlife inspectors with powers to take tissue samples from wildlife species for DNA analysis. Following a separate consultation exercise in Scotland, a process of pre-legislative consultation on reform of the law will take place in the near future.

Species Recovery and Reintroduction

Extensive research and management are carried out, principally by the four statutory nature conservation agencies, to encourage the recovery of populations of species threatened with extinction in the UK. Species recovery programmes form part of the UK Biodiversity Action Plan (see p. 311). Individual action plans cover a large number of plants and animals in need of conservation action, including some which are close to extinction. While some well-known species, such as the skylark and red squirrel, are still declining, others like the otter and red kite are recovering.

The Royal Botanic Gardens at Kew (see p. 446) has been successful for many years with reintroduction projects. The Millennium Seed Bank within the Wellcome Trust Millennium Building, at Wakehurst Place, West Sussex, has recently been completed. The Bank holds seeds of 1,312 native UK wildflowers, plants and trees—90 per cent of the entire UK population. It aims to hold 10 per cent of flowering plants from the arid regions of the world by 2010 and 25 per cent by 2025. The Royal Botanic Garden in Edinburgh (see p. 446) promotes conservation programmes for rare plants in Scotland and for coniferous trees worldwide, maintaining genetically diverse populations in cultivation at many sites, as pools for eventual reintroduction to the wild.

Tree Preservation and Planting

Tree Preservation Orders enable local authorities to protect trees and woodlands. Once a tree is protected, it is, in general, an offence to cut down or carry out most work to it without permission. Courts can impose substantial fines for breaches of such orders. Where protected trees are felled in contravention of an order or are removed because they are dying, dead or dangerous, replacement trees must be planted and local authorities have powers to enforce this.

Tree planting is encouraged through various grant schemes, including the Forestry Commission's Woodland Grant Scheme. Consequently, the planting of broad-leaved trees has greatly increased since the 1980s. Major afforestation projects involving the Forestry Commission, the Countryside Agency and 58 local authorities include the creation of 12 Community Forests in and around major cities, covering 450,000 hectares (1.1 million acres). The aims of these forests are: to increase woodland cover near the cities from 6.5 per cent to about 30 per cent; restore areas scarred by industrial dereliction; create sites for recreation, sport and environmental education; and form new habitats for wildlife.

NAfW is developing a woodland strategy—to be published in autumn 2000—which will focus upon community woodlands, the environmental management of existing woodland, and the contribution that woodlands make to rural, social and economic development.

The Woodland Trust is a voluntary body which protects existing woods, and plants new areas of woodland. It owns woods across the UK covering about 17,700 hectares (43,070 acres) and, since 1976, has planted over 3.25 million trees.

International Action

The UK's international obligations to conserve wildlife include membership of the World Conservation Union and of several international Conventions. Under the EC Wild Birds Directive, 216 UK sites have been designated as Special Protection Areas (SPAs). Under the EC Habitats Directive, 340 sites in the UK have been put forward to the European Commission as candidate Special Areas of Conservation (SACs). Collectively, SPAs and SACs form the European Union network of nature conservation sites known as Natura 2000.

The UK is party to the Ramsar Convention, an intergovernmental treaty which aims to stem the progressive encroachment on, and loss of, wetlands. The Convention covers all aspects of wetland conservation and use, recognising wetlands as ecosystems that are extremely important for biodiversity conservation and for the wellbeing of human communities. By March 2000, 147 Ramsar sites covering 680,000 hectares had been established within the UK. In addition, there are a further ten sites in the British Overseas Territories: seven in Bermuda and one each in the British Virgin Islands, the Cayman Islands and the Turks and Caicos Islands, collectively covering over 55,000 hectares.

The Darwin Initiative, launched at the 1992 'Earth Summit' in Rio de Janeiro, is designed to bring British expertise to bear on the biodiversity needs of developing countries. Eight rounds of funding have so far been approved for about 200 projects at a total cost of £24 million. The latest round of 20 projects, announced in March 2000, includes work to conserve big mammals, small invertebrates, tropical rainforests and soil diversity. The projects will examine:

- how to assess the impact of invasive species;
- the effect of tourism on the environment;
- exploring practical measures with indigenous people on how they can best use their local natural resources; and
- raising public awareness of biodiversity issues.

The UK is also party to the Convention on International Trade in Endangered Species of Wild Fauna and Flora (CITES), which strictly regulates trade in endangered species by means of a permit system. During 2000 the UK led an international mission to tiger habitats and to countries where trade of tigers occurs, to promote efforts to conserve the species. The mission's recommendations, which included the setting up of a global Tiger Enforcement Task Force, were agreed by the CITES conference in April 2000. The conference also endorsed a UK paper on Bushmeat (meat for human consumption derived from wild animals) and the Government announced that it would provide £30,000 towards the establishment of an international working group to identify ways to manage the trade. In September 2000 a UK listing of the basking shark came into force; this bans global trade in basking sharks taken from UK waters.

In November 1999 the latest Conference took place of the Parties to the Bonn Convention (the Convention on the Conservation of Migratory Species of Wild Animals). The Convention co-ordinates international action on a wide range of endangered migratory species. The UK was responsible for putting forward a resolution which commits all Parties to tackle the problem of fisheries by-catch (any species which are not part of the quota system) which is a particular risk to endangered migratory seabirds, turtles, and cetaceans.

Buildings and Monuments

In England lists of buildings of special architectural or historic interest are compiled by the Department for Culture, Media and Sport (DCMS) with advice from English Heritage. In Scotland and Wales buildings are listed by Historic Scotland and Cadw: Welsh Historic Monuments, an executive agency within NAfW. It is against the law to demolish, extend or alter the character of any 'listed' building without prior consent from the local planning authority or the appropriate Secretary of State, Scottish minister or NAfW. A local planning authority can issue a 'building preservation notice' to protect for six months an unlisted building—which it considers to be of special architectural or historic interest and is at risk—while a decision is taken on whether it should be listed. In Northern Ireland, the EHS has responsibility for historic buildings, following consultation with the advisory Historic Buildings Council (HBC) and the relevant local district council.

Ancient monuments are protected through a system of scheduling. English Heritage is assessing all known archaeological sites in England in order to identify those sites—of a total 600,000—that should be afforded statutory protection. English Heritage will then make its recommendations to DCMS, which maintains the schedule of ancient monuments. Similar efforts are being made to identify buildings and ancient and historic monuments eligible for statutory protection in Scotland, Wales and Northern Ireland.

In England details of all listed buildings are contained in about 2,000 volumes which can be inspected at the English Heritage offices in Swindon (National Monuments Record Centre) and London. The lists for particular areas are also held by the relevant local planning authorities, where they are available for inspection, and at some public libraries. In Wales records are kept at Cadw: Welsh Historic Monuments in Cardiff, and in

Table 20.3: Scheduled Monuments and Listed Buildings, May 2000

	Listed buildings	Scheduled monuments
England	370,742[1]	18,382[2]
Wales	23,500	3,300
Scotland	45,155[3]	7,240[3]
Northern Ireland	8,357	1,435

[1] This is the number of list entries, some of which include more than one building. There are about 450,000 listed buildings in England.

[2] This is the number of scheduled entries, some of which cover more than one site. There are approximately 31,500 individual sites scheduled in England.

[3] As at July 2000.

Sources: Department for Culture, Media and Sport, National Assembly for Wales, Scottish Executive and Environment and Heritage Service (NI).

Scotland they are kept at Historic Scotland's head office in Edinburgh or the relevant local planning authority. EHS's Monuments and Buildings Record in Belfast holds information on all historic monuments and buildings in Northern Ireland.

English Heritage is responsible for the maintenance, repair and presentation of 409 historic properties in public ownership or guardianship, and gives grants for the repair of ancient monuments and historic buildings in England. Most of its properties are open to the public, and there were nearly 6 million visitors to its staffed properties alone in 1999–2000. Government funding for English Heritage is £114 million in 2000–01.

In Scotland and Wales, Historic Scotland, which cares for over 330 monuments, and Cadw, with 130 monuments, perform similar functions. There were nearly 3 million visitors to Historic Scotland's properties in 1999–2000. An Ancient Monuments Board and the HBC advise the Scottish First Minister and similar arrangements exist in Wales. The DOE in Northern Ireland has 181 historic monuments in its care, managed by the EHS (another 1,435 are scheduled). It is also advised by a Historic Monuments Council.

Local planning authorities have designated more than 9,000 'conservation areas' of special architectural or historic interest in England; there are 504 in Wales, 602 in Scotland and 53 in Northern Ireland. These areas receive additional protection through the planning system, particularly over the proposed demolition of unlisted buildings.

The National Heritage Memorial Fund (NHMF) helps towards the cost of acquiring, maintaining or preserving land, buildings, objects and collections that are of outstanding interest and of importance to the national heritage. Trustees are responsible for distributing the heritage share of the proceeds from the National Lottery (see p. 117). By August 2000, over £1.5 billion had been awarded from the Heritage Lottery Fund for 5,627 projects.

Many of the royal palaces and all the royal parks are open to the public; their maintenance is the responsibility of the Secretary of State for Culture, Media and Sport, and Historic Scotland. Historic Royal Palaces and the Royal Parks Agency carry out this function on behalf of the Secretary of State in England.

> The Local Heritage Initiative, devised by the Countryside Agency, is an English grant scheme that helps community groups investigate, explain and care for the local landscape, landmarks, traditions and culture. It was set up in February 2000, with £1 million funding from the Nationwide Building Society and £8 million from the Heritage Lottery Fund, with a commitment to continue funding until 2010. This money is expected to help establish about 3,000 individual projects covering natural, built, archaeological and industrial heritage, plus traditions and customs. There are plans to develop similar schemes for communities in Scotland, Wales and Northern Ireland.

Industrial, Transport and Maritime Heritage

As the first country in the world to industrialise on a large scale, the UK has a rich industrial heritage, including such sites as the Ironbridge Gorge, where Abraham Darby (1677–1717) first smelted iron using coke instead of charcoal (now a World Heritage Site—see p. 323). Several industrial monuments in Scotland are in the care of the First Minister, including Bonawe Iron Furnace, the most complete charcoal-fuelled ironworks surviving in Britain; the working New Abbey Corn Mill; and Dallas Dhu Malt Whisky Distillery.

The UK pioneered railways, and has a fine heritage of railway buildings and structures. A large number of disused railway lines have been bought by railway preservation societies, and several railway museums have been established.

Reminders of the UK's maritime past are also preserved. Portsmouth is home to HMS *Victory* (Admiral Nelson's flagship), HMS *Warrior* (the world's first iron battleship, launched in 1860), and the remains of King Henry VIII's *Mary Rose*, the world's only surviving 16th-century warship.

A voluntary body, the Maritime Trust, preserves vessels and other maritime items of historic or technical interest. The Trust's vessels include the clipper *Cutty Sark* (launched in 1869) at Greenwich, in London. In all, about 400 historic ships are preserved in the UK, mostly in private hands.

World Heritage Sites

The UK has 18 sites in the World Heritage List (see map at the front of the book), which was established under the United Nations Educational, Scientific and Cultural Organisation's (UNESCO) 1972 World Heritage Convention to identify and secure lasting protection for sites of outstanding universal value.

The UK is seeking election in 2001 to become one of the 21 members of the World Heritage Committee. The UK has drawn up a tentative list of potential World Heritage sites. Nomination for World Heritage Status will be drawn from the 25 sites included in this list over the next five to ten years. Three sites from the tentative list were formally nominated in 1999: the Heart of Neolithic Orkney in Scotland; Blaenavon Industrial Landscape in south Wales; and the town of St George in Bermuda. Four further sites—Derwent Valley Mills in Derbyshire; Saltaire in West Yorkshire; New Lanark in Central Scotland; and the Dorset and East Devon Coast—were nominated in June 2000.

The Voluntary Sector

Voluntary organisations are well represented in conservation work. Although they are funded largely by subscription, private donations and entrance fees, many receive government support and grants, sometimes in recognition of statutory responsibilities that they perform.

The National Trust, a charity with nearly 2.7 million members, owns and protects places of historic interest and natural beauty for the benefit of the nation. It looks after around 270,000 hectares (667,000 acres) of land in England, Wales and Northern Ireland, including: 200 historic houses; 160 gardens; 40,000 ancient monuments and archaeological remains; forests; woods; fens; farmland; downs; moorland, islands; nature reserves; coastline; and 46 villages. Some 12 million people visit National Trust 'pay for entry' properties each year and an estimated 50 million visits are made annually to its coasts and countryside properties. The separate National Trust for Scotland owns 125 properties and 75,000 hectares (185,000 acres) of countryside.

Pollution Control

Administration

Executive responsibility for pollution control is divided between local authorities and central government agencies. The central administration makes policy, promotes legislation and advises pollution control authorities on policy implementation. In England, the Secretary of State for the Environment, Transport and the Regions has general responsibility for co-ordinating the work of the Government on pollution control. Similar responsibilities are exercised in Scotland by the Minister for Transport and the Environment, in Wales by the National Assembly Environment Secretary and in Northern Ireland by the DOE.

Local authorities also have important duties and powers. They are responsible for:

- collection and disposal of domestic wastes;
- keeping the streets clear of litter;
- control of air pollution from domestic premises and, in England and Wales, from many industrial premises;
- review, assessment and management of local air quality; and
- noise and general nuisance abatement.

The Environment Agency and the Scottish Environment Protection Agency (SEPA) regulate the major pollution risks to air, water and land, and waste. In Northern Ireland, the EHS exercises similar functions.

There is an extensive framework of national and EC legislation on the manufacture, distribution, use and disposal of hazardous chemicals. New and existing chemicals are subject to notification and assessment procedures under EC legislation. Pesticides, biocides and veterinary medicines are subject to mandatory approval procedures. International controls on the movement of hazardous waste were strengthened under the Basel Convention in 1998.

The Royal Commission on Environmental Pollution is an independent standing body that advises the Government on dangers to the environment, and suggests ways of integrating environmental objectives with other economic and social objectives in order to achieve sustainable development. It has produced 22 reports so far on a variety of topics; the most recent, entitled *Energy—the changing climate*, was published in June 2000. A report on environmental planning is expected be published in 2001.

In 2000 the Environment Agency published *Spotlight on Business Environment Performance*, its 1999 report which highlights good and poor performance by industry in England and Wales. The report provides league tables of good performers that have reduced the amount of pollution they produce and league tables of poor performers which have been fined and prosecuted for pollution offences. Key achievements highlighted, include: a 20 per cent cut in the chemical industries' emissions of volatile organic compounds; a 29 per cent cut in sulphur dioxide released by fuel and power stations; a 20 per cent reduction in particulate emissions from metal production and processing industries; and a 10 per cent reduction in particulate emissions from the mineral industries. In all, 566 businesses and individuals were prosecuted for pollution offences in 1999. The average fine imposed was £3,500—or £4,750 if the £750,000 fine for the Milford Haven *Sea Empress* disaster in 1996 is included.

Industrial Pollution Control

The Environmental Protection Act 1990 established two pollution control regimes for Great Britain: Local Air Pollution Control (LAPC), which regulates emissions to air; and Integrated Pollution Control (IPC), which regulates emissions to land and water, as well as air.

In England and Wales, LAPC is operated by local authorities and IPC by the Environment Agency. In Scotland SEPA operates both IPC and LAPC. In Northern Ireland the EHS exercises broadly similar controls, and a regime similar to IPC was introduced in 1998.

At the beginning of 2000 the Environment Agency published the fourth and final report in a series of initial evaluations of the state of the environment of England and Wales. This publication reviews the state of the atmosphere while the previous three reports addressed the state of the freshwater environment, the coastal environment and the state of the land. The reports are intended to both inform and to highlight those areas in which the Agency has a particular role to play. Within the report on the state of the atmosphere, the Agency lists its priorities which include: continuing to reduce emissions from the industrial and waste sectors by encouraging them to self-improve; and improving air quality information available to the public by expanding the Pollution Inventory (see p. 325).

A new Pollution Prevention Control (PPC) regime, which implements an EC Directive on Integrated Pollution Prevention and Control (IPPC), came into force in England and Wales in August 2000, and in Scotland in September 2000. PPC will succeed IPC and LAPC and will be fully established by 2007.

Under both regimes, regulators are required to ensure pollution from industry is prevented or reduced through the use of best available techniques, subject to assessment of costs and benefits. Both regimes require regulators to take account of the special characteristics of an installation and its local environment.

Under PPC, the issuing of integrated permits will apply to a larger number of industrial activities. These include, for example, animal rendering, currently regulated under LAPC, as well as some, such as food and drink and intensive livestock installations, which have not been controlled under this type of regime. Regulators are also required to take into account a wider range of environmental impacts (including noise, energy efficiency and site restoration) when issuing integrated permits. Those LAPC installations not covered by the IPPC Directive will continue to have emissions to air only regulated under PPC.

Existing installations are being phased into the new PPC regime on a sectoral basis until 2007. Regulators, with some exceptions, continue to be responsible for those installations they currently regulate under IPC and LAPC. In Scotland, SEPA will continue to regulate all installations falling within the regime.

In May 1999 the Environment Agency launched a Pollution Inventory, which provides details of emissions to air, water and land from processes regulated under PPC and their contributions to national emission levels. In 2000 it published the results. The data is updated annually and can be found on the Agency's website: www.environment-agency.gov.uk.

Land, Waste, Recycling and Litter

Soil quality in the UK is relatively good, but faces pressure from a range of factors, including urbanisation, localised erosion, declining organic content and contamination. The DETR plans, jointly with MAFF, to publish a draft strategy for England to promote the sustainable use of soil and to raise public awareness of the importance of soil as part of the environment.

The UK's legacy of contaminated land results from an industrial age that generated wealth but also caused much pollution. The Environment Agency estimates that some 300,000 hectares of land are contaminated in Great Britain. Government policy emphasises the importance of voluntary action to clean up contaminated land, and most attempts to clean up sites occur when they are redeveloped. A strengthened regulatory regime for dealing with contaminated land came into force in England in April 2000, and in Scotland in July 2000.

Waste regulation in England and Wales is the responsibility of the Environment Agency, while local authorities in England and Wales are responsible for the collection and disposal of all household waste and some commercial waste. In 'two-tier' areas district councils are responsible for waste collection and county councils for waste disposal, while in unitary areas the council has both roles. In Scotland local authorities carry out both roles and waste regulation rests with SEPA, while in Northern Ireland responsibility for waste regulation is being transferred from district councils to the DOE.

The Environmental Protection Act 1990 (as amended) and the Waste Management Licensing Regulations 1994 regulate waste management. A waste management licence is required by anyone wanting to deposit, recover, or dispose of waste. Licences are issued by the Environment Agency and SEPA. A duty of care requires waste producers, and anyone else with responsibility for waste, to take all reasonable steps to keep their waste safe. If they give their waste to someone else they must be sure that those people are authorised to take it and can transport, recycle or dispose of it safely. Failure to comply with either the licensing requirements or the duty of care is an offence. Policies on waste shipment into and out of the UK are under review.

Final disposal, generally through landfill, makes little practical use of waste, although recovery of the landfill gas for energy generation can occur. The Government has said that it wants to reduce reliance on landfill and in 1999 increased the standard rate of landfill tax from £7 to £10 a tonne, with a further rise of £1 a tonne a year until at least 2004, to encourage less disposal of waste to landfill and more recycling.

In May 2000 the Government published *Waste Strategy 2000 for England and Wales*, explaining its views on managing waste and resources better and setting out the changes needed to deliver more sustainable waste management during the next 20 years, as well as significant reductions in the amount of biodegradable waste sent to landfill in line with the relevant EC Landfill Directive. Key measures include:

- new plans to require government departments to buy recycled products;

- statutory local authority recycling and composting targets, which will double recycling and composting by 2003;
- more use of the landfill tax credit scheme to deliver an increase in recovery, particularly of household waste;
- a new Waste and Resources Action Programme for developing the new markets and end uses for recycled waste;
- tradable permits, limiting the amount of biodegradable municipal waste that local authorities can send to landfill sites;
- extending producers' responsibilities to recover their product, for example newspapers and direct mail; and
- continuing to raise public awareness, working with the National Waste Awareness Initiative.

By 2005 the Government aims to reduce the amount of industrial and commercial waste landfilled to 85 per cent of 1998 levels and to recycle or compost at least 25 per cent of household waste, increasing to 33 per cent by 2015. To ensure that all local authorities contribute to achieving these targets, the Government has set statutory performance standards for local authority recycling in England. Nine per cent of municipal waste in England and Wales, 5 per cent in Scotland and 4 per cent in Northern Ireland were recycled in 1998–99.

A similar waste management strategy in Northern Ireland was launched in March 2000. This strategy was designed as a framework against which planning and developments will be shaped to achieve sustainable waste management and to meet the targets for diversion away from landfill. The main goals for the term of the strategy are: by 2010 a reduction of 25 per cent for biodegradable municipal waste going to landfill (set against 1995 levels); a reduction of 50 per cent by 2013; and a reduction of 75 per cent by 2020.

Scotland also has its own waste strategy, launched in 1999. The strategy's objectives include: ensuring that waste is disposed of without endangering human health and without harming the environment; establishing an integrated and adequate network of waste disposal installations; encouraging the prevention or reduction of waste production and encouraging the recovery of waste. SEPA aims to fulfil the objectives set out in its waste strategy by a number of measures, including:

- establishing an integrated waste management data system to enable changes in waste management to be monitored;
- greater investment;
- new markets for recycled goods;
- publishing guidance on general technical requirements for particular wastes;
- encouraging producers of special waste to minimise waste and undertake pre-treatment prior to disposal;
- supporting the use of targets as a method of changing behaviour; and
- commissioning waste management research.

Under the EC Directive on packaging and packaging waste, at least 50 per cent of the UK's packaging waste must be recovered and at least 25 per cent recycled by the year 2001. Regulations that came into force in 1998 in Great Britain and in 1999 in Northern Ireland stipulate, among other things, that all packaging must be 'recoverable' through at least one of the following: recycling; incineration with energy recovery; composting or biodegradation.

Across the United Kingdom, banks are available for the public to deposit various waste material for recycling. In 1999 there were over 14,000 bottle bank sites provided by local authorities. In 1998 there were over 9,000 can banks accepting aluminium cans. A variety of other materials, such as textiles, paper and plastics, are also recycled. In addition, some local authorities provide kerbside collection of recyclable material.

Litter and Dog Fouling

It is a criminal offence to leave litter in any public place in the open air or to dump rubbish except in designated places. The maximum fine upon successful prosecution is £2,500. The optional litter fixed penalty fine, which discharges a person's liability to prosecution, is £25.

Local authorities have a duty to keep their public land free of litter and refuse, including dog faeces, as far as is practicable. Members of the public have powers to take action against authorities which fail to comply with their responsibilities. In England, Wales and Northern Ireland local authorities also have powers to make it an offence not to clear up after one's dog in specified places, and may issue a fixed penalty fine of £25 under the Dogs (Fouling of Land) Act 1996. In Scotland it is an offence to allow a dog to foul in specified places.

The Tidy Britain Group and Keep Scotland Beautiful are the national agencies for tackling litter in collaboration with local authorities and the private sector. The environment agencies, local authorities, police and the Tidy Britain Group have been monitoring the incidence of 'fly tipping' (illegal dumping of waste) since the introduction of the landfill tax and found that fly tipping has increased since 1994–95. The maximum penalty for fly tipping (and other offences relating to waste) is up to five years' imprisonment and/or an unlimited fine.

Water

In the UK, 94 per cent of the population live in properties connected to a sewer, and about 90 per cent of the population receive primary treatment and above. In England and Wales the water industry is planning an investment programme of some £7.4 billion during the period 2000 to 2005 for improvements to water quality. Progressively higher treatment standards for industrial waste effluents and new measures to combat pollution from agriculture are expected to bring further improvements in water quality.

In Scotland responsibility for the provision of all water and sewerage services lies with three Water Authorities, covering the north, east and west of the country. For details on the water supply industry and the Drinking Water Inspectorate, see pp. 505-7.

In the UK, all discharges to water require the consent of the appropriate regulatory authority. For England and Wales this is the Environment Agency, which controls water pollution through the regulation of all effluent discharges into controlled waters (groundwaters, inland and coastal waters). The Agency maintains public registers containing information about water quality, discharge consents, authorisations and monitoring. Applicants for consents to discharge have the right of appeal if they are dissatisfied with the Agency's decision—most of these appeals are dealt with by the Planning Inspectorate, an executive agency of the DETR. Trade effluent discharges to the public sewers are controlled by the sewerage undertakers. In Scotland controlling water pollution is the responsibility of SEPA, appeals are dealt with by the Scottish Executive and trade effluent discharges to the public sewer are controlled by the Water Authorities. In Northern Ireland the EHS is responsible for controlling water pollution.

The Environment Agency reported 17,863 substantiated water pollution incidents in 1998, of which 3,600 were industrial. The biggest polluter was the construction industry, with 625 incidents. In Scotland SEPA reported 2,168 water pollution incidents in 1998–99, of which 188 were significant. Pollution by sewage remained the most important source of pollution, with 615 incidents. In Northern Ireland of 1,506 substantiated incidents, 438 and 347 were attributed to the agricultural and industrial sectors respectively.

In 1999 new regulations came into force to further protect groundwater. The regulations are aimed at ensuring that groundwater is not polluted by disposals to land of a wide range of dangerous substances. Under the regulations, certain such substances may not be disposed of to land, and others may only be disposed of following prior authorisation. The regulations also give the Environment Agency powers to stop activities which might cause groundwater pollution.

There are 68 Nitrate Vulnerable Zones (NVZs) in England and Wales, designated under the EC Nitrates Directive, covering 8 per cent of the total agricultural land area. There are a further two zones in Scotland and three in Northern Ireland. Farmers in NVZs are required to follow rules on timing and rate of application of fertilisers and organic manures. The aim is to protect vulnerable waters against agricultural nitrate pollution as nitrates can disturb the natural ecological balance of water systems if they become overabundant. This can lead to eutrophication (enrichment of water by nutrients causing growth of algae) and—in drinking waters—pose a risk to human health. Farmers in NVZs are also required to keep formal records of their cropping and stocking densities together with details of fertiliser and organic manure use.

Bathing Waters and Coastal Sewage Discharges

Bathing water quality is influenced by natural factors such as temperature, salinity and sunlight, discharges from coastal sewerage treatment works, the operation of combined sewer overflows (CSOs) in wet weather, and run-off from agricultural land. Over the past 11 years the overall quality of UK bathing waters has improved considerably; 91 per cent of waters complied with the mandatory coliform standards of the EC Bathing Water Directive in 1999, compared with 66 per cent in 1988. The Thames region and Northern Ireland achieved 100 per cent compliance, compared with the North West of England which had the lowest compliance rate—just over two-thirds of bathing waters met the required standard. In 1999 the Government announced measures designed to bring further improvements to bathing water quality over the next five years. There will be secondary treatment for all significant sewage discharges—higher levels of treatment where this is needed to protect bathing waters—and the process of improving CSOs will be speeded up, with around 3,800 (80 per cent) to be tackled by March 2005. These measures will be implemented with the help of £600 million from the water companies of England and Wales. Consistent compliance with the mandatory standards of the Directive is expected to increase from 91 per cent in 1999 to 97 per cent by 2005, with further improvement in compliance, particularly at major holiday resorts. A record 57 beaches in the UK were awarded Europe's 'Blue Flag' in 2000, a substantial increase on the 41 beaches that received an award in 1999, and the number of marinas gaining the award rose from 26 to 29. Blue Flag awards recognise bathing water quality, beach cleanliness, dog control, wheelchair access and the provision of life-saving equipment and other facilities. In 2000 the Tidy Britain Group gave Seaside Awards to 272 beaches in the UK for meeting appropriate standards of water quality and beach management.

Percentage of Bathing Waters complying[1] with the EC Bathing Waters Directive, UK

[1] The small number of designated bathing waters in Scotland (60 in 1999 and 23 previously) and Northern Ireland (16) causes greater fluctuations in percentage compliance than in England and Wales (over 400 sites).

Sources: Environment Agency, Scottish Environment Protection Agency, and Environment and Heritage Service, Northern Ireland

Marine Environment

The Maritime and Coastguard Agency (see p. 372) is responsible for dealing with spillages of oil or other hazardous substances from ships at sea. The various counter-pollution facilities for which it is responsible include: remote-sensing surveillance aircraft; aerial and seaborne spraying equipment; stocks of oil dispersants; mechanical recovery and cargo transfer equipment; and specialised beach cleaning equipment. The Agency has an Enforcement Unit at its headquarters in Southampton for apprehending ships making illegal discharges of oil and other pollutants off the British coast. In 1997, the maximum fine for pollution from ships was raised to

£250,000 in cases which are heard in magistrates' courts.

Decisions about which areas of the UK Continental Shelf should be made available for petroleum licensing take account of advice from the JNCC. Where areas are made available for exploration and development, special conditions may be imposed on the licence holders to minimise or avoid any impact on the marine environment. These conditions are agreed with the JNCC.

Government policy is not to permit any deposit of waste in the sea where there is a safe land-based alternative unless it can be demonstrated that disposal at sea is the best practicable option. Under the OSPAR Convention, the Government is working towards achieving substantial reductions of radioactive discharges to near background values for naturally occurring substances and close to zero for artificial substances. Disposal of sewage sludge at sea ceased at the end of 1998. The only types of waste that are now routinely considered for deposit in the sea are dredged material from ports and harbours, and small quantities of fish waste.

Air and the Atmosphere

Air quality has improved considerably since the smogs of the 1950s. The first step towards these improvements was the introduction of the Clean Air Act in 1956, which controlled smoke from industrial and domestic coal burning, a major source of pollution at the time. Since then, better regulation of industry has led to considerable improvements in air quality. For example, in 1971, almost 8.5 million tonnes of carbon monoxide and over 6 million tonnes of sulphur dioxide were emitted into the air in the UK. By 1998 these emissions had fallen to under 5 million and under 2 million tonnes respectively.

Industrial processes with the greatest potential for producing harmful emissions are subject to IPC and the IPPC (see p. 324). Processes with a significant but lesser potential for air pollution require approval, in England and Wales from local authorities, in Scotland from SEPA and in Northern Ireland from the EHS. Local authorities also control emissions of black smoke from commercial and industrial premises, and implement smoke control areas to deal with emissions from domestic properties. The Department of Trade and Industry has a major influence on air pollution through its regulation of company matters, through licensing of electricity generation and supply, and through promoting the development of cleaner technologies.

A new UK-wide air quality strategy was published in January 2000. This sets air quality objectives for the air pollutants of main concern to health: nitrogen dioxide, PM_{10}, sulphur dioxide, carbon monoxide, lead, benzene and 1,3-butadiene. It sets out a programme of action to reduce air pollution and so protect people's health, particularly the elderly and those with conditions such as asthma who are most vulnerable, and the natural and built environment. Measures to reduce pollution from road transport are seen as being key to achieving the objectives. Progressively tighter standards on fuels and vehicle emissions mean that urban road transport emissions of carbon monoxide, nitrogen oxides and particulates are projected to fall by around 70 per cent between 1995 and 2015 (see chart on p. 330).

The UK has an automatic air quality monitoring network with sites covering much of the country, in both urban and rural areas. In recent years this network has undergone a rapid expansion, and it now has 110 automated sites. Daily Air Quality Bulletins make air pollution data from the monitoring network available to the public. These give the concentrations of the main pollutants, together with an air pollution forecast. The information features in television and radio weather reports, and appears in many national and local newspapers. Information on the Internet may be accessed through the UK's National Air Quality Archive website (www.environment.detr.gov.uk/airq.aqinfo.htm).

Vehicle Emissions

All new petrol-engined passenger cars in the UK must be fitted with catalytic converters, which typically reduce emissions by over 75 per cent. Vehicle emissions standards are governed by a series of EC Directives enforced in the UK under the Motor Vehicles

Construction & Use and Type Approval Regulations. The latest EC Directives, which came into force in January 2000, will further reduce emissions from passenger cars and light commercial vehicles. The European Commission has set tighter standards for both car emissions and fuel quality, to be introduced in 2005.

A further directive, which will come into effect in October 2000, is designed to cut pollution from goods vehicles and buses by 60 per cent. As well as reductions in oxides of nitrogen, hydrocarbons and carbon monoxide, this involves cutting emissions of particulate matter by 86 per cent by 2005. Lorries and buses are responsible for 55 per cent of particulate transport emissions (and 39 per cent of oxides of nitrogen). The use of new 'particulate traps' will remove most of the smallest particles, which pose the greatest health risk.

These measures to reduce vehicle emissions from new vehicles have been accompanied by improvements in fuel quality with, for instance, reductions in components such as benzene and sulphur which have an environmental impact, and the phasing out of leaded petrol.

Compulsory tests of emissions from vehicles in use are a key element in the UK's strategy for improving air quality. Metered emission tests and smoke checks feature in the annual 'MoT' roadworthiness test (see p. 363). Enforcement checks carried out at the roadside or at operators' premises also include a check for excessive smoke. The Vehicle Inspectorate (see p. 363) carried out 119,441 roadside emissions checks in 1999–2000 (on cars, coaches, goods vehicles, buses and taxis), of which 2,680 failed. Under a trial scheme introduced in 1997, seven local authorities

Urban Road Transport Emissions and Projections in the UK

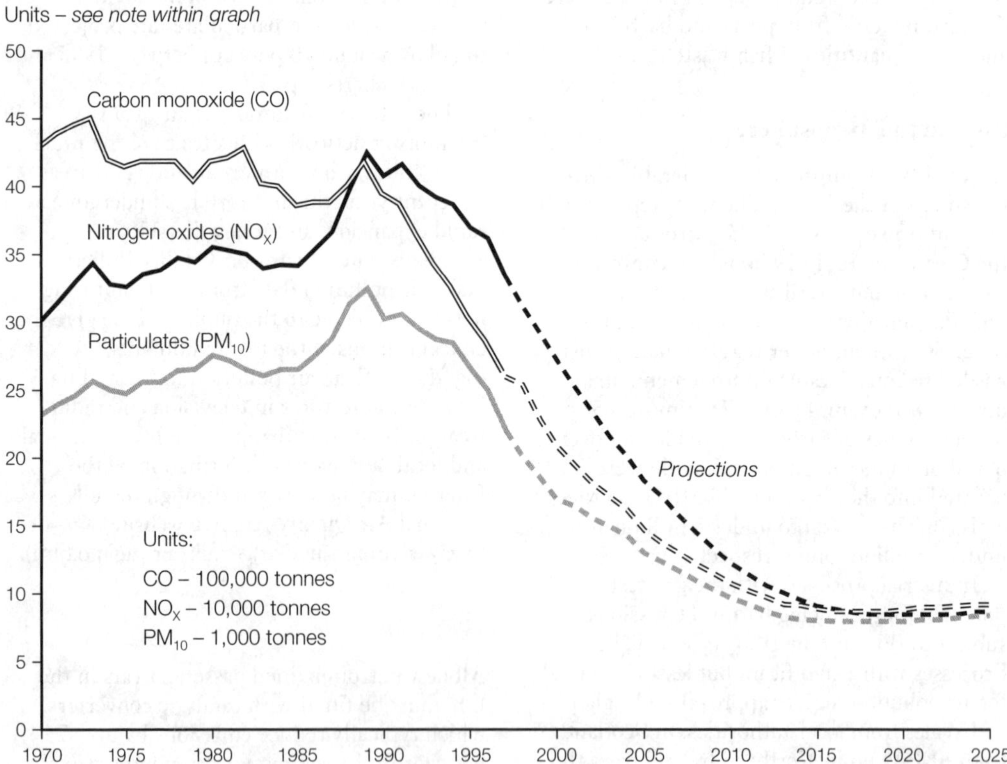

Source: Department of the Environment, Transport and the Regions

were given powers to enforce vehicle exhaust emissions standards by random testing at the roadside, with a £60 fixed penalty fine for offenders causing avoidable pollution. A consultation document, issued in June 2000, proposes an extension of these powers to local authorities in England and Wales which have designated air quality management areas.

The Cleaner Vehicles Task Force was established to encourage the manufacture, purchase and use of vehicles which are more fuel-efficient, quieter, cause less pollution and also use less resources in their manufacture. The Government, industry and non-governmental organisations worked together in partnership in the Task Force, and in June 2000 it produced its final report and recommendations entitled *The Way Forward*. Progress on implementing the Task Force's recommendations includes:

- a £6 million programme to take forward the recommendations on reducing pollution from existing vehicles;
- an increase in funding of the Powershift Programme to £10 million for 2000–01 (the Powershift Programme is a programme of the Energy Saving Trust (see p. 492), helping to establish a sustainable market for alternative fuel vehicles in the UK and encourage wider uptake of cleaner fuels);
- a voluntary environmental label was introduced by the motor industry to provide buyers of new cars with information on fuel consumption and emissions of carbon dioxide (CO_2), local pollutants and noise; and
- 'Motorvate', a government-backed scheme which sets targets for business vehicle fleets to cut their fleet travel costs and at the same time help the environment, was launched in June.

Climate Change

Several gases naturally present in the atmosphere keep the Earth at a temperature suitable for life by trapping energy from the sun—the 'greenhouse' effect. Emissions from human activities are increasing the atmospheric concentrations of several important gases, causing global warming and climate change. The most significant greenhouse gas in the UK is carbon dioxide, followed by methane and nitrous oxide. Some other greenhouse gases, such as hydrofluorocarbons (HFCs), have high global warming potential but comparatively low levels of emissions. However, there is an upward trend in HFC emissions from end uses, as consumption of HFCs has risen in response to the phasing out of ozone-depleting substances under the Montreal Protocol (see p. 332). HFCs were virtually unused before 1990, but their emissions accounted for 2 per cent of total UK greenhouse gas emissions in 1995 at 4 million tonnes of carbon.

Globally the temperature rose by about 0.6°C during the 20th century. In England, the 1990s experienced four out of the five warmest years since records began in 1659, with 1999 being the warmest year. Research at the Hadley Centre, part of the Meteorological Office, is focused on improving climate predictions and investigating the cause of recent climate change. Results from its latest climate model suggest that, with current levels of increase in greenhouse gases, the global mean sea level will rise about 20 cm by the 2050s, and there will be a rise in average global temperature of up to 3°C over the next 100 years.

The Government has set up the UK Climate Impacts Programme to allow detailed assessments of the impacts to be made, both at UK and regional levels. In Britain there may be more droughts in the south and east of England, more flooding in the north and west of England, more damage as a result of storm surges, threats to the coast and low-lying agricultural land, and changes in wildlife and habitats.

Solutions on a global scale require international co-operation and action. The first international action dealing with climate change dates from the 'Earth Summit' in Rio de Janeiro in 1992, where the UN Framework Convention on Climate Change called for the stabilisation of greenhouse gas concentrations in the atmosphere at a level which would prevent dangerous man-made interference with the climate system.

At the third Conference of the Parties to the Framework Convention, held in Kyoto

(Japan) in 1997, developed countries agreed legally binding targets to reduce emissions of the basket of six main greenhouse gases: CO_2; methane; nitrous oxide; HFCs; perfluorocarbons (PFCs); and sulphur hexafluoride. The Protocol committed developed nations to a 5.2 per cent reduction in greenhouse gas emissions below 1990 levels by 2008–12 (in 1990, the UK emitted 168 million tonnes of CO_2, 20.8 million tonnes of carbon equivalent of methane and 18 million tonnes of carbon equivalent of nitrous oxide). The EU agreed to a collective reduction target of 8 per cent. At a subsequent meeting in June 1998, the EU and member states agreed to share out the EU's target to reflect national circumstances. Individual country's targets range from a reduction of 28 per cent for Luxembourg to a permitted increase of 27 per cent for Portugal. The UK's target is a reduction of 12.5 per cent.

A key consultation document published in early 2000 was the Climate Change Draft UK Programme, which sets out how the UK intends to meet its Kyoto target. It sets out a framework for:

- moving the UK towards a more sustainable lower carbon economy;
- moving towards a domestic goal of a 20 per cent cut in CO_2 emissions by the year 2010;
- ensuring that all sectors of the UK's economy and all parts of the UK should play their part; and
- ensuring that the main polluters do what they can to cut emissions.

The integrated package of policies and measures contained in the Draft Programme include the climate change levy (see p. 490), agreements with energy-intensive sectors to meet challenging targets, extra money for improving business use of energy, carbon trading (where countries that have achieved emissions reductions over and above those required by their Kyoto target can sell the excess to countries finding it more difficult to meet their commitments), reform of the building regulations, EU-level voluntary agreements with manufacturers to increase fuel efficiency in vehicles and the promotion of energy efficiency in the domestic sector. The final Climate Change UK Programme will be published later in 2000, prior to the sixth Conference of the Parties to the Framework Convention due to be held in the Netherlands in November 2000.

Stratospheric Ozone Layer

Stratospheric ozone forms a layer of gas about 10 km to 50 km (6 to 30 miles) above the Earth's surface, protecting it from the more harmful effects of solar radiation. British scientists first discovered ozone losses over much of the globe, including a 'hole' in the ozone layer over Antarctica, in 1985. This 'hole' has been growing steadily and its edges now reach beyond the Antarctic continent to the tip of South America. Similar but less dramatic thinning of the ozone layer occurs over the North Pole each year as well. Ozone depletion is caused by man-made chemicals containing chlorine or bromine, such as chlorofluorocarbons (CFCs), hydrochlorofluorocarbons (HCFCs) or halons, which have been used in aerosol sprays, refrigerators and fire extinguishers.

In an effort to repair this damage, over 170 countries have ratified the Montreal Protocol, an international treaty for the protection of the stratospheric ozone layer. This is currently enforced in the UK by an EC Regulation. From 1 October 2000 a new EC Regulation will be introduced with tougher restrictions, including controls on the use of most ozone-depleting substances, production controls on HCFCs, a ban on new substances listed (currently bromochloromethane), trade controls and an export licensing system.

Following the implementation of the Protocol, total levels of CFCs in the lower atmosphere are now declining from a recent peak.

Acid Rain

The pollutant gases sulphur dioxide (SO_2) (mainly from power stations), oxides of nitrogen (NO_x) (from road transport and power stations), and ammonia (NH_3) (mainly from livestock), can be carried over long distances before being deposited directly on to vegetation and soil or being washed out as acid rain. Acidification results when sensitive ecosystems are not capable of neutralising the deposited acidity. In the UK, the ecosystems that are most sensitive to acidification are located in the northern and western uplands. The damaging effects of high levels of acid deposition on soils, freshwaters and trees, and on buildings, have been demonstrated by scientific research. Lower emissions of SO_2 over the past 25 years have led to the first signs of a decrease in acidification in some upland freshwaters, particularly in some lochs in Scotland.

The UK is a party to the UNECE (United Nations Economic Commission for Europe) Convention on Long Range Transboundary Air Pollution, which was set up in 1979 in response to evidence that acidification of lakes in Scandinavia was linked to European emissions of SO_2. Under the Convention, there have been a number of protocols to reduce emissions of acidifying pollutants. The latest 'Gothenburg' Protocol, signed in December 1999, tackles the three environmental problems of acidification, eutrophication (excess nitrogen deposition) and ground-level ozone (summer smog). Under the Protocol, the UK agreed annual emission ceilings of 625 kilotonnes for SO_2, 1,181 kilotonnes for NO_x and 297 kilotonnes for NH_3 to be achieved by 2010. By comparison, UK emissions in 1998 were 1,615 kilotonnes for SO_2, 1,753 kilotonnes for NO_x, and 350 kilotonnes for NH_3. The Protocol also set a ceiling of 1,200 kilotonnes for volatile organic compounds (VOCs) (for example, solvents used in industry, domestic products, dry cleaning and paints). This pollutant contributes to the formation of ground-level ozone.

Running in parallel to the UNECE Gothenburg Protocol is the National Emission Ceiling Directive (NECD), agreed in June 2000. The NECD aims to tackle the same three key environmental problems arising from transboundary air pollution and also sets ceilings for 2010 for the same four pollutants. The UK has committed to further cuts in SO_2 and NO_x emissions; by reducing the ceilings to 585 kilotonnes and 1,167 kilotonnes respectively.

Noise

The Air and Environmental Quality Division in the DETR is responsible for the co-ordination and development of policies and the promotion of initiatives to address the problem of noise in England and Wales and act as the UK lead in negotiations on environmental noise in Europe. In Scotland the Air Quality Team, part of the Environment Group in the Scottish Executive, has equivalent responsibility.

Local authorities have a duty to inspect their areas for 'statutory nuisances', including noise nuisance from premises and vehicles, machinery or equipment in the street. They must take reasonable steps to investigate complaints, and serve a noise abatement notice where it is judged to be a statutory nuisance. There are specific provisions in law to control noise from construction and demolition sites, to control the use of loudspeakers in the streets and to enable individuals to take independent action through the courts against noise nuisance.

The Noise Act 1996 strengthened the law in England, Wales and Northern Ireland on action that can be taken against noisy neighbours, and the Housing Act 1996 gave local authorities new powers to deal with anti-social behaviour by tenants, including noise. However, these two Acts do not apply in Scotland where action against noisy neighbours is taken under earlier legislation. The Crime and Disorder Act 1998 introduced Anti-Social Behaviour Orders in England and Wales, which can be used against any person who is causing harassment, alarm or distress to others.

Compensation may be payable for loss in property values caused by physical factors, including noise from new or improved public works such as roads, railways and airports. Highway authorities are required to make grants available for the insulation of homes when they are subject to specified levels of increased noise caused by new or improved roads. Equivalent regulations exist for railways.

National Noise Action Day on 7 June 2000 was co-ordinated by the National Society of the Impact of Environmental Noise Pollution to develop working partnerships with national organisations with an interest in noise to promote a harmonious society.

Sulphur Dioxide and Nitrogen Oxide Emissions and International Obligation Targets, UK

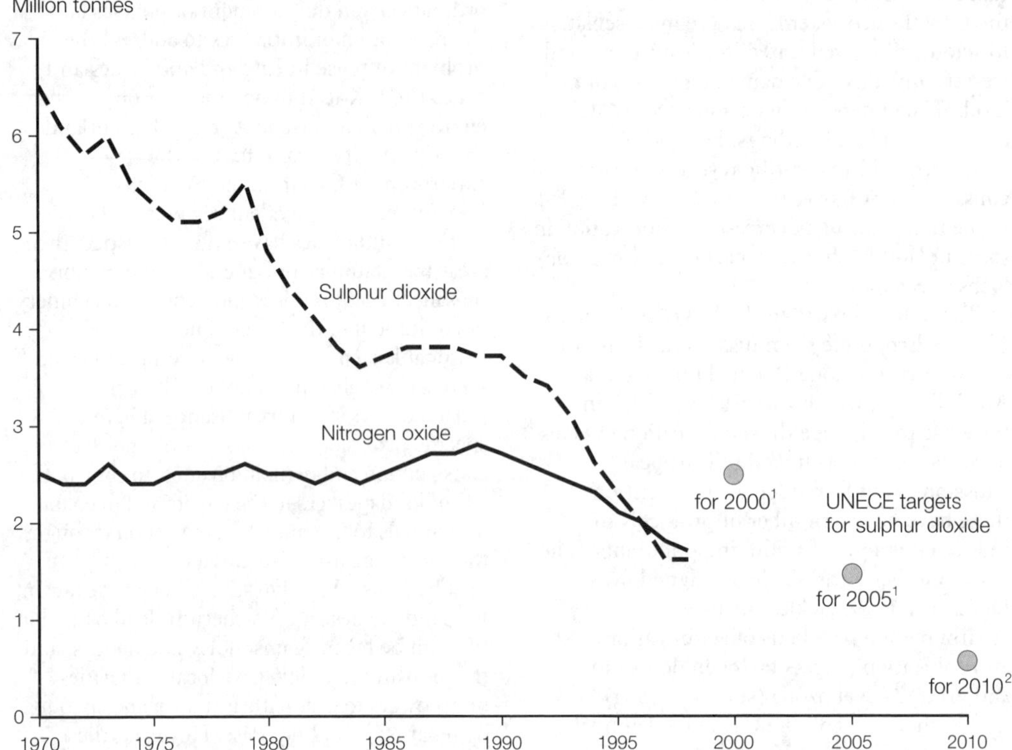

[1] Target set by the UNECE Oslo Protocol, 1994.

[2] Target set by the EC National Emissions Ceilings Directive, 2000.

Source: Department of the Environment, Transport and the Regions

The UK is committed to seeking further improvements in international aircraft noise standards with a target date for agreement of 2001. Under international agreements, noisier subsonic jet aircraft are due to be phased out by 2002. Already over 95 per cent of UK-registered jets are the quieter 'Chapter 3' types. Various operational restrictions, including at night, aim to reduce noise disturbance at the UK's major airports.

The National Noise Incidence Survey and the National Noise Attitude Study are surveys undertaken by DETR to establish a baseline for, and monitor changes in, the noise climate in Britain. The latest survey results are expected to be published in 2001.

Radioactivity

Man-made radiation represents about 15 per cent of the total exposure to ionising radiation of the UK population; most radiation occurs naturally. A large proportion of the exposure to man-made radiation comes from medical sources, such as X-rays. This and other man-made radiation is subject to stringent control. Users of radioactive materials must be registered by the Environment Agency in England and Wales, SEPA in Scotland and DOE in Northern Ireland. The Health and Safety Executive (HSE—see p. 160) is responsible for regulating safety at civil nuclear installations. The National Radiological Protection Board (NRPB) advises on health risks posed by radiation and how to guard against them.

International Commitments

An EC Directive lays down basic standards for the protection of the health of workers and the general public against the dangers arising from ionising radiation. The provisions of the Directive are implemented in the UK through a number of Acts including the Radioactive Substances Act 1993.

The UK has also ratified and will be implementing the International Joint Convention on the Safety of Spent Fuel Management and on the Safety of Radioactive Waste Management.

The contracting parties to the OSPAR Commission, including the UK, agreed at Sintra, Portugal, in 1998 to reduce radioactive discharges to levels whereby the additional concentrations of radioactive substances in the marine environment are close to zero by 2020.

In May 2000 the Government published a consultation paper, *UK Strategy for radioactive discharges 2001–2020*, which outlines the proposed framework of the UK to meet the Sintra commitments.

Radon

Radon is a naturally occurring radioactive gas which can accumulate in houses and accounts for half of the total average population radiation dose. Long-term exposure to the gas can increase the risk of lung cancer. The first measures to deal with the problem of radon were announced in 1987. In Scotland (where two radon affected areas were designated in 1983) data on radon levels are being collected to help draw up a detailed picture of the position. In 1998–99 the Government completed its programme of offering a free radon measurement to all households with a greater than 5 per cent probability of being above the radon 'Action Level', and is now working with local authorities to encourage building works that reduce radon levels in homes.

Radioactive Waste Disposal

Currently all solid radioactive waste in the UK is either disposed of safely in suitable facilities on land or stored pending such disposal. The UK has not disposed of any solid radioactive waste at sea since 1982.

The disposal of such waste is regulated by law. Under the Radioactivity Substance Act 1993, the Environment Agency is responsible for regulating the use and keeping of radioactive materials and disposal of the waste.

Radioactive wastes vary widely in nature and level of activity, and the methods of disposal reflect this. Most solid low-level waste—material of low radioactivity—is disposed of at the shallow disposal facility at Drigg in Cumbria. Some small quantities of very low-level waste are disposed of at authorised landfill sites. Intermediate-level waste is stored at nuclear licensed sites, usually those sites where it is generated. Most of the UK's inventory is at Sellafield in Cumbria. High-level or heat-generating waste is stored in either raw (liquid) or vitrified (glasslike) form. Once vitrified it will be stored for at least 50 years to allow it to cool to a safe temperature for disposal.

Environmental Research

Several government departments—such as the DETR and MAFF, the Department of Health and the Scottish Executive—have substantial environmental research programmes. In 1999–2000 they commissioned about 140 research contracts, with a total value of £19 million. An increasingly important area is research into the environmental effects of genetically modified crops and micro-organisms (see pp. 442 and 454).

The European Wildlife Division within the WACD manages a significant research effort, of which the biggest element is the *Countryside Survey 2000*. This is the fourth survey—carried out every ten years—of habitats and landscape features in Great Britain. However, this will be the first survey to combine both the latest satellite image analysis techniques with traditional field survey to obtain full national coverage and detailed information on vegetation, soils and freshwater. The results are expected to be published in a report towards the end of 2000.

Among the other organisations that carry out environmental research are the Meteorological Office (including the Hadley Centre); the Environment Agency, whose R&D budget for 2000–01 is £10.7 million; the Natural Resources Institute of the University of Greenwich at Chatham (Kent); and the Climatic Research Unit at the University of East Anglia. Around 100 British universities and colleges run courses on environmental studies or natural resource management; many also carry out research. In addition to research funded directly by SEPA and the EHS, the Scotland and Northern Ireland Forum for Environmental Research also commissions research.

Most of the government-funded Research Councils (see pp. 440–3) have a role in environmental science research, but the Natural Environment Research Council (NERC) takes the lead. NERC funds and carries out scientific research in the sciences of the environment and trains the next generation of scientists. It carries out research into five environmental and natural resource issues of priority to the UK: biodiversity; environmental risks and hazards; global change; natural resource management; and pollution and waste.

The UK is working on implementing the EC Directive on zoos, which came into operation in 1999 and which must be implemented in UK domestic legislation by April 2002. A zoos forum was set up in 1999 to advise ministers on all zoo matters and one of its first duties was to consider new standards for zoos, giving greater emphasis to animal welfare, conservation and education.

Further Reading

Digest of Environmental Statistics, No. 20. DETR. The Stationery Office, 1998.

Energy—the changing climate. Royal Commission on Environmental Pollution. The Stationery Office, 2000.

National Waste Strategy: Scotland. SEPA, 1999

The Scottish Environment Statistics, No. 6. 1998. Scottish Natural Heritage. The Stationery Office, 1998.

The state of the countryside 2000. The Countryside Agency, 2000.

Waste Management Strategy for Northern Ireland. The Stationery Office, 2000

Waste Strategy 2000: England and Wales. DETR. The Stationery Office, 2000.

The Way Forward: The Final Report of the Cleaner Vehicles Task Force. The Stationery Office, 2000.

Websites

Department of the Environment, Transport and the Regions: www.environment.detr.gov.uk

Countryside Agency: www.countryside.gov.uk

Countryside Council for Wales: www.ccw.gov.uk

The Countryside information system: www.cis-web.org.uk

English Nature: www.english-nature.org.uk

Environment Agency for England and Wales: www.environment-agency.gov.uk

Environment & Heritage Service: www.ehsni.gov.uk
Joint Nature Conservation Committee: www.jncc.gov.uk
Natural Environment Research Council: www.nerc.ac.uk
Royal Commission on Environmental Pollution: www.rcep.org.uk
Scottish Environment Protection Agency: www.sepa.org.uk
Scottish Natural Heritage: www.snh.org.uk

21 Planning, Housing and Regeneration

There are growing pressures on land use in the United Kingdom as a result of an increase in the population and the demands of a growing economy. The United Kingdom is a relatively densely populated country, with 245 people per sq kilometre in the UK in 1999. The number of dwellings in the UK was estimated at 25.0 million in 1998. The number of households in England is projected to increase from 20.2 million in 1996 to 24.0 million in 2021.

LAND USE PLANNING

Planning systems regulate the development of land use and contribute to the Government's strategy for promoting a sustainable pattern of physical development in cities, towns and the countryside.

Land use planning is the direct responsibility of local authorities in Great Britain. The Secretary of State for the Environment, Transport and the Regions has responsibility for the operation of the system in England, and in Wales and Scotland control now rests with the National Assembly for Wales and the Scottish Executive respectively. In Northern Ireland, the Planning Service, an executive agency within the Northern Ireland Executive, is responsible for the implementation of government policies for town and country planning in consultation with the district councils.

The Department of the Environment, Transport and the Regions (DETR) issues national planning policy guidance in England on housing, economic development, transport, retail and town centres, the countryside, green belts, sports and recreation, minerals and waste, and other topics. The DETR also provides guidance on the operation of the planning system at regional and local levels. Working with the Government Offices for the Regions (GORs), it ensures that regional planning guidance, local authorities' development plans and decisions on planning applications are consistent with national policies.

The National Assembly for Wales is responsible for the development of national planning policy in Wales. It ensures that development plans and decisions on planning applications are consistent with its national planning policy.

The Planning Inspectorate serves both the Secretary of State for the Environment, Transport and the Regions in England and the National Assembly for Wales on appeals and other casework under planning, housing, the environment, highways and related legislation. It also provides information and guidance to appellants and other interested parties about the appeal process. In 1999–2000, over 12,600 planning appeal cases were determined. A review of the Planning Inspectorate was announced in March 2000 to look at its organisation and identify means of improving efficiency.

The Government is committed to modernising the planning system. In general, in England the responsibility for regional planning is shifting from central government to the regions. Regional planning guidance (RPG) is issued by the Secretary of State and sets out policies for land use and development across the English regions. Although the RPG has no statutory force, it provides the framework for local authorities' preparation of development plans and local transport plans. Draft planning policy guidance, issued in 1999, on regional planning issues places a greater responsibility on the regional planning bodies to work together with the Government Offices, including the Regional Development Agencies (see p. 394) and the public to resolve planning issues at the regional level. The planning policy guidance provides advice on the main policy areas to be covered by the RPG. Draft RPGs are subject to a 'sustainability appraisal' (SA) to determine whether they deliver sustainable development. An SA considers the potential economic and social impacts of the plan, together with any environmental effects. It is expected that by the end of 2001 the majority of revised RPGs will have been issued in England.

The Greater London Authority Act 1999 introduced new arrangements for planning in London (see p. 63). The new Mayor has responsibility for the production of a 'spatial development strategy' that has a framework for development, regeneration and transport issues in London, and the strategy will require changes to the legislative background against which the unitary development plans are prepared.

The Government issued its revisions to South East local authorities draft regional planning guidance in March 2000. The revisions provide a framework for the planning, management and monitoring of future housing developments in the South East. Outside London, the Government proposes that the local authorities should plan to provide an additional 43,000 dwellings a year, subject to a regular review no less than every five years. Based on the advice of the London Planning Advisory Committee, the Greater London Authority should plan to provide 23,000 new homes a year, the vast majority of which will be on 'brownfield' (previously developed) sites. The revisions also include an extension of the Thames Gateway area that would become a hub for development and regeneration with fast links to London and the continent of Europe. Development projects previously undertaken in the Thames Gateway area include the Greenwich Millennium Village.

In both Wales and Scotland, operation of the planning system—including the determination of most planning applications, and the preparation of development plans—is the responsibility of local planning authorities.The National Assembly for Wales and the Scottish Executive regulate and provide guidance on the operation of planning systems. The Scottish ministers approve structure plans and take decisions on planning applications that raise issues of national importance. In Northern Ireland, the Planning Service is responsible for issuing planning guidance, for determining planning applications and for preparing development plans.

Land Use Development

The revised *Planning Policy Guidance Note 3 on Housing*, providing national planning guidance on the future of housebuilding and development in England, was issued in March 2000. The policies aim to take account of changing lifestyles and the projected increase in single–person households in the future. The guidance sets out proposals for planning authorities to recycle brownfield sites and empty properties in preference to 'greenfield' sites; for using land more efficiently; for assisting with the provision of affordable housing in both rural and urban areas; and for promoting mixed-use developments which integrate housing with shops, local services and transport.

A Planning Advice Note entitled *Improving Town Centres* was issued in Scotland in November 1999 providing advice on the future regeneration of town centres.

> The Government's national target is that, by 2008, 60 per cent of additional housing in England should be provided on previously developed land or by re-using existing buildings. In 1998 the proportion of new dwellings built on previously developed land or provided by conversions of existing buildings was 57 per cent. Over the period 1994 to 1998, the average density on previously developed land was 28 dwellings per hectare, compared with 22 dwellings per hectare on land not previously developed.

Green Belts

Green Belts are areas of land that are intended to be left open and protected from inappropriate development. They aim to control the unrestricted sprawl of large built-up areas, prevent towns from merging with one another, preserve the heritage of historic towns and encourage the recycling of derelict and other urban land, thereby encouraging urban regeneration. Not all Green Belt land is countryside. It can cover small villages comprising a mixture of residential, retail, industrial and recreational land as well as fields and forests.

The first major Green Belt was established around the fringes of Greater London, under the London and Home Counties Green Belt Act 1938. Green Belts have also been established around Glasgow, Edinburgh, Aberdeen, Greater Manchester, Merseyside and the West Midlands, as well as several smaller towns. In 1997, there were 14 separate designated Green Belt areas in England, amounting to 1.65 million hectares, about 13 per cent of the land area. In Scotland there were six Green Belt areas totalling 156,000 hectares. There are no Green Belts at present in Wales, but their creation is under consideration. Development on Green Belts is only permitted under exceptional circumstances.

Where greenfield development is necessary to accommodate housing growth, the Government prefers extending existing urban areas. The potential for investigating the further development of two areas in the South East—Milton Keynes in Buckinghamshire and Ashford in Kent—and a study to examine the longer-term possibility of major growth in the area around Stansted and the M11 corridor in Essex were proposed under the Government's draft changes to the draft revised planning guidance for the South East.

National Land Use Database

The National Land Use Database is a partnership project between the DETR, English Partnerships (see p. 353), the Improvement and Development Agency (representing the interests of local government) and Ordnance Survey. It aims to establish a complete, consistent and detailed geographical record of land use in England.

The first phase of the project focused on previously developed vacant and derelict land and other previously developed land which may be available for redevelopment. This provided a snapshot for 1998, which showed an estimated 57,710 hectares, in England, of previously developed land that was unused or potentially available for redevelopment, of which 27,320 hectares either had planning permission for housing or was judged suitable for housing. According to density assumptions current at the time, it was estimated that this land could accommodate over 733,000 new dwellings. The previously developed land comprised 14,860 hectares of vacant previously developed land, 19,340 hectares of derelict land and buildings, 4,310 hectares of land occupied by vacant buildings, 10,960 hectares of land in current use but allocated in the local plan for a change of use or with planning permission for housing, and 8,240 hectares of land with known development potential but without planning permission.

Development Plans

Development plans play an integral role in shaping land-use development in an area, and provide a framework for consistent decision-making. Planning applications are determined in accordance with relevant development plan policies unless 'material considerations' indicate otherwise. In England, local planning authorities are required to prepare development plans in line with the Town and Country Planning Act 1990. Regulations, which took effect in January 2000, provide a statutory framework for new procedures designed to improve the delivery of development plans. The Government expects plans to be prepared and updated more quickly and efficiently than they were in the past. *Planning Policy Guidance Note 12 (December 1999)* emphasises that plans should be clear and succinct, and highlights the importance of integrating sustainable development and transport with land-use policies in development plans. Unless justified by specific local considerations, plans should not conflict with either national or regional policies.

In England, outside metropolitan areas and certain non-metropolitan unitary authority areas, the development plan comprises:

- *structure plans*, which are produced by county councils, some unitary authorities and National Park authorities (in many cases on a joint basis) and set out the key strategic policies and provide a framework for local plans;
- *local plans*, which are produced by district councils, some unitary authorities and National Park authorities in which more detailed policies are set out to guide development in a particular local authority area. The plans cover the whole of a local authority area and may include proposals for specific sites; and
- *minerals and waste local plans,* which are produced by county councils, some unitary authorities and National Park authorities (which are usually the development control authorities for these issues).

Within metropolitan areas and in some non-metropolitan unitary authorities, the development plan comprises a single *unitary development plan (UDP)*. There are two parts to the UDP: Part I consists of the local authority's strategic policies for the development and use of land in its area, and forms the framework for the detailed proposals for the use and development of land set out in Part II. By the end of 1999, 79 per cent of local authorities had a local plan or UDP in place.

All unitary authorities and National Park authorities in Wales are preparing their first unitary development plans based upon the requirement in the Town and Country Planning Act 1990, as amended by the Local Government (Wales) Act 1994, for each local planning authority to prepare a UDP for its area. The UDP will be the development plan for each county or county borough council and each National Park, replacing the structure plan, local plan and any other existing plan. It is expected that adopted UDPs will be reviewed in full at least once every five years and partial reviews may be more appropriate (for example on particular topic areas) on a more frequent basis.

The planning system in Scotland is governed by the Town and Country Planning (Scotland) Act 1997. Development plans are prepared by councils and consist of structure and local plans. Councils are also responsible for making decisions on most applications for planning permission and for taking action against development that has not been approved. In November 1999, the Minister for Transport and the Environment in Scotland announced proposals designed to improve the efficiency and effectiveness of the planning process. The Planning Audit Unit has been reviewing how local authorities handle planning applications with a view to improving performance and disseminating practical advice.

In Northern Ireland, the Planning Service put in place the Development Plan

Programme in 1998. The programme is reviewed and rolled forward annually, and is designed to meet the development planning needs of all districts.

Development Control

Most development requires specific planning permission. Applications are dealt with on the basis of the development plans and other relevant considerations, including national and regional guidance. In England, 480,000 planning applications were determined in 1999–2000, of which 63 per cent were decided within eight weeks. The Government's target is for 80 per cent of applications to be dealt with within this time frame, with the remainder within three months. In Wales, 26,000 planning applications were received of which over 67 per cent were decided within eight weeks. In Scotland, 65 per cent of applications had been processed within two months in 1998–99, when Scottish councils decided 42,400 planning applications. In Northern Ireland, 20,000 district planning applications were received in 1998–99, of which 70 per cent were decided within eight weeks.

If a local authority refuses to grant planning permission, grants it with conditions attached or fails to decide an application within eight weeks, or two months in Scotland, the applicant has a right of appeal to the Secretary of State in England, the National Assembly in Wales and Scottish ministers in Scotland. In August 2000, a package of revised rules and guidance was introduced aimed at speeding up decisions on planning appeals in England. New arrangements are expected to come into effect in Wales in early 2001. In Northern Ireland, the applicant has the right of appeal to the Planning Appeals Commission.

> A pilot study undertaken by the Planning Inspectorate during December 1998 and December 1999 investigated the use of mediation to resolve planning disputes between local authorities and developers or housebuilders. The study held 48 mediations, of which 65 per cent achieved a successful outcome, and in 73 per cent of cases there were no subsequent appeals.

In England, a small number of planning applications are called in by the Secretary of State each year for his decision, rather than being decided by the local planning authority. Generally this only happens where the planning issue is of national or regional importance. A small number of cases end up as public inquiries; for example, the public inquiry that began in June 2000 into Railtrack's Thameslink 2000 project, which aims to expand and enhance the existing North–South rail network affecting London, the South East and East of England.

In certain circumstances, some categories of planning application will have to be notified to the appropriate ministerial authority; for example, those involving a significant departure from the approved development plan. In Wales, a small number of cases are called in for determination by the National Assembly.

In Scotland, the Scottish Executive Inquiry Reporters Unit is responsible for the determination of the majority of planning appeals and it organises public local inquiries into planning proposals and related matters. In Northern Ireland, major planning applications can be referred to a public inquiry in certain circumstances.

Certain projects must be accompanied by an 'environmental assessment', which should identify the likely environmental effects and describe measures to minimise any adverse effects. Before planning permission can be granted, local planning authorities must consider the assessment and any representations received. New environmental impact assessment regulations came into force in Scotland in 1999.

The Architects Registration Board, together with the architects' professional bodies, exercises control over standards in architectural training, and encourages high standards in the profession. The Royal Town Planning Institute carries out similar functions for the planning profession.

HOUSING

In England, the Secretary of State for the Environment, Transport and the Regions has responsibility for determining housing policy and supervising the housing programme. Responsibility for housing policy in Wales, Scotland and Northern Ireland has passed, respectively, to the National Assembly for Wales, the Scottish Executive and the Northern Ireland Executive.

In Great Britain, the Government works with local authorities (which are responsible for preparing local housing strategies) and with the private and voluntary sectors. In England, the DETR also works with the Housing Corporation, which regulates registered social landlords (RSLs—see p. 348) and provides financial support to help them supply affordable housing. In Wales, the National Assembly for Wales has responsibility for funding and regulation of RSLs. In Northern Ireland, the Northern Ireland Housing Executive (NIHE) is accountable to the Department for Social Development and is the single housing authority in the Province.

The administrations across the UK have set out their respective draft strategies for housing policies for the future. In England, the Housing Green Paper—*Quality and Choice: A Decent Home for All*—was published in April 2000. The policies are aimed at improving the provision, maintenance and management of homes and include:

- a new Starter Home Initiative to provide special target support for key workers on lower incomes to help them into home ownership in high price, high-demand areas. Some £250 million will be provided for this initiative over the next three years (2001–02 to 2003–04);
- increased help with housing costs to assist unemployed people back to work;
- action to prevent landlords neglecting their responsibilities;
- assistance to homeowners for maintenance and modernisation;
- short-term and long-term reform of the Housing Benefit (see p. 178) and rent systems to improve efficiency and fairness and reduce fraud and error;
- raising the standard of social housing within ten years; and
- assistance for a wider group of homeless people such as 16–17 year olds and those who are vulnerable because they are leaving care.

Housing Stock and Housebuilding

It was estimated that there was a stock of 25.0 million dwellings in the UK at the end of 1998. Completions of dwellings in Great Britain numbered 169,700 in 1998 and rose by 1 per cent to 171,400 in 1999.

The number of households in England is projected to increase from 20.2 million in 1996 to 24.0 million in 2021, an increase of 19 per cent over the 25-year period, according to household projections produced by the DETR. The biggest increase is expected in the number of one-person households which are projected to grow by 2.7 million, from 5.8 million in 1996 to 8.5 million by 2021—71 per cent of the total increase in the number of households. The size of the projected increases in the number of households varies across England. The South East, East of England and the South West are all projected to have around a quarter more households in 2021 than in 1996. For London and the East Midlands growth is around a fifth and in other areas projected growth is significantly lower. The North East has the lowest projected growth of just 8 per cent. In Wales, the number of households is projected to increase from 1.2 million in 1996 to 1.3 million in 2021. In Scotland, the number of households is projected to increase by 12 per cent from 2.2 million in 1998 to 2.4 million in 2012. One-person households accounted for an estimated 32 per cent of all households in 1998 and this proportion is projected to increase to 38 per cent by 2012.

In 1998–99, 22 per cent of households in the United Kingdom lived in a detached home, while 30 per cent and 28 per cent lived in semi-detached or terraced accommodation respectively (see chart on p. 345). A further

Stock of Dwellings[1] by Tenure, UK

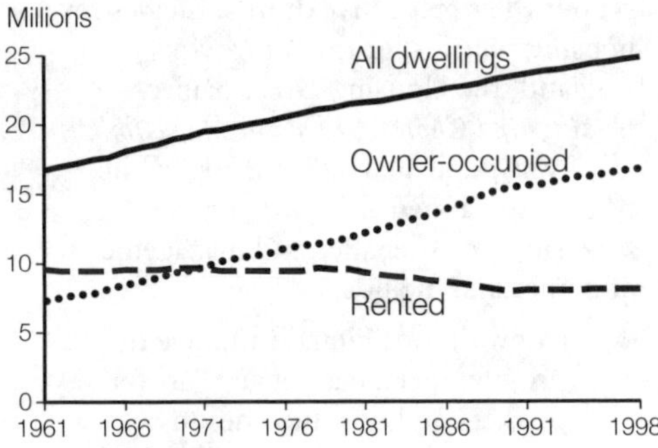

[1] At December each year.

Sources: Department of the Environment, Transport and the Regions, National Assembly for Wales, Scottish Executive and Department for Social Development, Northern Ireland

14 per cent lived in a purpose-built flat or maisonette.

Home Ownership

At the end of 1998, it was estimated that the number of owner-occupied dwellings in England was 14.2 million, 68 per cent of all dwellings. Homes rented from local authorities or new town corporations represented 16 per cent; those rented from private owners or attached to a job or business 11 per cent; and those rented from registered social landlords 5 per cent.

In England, provisional data for 1998 show owner-occupation was highest in the South East, at 75 per cent, followed by the South West (73 per cent) and the East (72 per cent), while the lowest level was in Greater London (56 per cent). Owner-occupation was 71 per cent in Wales and Northern Ireland, while in Scotland, where owner-occupation has traditionally been lower, the proportion was 61 per cent in 1998.

There are a number of schemes that exist which aim to increase low-cost home ownership. In England, these include the Right to Buy, Right to Acquire and Voluntary Purchase Grants, which offer tenants in social housing a discount against the market value of the homes they rent if they choose to buy them. In addition, funding to support low-cost ownership is also provided through the Housing Corporation and local authorities, including:

- *Conventional Shared Ownership*, which allows people to part buy and part rent homes developed by RSLs. The scheme allows people to increase their share of ownership in their home over time;
- *Do-It-Yourself Shared Ownership*, which enables people to select a house in the private market and then part own and part rent it, with the RSL taking on ownership of the rented share of the property;
- *Homebuy*, which allows people to buy a home in the private market with an interest-free equity loan from an RSL for 25 per cent of the value of the property. The loan is repayable, at 25 per cent of the current market value, when the home is sold; and
- the *Cash Incentive Scheme*, where local authorities offer cash grants for the purchase of a home in the private market.

In Wales, local authorities and housing associations operate a low-cost home ownership scheme allowing purchasers to buy a home for 70 per cent of its value, the balance being secured as a charge on the property. Scottish Homes operates a scheme to encourage private developers to build for owner-occupation in areas they would not normally consider. The Northern Ireland Co-ownership Housing Association administers the 'buy half, rent half' (shared ownership) scheme operating in the Province.

Mortgage Loans

A feature of home ownership in the UK is the relatively high proportion of homes purchased with a mortgage. Most people buy their homes with a mortgage loan, using the property as security. In 1999 loans for home purchase were obtained mainly through banks (756,000) and building societies (304,000), with 122,000 loans being obtained from other lenders. Some companies offer low-interest loans to their employees.

Table 21.1: Tenure of Dwellings in the UK, 31 December 1998				*Per cent*
	Owner-occupied	Rented from local authority or New Town[1]	Rented from private owners or with job or business	Rented from registered social landlord
Great Britain	**68**	**17**	**11**	**5**
England	68	16	11	5
Wales	71	16	8	4
Scotland	61	27	7	5
Northern Ireland[2]	71	22	4	3

[1] Including Scottish Homes and Northern Ireland Housing Executive.
[2] Figures for Northern Ireland are not directly comparable with those for the rest of the UK.
Sources: Department of the Environment, Transport and the Regions, National Assembly for Wales, Scottish Executive and Department for Social Development, Northern Ireland.

Type of Dwelling, UK, 1998–99

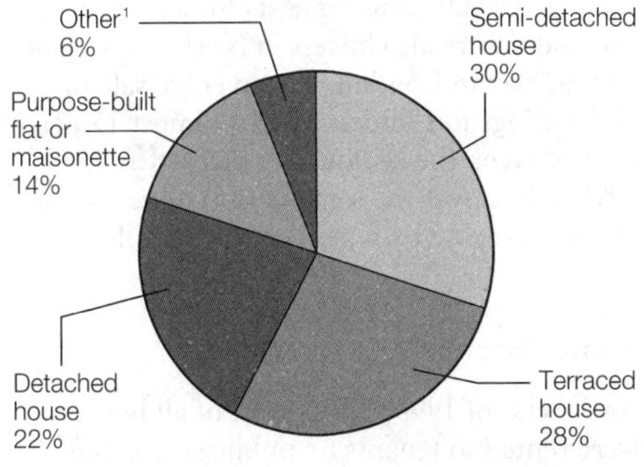

[1] Includes converted flats, which are particularly common in London.

Sources: Department of the Environment, Transport and the Regions, Office for National Statistics and Northern Ireland Statistics and Research Agency

Lenders differ in the amount they will lend relative to annual income but will commonly be prepared to lend up to three times earnings. There are two main types of mortgage: a repayment mortgage, which provides for regular monthly repayments so that, over the life of the mortgage (usually 25 years), the debt, together with interest, is entirely repaid. The second type of mortgage is the investment-linked mortgage. With this type of mortgage, only the interest on the loan is paid from the beginning, so that the capital sum borrowed does not decrease. Usually the borrower makes a long-term investment at the same time as taking out the mortgage which should produce a capital sum sufficient to repay the mortgage loan. Different types of investments can be taken out including endowment policies, personal pensions or ISAs (Individual Savings Accounts). In addition to the different ways in which a mortgage loan can be repaid, there are also a number of ways that the interest is charged:

- *fixed rate*, where the interest rate remains fixed for a period of time, after which it changes to the current variable rate or to a new fixed rate;
- *variable rate mortgage*, where payments vary according to mortgage rate changes. Some lenders adjust the amount that is paid on an annual basis, so that changes which occur during the year are incorporated when calculating the following year's repayment;
- *discounted rate mortgage*, where a discount to the lender's standard variable rate of interest is offered. Some lenders also offer cashbacks where a specified sum of money is returned to the borrower on completion of the mortgage; and
- *cap-and-collar mortgage*, where the maximum and minimum rates of interest which may be charged on the loan for a given term are fixed.

Other types of mortgages exist for those who wish to retain flexibility over their payments to allow for variations in their personal circumstances, and accelerated schemes to provide the opportunity to repay the debt more quickly.

Endowment mortgages have recently become less popular with borrowers because of the possibility that investments may not grow fast enough to repay the capital borrowed. In 1988, endowment policies reached a peak of popularity when 83 per cent of new mortgages for house purchase were of this type. By 1999, this had fallen to 27 per cent. Since 1988 there has been a revival of the repayment mortgage. Around 46 per cent of new mortgages were repayment mortgages in 1999. The take-up of interest-only mortgages has also increased since 1992 to 27 per cent in 1999.

There has also been an increase in the take-up of fixed-rate loans and a greater willingness to remortgage in order to take advantage of price differentials between lenders. Over one-third of loans in 1999 were at a fixed rate. In October 1999, the Government announced measures aimed at improving the home buying and selling process in England and Wales. The proposals include a requirement for sellers to provide a pack of standard documents and information for prospective buyers before the property is marketed for sale. The components of the seller's information pack were tested in a pilot study of around 200 home sales in Bristol. The study began in December 1999 and finished in August 2000. Further measures to improve the home buying and selling process include changes to the law to permit electronic conveyancing, encouraging local authorities to increase the speed of the search process and asking lenders to accelerate the provision of deeds and the processing of mortgage applications. The proposals seek to reduce the time between offer acceptance and contractual commitment, the period during which gazumping (whereby the seller raises the price of a property after having accepted an offer by an intending buyer) and other problems most commonly occur. Different arrangements for home buying and selling operate in Scotland, where the contract of sale becomes binding once an offer has been accepted.

Under the Financial Services and Markets Act 2000, the Financial Services Authority (FSA) will have statutory responsibility from 2001 for regulating certain aspects of mortgage lending for residential purposes. The FSA will authorise lenders to carry out mortgage lending, regulate mortgage advertising and require lenders to disclose the main features of loans clearly and openly. The FSA will also have a statutory objective to improve public awareness and understanding of all financial products.

New benchmark standards for variable rate and fixed or capped rate mortgages to enable borrowers to identify mortgage products which meet minimum standards on charges, access and terms (CAT) were introduced by HM Treasury in April 2000. The CAT standards for mortgages are voluntary.

In 1998–99, average weekly mortgage payments for owner-occupiers ranged from £38 in Northern Ireland to £88 in London. Average weekly housing costs for all owner-occupiers were also lowest in Northern Ireland and highest in London. The average sale price of dwellings in London rose by almost 17 per cent between the last quarter of 1998 and 1999, while over the same period prices in the North East rose by 6 per cent (see Table 21.2).

Rented Sector

At the end of 1998, 21 per cent of all homes were rented to tenants by public sector and non-profit-making bodies (such as housing associations) in England, compared with 20 per cent in Wales and 25 per cent in Northern Ireland. The highest level in the United Kingdom was in Scotland, with around 30 per cent of homes.

Private Rented Sector

The Government wants to see a healthy private rented sector. It funds two independent statutory housing services in England. The Rent Service Agency, which was established in October 1999 as an executive agency of the DETR, provides impartial rental valuations, which are designed to be fair to tenants and landlords. Rent Assessment Panels deal mainly with appeals against rent officers' determinations and disputes between

Table 21.2: Average Dwelling Price[1] in England and Wales, 1999

	Average sale price (£)					Per cent
	Detached houses	Semi-detached houses	Terraced houses	Flats/ maison-ettes	All dwellings	increase on last quarter of 1998
England	146,637	84,546	74,745	96,127	98,252	*14.4*
North East	101,214	55,044	42,463	44,124	59,442	*6.0*
North West	116,972	60,735	39,787	57,776	65,543	*7.0*
Yorkshire and the Humber	103,493	55,694	41,987	54,101	63,524	*6.8*
East Midlands	101,609	54,105	43,840	47,215	69,500	*7.0*
West Midlands	126,302	64,941	50,350	51,622	76,633	*11.9*
East	142,803	84,698	70,387	58,097	94,679	*8.1*
London	284,789	168,159	151,204	131,475	150,094	*16.7*
South East	196,487	106,101	84,186	68,910	118,385	*12.4*
South West	134,592	78,734	65,118	65,623	90,274	*9.7*
Wales	92,412	55,344	42,563	51,253	62,424	*6.9*
England and Wales	**139,760**	**80,599**	**71,367**	**92,567**	**94,581**	***11.6***

1 Excludes those bought at non-market prices. The average sale price for 1999 is taken from the last quarter.
Source: HM Land Registry

leaseholders and their landlords. A report on a review of the Panels in England was published in July 2000, recommending a range of measures for improving the quality and effectiveness of the Panel service.

The Government published a draft Bill on leasehold reform, for consultation in summer 2000, which included a range of proposals to improve the rights of leaseholders to purchase their freehold and protect themselves against abuse by unscrupulous landlords.

Social Housing

Much of the Government's expenditure on social housing (rented housing at below market rent) is provided as subsidies to local authorities to help pay for the costs of over 3 million rented council homes. More than 2,000 housing associations (most of them RSLs) provide other social housing. The RSLs manage and build new homes for rent and sale with the aid of government grants.

Most social housing in England is provided by local housing authorities that are responsible for preparing local housing strategies. The finance for authorities' housing capital programmes comes partly from local authorities' own resources (mainly from receipts from sales of assets not used to repay debt and from contributions from the authorities' Housing Revenue Account and general fund) and partly from central government. In recent years, around £1 billion (about 40 per cent) of housing capital expenditure by local authorities has been financed by their own resources.

Central government resources are allocated annually through the housing investment programme (HIP) in England, based on indices of the relative need for housing investment in each authority and assessments by Government Offices for the Regions of the quality of authorities' housing strategies and their performance in delivering housing services. Allocations for 2000–01 total just under £2.1 billion, around 50 per cent more than the 1999–2000 total. The extra resources have been provided mainly to improve the quality of local authority housing, but they can also be used to fund private sector renovation grants or to support the building or acquisition of homes by housing associations where this is a local priority.

The Housing Inspectorate has been established to assess local authorities' performance in achieving 'best value' in the provision of housing services. It will inspect all local authorities in England and Wales over a five-year cycle commencing in 2000–01. From April 2001, the Housing Revenue Account will be in a new more transparent form, based on resource accounting (see p. 404), as part of a new financial framework for local authority housing.

Between 1988 and 2000, 103 local authorities in England transferred all or part of their housing stock to new landlords, with the support of tenants and the approval of the Secretary of State for the Environment, Transport and the Regions. The transfers, involving over 457,000 dwellings, generated over £3.75 billion in capital receipts, and raised over £7.59 billion of private finance. Plans for the housing transfer programme for 2000–01 involving 22 local authorities were announced in March 2000. It is expected that the programme will involve over 160,000 dwellings in large-scale voluntary transfers, generating capital receipts of over £940 million.

Housing revenue accounts are kept separate from other council funds. The Government grants English and Welsh local authorities Housing Revenue Account Subsidy, planned at £3.1 billion in England and £188 million in Wales in 2000–01. In Scotland, Housing Support Grant of £9.6 million and £272 million grant-in-aid to Scottish Homes are planned for 2000–01.

Local authorities in Wales own around 200,000, or approximately 16 per cent, of all Welsh homes. By law they have to manage their own stock efficiently and in consultation with their tenants, address current housing needs in their area and plan to meet future needs and demands. Planned provision for local housing capital expenditure in 2000–01 is £194 million.

The Scottish Executive has provided local authorities with nearly £155 million in capital allocations for 2000–01. Public housing in Scotland is also provided by Scottish Homes whose main purpose is to help provide housing and contribute to the regeneration of local communities. It works in partnership with local authorities, housing associations, the voluntary sector, private developers, economic development agencies, financial institutions and local communities to tackle Scotland's housing problems. Funded through an annual grant from the Scottish Executive, rental income, and receipts from the sale of its own houses, Scottish Homes plans to invest substantially in its housing development programme in 2000–01. Investment will fund the provision of around 6,600 new and improved homes by housing associations and private developers. Scottish Homes currently manages its own 12,000 social rented houses. Arrangements are being made to transfer these to other landlords.

New Housing Partnership projects are making an impact in urban and rural Scotland. Around £170 million has been set aside between 1998 and 2002 to develop community ownership proposals and tackle outstanding debt. A further £200 million has been invested in development and regeneration partnerships.

The Northern Ireland Housing Executive (NIHE) is the landlord of nearly one-third of homes in Northern Ireland—over 128,000 properties. The Housing Executive, as the strategic housing authority in Northern Ireland, is responsible for the assessment of the need for, and arranging for the supply of, social housing while construction is undertaken by housing associations. The NIHE's capital programme is financed mainly by borrowing from government and receipts from house sales; in 2000–01 plans for borrowing are £18 million. Revenue expenditure is funded from rental income and by a government grant, which in 2000–01 is about £197 million.

Registered Social Landlords

Registered Social Landlords (RSLs) are the major providers of new subsidised homes for those in housing need. They own and manage 1.4 million self-contained units in England and are diverse bodies, ranging from small almshouses to very large housing associations managing many thousands of homes. They also include large-scale voluntary transfer and local housing companies, set up to own and manage council houses transferred out of local authorities.

In England, RSLs are regulated by the Housing Corporation, a non-departmental public body sponsored by the DETR. RSLs are non-profit-making bodies run by voluntary committees, and over 2,100 are registered with the Housing Corporation. The Housing Corporation gives capital grants to RSLs to provide homes for rent and for sale under shared ownership terms. The rental programme includes building new homes and the purchase or rehabilitation of existing dwellings. The home ownership initiatives help tenants (and other first-time buyers) to buy homes of their own. The capital comes from the Approved Development Programme (ADP). In 1999–2000, the ADP provided over 25,000 homes for rent and sale to those in housing need, and the transfer of 97,000 dwellings generated more than £650 million in capital receipts for local authorities and raised nearly £1.2 billion in private finance.

Similar arrangements apply in Wales with the National Assembly's Housing department and in Scotland with Scottish Homes.

The Northern Ireland Housing Executive has continued to transfer its new build programme to registered Housing Associations. The 2001–02 transfer programme involves 29 schemes, representing a total of 519 dwellings. The Housing Executive only builds where the housing associations are unwilling to do so.

Tenant Participation

Local authority tenants in England, Wales and Scotland have security of tenure and statutory rights, which are set out in the Council Tenant's Charter. All local housing authorities in England are expected to have been introducing tenant participation compacts since April 2000. These are agreements between local councils and their tenants on how tenants can be involved in decisions about managing their homes in a way that meets their needs and priorities. In 2000–01, £6 million of extra funding has been provided to local authorities in England, with a further £6 million being made available in 2001–02 to help them develop compacts with their tenants. In Wales, RSLs are expected to establish compacts by April 2001.

Rural Housing

If a clear need exists for low-cost housing in rural areas, local authorities can permit housing in localities where development would normally not be allowed, as long as the new housing can be reserved to meet that need. The Housing Corporation finances a special rural programme to build houses in villages with a population of 3,000 or less; funding for the building of almost 17,000 such homes was approved between 1989–90 and 1999–2000. The National Assembly for Wales supports the development of housing in rural areas if it is regarded as a strategic priority by the local authority. In Scotland, the Rural Partnership for Change Initiative, announced in March 2000, is a pilot scheme, bringing together Highland Council, Scottish Homes and local housing providers. The scheme is designed to tackle rural housing problems and target resources more effectively. The Scottish Homes Development Programme was increased for 2000–01 by over 10 per cent to £45 million. Funding will provide over 1,550 new homes and improved homes across rural Scotland, of which 1,250 are planned for social rent. A further 1,500 new or refurbished homes are planned to be provided by attracting new private investment into former council housing. In Northern Ireland, a revised rural housing policy was introduced in April 2000. This policy reflects a wide range of topics related to rural housing, including assessment of need, improving housing conditions and closer working with rural communities. It includes a programme of around 260 new rural dwellings a year, improvement or replacement of some 900 rural cottages over the next three to five years and provision of central heating in some 7,000 rural dwellings within three years.

Improving Existing Housing

Slum clearance and large-scale redevelopment used to be major features of housing policy in urban areas in the UK. The modernisation and conversions of sub-standard homes in order to help maintain existing communities is now undertaken wherever practicable. In some cases, however, clearance may still occur. To help overcome objections to clearance, local authorities can pay a discretionary relocation grant together with home loss and disturbance payments to those with an interest in the property to help them to buy a comparable home in or near the same area.

Social Housing

Most of the capital expenditure on housing goes towards renovating and improving existing council housing. In July 2000 the Government announced an additional £1.8 billion for investment in housing. This is on top of the extra £5 billion already being made available through the Capital Receipts Initiative and Comprehensive Spending Review. These extra resources are expected to help to bring all social housing up to a decent standard by 2010. A new major repairs allowance will be introduced from April 2001 to ensure that authorities have the resources necessary to maintain their stock. In Wales, £140 million of the £200 million capital expenditure is spent on private renovation grants.

Rundown estates are being improved through various initiatives including Housing Action Trusts, Estate Action, the Single Regeneration Budget Challenge Fund (see p. 352). Where a local authority's housing strategy includes the transfer of negative value stock and tenants support this, the authority may consider funding it through its main housing investment programme or seek to fund it from the New Deal for Communities Programme (see p. 352) or the Single Regeneration Budget. The Private Finance Initiative is another important option for improving local authority housing. The DETR's new spending plans provide £160 million in 2001–02 to fund eight existing schemes and an extra £600 million over the following two years to fund new schemes. In Wales, Estate Partnership was set up to assist local authorities in tackling the worst problems on local authority housing estates by co-ordinating efforts to raise the quality of the housing stock, along with social and environmental improvements. Options include transferring ownership to the private sector.

Private Housing

Local authorities in England have powers to help home owners and tenants to improve the worst quality housing and to assist with the regeneration of communities. Local authorities are expected to invest about £275 million in private housing renewal in 2000–01 providing repairs for some 75,000 households. Local authorities also pay disabled facilities grants (DFG) to disabled people so that they can live more independently. Subsidy of £72 million, generating £120 million of local authority investment, is expected to provide adaptations for over 25,000 households.

In Scotland, local authorities have powers to provide grants for the improvement and repair of private sector housing. Scottish Homes also has the power to provide grants to complement the role of local authorities in private house renewal. In Northern Ireland, funding is allocated through the house renovation grants scheme, administered by the NIHE, on a similar basis to that in England and Wales. In rural areas, financial assistance to replace isolated dwellings that cannot be restored is also on offer.

Home Improvement Agencies

Home improvement agencies (HIAs) provide independent advice and help to assist elderly people, people with disabilities and those on low incomes to carry out repairs, improvements and adaptations to their properties. They are usually small-scale bodies operating on an authority-wide basis. HIAs are managed by a variety of organisations, often housing associations but also local authorities and independent bodies such as Age Concern. Local authorities in England have been allocated £6.7 million for 2000–01 to support agencies operating in their areas. In Scotland a Care and Repair service provides similar assistance to that provided by HIAs. The scheme is overseen by Scottish Homes.

Homelessness

Local authorities have legal duties to provide housing assistance for families and vulnerable people who are eligible for assistance, unintentionally homeless and in priority need. The priority need group includes households with dependent children or containing a pregnant woman; people who are vulnerable as a result of old age, mental or physical illness or disability or other special reason; and people who are homeless in an emergency.

In 1999–2000, local authorities in England made a total of 243,600 decisions on applications for housing from households eligible under the homelessness provisions of the 1985 and 1986 Housing Acts. They accepted around 105,500 households as meeting the conditions of eligibility for assistance. Over a quarter of all households accepted as homeless in England were in their situation because parents, other relatives or friends were no longer able or willing to accommodate them. A further quarter arose following a relationship breakdown.

The Government's target is to reduce rough sleeping in England to as close to zero as possible, and by at least two-thirds by 2002, compared with the level of 1999. The Rough Sleepers Unit has a budget of £160 million for London over three years, of which nearly £88 million is administered by the Housing Corporation for capital and revenue projects for re-housing rough sleepers. Outside London, where the local authorities are responsible for developing local strategies, the Unit has a programme of grants for the voluntary sector of around £36 million. A government strategy for homelessness in England, *Coming in from the Cold*, was published in December 1999. The strategy proposed a new approach to helping vulnerable rough sleepers off the streets, preventing new rough sleepers and rebuilding the lives of former rough sleepers. Between June 1998 and June 2000, there was a reduction of more than one-third in the numbers of rough sleepers.

Responsibility for rough sleeping initiatives in Scotland and Wales has been devolved to the Scottish Executive and National Assembly for Wales respectively. The Homelessness Task Force was established in 1999 to review the causes and nature of homelessness in Scotland, to examine current practice in dealing with cases of homelessness, and to make recommendations on how this can best be prevented and, where it does occur, tackled effectively. Funding is provided through the Rough Sleepers Initiative which received an additional £12 million funding in June 2000, on top of £30 million already allocated to projects to March 2002. In addition, a further £6 million has been made available to reduce the use of 'bed and breakfast' temporary accommodation for the homeless. In Wales, £1.85 million has been allocated in 2000–01 to support voluntary organisations. The funding will establish emergency night-shelters, outreach support, bond schemes (a guarantee fund held by the National Assembly for Wales and managed by the Housing and Community Renewal Division), tenancy support schemes and direct access hotels.

REGENERATION

Regeneration policies aim to enhance economic development and social cohesion through effective regional action and integrated local regeneration programmes. These programmes work through partnership between the public and private sectors and involve a substantial contribution from the latter. They support and complement other programmes tackling social and economic decline, and initiatives such as Sure Start (see p. 121), Health Action Zones (see p. 190), the Crime Reduction Programme (see p. 213) and the work of the Cabinet Office Social Exclusion Unit (see p. 113). Rundown areas in the UK benefit from European Union Structural Funds, notably the European Regional Development Fund (ERDF) which assists a wide variety of projects in the least prosperous urban and rural areas of the European Union. Around £10 billion of total structural funds, with £3 billion covering Objective 1 areas (see p. 396) have been allocated to the UK for the period 2000–06.

England

In England, government departments and public agencies work together to develop national regeneration policies. The government and the new Regional Development Agencies (RDAs) set out the priorities for regeneration and ensure that programmes aim to enhance and complement those already in place.

Eight RDAs in the English regions outside London were established in 1999, and the ninth in London was created in July 2000.

Regeneration objectives are administered by the DETR and the GORs and many programmes are delivered by the RDAs (see p. 394). In April 1999, the first eight RDAs took over responsibility for administering several regeneration programmes, including the Single Regeneration Budget (SRB) from the GORs, the land and property budgets from English Partnerships and the Rural Development Commission's rural regeneration programme. The new Mayor for London, supported by the London Development Agency, assumed responsibility for the SRB in London in July 2000. The RDAs are also responsible for co-ordinating inward investment in their own regions. Following consultation, RDAs outside London prepared their regional strategies which provide a regional framework for economic development and regeneration.

The Government Offices for the Regions liaise with the RDAs on behalf of the Government in providing advice as to whether strategies are consistent with national policies. They are also responsible for administering regeneration programmes including the New Deal for Communities and Estate Action.

The SRB provides funding for regeneration schemes, which are developed and implemented by local partnerships, and it supports a range of economic, physical and social regeneration activities. It is seen by the Government as an important instrument in its policy of tackling social exclusion.

Regeneration partnerships, consisting of key local organisations including the voluntary sector, are able to bid for resources from the SRB at annual bidding rounds. The successful bids from the first five rounds of the SRB are expected to involve expenditure of more than £17.6 billion over their lifetime, including more than £4.4 billion from the SRB, £6.5 billion from other public service support and an estimated £6.7 billion of private sector investment. The 163 successful fifth round bid schemes, announced by the Government in July 1999, have more than £1 billion to spend over their lifetime of up to seven years and are expected to create or safeguard 118,000 jobs. Sixteen of the 163 successful bids are major new SRB schemes in the most deprived areas. A target of the funding of 50 new major projects by March 2002 has been set. It is projected that funding from the first five rounds will see the creation or safeguarding of 696,000 jobs, with 775,000 people trained and obtaining qualifications; over 87,000 business start-ups; nearly 310,000 dwellings built or improved; and 136,000 voluntary groups supported. A sixth SRB round was launched in December 1999 and the announcement about the successful bids was made in August 2000. This round has focused 81 per cent of its resources on England's most deprived areas. The £931 million of SRB schemes outside London will help to secure a further £1.2 billion from the private sector and more than £2 billion from other public sector programmes, including European funds. London's £300 million will help to secure £700 million of private sector funding and £430 million from other public sector and European funds.

As part of the Government's strategy to tackle social exclusion, 17 partnerships were set up at the end of 1998 under the New Deal for Communities (NDC); a further 22 areas were invited to bid for funding in November 1999 as part of the second round. The NDC programme builds on the Social Exclusion Unit's report *Bringing Britain Together: a national strategy for neighbourhood renewal*. The NDC programme plans vary according to local circumstances, but in the main focus on unemployment, crime, educational under-achievement and poor health; for example, several Partnerships plan to introduce neighbourhood warden schemes, to provide a community presence on the streets. Resources of £800 million are available to support the NDC over the three years 1999–2000 to 2001–2002.

In April 2000, the Government issued a consultative document containing a draft strategy to tackle some of the worst problems experienced in neighbourhoods. This plan suggests ways to tackle many of the issues surrounding social deprivation, such as crime, unemployment and lack of services. Consultation on the document ended in June 2000 and a summary of the responses is expected to be published by the end of the year.

Manchester Millennium is a task force of public and private sector partners set up to help the redevelopment of Manchester's city centre after the terrorist bomb explosion in June 1996. The city centre was officially reopened in November 1999 and further work will continue over the next two years. The majority of funding for the redevelopment comes from the private sector (£438 million), with public expenditure of around £83 million, including £44 million from the DETR, 25 million ECU from the European Regional Development Fund and a £20 million Millennium Commission scheme.

Urban Renaissance

The Urban Task Force was formed in April 1998 to examine the causes of urban decline and recommend ways of encouraging people to return to urban neighbourhoods. The report *Towards an Urban Renaissance,* published in June 1999, included over 100 recommendations for improving towns and cities. Following the Task Force's recommendation for setting up urban regeneration companies (URCs), three pilot URCs were launched in 1999 in Liverpool, East Manchester and Sheffield. A preliminary assessment of the potential impact on the regeneration of each area has been carried out. Another recommendation of the Task Force was for the setting up of Home Zones, which aim to improve the quality of life in residential areas. Nine pilot Home Zones have been established. The Government has also published a revised *Planning Policy Guidance Note 3 (Housing)*, which addresses a number of the Task Force's recommendations on the management of land supply.

The Government has announced plans to publish a White Paper on urban policy towards the end of 2000, which is intended to address many of the Task Force's recommendations.

English Partnerships

By working together with central and local government, the RDAs, local authorities and other partners in public and private sectors, English Partnerships seeks to create new jobs and investment through sustainable economic regeneration and development in the English regions. EP has promoted, in partnership with the public and private sectors, job creation, inward investment, creation of workspace and environmental improvement, through the reclamation of vacant, derelict or contaminated land in areas of need throughout England. EP has provided support to the pilot urban regeneration companies, launched the Network Space programme (see p. 354) and continues to develop and co-ordinate the Millennium Communities Competition Programme. EP has been funded through grant-in-aid and through its own activities. Direct expenditure in 2000–01 (including that provisionally set aside for the London Development Agency) is planned to be in excess of £500 million. Following a European Commission decision that the EP's current Partnership Investment Programme (PIP) needs to be amended to comply with the European Commission rules on state aid, the Government announced in December 1999 that it would produce new proposals for how projects aimed at regenerating deprived areas could use Public-Private Partnerships. The PIP, managed by EP and delivered by the RDAs, supports non-commercially viable regeneration projects where the cost of development exceeds the likely final value. Under the present arrangements, payments made are the minimum necessary to allow regeneration schemes to proceed. During 1998–99, PIP provided over £200 million of support to projects, which over their lifetime are expected to secure £567 million of private investment, regenerate 1,300 hectares of land, create or safeguard 29,000 jobs, help build 7,500 housing units and create 860,000 sq metres of industrial or commercial floorspace.

Coalfields Regeneration

The Coalfields Regeneration Trust, an independent grant–giving body, provides support for coalfield communities, projects which generate work and training opportunities and support community enterprise, provides welfare advice and supports credit unions. It was set up as part of the Government's major long-term programme of action for coalfield areas, in response to the Coalfields Task Force Report. An investment package for the areas worth over £354 million over three years was announced in 1998. The Trust is being provided with more than £50 million for regenerating communities in former mining areas across England, Scotland and Wales.

The Network Space programme, a public/private partnership venture between English Partnerships and Langtree Group plc, will provide new managed workspace for small businesses across English coalfield areas. Over 45,000 sq metres of workspace will be developed on up to 17 sites, providing more than 1,000 jobs over three years.

The Coalfields Enterprise Fund, under development by EP, will support small and medium-sized firms with high growth potential in the English coalfield areas. It aims to secure funding of more than £50 million in partnership with the private sector. The Government will invest £15 million in the fund over three years.

Groundwork

Groundwork consists of a national co-ordinating body, Groundwork UK, and over 40 independent trusts, operating throughout England, Wales and Northern Ireland. The organisation supports programmes covering physical environmental improvements, education and community involvement, and integration of the economy with the environment. In 1999–2000, £12.9 million of private sector funding was attracted which helped to support almost 4,000 projects undertaken by nearly 3,000 private and voluntary sector partners.

Rural Regeneration

Although most problems arising from dereliction and unemployment occur in urban areas, some rural areas have also been affected as employment in traditional sectors, such as mining and rurally based defence establishments, has declined. Low wages and a decline in local public transport and other services have caused problems for some rural residents. The movement of people into the countryside has increased the demand for housing and local services. However, some rural areas have been successful in recent years in attracting high-technology industries, while the spread of modern telecommunications facilities and information technology has made it easier for people to work from home. The Government will set out its objectives and policies for rural areas in a White Paper to be published later in 2000.

Since April 1999, the RDAs outside London have been responsible for rural regeneration. Funding of over £22 million is allocated to the rural development programme (RDP) for 2000–01. Previously, the Rural Development Commission (RDC) had acted both as the Government's statutory adviser on the economic and social development of England's rural areas and as lead provider of regeneration projects. Rural challenge, one of the former RDC programmes, has been absorbed into the SRB (see p. 352). The RDAs manage both rural and non-rural aspects of the SRB and it is estimated that in addition to the RDP funds, the fifth round of SRB resulted in some 7 per cent of its funding (some £70 million over seven years) being allocated to either wholly rural schemes or the rural parts of mixed area schemes.

Parts of the former RDC were merged with the Countryside Commission to form the new Countryside Agency in April 1999 (see p. 314), which also inherited the RDC's advisory role. The Agency promotes and advises on conserving and enhancing the countryside, people's access to the countryside for recreation, and the economic and social development of England's rural areas. The Agency set out its policies in *Tomorrow's Countryside—2020 Vision*. It works with local communities to promote social inclusion, by helping to improve the mobility of, and services available to, the less well-off sections of the community and by tackling the problems of a lack of job opportunities, low wages and relative economic weakness in more isolated areas.

Wales

Parts of Wales have been adversely affected by the decline in traditional industries, especially the coal industry.

The Welsh European Funding Office was set up in April 2000 as an executive agency of the National Assembly for Wales to manage all aspects of European Structural Fund Programmes in Wales, the Rural Development Plan and the Local Regeneration Fund. Wales will receive up to £1.4 billion from the European Union to fund a variety of programmes until 2006. These include Objective 1 (see p. 396) for the west of Wales and the Valleys and Objectives 2 'Supporting the economic and social conversion of areas facing structural difficulties' and 3 'Supporting the adaptation and modernisation of policies and systems of education, training and employment' in East Wales. This money will be allocated in line with plans agreed with the European Commission. The programmes will be aimed at developing a stronger, more sustainable economy (especially with an expanded small and medium-sized company sector), better infrastructure, a more highly skilled workforce, and at securing the regeneration of urban and rural communities.

The Assembly plans to regenerate rural communities by encouraging new forms of rural enterprise, including forestry, and assisting farming families to diversify through the Rural Development Plan. The Plan is based on ten possible measures, including agri-environment, support for Less Favoured Areas, the wider adaptation and development of rural communities, and processing and marketing of agricultural products.

The new Local Regeneration Fund has been established by merging the Welsh Capital Challenge with the Local Authority Rural Scheme, which will be phased out over the next two years. The National Assembly for Wales has allocated £36 million for 2000–01. Wales is contributing £3.5 million over three years to the Coalfields Regeneration Trust.

There are currently four Groundwork Trusts operating in five local authorities in Wales. The Trusts aim to promote conservation, and improvement of the environment, and have been involved in the improvement of many derelict and run-down areas. They work with local partnerships, particularly local communities, in developing and implementing local projects. Groundwork Wales has been established as an umbrella body to co-ordinate activities and promote the Groundwork movement in Wales. The National Assembly for Wales provides a contribution to the funding of the Welsh Groundwork Trusts and Groundwork Wales. The Groundwork Trusts' funding is provided via the local authorities in which they are based and operate.

The Rural Partnership for Wales is an advisory body that contributes to the future development of rural policies and programmes in Wales. It comprises 27 organisations including the National Assembly for Wales, the Welsh Development Agency, the Welsh Local Government Association, the farming unions and others active in the field of rural development. It covers economic, social, environmental, equal opportunities and cultural issues of concern to rural Wales. In 1999, the Partnership published its statement *Rural Wales*.

There are four economic fora in Wales, for north Wales, south-west Wales, south-east Wales and mid-Wales. They aim to promote economic growth and development by developing close working relationships between the primary economic agencies, and between the private and public sectors. The fora are completely independent of the National Assembly.

The Welsh Development Agency contributes to economic regeneration across Wales. Its programmes include physical and environmental regeneration activities, such as land reclamation, urban, rural and environmental improvements; activities to provide site development works to assist with business infrastructure; and financial support for community initiatives such as the Market Towns Initiative and the Small Towns and Villages programmes.

Funding is also provided through the People in Communities programme, which was launched in June 1998 with a budget of £750,000 as a response to tackling social exclusion in deprived communities in Wales. Eight deprived communities across Wales were selected to take part in the Programme.

During 1999–2000, £1 million was allocated to enable the eight existing projects to expand and develop their work. A second round, involving a further eight projects, was announced in June 2000.

Communities First is a new approach designed to meet the needs and priorities determined by communities. Consultation on the programme has begun and it is expected that communities will be identified by the start of 2001, with implementation in April 2001.

Scotland

The Social Inclusion Partnership (SIP) programme was established in April 1999, and now involves a network of 48 local partnerships tackling the problems that disadvantaged groups and communities face across rural and urban Scotland. The SIPs are multi-agency partnerships, consisting of all relevant local public agencies, the voluntary and private sectors, and representatives from the community. The 48 SIPs are supported by £150 million over the three years from 2000–01 from the Social Inclusion Partnership Fund. The Coalfields Regeneration Trust will receive funding of £4.5 million from the Scottish Executive over the three years from 1999–2000.

Funding is also provided through the Working for Communities and Listening to Communities programmes. These programmes are testing and developing new models for delivering integrated local services in deprived areas, and for developing the capacity of excluded communities to influence decisions about their lives.

Local Enterprise Companies (LECs, see p. 149), working as part of the Highlands and Islands Enterprise Network (in the north of Scotland) and the Scottish Enterprise Network (in the south), have a range of powers and functions to engage in regeneration and encourage business and employment in their areas. A wide range of regeneration projects are ongoing around Scotland. For example, in Edinburgh, a partnership between Scottish Enterprise Edinburgh and Lothian and the City of Edinburgh Council, Waterfront Edinburgh Limited, has been established to co-ordinate and promote the regeneration of Edinburgh's waterfront. It is expected that the 15-year project, with public funding of over £33 million, will lead to private sector investment of £500 million providing 5,000 new homes, new business and retail developments, two new schools, a university college campus and a new marina. It is anticipated that the project will support between 4,000 and 7,000 new jobs.

In Lanarkshire, the site of the former Ravenscraig steelworks, which closed in 1992, and the adjacent site of another former steelworks form the largest single derelict site in the UK, and one of the biggest brownfield sites in Europe. Since its closure, the Corus Group (formerly British Steel) has spent over £20 million clearing and de-contaminating the site. In January 2000, work began on the first stage of a regeneration plan for Ravenscraig which has been prepared by Scottish Enterprise Lanarkshire, North Lanarkshire Council and the Corus Group working together as the Ravenscraig Regeneration partnership. The initial stage has funding of over £12 million and will include the construction of a 2.5-kilometre road with public footways and a cycleway.

Northern Ireland

The Department for Social Development (DSD) has been created as part of the new departmental arrangements for the devolved administration (see p. 18). It amalgamates some of the agencies and functions previously associated with the Department of Health and Social Services and the Department of the Environment for Northern Ireland. The aim of the Department is to promote individual and community wellbeing of the people of Northern Ireland through integrated social and economic action.

The Urban Generation and Community Development Group is responsible for the establishment of policy and strategy, implementation of programmes targeting resources to areas of social need, addressing the social, economic and physical regeneration of cities, towns and villages in Northern Ireland and promoting partnership between the Government and the voluntary and community sector. Over £40 million has been allocated for expenditure on urban regeneration and community development, including grants to voluntary bodies, certain grants-in-aid and on other services for the year ending 31 March 2001.

The Northern Ireland Partnership board was established in 1996 as one of the intermediary funding mechanisms for the delivery of the European Union Special Support Programme of Peace and Reconciliation in Northern Ireland. The overall aim of the programme is to help build a stable society, develop the economy and encourage cross-community and community relation based activities. There are 26 partnerships, one for each district council area, which are composed of one-third elected representatives, one-third from the community and voluntary sector, and one-third from the business, trade union and statutory agency sector. By January 2000, around £35 million had been spent by district partnerships.

The Belfast Regeneration Office is responsible for the functions previously carried out by Belfast Development Office and Making Belfast Work. Making Belfast Work was launched in 1988 to advance efforts being made by community interests, the private sector and the Government to address problems faced by the most disadvantaged areas of Belfast. The Londonderry Development Office, which is also part of the DSD's Urban Generation and Community Development Group aims to play a leading role in promoting comprehensive social, economic and physical regeneration and the redress of disadvantage in Londonderry. A new programme by Business in the Community to help develop the role of the private sector in regeneration partnerships in Belfast and Londonderry was launched in September 1999.

Regeneration of the centre of Lisburn announced in June 2000 will involve investment of more than £60 million on projects such as the Historic Quarter, Lisburn Square and the new Civic Centre.

Further Reading

DETR Annual Report 2000: The Government's Expenditure Plans 2000–01 to 2001–02. The Stationery Office, 2000.

Housing and Construction Statistics 1988–1998, Great Britain. The Stationery Office, 1999.

The Housing Corporation: Annual Report. The Housing Corporation.

Quality and Choice: A Decent Home for All. DETR, 2000.

Social Trends (Annual). Office for National Statistics, The Stationery Office.

Websites

Department of the Environment, Transport and the Regions: www.detr.gov.uk

National Assembly for Wales: www.wales.gov.uk

Northern Ireland Executive: www.nics.gov.uk

Scottish Executive: www.scotland.gov.uk

22 Transport and Communications

Following the establishment of the Scottish Parliament, the National Assembly for Wales and the Northern Ireland Assembly, responsibility for a range of transport functions has been transferred from the UK Government to the devolved administrations. In July 2000 the UK Government announced a ten-year investment plan, involving public and private expenditure of £180 billion, for modernising the nation's transport system. This primarily relates to investment in England, although it also covers investment in the railways in Scotland and Wales. The plan sets out the Government's intention to provide greater investment in railways and light rail systems, more by-passes and road widening schemes, and measures to encourage greater use of buses. Telecommunications services are expanding rapidly, and now more than half the population—over 33 million people—have a mobile telephone, while use of the Internet is also rising quickly and nearly half of adults have accessed it at some time.

Transport

TRAVEL TRENDS

Passenger travel was 728 billion passenger-kilometres in Great Britain in 1999 (see Table 22.1). Travel by car, van and taxi has more than doubled in the past 30 years, but recently the rate of growth has slowed, and car traffic grew by just 1.7 per cent in 1999. On the other hand, motorcycling was 16 per cent higher in 1999 than in 1998. Cycling also rose in 1999, being 6 per cent higher than in 1998, reversing the previous decline, which had averaged 4 per cent a year between 1995 and 1998. Travel by bus has shown a steady decline since the 1950s. Rail travel rose by around 6 per cent in 1999–2000, and is at its highest level since 1946, while travel on the various light rail/supertram systems is also growing. Air travel, particularly international traffic, is continuing to grow substantially.

Travel by car accounted for 85 per cent of passenger mileage within Great Britain in 1999. Over the last ten years, the proportion of households with regular use of one car has remained relatively constant, at 45 per cent (see chart on p. 118), but there has been an

Table 22.1: Passenger Transport in Great Britain by Mode

Billion passenger-kilometres

	1989	1994	1997	1998	1999
Buses and coaches	47	44	44	45	45
Cars, vans and taxis	581	591	614	617	621
Motorcycles, mopeds and scooters	6	4	4	4	5
Pedal cycles	5	5	4	4	4
All road	**639**	**643**	**666**	**671**	**675**
Rail[1]	39	35	42	44	46
Air[2]	5	5	7	7	7
All modes[3]	**683**	**684**	**715**	**722**	**728**

[1] Financial years. Former British Rail companies and urban rail systems.
[2] Scheduled and non-scheduled services. Excludes air taxi services, private flying and passengers paying less than 25 per cent of the full fare. Includes Northern Ireland and the Channel Islands.
[3] Excluding travel by water within the UK (including the Channel Islands), estimated at 0.6 billion passenger-kilometres in 1999.
Source: *Transport Statistics Great Britain 2000 Edition*

increase in households with two cars (from 18 per cent in 1989 to 22 per cent in 1999), while in 1999, 5 per cent of households had regular use of three or more cars. Most freight is carried by road, which accounts for 81 per cent of goods by tonnage and 65 per cent in terms of tonne-kilometres.[1]

At the end of 1999 there were 28.4 million vehicles licensed for use on the roads of Great Britain, according to the Driver and Vehicle Licensing Agency, which maintains official records of drivers and vehicles in Great Britain. There were 24.0 million cars (of which 2.4 million were company-owned); 2.4 million vans and light goods vehicles; 415,000 goods vehicles over 3.5 tonnes; 760,000 motorcycles, scooters and mopeds; and 84,000 public transport vehicles with nine or more seats.

TRANSPORT POLICY

In 1998 the Government issued a White Paper, *A New Deal for Transport: Better for Everyone*, setting out its policy for creating an integrated transport system to tackle the growing problems of congestion and pollution by improving all types of transport. The White Paper's approach covered the whole of the UK, but complementary White Papers/ policy documents have been issued for Scotland, Wales and Northern Ireland, and a selection of the main points and recent developments is given below. Transport safety is a high priority, and measures have been taken to improve safety in several sectors, including road safety (see p. 363) and railway safety (see p. 369). The Commission for Integrated Transport was set up to provide independent advice to the UK Government on implementing an integrated transport policy, review progress towards meeting government objectives, and identify best practice on transport issues from the UK and overseas. Public-Private Partnerships (see p. 405) will have an increasingly important role in transport, notably for the Channel Tunnel Rail Link, the London Underground and air traffic control.

The Transport Bill, now before Parliament, contains provisions to implement some of these measures, including:

- establishing the Strategic Rail Authority (see p. 367);
- requiring local authorities to prepare five-year plans to improve their local transport;

[1] A tonne-kilometre is equivalent to 1 tonne transported for 1 kilometre.

- enabling local authorities to introduce road charges or a levy on workplace parking, to tackle congestion and pollution;
- giving local authorities new powers to improve local bus services, and requiring them to offer concessionary fares for pensioners; and
- providing for a new Public-Private Partnership for air traffic services (see p. 375).

The powers allocated to local authorities under the Bill would cover only those authorities in England and Wales. Local transport plans have already been drawn up on a provisional basis by local authorities in England and Wales; in Scotland there are local transport strategies. In England full local transport plans were submitted in July 2000 for consideration by the Department of the Environment, Transport and the Regions (DETR). In London a second round of interim transport plans has been submitted to Transport for London (set up by the Greater London Authority—see p. 63), which took up its new powers in July 2000. The new Mayor of London and the London Assembly are responsible for delivering integrated transport in London, and the Mayor has responsibility for producing a transport strategy covering all modes of transport to, from and within London. In Wales full local transport plans were submitted to the National Assembly in August 2000.

Ten-year Plan

In July 2000 the Government issued its ten-year transport investment plan.[2] It envisages investment in transport of some £180 billion: £60 billion for railways in Great Britain, £59 billion for local transport in England, £25 billion for transport in London, £21 billion for strategic roads in England and £15 billion on future projects and other sectors. The total includes capital investment of £121 billion, which the Government intends should be delivered through a partnership between the private and public sectors. The investment is intended to:

- provide 100 new by-passes, enable 580 kilometres (360 miles) of the motorway and trunk road network to be widened, and eliminate a backlog of road maintenance and reduce road congestion;
- modernise and upgrade the railway network;
- improve services on the London Underground and London buses;
- provide up to 25 new tram lines in major cities and conurbations;
- improve rural transport; and
- make the transport system safer and more secure.

Wales

The integrated approach to transport policy in Wales, now being taken forward by the National Assembly for Wales, envisages improved public transport in both urban and rural areas—grants of £5 million are available in 2000–01 to support non-commercial bus services and £250,000 is available for community transport schemes in rural areas. Both schemes are under review to see how they can be refined so that services more closely match community needs, and a revised approach will take effect from 2001–02. To reduce congestion, the Assembly is encouraging employers to develop travel plans, and the adoption of traffic management measures. Funding is also provided to schemes which reduce use of the car for journeys to school. The Assembly is considering a report issued in June 2000 on improving transport links between north and south Wales. The report's recommendations include improvements to the strategic trunk road network, new direct rail services, better car parking facilities at railway stations, better connections between trains and local buses, and further investigation of a north–south coach service.

---

[2] *Transport 2010: The 10 Year Plan* focuses on surface transport, and improvements in surface access to ports and airports. It mainly covers England, although for the railways the plan covers the network in Great Britain.

The National Cycle Network

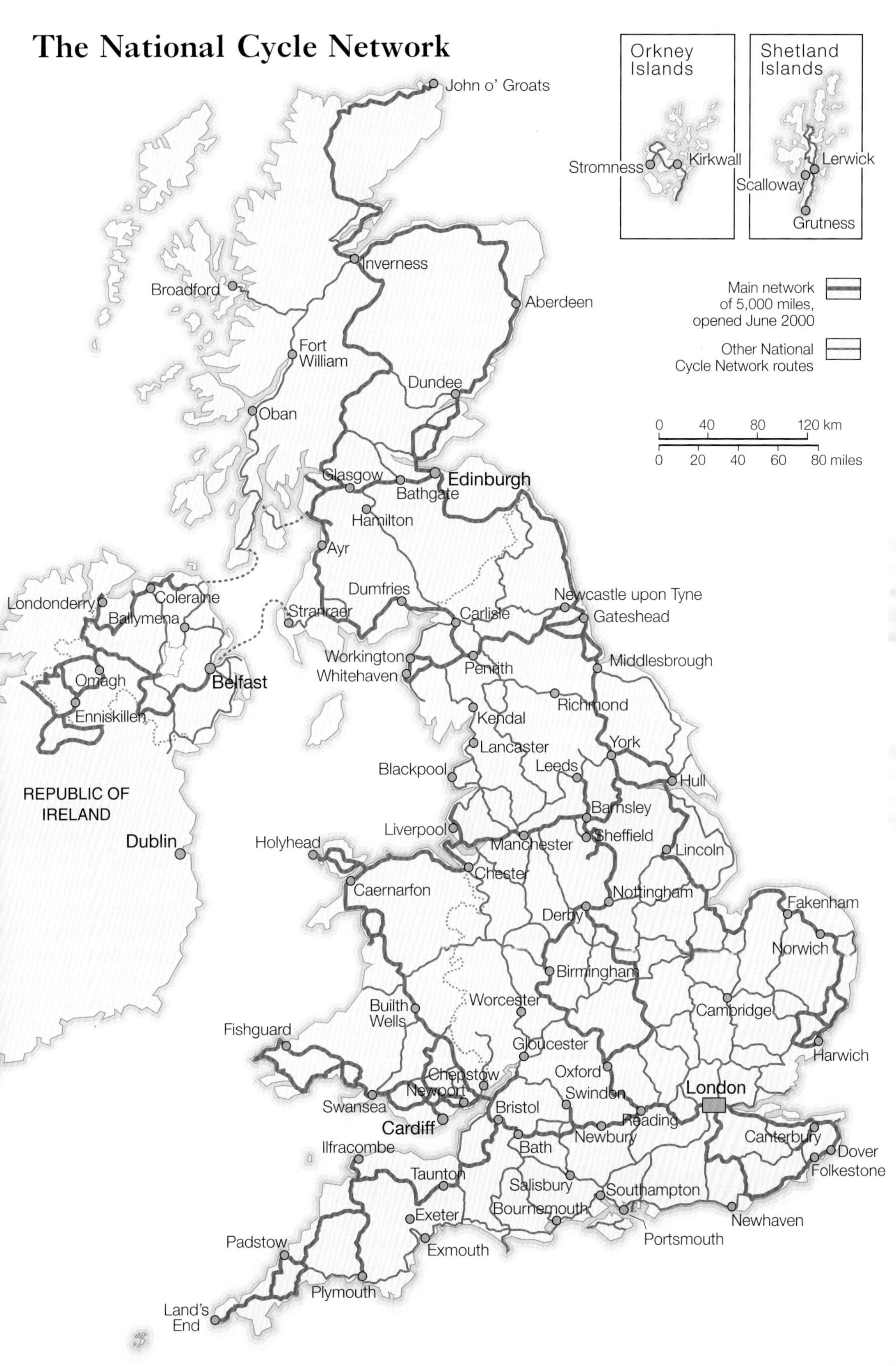

Orkney Islands
Stromness
Kirkwall
Shetland Islands
Lerwick
Scalloway
Grutness
Main network of 5,000 miles, opened June 2000
Other National Cycle Network routes
0 40 80 120 km
0 20 40 60 80 miles
John o' Groats
Inverness
Broadford
Aberdeen
Fort William
Dundee
Oban
Glasgow
Edinburgh
Bathgate
Hamilton
Ayr
Dumfries
Stranraer
Londonderry
Coleraine
Ballymena
Omagh
Belfast
Enniskillen
REPUBLIC OF IRELAND
Dublin
Carlisle
Newcastle upon Tyne
Gateshead
Workington
Whitehaven
Penrith
Middlesbrough
Richmond
Kendal
Lancaster
York
Leeds
Hull
Blackpool
Barnsley
Liverpool
Manchester
Sheffield
Lincoln
Holyhead
Chester
Caernarfon
Nottingham
Derby
Fakenham
Norwich
Birmingham
Builth Wells
Worcester
Cambridge
Fishguard
Gloucester
Harwich
Oxford
Chepstow
Newport
Swindon
London
Swansea
Bristol
Reading
Cardiff
Bath
Newbury
Canterbury
Dover
Folkestone
Ilfracombe
Taunton
Salisbury
Southampton
Bournemouth
Exeter
Newhaven
Portsmouth
Exmouth
Padstow
Plymouth
Land's End

THE NATIONAL CYCLE NETWORK

The National Cycle Network is a UK-wide project supported by £43.5 million of National Lottery funding from the Millennium Commission and co-ordinated by the civil engineering charity Sustrans. Some 400 local authorities and other partners have been involved in developing the network which, by 2005, will comprise 10,000 miles (16,000 km) of cycle route. The first 5,000 miles (8,000 km) were officially opened for use in June 2000. The network is made up of approximately 60 per cent lightly trafficked or calmed minor roads and 40 per cent traffic-free routes which are often also suitable for pedestrians, wheelchair users and horse riders.

Blackpool: The first electric trams in Great Britain ran in Blackpool in 1885. The 18 km Blackpool and Fleetwood Tramway has remained in continuous operation since the line to Fleetwood opened in 1898. Up to 65 trams operate during Blackpool's summer season and the service runs throughout the year.

Tram 660, 'Coronation Car', built for the Queen's Coronation by Roberts of Wakefield. Entered service in 1952.

Tram 626, single decker in service since 1937.

Tram 606, 'open boat' design, entered service in 1939 and left Blackpool Transport in 2000 to be displayed in a Transport Museum in Cleveland, Ohio.

Trams 700 and 711, double deckers in service since 1934.

Manchester: Officially opened in 1992, Manchester's Metrolink became Britain's first modern street operating light rail system. By early 1998 the expanded route network, linking the city centre with Altrincham and Bury, was carrying around 14 million passengers a year. It is estimated that Metrolink has saved about 2 million car journeys a year, reducing vehicle emissions by around 3,600 tonnes of carbon dioxide, 487 tonnes of carbon monoxide and 15 tonnes of nitrous oxide.

Birmingham: The Metro in Birmingham, opened in 1999, follows the route of the former Great Western Railway line connecting five towns between Wolverhampton and Snow Hill. In its first year of operation the Metro has carried over 5 million passengers.

Croydon: Work on Croydon's Tramlink system was completed in spring 2000, bringing trams back to the town for the first time since 1951. The network has 38 stops and currently operates 24 trams, 21 of which are in service during the peak period. Each tram can carry over 200 passengers and has a maximum speed of 80 km per hour.

Scotland

The Transport (Scotland) Bill, now being considered by the Scottish Parliament, would provide local authorities with additional powers to enable them to obtain an integrated transport system at the local level. The Bill would allow:

- Scottish ministers to require designated public bodies to prepare a joint plan for particular transport issues;
- the establishment of statutory bus 'quality partnerships' and 'quality contracts' between local authorities and bus operators;
- local authorities to introduce statutory ticketing schemes and set minimum standards of information for bus passengers;
- Scottish ministers to establish a national minimum level of concessionary fares for pensioners and people with disabilities; and
- local authorities to introduce local road user charging and workplace parking schemes to tackle congestion in cities, with all the revenue to be set aside for transport.

Expenditure on transport of £283 million is planned in 2000–01, rising to £311 million in 2001–02. Following a review of strategic roads, the Scottish Executive announced that over the next three years construction work would start on five major trunk road schemes, with an estimated capital cost of £140 million. These schemes are part of a two-year package costing £444 million of improvements and repairs to the motorway and trunk road network.

Rail services in Scotland receive an annual subsidy of over £200 million. The Public Transport Fund is providing £90 million over the three years to 2001–02 to assist local authorities in improving the provision of public transport across Scotland. Projects supported have included new railway stations, 'park and ride' facilities, and bus priority schemes.

The Scottish Executive is also providing £14.6 million over the three years to 2000–01 through the Rural Transport Fund to help improve transport in rural Scotland. The fund has supported over 350 new and improved public transport services, 71 community transport projects and 18 refurbished petrol stations. Support is also being given to essential services to the Scottish Islands, including a £3 million contribution towards the cost of replacing airport terminals at Kirkwall (Orkney) and Stornoway and installing an instrument landing system at Kirkwall.

Northern Ireland

The transport policy statement for Northern Ireland *Moving Forward*, published in November 1998, acknowledged that much needed to be done to deliver a sustainable and inclusive transport system for Northern Ireland. The statement contained an interim regional transport plan, designed to continue a programme of measures arising from a previous statement. The Department for Regional Development has now begun preparing a regional transport strategy to facilitate the future development of local transport plans and consider how they can be adequately resourced. Until this strategy comes into effect, the Department's policy is to follow the principles of *Moving Forward* through the implementation of the interim regional transport plan.

A task force, established to look at a range of strategic options for the future of the railway network, reported to the Minister for Regional Development in September 2000.

ROADS

The total road network in Great Britain in 1999 was 371,900 kilometres (231,100 miles). Trunk motorways[3] accounted for 3,316 kilometres (2,060 miles) of this, less than 1 per cent, and other trunk roads for over 12,150 kilometres (7,550 miles), or 3.3 per cent. However, motorways carry 18 per cent of all traffic, and trunk roads another 17 per cent.

---

[3] That is, those motorways that are the direct responsibility of the central administration rather than the local authority.

Road Traffic in Great Britain by Vehicle Type, 1999

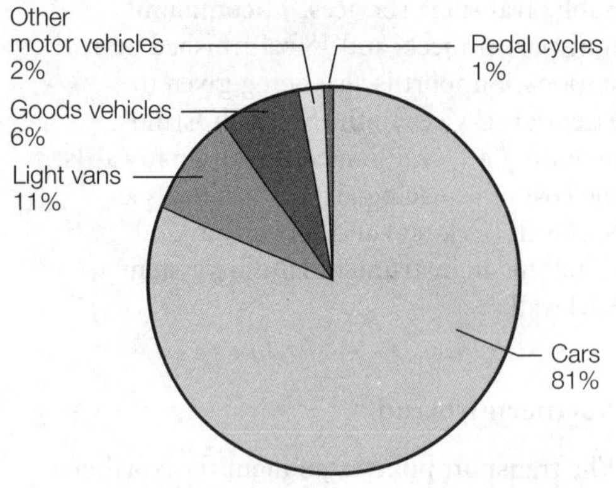

Note: Light vans = goods vehicles under 3.5 tonnes gross weight. Goods vehicles = goods vehicles over 3.5 tonnes gross weight. Other motor vehicles include two-wheel motor vehicles and large buses and coaches.

Source: Department of the Environment, Transport and the Regions

Combined, they carry over half of all goods vehicle traffic in Great Britain. In Northern Ireland the road network is over 24,000 kilometres (15,000 miles), of which motorways represent 114 kilometres (71 miles).

Motor traffic in Great Britain was 1.7 per cent higher in 1999 than in 1998, rising to an estimated 467 billion vehicle-kilometres (see Table 22.2). Traffic on motorways was up by 3 per cent, to 83.6 billion vehicle-kilometres.

Road Programme

The Highways Agency—an executive agency of the DETR—is responsible for maintaining, operating and improving the national road network in England, except for London where responsibility has been transferred to the Greater London Authority. In Wales the motorway and trunk road network is the responsibility of the National Assembly. In Scotland responsibility rests with the Scottish Executive. In Northern Ireland responsibility rests with the NI Assembly. The Roads Service, an agency within the Department for Regional Development, maintains and improves the road network on behalf of the Assembly.

The Highways Agency is responsible for about 70 per cent of the motorway and trunk road network in England, with the other 30 per cent being the responsibility of local authorities. Its budget is £1.5 billion in 2001–02 when it expects to spend £672 million on motorway and trunk road maintenance, £494 million on major network improvements and £208 million for making better use of the network. In addition, local authorities have a budget of nearly £2.2 billion for maintaining local roads.

The ten-year plan envisages public investment of £21.3 billion in the Highways Agency's strategic road network, together with £2.5 billion of private capital investment. Investment will help to tackle the main congestion pressures. Extra capacity will be provided through 30 trunk road by-passes, 80 major schemes to tackle bottlenecks at junctions, and the widening of some 5 per cent of the strategic road network and associated junction improvements. For example, one major scheme is planned to widen to 12 lanes the sections of the M25 near Heathrow Airport, the most heavily used sections of the UK motorway network. Some £130 million a year will be spent on smaller-scale improvements, while new technology will be extended to provide better network management to reduce traffic delays (see p. 364).

Table 22.2: Motor Vehicle Traffic in Great Britain *Billion vehicle-kilometres*

	1989	1994	1997	1998	1999
Motorways	59.0	66.7	77.9	81.3	83.6
Trunk roads	68.5	69.8	74.1	75.0	78.6
Principal roads	122.6	130.1	134.6	136.4	136.0
Minor roads	156.7	155.9	166.0	166.6	168.8
All roads	**406.9**	**422.6**	**452.5**	**459.2**	**467.0**

Source: *Transport Statistics Great Britain 2000 Edition*

Private sector finance is playing a role through 'Design, Build, Finance and Operate' (DBFO) contracts, under which the private sector provides the funding for construction and maintenance, and receives government payments linked to usage and performance. About 25 per cent of current and new major schemes are expected to be built using DBFO contracts. Work on the privately financed A55 across Anglesey is due for completion early in 2001 and work on the Birmingham northern relief road is due to start in late 2000.

Standards

Minimum ages for driving are:

- 16 for riders of mopeds, drivers of small tractors, and disabled people receiving a mobility allowance;
- 17 for drivers of cars and other passenger vehicles with nine or fewer seats (including that of the driver), motorcycles and goods vehicles not over 3.5 tonnes maximum authorised mass (MAM);
- 18 for goods vehicles weighing over 3.5, but not over 7.5, tonnes MAM; and
- 21 for passenger-carrying vehicles with more than nine seats and goods vehicles over 7.5 tonnes MAM.

New drivers of motor vehicles must pass both the computer-based touch screen theory test and the practical driving test in order to acquire a full driving licence. In 1999, 1.2 million driving tests were conducted in Great Britain by the Driving Standards Agency (DSA), the national driver testing authority. The average pass rate was nearly 44 per cent. About 32.7 million people hold a car full driving licence. The DSA also supervises professional driving instructors, the compulsory basic training scheme for learner motorcyclists and a voluntary register for instructors of drivers of large goods vehicles.

Before most new cars and goods vehicles are allowed on the roads, they must meet safety and environmental requirements, based primarily on standards drawn up by the European Union (EU). The Vehicle Certification Agency is responsible for ensuring these requirements are met through a process known as 'type approval'.

The Vehicle Inspectorate is responsible for ensuring the roadworthiness of vehicles, through their annual testing. It also uses roadside and other enforcement checks to ensure that drivers and vehicle operators comply with legislation. In Northern Ireland the Driver and Vehicle Testing Agency is responsible for testing drivers and vehicles.

Road Safety

Since 1981–85 there has been a significant decline in road deaths and serious casualties in Great Britain, by 39 per cent and 48 per cent respectively, while road traffic has risen by 59 per cent. In 1999 there were 235,000 road accidents involving personal injury in Great Britain, 2 per cent fewer than in 1998, of which 36,400 involved death or serious injury. There were 3,423 deaths in road accidents, 39,100 serious injuries and nearly 277,800 slight injuries.

In March 2000 the Government launched *Tomorrow's Roads: Safer for Everyone*, its new road safety strategy. It has set a target of reducing the number of people killed or seriously injured on the roads of Great Britain by 40 per cent by 2010, compared with the average levels for 1994–98. A higher target reduction, of 50 per cent, has been set for deaths and serious injuries to children. Measures include:

- creating more 20 mph (32 km/h) zones around schools and in residential areas;
- enforcing road traffic law more effectively, with greater use of speed cameras;
- improving driver training;
- consulting on the mandatory fitting of seat belts in new coaches and minibuses;
- setting appropriate speed limits for local conditions;
- supporting the development of safer car design; and
- improving road safety education.

In June 2000 the Government announced a new approach to its road safety campaign, on which it spends about £9 million a year. The campaign aims to create greater public awareness of all road safety issues and encourage everyone to use the roads safely.

Local authorities in England and Wales are now required to plan specific road safety measures as part of their local transport plans, while local authorities in Scotland are expected to set out in their local transport strategies their plans for reducing road casualties. The DETR has funded a £5 million project in Gloucester to test a strategic approach to road safety in an average-sized local authority. Work began in 1996 and is due to be completed in 2001. The objective is to cut casualties in the city by a third; initial results in certain areas affected by the scheme show an average fall of 60 per cent.

Congestion

About 7 per cent of the Highways Agency's network experiences regular heavy peak and occasional non-peak congestion, and a further 13 per cent sees heavy congestion on at least half the days in the year. Traffic congestion also occurs in many towns and cities in the main morning and evening peak periods and for much of the day in central London. Traffic management schemes aim to reduce congestion through measures such as traffic-free shopping precincts, bus lanes and other bus priority measures, and parking controls. In London a 512-km (318-mile) network of priority 'red routes', with special stopping controls, is designed to improve traffic flow.

Under the Greater London Authority Act 1999 and the Transport Bill, local authorities in London and the rest of England and Wales respectively would be able to introduce congestion charging schemes for road users and a levy on workplace parking, as part of their local transport plan, and to retain the net revenue generated from charges for at least ten years, provided that these are used to fund local transport improvements. The Transport (Scotland) Bill provides for similar powers in Scotland, but would not involve any time limit on the retention of revenue. Local authorities would need to consult local people and businesses and to make improvements to public transport before starting such schemes. Leeds and Edinburgh will host the first full-scale demonstrations of electronic road user charging equipment in the UK, starting around the end of 2001.

The Government is encouraging major employers to adopt travel plans to reduce car use for travel to work and on business, for example, by promoting alternatives such as car sharing, cycling and use of public transport.

Traffic Information

Traffic information is provided throughout Great Britain by a variety of means, such as the media, roadside signs and in-vehicle systems. Information originates from a range of sources, such as roadside sensors, the traffic police and highway authorities. It is collated by motoring organisations, such as the Automobile Association (AA) and the Royal Automobile Club (RAC), and by information service providers, such as Integrated Traffic Information Services (ITIS), Metro Networks and Trafficmaster. Local traffic control centres across Great Britain help to manage traffic and provide information about traffic conditions. Centres covering wider areas exist in Scotland and Wales. A new national traffic control centre planned for England is due to enter service in 2001 and to be fully operational by 2003. In the next ten years the Highways Agency intends to introduce new roadside monitoring and communications equipment to improve traffic management on the strategic road network in England to ensure more reliable journey times and improve safety.

Cycling

The National Cycling Strategy, launched in 1996, aims to increase the number of cycling journeys fourfold by 2012. The National Cycling Forum is co-ordinating the implementation of the strategy which has been endorsed by the Government. The DETR announced its own target of trebling the number of cycling journeys by 2010, as part of its ten-year transport investment plan. Local authorities are expected to develop local cycling strategies and incorporate them in their local transport plans and strategies. The cycling strategies will set out measures to give greater priority to cycling, such as establishing safe and convenient cycle routes.

The first 5,000 miles (8,000 kilometres) of the National Cycle Network (see map opposite p. 360), which is being developed by the transport charity Sustrans, were officially opened in June 2000. When completed in 2005, the network will cover 10,000 miles (16,000 kilometres). Funds of up to £43 million from the Millennium Commission are contributing towards the cost. Nearly two-thirds of the network will follow existing roads, with traffic calming and cycle lanes being implemented where necessary. Over a third of the network will be entirely free from motor traffic by utilising old railway lines, canal towpaths, river paths and derelict land. Information on the network is on the Sustrans website (www.nationalcyclenetwork.org.uk).

Walking

People in the UK are walking significantly less than in the past, with fewer journeys on foot and many more by car. The Government wishes to reverse this trend, and is expecting local authorities to give more priority to walking by providing, for example, wider pavements, pedestrianisation schemes and more pedestrian crossings.

The DETR is monitoring the effectiveness of nine pilot schemes for 'home zones', and a similar study monitoring four sites in Scotland is about to start. Home zones aim to improve the quality of life in residential areas by making them places primarily for people and not just for traffic.

Road Haulage

An operator's licence is required for operating goods vehicles over 3.5 tonnes gross weight in the UK. About 88 per cent of the 111,000 licences in issue are for fleets of five or fewer vehicles, and there are around 424,000 heavy goods vehicles. Road haulage traffic by heavy goods vehicles amounted to 149 billion tonne-kilometres in Great Britain in 1999, 14 per cent more than in 1990. Road hauliers are tending to use larger vehicles carrying heavier loads—85 per cent of the traffic, in terms of tonne-kilometres, is now carried by vehicles of over 25 tonnes gross weight.

International road haulage has grown rapidly and in 1999 about 2.2 million road goods vehicles travelled by ferry or the Channel Tunnel to mainland Europe, of which 563,000 were powered vehicles registered in the UK. In 1999 UK vehicles carried 15.9 million tonnes internationally, and about 96 per cent of this traffic was with the EU.

In 1999 the Government issued a long-term strategy for freight in the UK, with the aim of promoting a competitive and efficient distribution sector to support future economic growth while minimising the effects on society and the environment. The strategy seeks to reduce the extent to which economic growth generates additional lorry movements, by improving efficiency, making the most of rail, shipping and inland waterways, and improving interchange links between the different types of transport. Following a report by the Commission for Integrated Transport in March 2000, the maximum weight for lorries on domestic journeys with six or more axles will be raised from 41 to 44 tonnes in February 2001.

Bus Services

In 1998–99 some 4,248 million passenger journeys were made on local bus services in Great Britain, nearly 19 per cent fewer than in 1988–89. Usage has been declining in nearly all areas, although in London (which accounts for nearly a third of bus journeys in Great Britain) passenger journeys in 1998–99 were higher than ten years earlier. There are around 80,000 buses and coaches in Great Britain, of which 32 per cent are minibuses or the slightly larger midibuses (which are becoming more widespread) and 22 per cent double-deckers.

Most local bus services are provided commercially, with 83 per cent of bus mileage outside London operated on this basis. Local authorities may subsidise services which are not commercially viable but are considered socially necessary.

Operators

Almost all bus services in Great Britain are provided by private sector concerns, apart from 17 bus companies owned by local authorities. In July 2000 Transport for London (see p. 63) succeeded London Transport as the authority responsible for providing or procuring public transport in London. It oversees about 750 bus routes run by about 30 companies under contract.

Five main groups operate bus services: Arriva, FirstGroup, Go-Ahead Group, National Express and Stagecoach. Most of these groups have diversified into running other transport services, such as rail services and airports, while some have also expanded into transport services in other countries, notably the United States.

In Northern Ireland almost all road passenger services are operated by subsidiaries of the publicly owned Northern Ireland Transport Holding Company (NITHC), collectively known as 'Translink'. Citybus Ltd operates services in Belfast, and Ulsterbus Ltd runs most of the services in the rest of Northern Ireland, carrying respectively 21 million and 48 million passengers a year.

Services

The Transport Bill and the Transport (Scotland) Bill would introduce, subject to parliamentary approval, a new statutory framework which aims to improve bus services other than in London. Local authorities in England and Wales would be required to develop bus services as part of their local transport plans. In Scotland there would be no such statutory requirement, but the Scottish Executive would expect local authorities to set out their views on bus services in their local transport strategies. The Bills would also provide statutory backing for 'bus quality partnerships' and 'quality contracts', between local authorities and bus operators. Similar partnerships have been developed voluntarily in around 130 towns and cities, and have led to better services with higher-quality buses, and increased passenger use of typically 10 per cent to 20 per cent. At the first National Bus Summit in November 1999 the industry agreed new targets on reliability and quality, including a target of reducing the average age of buses to eight years by 2001.

Extra funding for rural bus services has led to 1,800 new or improved services in England. In addition, a 'rural bus challenge' has been held in England to stimulate the development of innovative services in rural areas, and over 100 schemes have been introduced. A similar challenge fund is now being developed to support improved public transport links to deprived urban estates.

The Bills include measures to improve bus ticketing and information. Later in 2000 'Traveline', a telephone service providing integrated timetable information on all public transport modes from a single national number, will be launched. This will be followed by the development, involving transport operators, local and central government, of a more extensive system, known as 'Transport Direct', and by 2003 this is expected to be available on the Internet.

Bus priority measures, such as bus lanes, are becoming more extensive, while in some areas innovative measures, such as guided busways (with buses travelling on segregated track), are being adopted, and there is growing interest in expanding tram or light rail services (see p. 370). Around 70 park and ride schemes, in which car users park on the outskirts of towns and travel by public transport to the central area, are in operation in England and are being increasingly used to relieve traffic congestion in busy urban centres; up to 100 new schemes are envisaged over the next ten years.

Coaches

Coaches account for much of the non-local mileage operated by public service vehicles—this rose by about 6 per cent in 1998–99 to 1,657 million vehicle-kilometres. Organised coach tours and holiday journeys account for about 60 per cent of coach travel in Great

Britain. High-frequency scheduled services, run by private sector operators, link many towns and cities, and commuter services run into London and some other major centres each weekday. The biggest coach operator, National Express, has a national network of scheduled coach services and in 1999 carried 19 million passengers.

Taxis

There are about 63,000 licensed taxis in England and Wales, mainly in urban areas, around 9,000 in Scotland, and about 11,000 in Northern Ireland. In London (which has over 19,000 taxis) and several other major cities, taxis must be purpose-built to conform to strict requirements. In many districts, taxi drivers have to pass a test of their knowledge of the area.

Private hire vehicles with drivers ('minicabs') may be booked only through the operator and not hired on the street. Outside London, private hire vehicles are licensed; there are about 66,000 in England and Wales outside the capital and 8,000 in Scotland. Implementation of the Private Hire Vehicles (London) Act 1998, which for the first time provides the basis for regulating minicab operators, drivers and vehicles in London, is in progress.

RAILWAYS

Railways were pioneered in Britain: the Stockton and Darlington Railway, opened in 1825, was the first public passenger railway in the world to be worked by steam power. Privatisation of railway services in Great Britain was completed in 1997.

Railtrack is responsible for operating all track and infrastructure in Great Britain. Its assets include 32,000 kilometres (20,000 miles) of track; 40,000 bridges, tunnels and viaducts; 2,500 stations; and connections to over 1,000 freight terminals. Apart from 14 major stations operated directly by Railtrack, nearly all stations and passenger depots are leased to the 25 passenger train operating companies which run passenger services under franchise. Operators with two or more franchises include National Express, Prism Rail (which is being taken over by National Express), Virgin Rail, FirstGroup, Connex, Arriva and Stagecoach. The operators lease their rolling stock from the three main rolling stock companies: Angel Trains, HSBC Rail and Porterbrook Leasing. Four companies run freight services. There are a number of infrastructure maintenance companies.

There are also over 100 other passenger-carrying railways, often connected with the preservation of steam locomotives. Services are operated mostly on a voluntary basis and cater mainly for tourists and railway enthusiasts. They generally run on former branch lines, but there are also several narrow-gauge lines, mainly in north Wales.

Rail Regulation

Under the Transport Bill, a new Strategic Rail Authority (SRA) would be established to promote rail use, plan the strategic development of the rail network, work closely with transport providers and promote integration between different types of transport. The SRA would subsume OPRAF (the Office of Passenger Rail Franchising) and the British Railways Board, which are currently operating as the Shadow Strategic Rail Authority (SSRA). It would also acquire the consumer protection functions of the Office of the Rail Regulator, including responsibility for sponsoring the rail users' consultative committees that represent the interests of passengers. The Rail Regulator's other current functions include licensing the railway operators, dealing with agreements governing access by operators to track and stations, and enforcing competition law in connection with the provision of rail services.

The SSRA is currently responsible for negotiating, awarding and monitoring the franchises for operating rail services. Financial support for passenger rail services amounted to approximately £1 billion in 1999–2000. Most franchises are for around seven years, but some are for ten, 12 or 15 years. In June 2000 the SSRA announced changes to the franchise map for Great Britain, in connection with the development of a 20-year strategy for the railways. Three main service groupings (covering long-distance, high-speed services,

Table 22.3: Passenger Traffic on Rail,[1] Underground and Selected Light Rail Services in Great Britain *Million passenger-kilometres*

	1989–90	1994–95	1997–98	1998–99	1999–2000
National railways	33,300	28,700	34,700	36,300	38,300
London Underground	6,016	6,051	6,479	6,716	7,171
Glasgow Underground	39	43	45	47	49
Docklands Light Railway	38	55	103	144	172
Greater Manchester Metro	—	79	88	117	153
Tyne and Wear Metro	319	271	249	238	230
Stagecoach Supertram	—	8	34	35	37

[1] Excludes Heathrow Express.
Source: *Transport Statistics Great Britain 2000 Edition*

London commuter services, and regional services) are being created, which will eventually result in a reduction in the number of franchises to 22. The SSRA's objective is to establish stronger train operating companies with longer franchises and the ability to invest to provide extra capacity to meet the growing demand for travel by rail. Renegotiation of the shorter-term franchises, due to expire by 2004, is expected to be completed by the end of 2001.

Passenger Services

The passenger network (see map facing inside back cover) comprises a fast inter-city network, linking the main centres of Great Britain; local and regional services; and commuter services in and around the large conurbations, especially London and the South East. Passenger traffic is growing (see Table 22.3) and on the national railways rose by 5.5 per cent in 1999–2000 to 38,300 million passenger kilometres, the highest level for over 50 years, representing some 947 million passenger journeys.

Investment

The Government's ten-year plan envisages substantially increased rail investment to provide a large expansion of rail services to meet the growing demand and improve the quality of service to passengers. Over £34 billion of capital investment is envisaged from the private sector and nearly £15 billion from the public sector, of which £7 billion will be provided through the Rail Modernisation Fund. The Fund will allow the SRA and the railway industry to formulate a long-term investment programme and is designed to encourage a much greater level of private sector capital investment. Investment will go towards new rolling stock, modern signalling, safety improvements and the provision of greater capacity by removing bottlenecks. Major projects include modernising the West Coast and East Coast main lines, the Thameslink 2000 project to increase the capacity of north-south services through London, and improved rail links to airports (such as Heathrow and Stansted).

Freight

Rail freight traffic totalled 18.4 billion tonne-kilometres, representing the carriage of 102.8 million tonnes, in 1999–2000. Over 80 per cent of traffic by volume is bulk commodities, mainly coal, coke, iron and steel, building materials and petroleum. The two largest operators are English, Welsh & Scottish Railway (EWS), which also runs trains through the Channel Tunnel to the continent of Europe; and Freightliner, which operates container services between major ports and inland terminals.

The UK Government and the devolved administrations are keen to encourage more freight to be moved by rail, to relieve pressure on the road network and to bring environmental benefits. Grants are available to

Safety

In October 1999 two trains collided at Ladbroke Grove, near London's Paddington station, resulting in 31 deaths and 227 injuries. A public inquiry into the accident is now in progress. The industry is implementing a number of safety measures in the light of two rail safety summits convened by the Government, the report of the public inquiry into an earlier fatal rail accident at Southall in 1997, and regulations already being implemented by the Government. Action includes:

- the fitting of the train protection and warning system (TPWS), which is designed to reduce the risk associated with signals passed at danger, to the Railtrack network by the end of 2003;
- the introduction of automatic train protection (ATP) as lines that are included in the European high-speed network are upgraded;
- the removal of all Mark 1 rolling stock (which does not meet the crash resistance standards of modern rolling stock) by the end of 2002, with some modified stock allowed to remain in service until the end of 2004, by which time all trains with slam doors but without central locking doors will also have been phased out;
- more consistent and better standards for driver training;
- development of a new national safety plan to improve safety management and ensure best practice across the rail network; and
- the transfer from Railtrack to the Health and Safety Executive of responsibility for deciding whether train companies are safe to operate.

encourage companies to move goods by rail or water rather than by road. In 1999–2000, 14 grants were awarded in England and Wales (representing support of nearly £12.5 million). Since July 1999 in Scotland the Scottish Executive has awarded seven grants totalling about £13 million.

Northern Ireland

In Northern Ireland, Northern Ireland Railways, a wholly owned subsidiary of the NITHC (see p. 366), operates the railway service on about 336 kilometres (211 miles) of track and handled 6 million passenger journeys in 1999–2000. A review of rail safety, published in March 2000, found that safety levels were not unreasonable but made a number of recommendations for improvement. In view of the substantial investment required to implement these recommendations, a task force was set up to advise on the options for the future of the rail network in Northern Ireland. An interim report was published in September 2000 and provided advice on four options, which are being considered by the Minister for Regional Development.

Channel Tunnel

The Channel Tunnel was opened to traffic in 1994. It cost about £9 billion and was undertaken by TML (Transmanche Link) on behalf of Eurotunnel, a British-French group, under an operating concession from the British and French governments.

Eurotunnel Services

Eurotunnel operates a drive-on, drive-off shuttle train service, with separate shuttles for passenger and freight vehicles, between terminals near Folkestone and Calais. In 1999 the service carried nearly 3.3 million cars (54 per cent of car traffic on the Dover/Folkestone–Calais route), 839,000 goods vehicles (39 per cent of freight traffic) and 82,000 coaches (34 per cent of coach traffic).

Eurostar Passenger Services

Eurostar high-speed train services are operated jointly by Eurostar (UK) Ltd, French Railways and Belgian Railways under the commercial direction of Eurostar Group.

Frequent services connect London (Waterloo) and Paris or Brussels, taking less than 3 hours and 2 hours 40 minutes respectively. Trains also serve Ashford (Kent), Calais, Lille, Disneyland Paris and, during the winter, Bourg St Maurice in the French Alps. Eurostar handled 7 million passengers in 1999.

The first section of the Channel Tunnel Rail Link is under construction between the Channel Tunnel terminal and Ebbsfleet, near Gravesend (Kent), and should be completed in 2003. Construction work on the second section, from Ebbsfleet to St Pancras (London), is due to begin in summer 2001, and is due for completion by 2007. The whole project is forecast to cost some £5.2 billion. Eurostar trains will be able to travel at speeds of 300 km/h (180 mph), reducing the times for the London–Paris and London–Brussels services to 2 hours 20 minutes and 2 hours respectively.

Underground Railways

In 1863 the world's first Underground railway opened in London. Today London Underground is a major business, serving 275 stations over 408 kilometres (253 miles) of railway. London Underground Ltd will become part of Transport for London in 2001. In 1999–2000, 927 million passenger journeys were made. In 1999 the Jubilee Line Extension was opened, providing a fast link from central London to Stratford (east London) via Docklands and the Millennium Dome at North Greenwich, and is expected to play a major role in the continuing regeneration of the Docklands area.

Under a proposed Public-Private Partnership (PPP), responsibility for maintaining and upgrading London Underground's infrastructure would transfer to the private sector, while London Underground would continue to have responsibility for safety and all aspects of operating passenger services across the Underground network. The private sector would work under contract to London Underground for a 30-year period, after which all the assets would return to the public sector. The PPP is expected to deliver about £8 billion of investment in the network and up to £5 billion of maintenance over 15 years.

The Glasgow Underground, a heavy rapid transit system, operates on a 10-km (6-mile) loop in central Glasgow.

Light Railways and Tramways

Tramways carried over 1 billion passengers in the UK (including Ireland) in 1900, but by around the middle of the 20th century nearly all the tramways had closed, leaving two operators, in Blackpool and Llandudno. However, there has been a revival of interest in tram/light rail services, and the ten-year plan indicates a growing role for tramways, with the provision of up to 25 new lines in major cities and conurbations. A selection of pictures is given between pp. 360 and 361.

The latest operation, opened in May 2000, is the Croydon Tramlink, a 28-km (18-mile) light rail network in south London, linking Wimbledon, Beckenham, Elmers End and New Addington with Croydon town centre. Tramtrack Croydon Ltd (a private sector consortium) built and is operating the network, as a joint undertaking with Transport for London. Also in London the Docklands Light Railway (DLR) connects Docklands with surrounding areas, and is operated under franchise by Docklands Railway Management Ltd. A £200 million extension to Lewisham opened in 1999, extending the network to 26 kilometres (16 miles) with 36 stations. A link to London City Airport is planned and could be opened by 2004.

Four other light rail systems are in operation: the Tyne and Wear Metro, Manchester Metrolink, Stagecoach Supertram (in South Yorkshire) and the Midland Metro. The first stage of the Midland Metro, between Birmingham and Wolverhampton, opened in May 1999, and the extension of the Manchester Metrolink to Salford Quays and Eccles was completed in July 2000. DETR approval has been given for the £100 million extension of the Tyne and Wear Metro to Sunderland, and for the £180 million Nottingham Express Transit system, which will run for 13 kilometres (8 miles) and link Hucknall to the centre of Nottingham from 2003. Approval has also been given for three further extensions, costing over £500 million, of the Manchester Metrolink to Manchester Airport, Oldham and Rochdale, and to Ashton-under-Lyne.

INLAND WATERWAYS

Inland waterways are now used mainly for leisure and general recreation, but they also have a number of other important roles: as a heritage and environmental resource, as a catalyst for regeneration and in land drainage and water supply. Some inland waterways still carry freight.

The inland waterways are managed by about 30 navigation authorities. British Waterways, a public corporation sponsored by the DETR and the Scottish Executive, is the largest, responsible for some 2,600 kilometres (1,600 miles) of fully navigable waterways (see map opposite p. 72), about half the UK total.

In June 2000 the DETR issued *Waterways for Tomorrow*, a policy document setting out the Government's proposals for the future of the waterways. The DETR envisages greater recreational use of, and enhanced access to, the waterways; their wider use as a catalyst for regeneration; encouragement for the transfer of freight from road to waterway; and closer links between British Waterways and other navigation authorities. *Waterways for Tomorrow* encourages partnerships between navigation authorities and the private and voluntary sectors. British Waterways is developing a number of Public-Private Partnerships, including a project to transfer water from the wetter areas in the north-west to drier regions in the south-east of England in times of drought. The Waterways Trust has been created as a charitable trust to promote waterways and raise funds for restoration. The Scottish Executive is planning to publish a policy document for Scottish waterways in 2001. For some examples of waterway use and restoration see the picture section between pp. 72 and 73.

> The Millennium Link project, the largest heritage project in Scotland, will reopen in 2001 the Forth & Clyde Canal and the Union Canal to navigation. New sections of canal are being created, locks refurbished, bridges constructed and a tunnel is being built. The 35-metre high 'Falkirk Wheel' will allow boats to pass between the two canals, so connecting Glasgow and Edinburgh by canal. The total cost of the project is some £78 million, of which £32 million is being financed by a grant from the Millennium Commission and £16 million comes from Scottish Enterprise.

SHIPPING

It is estimated that about 95 per cent by weight (75 per cent by value) of the UK's foreign trade is carried by sea. The UK fleet has declined considerably in tonnage terms in the last 25 years, reflecting changing trade patterns, removal of grants, and greater competition.

At the end of 1999 there were 617 UK-owned merchant trading ships of 100 gross tonnes or more, with a total tonnage of 7.2 million deadweight tonnes. There were 155 vessels totalling 2.7 million deadweight tonnes used as oil, chemical or gas carriers, and 428 vessels totalling 4.4 million deadweight tonnes employed as dry-bulk carriers, container ships or other types of cargo ship, together with 34 passenger ships. In all, 70 per cent of UK-owned vessels (and the same percentage by tonnage) are registered in the UK, the Crown Dependencies or British Overseas Territories such as Bermuda.

The Government is implementing a series of measures which aim to revive the shipping industry and reverse the downward trend in the UK fleet. The Finance Act 2000 provides for a new fiscal regime, under which shipping will be taxed on the basis of tonnage, as occurs in a number of other countries. Other measures include more training and career opportunities for seafarers, and a new 'minimum training obligation', involving a formal commitment by shipping companies to train seafarers as a condition of owners' eligibility for the new tax on tonnage.

Cargo Services

International revenue earned by the UK shipping industry in 1999 was £3.4 billion: £2.7 billion from freight—£2.3 billion on dry cargo and passenger vessels and £429 million on tankers and liquefied gas carriers—£177 million from charter receipts and £463 million from passenger revenue.

Nearly all scheduled cargo-liner services from the UK are containerised. British tonnage serving these trades is dominated by a relatively small number of companies. Besides the carriage of freight by liner and bulk services between the UK and the rest of Europe, many roll-on, roll-off services carry cars, passengers and commercial vehicles.

Passenger Services

Over 50 million passenger journeys a year take place on international and domestic ferry services linking the UK with Ireland and with mainland Europe. Domestic passenger and freight ferry services run to many of Britain's offshore islands, such as the Isle of Wight, Orkney and Shetland, and the islands off the west coast of Scotland. Traffic from southern and south-eastern ports accounts for a large proportion of traffic to the continent.

P&O Ferries is the UK's largest ferry operator, with a fleet of 50 ships operating on 18 routes around the UK coast. Cross-Channel services are operated by roll-on, roll-off ferries, high-speed catamarans and high-speed monohulls. Capacity has been reduced following the merger in 1998 of P&O's cross-Channel operations with those of Stena Line to form P&O Stena Line.

Maritime Safety

The DETR's policies for improving marine safety and pollution control are implemented by the Maritime and Coastguard Agency (MCA), which inspects UK ships and foreign ships using UK ports to ensure that they comply with international safety, pollution prevention and operational standards. In 1999–2000, 106 foreign-flagged ships were detained in UK ports.

In 1999 MCA was alerted to 12,220 incidents, of which 6,721 were accidents requiring search and rescue assistance. In an emergency HM Coastguard co-ordinates facilities, such as its own helicopters; cliff rescue teams; lifeboats of the Royal National Lifeboat Institution (a voluntary body); aircraft, helicopters and ships from the armed forces; and merchant shipping and commercial aircraft.

Some locations around the UK are potentially hazardous for shipping. Measures to reduce the risk of collision include the separation of ships into internationally agreed shipping lanes, as applies in the Dover Strait, one of the world's busiest seaways, which is monitored by radar from the Channel Navigation Information Service near Dover. There are over 1,000 marine aids to navigation around the UK coast and responsibility for these rests with the general lighthouse authorities: Trinity House Lighthouse Service (for England and Wales), the Northern Lighthouse Board (for Scotland and the Isle of Man) and the Commissioners of Irish Lights (which covers the whole of Ireland).

In March 2000 the Government launched the Port Marine Safety Code, designed to ensure the highest standards of marine safety in UK ports. All harbour authorities are being asked to implement the code by the end of 2001.

PORTS

There are about 80 ports of commercial significance in Great Britain, while several hundred small harbours cater for local cargo, fishing vessels, island ferries or recreation. There are three broad types of port: over 90 trust ports owned and run by boards constituted as trusts; those owned by local authorities (predominantly small ports, but including a few larger ones, such as Sullom Voe in Shetland and Portsmouth); and company-owned facilities. Major ports controlled by trusts include Aberdeen, Dover, Milford Haven and Tyne.

Associated British Ports (ABP) is the UK's largest port owner and operates 23 ports, including Cardiff, Grimsby and Immingham, Hull, Ipswich, Newport, Port Talbot, Southampton and Swansea. Altogether they

Table 22.4: Traffic through the Principal Ports of Great Britain *Million tonnes*

	1995	1996	1997	1998	1999
London	51.4	52.9	55.7	57.3	52.2
Grimsby and Immingham	46.8	46.8	48.0	48.4	49.7
Tees and Hartlepool	46.1	44.6	51.2	51.4	49.3
Forth	47.1	45.6	43.1	44.4	45.4
Sullom Voe	38.3	38.2	32.1	31.1	37.7
Southampton	32.4	34.2	33.1	34.3	33.3
Milford Haven	32.5	36.6	34.5	28.8	32.2
Felixstowe	24.0	25.8	28.9	30.0	31.5
Liverpool	30.0	34.1	30.8	30.4	28.9
Dover	12.7	13.2	19.1	17.7	19.4

Source: Department of the Environment, Transport and the Regions

handled 119 million tonnes of cargo in 1999, when ABP invested £65 million in its ports and transport business. Other major facilities owned by private sector companies include Felixstowe, Harwich and Thamesport (all owned by the Hong Kong group Hutchison Whampoa), Clyde, Forth, Liverpool, Medway and Manchester.

The Government is preparing a strategy for the future of the UK ports industry.

Port Traffic

In 1999 traffic through major UK ports (those handling over 2 million tonnes a year) amounted to 533 million tonnes: 194 million tonnes of imports, 178 million tonnes of exports and 161 million tonnes of domestic traffic (which included offshore traffic and landings of sea-dredged aggregates). Minor ports handled an additional 33 million tonnes.

The main ports, in terms of total tonnage handled, are shown in Table 22.4. Forth, Milford Haven and Sullom Voe mostly handle oil, while the principal destinations for non-fuel traffic are London, Felixstowe, Grimsby and Immingham, Tees and Hartlepool, and Liverpool.

Container and roll-on, roll-off traffic through the major ports in the UK was 132 million tonnes in 1999 and now accounts for 85 per cent of non-bulk traffic. The number of units handled rose by 5 per cent in 1999 to 9.8 million: 5.4 million road goods vehicles and unaccompanied trailers, and 4.4 million containers. By far the most important port for container traffic is Felixstowe (which handles 41 per cent of this type of traffic), while Dover is the leading port for roll-on, roll-off traffic. Dover is also the major arrival and departure point, handling around half of international sea passenger movements to and from the UK.

Northern Ireland has four main ports, at Belfast, Larne, Londonderry and Warrenpoint. Belfast handles over 56 per cent of Northern Ireland's seaborne trade.

CIVIL AVIATION

In 1999 UK airlines flew a record 1,381 million aircraft kilometres, 66 per cent higher than in 1989: 947 million kilometres on scheduled services and 434 million kilometres on non-scheduled flights. They carried 65 million passengers on scheduled services and 33 million on charter flights. Passenger seat occupancy was 76 per cent, being much higher on charter flights (89 per cent) than on scheduled services (71 per cent). It is also higher for international flights (77 per cent) than internal services (61 per cent). The DETR is forecasting that demand for air travel at UK airports will grow to between 348 million and 461 million terminal passengers in 2020, with the mid-point of 401 million passengers representing an increase of 150 per cent compared with 1998.

UK airlines are entirely in the private sector, as are many of the major airports. Day-to-day responsibility for the regulation of civil aviation rests with the Civil Aviation Authority (CAA). A series of studies on regional airports has been undertaken, and a study of airport issues in south-east and east England is in progress. These will contribute to the development of a White Paper which will provide a long-term framework for the future of civil aviation and airports in the UK.

Airlines

British Airways

British Airways is the UK's biggest airline and one of the world's largest international airlines. During 1999–2000 its turnover from airline operations was £8.9 billion, and the British Airways group carried 46.6 million passengers, achieving a passenger load factor of 70 per cent on its main scheduled services. The airline's scheduled route network serves 188 destinations and its main operating bases are London's Heathrow and Gatwick airports.

British Airways was one of the founders, together with American Airlines, Canadian International Airlines, Cathay Pacific and Qantas, of the 'Oneworld' alliance in February 1999. The alliance now has nine member airlines and serves 641 scheduled destinations in 135 countries.

The British Airways group has a fleet of 366 aircraft, including seven Concordes, 85 Boeing 737s, 72 Boeing 747s, 53 Boeing 757s, 33 Boeing 777s and 27 Boeing 767s. Ten Airbus A320s and 20 A319s are in service, with a further 20 and 33 respectively on order.

Other UK Airlines

British Midland is the second largest scheduled carrier and operates an extensive network of scheduled services with 40 aircraft, which carried 6.5 million passengers in 1999. Britannia Airways is the world's biggest charter airline and carried 8.2 million passengers in 1999 on its 28 aircraft. Virgin Atlantic operates scheduled services to 20 overseas destinations with 29 aircraft. Low-fare, 'no-frills' airlines are expanding their services. Operators in the UK include EasyJet (which operates 28 routes in six European countries and has three European hubs—Luton, Liverpool and Geneva) and the British Airways subsidiary Go.

Airports

Of over 150 licensed civil aerodromes in the UK, nearly one-quarter handle more than 100,000 passengers a year each. In 1999 the UK's civil airports handled a total of 169.6 million passengers (168.5 million terminal passengers and 1.2 million in transit), and 2.2 million tonnes of freight.

Passenger traffic has been growing at the UK's main airports (see Table 22.5). Heathrow is the world's busiest airport for international travellers and is the UK's most important for passengers and air freight, handling 62 million passengers (excluding

Table 22.5: Passenger Traffic at the UK's Main Airports[1] *Million passengers*

	1989	1994	1997	1998	1999
London Heathrow	39.6	51.4	57.8	60.4	62.0
London Gatwick	21.1	21.0	26.8	29.0	30.4
Manchester	10.1	14.3	15.7	17.2	17.4
London Stansted	1.3	3.3	5.4	6.8	9.4
Birmingham	3.3	4.8	5.9	6.6	6.9
Glasgow	3.9	5.5	6.0	6.5	6.8
Luton	2.8	1.8	3.2	4.1	5.3
Edinburgh	2.4	3.0	4.2	4.5	5.1
Belfast International	2.2	2.0	2.5	2.6	3.0
Newcastle	1.5	2.4	2.6	2.9	2.9
Aberdeen	1.7	2.2	2.6	2.7	2.5
East Midlands	1.5	1.6	1.9	2.1	2.2

[1] Terminal passengers, excluding those in transit.
Source: Civil Aviation Authority

those in transit) and 1.3 million tonnes of freight in 1999. Gatwick is the world's sixth busiest international airport and has the world's busiest single runway.

Ownership and Control

BAA plc is the world's largest commercial operator of airports. Its airports handle almost 200 million passengers a year. In 1999–2000 its seven UK airports—Heathrow, Gatwick, Stansted and Southampton in southern England, and Glasgow, Edinburgh and Aberdeen in Scotland—handled 116.8 million passengers. Overseas, BAA manages all or part of eight airports: four in the United States, Naples Airport in Italy, Melbourne and Launceston airports in Australia, and Mauritius. It also manages commercial facilities at its airports, and is a major international duty-free retailer.

The UK's second largest operator is TBI, which has an interest in 29 airports worldwide, including Belfast International and Cardiff. Manchester and Newcastle airports are among those owned by local authorities.

All UK airports used for public transport and training flights must be licensed by the CAA for reasons of safety. Stringent requirements, such as adequate fire-fighting, medical and rescue services, have to be satisfied before a licence is granted.

Airport Development

Investment to expand passenger facilities is in progress at many UK airports. At Heathrow BAA has invested over £960 million in the last five years. A £100 million redevelopment of departure facilities at Terminal 3 is scheduled for completion in 2002. BAA's plans for a fifth terminal, which could eventually cater for 30 million passengers a year, have been considered by a public inquiry. If approval is granted, the new terminal could be operational by 2007. Expansion at Gatwick's two terminals over the next ten years is designed to raise annual capacity to around 40 million passengers. A second runway at Manchester Airport is expected to be operational early in 2001.

Stansted is the fastest growing major airport in Europe. Traffic rose by over a third in 1999 to 9.4 million passengers, and has doubled in the last four years. It now serves 90 destinations, including 25 new routes added during 1999–2000. Five low-cost scheduled carriers operate from the airport, accounting for 53 per cent of flights, and have made a significant contribution to increased traffic. BAA is investing over £200 million at Stansted in the next five years to increase its capacity to around 15 million passengers a year. Work began in February 2000 on an extension to the terminal and this is due to open in 2002, while a further extension is due for completion in 2004.

Among other large-scale improvements at UK airports are:

- a major £260 million expansion plan at Birmingham Airport, which will increase its capacity to 10 million passengers a year;
- a £54 million redevelopment programme at Edinburgh Airport; and
- a £30 million expansion scheme at Belfast City Airport over the next five years.

Air Traffic Control

Civil and military air traffic control over the UK and the surrounding seas, including much of the North Atlantic, is undertaken by National Air Traffic Services Ltd (NATS), working in collaboration with military controllers. NATS is currently a subsidiary of the CAA. Under the Transport Bill, it would be separated from the CAA (which would retain responsibility for air safety regulation) and established as a Public-Private Partnership. The Government's intention is to sell 51 per cent of NATS to the private sector, and this is planned for early 2001.

To cope with the rapid growth in air traffic, NATS is planning to replace the three existing UK centres for civil and military *en route* air traffic control operations at Prestwick, Manchester and West Drayton (near Heathrow) by two major centres. Swanwick (Hampshire) is due to open in 2002, while a new Scottish centre at Prestwick will replace the existing centre in 2006–07.

Air Safety

The CAA is responsible for safety standards on UK airlines. It certifies aircraft and air crews, licenses air operators and air travel organisers, and approves certain air fares and airport charges. To qualify for a first professional licence, a pilot must undertake a full-time course of instruction approved by the CAA—or have acceptable military or civilian flying experience—and pass ground examinations and flight tests. Every company operating aircraft used for commercial air transport purposes must possess an Air Operator's Certificate, which the CAA grants when it is satisfied that the company is competent to operate its aircraft safely. All aircraft registered in the UK must be granted a certificate of airworthiness by the CAA before being flown. The CAA works closely with the Joint Aviation Authorities (JAA), a European grouping of aviation safety regulation authorities.

The DETR's Air Accidents Investigation Branch investigates accidents and serious incidents occurring in UK airspace and those that happen overseas to aircraft registered or manufactured in the UK.

Communications

TELECOMMUNICATIONS

Telecommunications is one of the most rapidly expanding sectors of the UK economy. Growth has been particularly strong in new services, notably mobile telephones and services provided over the Internet. In the UK nearly 400 licences have been issued to more than 300 different providers. According to OFTEL (see below), turnover of the UK telecommunications market (including fixed and mobile networks and telecommunications equipment companies) was some £31.5 billion in 1999–2000, 17 per cent higher than in 1998–99. The market has become more competitive, with greater choice of suppliers for consumers, an expanding range of services and lower prices. Competitors to BT have increased their share of the market, especially the business market.

Services

Telephone traffic is growing quickly. Calls from fixed links were 13 per cent higher in 1999–2000, at 196.6 billion call minutes, than in 1998–99 (see Table 22.6). There are nearly 34 million fixed lines. A telephone is one of the most widely available consumer durable goods in the home. According to the 1998 ONS General Household Survey, an estimated 96 per cent of households had a telephone. In a survey for OFTEL, published in April 2000, over 97 per cent of the UK population had access to either a fixed or mobile telephone at home. This survey found that a significant and growing number of people preferred to use a mobile telephone rather than a fixed-line telephone as they favoured the former's flexibility and the ability to be contactable at all times. Around 5 per cent of homes now have a mobile telephone instead of a fixed line. By the end of March 2000 there were over 27 million mobile telephone users, 83 per cent more than a year earlier (see Table 22.6), and by September 2000 the number had risen to over 33 million.

Regulation

OFTEL (the Office of Telecommunications), a non-ministerial government department headed by the Director General of Telecommunications, is the independent regulatory body for the telecommunications industry. Its functions include ensuring that licensees comply with the conditions of their licences and promoting effective competition. Two major recent projects have been encouraging the early introduction of high-speed information services and cheaper Internet access for consumers.

Rapid developments in the sector are changing the emphasis of OFTEL's work. In

The use of the Internet in the UK is growing very rapidly. According to the ONS Family Expenditure Survey, over the first three months of 2000 an average of 6.5 million households (25 per cent of households) in the UK could access the Internet from a home computer, about twice the number a year earlier. However, many more people use the Internet, for example, at work, in education establishments and in libraries; 98 per cent of secondary schools and 86 per cent of primary schools in England are connected to the Internet, according to the Department for Education and Employment.

According to a separate ONS survey, the Omnibus Survey, conducted in July 2000, 45 per cent of adults have accessed the Internet, equivalent to 20.4 million adults. In this latter survey, among those who had accessed the Internet for personal use only, about seven in ten had used the Internet for e-mail and a similar proportion to find information about goods and services, with just over a quarter buying or ordering tickets, goods or services, and around two-thirds had used the Internet for general browsing or surfing.

There are over 400 Internet service providers (ISPs). Freeserve is the biggest ISP and has some 2 million registered users. Internet access is now becoming available by other means, for example, through the television, while ADSL (asymmetric digital subscriber line) technology will provide residential and business customers with much faster services.

Table 22.6: Telecommunications Statistics

	Call minutes 1999–2000 (million)	Per cent increase in call minutes 1999–2000 over 1998–99	Per cent increase in revenue 1999–2000 over 1998–99
Fixed link[1]			
Local calls	87,827	*–4.5*	*–8.5*
National calls	46,664	*–0.6*	*–6.1*
International calls	6,066	*4.2*	*–3.9*
Calls to mobile telephones	8,741	*53.3*	*17.3*
Other calls	47,314	*97.6*	*17.0*
All calls[2]	196,612	*12.7*	*2.0*
Cellular services			
UK calls	24,503	*74.8*	
Outgoing international calls	291	*78.5*	
Calls while abroad	655	*44.9*	
All calls	25,449	*73.9*	

	Number (thousands)		
	31 March 1999	31 March 2000	Per cent increase
Fixed link exchange connections	32,829	33,750	*2.8*
Cellular network subscribers	14,878	27,185	*82.7*

[1] Local, national and international only calls include simple voice calls. Other calls include number translation services, premium rate calls, directory enquiries, operator calls, the speaking clock, public payphones and calls to ISPs.

[2] Figures may include a small amount of double counting, as in some instances calls supplied by an operator to a reseller may be counted by both operator and reseller.

Source: *OFTEL Annual Market Information Report 1999–00*

January 2000 it announced a new strategy for regulation, looking particularly at circumstances where some formal or informal regulatory action is needed to protect consumers' interests.

Government proposals for changing the regulatory framework will be included in a White Paper on communications, due to be issued later in 2000. The Government's aim is to create a dynamic market for the UK's broadcasting and telecommunications industries and to promote their global competitiveness (see p. 268).

Service Providers

The three largest UK telecommunications companies are:

- *BT*, which became a private sector company in 1984, runs one of the world's largest public telecommunications networks, including about 20 million residential lines and 8.5 million business lines. It has over 6,000 local telephone exchanges and an optical fibre network of 4.6 million kilometres, and employs 136,000 people. Turnover in 1999–2000 totalled £21.9 billion. In April 2000 it announced a major restructuring of its global operations, including creating six new operations: Ignite (an international broadband network); BTopenworld (its international Internet business); BT Wireless (international mobile communications, including BT Cellnet—see p. 379); Yell (international directory enquiries and e-commerce operations); BT Wholesale (the UK network business) and BT Retail (serving UK business and residential customers). These new businesses operate both within the UK and internationally, working alongside Concert, BT's global venture with AT&T of the United States. Concert's global network reaches a total of 237 countries and territories.
- *Vodafone* has become the UK's biggest company by market capitalisation (see p. 386), following two main takeovers: the acquisition in 1999 of the US mobile telephone group AirTouch and the takeover in February 2000 of the German group Mannesmann. It is the UK's largest mobile telephone operator in terms of the number of subscribers (see p. 379) and has over 50 million customers worldwide through its operations in 25 countries. Turnover in 1999–2000 was £12.5 billion. Vodafone is working on developing advanced Internet application technologies so that customers will be able to access a much wider range of services on its mobile telephones.
- *Cable & Wireless* has operations in 70 countries and employs over 35,000 people. The company has adopted a new strategy to concentrate on the business sector, especially in Internet Protocol (IP), data and other advanced services, and has sold other non-strategic parts of the business, including its interest in Hongkong Telecom and the consumer business of Cable & Wireless Communications. It now has three main divisions: Cable & Wireless Global, as its main operation for delivering services to business customers in the United States, Europe (including the UK) and Japan; Cable & Wireless Optus (its Australian business); and Cable & Wireless Regional (for its businesses in the Caribbean and other areas of the world). In May 2000 it completed the first stage of its single global high-capacity IP network for delivering integrated IP, data, voice and messaging communications. The company has acquired 13 ISPs in Europe as well as other IP-related assets, and expects to have at least 20 web-hosting centres in operation around the world within two years, designed to provide customers with faster and better websites and advanced e-commerce applications.

Following a substantial consolidation among the cable operators, the two main companies are NTL (which acquired the residential interests of Cable & Wireless Communications in 2000) and Telewest. By the end of March 2000 cable operators had installed around 4.8 million telephone lines in the UK, and over 12 million homes were able to receive broadband cable services.

Mobile Communications

Mobile telephony continues to grow strongly. This rapid growth can be put down to the introduction of easier methods of payment, such as pre-paid, and the reduction in the cost of handsets. Pre-paid telephones now account for 80 per cent of sales, with a typical handset selling for less than £50. The first 'wireless application protocol' (WAP) telephones, which enable users to access the Internet and information services, are now on sale.

There are four network suppliers:

- Vodafone (with 9.4 million customers in mid-2000);
- BT Cellnet (8.1 million);
- Orange (7.2 million), which has been acquired by France Telecom; and
- One 2 One (6.0 million), a subsidiary of Deutsche Telekom.

In addition, there are around 50 independent service providers.

In 2000 the Government held an auction for licences to run systems to provide the next generation of mobile telephone services, known as 'third generation'. These will provide users with high-speed access to the Internet, e-mail facilities, video conferencing and access to a large number of information services. Bids for the five licences available totalled £22.5 billion. Licences were won by the four existing operators, with the licence reserved for a new entrant going to a subsidiary of TIW of Canada.

In 1999 Dolphin Telecommunications, the fifth mobile operator, launched the first mobile telephone network using the TETRA (Trans European Trunk Radio) technology, which allows enhanced services and functionality, including advanced speech, data facilities and direct mode communications.

POSTAL SERVICES

The Post Office, founded in 1635, pioneered postal services and was the first to issue adhesive postage stamps as proof of advance payment for mail. Today, its Royal Mail service delivers to 26 million addresses in the UK, handling around 80 million items each working day. In 1999–2000 it processed 18.9 billion inland letters and 861 million outgoing international letters. Mail is collected from about 113,000 posting boxes, and from post offices and large postal users. Its International Services uses 1,400 flights a week to send mail direct to 280 postal 'gateways' worldwide. The Post Office employs 200,000 people.

The rapid growth of electronic communications is having only a limited effect on Royal Mail traffic, mainly in the consumer market. The volume of domestic letters rose by about 4.6 per cent in 1999, and direct mail was up by 10 per cent. High-speed mail-handling machinery—the Integrated Mail Processor—has cut substantially the sorting time for processing letters. Automatic sorting utilises the information contained in the postcode; the UK postcode system allows mechanised sorting down to part of a street on a delivery round and, in some cases, to an individual address.

Parcelforce Worldwide provides a door-to-door overnight delivery service throughout the UK and an international service to 239 countries and territories. It handles 140 million items a year. Parcelforce Worldwide is modernising the facilities for handling parcels. Two new sorting centres in Coventry—one for international parcels and the other for domestic traffic—were opened in autumn 1999 and April 2000 respectively. When fully operational, they will form one of the largest and most modern distribution centres in Europe, handling some 50,000 items an hour.

In 1999 the Post Office acquired German Parcel, the third largest private carrier in Germany. In March 2000 it announced a joint venture with TNT Post Group of the Netherlands and Singapore Post to create the world's biggest international mail partnership; the Post Office will have a 24.5 per cent stake in the venture.

Postal Services Policy

Government reforms for the modernisation of the Post Office and for giving it greater commercial freedom were set out in a White Paper in July 1999 and are being implemented through the Postal Services Act 2000. The Act will establish the Post Office as a public limited company under government ownership, promote competition and stronger regulation, and define the duties and powers of a new independent regulator, the Postal Services Commission. Other measures in the Act will provide for the protection of the obligation to offer a universal postal service at a uniform tariff with daily weekday deliveries to every UK address, protect the nationwide network of post offices, and create a new Consumer Council for Postal Services.

Post Offices

The nationwide network of Post Office branches handles a wide range of transactions, with a total value of £160 billion in 1999–2000. It acts as an agent for Royal Mail and Parcelforce Worldwide, government departments, local authorities and Alliance & Leicester Giro and other banks' banking services. There are about 18,400 post offices in the UK, of which nearly 600 are operated directly by the Post Office. The remainder are franchise offices or are operated on an agency basis by sub-postmasters. A £1 billion investment programme in automation will involve the installation of modern computer systems in all post offices by spring 2001. In June 2000 the Government announced financial support for modernising the Post Office network, including the creation of a new Universal Bank aimed particularly at those who do not currently have a bank account, and support to prevent further closures of post offices in rural areas and deprived urban areas.

Private Courier and Express Services

Private sector couriers and express operators are allowed to handle time-sensitive door-to-door deliveries, subject to a minimum fee, currently of £1. The Government has asked the Postal Services Commission to advise on the size of the 'reserved area' (that part of the postal market which will require a licence from the Commission).

Further Reading

The Integrated Transport Bill: The Executive's Proposals. Scottish Executive, 2000.

Moving Forward. Northern Ireland Transport Policy Statement. Department of the Environment for Northern Ireland, 1998.

A New Deal for Transport: Better for Everyone. Cm 3950. The Stationery Office, 1998.

Post Office Reform: A world class service for the 21st century. Department of Trade and Industry. Cm 4340. The Stationery Office, 1999.

Tomorrow's Roads: Safer for Everyone. DETR, 2000.

Transport 2010: The 10 Year Plan. DETR, 2000.

Transporting Wales into the Future. Welsh Office, 1998.

Transport Statistics Great Britain, annual report. The Stationery Office.

Travel Choices for Scotland. Cm 4010. The Stationery Office, 1998.

Waterways for Tomorrow. DETR, 2000.

Websites

Department of the Environment, Transport and the Regions: www.detr.gov.uk

National Assembly for Wales: www.wales.gov.uk

Northern Ireland: www.nics.gov.uk

Scottish Executive: www.scotland.gov.uk

23 The Economy

The Government's economic policies are directed towards the achievement of high and stable levels of growth and employment, with the aim of increasing opportunity and enabling everyone to share in rising living standards. From a platform of economic stability, the Government is seeking to raise productivity and sustainable growth—by increasing skills, promoting enterprise and innovation, creating strong and competitive markets, and enhancing the legal and regulatory framework for the protection of consumers.

Growth in the UK economy continued for the eighth consecutive year in 1999. Gross domestic product (GDP) at constant market prices strengthened during the year, with quarterly growth rising from 0.3 per cent at the beginning of 1999 to an average of 0.9 per cent in the third and fourth quarters. Employment growth remained firm throughout, even during the temporary slowdown in GDP growth at the start of the year which stemmed, at least in part, from the global economic slowdown in 1998. Retail price pressure remained subdued in 1999. Underlying inflation was below the Government's target from April onwards, and averaged 2.3 per cent in the year as a whole.

STRUCTURE AND PERFORMANCE

The value of all goods and services produced in the UK economy for final consumption is measured by gross domestic product. In 1999 GDP at current market prices—'money GDP'—totalled £891 billion. Average annual growth in GDP at 1995 market prices over the past five years has been 2.9 per cent a year (see also Table 23.1). Values for two of the main economic indicators, inflation and GDP, are shown in the charts on p. 382.

Output

GDP grew by 2.1 per cent in 1999. Rapid growth in domestic demand was partly offset by a weaker net trade position. The actions of the Bank of England in progressively reducing interest rates from 7½ per cent in mid-1998 to 5 per cent in summer 1999 helped to buoy consumer confidence at a time when global and UK prospects had deteriorated.

HM Treasury, and independent forecasters, expect higher growth in 2000: GDP is forecast in the 2000 Budget to rise by between 2¾ and 3¼ per cent in 2000 as a whole, and by between 2¼ and 2¾ per cent in both 2001 and 2002. Over the long term, economic growth has averaged around 2¼ per cent a year.

In 1999, at constant basic prices—that is, adjusted for inflation, and excluding taxes and subsidies on products—the output of the

RPI Inflation, UK (All Items)

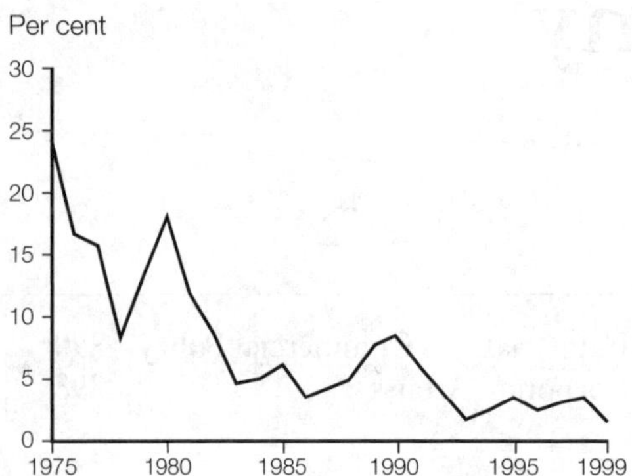

Source: Office for National Statistics

Percentage Change in GDP at 1995 Market Prices, UK

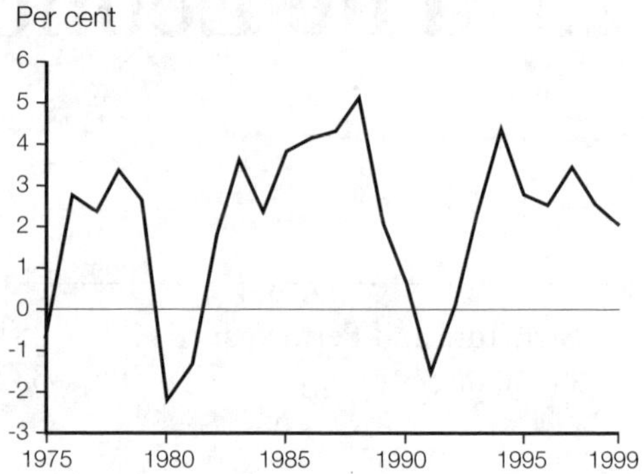

Source: Office for National Statistics

Table 23.1: Gross Domestic Product and Gross National Income *£ million*

	1989	1994	1998	1999
Final consumption expenditure	420,366	570,923	706,590	750,027
Gross capital formation	113,719	111,234	153,019	156,772
Total exports	121,883	178,767	225,474	229,649
Gross final expenditure	655,968	860,924	1,085,083	1,136,448
less Total imports	–142,690	–183,330	–233,429	–244,878
Statistical discrepancy	—	—	—	–464
GDP at current market prices	**513,278**	**677,594**	**851,654**	**891,106**
Gross national income at current market prices	**509,047**	**682,300**	**862,462**	**896,257**
GDP at 1995 market prices	**655,174**	**694,616**	**777,937**	**794,366**
GDP index at 1995 market prices (1995 = 100)	**91.8**	**97.3**	**109.0**	**111.3**

Source: *United Kingdom National Accounts 2000—the Blue Book*

service industries increased by 2.9 per cent, with particularly strong growth in transport, storage and communication (7.7 per cent) and business services and finance (3.7 per cent). The situation in manufacturing, in contrast, was less strong: although manufacturing output grew in each of the three quarters after the first quarter, output for 1999 as a whole was unchanged on the previous year.

Recent decades have generally seen the fastest growth in the service sector (see chapter 30) and this pattern continued during the 1990s. Manufacturing (see chapter 28) now contributes around 22 per cent of GDP, compared with over a third in 1950.

Over the past 25 or so years the UK has experienced lower economic growth than its major competitors. In the 1970s, according to OECD figures, average annual GDP growth was 1.9 per cent compared with 3.0 per cent in the EU and 3.3 per cent in the G7 countries. In the 1980s, annual growth of 2.7 per cent was slightly above the EU average of 2.4 per cent but a little below the G7 average of 3.0

Table 23.2: Output by Industry

	Gross value added at current basic prices 1999 (£ million)	% of gross value added 1999	% change in gross value added 1990–99 at 1995 basic prices
Agriculture, hunting, forestry and fishing	9,332	1.2	2.4
Mining and quarrying	17,976	2.3	47.3
Manufacturing	147,699	18.8	4.6
Electricity, gas and water supply	17,944	2.3	26.4
Construction	41,273	5.2	–4.4
Wholesale and retail trade	92,539	11.8	26.9
Hotels and restaurants	25,015	3.2	0.0
Transport, storage and communication	69,208	8.8	53.7
Financial intermediation	45,303	5.8	14.7
Adjustment for financial services	–30,411	–3.9	27.0
Real estate, renting and business activities	176,568	22.4	41.2
Public administration and defence	40,199	5.1	–7.2
Education	41,788	5.3	16.4
Health and social work	51,453	6.5	42.1
Other services	41,498	5.3	38.3
Total gross value added	787,386	100.0	21.2
Intermediate consumption at purchasers' prices	895,425		
Total output at basic prices	1,682,811		

Source: *United Kingdom National Accounts 2000—the Blue Book*

per cent. By the 1990s, UK growth was the same as for the EU, at 2.0 per cent a year in the period 1990–97, although slightly below the G7 average of 2.4 per cent.

Household Income and Expenditure

Total resources of the households sector—including non-profit institutions serving households—rose by 5.2 per cent in 1999 to £874 billion. Gross disposable income—after deductions, including taxes and social contributions—totalled £600 billion. In 1995 prices, real households' disposable income—that is, the amount of money the household sector has available for spending after taxes and other deductions—was 3.4 per cent higher, at over £543 billion, in 1999 than in 1998. Household net financial wealth grew strongly in 1999, amounting to £2,233 billion. Wages and salaries accounted for almost 60 per cent of household primary income in 1999 and rose by 6.2 per cent during the year.

In 1999, 95.0 per cent of after-tax household income was spent. Households' saving ratio—saving as a percentage of total available households' resources—fell slightly between 1998 and 1999, from 5.8 to 5.0 per cent, after the higher levels seen in previous years.

Household final expenditure—that is, spending by the household sector on products or services to satisfy their immediate needs or wants—accounted for just over 75 per cent of the total £750 billion final consumption expenditure in 1999, amounting to £564 billion at current market prices. In constant price terms, it grew by 4.4 per cent. Expenditure on services remained relatively strong, rising by 4.3 per cent in 1999, and expenditure on durable goods was 6.8 per cent higher than in 1998.

Table 23.3: Household Final Consumption Expenditure

	Expenditure in 1990 (£ million)[1]	Expenditure in 1999 (£ million)[1]	% of expenditure in 1999[1]	% change in expenditure at constant 1995 prices, 1990–99
Durable goods				
Cars, motorcycles and other vehicles	19,034	27,649	4.9	13.9
Other durable goods	15,483	27,218	4.8	86.5
Total	**34,517**	**54,867**	**9.7**	**45.2**
Non-durable goods				
Food	41,817	54,862	9.7	11.1
Alcohol and tobacco	30,009	44,611	7.9	–11.7
Clothing and footwear	21,212	33,530	5.9	56.8
Energy products	22,422	28,861	5.1	–1.5
Other goods	39,659	72,867	12.9	42.7
Total	**155,119**	**234,731**	**41.6**	**18.5**
Services				
Rent, water and sewerage charges	36,543	77,916	13.8	11.6
Catering	30,076	48,708	8.6	9.9
Transport and communication	30,969	54,390	9.6	37.1
Financial services	13,856	25,917	4.6	28.7
Other services	35,412	67,840	12.0	34.3
Total	**146,856**	**274,771**	**48.7**	**22.9**
Total	**336,462**	**564,369**	**100.0**	**23.3**

[1] At current market prices.
Source: *United Kingdom National Accounts 2000—the Blue Book*

Table 23.3 shows the changing pattern of households' final consumption expenditure. Over the longer term, as incomes rise, people tend to spend increasing proportions of their disposable income on durable goods and certain services. Spending on leisure pursuits and tourism, communications, health and financial services have all shown significant growth in recent years. Declining proportions are being spent on alcohol and tobacco, and energy products.

Investment

Gross fixed capital formation represents investment in assets which are used repeatedly or continuously over a number of years to produce goods, such as machinery used to create a product. Following growth of 10.1 per cent in 1998, investment at constant 1995 prices increased by 6.1 per cent in 1999 to £153.3 billion (see Table 23.4). Business investment, at constant prices, grew by 7.6 per cent in 1999 to reach a record high proportion of GDP, at 14.3 per cent. Within business investment, the 24.9 per cent rise in private sector other services more than offset a 14.7 per cent fall in manufacturing investment.

UK whole economy investment has accounted for a smaller share of GDP than other industrialised countries—around 17 per cent of GDP, compared with the OECD average of 21 per cent—but high levels of business investment in recent years have helped to narrow the gap.

General government investment rose by 3.1 per cent in 1998 and by 0.5 per cent in 1999, and is forecast by HM Treasury to rise at between 17.5 and 20 per cent in each of the next three years, reflecting the Government's

Table 23.4: Gross Fixed Capital Formation at Constant 1995 Prices *£ million*

	1989	1994	1998	1999
New dwellings, excluding land	27,096	22,267	23,231	23,522
Other buildings and structures	29,966	32,923	33,952	36,136
Transport equipment	13,734	11,927	14,913	16,256
Other machinery and equipment and cultivated assets	44,665	38,171	63,833	68,701
Intangible fixed assets	3,645	3,631	4,156	3,988
Costs associated with the transfer of ownership of non-produced assets	4,810	4,123	4,352	4,669
Gross fixed capital formation	**122,158**	**113,042**	**144,437**	**153,272**
of which:				
Business investment	80,671	70,947	105,866	113,899
General government	11,152	15,255	9,993	10,038
Public corporations	–297	2,059	1,679	1,698
Private sector	31,863	24,781	26,899	27,637

Source: *United Kingdom National Accounts 2000—the Blue Book*

commitment to the renewal and modernisation of the public sector capital stock (see also p. 402).

International Trade

International trade plays a key role in the UK economy (see chapter 25). The UK is the fifth largest exporter of goods and services, and exports accounted for 25 per cent of GDP in 1999. Other EU countries took nearly 59 per cent of UK exports of goods in 1999 and supplied almost 54 per cent of imported goods.

The UK's current account deficit (see p. 414) deteriorated sharply from £0.1 billion in 1998 to £11.0 billion in 1999. This partly reflected a reduction in exports to economies affected by the South East Asia crisis, but more recently strong imports as well. The deficit on trade in goods rose to £26.8 billion, but was partly offset by the combined effects of surpluses on both trade in services (£11.5 billion) and on investment income (£8.1 billion).

Business Structure

The UK has around 3.7 million businesses. They include many big companies. According to a *Financial Times* survey of the top 500 European companies in January 2000, 146 were UK-based, with a market capitalisation of some $2,269 billion (£1,380 billion). There are around 3,500 UK businesses employing over 500 people, representing 39 per cent of total employment by UK businesses and 41 per cent of turnover. A small number of large companies and their subsidiaries are responsible for a substantial proportion of total production in some sectors. This is particularly true for chemicals, pharmaceuticals, motor vehicle assembly and aerospace. Of the top 20 UK companies by market capitalisation (as at 24 April 2000), four are in the retail banking sector, five in telecommunications and three in pharmaceuticals (see Table 23.5).

Expenditure on company acquisitions overseas by UK companies reached a record level of £108.8 billion in 1999, almost double the amount in 1998, which had itself been a record. The largest reported transactions included the acquisition of AirTouch Communications Inc of the United States by Vodafone Group plc and of Astra AB of Sweden by Zeneca plc. Acquisitions in the UK by overseas companies also reached a record level—£60.1 billion—almost twice that achieved in 1998, the major acquisition being that of Orange plc by Mannesmann AG. Mannesmann was subsequently acquired in

Table 23.5: Top UK Companies by Market Capitalisation, 2000[1]

Company/ business sector	Market capitalisation (£ million)[2]
Vodafone AirTouch[3]/ telecommunications	184,780.7
BP Amoco/oil and gas	120,939.0
British Telecommunications/ telecommunications	72,289.5
Glaxo Wellcome[4]/ pharmaceuticals	71,349.4
HSBC Holdings/retail banking	60,689.2
AstraZeneca/ pharmaceuticals	50,232.6
SmithKline Beecham[4]/ pharmaceuticals	49,445.5
Shell Transport & Trading Company/oil and gas	47,917.5
Lloyds TSB Group/ retail banking	36,219.3
British Sky Broadcasting Group/cable and satellite	29,221.5
Royal Bank of Scotland/ retail banking	24,842.2
Cable & Wireless/ telecommunications	24,717.2
Barclays/retail banking	24,374.9
Marconi/IT hardware	20,430.0
COLT Telecom Group/ telecommunications	19,522.6
Prudential/life assurance	18,367.7
Diageo/alcoholic beverages	18,352.9
Reuters Group/publishing & printing	16,008.8
Tesco/food & drug retailers	14,483.9
Cable & Wireless Communications[5]/ telecommunications	13,730.9

[1] As at 24 April.
[2] Market capitalisation represents the number of shares issued multiplied by their market value.
[3] Now Vodafone.
[4] Due to merge later in 2000.
[5] See p. 378 for the change in status of this company.
Source: *FT 500 Survey*

2000 by Vodafone AirTouch for a reported £101.2 billion.

Small firms play an important part in the UK economy: around 44 per cent of the workforce work for companies employing fewer than 50 people. Around 2.3 million businesses are sole traders or partners without employees, while a further 963,600 businesses employ one to four people. Together these 3.3 million enterprises account for 89 per cent of the number of businesses, over 23 per cent of business employment and 16 per cent of turnover.

Private sector firms predominate in the economy. The public sector has become much less significant following the privatisation since 1979 of many public sector businesses, including gas, electricity supply, coal and telecommunications. The remaining major nationalised industries are the Post Office, BNFL (British Nuclear Fuels) and the Civil Aviation Authority.

Inflation

There are three main measures of retail price inflation used in the UK:

- the Retail Prices Index (RPI), which is the main domestic measure of inflation in the UK. It measures the average change from month to month in the prices of goods and services purchased by most households in the UK and is commonly called 'headline' inflation;
- the RPI excluding mortgage interest payments (RPIX), which is used to calculate 'underlying' inflation and is the target measure set by the Government (see p. 388); and
- the harmonised index of consumer prices (HICP), which is calculated for each member state of the European Union for the purposes of European comparisons; it is also used to derive inflation rates for the eurozone and the EU as a whole.

Underlying annual inflation (RPIX) in the last 20 years or so has fluctuated considerably, with a peak of 20.8 per cent in the year to May 1980. However, it was much lower in the

1990s, and since 1993 has been in a relatively narrow range, from around 2 per cent to 3.5 per cent. In 1999 it averaged 2.3 per cent—the RPI was only 1.5 per cent—and it has been consistently below the Government's target of 2.5 per cent since April 1999.

Producer input prices for materials and fuel purchased by manufacturing industry rose by 12.5 per cent in the year to December 1999 having fallen by around 9 per cent in each of the two previous years. Generally the index has risen since then, and is approaching levels last seen early in 1997, which largely reflects rises in crude oil prices. Producer output price inflation has been gradually rising since the end of 1998, with prices of UK manufactured goods rising at an annual rate of between 2½ and 3 per cent in mid-2000.

During 1999, the 'all items' RPI low average percentage change reflected falling prices for household goods, clothing and footwear, leisure goods, fuel and light, and food, some of which were lower than the previous year. Housing costs also rose considerably less than in 1998, mainly due to reductions during the first half of the year in mortgage interest payments. The higher levels of duty and increases in manufacturers' prices counteracted these falls and gave above average rises in prices for tobacco, and petrol and oil. Towards the end of 1999 and the beginning of 2000, mortgage interest payments were increasing.

In 1999 inflation according to the HICP for the UK was 1.3 per cent, compared with an EU average of 1.2 per cent. During the first half of 2000 the UK's HICP was well below the EU average, averaging 0.8 per cent compared with 2.1 per cent in the EU as a whole, partly as a consequence of the weak euro.

Labour Market

Employment in the UK continued to grow in the year to July 2000, with ongoing falls in unemployment. Latest figures show that employment—at 28.0 million in the three months to July—was at a record high level, 354,000 higher than in the same period a year earlier (see chapter 11). Economic inactivity fell as more people found jobs or sought work. Unemployment also continued to fall, and at 1,580,000 in the three months to July 2000 was 166,000 lower than a year earlier, according to International Labour Organisation (ILO) measures. This represented 5.3 per cent of the workforce, well below the latest figure currently available (8.3 per cent) for all European Union countries and the lowest UK rate since 1984. Long-term (over two years) and youth unemployment have both declined.

ECONOMIC STRATEGY

The main elements of the Government's economic strategy, set out in the November 1999 Pre-Budget Report, which is designed to deliver high and stable levels of economic growth and employment, are:

- delivering macroeconomic stability;
- meeting the productivity challenge;
- increasing employment opportunity for all (see chapter 11);
- ensuring fairness for families and communities; and
- protecting the environment.

HM Treasury is the department with prime responsibility for the Government's monetary and fiscal frameworks. It is also responsible for wider economic policy, which it carries out in conjunction with other government departments, such as Trade and Industry; Education and Employment; and the Environment, Transport and the Regions.

Government policy on UK membership of the European single currency (see p. 79) remains as set out by the Chancellor of the Exchequer in 1997, and restated by the Prime Minister in February 1999. The determining factor underpinning any government decision is whether the economic case for the UK joining is clear and unambiguous. The Government has set out five economic tests which will have to be met before any decision to join can be taken. These tests are:

- sustainable convergence between Britain and the economies of the single currency;
- whether there is sufficient flexibility to cope with economic change;

- the effect on investment;
- the impact on the UK financial services industry; and
- whether it is good for employment.

The Government has said that making a decision, during this Parliament, to join, is not realistic. It intends to make another assessment of the five economic tests early in the next Parliament.

Economic Stability

The Government considers that economic stability is vital for the achievement of its central economic objective of high and stable levels of growth and employment. It has introduced new frameworks for the operation of both monetary and fiscal policy to achieve low and stable inflation and sound public finances. In the Government's view, the co-ordination of monetary and fiscal policy is very important. The Government ensures co-ordination by setting mutually consistent objectives for monetary and fiscal policies.

The Bank of England's Monetary Policy Committee (see p. 511) is responsible for setting interest rates to meet the Government's inflation target of 2.5 per cent, as defined by the 12-month change in RPIX.

Interest rates peaked at $7\frac{1}{2}$ per cent in 1998, compared with a peak of 15 per cent in 1990 in the previous economic cycle. Interest rates have remained at 6 per cent since February 2000.

International Stability

The UK Government plays an active role in international efforts to maintain global prosperity, and prevent and resolve crises. The G7 Declaration of October 1998, under the UK presidency, provided a comprehensive blueprint for reform of the international financial architecture, designed to promote economic and financial stability. The key reforms include measures to:

- strengthen and reform the international financial institutions, including the International Monetary Fund, World Bank and multilateral development banks;
- enhance transparency and promote best practices, by implementing a range of agreed codes and standards;
- strengthen financial regulation, including the establishment of the Financial Stability Forum (see p. 511);
- strengthen macroeconomic policies and financial systems in emerging markets;
- improve crisis prevention and management, and involve the private sector; and
- promote social policies to protect the poor and most vulnerable.

The G7 Finance Ministers' report from Fukuoka (Japan) in July 2000 shows that much progress has been achieved. The UK is committed to ensuring that the reform process continues.

Fiscal Policy

The *Code for Fiscal Stability*, set up under the Finance Act 1998, requires fiscal and debt management policy to be carried out in accordance with five key principles:

- *transparency* in setting fiscal policy objectives, the implementation of fiscal policy and the presentation of the public accounts;
- *stability* in the fiscal policy-making process and in the way that fiscal policy affects the economy;
- *responsibility* in the management of the public finances;
- *fairness*, including between present and future generations; and
- *efficiency* in the design and implementation of fiscal policy, and in managing both sides of the public sector balance sheet.

Consistent with these principles, the Government established objectives for fiscal policy as:

- over the medium term, to ensure sound public finances and that spending and taxation have an impact fairly, both within and across generations; and

- over the short term, supporting monetary policy where possible through the operation of the 'automatic stabilisers' and, where prudent and sensible, changes in the fiscal stance.

To meet these objectives, the operation of fiscal policy is guided by two strict rules, set out in HM Treasury's Economic and Fiscal Strategy Report (see below), against which its performance may be judged:

- the golden rule—over the economic cycle, the Government will borrow only to invest and not to fund current spending; and
- the sustainable investment rule—public sector net debt as a proportion of GDP will be held over the economic cycle at a stable and prudent level.

These rules aim to ensure that, over the course of an economic cycle, each generation pays for the public services they use, and that public borrowing is kept under firm control.

The fiscal policy framework is being strengthened by a new way of planning and controlling public expenditure—Resource Accounting and Budgeting (RAB). RAB will ensure that the full economic cost of government activities is measured properly by including other costs not reflected in cash-based accounts. RAB will, for the first time, require departments to report systematically on how their resources are allocated to their aims and objectives, and on what is achieved as a result. This is intended to provide the Government with a better basis for deciding on the allocation of resources and improve transparency, by making it easier to see what taxpayers are getting for their money.

The Budget

The Budget is the Government's main economic statement of the year and is usually issued in March. In a major speech to Parliament, the Chancellor of the Exchequer reviews the nation's economic performance and describes the Government's economic objectives and economic policies it intends to follow in order to achieve them. The 2000 Budget report comprised two documents:

- the *Economic and Fiscal Strategy Report*, setting out the Government's long-term strategy and objectives; and
- the *Financial Statement and Budget Report*, providing a summary of each Budget measure and an analysis of the economic and public finance forecasts.

In advance of the spring Budget, the Government now publishes a Pre-Budget Report, usually in the previous November. As well as setting out economic and fiscal developments and prospects, it describes the direction of government policy and sets out for consultation measures under consideration for the forthcoming Budget.

The Spending Review

In the 1998 Comprehensive Spending Review, the Government introduced a new framework for public spending. The main elements of the reforms (see also chapter 24) are set out below:

- the annual Public Spending Survey has been replaced with firm plans set for three years, through Departmental Expenditure Limits. Where expenditure cannot be planned on a multi-year basis, it is subject to annual scrutiny as part of the Budget process; such expenditure is denoted Annually Managed Expenditure. This gives departments greater certainty when planning expenditure and allows the Government to take a more strategic look at the effectiveness of public spending;
- spending is separated into capital and resource (formerly current) budgets with tight controls on transfers from capital to resource spending to ensure short-term pressures do not squeeze out essential investment;
- underspending within Departmental Expenditure Limits in a given year can be carried over to the following year, assisting departments in managing their budgets and avoiding wasteful end-of-year spending surges;
- the National Asset Register and departmental investment strategies will help to improve the utilisation of existing assets and the planning of new capital

investment and ensure that the public sector does not hold on to assets which are surplus to its requirements;

- public service agreements detail the outcomes departments will deliver with the funds provided; and
- cross-departmental reviews have been introduced to tackle problems such as crime, drugs and social exclusion, with joint working across departments. Fifteen cross-departmental reviews were conducted in the 2000 Spending Review.

INDUSTRIAL AND COMMERCIAL POLICY

The Department of Trade and Industry (DTI) aims to increase UK competitiveness and scientific excellence in order to generate higher levels of sustainable growth and productivity. It has four specific objectives:

- to promote enterprise, innovation and higher productivity;
- to make the most of the UK's scientific, engineering and technological capabilities;
- to create strong and competitive markets; and
- to develop a fair and effective legal and regulatory framework.

Measures to help achieve these objectives are described below. DTI responsibilities on export promotion are covered in chapter 25, technology and innovation in chapter 26, and consumer protection in chapter 30, while those on industrial relations are described in chapter 11.

Competitiveness

The Government set out its industrial policy in the White Paper on competitiveness, *Our Competitive Future: Building the Knowledge Driven Economy*, published in 1998. The Government's aim is for UK business to close the performance gap with its competitors, both in terms of productivity and its ability to produce innovative new products and create high-value services.

In December 1999 the DTI published the first in an annual series of UK competitiveness indicators. The indicators are to be used to track the UK's performance as a knowledge-driven economy and monitor progress in closing the productivity gap with other advanced economies. The first assessment showed that in many respects the UK was beginning to succeed as a knowledge-driven economy, but in some areas it still had some way to go to achieve the standards of the best. Overall the assessment showed that the UK's GDP per head was around the EU average but 18 per cent below the average for the G7 group of countries. Although the UK had a relatively good performance on employment, its productivity performance was disappointing. Among the UK's strengths highlighted in the report were:

- improved prospects for economic stability;
- an economy open to international trade and investment;
- a high proportion of people in work;
- a strong science base, with UK research highly regarded around the world;
- good performance in some key knowledge-intensive sectors (such as aerospace, pharmaceuticals and the creative industries); and
- a growing recognition by business of the importance of information and communications technology (ICT) and of investing in ICT.

Areas identified as having scope for improvement included innovation performance, management skills, basic skills (such as literacy and numeracy), and attitudes to entrepreneurship.

Enterprise, Innovation and Business Support

The DTI promotes enterprise and innovation through encouraging successful business start-ups and offering businesses a number of support services. Most support is designed to assist business, especially small and medium-sized enterprises (SMEs), to expand and invest, and to adopt best practice.

The Small Business Service (SBS), a new DTI agency, was established in April 2000. Its main tasks are to:

- act as a strong voice for small businesses within government;
- simplify and improve government support for small firms; and
- help small businesses deal with regulation, and ensure that their interests are considered in future regulations.

The SBS is responsible for the future development of the 'Business Link' network of local partnerships that are the main mechanism for delivering business information, advice and support in England. The network brings together the business support activities of many chambers of commerce, enterprise agencies, training and enterprise councils (see p. 149), and local authorities to provide a single local point of access for integrated information and advisory services tailored to the needs of businesses. It has nearly 1,000 personal business advisers and specialist counsellors for export development, design, and innovation and technology. From April 2001 the SBS will have a network of 45 local outlets.

In the March 2000 Budget the Government announced a £60 million series of measures to encourage SMEs to adopt information technology (IT) and electronic commerce ('e-commerce'). This includes £20 million for the SBS to develop a new business advice service, which will be available on the Internet and by telephone from April 2001.

Elsewhere in the UK similar business support arrangements apply:

- in lowland Scotland, the new Small Business Gateway offers a package of measures designed to improve on the quality and consistency of public sector support for new and small businesses in the Scottish Enterprise area, while Highlands and Islands Enterprise, through its Business Information Source, operates equivalent services to those that are available through the Small Business Gateway;
- in Wales, Business Connect covers all the main business support agencies and has a network of business support and front-line advice centres; and
- in Northern Ireland small firms are helped by the Local Enterprise Development Unit's network of regional offices.

Queen's Awards for Enterprise

The Queen's Awards Scheme was originally instituted in 1966 to recognise outstanding performance by UK firms. Following a review in 1999, the Scheme was renamed The Queen's Awards for Enterprise. Under the first of the new Awards, announced in April 2000, 116 companies received Awards: 77 for International Trade, 32 for Innovation and seven for Environmental Achievement (see picture section between pp. 488 and 489 for some examples of Award winners). Awarded annually, they are valid for five years and are granted by the Queen on the advice of the Prime Minister, who is assisted by an advisory committee consisting of senior representatives from business, trade unions and government departments. Any self-contained 'industrial unit' in the UK with at least two full-time employees is eligible to apply so long as it meets the Scheme's criteria. Winners are entitled to display the Award Emblem on their goods, packaging, advertising and letter headings.

Business Finance

An Enterprise Fund has been established to provide financial support for SMEs with growth potential. It consists of three elements:

- the Small Firms Loan Guarantee Scheme which, by offering a government guarantee against default by the borrower, aims to encourage banks and others to lend to people lacking security or a business track record;
- a UK High Technology Fund to make investments in existing funds that support growth businesses in the high-technology sector; and
- Regional Venture Capital Funds to provide smaller amounts of equity finance to growth businesses.

Other measures aimed at improving small firms' access to finance include:

- providing capital to new and existing Community Finance Initiatives—these are usually local non-profit-making organisations that lend to people starting and running businesses in disadvantaged areas who cannot obtain bank loans;
- supporting the National Business Angels Network to enable it to become the national network through which SMEs seeking smaller equity investments can be put in touch with informal investors, or 'business angels';
- consulting on a range of options for supporting new knowledge-based businesses (which, as they may not have tangible assets to support them, face particular difficulties in obtaining bank finance and are generally too young and small to be of interest to venture capitalists); and
- working to raise awareness of corporate venturing.

These initiatives are being taken forward by the Small Business Service with the support and advice of a Small Business Investment Taskforce composed of representatives of banks and other finance providers, accountancy bodies, academics and representatives of small firms.

Information and Communications Technology

The Government is keen to ensure that the UK benefits fully from the rapid developments in ICT, including the growth of the Internet (see p. 377) and of 'e-commerce'. Already, the UK leads the world in some areas, such as digital terrestrial broadcasting and the implementation of third generation mobile telephone services. Around 1.7 million SMEs are online, compared with 600,000 in 1999.

The Government's e-commerce strategy is to ensure that the UK is the best environment in the world to do business electronically, and that, by 2005, there will be universal access within the UK, with everyone who wants it having access to the Internet. The Office of the 'e-Envoy' was set up to take forward this strategy. Its work will include developing and reviewing strategic thinking on e-commerce, involving business in facing the challenges of e-commerce, spreading the benefits throughout society, ensuring e-Government, promoting the UK's e-commerce strategy overseas and monitoring progress.

> Public services are being modernised to take advantage of the benefits of ICT. More services, such as NHS Direct (see p. 189), are being provided online. A Cabinet Office Performance and Innovation Unit study of public services, launched in September 2000, is looking at how to accelerate the electronic delivery of better services. Government purchasing arrangements are increasingly using electronic means (see p. 403). The Office of the e-Envoy's e-Communications Team (which is responsible for the strategy and marketing of the Government's online presence, 'UK online') is working closely with other government departments to improve the design, access to, and navigation around government websites. A portal, or a single electronic point of access, for government information and services—ukonline.gov.uk—will be launched in autumn 2000.

The DTI is working to ensure that all UK businesses make the best use of ICT to enhance their competitiveness. Some £60 million is being invested to encourage more SMEs to connect to the Internet. This includes £30 million to develop a secure electronic interface linking government, business and the public and an extra £10 million for the DTI's UK online for business initiative (previously known as the Information Society Initiative), which is providing businesses with practical advice and training to enable them to exploit the opportunities for doing business electronically.

Substantial investment in education and training is being undertaken to improve the level of skills and give everyone the opportunity to obtain the skills required for ICT. The Government is providing £1.7 billion for its national IT strategy, including support from the New Opportunities Fund (see p. 117). Many schools already have access to the Internet, and by 2002 all the UK's 23,000 schools should be connected, with training in computers available for 400,000 teachers. Up to 1,000 ICT learning centres are to be established, and all schools, libraries, colleges and universities are to be linked via the Internet through the National Grid for Learning (see p. 131) by 2002. The University for Industry (see p. 140), to be launched in autumn 2000, is creating a national online and distributed learning network aimed at both individuals and businesses. Its initial priorities are basic skills, ICT skills, and business skills for SMEs.

The Electronic Communications Act 2000 has modernised the law to facilitate the development of electronic trading. By giving legal recognition to electronic signatures, it allows electronic communications and storage as a substitute for pen and paper. It also creates a voluntary approvals system for businesses providing electronic signature and similar services, to ensure that messages remain confidential and cannot be changed in transit. The Act contains reserve powers for the Government to introduce a statutory scheme if self-regulation does not work satisfactorily.

The Government is promoting a co-ordinated approach to e-commerce in the European Union. The EU is working towards having a basic regulatory framework governing e-commerce in place by the end of 2000. Within the UK the Government is reviewing barriers to competition in e-commerce, and taking action to remove them and enhance competition.

Millennium Bug

Action was taken to deal with the 'Millennium Bug', the potentially serious problem primarily affecting some older IT systems and electronic equipment when the year changed from 1999 to 2000. A report by the Cabinet Office,[1] published in April 2000, outlined the detailed planning across the Government and the national infrastructure, and found that no material disruption occurred in the UK. Central government spent some £380 million, and over 300,000 critical systems were checked. Some 39 per cent of expenditure was by the Ministry of Defence, where 35 per cent of systems needed to be fixed and 18 per cent required major work. The Government also spent £58 million on 'Action 2000', a company which raised awareness and provided practical advice to businesses. Action 2000 set up a National Infrastructure Forum bringing together the major providers of essential services to share best practice. The Cabinet Office is now taking into account the experience obtained in tackling the Millennium Bug in pursuing the reforms in the 'Modernising Government' programme (see p. 57).

Design

The Design Council, funded by the DTI, is the UK's national authority on design. It is an independent organisation promoting the effective use of design and design management techniques for the creation of successful new products, services, processes and opportunities. The Design Council's activities are directed towards developing tools and initiatives for business, education and government to enhance their design practice. It works with Business Links, Scottish Design, the Welsh Design Advisory Service and the Northern Ireland Design Directorate on national initiatives.

From 2000 onwards one of its main initiatives will be 'Sharing Innovation', a nationwide programme that aims to help organisations learn from each other. The programme is based on the analysis of over 1,000 'Millennium Products', an initiative launched in 1997 which demonstrates the range of innovative British products and services. The Millennium Products and the stories behind them are being featured in international exhibitions during 2000 and 2001.

---

[1] *Modernising Government in Action: Realising the Benefits of Y2K.* Cabinet Office. The Stationery Office, 2000.

Quality and Standards

Quality is important throughout the business cycle—design, production, marketing and delivery to customers. Conformity assessment is a key part of the quality infrastructure encompassing certification of products, processes, services and personnel to indicate that they meet certain criteria, such as standards and technical regulations. Conformity assessment conducted by third-party organisations can provide an impartial assessment, which is given greater emphasis when these bodies are themselves accredited by an authoritative body. In the UK the United Kingdom Accreditation Service is recognised by the Government as the sole national accreditation body, and companies that use accredited conformity assessment bodies in certain areas are entitled to use the national accreditation mark—the 'tick and crown'.

The DTI is responsible for policy relating to the National Measurement System, which provides many of the measurement standards and associated calibration facilities necessary to ensure that measurements in the UK are made on a common basis and to the required accuracy in order to meet the needs of UK business, innovation and science (see p. 435).

British Standards Institution

The British Standards Institution (BSI) is the national standards body and is independent of the Government. It works with business, consumers and the Government to produce standards relevant to the needs of the market and suitable for public purchasing and regulatory purposes. The Kitemark is BSI's registered product certification trade mark. Government support for BSI is directed particularly towards European and international standards, which account for over 90 per cent of its work.

Regional Development

The Government's regional policy is designed to promote economic growth and competitiveness in all areas of the UK, working in partnership with businesses, local authorities, voluntary groups and others. A key element is the promotion of inward investment (see p. 423). Where additional help is needed, it is focused on the Assisted Areas.

Regional Selective Assistance (RSA), the main instrument of government support to industry in the Assisted Areas in Great Britain, is now focusing support more on high-quality, knowledge-driven projects providing skilled jobs. In 1999–2000 the DTI offered an estimated £111 million on RSA grants in England, covering 838 projects with the expected creation or safeguarding of around 35,270 jobs; total investment in the projects is expected to be £1.2 billion. A new Enterprise Grant scheme has been established in England, with a budget of £45 million over three years to provide grants to growing SMEs investing in the Assisted Areas and other specified areas with particular needs. Following a review of the Assisted Areas, the new areas took effect in July 2000, covering some 16.5 million people in Great Britain as well as the whole of Northern Ireland.

England

Nine new Regional Development Agencies (RDAs) are now operating in England (see also chapter 2), including the London Development Agency, which was established in July 2000. Their statutory purpose is to further enhance economic development and regeneration; to promote business efficiency, investment, competitiveness and employment; to enhance the development and application of skills and to contribute to the achievement of sustainable development. The eight RDAs outside London have developed regional economic strategies demonstrating how they plan to improve regional economic performance. The strategies include proposals for regional activity to support business clusters and networks, to promote enterprise and growing SMEs, to encourage inward investment, to develop business–university links, and promote e-commerce. RDAs are working with other bodies, such as the Government Offices for the Regions, chambers of commerce, the SBS and Business Links.

Financial support available to the RDAs to stimulate development includes:

- a Competitiveness Development Fund, providing £10 million over the three years to 2002, for RDAs to address priorities for improving business competitiveness in their regions;
- an Innovation Clusters Fund to provide support of £50 million in 2000–02 for the development of business 'clusters'—businesses can benefit from shared infrastructure and close links to training and research institutions, and clusters tend to be conducive to the creation and development of small start-up firms;
- a Regional Innovation Fund providing £115 million in 2001–04 for RDAs to promote regional competitiveness, including key innovative clusters, innovation and economic development; and
- new regional venture capital funding (see p. 391).

Scotland

In Scotland the Scottish Executive Enterprise and Lifelong Learning Department, which has overall responsibility for development of the Scottish economy, operates a range of schemes to support business. Emphasis is given to the links between education and enterprise. Scottish Enterprise and Highlands and Islands Enterprise are the lead economic development agencies in lowland and highland Scotland respectively, operating mainly through the network of LECs (see p. 149). Their duties include:

- promoting industrial efficiency and competitiveness;
- attracting inward investment and encouraging exports;
- giving financial and management support to new businesses and helping existing ones to expand;
- improving the environment by reclaiming derelict and contaminated land; and
- increasing job opportunities and skills.

In February 2000 the Scottish Executive launched a wide-ranging review on the future of the enterprise networks, including their structure, functions and activities. In June 2000 it published the first Framework for Economic Development in Scotland. The interim conclusions of the review of enterprise networks were presented to the Scottish Parliament in July 2000. A strategy on enterprise is to be produced, while access to business support services will be improved through the new Small Business Gateway (see p. 391) and local economic forums will be developed to consider local needs within the national framework.

Wales

The purposes of the Welsh Development Agency (WDA—see p. 355) are to further economic and social development, promote efficiency in business and international competitiveness, and improve the environment of Wales. It is focusing on developing stronger regional 'clusters' of firms, increasing standards and efficiency, and helping Welsh companies to exploit new technology. The WDA's programmes are being developed in line with *A Better Wales* (see p. 31) and the new national economic development strategy, due to be issued in the first half of 2001. It is co-ordinating an Entrepreneurship Action Plan, with the aim of fostering a stronger enterprise culture in Wales; this is being linked to the Enterprise Insight campaign (see p. 400).

In January 2000 the National Assembly for Wales announced a major review of business support and development programmes. The review is considering their effectiveness, the roles of the WDA and Business Connect, how to achieve the maximum benefit from inward investment, and proposals for a development bank and the financial needs of new and growing businesses. The Assembly is currently setting up a development fund, to be called Finance Wales (which is expected to be in operation by December 2000), to offer appropriate finance and management support to SMEs in Wales.

Northern Ireland

In Northern Ireland support for industrial development is implemented through:

- the Industrial Development Board, which deals with overseas companies considering Northern Ireland as an investment location, as well as the development of local companies with more than 50 employees;
- the Local Enterprise Development Unit, which promotes enterprise and the development of small businesses;
- the Industrial Research and Technology Unit, which provides advice and assistance on R&D, innovation and technology transfer; and
- the Business Support Division of the Department of Enterprise, Trade and Investment, which helps with in-company training and management development.

European Union Regional Funding

The EU seeks to promote economic and social cohesion, reducing disparities between the regions and countries of the Union. The principal responsibility for helping poorer areas remains with national authorities, but the EU complements schemes, targeting the worst affected areas through its Structural Funds, including the European Regional Development Fund (ERDF), which support regional competitiveness, training, economic development and innovation.

The UK is due to receive over £10 billion from the Funds in 2000 to 2006. Funding will support a range of projects, designed to encourage businesses to grow, create suitable conditions for inward investment and new jobs, assist the most disadvantaged areas and the socially excluded, and help people to learn new skills.

The highest level of assistance is available to areas with 'Objective 1' status, where GDP is less than 75 per cent of the EU average. In the UK about £3 billion is allocated to four Objective 1 areas: Cornwall, Merseyside, South Yorkshire, and West Wales and the Valleys. In recognition of the special position of Northern Ireland and the structural problems faced by the Highlands and Islands, both of which used to have Objective 1 status, they are eligible for special transition packages, with funding levels broadly equivalent to Objective 1 status.

Aid is also available to areas qualifying for 'Objective 2' status, which cover industrial and urban areas in need of regeneration, declining rural areas, and depressed areas dependent on fisheries. About 13.8 million people in the UK are in Objective 2 areas and a further 6 million benefit from transitional programmes.

Competitive Markets

The Government seeks to improve the openness and effectiveness of markets, both within the UK and internationally, and believes that effective competition is the best stimulus to innovation and efficiency.

Competition Act 1998

The Competition Act 1998, which came fully into effect in March 2000, strengthened competition law. It is modelled on EC competition law and provides a strong deterrent against anti-competitive practices and agreements such as cartels, and against abuse of a dominant market position. The Act prohibits agreements, practices and conduct which have a damaging effect on competition. Where necessary, anti-competitive action can be halted while detailed investigations are made. The main enforcement authority is the Director General of Fair Trading (head of the Office of Fair Trading—OFT). The Act is also enforced by the utility regulators in their sectors. A company found to be infringing the Act may be liable to a maximum penalty of up to 10 per cent of its UK turnover for each year of the infringement, up to a maximum of three years. Competing firms and customers adversely affected by anti-competitive behaviour in breach of the law are entitled to claim for damages in the courts.

Agreements do not fall within the scope of the Act unless they have as their object or effect an appreciable prevention, restriction or distortion of competition. In general, an agreement is unlikely to be considered as having an appreciable effect if the combined market share of the parties to the agreement is less than 25 per cent, unless it is one of a network of agreements that have a cumulative effect on the market concerned. Agreements to fix prices, to impose minimum resale prices or to share markets are generally seen as capable of having an appreciable effect even where the combined market share is below 25 per cent. In determining whether or not an undertaking is in a dominant market position, the OFT, as a general rule, is unlikely to consider an undertaking as dominant if its market share is under 40 per cent.

The Competition Commission, which replaced the Monopolies and Mergers Commission (MMC) in 1999, has two main arms:

- a reporting arm, which took on the existing investigatory functions on monopolies and mergers previously exercised by the MMC; and
- an Appeal Tribunals arm, which hears appeals against decisions of the Director General of Fair Trading and the regulators on the prohibitions of anti-competitive agreements and abuse of a dominant position.

Monopolies

The framework under the Fair Trading Act 1973 for dealing with scale and complex monopolies[2] has been retained alongside the Competition Act. The Director General of Fair Trading and those utility regulators which have parallel powers to apply the monopoly provisions of the 1973 Act may examine such monopolies and make a reference to the Competition Commission to establish whether a monopoly operates, or may be expected to operate, against the public interest.

[2] A scale monopoly situation exists where a single company (or a group of interconnected companies) supplies or acquires at least 25 per cent of the goods or services of a particular type in all or part of the UK. A complex monopoly situation exists where a group of companies which are not connected and together account for at least 25 per cent of the supply of, or acquisition of, any particular description of goods or services in all or part of the UK engage in conduct which has, or is likely to have, the effect of restricting, distorting or preventing competition.

The Competition Commission's report on the supply of cars, published in April 2000, found that prices of new cars in the UK had recently been about 10 to 12 per cent higher than in similar European countries—France, Germany and Italy—and that, after taking account of discounts and other finance deals, private car buyers were paying about 10 per cent too much for a new car. A complex monopoly situation operated in favour of 17 suppliers, each with 1 per cent or more of the total supply of new cars in the UK. The Commission recommended substantial changes to the distribution of new cars, especially in the relationship between manufacturers and dealers. In response to the report, the Government introduced measures, which came into force in September 2000, to bring more competition to the supply of new cars and so help reduce prices. It is also discussing with the European Commission some of the issues raised, as there is an EC block exemption which permits many of the practices criticised by the Competition Commission.

Mergers

A merger generally qualifies for investigation if it involves the acquisition of assets of more than £70 million or the creation or enhancement of a 25 per cent share of the supply or acquisition of a particular good or service in the UK or a substantial part of it. Qualifying mergers are considered by the Director General of Fair Trading, who then advises the Secretary of State for Trade and Industry on whether the merger should be referred to the Competition Commission. There is a voluntary procedure for pre-notification of proposed mergers. In general, the Secretary of State will make a reference to the Competition Commission where the merger raises competition concerns. In rare cases a merger reference may be based on other public interest issues. Alternatively, the Secretary of State may ask the Director General to obtain suitable undertakings from the companies involved to remedy the adverse effects identified. Most mergers are cleared without being referred to the Competition Commission.

If the Competition Commission finds that a merger could be expected to operate against the public interest, the Secretary of State can prohibit it, allow it, or allow it subject to certain conditions being met. Where the merger has already taken place, action can be taken to reverse it. There are special provisions for newspaper and water company mergers.

In October 2000 the Goverment published its response to the consultative document issued in 1999 on reforming the regulation of mergers. It confirmed that, as proposed in the consultative document, it will reform the system so that decisions will normally be taken by the competition authorities against a competition-based test. Ministers will only be involved in making decisions in a small minority of cases where specified exceptional public interests, such as national security, are at issue.

Certain mergers with an EC dimension, assessed by reference to turnover, come under the exclusive jurisdiction of the European Commission. The Commission can ban mergers if it concludes that they would create or strengthen a dominant position which would significantly impede effective competition within the EU or a substantial part of it; alternatively, it may negotiate undertakings to correct the adverse effect.

Utility Competition and Regulation

The Government is reforming competition and regulation among the privatised utilities, with the aim of promoting the interests of consumers and delivering further price reductions. The Government expects the Utilities Act 2000 to deliver these aims in the electricity and gas industries (see p. 499); changes are also being made to the regulatory arrangements for the railways (see p. 367).

EU Single Market

The Government is working with the European Commission and other member states to ensure effective competition within the single market. It is looking to improve the functioning of the single market (see p. 420) through wide-ranging economic reforms, which target 'weak areas' (those areas where the single market does not work as well as it could) identified by the Commission. On the transposition of EC legislation into UK law, the Government is working towards meeting its target of implementing 98 per cent of single market measures by the end of 2000.

CORPORATE AFFAIRS

Corporate Structure

There are just over 1.5 million 'live' companies registered in Great Britain with the Registrar of Companies. Companies incorporated overseas with a place of business or branch in Great Britain must also register. Most corporate businesses are 'limited liability' companies, where the liability of members is restricted to contributing an amount related to their shareholding (or to their guarantee where companies are limited by guarantee). The Limited Liability Partnerships Act 2000 will allow firms the flexibility to incorporate with limited liability while organising themselves as partnerships; the legislation is likely to come into force in early 2001.

Companies may be either public or private; just over 15,000 are public limited companies (plcs). A company must satisfy certain conditions before it can become a plc. It must be limited by shares and meet specified minimum capital requirements. Private companies are generally prohibited from offering their shares to the public.

Company Law and Corporate Governance

Company law is designed to meet the need for proper regulation of business, to maintain open markets and to create safeguards for those wishing to invest in companies or do business with them. It takes account of EC Directives on company law, and on company and group accounts and their auditing.

The DTI has initiated a fundamental review of company law to produce a modern framework which encourages both competitiveness and accountability. The review is overseen by an independent steering group of experts, which will present its final report and recommendations to the Government in spring 2001. In March 2000 the steering group issued its second strategic consultative document. It contained proposals on company governance (the main rules governing the operation and control of companies, including directors' duties, the role of shareholders in company governance, and the accounting and reporting regime) for reforming the law for private companies and for a separate form of incorporation for charitable companies.

The Government is proposing to improve the arrangements for company insolvency. Under the Insolvency Bill now before Parliament, small firms in short-term financial difficulties would be given time to produce a rescue plan for their creditors without fear of legal action, and the process of disqualifying unfit company directors would be speeded up. In April 2000 the Government announced proposals to modernise the law on bankruptcy, to distinguish between the dishonest and those who fail to save their business for reasons beyond their control (such as insufficient funds) despite their best efforts; for the large majority of bankrupts whose failure is honest, a much earlier discharge from bankruptcy is envisaged.

The Government believes that greater business involvement in corporate social responsibility (CSR) can make an important contribution to addressing social problems, can help to tackle deprivation and promote a fairer, more inclusive society. Some businesses have found that greater involvement in CSR can be linked to improved competitiveness. Many government departments are engaged in work to promote CSR. In March 2000 one of the DTI's ministers was given additional responsibilities for work across government to promote Corporate Social Responsibility, help make the business case for CSR; and co-ordinate activity across the Government to promote CSR.

Regulation of Business

In its *Modernising Government* White Paper, issued in 1999 (see p. 57), the Government announced a new policy on removing unnecessary regulation. The proposed Regulatory Reform Bill would provide a new mechanism for reforming regulatory regimes affecting business and other sectors. The Cabinet Office's Regulatory Impact Unit ensures that all proposals for regulations are fully assessed before their introduction and that the benefits justify the costs. Each government department has a minister responsible for its regulatory reform programme, and these ministers are called to account by the Panel for Regulatory Accountability, which is chaired by the Minister for the Cabinet Office. An independent Better Regulation Task Force advises the Government on action to improve the effectiveness and quality of existing regulations, while making sure that they remain necessary, are fair, affordable, and simple to understand and administer.

Industrial Associations

The Confederation of British Industry (CBI) is the largest business organisation in the UK. With a membership comprising companies and trade associations, it directly and indirectly represents some 200,000 firms which employ some 7.5 million people. The CBI's objective is to help create and sustain the conditions in which business can compete and prosper. Examples of its work include lobbying to minimise the burden of regulation and campaigning to spread best practice. The CBI also offers a wide range of advisory services, including a series of regular surveys on the outlook for the UK economy. It is the British member of the Union of Industrial and Employers' Confederations (UNICE). In addition to its London headquarters, the CBI has 13 regional offices and an office in Brussels.

Chambers of commerce represent business views to the Government at national and local levels. They promote local economic development, for example, through regeneration projects, tourism, inward investment promotion and business services, including overseas trade missions, exhibitions and training conferences. The British Chambers of Commerce represents about 120,000 businesses through 60 approved chambers of commerce. It offers commercial and export-related services to its members.

The Institute of Directors (IOD) has around 53,000 members in the UK. It provides business advisory services on matters affecting company directors, such as corporate management, insolvency and career counselling, and represents the interests of members to authorities in the UK and EU. In May 2000 it announced a plan to provide business centres for SMEs in over 20 UK cities; the first is expected to open in Bristol in autumn 2000.

The Federation of Small Businesses is the largest pressure group promoting the interests of the self-employed and small firms. The Federation has 155,000 members, and provides them with expert information and guidance on subjects such as taxation, employment, health and safety, and insurance.

Enterprise Insight

Enterprise Insight is a new initiative launched in 2000 to encourage more entrepreneurial attitudes among young people aged five to 30 and develop their entrepreneurial skills. The initiative, which is supported by the Government, is led by a company owned jointly by the British Chambers of Commerce, the Institute of Directors and the Confederation of British Industry. Up to 1,000 'ambassadors' from business will help to develop closer links between schools and the business community.

Trade associations represent companies producing or selling a particular product or group of products. They exist to supply common services, regulate trading practices and represent their members in dealings with government departments. For information on trade associations and trade unions see chapter 11.

Further Reading

Prudent for a Purpose: Working for a Stronger and Fairer Britain: Economic and Fiscal Strategy Report and Financial Statement and Budget Report March 2000. HM Treasury. The Stationery Office, 2000.

Our Competitive Future: Building the Knowledge Driven Economy. Cm 4176. The Stationery Office, 1998.

Our Competitive Future: UK Competitiveness Indicators 1999. Department of Trade and Industry, 1999.

Trade and Industry: The Government's Expenditure Plans 2000–01 to 2001–02. Cm 4611. The Stationery Office, 2000.

United Kingdom National Accounts—the Blue Book (annual). Office for National Statistics. The Stationery Office.

Websites

Department of Trade and Industry: www.dti.gov.uk

HM Treasury: www.hm-treasury.gov.uk

National Statistics: www.statistics.gov.uk

24 Public Finance

The UK public sector is forecast to spend around £372 billion in 2000–01, about 39 per cent of national income. Plans for public expenditure to grow by 3¼ per cent a year in real terms in the three years to 2003–04 were set out in the Spending Review in July 2000. Above average rises in expenditure are planned in the Government's priority areas, including health, education, law and order, transport, and tackling deprivation.

MAIN PROGRAMMES

The Spending Review (SR) 2000 rolled forward the three-year planning cycle, established in the Comprehensive Spending Review in 1998, and set new departmental spending plans for 2002–03 and 2003–04. Current spending is planned to grow by 2½ per cent a year in real terms, in line with the UK's economic growth rate, while net public sector investment is expected to rise to 1.8 per cent of gross domestic product (GDP) by 2003–04.

The Government is allocating more to key public services (see p. 402), reflecting the relatively low growth in social security spending and tax credits (one of the main elements of public expenditure) and the lower cost of interest payments on government debt.

For the first time the SR was conducted on a resource budgeting basis (see p. 404), taking account of all the resources used by departments. A feature was the holding of 15 cross-departmental reviews in issues involving more than one department (such as government intervention in deprived areas, crime reduction and illegal drugs). These identified ways of improving interdepartmental co-operation and co-ordination.

The main categories of expenditure are shown in the chart on p. 403. Social security is the biggest single element, involving expenditure of £103 billion (nearly 28 per cent of spending) in 2000–01, followed by spending on the National Health Service (NHS) of £54 billion and on education of £46 billion.

Local authorities are estimated to spend about £86.7 billion in 2000–01, around a quarter of public expenditure. The main categories of expenditure are education, law and order, personal social services, housing and other environmental services, and roads and transport.

Net public investment is planned to rise to £19.0 billion by 2003–04 (see Table 24.1). The Capital Modernisation Fund, with funds of £2.7 billion, has been set up to support innovative capital projects aiming to improve delivery of public services, and funds are allocated to departments on a competitive basis. The Invest to Save Budget allocates funds to projects that improve public service operations through partnership between public sector bodies. Two rounds of bidding

Key Government Priorities

Significant improvements in key public services are planned in areas including:

- education, where expenditure will rise by 5.4 per cent a year on average in real terms over the next three years with the aim of modernising schools and improving attainment in literacy, numeracy, science, and information and communications technology;
- health, where there is provision for average annual real growth in spending of 6.1 per cent over the four years from 1999–2000, which is intended to help to reform and modernise the National Health Service and implement the NHS Plan (see p. 184), also announced in July 2000;
- transport, where substantially higher investment is envisaged to implement the first stage of the ten-year plan (see chapter 22);
- law and order, which will see an average annual increase in spending on the police of 3.8 per cent in real terms over the next three years;
- deprived areas, where a new strategy will be adopted to tackle the problems experienced by these areas and a Neighbourhood Renewal Fund will be established (see chapter 21); and
- science, where a £1 billion Science Research Investment Fund, in partnership with the Wellcome Trust, will renew outdated science laboratories and equipment (see chapter 26).

Table 24.1: Resource and Capital Budgets *£ billion*

	1999–2000	2000–01	2001–02	2002–03	2003–04
Resource budget	**287.2**	**305.3**	**322.7**	**338.9**	**356.3**
Locally financed current expenditure	16.4	17.3	18.2	19.0	19.8
Central government debt interest	25.6	27.0	26.1	25.3	24.7
Other current spending and adjustments[1]	–5.7	–0.2	–0.2	1.3	3.5
Public sector current expenditure	**323.5**	**349.4**	**366.8**	**384.5**	**404.3**
Capital budget	**21.7**	**25.8**	**29.8**	**34.7**	**39.3**
Locally financed capital expenditure	0.8	0.7	0.7	0.8	0.8
Other capital spending and adjustments[1]	–5.3	–4.2	–4.4	–4.6	–4.7
Public sector gross investment	**17.2**	**22.3**	**26.1**	**30.9**	**35.4**
less depreciation	–14.6	–15.0	–15.4	–15.9	–16.3
Public sector net investment	**2.6**	**7.3**	**10.6**	**15.0**	**19.0**

[1] Adjustments include accounting adjustments and classification changes to the national accounts.

Source: *Prudent for a Purpose: Building Opportunity and Security for All. 2000 Spending Review: New Public Spending Plans 2001–2004*

have been held, and some £183 million has been allocated to nearly 140 projects. Two examples of projects announced in the second round in February 2000 are a website being developed by the Lord Chancellor's Department to offer legal information and advice in seven languages, and a database system being developed by the Driver Vehicle and Licensing Agency to track the movement of vehicles between motor dealers.

Forecast UK Government Expenditure and Revenue 2000–01

Main Sources of Revenue

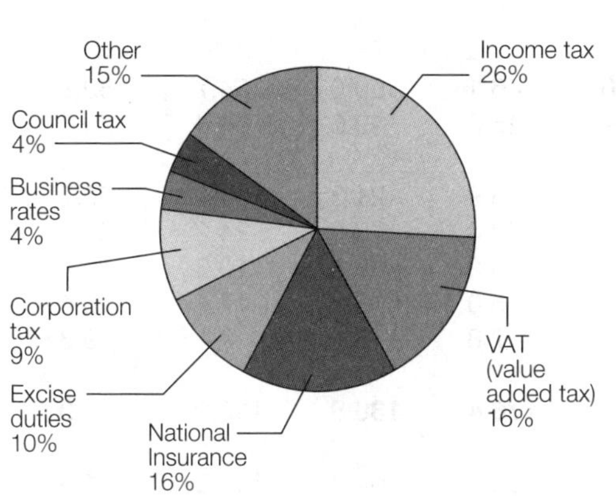

Expenditure

Transport
2%
Other
16%
Housing
and the
environment
4%
Social
security
28%
Industry,
agriculture
and
employment
4%
Law
and order
5%
Defence
6%
Debt interest
7%
National
Health
Service
15%
Education
12%

Source: HM Treasury

> The auction of five licences allowing spectrum use by third generation mobile telephone companies (see p. 379) will raise £22.5 billion, substantially more than originally expected. The Government has indicated that the proceeds, representing about £1 billion a year over the life of the licences, will be used to reduce net government debt.

Control of Spending

The main concept in the measurement of public expenditure is Total Managed Expenditure (see Table 24.2). Within this concept, current and capital expenditure are planned and managed separately. Around half of Total Managed Expenditure is managed through Departmental Expenditure Limits, involving a tightly drawn control figure for each department. The other half is Annually Managed Expenditure, covering expenditure such as social security benefit payments, which cannot reasonably be subject to limits covering more than one year. However, this type of expenditure is subject to rigorous scrutiny each year as part of the Budget process.

Other reforms have been introduced with the aim of improving the effectiveness of public spending. In connection with the SR 2000, departments have prepared new public service agreements (PSAs), listing specific targets for improving service delivery and departmental efficiency. Departmental performance against the targets is scrutinised by a Cabinet Committee, which is chaired by the Chancellor of the Exchequer, and supported by a Public Services Productivity Panel of experts from outside government. From autumn 2000 new service delivery agreements will be set for every government

> The Office of Government Commerce (OGC) was established as an office of HM Treasury in April 2000. It aims to work with civil departments, agencies and non-departmental public bodies as a catalyst to achieve best value for money in their commercial activities; these activities involve annual expenditure of around £13 billion. The OGC's current activities include development of best practice, the management of strategic suppliers, wider use of 'e-procurement', improving the management of major projects, and raising the professionalism and skills of the Government's staff involved in procurement and projects.

Table 24.2: Total Managed Expenditure *£ billion*

	1999–2000	2000–01	2001–02	2002–03	2003–04
Departmental Expenditure Limits	**176.8**	**195.2**	**212.1**	**229.3**	**245.7**
of which:					
Department of the Environment, Transport and the Regions	44.0	46.1	50.0	54.7	59.8
Department of Health	40.9	45.3	49.5	54.4	59.0
Department for Education and Employment	15.5	18.9	21.3	23.5	25.7
Ministry of Defence	21.9	23.0	23.6	24.2	25.0
Home Office	7.5	8.2	9.6	10.3	10.6
Scotland	13.9	15.0	16.2	17.4	18.4
Wales	7.1	7.8	8.4	9.1	9.8
Annually Managed Expenditure	**163.9**	**176.4**	**180.8**	**186.2**	**193.9**
of which:					
Social security benefits	97.1	99.5	104.4	107.3	111.9
Locally financed expenditure	17.2	18.0	18.9	19.8	20.6
Central government debt interest	25.6	27.0	26.1	25.3	24.7
Total Managed Expenditure	**340.7**	**371.6**	**392.9**	**415.4**	**439.6**

Source: *Prudent for a Purpose: Building Opportunity and Security for All. 2000 Spending Review: New Public Spending Plans 2001–2004*

department, setting out how the PSAs will be delivered. Each department has produced its own investment strategy, to demonstrate that capital investment is being used efficiently and effectively. These strategies are taken into account in the allocation of resources from the Capital Modernisation Fund.

Government Accounts

Under the Government Resources and Accounts Act 2000, new 'resource accounting' and budgeting procedures are being adopted, applying the financial reporting practices of the private sector and much of the rest of the public sector to government departments' accounts, Estimates and Budgets. The changes are designed to improve efficiency and focus more on departmental objectives and outputs in terms of resources used rather than the money available for spending. Eventually the principles of the new system will be applied to the consolidated accounts covering the whole public sector. The 2000 Spending Review was conducted on the new resource basis.

Examination of Public Expenditure

Examination of public expenditure is carried out by select committees of the House of Commons. These study in detail the activities of particular government departments and question ministers and officials. The Public Accounts Committee considers the accounts of government departments, executive agencies and other public sector bodies, and reports by the Comptroller and Auditor General on departments and their use of resources.

Audit of the Government's spending is exercised through the functions of the Comptroller and Auditor General, the head of the National Audit Office (NAO). The NAO's responsibilities include certifying the accounts of all government departments and executive agencies, and those of a wide range of other public sector bodies; scrutinising the efficiency and effectiveness of their operations; examining revenue accounts and inventories; and reporting the results of these examinations to Parliament. In February 2000 the Government announced a review of central government audit arrangements, taking account of factors including the 'Modernising Government' programme (see p. 57), the implications of devolution and the relationship with other audit and regulatory bodies.

Public-Private Partnerships

The Government sees Public-Private Partnerships as a key factor in the delivery of high-quality public services, by bringing in private sector management, finance and ownership with the intention of improving the value for money, efficiency and quality of these services. The partnerships cover a variety of arrangements, including joint ventures; outsourcing; the sale of equity stakes in government-owned businesses; and the Private Finance Initiative (PFI), in which the public sector specifies, in terms of the outputs required, the service needed, and private sector companies compete to meet the requirements.

In March 2000 the Government issued *Public Private Partnerships: The Government's Approach*, its strategy for increasing investment in the public sector. The Government expects that this will involve a £20 billion expansion of the partnerships over the next three years, bringing to £32 billion the level of capital investment allocated since mid-1997. Capital investment will be concentrated on the Government's priority areas of health, education and transport. Existing projects in progress include the Channel Tunnel Rail Link and 35 major hospital projects. Additional projects envisaged include:

- a scheme to modernise the London Underground (see p. 370), in which private sector partners will become responsible for the infrastructure and undertake some £8 billion of investment over a 15-year period;
- the sale of 51 per cent of the National Air Traffic Services (see p. 375) to the private sector through a flotation or trade sale, with the new company taking responsibility for an estimated £1 billion modernisation programme;
- a new partnership for the Defence Evaluation and Research Agency (see p. 435), involving the transfer of around three-quarters of the current Agency to a new company which would eventually be sold;
- over 60 new education projects;
- 25 new health projects; and
- 12 other transport projects.

In June 2000 Partnerships UK was set up to help the public sector to build more effective partnerships with the private sector. It is building on the work previously carried out by a task force within HM Treasury and, in due course, will itself become a public-private partnership, as a joint venture, with the public sector owning a majority stake and the private sector having a minority interest.

DEBT MANAGEMENT

The Government finances its borrowing requirement by selling debt to the private sector. At the end of March 2000 public sector net debt was £339 billion, 36.6 per cent of gross domestic product (GDP), compared with 39.6 per cent at the end of March 1999 and it has been falling since 1996–97 (see chart on p. 406). Significant repayments of borrowing contributed to the fall in the net debt ratio in 1999–2000 when there was a net repayment of £17.3 billion.

The Government's debt management policy is to minimise the cost of meeting its financing needs over the long term, taking risk into account. Major changes in the management of government debt have been implemented, with the transfer of government responsibility for debt and cash management from the Bank of England to HM Treasury. Responsibility now rests with a Treasury agency, the United Kingdom Debt Management Office (DMO).

Gilt-edged Stock

The major debt instrument, government bonds, is known as gilt-edged stock ('gilts') as there is no risk of default. Gilts are widely traded, with pension funds and life assurance companies having the largest holdings. The annual Debt Management Report sets out the framework for issuing gilts in the coming year.

Public Sector Net Debt as a Percentage of Gross Domestic Product, UK

Source: Office for National Statistics

Gilt issues are primarily by auction. This used to be broadly monthly, but the frequency has been reduced, reflecting lower government borrowing. Gilts include 'conventionals', which generally pay fixed rates of interest and redemption sums; and index-linked stocks, on which principal and interest are linked to movements in the Retail Prices Index. At the end of March 2000 holdings of marketable gilts were estimated at £283 billion: over £217 billion of conventional gilts and £66 billion of index-linked gilts. The DMO is continuing with a series of reforms designed to improve the efficiency of the gilts market.

MAIN SOURCES OF REVENUE

Government revenue is forecast to be £376 billion in 2000–01. The main sources of revenue (see chart on p. 403) are:

- taxes on income (together with profits), which include personal income tax, corporation tax and petroleum revenue tax;[1]
- taxes on capital, which include inheritance tax, capital gains tax, council tax and non-domestic rates;
- taxes on expenditure, which include VAT (value added tax) and customs and excise duties; and
- National Insurance contributions (see chapter 12).

Taxation Policy

The primary aim of tax policy is to raise sufficient revenue for the Government to pay for the services that its policies require, and to service its debt, while keeping the overall burden of tax as low as possible. The Government has based its tax policy on the principles of encouraging work, raising investment, and promoting fairness and opportunity.

The March 2000 Budget included:

- action designed to increase productivity and boost enterprise, including reforms to capital gains tax (see p. 410) and steps to support electronic commerce (see p. 409);
- support for families and children, including increases in the new tax credits (see p. 408), and for pensioners (see chapter 12); and
- measures to tackle climate change, improve air quality, regenerate urban areas and protect the countryside (see chapter 19).

Collection of Taxes and Duties

The Inland Revenue assesses and collects taxes on income, profits and capital, and stamp duty, and its Contributions Office is responsible for collecting National Insurance contributions. HM Customs and Excise collects the most important taxes on expenditure (VAT and most duties). Local authorities collect the main local taxes, such as council tax.

Most wage and salary earners pay their income tax under a Pay-As-You-Earn (PAYE) system whereby tax is deducted and accounted

[1] The windfall tax, a one-off tax on the excess profits of the privatised utilities, was levied in 1997, but collected in two equal parts in 1997 and 1998, bringing in some £5.2 billion which financed the Welfare-to-Work programme (see p. 151).

The Budget contained a package of measures designed to improve incentives for people to give to charity and to make the tax system more suitable for charities (see p. 115), including:

- abolition of the £250 minimum limit on donations under the Gift Aid scheme—in future, relief will apply to any donations;
- abolition of the £1,200 maximum limit on the Payroll Giving Scheme, under which employees authorise their employer to deduct charitable donations from their earnings and receive tax relief on the donation at the highest rate of tax;
- encouraging the take-up of Payroll Giving through a promotional campaign and a 10 per cent supplement, paid for by the Government, on donations;
- a new tax relief on gifts of certain shares and securities to charity; and
- measures to simplify and ease both the administration and tax burdens of charities.

for to the Inland Revenue by the employer, in a way which enables most employees to pay the correct amount of tax during the year.

Under the self-assessment system for collecting personal taxation, over 8 million people—primarily higher-rate taxpayers, the self-employed and those receiving investment income (particularly where this is paid without tax being deducted)—are required to complete an annual tax return for the Inland Revenue. Taxpayers may calculate their own tax liability, although they can choose to have the calculations done by the Inland Revenue if they return the form by the end of September.

Electronic transmission is already used to a limited extent in the collection of taxes and duties. To encourage greater use, in February 2000 the Government announced tax discounts for electronic filing of tax returns and payment of tax:

- individuals who file their tax returns over the Internet in 2000–01 and pay electronically any tax due will receive a discount of £10; and
- from April 2001 small businesses that file their VAT returns or PAYE end-of-year returns over the Internet and pay electronically the tax due will receive a discount of £50, or £100 for both PAYE and VAT.

The UK has agreements governing double taxation with over 100 countries, the largest network of tax treaties in the world. They are intended to avoid double taxation arising, deal with cross-border economic activity, and prevent fiscal discrimination against UK business interests overseas, and they include provisions to counter tax avoidance and evasion.

Taxes on Income

Income Tax

In general, income tax is charged on all income originating in the UK—although some forms of income, such as child benefit, are exempt—and on all income arising abroad of people resident in the UK. Income tax is imposed for the year of assessment beginning on 6 April. The tax rates and bands for 1999–2000 and 2000–01 are shown in Table 24.3. Recent changes have included a new 10 per cent starting rate of income tax, which took effect in April 1999, and a reduction in the basic rate from 23 to 22 per cent from April 2000, representing the lowest basic rate for nearly 70 years. Of around 28 million income taxpayers, 2.7 million are expected to pay tax only at the starting rate of 10 per cent in 2000–01, 21.4 million at 22 per cent and 2.7 million at 40 per cent, while 1.1 million 'savers' will have a marginal rate of 20 per cent or 10 per cent.

Allowances and reliefs reduce an individual's income tax liability. All taxpayers are entitled to a personal allowance against income from all sources, with a higher allowance for the elderly (see Table 24.3). One of the most significant reliefs covers employees' contributions to their pension schemes, which is designed to encourage people to save towards their retirement.

Informal Economy
According to a report to HM Treasury published in March 2000, substantial sums have been lost to the Exchequer from the informal economy. For example, the report estimated that 120,000 people were working while claiming to be unemployed, while other people concealed income or sales in order to evade income tax and VAT, and HM Customs and Excise has estimated the loss of £2.5 billion a year of revenue as a result of illegal smuggling into the UK of tobacco.

The report recommended measures to help people move into legitimate work, prevent people joining the informal economy (such as tightening the registration requirements for those starting up in business and for issuing National Insurance numbers), improve the detection of offenders, and increase the effectiveness of punishment through, for example, creating a new statutory offence of fraudulent evasion of income tax, to be tried in magistrates' courts. The Government has adopted a range of measures designed to ensure that both individuals and businesses pay their fair share of taxes and duties. For example, in March 2000 it announced a strategy to tackle tobacco smuggling through deploying extra Customs officers, additional specialist investigators, X-ray scanners to examine lorries and freight containers, tougher penalties, and introducing a public awareness campaign.

Personal tax-free saving is also encouraged through the Individual Savings Account (ISA) (see p. 520).

In line with its policies of improving work incentives, promoting a fair and efficient tax system, and supporting families, the Government is changing the system of allowances and introducing a series of tax credits. Mortgage interest relief, which used to be 10 per cent on loans used for house purchase up to a limit of £30,000, was withdrawn in April 2000. Except for couples where at least one of the spouses was aged 65 or over on 5 April 2000, the married couple's allowance was also abolished. It will be replaced from April 2001 by a new Children's Tax Credit (CTC), which will provide an allowance worth up to £442 a year to families with one or more children under 16 living with them. To target this on the most needy families, the credit will gradually be withdrawn where the person claiming the credit is liable to tax at the higher rate. The Working Families Tax Credit (WFTC) replaced Family Credit in October 1999 (see chapter 12) and is designed to provide a guaranteed minimum income for working families. From 2003 a new integrated child credit will bring together the support for children in the WFTC, the CTC and Income Support. A new employment tax credit will also be introduced in 2003, to extend the principles of the WFTC to people without children.

Corporation Tax

The UK rate of corporation tax, payable by companies on their income and capital gains, is the lowest among major industrial countries. The main rate of tax is 30 per cent. A reduced rate of 20 per cent is levied on small companies (those with profits below £300,000 in a year), and from 2000–01 a new starting rate of 10 per cent will apply to the smallest firms (those with annual profits of up to £10,000). Marginal relief is allowed for companies with profits between £300,000 and £1.5 million, so that their overall average rate is between the main rate and the small companies' rate, and from 2000–01 similar marginal relief will apply to firms with profits between £10,000 and £50,000.

Some capital expenditure—on machinery and plant, industrial buildings, agricultural buildings and scientific research, for example—may qualify for relief in the form of capital allowances. To boost investment in manufacturing and services, the Government has made permanent the 40 per cent first-year allowance, which had been due to expire in July 2000, for expenditure on machinery or plant by small or medium-sized businesses. In addition, to encourage more companies to

Table 24.3: Tax Bands and Allowances £

	1999–2000	2000–01
Income tax allowances:		
Personal allowance:		
age under 65	4,335	4,385
age 65–74	5,720	5,790
age 75 and over	5,980	6,050
Married couple's allowance:[1]		
age 65 before 6 April 2000	5,125	5,185
age 75 and over	5,195	5,255
minimum amount[2]	1,970	2,000
Income limit for age-related allowances	16,800	17,000
Widow's bereavement allowance[1]	1,970	2,000
Blind person's allowance	1,380	1,400

Bands of taxable income:[3]

	1999–2000		2000–01
Starting rate of 10 per cent	0–1,500	Starting rate of 10 per cent	0–1,520
Basic rate of 23 per cent	1,501–28,000	Basic rate of 22 per cent	1,521–28,400
Higher rate of 40 per cent	over 28,000	Higher rate of 40 per cent	over 28,400

[1] The married couple's allowance for couples in which neither partner had reached the age of 65 before 6 April 2000 and associated reliefs (including the widow's bereavement allowance) were withdrawn in April 2000. However, women widowed during 1999–2000 retain their widow's bereavement allowance in 2000–01 for the second year of their entitlement. The rate of relief for the married couple's and widow's bereavement allowance is restricted to 10 per cent.

[2] The minimum amount of married couple's allowance is the level at which the tapered withdrawal of the allowance ceases for taxpayers who have income over the income limit.

[3] The rate of tax applicable to savings income in the basic rate band is 20 per cent. For dividends the rates applicable are 10 per cent for income below the basic rate upper limit and 32.5 per cent above that.

Source: Inland Revenue

invest in information and communications technology (ICT) and adopt electronic commerce, small businesses are able to claim 100 per cent first-year allowances on investments between 1 April 2000 and 31 March 2003 in ICT, so enabling them to write off immediately the entire cost against their taxable income. A new research and development (R&D) tax credit also took effect in April 2000, benefiting small and medium-sized firms by reducing the cost of R&D.

Petroleum Revenue Tax

Petroleum revenue tax (PRT), deductible in computing profits for corporation tax, is charged on profits from the production—as opposed, for example, to the refining—of oil and gas in the UK and on its Continental Shelf under licence from the Department of Trade and Industry. Each licensee of an oilfield or gasfield is charged at a rate of 50 per cent on the profits from that field after deduction of certain allowances and reliefs. New fields given consent for development on or after 16 March 1993 are not liable to PRT.

Taxes on Capital

Capital Gains Tax

Capital gains tax (CGT) is payable by individuals and trusts on gains realised from the disposal of assets. It is payable on the amount by which total chargeable gains for a year exceed the exempt amount (£7,200 for individuals and £3,600 for most trusts in 2000–01). Gains on some types of asset are exempt from CGT, including the principal private residence, government securities, certain corporate bonds, and gains on holdings of Personal Equity Plans and ISAs. For individuals, CGT in 2000–01 will be payable at 10, 20 or 40 per cent, according to a person's marginal income tax rate.

CGT taper relief, introduced in 1998 to succeed the previous system of indexation relief to take account of inflation, reduces the amount of the chargeable gain depending on how long an asset has been held. For a business asset the percentage of the gain that is chargeable is reduced from 100 per cent for assets held for less than one year to 25 per cent for assets held for ten years or more. For non-business assets the chargeable gain falls from 100 per cent for assets held for less than three years to 60 per cent for assets held for ten years or longer.

In the March 2000 Budget the Government announced changes to the CGT taper relief with the intention of boosting productivity, stimulating employee share ownership, and encouraging outside 'business angel' investors to provide risk capital for growing companies. The holding period for relief for business assets will be reduced from ten years to four years, and the definition of business assets will be extended by reducing current qualifying thresholds. All shareholdings in unquoted trading companies (companies which have no shares or securities listed on a recognised stock exchange) will qualify for the business assets taper, while in quoted companies all employee shareholdings will qualify, as will shareholdings held by outside investors above a 5 per cent threshold.

Inheritance Tax

Inheritance tax is charged on estates at the time of death and on gifts made within seven years of death; most other lifetime transfers are not taxed. There are several important exemptions, including transfers between spouses, and gifts and bequests to UK charities, major political parties and heritage bodies. In general, business assets and farmland are exempt from inheritance tax, so that most family businesses can be passed on without a tax charge.

Tax is charged at a single rate of 40 per cent above a threshold: £234,000 in 2000–01. Only about 4 per cent of estates a year become liable for an inheritance tax bill.

Taxes on Expenditure

Value Added Tax (VAT)

VAT is a broadly based expenditure tax, which is collected at each stage in the production and distribution of goods and services. The final tax is payable by the consumer. The standard rate is 17.5 per cent, with a reduced rate of 5 per cent on domestic fuel and power, on the installation of energy-saving materials in homes and, from 1 January 2001, on women's sanitary products.

The annual level of turnover above which traders must register for VAT was raised to £52,000 from April 2000. Certain goods and services are relieved from VAT, either by being charged at a zero rate or by being exempt.

- Under zero rating, a taxable person does not charge tax to a customer but reclaims any VAT paid to suppliers. Among the main categories where zero rating applies are goods exported to other countries; most food; water and sewerage for non-business use; domestic and international passenger transport; books, newspapers and periodicals; construction of new residential buildings; young children's clothing and footwear; drugs and medicines supplied on prescription; specified aids for handicapped people; and certain supplies by or to charities.
- For exempt goods or services, a taxable person does not charge any VAT but is not entitled to reclaim the VAT on goods and services bought for his or her business. The main categories where exemption applies are many supplies of land and buildings; financial services; postal services; betting; gaming (with certain important exceptions); lotteries; much education and training; and health and welfare.

Customs Duties

Customs duties are chargeable on goods from outside the EU in accordance with its Common Customs Tariff. Goods can move freely across internal EU frontiers without making customs entries at importation or stopping for routine fiscal checks. For commercial consignments, excise duty and VAT are charged in the member state of destination, at the rate in force in that state.

Excise Duties

Mineral oils used as road fuel are subject to higher rates of duty than those used for other purposes, although there are reduced rates to encourage the use of more environmentally friendly fuels, such as ultra low sulphur petrol, ultra low sulphur diesel, and gas used as road fuel. Kerosene not used as road or motor fuel, most lubricating oils and oils used for certain industrial, horticultural and marine uses are free of duty or attract very low rates. Fuel substitutes are taxed at the same rate as the corresponding mineral oil.

The annual vehicle excise duty (VED) on a privately owned motor car, light van or taxi is £155, with a lower rate of £100 for small cars with engines up to 1,100 cc. From March 2001 the rates will be £160 and £105 respectively, with the latter applying to cars with engines up to and including 1,200 cc. A graduated VED system will apply to new cars, with four VED bands according to the rate of carbon dioxide emissions and a discount of £10 within each band for cars using cleaner fuels and technology. The Government is also reforming from April 2002 company car taxation with the intention of helping to protect the environment, for example, by removing incentives to drive extra miles on business.

The VED on goods vehicles is levied on the basis of gross weight and, if over 12 tonnes, according to the number of axles. The March 2000 Budget contained a series of cuts in VED on certain lorry weights, with the intention of boosting the competitiveness of the UK road haulage industry. Duty on taxis and buses varies according to seating capacity, and duty on motorcycles according to engine capacity.

Cigarette duty is charged partly as a cash amount per cigarette and partly as a percentage of retail price. Duty on other tobacco products is based on weight. In the Government's view, there is a strong case for annual increases in tobacco duty in real terms. It has decided that the extra revenue raised from such increases will be allocated for NHS expenditure.

Duties are levied on spirits, beer, wine, cider and other alcoholic drinks according to alcoholic strength and volume. Spirits used for scientific, medical, research and industrial processes are generally free of duty.

Duties are charged on off-course betting, pool betting, gaming in casinos, bingo and amusement machines. Rates vary with the particular form of gambling. HM Customs and Excise is reviewing general betting duty levied on bets placed with off-course bookmakers, in the light of the rapid growth of offshore bookmakers offering services over the Internet and telephone. On the National Lottery (see p. 117) there is a 12 per cent duty on gross stakes, but no tax on winnings.

Insurance premium tax is levied on most general insurance at a rate of 5 per cent, with a higher rate of 17.5 per cent on travel insurance and on insurance sold by suppliers of cars and domestic appliances.

Air passenger duty is charged at £10 for flights to internal destinations and to those in the European Economic Area (EEA) and £20 elsewhere. A new structure will take effect from April 2001, introducing a differential between standard and economy flights, so that, for example, the duty on economy flights to EEA countries will be reduced to £5. The duty on flights from airports in the Highlands and Islands of Scotland will be removed in recognition of their remoteness and dependence on air travel.

A landfill tax is levied at £11 a tonne, and this will rise by £1 a tonne each year until 2004 when it will be reviewed; a lower rate of £2 a tonne applies for inert waste. The Government has decided to introduce from April 2002 an aggregates levy of £1.60 a tonne on the extraction of sand, gravel and crushed rock.

The climate change levy will be introduced in April 2001. It will apply to sales of electricity, gas, coal and liquefied petroleum gas to the business and public sectors. It is designed to improve energy efficiency in, and decrease carbon emissions from, these sectors. Revenues from the levy will be recycled back to business through a reduction in employers' National Insurance contributions and additional support for energy efficiency measures (see chapter 29).

Stamp Duty

Some transfers are subject to stamp duty. Transfers of shares generally attract duty at 0.5 per cent of the cost, while certain types of document, such as declarations of trust, generally attract a small fixed duty of £5. Transfers by gift and transfers to charities are exempt. Recent Budgets have raised the rate of stamp duty on the transfers of land and property worth over £250,000. Duty on land and property is now payable at 1 per cent of the total price when above £60,000, 3 per cent above £250,000 and 4 per cent over £500,000.

Other Revenue

National Insurance Contributions

Details of the five classes of National Insurance contribution and the rates of contribution are given in chapter 12 on p. 171.

Local Authority Revenue

Local authorities in Great Britain have four main sources of revenue income: grants from central government; council tax; non-domestic rates (sometimes known as business rates); and sales, fees and charges. About 75 per cent of expenditure (excluding sales, fees and charges) is financed by government grants and redistributed non-domestic rates.

Non-domestic rates are a tax on the occupiers of non-domestic property. The rateable value of property is assessed by reference to annual rents and reviewed every five years. The non-domestic rate is set nationally by the central bodies in England, Wales and Scotland, and collected by local authorities. It is paid into a national pool and redistributed to local authorities in proportion to their population.

Domestic property in Great Britain is generally subject to the council tax. Each dwelling is allocated to one of eight valuation bands, based on its capital value (the amount it might have sold for on the open market) in April 1991. Discounts are available for dwellings with fewer than two resident adults, and those on low incomes may receive council tax benefit of up to 100 per cent of the tax bill (see p. 178).

In Northern Ireland, rates—local domestic property taxes based on the value of the property—are collected by local authorities.

Further Reading

Prudent for a Purpose: Building Opportunity and Security for All. 2000 Spending Review: New Public Spending Plans 2001–2004. Cm 4807. HM Treasury. The Stationery Office, 2000.

Prudent for a Purpose: Working for a Stronger and Fairer Britain: Economic and Fiscal Strategy Report and Financial Statement and Budget Report March 2000. HM Treasury. The Stationery Office, 2000.

Public Private Partnerships: The Government's Approach. HM Treasury. The Stationery Office, 2000.

Annual Report

Debt Management Report, HM Treasury.

Websites

HM Treasury: www.hm-treasury.gov.uk
Inland Revenue: www.inlandrevenue.gov.uk

25 International Trade and Investment

Trade has been of vital importance to the British economy for hundreds of years. Although it has less than 1 per cent of the world's population, the UK is the fifth largest trading nation, accounting for around 5.6 per cent of world trade in goods and services in 1998. As one of 15 member states of the European Union (EU), the world's largest established trading group, 53 per cent of the UK's trade in goods and services in 1999 was with fellow EU members. The UK has a higher degree of inward and outward investment than any of the other G7 economies, relative to gross domestic product (GDP), and was second only to the United States as a destination for international direct investment in 1998. Within the World Trade Organisation (WTO), the UK is calling for a new round of negotiations aimed at lowering tariffs, eliminating non-tariff barriers and liberalising world markets, as well as supporting work on international competition policy principles and investment liberalisation in the Organisation for Economic Co-operation and Development (OECD).

The UK exports more per head than the United States and Japan. Its sales abroad of goods and services were just over 20 per cent of gross final expenditure in 1999. Receipts from trade in services (such as financial services, business services, travel, transport and communications) and investment income make up about half of total British external earnings, and the UK consistently runs large surpluses on these accounts. The UK was the world's second biggest foreign investor in 1998 and UK direct investment abroad significantly exceeds direct investment in the UK.

BALANCE OF PAYMENTS

The United Kingdom balance of payments measures the economic transactions between UK residents and the rest of the world. It also draws a series of balances between inward and outward transactions, provides an overall net flow of transactions between UK residents and the rest of the world, and reports how that flow is funded. Economic transactions include:

- exports and imports of goods, such as oil, agricultural products, other raw materials, machinery and transport equipment, computers, white goods, such as refrigerators and washing machines, and clothing;
- exports and imports of services, such as international transport, travel, financial and business services;
- income flows, such as dividends and interest earned by non-residents on investments in the UK and by the UK investing abroad;

- financial flows, such as investment in shares, debt securities, loans and deposits; and
- transfers, such as payments to, and receipts from, EU institutions, foreign aid and funds brought by migrants to the UK.

The balance of payments classification comprises the following groups of accounts:

- the *current account*, which comprises trade in goods and services, income (compensation of employees and investment income) and current transfers;
- the *capital account*, which comprises capital transfers and the acquisition and disposal of non-produced, non-financial assets (such as copyrights);
- the *financial account*, which covers direct, portfolio and other investment and reserve assets; and
- the *international investment position*, which measures the UK's stock of external financial assets and liabilities.

Table 25.1 summarises the UK's balance of payments position over recent years. In 1999 the current account moved into deficit, at £11.0 billion, the highest since 1990, compared with a very small deficit of £0.1 billion in 1998. There were sharp deteriorations in both the deficit on goods and services and in the surplus on income. The capital account surplus rose from £473 million in 1998 to £776 million in 1999.

Trade in Goods and Services

Table 25.2 summarises the UK's trade in goods and services over recent years. More detailed analyses for 1999 can be found in subsequent tables. In 1999, exports of UK goods amounted to £165.7 billion and imports £192.4 billion, giving a deficit on trade in goods of £26.8 billion, up from £20.5 billion in 1998 and the largest deficit on record. The trade in services surplus in 1999 of £11.5 billion was slightly lower than the record £12.6 billion achieved in 1998.

Commodity Composition

UK exports of goods are dominated by manufactures—finished manufactures and semi-manufactured goods. In 1970 they accounted for 84 per cent of UK exports of goods. Although the advent of North Sea oil meant their share declined in the 1970s, they have subsequently recovered and by 1999 stood at 86 per cent of goods (see Table 25.3).

Historically the UK was an importer of foods and basic materials. However, over the last 30 years, imports of manufactures have grown rapidly. Between 1970 and 1999 the share of finished manufactures in total imports rose from 25 per cent to 61 per cent, while the share of basic materials fell from 15 per cent to just 3 per cent. The percentage of food, beverages and tobacco has been dropping since the 1950s, down to under 9 per cent in 1999. The UK has not had a surplus on manufactured goods since 1982.

Table 25.1: UK Balance of Payments Summary, 1989–99[1] *£ million*

	1989	1994	1997	1998	1999
Current account					
Trade in goods and services	–20,807	–4,563	504	–7,955	–15,229
Income	–64	7,770	11,170	14,245	8,332
Current transfers	–2,620	–4,665	–5,051	–6,370	–4,084
Current balance	**–23,491**	**–1,458**	**6,623**	**–80**	**–10,981**
Capital account	270	33	804	473	776
Financial account	19,024	–6,082	–13,186	–4,677	5,853
Net errors and omissions[2]	4,197	7,507	5,759	4,284	4,352

[1] Balance of payments basis.
[2] Amount necessary to bring the sum of all balance of payments entries to zero.
Source: *United Kingdom Balance of Payments—the Pink Book 2000*

UK Balance of Payments in Goods and Services

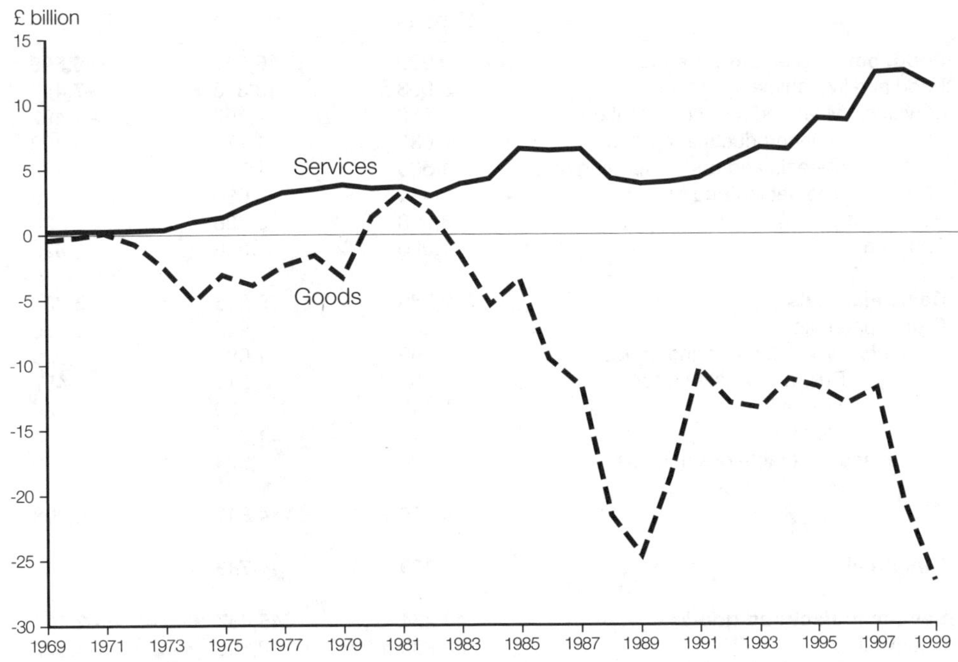

Source: Office for National Statistics

Table 25.2: External Trade in Goods and Services, 1989–99[1] *£ million*

	1989	1994	1997	1998	1999
Exports of goods	92,611	135,260	171,783	164,092	165,667
Exports of services	29,272	43,507	57,543	61,382	63,982
Exports of goods and services	**121,883**	**178,767**	**229,326**	**225,474**	**229,649**
Imports of goods	117,335	146,351	183,693	184,629	192,434
Imports of services	25,355	36,979	45,129	48,800	52,444
Imports of goods and services	**142,690**	**183,330**	**228,822**	**233,429**	**244,878**
Balance of trade in goods	–24,724	–11,091	–11,910	–20,537	–26,767
Balance of trade in services	3,917	6,528	12,414	12,582	11,538
Balance of trade in goods and services	**–20,807**	**–4,563**	**504**	**–7,955**	**–15,229**

[1] Balance of payments basis.
Source: *United Kingdom Balance of Payments—the Pink Book 2000*

Machinery and transport equipment accounted for 48 per cent of exports in 1999 and 46 per cent of imports. Aerospace, chemicals and electronics have become increasingly significant export sectors, while textiles have declined in relative importance. Sectors with a positive balance of trade in 1999 included chemicals, fuels, and beverages and tobacco.

Geographical Distribution

Most of the UK's trade in goods is with other developed countries (see Table 25.4). In 1999,

Table 25.3: Commodity Composition of Trade in Goods, 1999[1] *£ million*

	Exports	Imports	Balance
Food, beverages and tobacco	**9,929**	**16,527**	**–6,598**
Food and live animals	5,903	13,343	–7,440
of which: Meat and meat preparations	660	2,152	–1,492
Dairy products and eggs	683	1,176	–493
Cereals and animal feeding stuffs	1,560	1,722	–162
Vegetables and fruit	434	4,030	–3,596
Beverages	3,006	2,786	220
Tobacco	1,020	398	622
Basic materials	**2,280**	**5,516**	**–3,236**
Crude materials	2,082	4,942	–2,860
of which: Wood, lumber and cork	69	1,089	–1,020
Pulp and waste paper	54	511	–457
Textile fibres	446	420	26
Metal ores	516	1,319	–803
Animal and vegetable oils and fats	198	574	–376
Oil	**9,050**	**4,842**	**4,208**
Other fuels	**803**	**783**	**20**
Semi-manufactured goods	**43,234**	**45,437**	**–2,203**
Chemicals	22,999	18,622	4,377
of which: Organic chemicals	5,483	4,803	680
Inorganic chemicals	1,124	1,056	68
Colouring materials	1,536	958	578
Medicinal products	6,261	4,124	2,137
Toilet preparations	2,457	1,756	701
Plastics	3,145	3,819	–674
Manufactures classified chiefly by material	20,235	26,815	–6,580
of which: Wood and cork manufactures	275	1,145	–870
Paper and paperboard manufactures	2,021	4,323	–2,302
Textile manufactures	3,004	4,385	–1,381
Iron and steel	2,571	2,466	105
Non-ferrous metals	2,123	2,942	–819
Metal manufactures	3,527	3,763	–236
Finished manufactured goods	**98,876**	**117,540**	**–18,664**
Machinery and transport equipment	78,711	88,550	–9,839
Mechanical machinery	21,857	17,289	4,568
Electrical machinery	35,838	40,843	–5,005
Road vehicles	15,040	24,080	–9,040
Other transport equipment	5,976	6,338	–362
Miscellaneous manufactures	20,165	28,990	–8,825
of which: Clothing	2,768	7,475	–4,707
Footwear	529	2,036	–1,507
Scientific and photographic	6,726	6,177	549
Unspecified goods	**1,495**	**1,789**	**–294**
Total	**165,667**	**192,434**	**–26,767**

[1] Balance of payments basis.

Sources: *United Kingdom Balance of Payments—the Pink Book 2000 and Monthly Digest of Statistics*

Table 25.4: Distribution of Trade in Goods, 1999[1]

	Value (£ million)			%	
	Exports	Imports	Balance	Exports	Imports
European Union	97,283	103,719	–6,436	58.7	53.9
Other Western Europe	6,514	10,629	–4,115	3.9	5.5
North America	27,872	28,116	–244	16.8	14.6
Other OECD countries	9,159	15,934	–6,775	5.5	8.3
Oil-exporting countries	5,552	3,269	2,283	3.4	1.7
Rest of the world	19,286	30,765	11,479	11.6	16.0
Total	**165,667**	**192,434**	**–26,767**	**100.0**	**100.0**

[1] Balance of payments basis.
Source: Office for National Statistics

85 per cent of UK exports were to other OECD countries, and over 82 per cent of imports came from the same countries. The proportion of export trade with the European Union was almost 59 per cent, while imports from the EU accounted for around 54 per cent of the total. Western Europe as a whole took almost 63 per cent of UK exports in 1999.

EU countries accounted for eight of the UK's top ten export markets in 1999—the United States and Japan took the other two places—and seven of the top ten leading suppliers of goods to the UK (see Table 25.5); the other three places were taken by the United States, Japan and Switzerland. The United States maintained its position as the UK's largest external market for the third year running and was again the UK's second largest single supplier, with Germany the largest supplier. Total exports were little changed from the level seen in 1998, although they were around 12 per cent higher to both the United States and the Irish Republic, and almost 9 per cent higher to Belgium and Luxembourg. Within the EU, however, UK exports to Italy fell by almost 10 per cent and were over 1 per cent lower to Germany. In South East Asia, growth in 1999 was strong, but export levels were still below those seen in 1997.

Services

There has been a surplus recorded for trade in services every year since 1966. In 1999 this was £11.5 billion (see Table 25.6), slightly down on the £12.6 billion surplus achieved in 1998. Exports of services grew by 4.2 per cent to £64.0 billion in 1999, with particularly strong growth in insurance, computer and information services, and communications. Imports of services grew by 7.5 per cent to £52.4 billion, with exceptionally strong growth in the government sector and, to a lesser degree, in financial services, communications, and travel.

Income and Transfers

Earnings on UK investment assets overseas fell marginally to £108.1 billion in 1999, while debits (earnings of foreign-owned assets in the UK) increased by 6.2 per cent to £100.0 billion, giving a surplus of £8.1 billion (see Table 25.7), down significantly on the record surplus of £14.3 billion in 1998. The surplus on direct investment income of £11.5 billion, down £8.8 billion from the record £20.3 billion surplus in 1998, was partly offset by a deficit of £4.7 billion on other investment income, the lowest since 1990. Earnings on reserve assets in 1999 at £1.2 billion were little changed from 1998. The deficit on current transfers fell from £6.4 billion in 1998 to £4.1 billion in 1999.

Financial Account and International Investment Position

The financial account (see Table 25.8) shows that UK direct investment abroad was £125.3 billion in 1999, and foreign direct investment in the UK was £52.3 billion. These levels

Table 25.5: Trade in Goods—Main Markets and Suppliers, 1999[1]

	Value (£ million)	Share of UK trade in goods (%)
Main markets		
United States	24,297	14.7
Germany	20,350	12.3
France	16,809	10.1
Netherlands	13,544	8.2
Irish Republic	10,716	6.5
Belgium and Luxembourg	9,188	5.5
Italy	7,781	4.7
Spain	7,484	4.5
Sweden	4,012	2.4
Japan	3,303	2.0
Main suppliers		
Germany	26,468	13.8
United States	24,431	12.7
France	17,851	9.3
Netherlands	13,401	7.0
Belgium and Luxembourg	9,471	4.9
Italy	9,311	4.8
Japan	9,251	4.8
Irish Republic	8,478	4.4
Spain	5,894	3.1
Switzerland	5,329	2.8

[1] Balance of payments basis.
Source: *Monthly Digest of Statistics*

Table 25.6: Trade in Services, 1999 *£ million*

	Exports	Imports	Balance
Transportation	11,538	13,930	–2,392
Travel	14,293	22,634	–8,341
Communications	1,484	1,694	–210
Construction	267	85	182
Insurance	4,111	569	3,542
Financial services[1]	6,992	205	6,787
Computer and information services	1,928	500	1,428
Royalties and licence fees	4,387	3,840	547
Other business services	17,083	6,130	10,953
Personal, cultural and recreational services	782	490	292
Government	1,117	2,367	–1,250
Total	**63,982**	**52,444**	**11,538**

[1] Service earnings of financial institutions are recorded net of their foreign expenses. Imports of financial services only cover imports by non-financial institutions.
Source: *United Kingdom Balance of Payments—the Pink Book 2000*

Table 25.7: Income and Transfers, 1999 £ *million*

	Credits	Debits	Balance
Income			
Compensation of employees	960	759	201
Investment income	108,139	100,008	8,131
of which:			
Earnings on direct investment	33,820	22,302	11,518
Earnings on portfolio investment	27,928	27,819	109
Earnings on other investment[1]	46,391	49,887	–3,496
Total	**109,099**	**100,767**	**8,332**
Current transfers			
Central government	9,464	7,278	2,186
Other sectors	8,814	15,084	–6,270
Total	**18,278**	**22,362**	**–4,084**

[1] Including earnings on reserve assets.
Source: *United Kingdom Balance of Payments—the Pink Book 2000*

Table 25.8: Financial Account Summary, 1989–99[1] £ *billion*

	1989	1994	1997	1998	1999
UK investment abroad (net debits)					
Direct investment abroad	21.4	22.2	38.9	71.9	125.3
Portfolio investment abroad	38.9	–21.8	51.9	36.7	5.4
Other investment abroad	35.5	28.9	168.4	15.9	50.1
Reserve assets	–5.4	1.0	–2.4	–0.2	–0.6
Total	**90.4**	**30.4**	**256.8**	**124.4**	**180.1**
Investment in the UK (net credits)					
Direct investment in the UK	18.6	6.1	22.6	38.4	52.3
Portfolio investment in the UK	18.2	33.2	27.2	17.9	115.6
Other investment in the UK	72.6	–15.0	193.9	63.4	18.1
Total	**109.4**	**24.3**	**243.7**	**119.7**	**186.0**
Net transactions (net credits less net debits)					
Direct investment	–2.9	–16.1	16.3	–33.5	–73.0
Portfolio investment	–20.7	55.0	–24.7	–18.8	110.2
Other investment	37.1	–44.0	25.5	47.5	–32.0
Reserve assets	5.4	–1.0	2.4	0.2	0.6
Total	**19.0**	**–6.1**	**–13.2**	**–4.7**	**5.9**

[1] Balance of payments basis.
Source: *United Kingdom Balance of Payments—the Pink Book 2000*

represent very significant growth over 1998 and were the highest direct investment flows on record. There was substantial merger and acquisition activity by UK companies in 1999; many of these deals were financed by the issue of equity to the original shareholders of the foreign companies, resulting in a significant rise in portfolio investment in the UK—up from £17.9 billion in 1998 to a record £115.6 billion in 1999. Portfolio investment abroad decreased very sharply in 1999 to £5.4 billion from £36.7 billion in 1998. Other investment abroad rose significantly from £15.9 billion in 1998 to £50.1 billion in 1999, while other

Table 25.9: International Investment Position, 1989–99[1]					*£ billion*
	1989	1994	1997	1998	1999
UK assets					
Direct investment abroad	123.2	173.9	226.5	301.1	418.5
Portfolio investment abroad	227.3	414.4	626.7	685.5	771.6
Other investment abroad	566.0	719.0	1,066.2	1,102.6	1,130.9
Reserve assets	26.3	30.7	22.8	23.3	22.2
Total	**942.8**	**1,337.9**	**1,942.2**	**2,112.5**	**2,343.2**
UK liabilities					
Direct investment in the UK	100.1	122.6	167.1	192.8	243.1
Portfolio investment in the UK	194.1	320.0	588.4	686.7	882.9
Other investment in the UK	597.5	873.1	1,269.3	1,351.2	1,365.4
Total	**891.8**	**1,315.6**	**2,024.8**	**2,230.7**	**2,491.4**
Net international investment position					
Direct investment	23.1	51.3	59.4	108.3	175.4
Portfolio investment	33.2	94.4	38.3	–1.2	–111.3
Other investment	–31.5	–154.1	–203.1	–248.5	–234.5
Reserve assets	26.3	30.7	22.8	23.3	22.2
Total	**51.0**	**22.2**	**–82.6**	**–118.1**	**–148.3**

[1] Balance of payments basis.
Source: *United Kingdom Balance of Payments—the Pink Book 2000*

investment in the UK fell sharply from £63.4 billion to £18.1 billion. Reserve assets decreased slightly by £0.6 billion in 1999.

Table 25.9 shows the UK's international investment position. At the end of 1999, direct investment in the UK stood at £243.1 billion, while direct investment abroad amounted to £418.5 billion, giving a net balance of £175.4 billion. Inward portfolio investment stood at £882.9 billion, while the stock of UK portfolio investment abroad amounted to £771.6 billion. In total, UK external liabilities exceeded assets by £148.3 billion.

INTERNATIONAL TRADE POLICY

Government policy is to promote open world markets in goods and services and the further liberalisation of international direct investment, and to improve the transparency of international trade agreements and the World Trade Organisation (WTO). The UK plays an active role in achieving these objectives through work in the WTO, the International Monetary Fund (IMF) and the OECD, as well as the EU.

European Union

The promotion of the Single European Market (SEM) (see p. 79) has been one of the key policies of the European Union. Although progress has been made in abolishing barriers to trade, the Government's view is that further reform is needed in several important areas, including utilities, public procurement, state aid, and financial and other services. This and the improvement in the level of transposition and enforcement of single market legislation across the EU remain the UK's priorities. The Government is continuing to work with other EU member states and the European Commission to make the SEM a top priority within the EU's economic policy. The framework for its development over the next five years is set out in the Commission's Strategy for the Internal Market, which aims to make the SEM work more effectively. The EU's approach in this area is based on four strategic objectives:

- improving the quality of life of citizens;
- enhancing the efficiency of EU product and capital markets;

- improving the business environment; and
- exploiting the achievements of the single market in a changing world.

In December 1997 the Commission's 'Single Market Scoreboard' publication was introduced. This shows progress in implementing single market measures across the EU. Areas already identified in which the SEM could operate more strongly include financial services, public procurement and mutual recognition of standards. The Government is promoting a process of economic reform in the EU, with the goal of further improvements in productivity, investment and growth. It is also promoting the principles of competitiveness and the economic reform agenda to the EU applicant countries. Through the agreements each applicant has with the EU, these countries already enjoy many of the benefits of the single market in industrial goods, and the Government is working to ensure that by the time of entry each country has adopted the measures required of EU membership, and has the necessary administrative infrastructure.

The Treasury's Euro Preparations Unit is helping British business adjust to the introduction of the euro in 11 EU member states (see p. 79).

World Trade Organisation

The level of industrial tariffs in developed countries has fallen dramatically since 1948. This is one of the main outcomes of the General Agreement on Tariffs and Trade (GATT), which helped establish a multilateral trading system through successive rounds of trade negotiations. The eighth GATT Round (the Uruguay Round) of 1986–94 led to the formation of the World Trade Organisation and a new set of agreements, including the establishment of a dispute settlement system.

Although the WTO Ministerial Conference in Seattle in November 1999 was unable to reach agreement on the agenda and scope for further multilateral trade negotiations, the UK and its EU partners will continue to push for the launch of a comprehensive round of trade negotiations as soon as possible, with parallel work on reform of WTO operations. The Government, in partnership with UK businesses, has identified a number of priority areas for inclusion in such a round, including a further substantial reduction of tariffs, the removal of other barriers to trade, the simplification of trade procedures and the opening of global government procurement markets.

The DTI monitors actions by third countries which represent obstacles to UK exports and seeks to resolve problems bilaterally in conjunction with EU partners and ultimately through the initiation of WTO dispute settlement action. It seeks to ensure that bilateral agreements between the EU and third countries are established and implemented in a way which secures open markets. A similar approach is adopted in the negotiations with countries seeking to join the WTO, including the People's Republic of China, Russia, Saudi Arabia and the Ukraine.

Relations with Other Countries

The UK places great importance on developing strong relations with third countries, in particular through the EU. Examples include:

- the Transatlantic Economic Partnership (TEP), where at the US/EU summit in 1998 the two partners agreed to reinforce their close relationship. The TEP has led to agreement on the establishment of an early warning system to highlight potential problems and prevent them from becoming damaging trade disputes. The private sector is fully involved in this process through the Transatlantic Business Dialogue;
- the Asia-Europe Meeting (ASEM), which provides a forum for wide-ranging dialogue between 25 Asian and European countries together representing one-half of global wealth. The challenge for ASEM in the run-up to 'ASEM 3' in Seoul in October 2000 is to reinforce the pledge made at the London Leaders Summit, ASEM 2, in April 1998 to maintain open markets and reject protectionist pressures and to secure

tangible improvements in the trade and investment climate in the two regions. Business input to the ASEM process is provided via the Asia-Europe Business Forum (AEBF), which meets annually—its meeting in Vienna in September 2000 fed directly into ASEM 3 the following month; and

- the DTI works closely with the Department for International Development (DFID) to ensure that developing countries benefit more from, and participate more fully in, the world trade system. The EU is committed to implementing duty- and quota-free access for virtually all exports from the Least Developed Countries no later than 2005.

Special Trading Arrangements

The multilateral trading system provides the foundation for the EU's common commercial policy. However, the EU has preferential trading arrangements with a number of countries. These fall into three main categories:

- Those that prepare countries in Central and Eastern Europe for possible EU membership. Europe (Association) Agreements (see p. 83) are designed to facilitate closer political and economic ties and the eventual liberalisation of trade with a view to these countries becoming full members of the EU.
- The EU has association and co-operation agreements with virtually all non-member countries with a Mediterranean coastline, plus Jordan. These provide for the eventual setting up of a free trade area between the EU and these countries by 2010.
- Those that provide an economic dimension to its assistance to former dependent territories. Trade relations with these countries (known as ACP countries), which were formerly beneficiaries of the Lomé Convention, are now governed by the EU/ACP Partnership Agreement signed in Cotonou, Benin, which gives them tariff-free access, subject to certain safeguards, to the EU for industrial and agricultural products. The EU also operates a Generalised System of Preferences which is available to nearly all developing countries and applies to industrial products, including textiles and certain (mainly processed) agricultural products.

New trade relationships with countries and regions of Latin America are being pursued. A free trade agreement with Mexico came into force on 1 July 2000, and negotiations for new agreements with the Mercosur regional economic area (Argentina, Brazil, Paraguay and Uruguay) and Chile are under way.

Partnership and co-operation (non-preferential) agreements have been concluded with ten states of the former Soviet Union. Non-preferential co-operation agreements have also been made with countries in South Asia and Latin America, as well as the People's Republic of China, the Association of South East Asian Nations, the Andean Pact, and the Central American States.

Controls on Trade

Import Controls

Following the completion of the Single European Market, all national quantitative restrictions have been abolished. However, some EU-wide quotas have been imposed on a small range of products from the People's Republic of China, while EU imports of some steel products from Russia, the Ukraine and Kazakhstan are also restricted. Quantitative restrictions on textiles and clothing stem from the Multi-Fibre Arrangement (MFA), under which there is a series of bilateral agreements. Some quotas are also maintained for imports from non-WTO countries. The MFA restrictions will be eliminated by 2005 as part of the Uruguay Round agreement.

Imports from certain countries remain subject to sanctions or embargo agreed by, for example, the United Nations. Imports of certain other goods from all countries are prohibited or restricted in order to protect human, animal or plant life and health. These include firearms and ammunition; nuclear materials; certain drugs; explosives; endangered wildlife and derived products;

pornographic material; and certain agricultural, horticultural and food products.

Strategic Export Controls

Strategic export controls apply to a range of goods, components, spare parts and technology, including military goods, arms, ammunition and related materials, dual-use goods that can be used for civil and military purposes, nuclear-related goods and goods that can be used in weapons of mass destruction and their delivery systems. Some exports and other activities are only controlled where particular destinations are involved, for example where EU or UN trade sanctions or arms embargoes apply.

Strategic export controls are imposed for a variety of reasons, for example irresponsible transfers of arms, ammunition and related material contribute to internal repression or regional instability, while goods intended for civil purposes can also contribute to the development of weapons of mass destruction and the missiles to deliver them. Controls are also imposed to meet various international commitments.

Licences to export arms and other goods controlled for strategic reasons are issued by the DTI acting through its Export Control Organisation (ECO). All licence applications are circulated to other departments with an interest, as determined by them in line with their policy responsibilities, including the Foreign & Commonwealth Office (FCO), the Ministry of Defence and DFID. The ECO is also the licensing authority for applications to export most goods and services controlled because of trade sanctions imposed by the EU or UN.

A White Paper on *Strategic Export Controls* published in 1998 contained proposals for new primary legislation and would, among other things, provide for parliamentary scrutiny of secondary legislation, and introduce powers enabling government to impose controls on the transfer of technology by intangible means and trafficking and brokering.

Inward and Outward Investment

The UK has an open economy, and there are no restrictions on the outward flow of capital. Outward investment helps develop markets for UK exports while providing earnings in the form of investment income (see p. 417). Inward investment is promoted by Invest·UK (formerly the Invest in Britain Bureau), which reports jointly to the DTI and the FCO. Invest·UK (see p. 425) assists overseas companies with comprehensive arrangements for locating, relocating or expanding business anywhere within the UK. This inward investment is seen as a means of introducing new technology, products and management styles to the UK, and creating or safeguarding employment.

Inward Investment

The UK was ranked second in the world at attracting inward investment according to the latest (1999) United Nations World Investment Report. About 33 per cent of new investment comes from companies that already have a UK presence. North America continues to be the largest source of inward investment. Britain is the premier inward investment location in Europe and inward investment is a significant contributor to the economy. It attracted 29 per cent of all inward investment into the EU in 1998, and overseas businesses investing in Britain generate an estimated 40 per cent of UK exports. There are nearly 18,000 foreign investors in the UK, including 5,000 from the United States.

Inward investment into the UK has reached record levels, according to Invest·UK. In the year to March 2000, 757 inward investment projects were reported from 30 countries, creating 52,783 jobs. The largest single investor country was the United States, with 48 per cent of projects, followed by Germany (8.3 per cent), Japan (7.7 per cent), Canada (6.3 per cent) and France (6.2 per cent). The UK is particularly successful in attracting investment in industries linked to the knowledge-driven economy—computer software, Internet, telecommunications and e-business sectors—which, when taken together, form the largest category of foreign direct investment with some 205 projects (27 per cent). Other main sectors for UK inward investment are the automotive sector, speciality chemicals and financial services.

Britain is second only to the US in investment in IT and communications equipment.

Recent inward investment announcements have included:

- Toyoda Gosei of Japan is to invest £32 million by building its first European manufacturing plant at Rotherham, South Yorkshire, creating 400 new jobs. The factory will supply rubber seals for car doors and windows to Toyota plants in Derbyshire and northern France;
- General Motors—£200 million will be spent on a replacement for the Vauxhall Vectra car, safeguarding 4,400 direct and 4,360 indirect jobs;
- MCI Worldcom, the US telecommunications group, is establishing a service and marketing centre for Europe in central London, creating 1,000 jobs;
- Computer Associates International is investing US $160 million in a new European headquarters near Slough, Berkshire, which will be a centre for training and software development excellence across Europe; and
- Motorola is to invest US $2 billion in Europe's largest semi-conductor plant in Dunfermline, Fife. This is the company's largest ever investment in Europe. Motorola will also build a US $32 million R&D software and design centre in Livingston, Lothian.

Outward Investment

According to the latest United Nations Conference on Trade and Development (UNCTAD) report, the UK was the world's largest outward investor in 1999 (US $212 billion), surpassing the United States for the first time since 1988.

GOVERNMENT SERVICES

The Government provides a wide range of advice and practical support to meet the needs of exporters. This support is designed to help businesses, especially small and medium-sized enterprises, through all stages of the exporting process.

British Trade International

British Trade International (BTI), established in 1999, has lead responsibility within government for trade development and promotion services on behalf of British business. It brings together the joint work of the DTI and the FCO in support of British trade and investment overseas, for both the manufacturing and services sectors. It combines in a single operation all trade development and promotion work currently undertaken in the English regions by the Business Link network (see p. 391); trade support services provided nationally; the commercial work overseas of over 200 embassies and other diplomatic posts; and central co-ordination of trade promotion sponsored and undertaken by other government departments.

The Chief Executive reports to the Secretary of State for Trade and Industry and the Foreign Secretary, and to the Board of BTI, chaired jointly by DTI and FCO ministers. A majority of the Board's members are from business and have wide experience of international trade.

Key priorities over the next two years include:

- putting in place a new structure which will enable the team abroad and at home to function as a single organisation;
- establishing a strong brand for trade development and export promotion services to make sure that businesses know what BTI can offer to help them win business overseas;
- implementation of changes to the delivery of market information to British businesses, including delivery of the service through BTI's website; and
- greater focus on sectoral needs and development of a package of new trade development initiatives for delivery through the new regional and local network.

An early task for the Board of BTI was the preparation of a national trade development

SEASIDE PIERS

The history of piers began in the late 1700s when it became fashionable for the rich to visit developing seaside towns. The success of spa towns such as Bath dispelled the fear of water and people became fond of walking along jetties over the sea. During the 1860s and 1870s an average of two piers were opened each year, the growth in the numbers reflecting the rising popularity of the British seaside.
There are currently 55 pleasure piers in existence around the UK coastline.

Dunoon (Argyll and Bute): Opened 1898.

Paignton (Devon): Opened 1879.

Clevedon (North Somerset): Opened 1869.

Background picture: Bangor Garth (Gwynedd): Opened 1896.

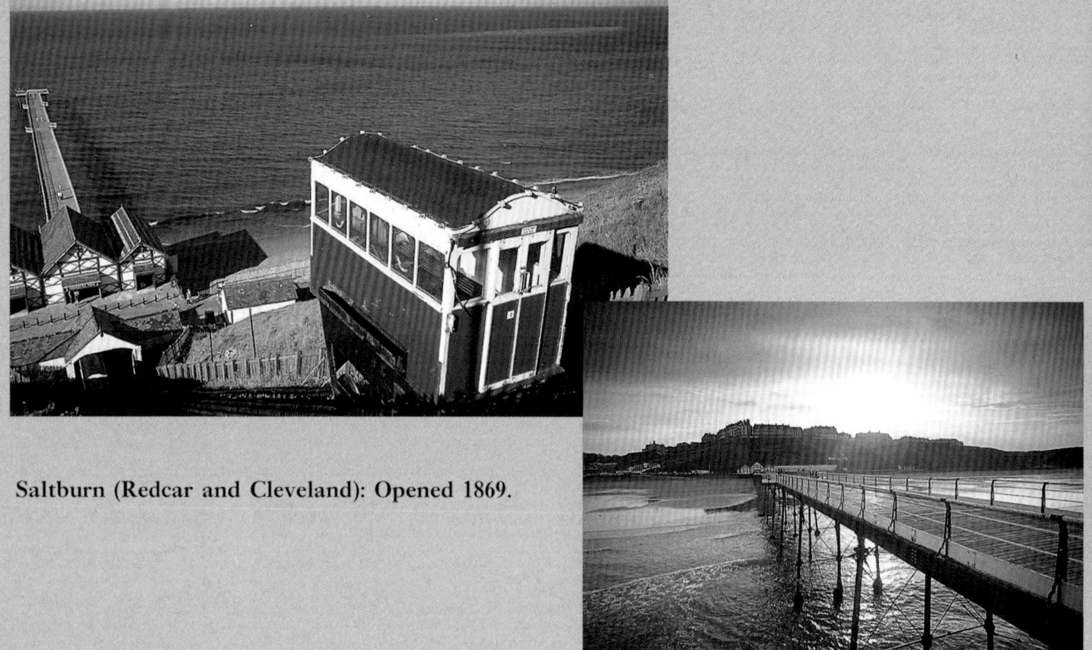

Saltburn (Redcar and Cleveland): Opened 1869.

Southend (Essex): Opened 1830.

GLASGOW

Millennium Spaces Project, Govanhill: part of Glasgow's year as UK City of Architecture and Design (1999) which transformed gap sites into spaces and was designed to bring a sense of community back into neighbourhoods.

Gorbals: St Francis Community Centre (a converted church) and Glasgow Central Mosque are both located in an ethnically diverse area of the city.

Provand's Lordship: restoration to protect the integrity of this house, a rare example of 15th century Scottish domestic urban architecture, is being carried out by Glasgow City Council.

CARDIFF

The development of Cardiff Bay is aimed at regenerating 1,100 hectares of former docklands in South Cardiff and Penarth.

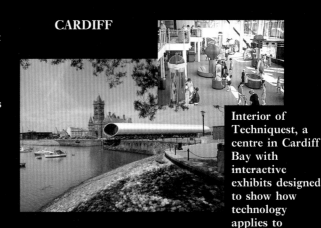

Interior of Techniquest, a centre in Cardiff Bay with interactive exhibits designed to show how technology applies to everyday life.

Mill Lane precinct has been redeveloped with a mix of cafés, restaurants, bars and pubs.

Bhatra Sikh centre: Built to cater for the religious and cultural needs of the Sikh community, it attracts several hundred users at any one time. The local community substantially funded the centre with assistance from the former Welsh Office and Cardiff City Council.

SHEFFIELD

Shirebrook Valley: a former sewage works has been sensitively converted into a nature reserve which is popular with local children.

Sheffield City Centre: low-quality open space has been transformed into an award-winning Peace Garden, a centerpiece of Sheffield's Heart of the City project.

Cornish Place: this derelict cutlery works has been turned into high-quality residential apartments designed to full mobility standards and capable of adaptation to meet the needs of people with disabilities.

BELFAST

Gasworks: clearance of old buildings and reclamation of 9 hectares of land —formerly the site of a 19th century gasworks—were followed by the development of accommodation for small business units. The area has been opened up to pedestrians and cyclists.

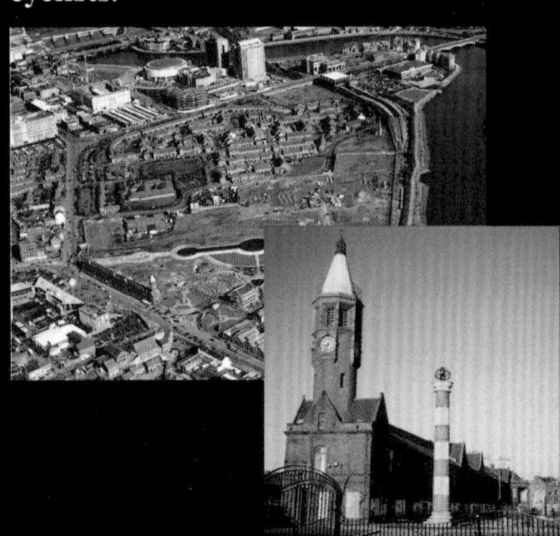

Waterfront Hall: one of Northern Ireland's premier entertainment venues attracting performances by local and international artists and also used for business events. The venue has won an award for its facilities for people with disabilities.

strategy to underpin the programmes and priorities of BTI and of other organisations working in support of Britain's exporters and overseas investors. This was published in November 1999.

BTI has a remit for the entire United Kingdom. Its strategy is a national one, and the devolved administrations in Scotland, Wales and Northern Ireland have played a full part in its development; each devolved administration is represented on BTI's Board.

Invest·UK

Invest·UK was launched in July 2000 as the new brand identity of the agency which promotes the whole of the UK as the first choice in Europe as an inward investment location. It operates through its network of offices in British diplomatic missions overseas and its development agency partners in the UK to assist new and existing investors with all aspects of locating and expanding in the UK.

Trade Partners UK

Launched at the end of May 2000, Trade Partners UK is a new unified brand for the export and international trade services provided to British business wishing to define and develop business opportunities overseas. The Trade Partners UK identity applies to all government-supported services whether from government departments with export interests, Business Links, chambers of commerce, export clubs or commercial sections in British embassies and consulates abroad.

Export Insurance

ECGD (Export Credits Guarantee Department), Britain's official export credit agency, is a separate government department reporting to the Secretary of State for Trade and Industry. It helps exporters of UK goods and services to win business, and UK firms to invest overseas, by providing medium-term and long-term export credit support for capital goods and projects. It also provides reinsurance for exports sold on short terms of payment, and political risk insurance for overseas investments. ECGD plays a key role in the Government's export strategy, and it works closely with BTI and other government departments involved in export promotion.

In 1998–99, ECGD issued guarantees for new business (exports and overseas investments) of £3.7 billion. It also made a cash contribution to the Exchequer of £363 million, achieved recoveries of £442 million and experienced a continued fall in claims to £143 million. ECGD aims to be flexible and innovative in developing solutions to individual problems, and offers simple packages for the more straightforward deals. ECGD has an extensive network of co-operation agreements with export credit agencies in other countries.

Further Reading

Trade and Industry. The Government's Expenditure Plans 2000–01. Cm 4611. The Stationery Office, 2000.

United Kingdom Balance of Payments—the Pink Book, annual report. Office for National Statistics. The Stationery Office.

Websites

Department of Trade and Industry: www.dti.gov.uk

British Trade International: www.brittrade.com

Invest·UK: www.invest.uk.com

Trade Partners UK: www.tradepartners.gov.uk

ECGD: www.ecgd.gov.uk

National Statistics: www.statistics.gov.uk

26 Science, Engineering and Technology

More Nobel Prizes for science (over 70) have been won by scientists from Britain than any country except the United States. The UK is responsible for about 4.5 per cent of global expenditure on science, produces about 8 per cent of scientific publications and receives 9 per cent of citations. UK scientists claimed about 10 per cent of internationally recognised prizes in the 20th century. Government policy aims to reinforce the UK's international scientific standing, and maximise the contribution of science, engineering and technology (SET) to economic competitiveness and the quality of life by promoting innovation.

BACKGROUND

The public sector is the prime funder of basic science in Britain. As well as playing a crucial part in advancing scientific knowledge and producing well-trained people, such research can often lead to exploitable results. Business has the prime responsibility for researching and developing new and improved products and services. The Government's aim is to create a knowledge-driven economy by building on the UK's science base and promoting the right climate to encourage innovation and the exploitation of new ideas.

The Government's policies for science, engineering and technology were set out in the July 2000 White Paper *Excellence and Opportunity—a science and innovation policy for the 21st century*. The White Paper set out the actions being taken by the Government to ensure that UK science remains world class, to open up opportunities for innovation throughout the economy and to increase public confidence in science. The Spending Review in July 2000 (see p. 401) provided for an average increase of 5.4 per cent a year in real terms between 2000–01 and 2003–04 for spending in this area. The European Union (EU) launched the Fifth Framework Programme, a further round of its collaborative research and development (R&D) programme, in March 1999. UK companies, higher education institutions and research organisations are playing an active role in this transnational collaborative research programme. EU proposals to create a European Research Area are expected to offer new opportunities for the UK to compete as part of the EU in global markets.

The Sanger Centre at Hinxton in Cambridgeshire funded mainly by the

Wellcome Trust has contributed a third of the sequence data to the international Human Genome Project, while the Medical Research Council (MRC) Human Genome Mapping Project Resource Centre on the same site also played a major role in supporting work on the human genome. The working draft of the human genome sequence was announced in June 2000 and has involved scientists working at 16 research institutes in six countries (see p. 441). The UK has been at the forefront of many other world-class advances in science. For example, in the latter part of the 20th century there was the discovery by Natural Environment Research Council (NERC) British Antarctic Survey scientists of the hole in the ozone layer over the Antarctic. Earlier, researchers at the Laboratory of Molecular Biology, Cambridge, had produced the first monoclonal antibodies—proteins with enormous potential in the diagnosis and treatment of disease. Among British breakthroughs in genetics research are the identification of the gene in the Y chromosome responsible for determining sex, and of other genes linked to diseases such as cystic fibrosis and a form of breast cancer. The world's first pig with a genetically modified heart was bred by scientists at Cambridge University. In 1997 scientists at the Roslin Institute in Edinburgh announced that they had succeeded in 'cloning' a sheep ('Dolly the Sheep') using a cell from an adult sheep's mammary gland. Professor Sir Harold Kroto of Sussex University shared the 1996 Nobel Prize for chemistry with two US scientists for discovering in 1985 the fullerene molecule—60 carbon atoms arranged in a symmetrical cage. Potential uses for fullerene and for materials derived from it include high-temperature superconductors, drugs, ultra-strong fibres, super-slippery lubricants, lightweight magnets and electronic superconductors.

Notable areas of UK achievement in R&D include biotechnology, materials, chemicals, electronics and aerospace. Among the British research achievements reported in the first half of 2000 are:

- The discovery by scientists at the NERC Southampton Oceanography Centre that young mussels living in the toxic, scalding waters of hot springs at hydrothermal vents—deep on mid-ocean ridges—are able to repair damage to their DNA quickly. DNA damage is one cause of ageing and cancers in humans and understanding how mussels repair their DNA may suggest ways to enhance human DNA repair.
- Chemists at The Queen's University, Belfast, have developed a faster way of detecting the illegal drug ecstasy (MDMA) in tablets. A technique called Raman scattering measures the spectrum of a laser beam bounced off the tablet being investigated. The characteristic spectra of several variants of MDMA have been identified. This test can be applied immediately to a suspect tablet, compared with existing methods which involve crushing and dissolving tablets and analysis by gas chromatography.
- Work at the MRC National Institute for Medical Research on malaria has demonstrated that a gene family, thought to be involved in red blood cell invasion, also allows the malaria parasite to adapt to changes in the (human) host environment as well as to evade the immune system. The parasite's ability to evade the host's immune system is one of the main problems in the development of an effective malaria vaccine.
- Researchers have realised that a gamma-ray camera originally developed for investigating the night sky could have another role, that of finding out how far breast cancer has spread within a patient's body and possibly eliminating the need for major surgery. The Particle Physics and Astronomy Research Council has awarded funding for the development of an item of medical equipment to take this idea forward.
- British scientists working with an international team from the United States, Italy and Canada have conducted an experiment that enabled them to create picture maps of the early Universe showing the pattern of hot spots and cold spots that collapsed to form clusters and

Table 26.1: UK Company Spending on R&D

	R&D expenditure 1999[1] (£ million)	R&D as % of sales	% change over 1998
AstraZeneca	1,814	16	18
Glaxo Wellcome[2]	1,269	15	9
SmithKline Beecham[2]	1,018	12	12
British Aerospace[3]	693	10	61
Unilever	616	2	11
Marconi	471	9	64
Invensys	378	4	17
Ford	372	5	–14
BT	345	2	29
Pfizer	329	37[4]	26

[1] Includes spending overseas.
[2] Due to merge to form Glaxo SmithKline later in 2000.
[3] Now BAE Systems.
[4] Pfizer's UK sales have been low, but much of their R&D is in Britain.
Source: *The 2000 UK R&D Scoreboard, DTI*

super clusters of galaxies or evolved into giant voids in space. The scientists obtained the maps by flying a robotic telescope on board a very large balloon which travelled around Antarctica for 11 days.

- Research at Oxford University has shown how genetically modified bacteria could help to clear some chlorobenzenes that contaminate derelict industrial 'brownfield' sites. The process changes chlorinated benzenes into phenols which can then be destroyed by common soil bacteria.
- Researchers at the John Innes Centre in Norwich have found a natural variant of a gene in the tiny weed thale cress that limits the plant's height. The significance of this is that it offers plant breeders a way of converting any locally adapted low-yielding variety of a crop into a higher-yielding form, without disturbing the plant's adapted background.
- Collaborative research between scientists at Oxford University and the Institute of Animal Health has helped to determine the structure of the Bluetongue virus which affects livestock. This information is providing new insight into how this virus, which is endemic in many parts of the world, attacks and penetrates cells.

RESEARCH AND DEVELOPMENT EXPENDITURE

Gross domestic expenditure in the UK on R&D in 1998 was £15.6 billion, 1.8 per cent of gross domestic product (GDP). Of this, £13.2 billion was on civil R&D, with the rest going to defence projects.

Industry provided 47 per cent of total funding of R&D and government 32 per cent in 1998; a further 17 per cent came from abroad. Other contributions were also made by private endowments, trusts and charities. As well as financing R&D carried out within industry itself, industry supports university research and finances contract research at government establishments. Some charities have their own laboratories and offer grants for outside research. Contract research organisations (see p. 444) carry out R&D for companies and are playing an increasingly important role in the transfer of technology to British industry.

Total spending on R&D in industry amounted to £10.2 billion in 1998. Of this total, industry's own contribution was 66 per cent, with 12 per cent coming from government and the rest from overseas. The three biggest investors in R&D (see Table 26.1)—AstraZeneca, Glaxo Wellcome and SmithKline Beecham—all operate in the pharmaceuticals sector, and pharmaceuticals account for 40 per cent of UK R&D

expenditure. The electronics and aerospace sectors are also big investors in R&D.

GOVERNMENT ROLE

Science, engineering and technology (SET) base issues are the responsibility of a Cabinet minister at the Department of Trade and Industry (DTI), assisted by a Minister for Science; they are supported by the Office of Science and Technology (OST). A Ministerial Science Group has been created across government to ensure that SET issues are taken into account in the development of government policy. The OST, headed by the Government's Chief Scientific Adviser, is responsible for policy on SET, both nationally and internationally, and co-ordinates science and technology policy across government departments. The Chief Scientific Adviser also reports directly to the Prime Minister. An independent Council for Science and Technology advises the Prime Minister on the strategic policies and framework for science and technology in the UK. Its members are drawn from academia, business and charitable foundations/institutions. The policy and management of some aspects of science and technology are reserved to the UK Government, while in other instances this has been devolved to the new administrations in Scotland, Wales and Northern Ireland.

The term 'science and engineering base' is used to describe the research and postgraduate training capacity based in the universities and colleges of higher education and in establishments operated by the Research Councils (see pp. 440–4), together with the national and international central facilities (such as CERN—see p. 439) supported by the Research Councils and available for use by British scientists and engineers. There are also important contributions from private institutions, chiefly those funded by charities. The science and engineering base is the main provider of basic research and much of the strategic research (research likely to have practical applications) carried out in the UK. It also collaborates with the private sector in the conduct of specific applied research.

The OST, through the Director General of Research Councils, has responsibility for the Science Budget, and for the government-financed Research Councils. Through the Research Councils, the Science Budget supports research in the following ways: by awarding research grants to universities, other higher education establishments and some other research units; by funding Research Council establishments to carry out research or provide facilities; by paying subscriptions to international scientific facilities and organisations; and by supporting postgraduate research students and postdoctoral Fellows. The Science Budget also funds programmes of support to the science and engineering base through the Royal Society and the Royal Academy of Engineering. The other main sources of funds for universities are the higher education funding councils (see p. 444).

Strategy and Finance

Planned total government expenditure on SET (both civil and defence) in 2000–01 is £7.2 billion. This represents an increase of about 6 per cent in real terms over the estimated outturn of expenditure in 1999–2000. Of the 2000–01 total, £4.3 billion is devoted to civil science, including £1.6 billion for the Science Budget.

In 1998 the Government announced that it would provide an additional £1 billion for the science and engineering base between 1999 and 2002—£700 million through the Science Budget and £300 million through the Department for Education and Employment. A further £400 million is being provided by the Wellcome Trust. About £700 million of the extra funding, including £300 million of the Wellcome contribution, is devoted to upgrading university laboratories and other essential equipment (see p. 431). Another £400 million is being used by the Research Councils to support research in priority areas such as life sciences (including genetic research, medical science and biotechnology). In July 2000 a further £1 billion investment partnership with the Wellcome Trust—for the years 2002–03 and 2003–04—was announced (see p. 431) as part of the Spending Review.

Key features of the Spending Review of July 2000 and the associated White Paper,

Excellence and Opportunity—a science and innovation policy for the 21st century, are:

- an average increase in spending on science and engineering of 5.4 per cent in real terms over the three years 2001–02 to 2003–04;
- a Science Research Investment Fund, in partnership with the Wellcome Trust, of £1 billion over two years (see p. 431);
- through the Higher Education Innovation Fund, increasing funding to £140 million over three years, to help universities to work with business to help create jobs and wealth from the science base;
- an extra £250 million to boost key research areas—genomics, e-science, nanotechnology, quantum computing and bioengineering;
- in partnership with the Wolfson Foundation and the Royal Society, a fund, initially of £4 million a year, to help in the recruitment of up to 50 top researchers;
- an annual £50 million Regional Innovation Fund to enable Regional Development Agencies (see p. 394) to support business incubators and clusters and new clubs of scientists, entrepreneurs, managers and financiers to collaborate more closely in the regions; and
- a new Small Business Research Initiative to encourage more high-technology small firms to start up or develop their research expertise by bidding for government research contracts.

The Foresight Programme

The funding and organisation of British SET aim to create a close partnership between government, industry and the scientific community in developing strengths in areas of importance to the future economic well-being of Britain. In particular, the Government's Foresight Programme encourages the public and private sectors to work together to identify opportunities in markets and technologies likely to emerge over the next ten to 20 years that would support sustainable growth, and the actions needed to exploit them. Government priorities in SET programmes, and in overall policy, regulation and education and training, are being guided by the Programme.

The Foresight Programme is co-ordinated by a joint industry/academic steering group headed by the Chief Scientific Adviser. Building on the first round (1994–99), a second Foresight round was launched in April 1999. This has three thematic panels and ten sectoral panels, made up of people from industry, academia and government. The panels will produce visions of the future which might drive wealth creation and shape the quality of life. The thematic panels are addressing the issues of ageing population, crime prevention and manufacturing in 2020. The sectoral panels are looking at business sectors or broader areas—they are carrying forward the work of earlier panels and tackling new issues.

Government departments, universities and higher education funding councils, as well as the Research Councils, are reflecting Foresight priorities in their research spending allocations. The private sector is being encouraged to take account of the priorities both in its participation in collaborative research programmes and in its own strategic planning. The Government provided £30 million over four years for the first round of the Foresight Challenge Competition, to fund collaborative R&D projects which address

> Faraday Partnerships are intended to improve the exploitation of SET in the UK. The partnerships bring together universities, independent research organisations, industry associations and manufacturers. Four new Faraday Partnerships were announced in 2000 following a competition. They are in the areas of plastics, aerospace and automotive materials, technical textiles, and the application of mathematics and computer science. It is intended to have a national network of about 20 Faraday Partnerships by 2003.

priorities identified by the Foresight panels. This was complemented by a further £62 million from private sector project participants. In addition, more than £400 million has already been channelled into other Foresight initiatives.

A new Foresight fund, initially of up to £15 million, has been announced to implement the best ideas from the current round quickly.

A 'Knowledge Pool' has been established as an integral part of the second round of Foresight. This is an electronic library of strategic visions, information and views about the future which can be accessed through the Internet at the www.foresight.gov.uk website.

LINK

The LINK scheme provides a government-wide framework for collaborative research in support of sustainable growth and improvements in the quality of life, in line with Foresight priorities. LINK aims to promote partnerships in commercially relevant research projects between industry and higher education institutions and other research base organisations. Under the scheme, government departments and Research Councils fund up to 50 per cent of the cost of research projects, with industry providing the balance.

Since 1988, 68 LINK programmes have supported over 1,300 projects with a total value of more than £600 million (over half of which comes from industry) and involving some 1,900 companies. Over 800 of these projects have been completed. The latest programmes deal with future integrated transport, applied genomics, optical systems, and people at the centre of communication and information technologies. Within LINK, Foresight Link Awards support projects outside areas covered by LINK programmes. New awards, with a total value of £16 million, include: reducing the environmental impact of wash from high-speed ships through hull design and ship operation; a new technique to enable strong human tissues, such as cartilage or bone, to be grown; 'smart-wired' houses with computer sensors to provide help for elderly people; and research into new types of plastic-encapsulated solar cells to reduce energy costs for portable electronics and domestic equipment.

Joint Research Equipment Initiative

The Joint Research Equipment Initiative brings together the higher education funding councils, the Department of Higher and Further Education, Training and Employment in Northern Ireland and the Research Councils. It directs funds for research equipment in strategic priority areas. Since 1996 over £275 million of public and private money has been committed for 'leading edge' equipment for UK universities and colleges.

Joint Infrastructure Fund

The Joint Infrastructure Fund (JIF) is a programme to address the infrastructure problems of universities and was created by the Wellcome Trust and the DTI, each contributing £300 million. The Higher Education Funding Council for England has also contributed £150 million, raising the total fund to £750 million. In the first round of awards in May 1999, £150 million was allocated to over 20 universities. By mid-2000, 109 projects had been awarded nearly £600 million. Successful bids have included an optical/infrared telescope capable of mapping huge tracts of the Universe, a state-of-the-art vaccine centre, a fire safety engineering research facility and a post-genomic research centre to make advances in healthcare using data amassed by the Human Genome Project.

A £1 billion initiative announced in July 2000 builds on the Joint Infrastructure Fund (which will continue until 2001–02). The Science Research Investment Fund—a two-year partnership between the Government and the Wellcome Trust—will finance new infrastructure schemes across the spectrum of science and engineering during 2002–04. The Government will provide £775 million and the Wellcome Trust £225 million.

There will be a further round of awards in 2001.

University Challenge Fund

The University Challenge Fund is a competitive scheme which offers financing to universities to help them in the early stages of turning research into commercial products. The first round involved over £65 million of investment funds: the Government contributed £25 million, the Wellcome Trust £18 million and the Gatsby Charitable Foundation £2 million, with the remainder raised by universities. Fifteen seed funds were established, allowing 37 institutions (28 universities and nine institutes) access to investment capital. A second round of the University Challenge Fund competition was announced in the Science and Innovation White Paper in July 2000. In this round, £15 million will be available to provide seed funding to develop researchers' ideas to the stage where they can be taken up by industry, or attract venture capital to form a spin-off company.

Science Enterprise Challenge

The Science Enterprise Challenge was launched in February 1999 as a £25 million competition to establish up to eight centres of enterprise in UK universities. Universities were invited to submit proposals for establishing world-class centres which would foster the commercialisation of research and new ideas, stimulate scientific entrepreneurialism, and incorporate the teaching of enterprise into the science and engineering curricula. The winners of the competition were announced in September 1999: the universities of: Bristol, Cambridge, Glasgow, Imperial College of Science, Technology and Medicine, London Business School, University of Manchester Institute of Science and Technology, Nottingham Business School and Sheffield—some in partnership with other universities. In a further round of the competition worth £4.5 million, four additional centres were announced in June 2000—at Durham, Warwick, Ulster and Oxford universities—and some of these centres are also in partnership with other universities.

Public Awareness

The Government seeks to raise the status of SET among the general public, by increasing awareness of the contribution of SET to the UK's economic wealth and quality of life. Raising awareness is important in encouraging young people to pursue careers in science and engineering. To this end, the Government supports activities such as the annual science festival of the British Association for the Advancement of Science (BAAS) and National Science Week. The Committee on the Public Understanding of Science (COPUS), set up by the Royal Society, the BAAS and the Royal Institution (see p. 445), acts as a co-ordinator for those fostering public understanding and promotes best practice in the field.

> More than 400 schoolchildren attended a one-day event *A Millennium of British Mathematics* at the 200-year-old Royal Institution in London in March 2000 to mark World Mathematics Year. Presentations at the event by eminent British mathematicians included a display of the butterfly effect in chaos theory, 'illegal' symmetries in crystalline structures and the catastrophe theorem—applications of this to the buckling of beams, the biting of dogs, the behaviour of nesting fish and a stock market crash were illustrated. In September 2000 a festival, 'creating Sparks', celebrated creativity at the frontiers of science and the arts, featuring over 400 events.

Science festivals are also a growing feature of local co-operative efforts to further understanding of the contribution made by science to everyday life. Schools, museums, laboratories, higher education institutions and industry contribute to a variety of special events. The longest-established single-location annual science festival is the Edinburgh International Science Festival.

Activities such as these are important in assuring continued interest in SET among young people making educational and career choices. They also help to enhance the public's ability to relate to scientific issues in general and to make informed judgments about scientific developments. The Government is increasing its understanding of public attitudes to science through public consultation. Examples are consultation on developments in biosciences, held in 1999, and a broader national survey on public attitudes to science, conducted by the Government in 2000 in partnership with the Wellcome Trust.

Women

The Promoting SET for Women Unit within OST at the DTI was established in 1994 in response to a report which found that women were under-represented in the SET sectors, especially at senior levels. The Unit has highlighted the benefits to business of providing a working environment sensitive to the needs of women scientists and engineers who combine a career and family responsibilities. It seeks to ensure that careers information for girls and women is widely available and to promote good employment practices, such as the provision of childcare facilities and job sharing. A website (www.set4women.gov.uk) has been launched promoting SET for girls and women and giving details of the Unit's activities.

Industrial and Intellectual Property

The Government supports innovation through the promotion of a national and international system for the establishment of intellectual property rights. These matters are the responsibility of the Patent Office, an executive agency of the DTI. The Office is responsible for the granting of patents, and registration of designs and trade marks. In 1999 it received over 30,000 applications for patents and more than 84,000 applications for trade marks. The Patent Office encourages worldwide harmonisation of rules and procedures, and the modernisation and simplification of intellectual property law. International patenting arrangements include the European Patent Convention and the Patent Co-operation Treaty. For trade marks the European Community Trade Mark System and the Madrid Protocol provide means of extending rights beyond the borders of the United Kingdom. The Patent Office website and Central Enquiry Unit offer detailed information about all aspects of intellectual property rights to its customers.

R&D's important role in a knowledge-driven economy is further recognised in an intellectual property rights action plan set out in the Competitiveness White Paper (see p. 390), which focuses on making these rights more affordable and accessible. Further impetus has been given to work on the exploitation of public sector research through the publication in August 1999 of the Baker report, *Creating Knowledge: Creating Wealth—Realising the Economic Potential of Public Sector Research Establishments.* The key recommendations were:

- overcoming the risk avoidance culture in central government that inhibits entrepreneurial behaviour;
- giving government laboratories greater financial and management freedom; and
- reforming Civil Service conduct rules so as to reward scientists for exploiting their work.

The Government has welcomed the report. In implementing its recommendations, it will maintain the balance between pursuing exploitation and preserving both propriety and a continuing source of independent advice on sometimes controversial scientific subjects.

GOVERNMENT DEPARTMENTS

Department of Trade and Industry

In 2000–01 DTI's planned expenditure on SET is £380 million: £267 million on R&D and £113 million on technology transfer. Expenditure covers innovation and technology for a number of industrial sectors, including aeronautics, biotechnology, chemicals, communications, engineering, environmental technology, IT, space (see p. 437), and nuclear and non-nuclear energy. DTI is committed to helping UK businesses successfully exploit their ideas, and to promoting a business environment to encourage this. DTI's Innovation Budget is being increased over three years by some 20 per cent to nearly £230 million by 2001–02.

Innovation embraces the development, design and financing of new products, services and processes, exploitation of new markets, creation of new businesses and associated changes in management of people and organisational practices. Through its Innovation Unit, a mixed team of business secondees and government officials, DTI seeks to promote a culture of innovation in all sectors of the economy. In Northern Ireland the Industrial Research and Technology Unit has a similar role to that of the DTI, supporting industrial R&D, technology transfer and innovation.

Technology and Knowledge Transfer

DTI aims to increase collaboration and the flow of knowledge between the SET base and businesses; improve access to sources of technology and technological expertise; improve the capacity of business to use technology effectively; and increase the uptake of the latest technology and best practice techniques.

One example of a technology and knowledge transfer mechanism is TCS (formerly known as the Teaching Company Scheme); this is funded by six government departments and five Research Councils as well as by the participating companies. At any one time there are nearly 700 TCS programmes, each involving one or more graduates working in a company on a project that is central to its business needs. Each TCS programme lasts for at least two years and projects are jointly supervised by personnel from the knowledge base and the company. Small and medium-sized enterprises (SMEs) are involved in around 90 per cent of TCS programmes. The Competitiveness White Paper announced a commitment by DTI to double its expenditure on TCS and the aim is to increase the number of schemes to around 1,000 at any one time by 2002. The TCS scheme now has a common advisory board with LINK (see p. 431) to help increase the number of TCS programmes following on from LINK-funded research.

To help UK companies remain competitive in an increasingly global market, the DTI's International Technology Service (ITS) enables UK companies to become aware of, and gain access to, new technological developments and management practices not present in the UK. The ITS highlights developments and opportunities overseas; and assists companies to access technology, set up licensing agreements and collaborative ventures, and to gain first-hand experience of new technology and leading management practices.

Smart

The 'Smart' scheme helps individuals and SMEs review their use of technology, access technology, and research and develop technologically innovative products and processes. Traditionally, help has been available for feasibility studies into innovative technology and for development projects, to develop up to prototype stage new products and processes. During 1999, three new elements were introduced to Smart:

- technology reviews, which provide grants towards the consultancy costs of an expert review of a company's use of technology compared to best practice in its industry sector;
- technology studies, which provide grants for a more in-depth consultancy to help a business identify technological opportunities leading to innovative products and processes; and
- micro projects, which provide grants of up to £10,000 to help individuals and small firms with fewer than ten employees to develop low-cost prototypes of products and processes involving technical advances and/or novelty.

Business Links (see p. 391) have an important role in providing advice on all aspects of Smart, generating suitable feasibility studies and development projects, and in helping firms to submit applications. Smart is managed in England by the Small Business Service (see p. 391). Separate Smart schemes are operated in Scotland, Wales and Northern Ireland.

Aeronautics

The DTI's Civil Aircraft Research and Technology Demonstration Programme (CARAD) supports research and technology demonstration in aeronautics. In 2000–01 the CARAD budget is £20 million. The programme is part of the national aeronautics research effort, with almost half of the supported research work being conducted in industry, and around a third at the Defence Evaluation and Research Agency (see below). Universities and other research organisations receive about 7 per cent of funding. CARAD and earlier programmes have supported a range of projects, including aluminium and composite airframe materials, more efficient and environmentally friendly engines, and advanced aircraft systems.

Measurement Standards

The DTI finances work on measurement standards under the National Measurement System (NMS—see p. 394) and materials metrology programmes, contributing £38 million and £8 million a year respectively. Although most of the work is carried out at the National Physical Laboratory, the Laboratory of the Government Chemist, the National Engineering Laboratory and the National Weights and Measures Laboratory, the DTI is taking steps to increase competition in these programmes and to work more closely with business in order to identify its future needs. The NMS provides the infrastructure to ensure that measurements can be made on a consistent basis throughout the UK.

Ministry of Defence

The Government has traditionally invested considerable sums in technological research for defence purposes, and about £450 million is currently being spent in this area to ensure that the UK's armed forces stay ahead of threats from potential adversaries. The MoD has a *research* budget and also a much larger *equipment procurement* budget. The latter includes development—the design and testing, which are normally carried out by industry for the MoD, of specific equipment—on which about £2 billion a year is spent.

Currently almost all MoD research is carried out through the Defence Evaluation and Research Agency (DERA), the largest single scientific employer in the UK. Its role is to supply scientific and technical services primarily to the MoD but also to other government departments. DERA has set up five dual-use (civil/military) technology centres in subjects ranging from structural materials to high-performance computing, to enhance the degree of collaboration between DERA, industry and the academic science base.

DERA subcontracts some research to industry and universities, and works closely with industry to ensure that scientific and technological advances are integrated at an early stage into development and production. This technology transfer is not just confined to the defence industry but has also led to important 'spin-offs' into civil markets, in fields ranging from new materials and electronic devices to advanced aerodynamics. These spin-offs are encouraged through the Defence Diversification Agency.

To enable DERA to continue to support the MoD and the wider science base, in July 2000 the Government announced its intention to adopt a Public-Private Partnership for DERA which could potentially take effect in 2001. This would result in around 75 per cent of DERA's staff transferring to a new private sector company, with the remaining 25 per cent continuing to work for government.

Department of the Environment, Transport and the Regions (DETR)

The DETR funds research in response to the requirements of all its major policy responsibilities: environmental protection; housing; construction; regeneration; the countryside; local and regional government; planning; roads and local transport; and railways, aviation and shipping. Total expenditure for 2000–01 is £191 million (including spending by executive agencies and non-departmental public bodies—NDPBs). Major programmes of industrial support aim to benefit the construction sector and to help British industry's adoption of energy-efficient technologies. Through the Darwin Initiative (see p. 320), British expertise is being made available to assist countries that are rich in biodiversity but have insufficient financial or technical resources to implement the Biodiversity Convention.

Ministry of Agriculture, Fisheries and Food (MAFF)

MAFF co-ordinates its research programme with devolved administrations, the Research Councils and other public bodies in related areas. The programme supports the Ministry's wide-ranging responsibilities for protecting the public in relation to farm produce and animal diseases transmissible to humans; protecting and enhancing the rural and marine environment; reducing risks from flooding and coastal erosion; improving animal health and welfare; and encouraging modern, efficient and competitive agriculture, fishing and food industries. The budget for research expenditure in 2000–01 is £118 million, including support for the Royal Botanic Gardens, Kew (see p. 446).

Department of Health (DH)

The DH supports R&D to provide the evidence needed to inform policy and practice in public health, healthcare and social care. It delivers this objective through:

- National Health Service (NHS) R&D Funding, which supports projects funded by other non-commercial R&D sources (including charities) carried out in the NHS, and also specific health and social care projects meeting identified research needs of the DH and the NHS;
- a Policy Research Programme (PRP), directly commissioned by the DH; and
- *ad hoc* project funding from other DH R&D budgets and support for NDPBs.

The DH expects to spend some £520 million on research in 2000–01: £449 million on NHS R&D, £30 million on the PRP and £41 million involving the NDPBs and *ad hoc* budgets.

Department for International Development (DFID)

DFID commissions and sponsors knowledge generation in natural resources, health and population, engineering, education and social sciences. Financial provision for this in 2000–01 is about £120 million, covering research projects addressing particular development problems and projects to improve research, and research capacity relevant to particular countries. DFID also contributes to international centres and programmes generating knowledge on development issues. These contributions include support for the EU Framework Programmes, which sponsor research and technological development in renewable natural resources, agriculture, health and information technologies, and for the Consultative Group on International Agricultural Research (CGIAR).

Scottish Executive

In many areas—electrical and electronic engineering, medicine, agriculture and biological sciences, fisheries and marine science—Scotland's science base has an international reputation for research excellence. The majority of the Scottish Executive's support for the science base is disbursed by the Scottish Higher Education Funding Council. In total this amounts to some £616 million for 2000–01, including £313 million for research and £23 million to support the strategic development of the sector. A further £75 million encourages and funds agricultural and fisheries research, and related biological, food, environmental, economic and social science—most of this goes to the Scottish Agricultural and Biological Research Institutes, the Fisheries

Research Service and the Scottish Agricultural College. In addition, about £135 million goes to Scottish research institutions from the UK Research Councils.

The Scottish Executive Enterprise and Lifelong Learning Department encourages the development of science-based industry, for example, by promoting and administering government and EU industrial R&D schemes. The enterprise network in Scotland—Scottish Enterprise, Highlands and Islands Enterprise and LECs (see chapter 11)—addresses the need for innovation and technology transfer, both through grant support for innovation and through a wide range of initiatives.

Scottish ministers have announced plans to produce a strategy for science in Scotland early in 2001.

Space Activities

The UK's civil space programme is brought together through the British National Space Centre (BNSC), a partnership of government departments and the Research Councils. BNSC's key aims are to develop practical and economic uses of space, to promote the competitiveness of British space companies in world markets, to maintain the UK's position in space science, to foster the development of innovative technology and to improve understanding of the Earth's environment and resources. These are realised primarily by collaboration with other European nations through the European Space Agency (ESA).

Through BNSC, the Government spends around £180 million a year on space activities. About three-quarters of this is channelled through ESA for collaborative programmes on Earth observation, telecommunications and space science, much of which returns to the UK through contracts awarded to British industry. The remaining quarter of the space budget is spent on international meteorological programmes carried out through the European Meteorological Satellite Organisation (EUMETSAT), developing experiments (such as the Beagle 2 Mars Lander) for ESA satellites, and on the national programme, which is aimed at complementing R&D supported through ESA. Around half of the British space programme is concerned with satellite-based Earth observation (remote-sensing) for commercial and environmental applications.

The UK is also a major contributor to ESA's latest Earth observation satellite, ENVISAT, due to be launched in 2001. This will carry a new generation of radar and radiometer systems as well as other scientific environmental instruments, some of which have been either designed or constructed in Britain. British companies are also active in the development of microsatellites.

A quarter of the UK's space budget is devoted to space science led by the Particle Physics and Astronomy Research Council, in support of astronomy, planetary science and geophysics. The UK is contributing substantially to the SOHO mission to study the Sun; to the Cluster mission (see p. 442) launched in mid-2000 to study solar-terrestrial relationships; to the Infrared Space Observatory, which is investigating the birth and death of stars; and to the Cassini Huygens mission, a seven-year programme to send a probe to Saturn and its moon Titan, launched in 1997. It is also participating in XMM, ESA's X-ray spectroscopy mission launched

Three small satellite projects have been announced under MOSAIC—BNSC's Small Satellite Programme. The projects offer innovative ways of demonstrating small satellite technology and may open up new markets for their use. They could make environmental disaster monitoring faster and cheaper.

- TOPSAT aims to deliver low-cost, relatively high-resolution images direct to local users wherever they need them;
- GEMINI will develop a low-cost small geostationary satellite for telecommunications; and
- the Disaster Monitoring Constellation project will develop a network of affordable microsatellites, which could provide daily imaging of disaster areas.

in December 1999 to investigate X-ray emissions from black holes.

The UK is taking an active role in the largest current international project in ground-based astronomy. The Gemini project involves building two 8 m telescopes at Mauna Kea (Hawaii) and Cerro Pachón (Chile): the former became operational in June 1999 and the latter is expected to be fully operational in August 2001. The other partners are the United States, Canada, Argentina, Brazil and Chile. The UK has a 25 per cent stake in the work, with major responsibility for the primary mirror support system and much of the control software.

ESA's £400 million Living Planet environmental research programme, to help scientists understand and predict the Earth's environment and humankind's effects upon it, was launched in 1999. BNSC will contribute £67 million to this programme. The first project to benefit from the programme will be the British CRYOSAT mission, to be launched in 2002, which will study the effects of global warming on the polar ice caps and floating Arctic sea ice. UK environmental scientists also have a significant interest in a second mission, which will measure soil moisture and ocean salinity.

Two new centres of excellence in Earth observation will use satellites and models to help forecast environmental change and play a role in exploiting data from ENVISAT and the Living Planet programme. The Data Assimilation Research Centre will forecast changes in the Earth's systems, while the Centre for Polar Observation Modelling will measure changes in polar ice which could cause rising sea levels and changes in ocean circulation.

The UK is also developing the Geostationary Earth Radiation Budget instrument, which is intended to provide accurate measurements of the energy source for the Earth's climate and, together with the National Aeronautics and Space Administration (NASA), the High Resolution Dynamics Limb Sounder, which will provide measurements of upper atmosphere trace chemicals and temperature.

The UK has many bilateral agreements for scientific research with other countries, such as Russia, Japan and the United States. For example, British scientists contributed to the high-resolution camera for Chandra (the NASA X-ray satellite).

Another major area of British space expertise is satellite communications and navigation. In Europe, the UK is both a leading producer and user of satellite communications technology (see p. 486). It is taking a leading role in preparations for future ESA satellite communications missions, including ARTEMIS, which will provide important communications links for the ENVISAT programme. Britain is also contributing to the Galileo global navigation satellite system.

INTERNATIONAL COLLABORATION

European Union

Since 1984 the EU has operated a series of R&D framework programmes, across a range of disciplines and sectors, to strengthen the scientific and technological basis of European industry and support the development of EU policies. The Fifth Framework Programme, which runs for four years (1999–2002), supports strategic and applied multidisciplinary research targeted at tackling pressing European problems, such as land transport and marine technologies, the ageing population, e-commerce and the 'city of tomorrow'. The Research Councils and the British Council maintain a joint office in Brussels to promote UK participation in European research programmes. The UK is actively engaged in the development of a common European Space Strategy involving the ESA, the EU and others.

Other International Activities

Over 800 UK organisations have taken part in EUREKA, an industry-led scheme to encourage European co-operation in developing advanced products and processes with worldwide sales potential. There are 30 members of EUREKA, including the 15 EU countries and the European Commission. Some 600 projects are in progress, involving firms, universities and research organisations. Over 500 projects have finished. One example was of a project involving software used to create special effects in films such as *Notting Hill* and a number of television advertisements.

The COST programme (European co-operation in the field of scientific and technical research) is a multilateral agreement involving 32 countries (including all the EU member states, many Mediterranean, Central European and Eastern European countries and Israel). Its purpose is to encourage co-operation in national research activities across Europe, with participants from industry, academia and research laboratories. Transport, telecommunications and materials have traditionally been the largest areas supported. New areas include physics, chemistry, neuroscience and the application of biotechnology to agriculture, including forestry. The UK participates in the majority of COST actions.

Another example of international collaboration is CERN, the European Laboratory for Particle Physics, based in Geneva, where the proposed Large Hadron Collider is due to be completed by 2005. Scientific programmes at CERN aim to test, verify and develop the 'standard model' of the origins and structure of the Universe. There are 20 member states. The Particle Physics and Astronomy Research Council (PPARC—see p. 442) leads UK participation in CERN and the Council for the Central Laboratory of the Research Councils co-ordinates the UK research community's involvement in the CERN project. Britain also contributes to the high-flux neutron source at the Institut Laue-Langevin and to the European Synchrotron Radiation Facility, both in Grenoble.

The PPARC is a partner in the European Incoherent Scatter Radar Facility within the Arctic Circle, which conducts research on the ionosphere. The Natural Environment Research Council (NERC) has a major involvement in international programmes of research into global climate change organised through the World Climate Research Programme and the International Geosphere-Biosphere Programme. It also supports the UK's subscription to the Ocean Drilling Program.

Through the Medical Research Council (MRC), the UK participates in the European Molecular Biology Laboratory (EMBL), at Heidelberg. The European Bioinformatics Institute, an outstation of the EMBL, at Hinxton, near Cambridge, provides up-to-date information on molecular biology and genome sequencing for researchers throughout Europe. The MRC pays Britain's contribution to the Human Frontier Science Programme, which supports international collaborative research into brain function and biological function through molecular-level approaches. It also pays Britain's subscription to the International Agency for Cancer Research.

The Research Councils have a number of bilateral arrangements to promote international collaboration. For example, the Biotechnology and Biological Sciences Research Council (BBSRC) has agreements with its equivalent organisations in France, the Netherlands, the United States, Canada, Japan, Korea and India, and provides travel funding and fellowships to encourage international linkages.

The UK is a member of the science and technology committees of such international organisations as the OECD and NATO, and of various specialised agencies of the United Nations, including the United Nations Educational, Scientific and Cultural Organisation (UNESCO). The Research Councils, the Royal Society and the British Academy are members of the European Science Foundation, and a number of British scientists are involved in its initiatives.

The British Government also enters into bilateral agreements with other governments to encourage closer collaboration in science, engineering and technology. Staff in British Embassies, High Commissions and British Council offices conduct government business on, and promote contacts in, SET between the UK and overseas countries; and help to inform a large number of organisations in the UK about developments and initiatives overseas. There are science and technology attachés in British Missions in Washington, Tokyo, Moscow, Ottawa, Paris, Bonn, Munich, Rome, Beijing (Peking), Taipei and Seoul, and the July 2000 White Paper included a proposal to extend the network. A number of British Council offices have designated Science Officer posts.

The British Council promotes the creativity and innovation of cutting-edge UK science through events, partnership programmes, seminars, exhibitions and information provision. It balances one-to-one scientific links with projects aimed at raising awareness of scientific issues among overseas public audiences through popular communication.

RESEARCH COUNCILS

Each Research Council is an autonomous body established under Royal Charter, with members of its governing council drawn from the universities, professions, industry and government. The Councils support research, study and training in universities and other higher education institutions, and carry out or support research, through their own institutes and at international research centres, often jointly with other public sector bodies and international organisations. They provide awards to about 15,000 postgraduate students in science, social sciences, engineering and technology. In addition to funding from the OST, the Councils receive income from research commissioned by government departments and the private sector.

Three Research Councils are sponsoring a new interdisciplinary centre to help society find sustainable solutions to the problems caused by climate change. The Tyndall Centre for Climate Change Research, based at the University of East Anglia in Norwich, will receive £10 million over five years from the Natural Environment Research Council, the Engineering and Physical Sciences Research Council, and the Economic and Social Research Council. Its research programme will include modelling of climate and related systems; assessment and regional analysis; impacts of, and adaptation to, climate change; energy technologies; and greenhouse gases.

Engineering and Physical Sciences Research Council (EPSRC)

The EPSRC, the Research Council with the largest budget (£413 million in 2000–01), has responsibility to promote and support high-quality basic, strategic and applied research and related postgraduate training in engineering and the physical sciences. It also has responsibility to provide advice, disseminate knowledge and promote public understanding in these areas. Its remit is delivered through nine programme areas: physics, chemistry, mathematics, the generic technologies of information technology and materials, three engineering programmes (general engineering, engineering for manufacturing and engineering for infrastructure, the environment and healthcare) and the life sciences. This last programme was set up in 1999 to cover research and training at the interface between the life sciences and all areas of engineering and the physical sciences.

EPSRC 'Partnerships for Public Awareness' awards were launched in 1998 to improve public awareness of leading research and its possible impact on society. The awards encourage researchers to communicate the value of their work to the public. In the first two years, 47 projects received awards totalling over £1.2 million. Two projects received EPSRC's 'Year 2000' accolade: a schools' robot league and an electron microscope which the public can operate by remote control over the Internet. The awards bring together scientists with industry specialists, schools, artists, poets, community groups and the media in a wide range of activities.

A series of posters on mathematics is being displayed on the London Underground during 2000. They have been developed by the Isaac Newton Institute for Mathematical Sciences at Cambridge University. Each poster shows the contribution of mathematics to everyday life. Themes chosen for the posters include weather, medicine, economics, plants and computer chips. The campaign is intended also to contribute to UNESCO's World Mathematics Year.

Medical Research Council (MRC)

The MRC, with an overall budget of £345 million for 2000–01, is the main source of public funds for biomedical and related sciences research. It supports research and training aimed at maintaining and improving human health. The MRC advances knowledge and technology to meet the needs of user communities, including the providers of healthcare and the biotechnology, food, healthcare, medical instrumentation, pharmaceutical and other biomedical-related industries. About half the MRC's expenditure is allocated to its own institutes and units, the rest going mainly on grant support of research in universities, including training awards. The Council has several large institutes, including the National Institute for Medical Research at Mill Hill in London and the Laboratory of Molecular Biology in Cambridge; it also runs the Clinical Sciences Centre at Imperial College, London. It has more than 50 research units and a number of smaller scientific teams in the UK.

> The Human Genome Project is an international project to identify all the genes of the human body and has involved thousands of scientists working at 16 centres across the world. Completion of the initial stage—mapping of 97 per cent of the human genome (of which 85 per cent has been accurately sequenced)—was announced at the end of June 2000. Nearly one-third of the genome was decoded by scientists working at the Sanger Centre at Hinxton in Cambridgeshire (see p. 427).

Natural Environment Research Council (NERC)

The NERC carries out Earth system science. In 2000–01 it will spend its budget of £223 million in the following areas: biodiversity; environmental risks and hazards; global change; natural resource management; and pollution and waste.

The Council supports research in its own and other research establishments as well as research and training in universities. It also provides a range of facilities for use by the wider environmental science community, including a marine research fleet. NERC establishments are the British Geological Survey, the British Antarctic Survey (which has taken delivery of a new ship, RRS *Ernest Shackleton*), the Centre for Ecology and Hydrology, the Plymouth and Dunstaffnage Marine and Proudman Oceanographic Laboratories, together with a number of university-based units. The Southampton Oceanography Centre, a partnership with Southampton University, undertakes research, training and support activities in oceanography, geology and aspects of marine technology and engineering. The NERC's Research Ships Unit is located at the Centre.

> Autosub, NERC's pioneering robot submarine, has now operated on eight autonomous missions, the first time any autonomous underwater vehicle has operated successfully beyond the range of its support vessel. Its missions included counting herring shoals with sonar; measuring turbulence near the sea floor; and detecting manganese in Scottish lochs. Future scientific missions include going under the Antarctic sea ice to measure ice thickness and the abundance of krill. Autosub has been awarded 'Millennium Product' status by the Design Council.

Biotechnology and Biological Sciences Research Council (BBSRC)

The BBSRC has a budget of £202 million for 2000–01. It supports basic and strategic research and research training related to the understanding and exploitation of biological systems, which underpin the agriculture, bioprocessing, chemical, food, healthcare, pharmaceutical and other biotechnology-related industries. The scientific themes are biomolecular sciences; genes and developmental biology; biochemistry and cell biology; plant and microbial sciences; animal sciences; agri-food; and engineering and biological systems. As well as funding research in universities and other research centres, the BBSRC sponsors eight research institutes.

The BBSRC funds research that provides the UK with world-class genetics resources, databases and genomics technologies for a variety of model laboratory species and for important microbes, crops and livestock. This research underpins many applications. For example, greater precision in drug design and in matching therapeutics to the genetic make-up of patients is expected to become possible, crops and livestock can be bred to meet environmental and welfare concerns, and newly identified molecules will form a basis for novel drugs, catalysts and fine chemicals for manufacturers.

The BBSRC has established six specialist Centres for Structural Biology, the science that underpins understanding of, and ability to predict how, the function of individual biological molecules and large molecular assemblies, such as virus particles, is determined by their structure.

The Bioscience Business Plan competition has been developed and piloted by the BBSRC with support from the MRC and private sector funding. It encourages the formation of new bioscience ventures by enabling participants to develop and submit ideas for new start-up businesses.

Fundamental research into the nature of genes, how they work and how they can be transferred between organisms, has underpinned the development of the technology of genetic modification (GM). As well as driving new applications of GM, the research is providing basic information about the behaviour of genes, and of genetically modified organisms (GMOs). In May 1999 the Government announced a new framework for overseeing developments in biotechnology. The Agricultural and Environment Biotechnology Commission and the Human Genetics Commission have been set up to advise on agricultural and environmental issues and on human genetics respectively. They are working alongside the Food Standards Agency (see p. 208) as part of the strategic framework.

Particle Physics and Astronomy Research Council (PPARC)

The main task of the PPARC, which has a budget of £200 million for 2000–01, is to encourage and support a balanced and cost-effective research programme into fundamental physical processes. Its three main areas of research are:

- particle physics—theoretical and experimental research into elementary particles and the fundamental forces of nature;
- astronomy (including cosmology and astrophysics)—the origin, structure and evolution of the Universe, stars and galaxies; and
- planetary science (including solar and terrestrial physics)—the origin and evolution of the solar system and the influence of the Sun on planetary bodies, particularly Earth.

The European Cluster II space mission, launched in 2000 and comprising four identical spacecraft, is part of an integrated series of experiments to learn more about how the Sun affects the Earth. The spacecraft will spend the next two years in close formation around the Earth, gathering information about how the Sun affects space weather—space weather has an impact on the satellites used for communications, navigation and weather forecasting.

The PPARC's support involves the provision of funds to universities to undertake research and the provision of facilities to enable that research to take place. Facilities are provided on a national and international basis, the latter including membership of ESA and CERN (see pp. 437 and 439).

A UK project at Boulby (North Yorkshire) is undertaking experiments underground to look for weakly interacting particles which may provide more clues to improve understanding of the total matter density of the Universe.

Economic and Social Research Council (ESRC)

The ESRC, with an R&D provision of £71 million for 2000–01, supports research and training to enhance the UK's economic competitiveness, quality of life, and the effectiveness of public services and policy. All research funded by the ESRC is conducted in higher education institutions or independent research establishments. The Council has nine priority themes: economic performance and development; environment and sustainability; globalisation, regions and emerging markets; governance, regulation and accountability; technology and people; innovation; knowledge, communication and learning; lifespan, lifestyles and health; and social inclusion and exclusion.

> The ESRC has launched the Millennium Cohort—a £2.2 million longitudinal study of 15,000 people born in the period July 2000 to June 2001. Data will be collected from this group of people over their lifetime on all aspects of their lives, providing a unique insight into the effects of change over the first half of the 21st century and beyond. It will also greatly enhance the capacity of current longitudinal studies to chart social change.

A major research programme on devolution and constitutional change in the UK has been launched. It will explore the political, economic, social and geographical effects of constitutional changes connected with the creation of the Scottish Parliament, the National Assembly for Wales, the Northern Ireland Assembly, Regional Development Agencies (see p. 394) and the London Assembly and Mayor (see p. 63). The programme's aim is to increase understanding of these processes of change and the consequent effects on people's lives.

Council for the Central Laboratory of the Research Councils (CCLRC)

The CCLRC promotes scientific and engineering research by providing facilities and technical expertise primarily to meet the needs of the research communities supported by the other Research Councils. Its R&D budget for 2000–01 is £115 million, of which £86 million comes through agreements with other Research Councils and another £24 million from contracts and agreements with the EU, overseas countries, and other industries and organisations. It covers a broad range of science and technology, including materials, structural and biomolecular science using accelerators, synchrotrons and lasers, satellite instrumentation and data processing, remote sensing, electronics, sensor technology, computing, mobile communications, micro-engineering, microsystems and particle physics.

> Research on game theory and mechanism design undertaken at the ESRC's Centre for Economic Learning and Social Evolution was behind the design and operation of the auction for mobile telephone licences that will raise £22.5 billion (see p. 379). Economists are now designing markets across a wide range of industries, including electricity, environmental emissions trading, TV rights for football, and business-to-business Internet transactions.

> A third generation synchrotron—'diamond'—will be the largest scientific facility to be built in the UK for over 30 years. It will be built at the Rutherford Appleton Laboratory and be funded by a partnership of the UK Government, the Wellcome Trust and the French Government. Its function will be to produce pinpoint ultraviolet and X-ray light beams that will feed into a suite of advanced instruments. The data from these instruments are expected to enable scientists and engineers to understand the basic structure of matter and materials with the intention of revealing, for example, the detail of the building blocks of life and the origin of Earth.

The CCLRC is responsible for three research establishments: the Rutherford Appleton Laboratory in Oxfordshire; the Daresbury Laboratory in Cheshire; and the Chilbolton Observatory in Hampshire. These centres provide facilities too large or complex to be housed by individual academic institutions. Among the facilities are ISIS (the world's leading source of pulsed neutrons and muons), some of the world's brightest lasers and the pioneering Daresbury synchrotron source.

RESEARCH IN HIGHER EDUCATION INSTITUTIONS

Universities carry out most of the UK's long-term strategic and basic research in science and technology. The higher education funding councils provide the main general funds to support research in universities and other higher education institutions in Great Britain. These funds pay for the salaries of permanent academic staff, who usually teach as well as undertake research, and contribute to the infrastructure for research. The quality of research performance is a key element in the allocation of funding. In Northern Ireland institutions are funded by the Department of Higher and Further Education, Training and Employment.

> In November 1999 the Government announced funding of £70 million for a joint institute involving the Massachusetts Institute of Technology and Cambridge University. The Institute will undertake education and research designed to improve the UK's entrepreneurship, productivity and competitiveness, and stimulate the development of technology-based business out of the academic base.

Basic and strategic research in higher education institutions are also financed by the Research Councils. Institutions undertaking research with the support of Research Council grants have the rights over the commercial exploitation of their research, subject to the prior agreement of the sponsoring Research Council. They may make use of technology transfer experts and other specialists to help exploit and license the results of their research. The other main channels of support are industry, charities, government departments and the EU. The high quality of research in higher education institutions, and their marketing skills, have enabled them to attract more funding from a larger range of external sources, especially in contract income from industry and charities.

Science Parks

The UK has a range of Science Parks—business support and technology transfer initiatives having formal or operational links to a higher education institution or other major research centre and encouraging and supporting the start-up, incubation and growth of innovation-led, high-growth, knowledge-based businesses. The UK Science Park Association numbers 60 such initiatives, which between them host over 1,300 firms employing over 26,000 people in total. Many of these firms are spin-offs from the associated institution or are start-up enterprises in fields of high-technology such as software, biotechnology, analytical services or consultancy.

OTHER ORGANISATIONS

Research and Technology Organisations (RTOs)

RTOs are independent organisations carrying out commercially relevant research and other services on behalf of industry, often relating to a specific industrial sector. Others are contract research organisations undertaking specific projects for any client. The Association of Independent Research and Technology Organisations has 44 members which together employ about 10,000 people.

Charitable Organisations

Medical research charities are a major source of funds for biomedical research in the UK.

Their combined contribution in 1999–2000 was about £540 million. The three largest contributors are the Wellcome Trust, the Imperial Cancer Research Fund and the Cancer Research Campaign.

Professional and Learned Institutions

There are numerous technical institutions, professional associations and learned societies in the UK, many of which promote their own disciplines or the education and professional well-being of their members. The Council of Science and Technology Institutes has ten member institutes representing biology, biochemistry, chemistry, the environment, food science and technology, geology, hospital physics and physics.

The Engineering Council promotes and regulates the engineering profession. It is supported by 125 industry affiliates, which include large private sector companies and government departments, 34 professional engineering institutions and eight affiliates. In partnership with the institutions, the Council accredits higher and further education courses and advises the Government on academic, industrial and professional issues. It also runs a number of promotional activities. Some 285,000 individuals have satisfied the Council's regulations through their institution for registration, as either Chartered Engineers, Incorporated Engineers or as Engineering Technicians.

Royal Society

The Royal Society, founded in 1660, is the UK's academy of science and has 1,200 Fellows and 100 Foreign Members. Many of its Fellows serve on governmental advisory councils and committees concerned with research. The Society has three roles: as the national academy of science, as a learned society and as a funding agency for the scientific community. It offers independent advice to government on science matters, acts as a forum for discussion of scientific issues, and fosters public awareness of science and science education. Its government grant for 2000–01 is £25 million.

Royal Academy of Engineering

The national academy of engineering in Britain is the Royal Academy of Engineering, which has 1,150 Fellows and 80 Foreign Members. It promotes excellence in engineering for the benefit of society, and advises government, Parliament and other official organisations. The Academy's programmes are aimed at attracting first-class students into engineering, raising awareness of the importance of engineering design among undergraduates, developing links between industry and higher education, and increasing industrial investment in engineering research in higher education institutions. It has a government grant of £4 million in 2000–01.

Other Societies

In Scotland the Royal Society of Edinburgh, established in 1783, promotes science by offering postdoctoral research fellowships and studentships, awarding prizes and grants, organising meetings and symposia, and publishing journals. It also acts as a source of independent scientific advice to the Government and others.

Three other major institutions publicise scientific developments by means of lectures and publications for specialists and schoolchildren. Of these, the British Association for the Advancement of Science, founded in 1831, is mainly concerned with science, while the Royal Society of Arts, dating from 1754, deals with the arts and commerce as well as science. The Royal Institution, founded in 1799, also performs these functions and runs its own research laboratories. It also arranges public programmes to bring science to a wider public, including the *Christmas Lectures* and the *Friday Evening Discourses*. Both programmes were started in 1826 by Michael Faraday in the Royal Institution's Albemarle Street lecture theatre. The *Christmas Lectures* now reach a worldwide audience, being broadcast in Britain, other parts of Europe, Japan and the United States.

Zoological Gardens

The Zoological Society of London (ZSL), an independent conservation, science and education charity founded in 1826, runs London Zoo, which occupies about 15 hectares (36 acres) of Regent's Park (London). It also owns and runs Whipsnade Wild Animal Park (243 hectares/600 acres) in Bedfordshire. ZSL is responsible for the Institute of Zoology, which carries out research in support of conservation. The Institute's work covers topics such as ecology, reproductive biology and conservation genetics. ZSL also operates in overseas conservation projects, and is concerned with practical field conservation, primarily in East and Southern Africa, the Middle East and parts of Asia. Other well-known zoos in the UK include those in Edinburgh, Bristol, Chester, Dudley and Marwell (near Winchester).

Botanic Gardens

The Royal Botanic Gardens, Kew, founded in 1759, covers 121 hectares (300 acres) at Kew in south-west London and a 187-hectare (462-acre) estate at Wakehurst Place (Ardingly, in West Sussex). They contain one of the largest collections of living and dried plants in the world. Research is conducted into all aspects of plant life, including physiology, biochemistry, genetics, economic botany and the conservation of habitats and species. During 1998–2000 Kew has been building the Millennium Seed Bank, containing the world's most comprehensive collection of seeds of flowering plants, at Wakehurst Place. Staff are also active in programmes to reintroduce endangered plant species to the wild. Kew participates in joint research programmes in some 50 countries.

The Royal Botanic Garden in Edinburgh was established in 1670, and is the national botanic garden of Scotland. Together with its three associated specialist gardens, which were acquired to provide a range of different climatic and soil conditions, it has become an internationally recognised centre for taxonomy (classification of species); for the conservation and study of living and preserved plants and fungi; and as a provider of horticultural education.

A national botanic garden and research centre for Wales has been developed on a 230-hectare (570-acre) site on the Middleton Hall estate at Llanarthne, near Carmarthen and was opened in May 2000—the first botanic garden to be built in Britain for two centuries.

> The Millennium Seed Bank Project is one of the largest international conservation projects ever undertaken. It aims to collect and conserve seeds of 24,000 species (10 per cent of the estimated total), principally from the world's drylands, by 2010. It also aims to collect and conserve seeds of the entire UK native seed-bearing flora by the end of 2000. The seeds are stored in large underground vaults held at –20° C in the Wellcome Trust Millennium Building at Wakehurst Place. By August 2000 the Seed Bank held 259,606,777 seeds. The Millennium Commission is donating up to £30 million of National Lottery funding towards the estimated £80 million cost of the project and the Wellcome Trust is granting £9 million. A public exhibition area opened at the end of August 2000.

Scientific Museums

The Natural History Museum is one of Britain's most popular visitor attractions (with

> The Millennium Commission is investing over £250 million in the creation of 14 new science and technology centres including Millennium Point, Birmingham; @Bristol; the National Space Science Centre, Leicester; The Odyssey, Belfast; and Our Dynamic Earth, Edinburgh.
>
> The National Space Science Centre in Leicester, Britain's first attraction dedicated to space, will open to the public in spring 2001. Half of the £46.5 million cost is being provided by the Millennium Commission with co-funding by the University of Leicester and Leicester City Council among others. The Centre aims to provide visitors with a journey of discovery, showing technology of the past and the present, to explain current understanding of space and its impact on the future.

1.7 million visitors in 1999–2000), with exhibitions devoted to the Earth and the life sciences. It is founded on collections of 68 million specimens from the natural world, has 350 scientists working in 60 countries, and has 500,000 historically important original works of art. It also offers an advisory service to institutions all over the world. The Science Museum, which had nearly 1.5 million visitors in 1999–2000, promotes the public understanding of the history of science, technology, industry and medicine. A new wing added 10,000 sq metres of display space to the Museum when it was opened in June 2000. This contains galleries on biomedical science and information technology and a 450-seat 3D IMAX (large format screen) theatre. These two museums are in South Kensington, London. Other important collections include those at the Museum of Science & Industry in Manchester, the Museum of the History of Science in Oxford, and the Royal Scottish Museum, Edinburgh.

Further Reading

Excellence and Opportunity—a science and innovation policy for the 21st century. Cm 4814. The Stationery Office, 2000.

The Forward Look 1999. DTI/OST. Cm 4363. The Stationery Office, 1999.

Our Competitive Future: Building the Knowledge Driven Economy (the Competitiveness White Paper). DTI. Cm 4176. The Stationery Office, 1998.

Creating Knowledge: Creating Wealth—Realising the Economic Potential of Public Sector Research Establishments. DTI, 1999.

Guidelines 2000: Scientific Advice and Policy Making. OST, 2000.

The Government's Response to the Baker Report: 'Creating Knowledge, Creating Wealth': Realising the Economic Potential of Public Sector Research Establishments. OST, 2000.

UK Space Strategy 1999–2002. BNSC.

Websites

Office of Science and Technology: www.dti.gov.uk/ost

Council of Science and Technology: www.cst.gov.uk

Foresight: www.foresight.gov.uk

Biotechnology and Biological Sciences Research Council: www.bbsrc.ac.uk

Council for the Central Laboratory of the Research Councils: www.cclrc.ac.uk

Economic and Social Research Council: www.esrc.ac.uk

Engineering and Physical Sciences Research Council: www.epsrc.ac.uk

Medical Research Council: www.mrc.ac.uk

Natural Environment Research Council: www.nerc.ac.uk

Particle Physics and Astronomy Research Council: www.pparc.ac.uk

27 Agriculture, Fishing & Forestry

The Government's long-term policy for agriculture is 'to secure a more competitive and sustainable industry with a stronger market orientation'. It seeks to integrate the social, economic and environmental objectives that will bring this about, and to encourage diversification. The Food Standards Agency was established in 2000.

Agriculture

Major issues in 1999 were the continued low level of farm incomes and the difficulties facing the farming industry, caused by the strength of the pound in relation to the euro; the aftermath of the BSE (bovine spongiform encephalopathy) crisis; and the fall in international commodity prices. Among government measures in response to these problems are:

- a programme involving £1.6 billion of expenditure over 2000–07 on rural improvement measures in England;
- an extra £60 million in support for hill farmers;
- securing £528 million in EU funds during 1999–2004 to compensate farmers for the strength of the pound;
- £6 million to aid improvements in marketing and development;
- an extra £10 million to aid organic conversion;
- deferral of charges for cattle passports (worth £22 million a year) and specified risk material inspections (worth £18 million); and
- an aid package announced in March 2000 worth £203.5 million over three years and including specific programmes to help hard-hit pig and dairy farmers.

In December 1999 the Government set out a strategy for the future of agriculture in the UK, stressing a competitive, diverse and flexible industry, responsive to consumer wishes, environmentally responsible, and an integral part of the rural economy. In Scotland the Scottish Executive is responsible for implementing UK-wide elements of the strategy. The Government regards farming as a vital part of the food chain, worth £55 billion a year, employing 3 million people.

Land Use

Agricultural land makes up 76 per cent of the UK's total land area, with 11.4 million

Table 27.1: EU Agricultural Comparisons

Country	Area farmed ('000 hectares) 1998	Number of farms ('000 holdings) 1997	UAA[1] per holdings (hectares) 1997	External trade balance[2] (ECU billion) 1998
United Kingdom	16,169	233	69.3	–11.1
Austria	3,415	210	16.3	–1.4
Belgium	1,383	67	20.6	1.6[3]
Denmark	2,689	63	42.6	4.2
Finland	2,172	91	23.7	–1.0
France	28,331	680	41.7	11.4
Germany	17,160	534	32.1	–14.4
Greece	3,499	821	4.3	–1.0
Irish Republic	4,342	148	29.4	4.1
Italy	14,833	2,315	6.4	–6.9
Luxembourg	127	3	42.5	1.6[3]
Netherlands	2,011	108	18.6	16.7
Portugal	3,822	417	9.2	–2.6
Spain	25,630	1,208	21.2	2.7
Sweden	3,109	90	34.7	–2.3
EU	**128,691**	**6,989**	**18.4**	**–3.4**

[1] Average utilised agricultural area.
[2] In food and agricultural products.
[3] Belgium and Luxembourg.
There are 100 hectares to a square kilometre; 1 hectare = 2.471 acres.
Sources: Eurostat and European Commission Directorate-General of Agriculture

hectares (28.2 million acres) under crops and grass in 1999. A further 5.8 million hectares (14.4 million acres) were used for rough grazing, most of it in hilly areas.

Farming

In 1999 there were some 239,600 farm holdings in the UK (excluding minor holdings in Great Britain but including all active farms in Northern Ireland). These holdings had an average area of 66.6 hectares (164.6 acres). About 47 per cent of them are smaller than eight European size units (ESUs).[1] About two-thirds of all agricultural land is owner-occupied; the rest is tenanted or rented.

Total income from farming (representing income to those with an entrepreneurial interest in the agricultural industry) was estimated at £2.3 billion in 1999, 1.2 per cent less in real terms than that of 1998. The value of output (including subsidies directly related to products) was 3.1 per cent lower than in 1998, despite a nearly 1 per cent increase in output volume. This fall in output value was offset by reduced costs. Productivity in the industry improved by 2.6 per cent in 1999 as farmers reduced inputs but maintained output levels. Paid labour was significantly reduced; as a result, labour productivity increased by 8.2 per cent.

[1] ESUs measure the financial potential of the holding in terms of the margins which might be expected from stock and crops: 8 ESU is judged the minimum for full-time holdings.

PRODUCTION

Home production of the principal foods is shown in Table 27.2 as a percentage by weight of total supplies. Total new supply is home production plus imports less exports.

Livestock

About half of full-time farms are devoted mainly to dairy farming or to beef cattle and

Agricultural Land Use, UK, 1999

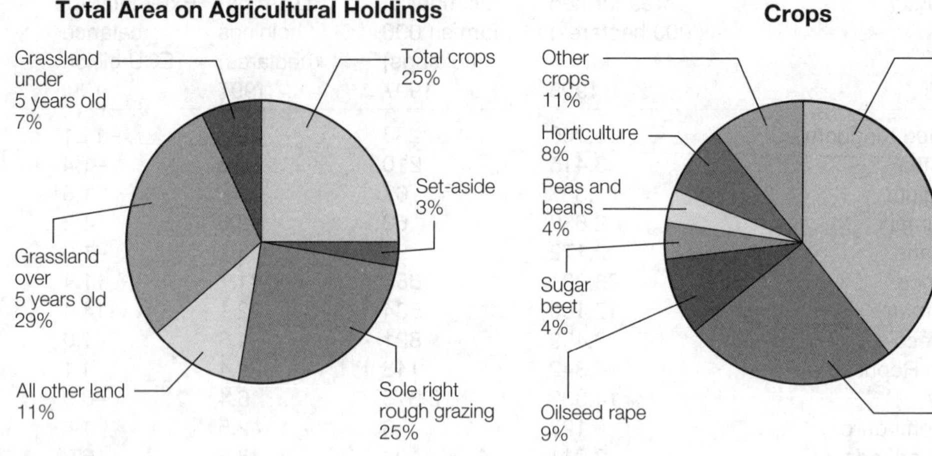

Source: Ministry of Agriculture, Fisheries and Food

Table 27.2: British Production as a Percentage of Total New Supplies

Food product	1988–90 average	1999 provisional
Beef and veal	92	80
Sheepmeat	90	103
Poultrymeat	97	90
Pork	100	102
Eggs	96	94
Milk for human consumption (as liquid)	100	102
Cheese	66	65
Butter	78	72
Sugar (as refined)	56	67
Wheat	120	114
Barley	142	127
Oats	100	105
Oilseed rape	102	97
Potatoes	89	91

Source: Ministry of Agriculture, Fisheries and Food

sheep. Most of the beef animals and sheep are reared in the hill and moorland areas of Scotland, Wales, Northern Ireland and northern and south-western England. Among world-famous British livestock are the Hereford, Welsh Black and Aberdeen Angus beef breeds, the Jersey, Guernsey and Ayrshire dairy breeds, Large White pigs and a number of sheep breeds. Livestock totals are given in Table 27.3.

Cattle and Sheep

Cattle and sheep constitute about 40 per cent of the value of Britain's gross agricultural output. Dairy production is the largest part of the sector, followed by cattle and calves, and then sheep and lambs. Most dairy cattle in the UK are bred by artificial insemination. In 1999 the average size of dairy herds was 73 (excluding minor holdings in Great Britain),

Table 27.3: Livestock and Livestock Products

	1988–90 average	1997	1998	1999 provisional
Cattle and calves ('000 head)	12,101	11,633	11,519	11,423
Sheep and lambs ('000 head)	43,184	42,823	44,471	44,656
Pigs ('000 head)	7,746	8,072	8,146	7,284
Poultry ('000 head)[1]	117,642	n.a.	152,886	153,590
Milk (million litres)	14,442	14,141	13,939	14,308
Hen eggs (million dozen)[2]	817	794	792	740
Beef and veal ('000 tonnes)	980	696	699	680
Mutton and lamb ('000 tonnes)	377	351	386	401
Pork ('000 tonnes)	773	888	931	832
Bacon and ham ('000 tonnes)	200	239	236	231
Poultrymeat ('000 tonnes)	1,137	1,510	1,532	1,500

[1] Includes ducks, geese and turkeys. In England and Wales a new approach to collecting poultry information has been used. The figures from 1998 are not therefore directly comparable with previous years.
[2] For human consumption only; does not include eggs for hatching.
n.a. = not available.
Source: Ministry of Agriculture, Fisheries and Food

while the average yield of milk for each dairy cow was 5,974 litres (1,314 gallons).

More than half of home-fed beef production originates from the national dairy herd, in which the Holstein Friesian breed predominates. The remainder derives from suckler herds producing high-quality beef calves, both in the hills and uplands and in lowland areas. The traditional British beef breeds (see p. 450) and, increasingly, imported breeds, such as Charolais, Limousin, Simmental and Belgian Blue, are used for beef production. The size of the beef-breeding herd expanded by 22 per cent during 1989–99, while the dairy herd decreased by 13 per cent.

The value of beef and veal production grew by 0.3 per cent in 1999 to £1,996 million as increased cattle prices offset a reduction in subsidy payments, but output fell by 2.8 per cent in 1999 to 680,000 tonnes.

The UK has more than 60 native sheep breeds and many cross-bred varieties. The size of the British breeding flock rose slightly in 1999 but the value of sheepmeat production fell by 11 per cent.

Pigs

The value of pigmeat production in 1999 was £782 million, 11 per cent down on 1998. Reductions in the breeding herd continued in 1999, and were particularly severe in some regions, notably Northern Ireland. Abundant supplies in Europe and the high value of the pound led to increased imports and helped to keep a downward pressure on UK prices. In 1999 UK pig farms made, on average, significant losses, and there was a substantial turnover of farms going out of pig production (about 20 per cent) and farms coming in.

Poultry

The total UK bird population in 1999 consisted of 101.6 million chickens and other table fowls; 29 million birds in the laying flock; 9.4 million fowls for breeding; and 13.3 million turkeys, ducks and geese.

Poultry production in 1999 was 1.5 million tonnes, a 2 per cent decrease on 1998, but prices continued to fall, because of lower feed prices, oversupply and cheap imports. The value of hen eggs for human consumption was 10 per cent down.

Farm Animal Welfare

In 1999 the UK achieved its aim of protecting laying hens by securing an EU Directive which bans the battery cage from 1 January

Table 27.4: Main Crops

	1988–90 average	1997	1998	1999 provisional
Wheat				
Area ('000 hectares)	1,994	2,036	2,045	1,859
Production ('000 tonnes)	13,272	15,018	15,465	15,104
Yield (tonnes per hectare)	6.65	7.38	7.56	8.12
Barley				
Area	1,684	1,359	1,255	1,162
Production	8,254	7,828	6,630	6,670
Yield	4.92	5.76	5.29	5.74
Oats				
Area	115	100	98	93
Production	536	577	587	575
Yield	4.64	5.78	6.00	6.17
Potatoes				
Area	178	166	164	178
Production	6,602	7,125	6,417	7,100
Yield	37.10	42.90	39.10	39.90
Oilseed rape				
Area	353	473	531	542
Production	1,062	1,527	1,570	1,665
Yield	3.01	3.23	2.96	3.08
Sugar beet				
Area	197	196	189	185
Production	8,056	11,084	10,002	10,328
Yield	40.86	56.55	52.92	55.83

Sources: *Agriculture in the United Kingdom 1999* and *Agricultural Census, June 1999*

2012. Among other advances during the year, a UK ban on close confinement stalls and tethers for pigs came into effect; new welfare standards, adopted by the Council of Europe, for ducks and geese, and for animals farmed for their fur, are now in place. The Welfare of Animals (Staging Points) Order 1998 lays down standards for the construction and operation of staging points in the transit of animals. New EU standards for vehicles carrying animals for over 8 hours were implemented in the Welfare of Animals (Transport) (Amendment) Order 1999.

The Welfare of Animals (Transport) Order 1997 was reviewed in 1999. New arrangements for pre-export inspections of food animals destined for other EU member states were introduced, to ensure that all animals are healthy and fit to travel. Certifying veterinarians are provided with clearer and more transparent instructions, including minimum inspection times. The State Veterinary Service assessed compliance with current legislation at livestock markets and the Government began a review of the Welfare of Animals (Markets) Order 1990.

Crops

The farms devoted primarily to *arable crops* are found mainly in eastern and central-southern England and eastern Scotland. The main crops are shown in Table 27.4. In the UK in 1999, the area planted to cereals—wheat, barley and oats—totalled 3.14 million hectares (7.76 million acres), a decrease of

8.3 per cent on 1998, mainly because of the increased compulsory set-aside area, raised from 5 to 10 per cent (see p. 458). Production was down by only 1.3 per cent to 22.5 million tonnes. Total value of cereals fell by 6.1 per cent to £2,349 million.

Large-scale *potato and vegetable cultivation* takes place on the fertile soils throughout the UK, often with irrigation. Principal areas are the peat and silt fens of Cambridgeshire, Lincolnshire and Norfolk; the sandy loams of Norfolk, Suffolk, West Midlands, Nottinghamshire, South Yorkshire and Lincolnshire; the peat soils of south Lancashire; and the alluvial silts by the river Humber. Early potatoes are produced in Shropshire, Pembrokeshire, Cornwall, Devon, Essex, Suffolk, Kent, Cheshire and south-west Scotland. Production of high-grade seed potatoes is confined mainly to east Scotland, Northern Ireland, the northern uplands and the Welsh borders. Total area for all potatoes rose by 8.2 per cent in 1999, with an overall increase in production of 11 per cent. The value of potato production increased by 21 per cent (£131 million) on 1998.

Sugar from *home-grown sugar beet* provides just over half of home needs.

Arable Area Payments Scheme (AAPS)

The AAPS, of which set-aside is a part and which originally aimed to cut cereals support prices, helps compensate farmers for these cuts. They are paid for the land under arable production, not the quantity of crop. To qualify for subsidy, all but the smallest farmers must set aside a proportion of their land (10 per cent for the 1999 harvest) to reduce cereals production. Where land is eligible, the subsidy is paid on cereals, oilseeds, proteins (including peas for harvesting dry) and linseed.

Set-aside payments compensate farmers for leaving part of their land fallow, while keeping it in good agricultural condition. They are encouraged to maximise the environmental benefit of the scheme and are allowed to count land entered into various environmental schemes (see p. 458) against their set-aside obligation. In addition to the compulsory set-aside rate, growers may set aside, on a voluntary basis, more than 50 per cent of the area claimed under the AAPS provided all of the set-aside land is used for the production of multiannual crops, such as short-rotation coppice, for biomass production. Farmers may also get grants of up to 50 per cent of the costs associated with the establishment of such crops on set-aside land.

In 1999, 60,632 AAPS claims for 4.5 million hectares (11.1 million acres) were received in the UK; £1,053 million was paid out. Payments were 14 per cent less than in 1998 owing to the end of the green pound and adoption of the euro. The Government and the devolved administrations paid £170 million to producers to compensate for the shortfall.

Horticulture

In 1999 the land used for horticulture (excluding hops, potatoes, and peas for harvesting dry) was 178,869 hectares (441,985 acres), compared with 178,249 hectares in 1998. Vegetables grown in the open accounted for 70.4 per cent of this, orchards for 15.6 per cent, soft fruit for 5 per cent, ornamentals (including hardy nursery stock, bulbs and flowers grown in the open) for 7.3 per cent and glasshouse crops for 1 per cent. More than one vegetable crop may be taken from the same area of land in a year, so that the estimated area actually cropped for horticulture in 1999 was 202,600 hectares (500,265 acres).

The output value of horticultural products (including seeds and peas harvested dry) was £1,899 million. Some 3.9 million tonnes of fruit and vegetables was imported.

Under the reformed EU fruit and vegetables regime, EU grants (up to 50 per cent of eligible expenditure) are payable to producer organisations (POs) which aim to improve cultivation techniques, with emphasis on environmentally sound practices, quality

> The first market of a new type, for farmers selling directly to the public, started in Bath in 1997. There are now more than 200 in the UK, estimated to be contributing £65 million to the farming economy in 2000.

improvements and marketing. Of 78 POs recognised in the UK, 60 had programmes running in 1999, with a total value of about £30 million.

Agri-Industrial Materials

The Agri-Industrial Materials Branch (AIMS) of the Ministry of Agriculture, Fisheries and Food (MAFF) seeks to encourage the marketing of renewable energy raw materials from crops. Under Agenda 2000 (see p. 458), farmers can continue to put all of their set-aside into biomass production, and the area of industrial crops planted on set-aside has risen to 21 per cent of set-aside land. MAFF, which promotes short-rotation coppice as an energy crop and miscanthus as a crop for energy and industry, intends to allocate £30 million to the growing of energy crops as part of the EU's Rural Development Regulation (see p. 457) in England.

Genetically Modified Crops

Now that the location and function of individual crop genes are being discovered, scientists have the chance to alter the genetic make-up of plants by adding or removing specific genes. Some 40 million hectares of genetically modified (GM) crops are estimated to have been planted throughout the world in 1999.

There is no general cultivation of GM crops in the UK at present. An agreement was reached between the Supply Chain Initiative on Modified Agricultural Crops (SCIMAC, a grouping of industry organisations) and the Department of the Environment, Transport and the Regions (DETR). A strictly limited programme of farm-scale evaluations of GM herbicide tolerant crops, on about 40 farms, to test their effects on the farmland environment, began in 1999 for spring and winter oilseed rape and for maize. This will compare GM with conventional crops for their effects on farmland biodiversity. Farmers growing these crops use SCIMAC guidelines, with MAFF support. These are designed to ensure best agricultural practice and that the crops are grown safely. The Government believes that they could form the basis of future legislation and intends to work with its EU partners in taking this forward.

The SCIMAC–DETR agreement, renewed in November 1999, stipulates that no unrestricted cultivation of GM crops can proceed until farm-scale evaluations are complete and that no direct commercial benefit will be sought from these plantings by the holders of consents for release or marketing of the GM organisms. The evaluations are expected to continue until 2002.

In May 2000 some 30,000 acres of Great Britain were accidentally affected by 1 per cent of herbicide resistant GM seed imported from Canada. After taking legal advice the Government directed the farmers concerned to destroy their crops or to sell them outside Europe. Advanta Seeds UK, the importing company concerned, agreed a £3 million compensation package for the 500 farmers affected. MAFF also advised farmers that oilseed rape, soya and maize seed imported from countries such as the United States and Canada should be regarded as potentially contaminated.

Among the tasks of the independent Agriculture and Environment Biotechnology Commission, which will advise the Government on a new GM strategy, are:

- to advise ministers on whether to continue the three-year moratorium on the commercial growing of GM crops in the UK;
- to decide separation distances between GM and non-GM crops; and
- to recommend the level of GM impurity in seeds.

FOOD SAFETY

The Food Standards Agency (FSA), a non-ministerial government department with powers to protect food safety and standards throughout the food chain, was launched in 2000. With an annual budget of £125 million, it is the primary source of advice to government throughout the UK on food safety and standards. Its remit covers the protection of public health and the interests of consumers in relation to food, and also food labelling and composition, and advice on nutrition. EU food law harmonisation covers food safety, fair trading and informative labelling.

BSE

The decline in the number of UK cases, starting in 1993, continues. In late 1999, about 45 suspect cases were being reported each week, compared with over 1,000 at the peak of the epidemic in early 1993. In October 2000 the Government published the report of an independent inquiry into the handling of the BSE epidemic between 1986 and 1996 and a possible link between it and a variant of Creutzfeldt-Jakob disease (vCJD) in humans. By 28 September 2000, the number of definite and probable cases of death from vCJD was 77. Among the measures introduced by government have been:

- a selective slaughter programme, to accelerate eradication of BSE from the national herd;
- introduction of an effective animal identification and movement recording system;
- legislation for removal of all mammalian meat and bone meal from farms and feedmills;
- strengthening and tightening controls on slaughterhouses to ensure removal of specified risk materials (SRM);
- a beef labelling scheme to provide customers with reliable information about the beef they buy; and
- effective implementation of the Over Thirty Month Scheme to remove meat from older bovine animals (of which some 4 million have so far been processed) from the food chain and destroy it.

A ban on the retail sale of beef-on-the-bone was lifted in December 1999, although the ban on the use of bones in manufacturing food products remains. Export from the UK of deboned beef produced under the Date-based Export Scheme (DBES) began in August 1999. A precondition was that the UK must slaughter all offspring born to confirmed BSE cases between 1 August 1996 and 25 November 1998, a process completed by June 1999. The UK is further required to slaughter offspring of BSE cases confirmed since 25 November 1998 without delay.

Application of the EU prohibition of the use of SRMs from cattle, sheep and goats over 12 months was postponed because of the unforeseen impact of the legislation on the supply of pharmaceuticals and cosmetics, and the failure of subsequent Commission proposals to achieve qualified majority support from member states, but is now in place. The UK forbids the import of SRMs except when delivered to approved premises for manufacture of technical products, such as bone china.

Tight hygiene rules on the production and marketing of fresh meat implement EU rules updated to allow hygiene controls to adapt to modern production methods and to make it possible to trace meat products back to their source for public health control. The Meat Hygiene Service (MHS) and its 1,700 veterinary surgeons and inspectors are responsible for enforcing legislation on meat hygiene, inspection, animal welfare at slaughter and SRM controls in all licensed abattoirs and cutting premises in Great Britain. The MHS Hygiene Assessment System score is a published guide to the hygiene performance of plants measured over a period. Irrespective of a plant's score, however, before any meat produced there enters the food chain, it must be inspected and health-marked as fit for human consumption. In addition, businesses making, selling or using animal feed additives have to apply for official approval or registration.

The EU is to set up a monitoring programme on a sample of animals that die on farms; this involves compulsory post-mortems on about 65,000 cattle over 2 years of age, a move welcomed by the UK which has already introduced such tests. The EU has also agreed to bring in, between September 2000 and January 2002, compulsory beef labelling, to show not only the country where the animal was slaughtered but also where it was born. Labels on minced beef will also have to show where the meat was processed.

EXPORTS

Food, feed and drink exports in 1999 dropped by 5 per cent to £8.8 billion (compared with £17.3 billion for imports). EU countries account for 63 per cent of all UK food and drink exports. In 1999 the main markets were the Irish Republic (£1.3 billion) and France (£1.2 billion). Sales to the United States increased by 10 per cent to £800 million and to Asia by 15 per cent, to £858 million.

Sales of soft drinks increased by over 30 per cent in 1999, fruit juices by 14 per cent, prepared vegetables by 8 per cent, cheese by 7 per cent, general groceries by 6 per cent and fish by 3 per cent. Beef exports were worth £18.4 million. In March 2000 the European Parliament ended a 25-year dispute between the UK and some other EU countries by approving the sale of British chocolate, made with vegetable fats other than cocoa butter, in Europe.

Export promotion for food and drink is headed by Food from Britain (FFB), an organisation funded by MAFF on behalf of the four agricultural departments (£5.4 million in 1999–2000) and industry (£6.1 million), which provides business development services for food and drink companies seeking expansion in international markets and within the UK speciality food and drink sector. It co-ordinates the British presence at ten or more international food and drink exhibitions each year and organises the annual FFB Export Awards. For all other agricultural products, services, livestock, machinery and processing equipment, the four agriculture departments (see p. 457) co-ordinate export promotion, participate in overseas trade fairs and arrange ministerial trade missions to other countries.

The annual Royal Agricultural Show, held at Stoneleigh in Warwickshire in early July, enables visitors to see the latest techniques and improvements in British agriculture. Some 160,400 visitors attended in 2000, of whom 9 per cent were from overseas. Other major agricultural events include the Royal Smithfield Show, held every other year in London, which exhibits agricultural machinery, livestock and carcases; the Royal Highland Show (June; 145,000 visitors in 2000) in Edinburgh, the largest trade exhibition of agricultural machinery in Great Britain; the Royal Welsh Show (late July) in Builth Wells; the Welsh Winter Fair for livestock and carcases (December), also at Builth Wells; and the Royal Ulster Agricultural Show (May) in Belfast.

MARKETING

The Government launched the Agriculture Development Scheme 1999 for England to improve competitiveness through better marketing. Some £2 million is available under this scheme and government funds must be matched by at least equal funding from private sources. In Scotland similar help is given under the Marketing Development Scheme—with some £0.9 million available in 2000–01—which requires matching funding from the private sector. MAFF has continued to help the UK speciality food industry through FFB and regional food groups. Speciality companies have an annual turnover of about £3.6 billion and a workforce of 52,000.

From June 2000 the British Farm Standard label (a tractor logo in red and blue), unveiled in over 4,000 supermarkets mostly in England, has enabled shoppers to support the British farming sector. It tells them that food has been produced under a farm assurance scheme and allows them to identify fruit, vegetables and meat produced to standards approved by the National Farmers' Union and to trace any item back to the farm of origin, check a beef herd's health record or verify pesticide use. Independent inspectors monitor the scheme. In Scotland, separate quality assurance marks, backed by certification and inspection regimes, already exist for beef, lamb, pork, cereals, trout and salmon. The British Farm Standard provides a complementary additional marketing tool for those Scottish companies that wish to use it rather than a replacement mark.

ROLE OF THE GOVERNMENT

MAFF, the Scottish Executive Rural Affairs Department (SERAD), the National Assembly for Wales, and the Department of Agriculture and Rural Development (DARD) in Northern Ireland have varying degrees of responsibility for agriculture and fisheries matters. The Government has responsibility for matters not devolved or transferred to the devolved administrations, such as relations with the EU and other international organisations. Concordats between MAFF and the new administrations cover arrangements since devolution. The work of MAFF's nine Regional Service Centres in England and SERAD's eight areas in Scotland relates to payments under domestic and EU schemes, licensing and other services for farmers and growers.

Common Agricultural Policy (CAP) Developments

Reform of the CAP has not gone as far as the UK would have liked. However, the EU's Agenda 2000 is still considered an important step forward. It emphasises the need to respond to further liberalisation of trade; a shift from price support to direct payments (accounting for about 60 per cent of the European Agricultural Guidance and Guarantee Fund's (EAGGF) £25 billion annual budget), thus reducing the CAP's economic distortions; and an integrated rural development policy, to bring about a change from support for food production to environmental and rural economy measures. Cross-compliance (under the EU Horizontal Measures Regulation) attaches environmental conditions to support payments. The Government looks for CAP reform to deliver annual net savings to the UK economy of £200 million in 2001, rising to £500 million in 2008: or £1 billion in savings to consumers when all the changes have been implemented.

In December 1999 the Government announced plans for England for a radical redirection of support for agriculture and a significant increase in expenditure under the EU Rural Development Regulation (RDR). Rural Development plans for the period

Public Expenditure[1] under the CAP by the Intervention Board and the Agricultural Departments, UK, 1999–2000

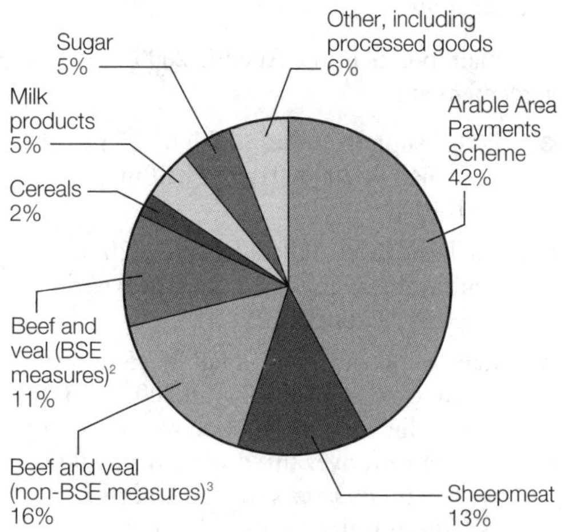

[1] Forecast.

[2] Payments to farmers under schemes to compensate for losses caused by BSE.

[3] Payments to farmers under schemes unrelated to BSE measures.

Source: Ministry of Agriculture, Fisheries and Food

2000–06 were submitted to the European Commission. Similar plans have been drawn up in Wales and Northern Ireland; in December 1999 Scotland also submitted its proposals under the RDR to the Commission.

The England Plan envisages regional implementation of measures to support marketing and processing of agricultural products, training and rural development. A system known as modulation will be introduced, which is a deduction at a flat rate from all direct payments to farmers under CAP commodity regimes from 2001, starting at 2.5 per cent, rising to 4.5 per cent in 2005 and 2006. Each pound contributed by farmers will be matched in funds by the Government. Among allocations to the Rural Development plans are £140 million to organic farming, £85 million to woodlands and £150 million to a new rural enterprise scheme. Proposed expenditure over seven years is put at more than £1.6 billion, of which about £1 billion will support agri-environment measures.

Among components of the Scottish Plan are proposals for supporting Less Favoured Areas (LFAs), forestry and diversification.

Agenda 2000

The main points in the Agenda 2000 agreement are:

- cereal support prices to fall by 15 per cent, half in 2000–01, and half in 2001–02;
- the basic price of beef to fall by 20 per cent in three steps, and the intervention price[2] by 25 per cent;
- dairy support prices to fall by 15 per cent in three steps, beginning in 2005, and quotas for milk production to increase by 1.5 per cent over three years from 2005, with extra increases for the UK (for Northern Ireland only), the Irish Republic, Spain, Italy and Greece.

The cuts in price support aim to bring market forces to bear on EU agriculture and make farmers more responsive to consumer wishes. Reductions in cereals support prices set the normal rate of compulsory set-aside at 10 per cent during 2000–06. The cut of 20 per cent for beef, though the most radical step since the beef regime was instituted in 1968, is not, in the UK's view, enough to bring EU beef prices to world levels, although at the new level the EU will provide private storage facilities, while not guaranteeing to buy in meat as in the existing intervention arrangements.

Under a system of 'national envelopes', a small part of the increase in direct payments to farmers will be given to member states to distribute according to national criteria suiting farmers' needs.

Agrimoney

Since 1 January 1999 CAP payments have been paid in euros or sub-denominations (participating currencies) in the 11 member states which have adopted the European single currency. The new agrimonetary regime uses daily market rates to convert CAP payments into national currencies in the four non-participating countries: the UK, Denmark, Greece and Sweden. The new measures allow for compulsory compensation, 100 per cent funded by the EU budget in 2000, for falls in the 1999 direct payments resulting from the transition. The Government announced compensation for the industry in the UK of £264 million in autumn 1999: £32 million to sheep producers; £62 million to beef producers; and £170 million to arable producers. Up to a further £132 million will be paid in 2000 and 2001.

[2] The price at which intervention authorities in member states buy commodities when their prices fall below certain agreed levels and store them for later resale.

Special Aid to Farmers

In March 2000 the Government announced extra aid of £203.5 million (including £16 million from the EU) to UK farmers to help towards offsetting recent losses in income:

- £26 million to the pig industry in the first year of a three-year scheme;
- £22 million for dairy farmers;
- £44 million for beef and sheep farmers;
- £60 million for hill farmers; and
- £20 million compensation for cattle banned from the food chain in the aftermath of the BSE crisis.

This aid is in addition to other recent government steps outlined above.

Agri-Environment Schemes

The UK's agri-environment programmes provide schemes to encourage environmentally beneficial farming and public enjoyment of the countryside. All are voluntary and offer payments to farmers who agree to manage their land for the positive benefit of wildlife, landscape, resource protection, historic features or public access. The payments are based on the agricultural income which farmers forgo by participating in the schemes and are partly funded by the EU. The Government normally evaluates and reviews these schemes every five years.

Table 27.5: ESAs at 31 March 2000

	Number of ESAs	Farmers with agreements	Land designated	Areas covered by agreements	Payments to farmers in 1999–2000 (£'000)
			'000 hectares		
England	22	10,000	1,100	531	34,000
Wales	6	2,257	429	169	6,219
Scotland	10	2,709	1,089	772	7,551
Northern Ireland	5	4,500	222	142	7,770

Sources: MAFF, National Assembly for Wales, SERAD and DARD

Environmentally Sensitive Areas (ESAs)

By the end of 1999 over 19,000 farmers throughout the UK had signed ESA management agreements to promote environmentally beneficial farming. Payments covering these agreements and conservation plans totalled some £60 million in 1999–2000. Sums range between £8 and £500 a hectare, and are designed to compensate for reduced profitability as a result of adopting less intensive production methods. They are generally funded half by the Government and half by the EAGGF. In Wales the ESA scheme closed to new applications in 1999. An all-Wales agri-environmental scheme, Tir Gofal (Land in Care), opened to applications in April 1999.

Countryside Stewardship

Countryside Stewardship is the main government incentive scheme for farmers in England for the wider English countryside outside the ESAs. Payments on over 8,600 agreements covering 152,800 hectares (377,570 acres) in operation at 31 March 2000 are expected to total some £26.1 million in 1999–2000. In 1999, 84 agreements in the Arable Stewardship pilot scheme aim to reverse the decline in a number of wildlife species in East Anglia and the West Midlands, with £0.5 million set aside for new agreements in each of the three years of the scheme. Two more experiments, to test an integrated approach to economic and environmental issues in the uplands, are taking place in Bodmin (Cornwall) and Bowland (Lancashire).

Organic Aid

Sales of organic food in the UK are rising by about 40 per cent a year, but 75 per cent is imported. In early 2000 the area of UK farmland organically managed or in the process of conversion was about 500,000 hectares, twice as much as in early 1999 (3 per cent of the agricultural area). The Organic Farming Scheme (OFS) in England and parallel schemes in Wales and Northern Ireland, launched in 1999, raised the payment rates to those farmers wishing to convert to organic methods from £250 to £450 a hectare over five years for most arable land and temporary grass, and from £50 to £350 for most improved land in the uplands. Total expenditure on UK organic schemes in 1999–2000 was £15.7 million (of which Wales accounted for £2.9 million, Scotland £1.8 million and Northern Ireland £170,000).

The Government also funds the Organic Conversion Information Service, which provides information and advisory visits to prospective organic farmers in England and Wales. The UK Register of Organic Food Standards is charged with overseeing standards of organic food production. MAFF's budget for R&D on organic agriculture was increased to £2.2 million in 1999.

Other Schemes

The final round of the Nitrate Sensitive Areas (NSA) Scheme in England (to run until September 2003) attracted applications covering 3,000 hectares (7,413 acres) and brought the total area of land subject to NSA undertakings to 28,000 hectares (69,190 acres), with payments of £6.2 million in 1999–2000. Under the UK Habitat Schemes, 1,616 farmers entered 17,143 hectares (42,360 acres) into agreements. Successful elements of the English Habitat Scheme were integrated into Countryside Stewardship from 1 January 2000. The Welsh, Scottish and Northern Ireland schemes have been closed to new applicants.

In Scotland there are three agri-environment schemes: the ESAs, the Organic Aid Scheme (OAS) and the Countryside Premium Scheme, with provision for £20.2 million expenditure in 2000–01. Wales has the ESAs, the OFS and Tir Gofal, with provision for £9.5 million expenditure over 2000–01. Northern Ireland has the ESAs, the OFS and the Countryside Management Scheme.

The UK-wide Farm Woodland Premium Scheme encourages farmers to convert agricultural land to woodland by providing annual payments for ten or 15 years to compensate for income forgone. Payments are 50 per cent funded by the European Commission under the CAP (75 per cent in disadvantaged areas). From April 1992 to March 2000 over 9,500 applications were approved to convert over 66,700 hectares (164,815 acres). Nearly 75 per cent of planting is broadleaved trees.

The Rural Economy and EU Structural Funds

Northern Ireland, the Highlands and Islands of Scotland and Merseyside qualified for assistance under Objective 1 of the EU Structural Funds for the period 1994–99. This aims to help those regions whose economic development lags behind the EU average. For the period 2000–06, four areas have been designated for Objective 1 support: Merseyside, Cornwall, South Yorkshire and West Wales and Valleys.

Eleven areas in Great Britain (including South West England, the English Northern Uplands, 70 per cent of the landmass of Wales, and Borders, Dumfries and Galloway and parts of Grampian, rural Stirling and Upper Tayside in Scotland) were eligible to receive funds under Objective 5b of the EU Structural Funds for the period 1994–99. This aims to promote the economic development of rural areas. To be eligible, areas must have a high share of agricultural employment in total employment, a low level of agricultural income and a low population density. In England by the end of 1999, 369 Objective 5b projects had been approved and nearly £102 million in EU and national public funding had been allocated to them. This included £4.83 million, comprising EU and MAFF and other public and private sector funding, to go towards the Bowland and Bodmin Moor upland pilot projects (see p. 460). In Scotland by the end of 1999, 100 marketing and processing projects had been approved and over £11.4 million committed, together with 427 projects and over £7.7 million under the Regional Development Programme. For the period 2000–06 the designation of rural areas falls under the new Objective 2 programme.

Integrated Administration and Control System (IACS)

The IACS, an EU-wide anti-fraud measure, requires farmers claiming payment under area-based CAP schemes to submit an annual application for aid giving field-by-field details of their farmed land. This provides the basis for administrative and on-farm checks on their entitlement to aid and for cross-checks between claims under the agri-environment and IACS schemes. Administrative verifications are done by computerised database, while those on the spot are done through farm visits by field officers and the use of observation satellites.

Hill Livestock Compensatory Allowances (HLCAs)

In LFAs, generally hills and uplands, farmers have traditionally received headage payments on breeding cattle and sheep to support the continuation of livestock farming, thus conserving the countryside and encouraging people to remain in the LFAs. Under Agenda 2000, HLCAs will be replaced in 2001 by a new area-based scheme which will have a clearer environmental, as well as socio-economic, objective.

Agricultural Trade Liberalisation

World Trade Organisation (WTO; see p. 421) negotiations on agricultural trade liberalisation in 2000 are likely to consider further commitments to improve access for agricultural products, cuts in subsidised exports and reductions in domestic support.

Ecuador, the world's largest banana exporter, has asked the WTO for permission to impose US$200 million-worth of trade retaliation against EU goods and services because of what it sees as the EU's discriminatory banana import regime. It accounts for 19 per cent of banana imports to the EU, compared with a 36 per cent average share in the rest of the world. The EU has yet to propose a solution, compatible with EU regulations, acceptable to its critics, while the WTO has upheld the complaint of the United States about the damage suffered by its own banana companies. EU member states have asked the Commission, after consultation with all interested parties, including the United States and Latin American, African, Caribbean and Pacific suppliers, to draft legislation for reform of the regime.

Hormone Growth Promoters

The UK, which has consistently voted against the EU ban on meat from animals treated with hormone growth promoters on the grounds that it is not scientifically justified, continues to work for a resolution of the dispute over meat imports between the EU and Canada and the United States which is based on sound science.

Price Guarantees, Grants and Subsidies

Expenditure in the UK in 1999–2000 under the CAP was £3,172 million, compared with £3,482 million in 1998–99; expenditure by the agriculture and other departments (including funding for special areas) on conservation measures is estimated at £248.5 million, £36.1 million less than in 1998–99.

Smallholdings and Crofts

In England and Wales county councils let smallholdings to experienced people who want to farm on their own account. Councils may lend working capital to them. At 31 March 1998 there were approximately 4,350 smallholdings in England and 780 in Wales. Land settlement in Scotland has been carried out by the Scottish Executive, which still owns and maintains about 105,000 hectares (259,455 acres) of land settlement estates, comprising 1,400 crofts and holdings.

In the Highlands and Islands of Scotland, much of the land is tenanted by crofters, who enjoy the statutory protection provided by crofting legislation and can benefit from government agriculture and livestock improvement schemes. Most crofters are part-time agriculturalists, using croft income to supplement earnings from other activities. The Crofters Commission has a statutory duty to promote their interests and to keep all crofting matters under review. The Transfer of Crofting Estates (Scotland) Act 1997 allows the Government to move some of its own crofting land to trusts set up by resident crofters, with the aim of giving them more responsibility for their own affairs. The Scottish Executive is planning legislation to allow other crofting communities to buy their own croft land.

Agricultural Landlords and Tenants

About 34 per cent of agricultural land in England and 21 per cent in Wales is rented. The Agricultural Tenancies Act 1995 provides a simplified legal framework for new tenancies entered into on or after 1 September 1995, known as farm business tenancies, on which landowners benefit from full income tax relief.

There is a similar proportion of rented land in Scotland, much of it under crofting tenure, including common grazings. The Scottish Executive is committed to changing the law relating to agricultural tenure.

Most farms in Northern Ireland are owner-occupied, but the conacre system allows owners not wishing to farm all their land to let it annually to others. Conacre land, about one-fifth of agricultural land, is used mainly for grazing.

Professional, Scientific and Technical Services

In England and Wales the Farming and Rural Conservancy Agency provides services to government on the design, development and implementation of policies on the integration of farming and conservation, environmental protection, rural land use and the diversification of the rural economy. In England and Wales ADAS provides professional, business, scientific and technical services in the agriculture, food and drink, and environmental markets. In Scotland the Scottish Agricultural College (SAC) provides professional, business, scientific and technical services in the agriculture, rural business, food and drink, and environmental markets. CAIS is a free and integrated service for Wales; DARD has a similar remit in Northern Ireland.

Lantra is the UK National Training Organisation for the land-based sector. It represents about 1.5 million individuals and 400,000 businesses, mostly in rural areas. It receives government support under contracts to MAFF and the Scottish Executive.

CONTROL OF DISEASES AND PESTS

Farm Animals

Britain enforces controls on imports of live animals and genetic material, including checks on all individual consignments originating from outside the EU and frequent checks on those from other EU member states at destination points. Measures can be taken to prevent the import of diseased animals and genetic material from regions or countries affected by disease. Veterinary checks also include unannounced periods of surveillance at ports.

The British Cattle Movement Service (BCMS) for Great Britain, at Workington (Cumbria), has provided over 6 million cattle with 'passports' since its launch in 1998. It has also processed over 5 million passports of slaughtered cattle and entered nearly 9 million cattle movements on to the Cattle Tracing System (CTS). The Government has met all BCMS and CTS costs and has undertaken not to introduce a central charge for passports before 2004.

Bovine tuberculosis (TB) in cattle, mainly in parts of south-west England and the Midlands, and south Wales, continues to increase. The Government spends over £30 million a year on TB in cattle. Two-thirds of this sum is spent on TB testing, slaughtering cattle that react to the test and on compensation. The other third is being spent on a comprehensive research programme aimed at reaching a better understanding of what causes the disease and how it is transmitted; on developing a vaccine; and on investigating the contribution that badger culling can make to reducing the incidence in cattle herds.

Professional advice and action on the statutory control of animal disease and the welfare of farm livestock are the responsibility of the State Veterinary Service. It is supported by the Veterinary Laboratories Agency (VLA), which also offers its services to the private sector on a commercial basis. Similar support is provided in Scotland by the SAC and in Northern Ireland by DARD's Veterinary Sciences Division.

The Pet Travel Scheme

Dogs and cats from the EU and certain other western European countries can, as long as they meet certain conditions, now enter the UK without quarantine under the Pet Travel Scheme (PETS). Animals from other countries will continue to be subject to quarantine, although the scheme is to be extended to certain rabies-free islands early in 2001. The position of dogs and cats from the United States and Canada will be reviewed in 2001. To enter the UK under the scheme, animals need to be resident in any of the qualifying countries for at least six months and be:

- microchipped;
- vaccinated against rabies;
- blood-tested at an approved laboratory;
- issued with an official PETS entry certificate confirming that these requirements have been met; and
- treated against certain parasites.

Animals can be brought into the UK under PETS only on prescribed routes.

Pesticides

The Pesticides Safety Directorate, an executive agency of MAFF, is responsible for the evaluation and approval of agricultural pesticides in England. It also carries out evaluations and approvals on behalf of the devolved administrations in Scotland, Wales and Northern Ireland. There is rigorous evaluation of new and existing pesticides under UK and EU legislation. Arrangements are currently in hand to put before Parliament regulations to strengthen enforcement and provide greater public access to information. Buffer zones for certain pesticides, to protect aquatic life from spray drift, allow farmers greater flexibility in the way the zones are applied while maintaining high environmental protection and encouraging the development of low-drift spray technology.

Veterinary Medicinal Products

The Veterinary Medicines Directorate, also an executive agency of MAFF, is responsible for ensuring that veterinary medicines are marketed only if they meet statutory standards for safety, quality and efficacy. The Government is advised by the independent scientific Veterinary Products Committee on the standards to be adopted in the authorisation procedures and, for example, on the use of organophosphorus (OP) compounds in veterinary medicines. In December 1999, the Government announced the withdrawal of OP sheep dips from the market pending improved container design to protect users against potential health hazards when handling the dip concentrate.

The Fishing Industry

The UK is one of the EU's largest fishing countries, taking about a quarter of the total catch in major species and committing £10 million in 1999 to fisheries science and to monitoring and developing stocks. It also has an interest in more than 100 allowable catches set by the Commission (see p. 464). In 1999 the British fishing industry provided about 40 per cent by quantity of total UK fish supplies, and household consumption of fish in the UK was provisionally estimated at 312,000 tonnes.

Fisheries departments are responsible for the administration of legislation, in partnership with the European Commission, concerning the fishing industry, including fish and shellfish farming. The Sea Fish Industry Authority, an industry-financed body, undertakes R&D, provides training and promotes the marketing and consumption of sea fish.

Fish Caught

In 1999 demersal fish (caught on or near the bottom of the sea) accounted for 48 per cent by weight of total landings by British fishing vessels, pelagic fish (caught near the surface) for 38 per cent and shellfish for 15 per cent. Landings of all types of fish (excluding salmon and trout) by British fishing vessels into the UK totalled 506,524 tonnes compared with 552,234 tonnes in 1998. Cod and haddock represented 21 per cent and 20 per cent respectively of the total value of demersal and pelagic fish landed. The quayside value of landings of all sea fish, including shellfish, by British vessels in 1999 was £586 million.

Catches of crabs, lobsters, scampi and other shellfish have increased to supply a rising demand. In 1985 British fishermen landed 76,000 tonnes of shellfish worth about £66 million. By 1999, the figures were 135,000 tonnes worth £153 million. From 2000 a national licensing scheme has limited the shellfish fleet at 3,000, mainly small boats. New minimum landing sizes for shellfish to be introduced across Europe in 2002, and which make it illegal to land a lobster smaller than 87 mm (3.4 in.), have applied in the UK from 2000.

The Fishing Fleet

The UK fisheries departments currently spend some £24 million a year on fisheries enforcement, primarily on monitoring the application of the Common Fisheries Policy (CFP—see p. 464) and ensuring that measures designed to conserve fish stocks are effective.

All British vessels fishing for profit must be licensed by the fisheries departments. To help conserve stocks and contain the size of the fleet, only replacement licences are issued. Quotas are allocated annually between producer organisations and other groups of fishermen, on the basis of the fixed quota units of vessels in their membership.

A satellite monitoring system, to track the movements of EU vessels over 24 m in length, as well as those from third countries fishing in EU waters, has been operating since 1 January 2000, as, since 5 January 1999, have new controls over the landing of fish. It is a condition of UK fishing licences that, subject to derogations for landings at designated ports during designated hours, at least four hours' notice must be given of all landings into UK ports by vessels 20 m in length and above. Measures to strengthen and improve standards of fisheries control throughout the EU provide for greater transparency of action taken by member states to monitor compliance with the CFP.

Britain aims to achieve the EU target for reducing its fleet through cutting its numbers and limiting the time some vessels spend at sea. At the end of 1999 the UK fleet consisted of 7,448 registered vessels, including 323 vessels greater than 27 m (88.5 ft) overall length, of which 196 are registered. There are an estimated 15,961 professional fishermen in Britain.

Fish Farming and Shellfish Production

There are over 1,000 fish and shellfish farming businesses in the UK, on 1,400 sites and employing more than 3,000 people. Total value is about £300 million at first sale. The main finfish species are salmon (115,000 tonnes, mainly in Scotland) and rainbow trout (16,000 tonnes), with a limited production of other species, such as carp and brown trout. There is also interest in farming marine species such as turbot and halibut.

Fishery Limits

British fishery limits extend to 200 miles or the median line (broadly halfway between the UK coast and the opposing coastline of another coastal state), measured from baselines on or near the coast of Britain.

Common Fisheries Policy (CFP)

The rise in demand for fish throughout the world by a growing population, and intensive fishing, have led over the years to overfishing and dwindling supplies.

The EU's CFP system for the management of fishing resources sets total allowable catches (TACs) each year in order to conserve stocks. TACs are then allocated as quotas between member states, taking account of traditional fishing patterns. In December 1999, the EU agreed substantial cuts in the number of fish caught in the North Sea and other UK waters to help rebuild stocks. These included a 60 per cent cut in the TAC for Irish sea cod; a 38 per cent cut for North Sea cod; and cuts of up to 20 per cent in English Channel catches.

In 1999–2000, new North Sea and Western approaches TACs were introduced to help conserve stocks of species hitherto less popular in the UK, such as spur dogfish in the North Sea.

The UK and Irish Republic have invoked the Hague preference, a deal struck in 1976 which allows them to demand a share of other countries' quotas with no penalties. They have also agreed to participate in a scheme to revive cod stocks in the Irish Sea.

Since 1997 the number of over 10 m UK vessels partly or wholly owned by overseas interests has fallen from 160 to 122. From 1999 all vessels fishing against UK quotas have been required, with Commission approval, to show that a satisfactory economic link is maintained with British coastal communities: by landing at least 50 per cent of their catch of quota stocks in the UK; by employing a crew of whom 50 per cent are resident in a UK coastal area; or by spending 50 per cent of operating expenses in UK coastal areas.

British vessels have exclusive rights to fish within 6 miles of the British coast. Certain other EU member states have historic rights in British waters between 6 and 12 miles. British vessels have similar rights in other member states' 6 to 12 mile belts. Between 12 and 200 miles, EU vessels may fish wherever they have access rights. Non-EU countries' vessels may fish in these waters if they negotiate reciprocal fisheries agreements with the EU.

Technical conservation measures supplement TACs and controls on the time spent at sea. They include minimum mesh sizes for nets and net configuration restrictions, minimum landing sizes and closed areas designed mainly to protect young fish.

Each member state is responsible for enforcement of CFP rules on its own fishermen and those of other member states in its own waters. EU inspectors monitor compliance.

Fisheries Agreements

CFP provisions are supplemented by a number of fisheries agreements between the EU and third countries, the most important for the UK being with Norway (for cod, haddock and saithe), Greenland and the Faroes. EU catch quotas, especially for cod, have also been established around Spitsbergen (Svalbard). New external waters licences are available to enable UK vessels to fish in those external waters not fully subscribed, in accordance with international conventions and agreements.

Salmon, Freshwater Fisheries and the Aquatic Environment

There is no public right to fish in freshwater lakes and non-tidal rivers in Great Britain. Those wishing to fish such waters must first obtain permission from the owner of the fishing rights and, in England and Wales, a licence from the Environment Agency. In Scotland salmon fisheries are managed locally by District Salmon Fishery Boards. In Northern Ireland fishing for freshwater species is licensed by the Fisheries Conservancy Board for Northern Ireland and the Foyle, Carlingford and Irish Lights Commission in their respective areas, and 62 public angling waters, including salmon, trout and coarse fisheries, are available to Department of Culture, Arts and Leisure permit holders.

Research

Departmental funding of R&D in agriculture, fisheries and food in 1999–2000 included £125 million commissioned by MAFF and £6 million conducted by DARD. In Scotland about £50 million is invested in the Agricultural and Biological Sciences-related research programme and £30.5 million in fishery research. Priority areas in the MAFF programme are public health (covering food safety, transmissible spongiform encephalopathies and zoonoses) and protection of the environment (improved sustainability in production methods, with benefits for the environment and agricultural efficiency).

Research Bodies

The BBSRC (see p. 441) supports research in biotechnology and biological sciences related to food and agriculture. The Natural Environment Research Council includes some agricultural aspects in its remit. Research institutes sponsored by these councils receive income from work commissioned by MAFF, industry and other bodies.

ADAS carries out R&D, at a network of research centres and on clients' premises, for MAFF and other organisations and companies. There are research centres across England and Wales. MAFF receives scientific expertise and technical support from its other agencies, the VLA and the Central Science Laboratory. Horticulture Research International, a non-departmental public body, transfers the results of its R&D to the British horticulture industry and the wider public.

SERAD support for agricultural, biological and related sciences is primarily through sponsorship of the five Scottish Agricultural and Biological Research Institutes, the SAC and the Royal Botanic Garden in Edinburgh. It contracts additional research through these bodies and provides funding for Education and Advisory Services at the SAC. In Northern Ireland DARD maintains an integrated Science and Technology programme to improve the economic performance of the agri-food, fishing and forestry sectors, to conserve the rural environment and to strengthen the economy and social infrastructure of disadvantaged rural areas. Fisheries research is undertaken by the Fisheries Research Service (FRS) in Scotland and by the Centre for Environment, Fisheries and Aquaculture Science (CEFAS) in England and Wales.

Forestry

Woodland covers an estimated 2.7 million hectares (6.6 million acres) in the UK: a little less than 8 per cent of England, nearly 17 per cent of Scotland, 14 per cent of Wales and 6 per cent of Northern Ireland. The EU's forests are estimated to be increasing by about 460 million cubic metres (17 billion cubic feet) a year, while the annual harvest has fallen to 300 million cubic metres (11 billion cubic feet) owing to cheaper imports and an over-supply of timber.

Britain's forestry programme aims to protect and expand forest resources and conserve woodland as a home for wildlife and for public recreation. The UK imports 85 per cent of its timber and wood products, which costs about £7.5 billion a year. Promoting the market for home-grown timber is an important part of the forestry programme.

The area of productive forest in Great Britain is 2.3 million hectares (5.7 million acres), just under 35 per cent of which is managed by the Forestry Commission. The rate of new planting (including natural regeneration) in 1998–99 was 96 hectares (237 acres) by the Commission and 15,914 hectares (39,323 acres) by other woodland owners, with the help of grants from the Commission. In 1998–99, 12,456 hectares (30,779 acres) of broadleaved trees were planted, both new planting and restocking.

Forestry and primary wood processing employ about 35,000 people. Great Britain's woodlands produced 9.02 million cubic metres (319 million cubic feet) of timber in 1998, 15 per cent of total UK consumption. The volume of timber harvested on Commission lands in 1998–99 was estimated at 5.35 million cubic metres (190 million cubic feet).

The Commission's Woodland Grant Scheme pays grants (£41.6 million in 1998–99) to help create new woodlands and forests, and regenerate existing ones. Under the scheme a management grant is available for work in woods of special conservation and landscape value or where the public are welcome.

The Forestry Commission and Forestry Policy

The Forestry Commission, established in 1919, is the government department responsible for forestry in Great Britain. With 1.06 million hectares of land (2.6 million acres), it is the UK's largest land manager and the biggest single provider of countryside recreation. The Commissioners advise on forestry matters and are responsible to the Scottish First Minister, the Minister of Agriculture, Fisheries and Food, and the National Assembly for Wales.

The Commission provides grants to private woodland owners for tree planting and woodland management, controls tree felling, and sets standards for forestry as a whole. Forest Enterprise, an agency of the Commission, develops and manages the Commission's forests and forestry estate, supplying timber and opportunities for recreation, and enhancing nature conservation and the forest environment. Forest Research is the R&D agency of the Commission.

Financed partly by the Government and partly by receipts from sales of timber and other produce, and from rents, the Commission's grant in aid for 1998–99 was £51.3 million, from which £400,000 was deducted for reimbursement of EU co-financing of private woodlands grants.

During 1981–99, 239,194 hectares (591,048 acres), worth £289.6 million, of Forestry Commission land were sold, of which over 62 per cent was forest land. The Government has imposed a moratorium on large-scale forest sales.

Forestry Initiatives

With an estimated 1,000 sq km (386 sq miles) of damaged land to be developed, the initial focus of the Commission's Land Regeneration Unit is on the creation of new woodlands (of 30 hectares—74 acres—or larger) in the central English coalfields and on wider plans to create working forests of about 800–1,200 hectares (1,980–2,970 acres). It has identified 175,000 hectares (432,400 acres) of derelict land suitable for trees that will stabilise and decontaminate the soil. The planned National Forest in England (520 sq km—200 sq miles) covers parts of Staffordshire, Derbyshire and Leicestershire, with the aim of increasing woodland from 6 per cent to a third of its area—16,500 hectares (40,775 acres). For Community Forests, see p. 320.

Forestry in Northern Ireland

Woodland and forest cover about 82,000 hectares (203,000 acres) of Northern Ireland. State-owned forest constitutes 61,000 hectares (150,700 acres).

Forest Service

The Forest Service is an executive agency within DARD and promotes the interests of forestry through sustainable management and expansion of state-owned forests. It encourages private forestry through grant aid for planting. The Forest Service offered 342,000 cubic metres (12 million cubic feet) of timber for sale during 1999–2000, with receipts of £4.1 million. Forestry and timber processing employ about 1,100 people.

Further Reading

Agriculture in the United Kingdom 1999. MAFF and the Agriculture Departments. The Stationery Office, 2000.

Economic Report on Scottish Agriculture 2000. The Stationery Office, 2000.

Report, Evidence and Supporting Papers of the Inquiry into the Emergence and Identification of Bovine Spongiform Encephalopathy (BSE) and Variant Creutzfeldt Jakob Disease (vCJD) and the action taken in response to it up to 20 March 2000. The Stationery Office, 2000.

Scottish Agriculture Facts and Figures 2000. Scottish Executive, 2000.

United Kingdom Sea Fisheries Statistics 1999. MAFF. The Stationery Office.

Annual Reports

MAFF and the Intervention Board. The Stationery Office.

Forestry Commission. The Stationery Office.

Websites

MAFF: www.maff.gov.uk

Forestry Commission: www.forestry.gov.uk

Food from Britain: www.foodfrombritain.com

Food Standards Agency: www.foodstandards.gov.uk

DARD: www.dani.gov.uk

Scottish Executive: www.scotland.gov.uk

28 Manufacturing and Construction

Manufacturing continues to play an important role in the modern economy, even though services now generate about three times as much gross domestic product (GDP) and four times as much employment. Important industries in the UK include chemicals, plastics, pharmaceuticals, electronics, motor vehicles and components, aerospace, offshore equipment, and paper and printing, where British companies are among the world's largest.

Introduction

Manufacturing accounted for 18.8 per cent of gross value added (at current basic prices) in 1999 and for 14.7 per cent of employment (just over 4 million people) in the UK at the end of 1999. The East Midlands and West Midlands have the highest proportion of manufacturing employees (around 24 per cent) and London the lowest (7 per cent). Almost all manufacturing is carried out by private sector businesses. Overseas companies have a strong presence (see p. 423), being responsible for about a quarter of manufacturing output in the UK.

The recession in the early 1990s led to a decline in manufacturing output, but it began to rise again in 1993. By 1999, the volume of output was 10.1 per cent above the level in 1991 and 1992, and rose a little into 2000. Some industries, notably electrical and optical equipment—where output was up by 54 per cent between 1992 and 1999—but also including chemicals, rubber and plastic products, and transport equipment, have achieved substantial growth following the recession. However, output of other sectors, including textiles, leather and wood products, remains well below their 1990 levels.

The construction industry contributed 5.2 per cent of gross value added in 1999. Following a period of marked decline as recession affected the industry in the early 1990s, output has picked up since 1993 and was 9.6 per cent higher in 1999 than in 1993, although still below pre-recession levels.

Sectors of Manufacturing

Relative sizes of enterprises are shown in Tables 28.1 and 28.2 and output and investment by sector in Table 28.3. An outline of the main manufacturing sectors follows. A brief statistical summary is included for most sectors, taken from the appropriate Office for National Statistics (ONS) sector review. In some circumstances, statistics in these summaries may differ from figures in the text where these have been obtained from the Department of Trade and Industry or the appropriate trade association. The variations usually reflect differences in coverage of the industry concerned. In addition, the value of

Table 28.1: Manufacturing—Size of Businesses by Turnover, 2000

Annual turnover (£'000)	Number of businesses
1–49	24,370
50–99	26,080
100–249	33,160
250–499	21,405
500–999	16,875
1,000–1,999	11,890
2,000–4,999	9,240
5,000–9,999	4,040
10,000–49,999	4,030
50,000+	1,140
Total	**152,230**

Source: ONS *Size Analysis of United Kingdom Business*. Business Monitor PA 1003

Table 28.2: Manufacturing—Size of Businesses by Employment, 2000

Employment size	Number of businesses
1–9	109,800
10–19	18,280
20–49	11,920
50–99	4,490
100–199	3,010
200–499	2,000
500–999	670
1,000+	450
Total	**150,620**

Not all businesses covered by the inquiry have been allocated by employment size—this accounts for the difference in totals between this table and Table 28.1 above.
Source: ONS *Size Analysis of United Kingdom Business*. Business Monitor PA 1003

exports can include that of re-exports of imported and factored goods, and can exceed the sales values quoted.

Food, Drink and Tobacco

Food and Drink

The UK's food and drink manufacturing and processing industry has accounted for a growing proportion of total domestic food supply since the 1940s. The largest concentration of enterprises is to be found in the production of bread, cakes and fresh pastry goods, followed by those engaged in processing and preserving fruit and vegetables. The greatest number of food and beverage manufacturing jobs are in Yorkshire (13 per cent of the total for Great Britain), the South East and London (12 per cent), and the East Midlands (12 per cent). Spirits production gives Scotland the highest concentration of employment in the alcoholic and soft drinks manufacturing industry (about 31 per cent of drinks manufacturing employment), with a significant proportion of jobs in its economically deprived rural areas; the South East and London has the second highest concentration (about 14 per cent) of drinks-related jobs. In 1999 by far the biggest food and drinks export category was alcoholic drinks, which accounted for £2.7 billion of the value of total food and drink sales overseas, £8.7 billion; the largest food exporting sector was biscuits and confectionery, worth £705 million.

Among the biggest companies involved in food and drink manufacturing and processing are Unilever, Cadbury Schweppes, Nestlé, Associated British Foods, Tate and Lyle, Unigate (the company announced in August 2000 that it would change its name to Uniq), Northern Foods, United Biscuits (part of which has been acquired by Heinz and a consortium, Finalrealm), Hillsdown Holdings, Hazlewood Foods, Ranks Hovis McDougall (RHM—see p. 470), Diageo and Allied Domecq. Specialist small and medium-sized firms in the food and drink manufacturing industry thrive alongside these large concerns, supplying high-quality 'niche' products, often to small retail outlets, such as delicatessens.

Frozen foods and chilled convenience foods, such as frozen potato products and ready-prepared meals, fish and shellfish dishes, salads and pasta, together with yogurts, desserts and instant snacks, have formed some of the fastest-growing sectors of the food market in recent years. The trend towards snacking—eating less, more often—and higher consumption outside the home means snacks are filling the gap left by the

Table 28.3: Output and Investment in Manufacturing, 1999 *£ million*

1992 Standard Industrial Classification category	Gross value added at current basic prices	Business investment at current prices
Food, beverages and tobacco	20,113	2,555
Textiles and textile products	6,382	338
Leather and leather products	722	49
Wood and wood products	1,826	221
Pulp, paper and paper products, publishing and printing	18,002	1,914
Coke, petroleum products and nuclear fuel	2,216	347
Chemicals, chemical products and man-made fibres	15,641	2,596
Rubber and plastic products	7,439	1,043
Other non-metal mineral products	5,145	672
Basic metals and fabricated metal products	14,729	1,392
Machinery and equipment not elsewhere classified	13,040	962
Electrical and optical equipment	19,876	1,772
Transport equipment	16,694	2,663
Other manufacturing	5,878	396
Total	**147,699**	**16,920**

Sources: ONS *United Kingdom National Accounts 2000—the Blue Book* and ONS *Quarterly Business Investment Inquiry*

decline of the traditional family meal. Consumption of pre-prepared meals in the UK was 5 kg a head in 1999, second only to Sweden within Europe. Many new low-fat and fat-free items are being introduced, ranging from dairy products to complete prepared meals, and organic foods are also becoming more widely available. There has been a substantial rise in sales of vegetarian foods (both natural vegetable dishes and vegetable-based substitutes of meat products, where soya plays a big role). For genetically modified foods, see chapter 27.

Just under one-third (30 per cent) of liquid milk supplies in Great Britain are distributed through a doorstep delivery system employing about 13,600 people. However, the proportion is declining (staff have declined by 60 per cent since 1991) as supermarkets increase their share of the market. Household consumption of liquid milk per head—2.2 litres (3.9 pints) a week—is among the highest in the world. Consumption of skimmed and semi-skimmed milk accounted for 58 per cent of total milk sales in 1999. The British dairy industry accounts for 81 per cent of butter and 63 per cent of cheese supplies to the domestic market, and achieves significant sales in overseas markets.

Bread production in 1999 was 1.8 million tonnes. The two largest producers are Allied Bakeries, owned by Associated British Foods, and British Bakeries which is part of RHM, owned by Doughty Hanson which acquired it from Tomkins in August 2000. The UK's largest plant cake producer (Manor Bakeries/Mr Kipling/Lyons) is also part of RHM. The morning goods market (including rolls, croissants, scones and teacakes) had an estimated retail value of £1.1 billion in 1998. A recent innovation—long-life bread—now accounts for 5 per cent of the plant bread market. Production of bagels grew by 50 per cent between 1998 and 1999 with UK sales of bagels worth £20 million in 1999. A feature of the bread-making market is a move towards production in in-store bakeries, notably in supermarkets. Part-baked bread (which allows

Food, Drink and Tobacco—statistics for 1999 unless indicated

	Sales[1] (£ million)	Index of production (1995 = 100)	Exports (£ million)	Number of enterprises	Investment (£ million, 1995 prices)
Sector	58,526	100.5	9,146	7,400	2,472
of which:					
Food and drink	*56,043*	*103.0*	*8,133*	*7,385*	*2,357*
Tobacco	*2,483*	*80.6*	*1,013*	*15*	*115*

[1] 1997.
Source: ONS Sector Review: *Food, Drink and Tobacco*

newly baked bread to be available throughout the day in a matter of minutes) is sold, for example, to in-store bakeries and restaurants. Sandwiches are the UK's most popular fast food, with consumers spending more on commercially made sandwiches than any other fast food. There has been a steady increase in the varieties available, and they are sold through major supermarkets, sandwich bars and other outlets. In 1999 the market for sandwiches was valued at £3.6 billion and is growing at around 11 per cent a year.

The brewing industry has four major national brewery groups—Scottish & Newcastle, Bass, Whitbread (both Bass and Whitbread brewery operations are being acquired by Interbrew of Belgium) and Carlsberg-Tetley—and 470 regional and local breweries. Brewers throughout the world use British malt, which is made almost entirely from home-grown barley. In 1998 lager accounted for 61 per cent of all beer sales, but there is still a demand for the vast range of traditional cask-conditioned and brewery-conditioned ales and stouts. Recently there has been a shift towards stronger bottled beers, a significant proportion of which is imported. Another recent trend has been a sizeable import of beer bought on the continent of Europe, mainly in Calais, by British travellers. The main brewers are modernising their brewing and distribution facilities to meet the changing pattern of demand, while also taking action to develop their public houses (pubs) and restaurants, concentrating increasingly on 'branded' or 'themed' pubs and restaurants.

The Scotch whisky industry is one of the UK's top export earners, with overseas sales worth £2.1 billion in 1999. About 90 per cent of production is exported to 200 markets worldwide, the European Union (EU) taking 40 per cent, the United States 13 per cent and Japan 6 per cent by volume. Some 12,000 people work in the Scotch whisky industry and a further 48,000 are employed in associated sectors, for instance supplying ingredients and materials. There are over 90 Scotch whisky distilleries in Scotland, producing either malt whisky or grain whisky. Most Scotch whisky consumed is a blend of malt and grain. Examples of well-known blended brands are J & B, Johnnie Walker, Chivas Regal, Ballantine's, Famous Grouse, Bell's and Teacher's. Glenfiddich, Glenmorangie, Glen Grant and Macallan are some of the best-known single malt Scotch whiskies. Gin and vodka production are also important parts of the spirits industry.

In a highly competitive market, English and Welsh wines have a distinctive local identity. Some 382 vineyards (including 125 wineries), mainly in the south, produce an average of 1.3 million litres of wine a year, most of which is white. Quality continues to improve with a combination of more experienced winemakers, modern technologies and better winemaking equipment. Cider is made primarily in south-west England, and in Gloucestershire, Herefordshire and Worcestershire.

The soft drinks industry produces still and carbonated drinks, dilutable drinks, fruit juices and juice drinks, natural mineral waters, and spring and table waters. The UK market was worth £7.4 billion by retail value in 1999, with Coca-Cola and Schweppes Beverages the largest supplier. It is one of the fastest-growing sectors of the grocery trade, responsible for introducing many innovative products each year. Bottled waters have experienced the fastest growth within the sector during the period 1994 to 1999, averaging increases in volume of 13 per cent a year and sales of £500 million in the UK in 1999. In 1999 UK consumption of soft drinks was 11.26 billion litres, compared with 8.33 billion litres in 1989—an increase of 35 per cent; there was a rise of 16 per cent in 1999 in the volume of the still fruit drinks market.

Tobacco

The British tobacco industry manufactures around 90 per cent of the cigarettes and tobacco goods sold legitimately in the UK. In recent years there has been a rapid growth in 'bootlegging' and smuggling. The Government acknowledges that since 1996 it has lost revenue in excess of £5.6 billion and that in 1999, 18 per cent of cigarettes and 75 per cent of handrolling tobacco were illegally sold. Three major manufacturers—Imperial Tobacco Ltd, Gallaher Ltd and Rothmans (UK) Ltd (now part of British American Tobacco)—supply the market. British American Tobacco, which mainly markets its products outside the UK, is now the second largest tobacco company in the world. The industry specialises in the production of cigarettes made from flue-cured tobacco, and achieves significant export sales—£1.02 billion in 1999. Europe, the Middle East and Africa are important overseas markets. The UK tobacco industry remains one of the top ten balance of payments earners in the UK economy.

Textiles, Clothing and Footwear

Annual turnover in the UK textiles, clothing and footwear industry is around £20 billion, and about 304,000 people were employed in December 1999. The sector has been significantly affected by a number of factors, including imports from low labour-cost suppliers, changing sourcing patterns in the UK high street and the weakness of the euro and related European currencies. In 1999 the volume of sales was 16 per cent below the level in 1995. To meet these challenges, UK textile, clothing and footwear manufacturers have had to modernise their domestic operations, and in some cases have invested in production facilities abroad. In addition, to compete on areas other than price, firms are shifting into higher-value products to benefit from the UK's strengths in fashion, design product and process innovation and information technology. New technologies, largely designed to improve response times and give greater flexibility in production, are being used throughout the industry.

For textiles, there is a high degree of regional concentration, reflecting the traditional centres for this sector: cotton textiles in the North West, fine knitwear in Scotland, linen in Northern Ireland, woollens

Textiles, Clothing and Footwear—statistics for 1999 unless indicated

	Sales (£ million)	Index of production (1995 = 100)	Exports (£ million)	Number of enterprises	Investment (£ million, 1995 prices)
Sector	n.a.	83.7	6,323	13,290	435
of which:					
Textiles	*9,548*[1]	*87.6*	*3,054*	*5,570*	*308*
Clothing	*4,561*[2]	*74.1*	*2,315*	*6,680*	*76*
Footwear and leather goods	*1,474*	*86.7*	*954*	*1,040*	*51*

[1] 1996.
[2] 1998.
n.a. = not available.
Source: ONS Sector Reviews: *Textiles* and *Clothing, Footwear and Leather Goods*

and worsteds in Yorkshire and Scotland, and knitted fabrics in the East Midlands. The clothing industry is more dispersed throughout the UK, but also has significant concentrations in the Midlands, north and east London and the North East.

The UK textile and clothing industry comprises a few multi-process companies, but in the main companies operate vertically. However, small and medium-sized firms dominate, some of which subcontract work to other companies or to home workers. Two of the mainstays of the UK's textile and clothing industry, Coats Viyella and Courtaulds Textiles, have undergone radical changes over the last 12 months. Courtaulds has now been taken over by the US conglomerate Sara Lee and Coats Viyella has taken a strategic decision to withdraw from a number of markets, including home furnishing and contract clothing.

The principal textile and clothing products are yarns, woven and knitted fabrics, interior (including printed) textiles, technical textiles, carpets and a full range of clothing (including knitwear).

The UK has a long established woollen and worsted sector, which remains well known for its quality and is moving more and more towards innovation. Worsted yarns are finely spun for use mainly in suit fabric and fine knitwear. As well as spinners, weavers and knitters, the sector supports a number of other processes, such as scouring of the raw wool and dyeing and finishing of the wool, yarn or fabric. British mills also process rare fibres such as cashmere and angora. In addition, the UK produces synthetic fibres, cotton/synthetic mixed yarns and fabrics and has a large dyeing and finishing sector (which includes fabric printing).

In woven carpets (Axminster and Wilton are the main types), the UK is recognised as a key player due to its high quality, variety of design and use of new technology. UK companies are also continually improving their capability in the manufacture of higher-volume, lower-value tufted carpets.

Technical textiles are usually defined as those for their performance characteristics. They include non-wovens for filtration and absorbency, textiles used in construction, automotive textiles, sewing thread, rope and medical textiles.

The clothing industry is more labour-intensive than textiles. Although a broad range of clothing is imported from overseas, British industry still supplies nearly two-fifths of domestic demand. Exports rose consistently until 1997 as a result of the rising prominence of the British fashion designer industry throughout the 1980s, and traditional design and high-quality production enabling branded clothing companies such as Burberry and Jaeger to compete successfully overseas. UK firms have also had success in the growing market for branded street and club-wear. Exports have, however, fallen by over 15 per cent between 1997 and 1999 to £2.7 billion.

Output of footwear has been particularly affected by the strength of sterling and increasing competitiveness of imports. Footwear manufacturers, with around 20,000 employees, are predominantly found in Northamptonshire, Leicestershire, Somerset and Lancashire. Nearly 60 per cent of production by value is exported, with the UK particularly renowned for classic men's Goodyear Welted shoes and youth/street fashion footwear.

Paper, Printing and Publishing

In total, the UK paper, printing and publishing industry employed some 471,000 people in December 1999. The paper and board sector has a relatively small number of medium and large firms—98 paper and board mills, employing 21,000 people—whereas printing in particular has a very large number of small businesses. Paper and board are produced for further industrial processing, corrugated paper, sacks, bags, cartons, boxes, household goods, stationery and a host of other articles. Production has been increasingly concentrated in large-scale units to enable the industry to compete more effectively. Over half the industry is made up of forestry product companies from Scandinavia, North America, Australia and elsewhere. Among the biggest British-owned groups in terms of production are St Regis, BPB Paperboard and Arjo Wiggins. There has been a significant trend towards waste-based packaging grades. Usage of recycled waste

Paper, Printing and Publishing—statistics for 1999 unless indicated

	Sales[1] (£ million)	Index of production (1995 = 100)	Exports[1] (£ million)	Number of enterprises	Investment (£ million, 1995 prices)
Sector	36,110	99.1	4,426	30,115	1,968
of which:					
Pulp, paper and paper products	*10,618*	*87.8*	*2,102*	*2,580*	*472*
Publishing and printing, etc.	*25,492*	*102.8*	*2,324*	*27,535*	*1,496*

[1] 1998.
n.a.= not available
Source: ONS Sector Review: *Paper, Publishing and Printing*

paper is increasing, and recycled paper made up over 55 per cent of the raw material for UK newspapers in 1999 (including imports).

Much publishing and printing employment and output is carried out in firms based in south-east England. Mergers have led to the formation of large groups in newspaper, magazine and book publishing. Pearson controls some of the world's leading educational publishing businesses. The British book-publishing industry is a major exporter; in 1999 it issued 83,997 new titles.

The UK printing industry has an annual turnover of around £11.8 billion and employs 196,700 people in Great Britain. It is undergoing significant technological change, with digital technology enabling much greater automation and standardisation, while colour printing is becoming cheaper and more widely available. Exports and imports are dominated by books and periodicals.

Chemicals and Chemical Products

The chemicals industry is one of the UK's major manufacturing sectors, directly employing over 256,000 people in December 1999 in over 4,000 companies. It had total product sales of £32 billion in 1999, of which over 70 per cent was exported. The sector does, however, also underpin much of the rest of UK manufacturing industry, with chemicals being essential feedstocks for most other industrial processes.

It is a diverse industry, with important representation in all primary chemical sectors—ranging from bulk petrochemicals to low-volume, high-value specialised organics. It includes key industrial materials such as plastics and synthetic rubber, and other products such as man-made fibres, soaps, detergents, cosmetics, adhesives, dyes and inks, and intermediates for the pharmaceutical industry.

Bulk Chemicals

The UK's North Sea oil and gas provide accessible feedstocks for its large organics sector, including such products as ethylene, propylene, benzene and methanol. These provide the basic building blocks for the manufacture of many downstream chemical products, including polymers used for the manufacture of plastics products; and synthetic fibres such as nylon, polyamide, polyester and acrylics used in the textiles, clothing and footwear industries.

There is substantial inorganics production, including sulphuric acid, chlorine and caustic soda, based upon minerals such as salt, sulphur, and phosphate ores or reaction between gases. These also serve many other downstream chemical processes.

Formulated Products

The UK is also strong in the 'formulation' of chemical products, in areas such as paints, inks, soaps and detergents, and cosmetics and

Chemicals and Chemical Products—statistics for 1999 unless indicated

	Sales[1] (£ million)	Index of production (1995 = 100)	Exports (£ million)	Number of enterprises	Investment (£ million, 1995 prices)
Sector	32,106	107.7	23,732	3,500	2,631

[1] 1997.
Source: ONS Sector Review: *Chemicals, Rubber and Plastic Products*

perfumes. Home decorative products include household names such as 'Dulux' (an ICI brand) and Crown Paints. The industrial coatings sector includes decoration on cans, and anti-fouling marine coatings.

Speciality Chemicals

For the chemicals industry, the last few years have brought increasingly rapid market and technological changes. Imperial Chemical Industries plc (ICI) is one of the world's largest producers of speciality products and paints, with a turnover of more than £8 billion in 1999 (with 50,000 products from more than 200 manufacturing sites in over 55 countries). The development of speciality chemicals to meet specific needs through the application of sophisticated 'chemistry' illustrates this dimension. The pharmaceutical and agrochemical sectors are at the forefront of such innovation. In recent years, the application of chirality[1] in synthesis has allowed firms to make drugs that are more closely tailored to targets.

Man-made Fibres

Synthetic fibres are supplied to the textiles, clothing and footwear industries. The main types of synthetic fibre are still those first developed in the 1940s: regenerated cellulosic fibres such as viscose, and the major synthetic fibres like nylon polyamide, polyester and acrylics. Extensive research continues to produce a variety of innovative products; antistatic and flame-retardant fibres are examples. More specialist products include the aramids (with very high thermal stability and strength), elastanes (giving very high stretch and recovery) and melded fabrics (produced without the need for knitting or weaving).

[1] Chiral compounds are mirror images of each other, analogous to left and right handed forms. One form may be more effective, or safer, than the other.

Pharmaceuticals

The UK pharmaceuticals industry, which is largely based in the South East and North West/North East England, is the world's second largest exporter of medicines, accounting for about 13 per cent of the developed world's export market. It researches and manufactures the complete range of medicinal products—human and veterinary medicines, medical dressings and dental materials. In recent times, the largest growth has been in medicines that act on the respiratory system, followed by cardiovascular, muscular and skeletal, anti-infective and alimentary tract remedies. Pharmaceutical exports in 1999 were £6.3 billion. The main overseas markets are Western Europe, North America and Japan.

Over 300 pharmaceutical companies operate in the UK, with indigenous and US parent multinationals dominating production. Glaxo Wellcome (employing some 13,400 people in the UK and 59,000 worldwide), AstraZeneca and SmithKline Beecham feature in the top ten UK-based companies (see p. 386); Glaxo Wellcome and SmithKline Beecham are merging in late 2000 to form Glaxo SmithKline.

Some 55,000 people are directly employed in the pharmaceutical industry, of whom about a third are engaged in R&D; another 250,000 are employed in related sectors. The industry invested approximately £2.7 billion in R&D in

1999, about 23 per cent of all UK commercial R&D. R&D expenditure in the UK on pharmaceuticals has grown by 108 per cent between 1990 and 1998. AstraZeneca, Glaxo Wellcome and SmithKline Beecham are the UK's top three companies in terms of R&D expenditure (see Table 26.1, p. 428) with Pfizer (US), Merck (US) and Novartis (Swiss) among the significant foreign investors.

Major developments pioneered in the UK are semi-synthetic penicillins and cephalosporins, both powerful antibiotics, and new treatments for ulcers, asthma, arthritis, migraine, coronary heart disease and erectile dysfunction (Viagra was developed in the UK by Pfizer). The UK pharmaceuticals industry has discovered and developed more leading medicines than any other country apart from the United States, including six of the world's current top 25 best-selling drugs. UK laboratories place about 20 new pharmaceutical products on the market each year. Among the best-selling drugs produced by the three largest UK-owned companies are:

- Glaxo Wellcome—Flixotide/Flovent (asthma), Zantac (anti-ulcer) and Imigran (migraine);
- SmithKline Beecham—Avandia (diabetes), Augmentin (infections) and Seroxat/Paxil (for depression); and
- AstraZeneca—Losec (anti-ulcer), Nexium (successor to Losec) and Zestril (heart disease).

Biotechnology

The UK biotechnology industry is second only to that of the United States, employing 14,000 people directly; 25,000 more jobs depend on providing services to the sector. As well as AstraZeneca, Glaxo Wellcome and SmithKline Beecham, there are some 275 smaller specialist dedicated biotechnology firms—about 20 per cent of the number in Europe—with particular strengths in biopharmaceuticals. Of the potentially new drugs under development in Europe, 70 per cent are from publicly quoted UK companies. Companies are clustered particularly around Cambridge, Oxford and southern Scotland. The industry benefits strongly from the UK's science base. Bioscience research in UK universities is of world renown, and the major research laboratories of leading pharmaceutical multinationals are based here. The UK has a number of world-class research institutes, such as the Sanger Centre in Cambridge which played an important part in the Human Genome project (see p. 441).

Rubber and Plastics Products

In December 1999 almost 237,000 people were employed by 6,740 enterprises in the rubber and plastics industries. Rubber products include tyres and tubes, pipes, hoses, belting and floor coverings, and many have applications in the automotive industry. The largest firms in this sector are major tyre manufacturers such as Goodyear and Michelin. The highest concentrations of plastics employment are in the West Midlands (with 29.6 per cent of the total), the South East, North West and the South West. Plastics have a multitude of applications in the packaging, building, electrical and electronic, transport, medical, household goods and clothing industries. The UK's plastics industry continues to be a world leader in material specification and design, with new

Rubber and Plastics Products—statistics for 1999 unless indicated

	Sales[1] (£ million)	Index of production (1995 = 100)	Exports (£ million)	Number of enterprises	Investment (£ million, 1995 prices)
Sector	16,062	101.1	4,042	6,740	1,049

[1] 1996.
Source: ONS Sector Review: *Chemicals, Rubber and Plastic Products*

processes allowing stronger plastics to replace traditional materials and develop new applications. Among the larger firms in a sector characterised by many small and medium-sized businesses is British Polythene Industries, manufacturing products such as carrier bags, sacks and shrink film. In the moulded plastics sector, Linpac's output includes food packaging and components for the automotive sector.

Glass, Ceramics and Building Materials

Almost 140,000 people were employed in this sector in December 1999.

The UK is a world leader in the manufacture of glass used in windows, doors and cladding. Flat glass is made through the float process, developed by Pilkington and licensed to glassmakers throughout the world. About half of Pilkington's sales are in glass products for buildings, while the company is the world's largest supplier of glass for cars, with about one-quarter of vehicles containing its glass. The manufacture and supply of windows and doors are carried out by a large number of other companies operating in one of three basic product sectors—timber, metal (aluminium and steel) and plastic (UPVC). The UK also has several leading lead crystal suppliers such as Waterford-Wedgwood, Dartington, Edinburgh Crystal and Royal Brierley.

The ceramics industry manufactures domestic ceramic tableware, as well as durables such as sanitaryware, tiles and clay pipes for the building trade. It is heavily concentrated in the West Midlands. Domestic tableware production includes fine china, bone china, earthenware and stoneware. Tableware is produced predominantly in Stoke-on-Trent. The UK is one of the world's leading manufacturers and exporters of fine bone china: Wedgwood, Spode and Royal Doulton are among the most famous names. Research is being conducted into ceramics use in housebuilding and diesel and jet engines. Important industrial ceramics invented in the UK include some forms of silicon carbide and sialons, which can withstand ultra-high temperatures.

Most crushed rock, sand and gravel quarried by the aggregates industry (some 208 million tonnes in Great Britain in 1999) is used in construction. In 1999, 2.94 billion bricks were produced by, and 3.02 billion bricks were delivered from, sites in Great Britain. Portland cement, a 19th-century British innovation, is the most widely used chemical compound in the world. Blue Circle Industries is the UK's largest producer of cement. Just over 91 million sq m of concrete building blocks were produced in Great Britain in 1999.

The UK is a major exporter of china clay, 80 per cent of which is used as coatings and fillers in paper-making, the remainder going into the ceramic, paint, rubber and plastics industries. Output of kaolin was 2.0 million tonnes in 1999. It accounted for 88 per cent of china clay output. The main producer is English China Clays International (ECCI), part of the English China Clays Group. ECCI was taken over by the French company Imetal in 1999. Imetal changed its name to IMERYS during 1999 and all the company's operations in Britain now trade under the name IMERYS Minerals Ltd. The combined company is the world's leading producer of high-quality kaolin.

Metals and Fabricated Metal Products

The Industrial Revolution in the UK was based to a considerable extent on the manufacture of

Glass, Ceramics and Building Materials—statistics for 1999 unless indicated

	Sales[1] (£ million)	Index of production (1995 = 100)	Exports (£ million)	Number of enterprises	Investment (£ million, 1995 prices)
Sector	9,624	95.3	1,856	4,800	638

[1] 1998.

Source: ONS Sector Review: *Glass, Ceramics and Building Materials*

iron and steel and heavy machinery. These sectors remain important parts of the industrial economy; some 520,000 people were employed in December 1999. The major areas of steel production are now concentrated in south Wales and northern England, with substantial processing in the Midlands and Yorkshire. Major restructuring in the steel industry took place during the 1980s and 1990s. Metals can be recycled many times; every year the British metals recycling industry processes about 8 million tonnes of scrap metal.

From total crude steel output of 16.3 million tonnes, British producers delivered 15.1 million tonnes of finished steel in 1999; nearly 50 per cent is exported to some 160 countries. Nearly three-quarters of UK steel exports go to other EU member states. Germany is the UK's biggest market. In the last 15 years annual steel industry exports have more than doubled to 7.6 million tonnes—worth £2.4 billion in 1999. British Steel merged with the Dutch steel producer Koninklijke Hoogovens during 1999 to create an international metals group. As Corus, it has become Europe's biggest steelmaker and the third largest in the world, employing 64,000 people worldwide (of whom 34,000 are in the UK) and producing 88 per cent of the UK's total crude steel. Its worldwide aluminium output is around 500,000 tonnes. Corus's UK steel output is based on strip mill products, plate, sections, specialist engineering steels, bars, wire rods and tubes. These are used principally in the construction, automotive, engineering, transport, metal goods, packaging and energy industries. Corus owns 51 per cent of Avesta Sheffield, the Anglo-Swedish stainless steel group.

Products manufactured by other UK steel companies include reinforcing bars for the construction industry, wire rod, hot rolled bars, bright bars, tubes, and wire and wire products. The production of special steels is centred on the Sheffield area and includes stainless and alloy special steels for the aerospace and offshore oil and gas industries.

Steel has had a notable success in UK construction, with its market share of buildings of two or more storeys more than doubling from 30 per cent in the early 1980s to 68 per cent today. It has 95 per cent of the single storey market. Total iron and steel sector sales are about £2.0 billion a year and consumption of constructional steelwork over 1.1 million tonnes.

Several multinational companies, including Alcan, Norsk Hydro, Kaiser, MIM and Quexco, have plants in Britain producing non-ferrous metals from both primary and recycled raw materials. The aluminium industry, which has raised its productivity and competitiveness significantly in recent years, supplies customers in the aerospace, transport, automotive and construction industries. Other important non-ferrous metal sectors are copper and copper alloys, used for electrical wire and cables, power generation and electrical and electronic connectors, automotive components, plumbing and building products, and components for industrial plant and machinery; lead for lead acid batteries and roofing; zinc for galvanising to protect steel; nickel, used principally as an alloying element to make stainless steel and high temperature turbine alloys; and titanium for high-strength, low-weight aerospace applications. Despite an overall decline in the castings industry, some foundries have invested in new melting, moulding and quality control equipment.

Fabricated metal products include pressure vessels, heat exchangers and storage tanks for chemical and oil-refining plant; steam-raising

Metals and Fabricated Metal Products—statistics for 1999 unless indicated

	Sales[1] (£ million)	Index of production (1995 = 100)	Exports (£ million)	Number of enterprises	Investment (£ million, 1995 prices)
Sector	27,784	94.3[2]	9,026	28,150	1,405

[1] 1998.
[2] Also includes other non-metallic mineral products.
Source: ONS Sector Review: *Metals and Fabricated Metal Products*

boilers; nuclear reactors; water and sewage treatment plant; and steelwork for bridges, buildings and industrial installations. Other products include central heating radiators and boilers, cutlery, tools and general hardware.

Machinery and Domestic Appliances

Some 380,000 people were employed in this sector in December 1999. The highest concentrations are found in the West Midlands, followed by the South East and the East region. Mechanical machine-building is an area in which British firms excel, especially internal combustion engines, power transmission equipment, pumps and compressors, wheeled tractors, construction and earth-moving equipment, and textile machinery.

The UK is a major producer of industrial engines, pumps, valves and compressors, and of pneumatic and hydraulic equipment. The Weir Group is the world's sixth biggest producer of pumps. Companies such as Mitsui-Babcock manufacture steam generators and other heavy equipment for power plants. ALSTOM, a global specialist in transport and energy infrastructure, is the world's leading supplier of major components for complete power station projects along with the transformers and switchgear needed in transmission and distribution of electricity. In the UK the company's strengths are steam turbine manufacture, switchgear manufacture, industrial gas turbines, and project design and management. The mechanical lifting and handling equipment industry makes cranes and transporters, lifting devices, escalators, conveyors, powered industrial trucks and air bridges, as well as electronically controlled and automatic handling systems. The commercial heating, ventilation, air-conditioning and refrigeration sector is served to a great extent by small and medium-sized firms, although several large multinational companies have sites in Britain.

Tractors and equipment used in agriculture, horticulture, forestry, sportsturf and gardens achieved export sales of almost £1.5 billion in 1999. Most exports were supplied by three major multinationals with tractor plants in Britain which, together with JCB Landpower, export to nearly every country in the world. A range of specialist golf, parks and sports field machinery, lawn and garden products, and agricultural equipment complement the tractor business.

Machine tools, most of which are computer controlled, are used in engineering, aerospace, automotive and metal goods industries. The global nature of the sector means that exports are important to this industry. In 1999, total turnover of the metalworking machine tools industry was £867 million, of which exports accounted for £382 million, or 44 per cent. Total orders on hand at the end of 1999 were around £200 million.

The mining and tunnelling equipment industry leads the world in the production of coal-cutting and road-heading (shearing) equipment, hydraulic roof supports, conveying equipment, flameproof transformers, switchgear, and subsurface transport equipment and control systems. JCB, Europe's biggest construction equipment manufacturer, is the world's largest producer of backhoe loaders and telescopic handlers, and a major exporter. The UK possesses one of the largest engineering construction sectors in the world. It serves the whole spectrum of process industries, although oil, gas and related industries are areas of particular strength. Most sales of textile machinery are to export markets.

Machinery and Domestic Appliances—statistics for 1999 unless indicated

	Sales[1] (£ million)	Index of production (1995 = 100)	Exports[1] (£ million)	Number of enterprises	Investment (£ million, 1995 prices)
Sector	27,252	90.0	16,388	12,955	1,038

[1] 1998.
Source: ONS Sector Review: *Machinery and Domestic Appliances*

British innovations include computerised colour matching and weave simulation, friction spinning, high-speed computer-controlled knitting machines and electronic jacquard attachments for weaving looms. British companies also make advanced printing machinery and ceramic processing equipment, and other types of production machinery.

The domestic appliance sector manufactures major appliances, such as washing machines, cookers, microwave ovens, refrigerators, tumble dryers and dishwashers, as well as heating, water heaters and showers, ventilation products, floor cleaners and vacuum cleaners, and small appliances for the kitchen and bathroom. There are around 100 companies of all sizes in the UK. Energy efficiency and water conservation are progressively improving in home laundry products, and new technology is being applied to all products. Visual design of what were traditionally 'white goods' is changing, giving a new look to kitchens, and modern design is also being applied to vacuum cleaners and small appliances such as kettles and toasters. The UK is Europe's largest manufacturer of tumble dryers, with an annual trade surplus in this product of around £22 million.

Electrical and Optical Equipment

In total, just over 504,000 people were employed in this sector in December 1999. There were 55,000 working in the office machinery and computers sector, 174,000 in electrical machinery, 128,000 in radio, TV and communications equipment and 147,000 in medical, precision optical equipment and watches. Production of office machinery and computers has more than trebled since 1990, while radio, television and communications equipment output is up by 74.9 per cent. However, output of medical and optical instruments fell by 7.3 per cent during the 1990s, while that of electrical machinery and apparatus has fallen by 7.1 per cent.

Southern England provides a substantial proportion of employment (especially sales and administrative jobs) in these sectors, with Scotland and Wales having become important areas for inward investors. Scotland's electronics industry ('Silicon Glen'—in reality all of central Scotland) directly employed about 42,500 people in 1997. In 1998 electrical and instrument engineering accounted for exports worth £10 billion, 54 per cent of Scotland's manufactured exports.

Many of the world's leading electronics firms have manufacturing plants in Britain. IBM, Sony, Compaq, Panasonic, Toshiba, NEC, Nortel, Seagate and Hewlett-Packard are among overseas-based multinationals with substantial manufacturing investment in the UK. The main electronic consumer goods produced are television sets. UK production is

Electrical and Optical Equipment—statistics for 1999 unless indicated

	Sales[1] (£ million)	Index of production (1995 = 100)	Exports[1] (£ million)	Number of enterprises	Investment (£ million, 1995 prices)
Sector	41,219	121.5	41,440	13,575	1,945
of which:					
Office machinery and computers	*8,432*	*165.8*	*13,708*	*1,300*	*205*
Electrical machinery and apparatus	*10,683*	*101.0*	*6,724*	*5,360*	*567*
Radio, television and communications equipment	*14,087*	*136.6*	*14,400*	*2,570*	*675*
Medical, precision and optical instruments	*8,017*	*93.6*	*6,608*	*4,345*	*498*

[1] 1998.
Source: ONS Sector Review: *Electrical and Optical Equipment*

concentrated in the high value market with an increasing proportion of widescreen and digital sets. High-fidelity audio and video equipment is also produced.

The computer industry in the UK is the largest in Europe, producing an extensive range of systems for all uses. For information on software, see p. 531. The multinational computer manufacturers in the UK include IBM, Compaq and Sun. Other companies, such as Psion (a pioneer of the 'palmtop' computer), have concentrated on developing new lines for specialised markets.

A broad range of other electrical machinery and apparatus is produced in the UK by both British and foreign companies, covering power plant, electric motors, generators, transformers, switchgear, insulated wire and cable, and lighting equipment. The UK is a world leader in the manufacture of generating sets. In the cables sector, AEI, BICC and Pirelli produce high-voltage transmission cables and optical fibre cables for telecommunications; other large cable manufacturers include Draka. TLG is the UK's largest manufacturer of lighting products.

The past ten years have seen the development of electronic service providers (contract electronic manufacturers) which manufacture and assemble products to the specification of another company. This global trend has encouraged some multinational producers to move away from manufacture to become designers, developers, marketers or sellers of their products. The UK is one of the leading locations in Europe for this type of business.

Communications Equipment

The domestic telecommunications equipment market is worth over £3 billion a year. Manufacturers have been investing heavily in facilities to meet the rapidly increasing demand for telecommunications services (see chapter 22). The main products are switching and transmission equipment, telephones and terminals. Marconi plc is the UK's foremost telecommunications manufacturer, with turnover of £3.8 billion in the year to March 1999. Its range includes PBXs (private branch exchanges), payphones, transmission systems and videoconferencing equipment.

Transmission equipment and cables for telecommunications and information networks include submarine and high-specification data-carrying cables.

There has been remarkable growth in mobile communications (see p. 376), where the UK is among Europe's leading markets and manufacturing bases. The main producers—Motorola, Nokia, Ericsson, Panasonic, NEC and Lucent—all have UK production or design centres. Fibre optics (invented in the UK) and other optoelectronic components are also experiencing rapid growth; Hewlett-Packard, Nortel, Pirelli and Corning have considerable UK facilities.

Another sector of the industry manufactures radio communications equipment, radar, radio and sonar navigational aids for ships and aircraft, thermal imaging systems, alarms and signalling apparatus, public broadcasting equipment and other capital goods. Radar was invented in the UK and British firms are still in the forefront of technological advances. Racal Avionics' X-band radar for aircraft ground movement control is in use at airports in several overseas countries. Solid-state secondary surveillance radar, manufactured by Cossor Electronics, is being supplied to numerous overseas civil aviation operators.

Medical Electronics

The high demand for advanced medical equipment in the UK stems from its comprehensive healthcare system and extensive clinical research and testing facilities in the chemical, biological, physical and molecular sciences. Important contributions have been made by British scientists and engineers to basic R&D in endoscopy, CT (computerised tomography) scanning, magnetic resonance imaging (MRI—pioneered in the UK), ultrasonic imaging, CADiagnosis and renal analysis. UK medical electronic firms are an integral part of the medical devices sector. Firms in the UK medical electronic sector continue their tradition of developing and manufacturing a range of medical equipment for domestic and overseas health sectors. About two-fifths of the medium to large companies in the UK have overseas parents.

Instrumentation and Control

A variety of electronic measurement and test equipment is made in the UK, as well as analytical instruments, process control equipment, and numerical control and indication materials, all for use in machine tools. The instrument engineering industry makes measuring, photographic, cinematographic and reprographic items; watches, clocks and other timing devices; and medical surgical instruments. The UK instrumentation and control sector has an estimated annual output of £9 billion, £4.6 billion of which is exported, and a trade balance of £884 million. The sector is diverse and exceeds 3,000 firms, employing 79,000 people. It is the fourth most important manufacturer of instrumentation and process control equipment in the World behind the United States, Japan and Germany.

Motor Vehicles

New car registrations in 1999 fell slightly by 2.2 per cent to 2.2 million, the fourth highest figure on record. Car production, at 1.79 million, was 2.2 per cent higher, the highest level since 1972, and has risen by about 38 per cent since 1990. Vehicle manufacturers are increasingly pursuing a global market, with production no longer dominated by their traditional home markets. This is reflected in the rise in both UK exports and imports of motor vehicles. Exports (including components) were valued at £16.9 billion in 1999. A total of 1.14 million passenger cars were produced for export in 1999, nearly three times as many as in 1990. Commercial vehicle production in 1999 was 186,000, significantly down on the last few years; 75,000 units were for export. Production is dominated by light commercial vehicles.

Around 790,000 jobs are dependent on the UK automotive industry, including 330,000 engaged in vehicle and component production and manufacturing activities. There are around 20 motor vehicle manufacturers in the UK. Six overseas groups, accounting for 74 per cent of the total now dominate car output: Ford (including Jaguar and Land Rover), Vauxhall/IBC, Peugeot, Honda, Nissan and Toyota. Rover, previously a subsidiary of the BMW group, has now been sold to the British Phoenix Consortium.

Despite the recent announcement of the closure of Ford's Dagenham, Essex, car plant, there are still many companies making cars and commercial vehicles in Britain. Table 28.4 shows 21 sites, many of them specialist manufacturers.

Capital investment continues on a large scale. Since 1997 motor vehicle manufacturers have announced over £3 billion in new investment in the UK. Since their arrival in the mid-1980s, Nissan, Toyota and Honda have invested substantial sums in the UK, which is their main base for the European market. All three are now producing at least two models of car in the UK. A period of major change has accompanied the arrival of the three Japanese car manufacturers. In the last 25 years UK vehicle production per person employed has increased by over 110 per cent.

Motor Vehicles—statistics for 1999 unless indicated

	Sales[1] (£ million)	Index of production (1995 = 100)	Exports (£ million)	Number of enterprises	Investment (£ million, 1995 prices)
Sector	31,235	109.0	16,853	2,420[2]	1,927

[1] 1997.
[2] Does not cover all firms regarded as being in the motor industry—the components sector (see p. 483), for example.
Source: ONS Sector Review: *Vehicles and Other Transport*

Rover Group ranges includes the highly successful Land Rover four-wheel drive vehicles and a full range of family cars. In 1998 Rolls-Royce began producing its first totally new model for nearly 20 years—the Silver Seraph—at its Crewe plant, and over 1,050 had been built by the end of 1999.

The main truck manufacturers are Leyland Trucks and ERF. Dennis, based in Guildford, Surrey, is also an important bus manufacturer. British-based bus companies achieve considerable sales in overseas markets. London Taxis International recently launched a new version of the famous London taxi.

The automotive components manufacturing sector, with an annual turnover of £8 billion and employing 100,000 in Great Britain, is a major contributor to the UK motor industry. There are 1,265 companies (some 19 per cent of them small and medium enterprises) involved, many of which also supply other sectors. Well-known British companies such as GKN, Pilkington, Unipart, Automotive Products, Johnson Matthey and TMD Friction have large automotive plants, as do other multinationals such as TRW, Federal Mogul, Valeo, Bosch and Johnson Controls. In recent years the sector has enjoyed strong growth and rising productivity.

The £3 billion of new investment announced since 1987 is expected to create over 9,700 new jobs in the UK car industry. This includes investment of £150 million by Toyota at its engine plant in Deeside, raising capacity to 400,000 engines a year; £189 million investment by GM in its Vauxhall and IBC plants for the new Vectra and van projects; four Unipart joint ventures totalling over £80 million; and investment of £128 million by Visteon on four facilities in the UK.

Shipbuilding and Marine Engineering

The UK merchant shipbuilding industry, located mainly in Scotland and northern England, consists of some 20 yards producing ships ranging from tugs and fishing vessels to fast ferries and large specialist craft for offshore exploration and exploitation work. The industry's order-book is between 25 and 30 vessels generating around £200 million. The merchant ship repair and conversion industry, which has a strong presence in the UK, consists of 30 companies employing 8,000 people. The turnover of the sector amounted to some £300 million in 1999. The three warship building and some of the repair and conversion yards are looking to extend their area of interest into the merchant vessel sector. Overall, shipyards employ about 26,000 people and tend to concentrate around the former major shipping and shipbuilding centres in Southampton, Liverpool, Newcastle upon Tyne, Glasgow and Belfast.

In addition, 1,000 firms are engaged in the manufacture and repair of pleasure and sporting boats. A few internationally known builders dominate the sector. The UK marine equipment industry has annual sales of about £1 billion and is estimated to employ more than 100,000 people in about 1,000 companies. The changing structure of manufacturing industry has resulted in a growing number of companies serving both the marine sector and other markets with their products. Production

Table 28.4: UK Vehicle Production in 1999

Company	Location	Number produced	Company	Location	Number produced
Nissan	Sunderland	271,157	Ford	Southampton	66,814
Ford	Dagenham	190,970	Rover (BMW)	Cowley	53,673
Vauxhall	Luton	184,243	Leyland Trucks	Leyland, near Preston	8,115
Toyota	Burnaston, near Derby	178,660	Lotus	Norwich	3,374
Rover (BMW)	Longbridge	172,099	London Taxis International	Coventry	3,142
Vauxhall	Ellesmere Port	168,035	TVR	Blackpool	1,460
Land Rover (BMW)	Solihull	166,101	Rolls-Royce/Bentley	Crewe	1,440
Peugeot	Coventry	162,921	Metrocab	Tamworth	624
Ford	Halewood	115,608	Aston Martin	Banbury	565
Honda UK	Swindon	114,479	Aston Martin	Newport Pagnell	57
Jaguar/Daimler	Coventry	86,317			

Source: Society of Motor Manufacturers and Traders Limited

ranges from traditional marine equipment to sophisticated navigational and propulsion systems, as well as the spectrum of equipment and supplies for the cruise industry. About 80 per cent of output is exported.

Over 25 years of oil and gas exploitation in the North Sea have generated a major offshore industry (see p. 495). Shipbuilders and fabricators build floating production storage and offload vessels (FPSOs) and semi-submersible units for drilling, production and emergency/maintenance support; drill ships; jack-up rigs; modules; and offshore loading systems. Harland and Wolff of Belfast is a world leader in the FPSO and drill ship fields, with potential Ropax/Freey contracts; Vosper Thornycroft and BAE Systems dominate warship production; and A&P and Cammell Laird are world leaders in the ship repair sector. UIE Scotland, Highlands Fabricators, John Brown and McDermott Scotland are among the larger contractors employed by the oil operators for the design and manufacture of jack-up oil rigs and semi-submersibles. Many other firms supply equipment and services to the offshore industry, notably diving expertise, consultancy, design, project management and R&D. A number have used their experience of North Sea projects to establish themselves in oil and gas markets throughout the world.

Railway Equipment

There are several hundred UK companies engaged in the manufacture of railway equipment for both domestic and overseas markets, mainly producing specialist components and systems for use in rolling stock, signalling, track and infrastructure applications. Three large multinational train builders—Adtranz (German-owned), Alstom (UK-French) and Bombardier (Canadian-owned)—have UK bases. After a period with a low level of orders in the early 1990s, the privatised rail operating companies are placing large orders for new rolling equipment.

Aerospace and Defence

The UK's aerospace industry is one of only three in the world with a complete capability across the whole spectrum of aerospace products and technology. On a wider definition of the aerospace industry, turnover in 1998 was about £17.6 billion, of which approximately £11.7 billion (66 per cent) was exported. The industry contributed £2.1 billion to the UK's balance of payments in 1999. Around 104,000 people are directly employed in the industry in Great Britain, with the North West, South West and East Midlands providing the highest number of jobs in 1998. The biennial Farnborough International Exhibition and Flying Display, organised by the Society of British Aerospace Companies, is one of the world's premier airshows.

Among the leading companies are BAE Systems—formed by the merger of British Aerospace with the Marconi Electronic Systems defence division of GEC—and Rolls-Royce, both of which are among the UK's top five exporters. BAE Systems is a global systems, defence and aerospace company. It employs more than 100,000 people in nine home markets around the world and has annual sales of some £12 billion and an order book of £37 billion. BAE Systems designs and manufactures civil and military aircraft, surface ships, submarines, space systems, radar, avionics, guided weapons systems, communications, electronics and a range of other defence equipment.

Industry activities cover designing and constructing airframes, aero-engines, guided weapons, simulators and space satellites, materials, flight controls including 'fly-by-wire' and 'fly-by-light' equipment (see p. 486), avionics and complex components, with their associated services.

The UK also has the Western world's second largest defence manufacturing industry after the United States. Exports were estimated at £4.8 billion in 1999, and the sector supported some 355,000 jobs in 1997–98.

Civil Aircraft

BAE Systems has a 20 per cent share of the European Airbus Integrated Company—EADS (European Aeronautic Defence and Space Company) controls the other 80 per cent. BAE Systems has responsibility for

Aerospace and Defence—statistics for 1999 unless indicated

	Sales[1] (£ million)	Index of production (1995 = 100)	Exports (£ million)	Number of enterprises	Investment (£ million, 1995 prices)
Sector	12,928	137.7	10,221	520	n.a.

[1] 1998.
n.a. = not available.
Source: ONS Sector Review: *Vehicles and Other Transport*

designing and manufacturing the wings for the whole family of Airbus airliners, from the short- to medium-haul A320 series (the first civil airliner to use fly-by-wire controls—see p. 486) to the large long-range four-engined A340. BAE Systems will also design and manufacture the wings for the new A3XX 'superjumbo', expected to create 22,000 jobs in the UK. Airbus and its related businesses support 62,000 UK jobs and contribute about £1.0 billion a year to the UK's balance of payments. In 1999 Airbus received firm orders for 476 new aircraft worth a total of US $30.5 billion from 34 customers around the world, and in the first half of 2000 it had 55 per cent of the world market for large civil aircraft.

Short Brothers, owned by Bombardier of Canada, employs about 6,000 people, mainly in Belfast. The company is mostly engaged in the design and production of major civil aircraft sub-assemblies, advanced engine nacelles and components for aerospace manufacturers as well as the provision of aviation support services.

Military Aircraft and Missiles

Among BAE Systems' military aircraft is the Eurofighter Typhoon, built by BAE Systems, EADS and Alenia of Italy. The company also has the Harrier, a vertical/short take-off and landing (V/STOL) military combat aircraft, and the Tornado combat aircraft (built jointly by BAE Systems and EADS) and the Hawk fast-jet trainer, being supplied to 17 customers worldwide. BAE Systems is involved in the Joint Strike Fighter programme teams of both Boeing and Lockheed Martin of the US.

BAE Systems is a major supplier of tactical guided weapon systems for use on land, at sea and in the air, having merged its missile business with that of France's Matra Corporation to form Europe's largest guided weapons concern, Matra BAe Dynamics. Shorts Missile Systems Ltd (SMS), which has been acquired by Thomson-CSF of France, operates in the area of very short-range air defence systems.

Helicopters

Agusta Westland (formed by the merger of GKN-Westland Helicopters and Agusta of Italy) manufactures the multi-role EH101 medium-lift helicopter for civilian and military markets and the Super Lynx light battlefield and naval helicopter. In addition, it is currently building the Apache attack helicopter for the UK Army, under licence from Boeing. It also has strong business in maintenance and support of its products, including the Sea King medium-size helicopter, which is no longer in production. Agusta Westland is, after Boeing, now the world's second largest helicopter manufacturer, when taking into account its product line inherited from Agusta and the manufacturing facilities in Italy.

Land Systems

The UK's main armoured fighting vehicle capability is concentrated in two companies: Rolls-Royce, which acquired Vickers (Defence Systems) in 1999, and Alvis. RO Defence, a division of BAE Systems, is the UK's only indigenous ordnance company.

Engines and Other Aviation Equipment

Rolls-Royce is one of the world's three prime manufacturers of aero-engines, with a turnover in 1999 of £3.8 billion for its aerospace business. More than 55,000 Rolls-Royce engines are in service, in over 150 countries. Customers include more than 500 airlines, 240 corporate and utility operators and 160 armed forces. Rolls-Royce is a partner in the low-emission V2500 aero-engine, now in service on the Airbus A320 family. Rolls-Royce produces military engines for both fixed-wing aircraft and helicopters, and is a partner in the EJ200 engine project for the Eurofighter and with GE on the alternative US Joint Strike Fighter programme.

Manufacturers such as BAE Systems, Cobham, Dowty Propellers, Dowty Aerospace, GKN-Westland Aerospace, Hunting, Meggitt, Messier-Dowty, Normalair-Garrett, TRW (Lucas Aerospace), Racal, Smiths Industries and Ultra provide aerostructures (doors, windows and aircraft body parts), equipment and systems for engines, aircraft propellers, navigation and landing systems, engine and flight controls, environmental controls and oxygen breathing and regulation systems, electrical generation, mechanical and hydraulic power systems, cabin furnishings, flight-deck controls and information displays. BAE Systems is the world's largest manufacturer of head-up displays (HUDs). British firms have made important technological advances, for example, in developing fly-by-wire and fly-by-light technology, where control surfaces on the wings and elsewhere are moved by means of automatic electronic signalling and fibre optics respectively. UK companies provide radar and air traffic control equipment and ground power supplies to airports and airlines worldwide (see also p. 481).

Space Equipment and Services

Over 400 organisations employing more than 5,400 people are engaged in industrial space activities (see pp. 437–8), with turnover of more than £365 million in 1998–99. Through its participation in the European Space Agency, the British National Space Centre (see p. 437) has enabled UK-based companies to participate in many leading space projects covering telecommunications, satellite navigation, Earth observation, space science and astronomy. The industry is strong in the development and manufacture of civil and military communications satellites and associated Earth stations and ground infrastructure equipment. In the field of Earth observation, it plays a major role in manufacturing platforms, space radar and meteorological satellite hardware, and in the exploitation of space data imaging products.

The largest British space company is Astrium Limited. Formed in May 2000 by the merger of Matra Marconi Space and the space divisions of Daimler Chrysler Aerospace, and jointly owned by BAE Systems and EADS, it is one of the world's major space companies. It has become the leading provider of direct broadcast television satellites, and is involved in all of Europe's space science and Earth observation projects and its launcher and navigation programmes.

Other firms supply satellite subsystems, and IGG is Europe's leading procurer and tester of space qualified components. UK companies such as Surrey Satellite Technology and Space Innovations are leaders in the field of micro and mini satellites, which provide relatively quick and cheap access to space. Major suppliers of satellite ground stations, space software and satellite imaging include Logica, Science Systems, SEA, Vega and NRSC.

Construction

The total value of work done in the construction industry in Great Britain during 1999 was £56.9 billion at constant 1995 prices, of which £30.6 billion was new work and £26.3 billion repair and maintenance. The volume of output at constant 1995 prices grew by almost 1 per cent. The main areas of construction work within the UK industry are:

- building and civil engineering—ranging from major private sector companies with diverse international interests to one-person enterprises carrying out domestic repairs;
- specialist work—companies or individuals undertaking construction work ranging from structural steelwork and precast concrete structures to mechanical and electrical services (including the design and installation of environmentally friendly building control systems);

- the supply of building materials and components—ranging from large quarrying companies, and those engaged in mass production of manufactured items, to small, highly specialised manufacturers; and
- consultancy work—companies or individuals engaged in the planning, design and supervision of construction projects.

In December 1999, 1,167,000 people in the UK were employed in the construction industry, less than 5 per cent of the total workforce; only about 15 per cent of employees were females. A large number—around 500,000—of people working in construction are self-employed.

Project Procurement, Management and Financing

Private and public sector projects are managed in a variety of ways. Most clients invite construction firms to bid for work by competitive tender, having used the design services of a consultant. The successful contractor will then undertake on-site work with a number of specialist sub-contractors. Alternative methods of project procurement have become more common in recent years—for example, contracts might include subsequent provision of building maintenance, or a comprehensive 'design-and-build' service where a single company oversees every stage of a project from conception to completion.

Financing of major projects has also been changing. Traditionally, clients raised the finance to pay for schemes themselves. Today, they often demand a complete service package that includes finance; as a result, larger construction companies are developing closer links with banks and other financial institutions. In public sector construction the Government's Private Finance Initiative/Public-Private Partnerships (see p. 405) have also heralded a move away from traditional financing.

Major Construction Projects in the UK

Major building schemes in hand or recently completed include the express rail link from central London to Heathrow Airport; the London Underground Jubilee Line Extension; the Channel Tunnel Rail Link (see p. 370); the M60 motorway in Manchester; the Midland Expressway; the refurbishment of GCHQ, Cheltenham; and the refurbishment of the Ministry of Defence Whitehall building.

The Channel Tunnel (see p. 369), which opened to traffic in 1994, remains the largest single civil engineering project ever undertaken in Europe. It is about 50 km (31 miles) long and 70 m (230 ft) below sea level at its deepest. Associated projects included new international stations at Waterloo in London and Ashford (Kent), and an international terminal at Folkestone (on the Kent coast).

In 1999, the public sector accounted for 22 per cent of construction industry contracts in the UK by value.

Many construction and renovation projects have received Millennium funding, and this can be seen all round the country.

Housing

In 1999 the total value of new housing orders in Great Britain was £6.9 billion, 1 per cent lower than in 1998—the private sector accounted for 86 per cent of the total compared with 75 per cent in 1993. In 1999 construction of 188,900 dwellings was started in the UK. Starts by private enterprise concerns were 165,900, by registered social landlords 22,600, and by the public sector 400. New dwellings completed by sector are shown in Table 28.5 on p. 488.

Overseas Contracting and Consultancy

UK companies operate worldwide and in any one year British consultants work in almost every country on the globe. Combined overseas earnings are in excess of £6 billion a year.

UK contractors have pioneered management contracting and design and build, and also the innovative financing mechanisms that have been developed in the domestic market through innovations such as the Private Finance Initiative. The contractors have been particularly successful in North

America and Hong Kong from where over 50 per cent of their new work came in 1999. Recent major contracts include:

- Bhairab Bridge, Bangladesh;
- New Valley Pumping Station, Egypt;
- Kowloon Railway Station, Hong Kong;
- liquid natural gas tanks in India;
- social housing and rural water supply in Romania;
- world leisure complex, Johannesburg, South Africa; and
- a tunnel for the Alps Transit project.

In 1999 the three main regions from which British consultants won new work were the Far East—notably Hong Kong, China, Japan and Korea—the Indian subcontinent and the countries of the EU. The main categories of work were structural commercial (roads, bridges, tunnels, and railways); electrical and mechanical services; chemical, oil and gas plants; and water supply. Recent major contracts include:

- Yokohama Airport in Japan;
- Marina Line in Singapore;
- Porto Metro in Portugal;
- a new rail tunnel in Sweden;
- Deep Bay Link and Route 9 in Hong Kong; and
- the A4 motorway in Poland.

UK building products companies export goods worth over £4 billion annually, with the EU being the main market. With the onset of globalisation, many of the major UK companies have entered into joint ventures with overseas companies, establishing production overseas, or undertaking major acquisitions to expand their scale and output.

Table 28.5: Permanent Dwellings completed by Sector in the UK, 1989–99

Number

	1989	1994	1997	1998	1999
Private enterprise	187,542	153,341	160,862	155,116	157,031
Registered social landlords	14,598	37,368	28,249	24,194	23,217
All public sector	19,381	2,882	1,474	1,058	349
Total	**221,521**	**193,591**	**190,585**	**180,368**	**180,597**

Sources: DETR, National Assembly for Wales, Scottish Executive and Department of the Environment (Northern Ireland)

Further Reading

ONS Sector Reviews.

Websites

Department of Trade and Industry: www.dti.gov.uk
Department of the Environment, Transport and the Regions: www.construction.detr.gov.uk

THE QUEEN'S AWARDS 2000

Each year the Queen makes awards to successful UK business units in recognition of outstanding achievement. Unlike personal honours, a Queen's Award recognises the contribution that management and employees of companies have made working as a team. There are three categories of Queen's Award: International Trade, Innovation and Environmental Achievement.

The Queen's Award for International Trade

KCL Enterprises Ltd: King's College, London's foreign earnings arise from overseas students' fees and research and consultancy services. Students come from all over the world to study at the College.

DANDO Drilling International Ltd: the 'Watertech 5' is one of a number of drilling rigs and equipment manufactured and exported for water extraction.

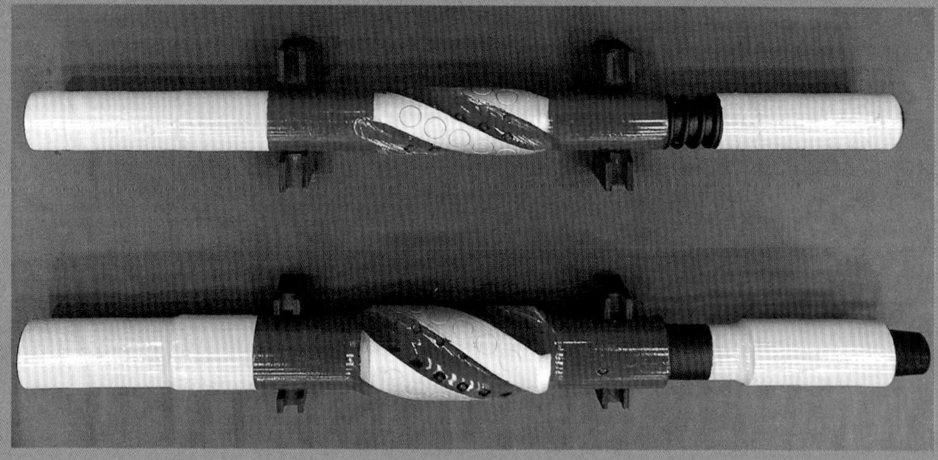

Andergauge Ltd: the Andergauge adjustable drilling stabiliser and other drilling products are exported to strategic locations around the world.

JCB Heavy Products Ltd: the company exports to more than 140 countries construction equipment such as the JCB 8016 Mini Excavator and the JCB JS330LC Tracked Excavator.

The Queen's Award for International Trade

John Ross Jnr (Aberdeen) Ltd: Scottish smoked salmon is produced by the traditional method of hand filleting, dry curing and smoking over open fires in brick kilns.

Macallan Distillers: almost two-thirds of the company's total sales of whisky go for export to around 50 countries worldwide.

The Queen's Award for Innovation

AVENT Isis Breast Pump (AVENT Group plc): designed to help mothers successfully combine breast and bottle feeding, this product proved in hospital trials to be as effective as large electric pumps. Achieving exports to 60 markets overseas, the pump gained a second Queen's Award in the International Trade category in 2000.

The Queen's Award for Innovation

High Temperature Hydraulic Nut
(Hydra-Tight Ltd Power Generation Group):
a hydraulic jack contained in a lockable nut.
Using the hydraulic nut reduces
maintenance time, saving millions of pounds
in the power generation industry.

The Gripple (Gripple Ltd):
a device for joining and tensioning
strands of wire and wire rope.
It has many uses in agriculture,
viticulture, construction and mining.

The Queen's Award for Environmental Achievement

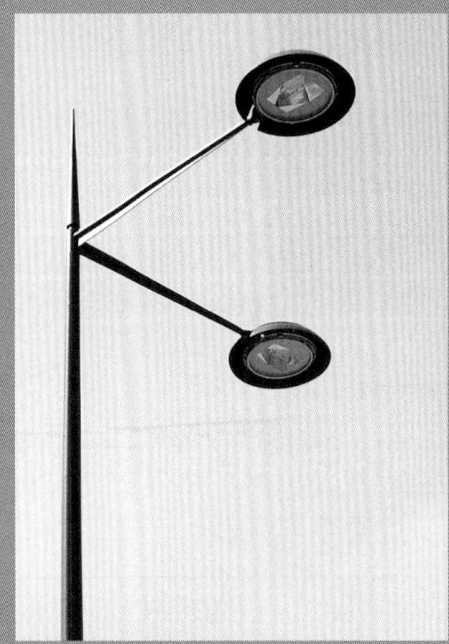

The 'Diamond Optic' (D W Windsor Ltd):
four controlled reflector elements
give unique light distributive patterns,
controlling light pollution and simultaneously
improving the effectiveness of street lighting.

Wind Turbine, Swaffham, Norfolk (Ecotricity):
'ecotricity' is electricity derived from sources
which are significantly less polluting and more
sustainable than conventional fuel sources.
These include wind power (shown here),
hydro power, landfill gas and sewage sludge.

29 Energy and Natural Resources

UK energy production was up by 3.9 per cent and primary energy consumption fell by 0.7 per cent in 1999. Oil production increased by 3.5 per cent to a new record level, while production and consumption of gas rose by 9.7 per cent and 0.5 per cent respectively, mainly because of a 19 per cent growth in the use of gas for electricity generation. The Government expects revenue from the proposed climate change levy of about £1 billion in 2001–02. Energy intensive sectors which agree energy efficiency targets will qualify for a discount on the main levy rates.

In April 2000 the Government announced that it would seek permission from the European Commission to pay up to £100 million of aid to the UK coal industry, which was facing exceptional challenges as a result of low international coal prices, coupled with changes in the UK electricity market.

Energy Resources

Production of coal continued to fall in 1999, by 10 per cent on 1998, to 36 million tonnes. Nuclear electricity output went down by 3.9 per cent to 96.2 terawatt hours. Production of natural gas rose to 105 billion cubic metres—a record level for the tenth consecutive year—in response not only to the growing demand for gas for electricity generation, but also to increased activity through the interconnectors to the Irish Republic and to Belgium, and to falling imports. Coal still supplied a significant, if declining, proportion of the country's primary energy needs: 29 per cent of the electricity supplied in 1999 was from coal, while gas supplied 40 per cent and nuclear 25 per cent.

For 1999, in value terms, total imports of fuels were 12 per cent higher than in 1998, largely owing to a 38.5 per cent increase in the value of petroleum product imports. Exports were 31.3 per cent higher, mainly because of a 33.6 per cent increase in the value of exports of crude oil. These increases reflect the rise in crude oil and petroleum product prices during 1999 (see p. 494).

Overall the UK remains a net exporter of all fuels, with a surplus on a balance of payments basis of £4.4 billion in 1999, nearly

£1.4 billion higher than in 1998. The trade surplus in crude oil and petroleum products was £4.6 billion. In volume terms, imports of fuel in 1999 were 7 per cent lower than in 1998, while exports were 2.4 per cent higher. The UK had a trade surplus in fuels of 46.9 million tonnes of oil equivalent—the seventh year in succession that it has had a trade surplus in volume terms.

ENERGY POLICY

The Government's energy policy is to ensure secure, diverse and sustainable supplies at competitive prices by setting out the framework in which competition can flourish, markets can operate efficiently for the benefit of suppliers and consumers, and the UK can make best use of its indigenous resources. The electricity market is open to full competition, with the aim of giving consumers a choice from a growing number of suppliers. Commercial gas supply is already unregulated. From 2001 UK domestic gas supply will no longer be regulated.

The 'climate change levy'—a tax on the business use of energy—will come into force in April 2001. The tax will be payable by energy suppliers who can be expected to pass it on to industrial and commercial customers. It is designed to encourage businesses to use energy more efficiently. The levy package itself, including support for energy efficiency measures and exemptions for electricity from renewables, and for good quality Combined Heat and Power (CHP—see p. 500), aims to cut carbon dioxide (CO_2) emissions by an estimated 2.5 million tonnes of carbon (mtc) a year. Further savings of at least 2.5 mtc a year should be produced by the levy's negotiated agreements. The levy is designed to contribute to meeting the Government's target under the Kyoto Protocol to reduce greenhouse gas emissions by 12.5 per cent by 2008–12 (see p. 332).

The Government announced its intention to introduce the levy in 1999. After consultation with business and other interested parties, a number of revisions to its design have been made. It will now raise about £1 billion annually (to be recycled to business, primarily through cuts in employer National Insurance contributions). In order to protect the international competitiveness of energy intensive industries, there will be an 80 per cent discount to major users of gas and oil willing to sign efficiency agreements, thus also increasing the levy's environmental effectiveness. New renewables and good quality CHP will be exempt. Changes announced in 2000 include:

- a lower rate of levy for liquefied petroleum gas (LPG; used in rural areas) to discourage switching from LPG to more environmentally damaging fuels;
- adding pipe insulation, refrigeration equipment and thermal screens to the technologies qualifying for enhanced capital allowances for companies making energy saving investments;
- an exemption of up to five years for natural gas use in Northern Ireland, to encourage the development of its gas marketing; and
- financial help and discounts for the horticultural sector to help its energy efficiency and protect its competitiveness while energy efficiency measures take effect.

International Developments

Since 1999 the Fifth Framework Programme of Research and Technological Development (see p. 438) has been the focus of research, development and demonstration of energy technologies in the EU. It has a non-nuclear budget of £120 million a year. The EU Energy Council adopted the Energy Framework Programme comprising the basic decision to rationalise a range of energy programmes run by DGTREN of the European Commission, and six separate components: ETAP (shared studies and analyses); SYNERGY (international co-operation); ALTENER (renewable energy); SAVE (strategic action for vigorous energy efficiency); SURE (safe transport of nuclear materials and safeguards); and CARNOT (clean and efficient use of solid fuels). The programme has a total budget of 170 million ecu (£119 million) over five years (1998–2002). Since 1999 eight agencies, which conduct research into, and promote, energy conservation, have been

Table 29.1: Inland Energy Consumption (in terms of primary sources)
Million tonnes oil equivalent

	1989	1995	1996	1997	1998	1999
Oil	76.3	75.7	77.9	75.4	74.9	73.4
Coal	67.0	48.9	46.2	41.1	41.4	36.7
Natural gas	49.5	69.2	80.9	82.7	85.8	90.9
Nuclear energy	17.7	21.2	22.1	23.0	23.6	22.7
Hydro-electric power[1]	0.4	0.5	0.3	0.4	0.5	0.5
Net imports of electricity	1.1	1.4	1.4	1.4	1.1	1.2
Total[2]	**212.8**	**216.9**	**230.3**	**226.2**	**229.4**	**227.8**

[1] Excludes pumped storage. Includes generation at wind stations.
[2] Total includes renewable fuels.
Source: Department of Trade and Industry

established in the UK under the SAVE II programme, which usually provides up to 150,000 euros of start-up funding.

The EC Oil Stocks Directive now requires all EU member states to hold contingency oil stocks. As an oil exporter, the UK is eligible for a reduction in its stocking obligation, which could save its oil industry about £10 million a year.

The EC collaborates with specialist international organisations, such as the International Energy Agency (IEA), which monitors world energy markets on behalf of industrialised countries and whose membership consists of all OECD members except Iceland and Mexico.

The EC Directive of February 1999 requires all EU members to open at least 33 per cent of their electricity supply markets to competition by 2003. By May 2000, however, over 60 per cent of the internal electricity market had been legally opened. Great Britain, Finland, Germany and Sweden have gone further and have introduced the right of consumer choice for all domestic, industrial and commercial customers. Since August 2000, EU member states have been required to open at least 20 per cent of their gas supply markets, rising to 28 per cent by 2003 and 33 per cent by 2008. The UK gas market has been fully open to competition since May 1998.

ENERGY CONSUMPTION

In 1999 consumption of primary fuels in the UK was only 7.2 per cent higher than in 1970, while in this period gross domestic product (at constant market prices) rose by 80 per cent. Energy consumption by final users in 1999, allowing for losses in conversion and distribution, and excluding non-energy use, amounted to 156.8 million tonnes of oil equivalent,[1] of which transport took 34.3 per cent, residential users 29.4 per cent, industrial users 22.6 per cent, commerce, agriculture and public services 12.1 per cent, and other users 1.6 per cent.

Primary energy demand in 1999 was 0.6 per cent lower than in 1998. Primary demand for coal and other solid fuels was 11.6 per cent lower than in 1998, reflecting the decline in the use of coal for electricity generation. Primary demand for oil fell by 1.5 per cent, but gas rose by 6 per cent, following marked increases in 1995–98. On a temperature corrected basis, which shows what the annual intake might have been if the average temperature during the year had been the same as the average for 1961–90, energy consumption grew by 0.3 per cent in 1999, compared with an average increase of 1.7 per cent a year between 1995 and 1998.

ENERGY EFFICIENCY

Government funding on energy efficiency programmes in the UK in 1999–2000 was £114.5 million. Some £50 million of the revenue from the climate change levy will go

[1] 1 tonne of oil equivalent = 41.868 gigajoules.

to support energy efficiency measures and renewables, including 100 per cent first-year capital allowances for energy-saving investments. They are an essential part of UK strategy for reducing greenhouse gas emissions (see p. 332). It has been estimated that by 2010, in the domestic sector, savings of up to 6.5 million tonnes of CO_2 a year could be achieved by improving the energy efficiency of buildings. The potential contribution of commercial and industrial buildings could be 5 million tonnes and of public sector buildings 1.1 million tonnes. These savings correspond to a reduction of 15–20 per cent on the estimated CO_2 emissions for 2010 for these sectors.

The Energy Efficiency Best Practice Programme (EEBPP) is the prime national source of independent authoritative information and advice on energy efficiency. Its target is savings of £800 million a year (at 1990 prices) by the end of 2000, or about 5 million tonnes of carbon, and it is currently saving about £650 million (about 3.25 million tonnes). Its budget was £16.6 million in 1999–2000.

The Energy Saving Trust (EST) was set up by the Government and the major energy companies. Its purpose is to work through partnerships towards the sustainable and efficient use of energy. In 1999–2000 it received £24.5 million in direct government funding for work with the domestic and small business sectors and £3.6 million on transport-related programmes, and its UK-wide programmes levered in an extra £99 million of investment. Under the government-funded programme of work, more than 284,000 installations of energy-saving measures have been made and advice given to some 907,000 individuals and organisations up to the end of March 2000. Since 1994 the public electricity suppliers (see pp. 497–9) have invested about £25 million a year in energy efficiency under the EST's Energy Efficiency Standards of Performance (EESOP). Since 1994 EESOP programmes have resulted in more than 383,000 insulation improvements and the sale of over 9.5 million energy-efficient light bulbs.

The new Home Energy Efficiency Scheme (HEES), with a budget of nearly £500 million over 2001–04, is aimed at people who are most at risk from ill health caused by fuel poverty: the elderly and families on low incomes, and the disabled and chronically sick. Data from the 1996 *English House Condition Survey* showed that there were at least 4.3 million of these fuel-poor households in England. The new HEES provides grants of up to £2,000 for home heating and insulation improvements. This includes central heating systems for low-income households aged 60 and over.

OIL AND GAS EXPLORATION AND PRODUCTION

The UK Continental Shelf (UKCS) comprises those areas of the seabed and subsoil beyond the territorial sea over which the UK exercises sovereign rights of exploration and exploitation of natural resources. It has been extended since the mid-1960s all around Great Britain, to over 300 km north of Shetland and some 1,500 km beyond the Hebrides into the North Atlantic. In 1999, either through direct use or as a source of energy for electricity generation, oil and gas accounted for over 70 per cent of total UK energy consumption, with UK production supplying 99 per cent of gas consumed. In 1999, output of crude oil and natural gas liquids (NGLs) in the UK averaged over 2.9 million barrels (about 384,100 tonnes) a day, keeping it as the world's ninth largest producer.

Taxation

The North Sea fiscal regime is a major mechanism for gaining for the UK the economic benefit from its oil and gas resources. The Government grants licences to private sector companies to explore for and exploit oil and gas resources (see p. 493). Its main sources of revenue from oil and gas activities are petroleum revenue tax (see p. 409), levied on profits from fields approved before 16 March 1993; corporation tax, charged on the profits of oil and gas companies—the only tax on profits from fields approved after 15 March 1993; and royalty, which applies only to fields approved before

Table 29.2: Oil Statistics *Million tonnes*

	1989	1995	1996	1997	1998	1999
Oil production						
Land	0.7	5.1	5.3	5.0	5.2	4.3
Offshore	91.0	116.7	116.7	115.3	119.1	124.0
Refinery output	81.4	86.1	89.9	90.4	87.1	82.0
Deliveries	73.0	73.7	75.4	72.5	72.0	71.0
Exports						
Crude, NGL, feedstock	51.7	84.6	81.6	79.4	84.6	91.8
Refined petroleum	16.7	21.6	23.7	26.8	24.3	21.7
Imports						
Crude, NGL, feedstock	49.5	48.7	50.1	50.0	48.0	44.9
Refined petroleum	9.5	9.9	9.3	8.7	11.4	12.3

Source: Department of Trade and Industry

April 1982 and is paid at 12.5 per cent of the value of petroleum 'won and saved'.

Licensing

No seaward licensing rounds occurred in 1999. By the end of 1999, some 7,400 wells had been, or were being, drilled in the UKCS: 2,100 exploration wells, 1,300 appraisal wells and 4,000 development wells. Only 16 exploration wells were started in 1999, the lowest number since 1965, compared with 47 in 1998. New appraisal wells numbered only 20, the lowest figure since 1971. The Government must approve all proposed wells and development plans.

Production and Reserves

Some 211 offshore fields were in production in March 2000: 107 oil, 88 gas and 16 condensate (a lighter form of oil). Production started at nine new offshore oil/condensate fields during 1999, and nine new development projects were approved. Offshore, these comprised three oilfields and three gasfields; onshore, two gasfields and one oilfield. In addition, approval for nine incremental offshore developments (elaborations to existing fields) was granted.

Cumulative UKCS stabilised crude oil production to the end of 1999 was 2,331 million tonnes, with Forties (324 million tonnes) and Brent (246.5 million tonnes) the largest producing fields. Britain's largest onshore oilfield, at Wytch Farm (Dorset), produces 85 per cent of the total crude oils and NGLs originating onshore. Possible maximum remaining UKCS reserves of oil are estimated at 1,665 million tonnes.

Offshore Gas

Natural gas now accounts for 40 per cent of total inland primary fuel consumption in the UK. In 1999 indigenous production amounted to a record 105 billion cubic metres.

Production from the three most prolific offshore gasfields—Leman, Indefatigable and the Hewett area—has accounted for 36 per cent of the total gas produced so far in the UKCS. Associated gas,[2] delivered by pipeline to land via the Far North Liquids and Associated Gas System (FLAGS), the Scottish Area Gas Evacuation System (SAGE) and the Central Area Transmission System (CATS), accounted for 35 per cent of gas production in 1999. The Southern Basin fields, the Morecambe Bay field and the Liverpool Bay fields in the Irish Sea produce more gas in winter to satisfy increased demand, with the North Sean and South Sean fields also augmenting supplies to meet peak demand on very cold days in winter. The

[2] Mainly methane, produced and used mostly on oil production platforms.

partially depleted Rough field is used as a gas store for rapid recovery during peak winter periods (see map at the end of the book).

Cumulative gas production to the end of 1999 is 1,490 billion cubic metres. Maximum possible remaining gas reserves in present discoveries now stand at just under 1,755 billion cubic metres.

Pipelines

Some 10,430 km (6,520 miles) of major submarine pipelines transport oil, gas and condensate from one field to another and to shore. Nine landing places on the North Sea coast bring gas ashore to supply a national and regional high- and low-pressure pipeline system some 273,000 km (170,625 miles) long, which transports natural gas around Great Britain. A pipeline (40 km; 25 miles) takes natural gas from Scotland to Northern Ireland; exports to the Irish Republic are conveyed by the Britain–Ireland interconnector. The pipeline (232 km; 145 miles) from Bacton to Zeebrugge in Belgium, opened in 1998 and costing £420 million, has a capacity of 20,000 million cubic metres a year.

Economic and Industrial Aspects

In December 1998 world oil prices hit a 50-year low in real terms, with only £50 a tonne received early in 1999; by late 1999 prices had increased to £108 a tonne. The average price received by producers from sales of UKCS oil in 1999 was about £80 a tonne, a third higher than in 1998. However, low levels of investment led to uncertainty for the contracting and supply sectors. In 1999 UKCS oil and gas production accounted for 1.8 per cent of the UK's gross value added. Total revenues from the sale of oil (including NGLs) produced from the UKCS in 1999 rose to some £11 billion, while those from the sale of gas fell slightly to £5.1 billion. Taxes and royalty receipts attributable to UKCS oil and gas remained at about £2.6 billion in 1999–2000.

The remit of the Oil and Gas Task Force, set up by the Government, with industry support, in 1998, was to recommend ways in which the UK industry can maintain competitiveness in the face of increasing maturity of its oil reserves and low oil prices. One recommendation was to increase the UK share of the world supplies market, currently worth £2.9 billion, by at least 50 per cent by 2005. Among the changes brought about by the Task Force's second phase, PILOT, have been a streamlined and more transparent and more predictable licensing process and longer production consents for both old and new fields, to increase company confidence when investing and encourage funding commitment. One of PILOT's work groups aims to aid commercial development of over 300 currently undeveloped discoveries.

> Since 1965 the oil and gas production industry has generated operating surpluses of some £250 billion, of which over £105 billion (including £23.5 billion of exploration and appraisal expenditure) has been reinvested in the industry, £90.9 billion paid in taxation, and about £54 billion retained by the companies. Total income of the oil and gas sector rose to over £19 billion in 1999.

Production investment in the oil and gas extraction industry fell back to some £3.2 billion in 1999. Including exploration and appraisal investment of a further £0.5 billion, it formed about 13 per cent of total British industrial investment and nearly 2.5 per cent of gross fixed capital investment. Some 27,200 people were employed offshore by the industry (which also supports about a third of a million jobs in related sectors) in 1999. PILOT has continued to build on the collaborative partnerships initiated by the joint industry/government Oil and Gas Task Force. Initiatives such as LOGIC (Leading Oil and Gas Industry Competitiveness); the Industry Technology Facilitator and the National Training Organisations Group; together with the LIFT (Licence Information for Trading) website; action on undeveloped discoveries; and improvements to the licensing and development approval processes, are aimed at making the UKCS more attractive to investors and sustaining activity through 2010 and beyond.

The Offshore Environment

Environmental impact assessments (under the EC Environmental Impact Directive) are mandatory for all field developments. An early result of the Government's public consultation in 1999 on improvements to the offshore environmental regime is Integrated Pollution and Prevention Control, already in force for large combustion plant operating on offshore installations.

During 1999, 300 hours of unannounced aerial surveillance of oil and gas rigs detected minimal amounts of oil on the surface of the sea. Offshore environmental inspections were also carried out. The 1999 figure for accidental oil spills (120 tonnes) was lower than that for 1998 (137 tonnes).

The Petroleum Act 1998 places a decommissioning obligation on the co-venturers of every offshore installation and the owners of every offshore pipeline on the UKCS. Companies have to submit a decommissioning programme for ministerial approval and ensure that its provisions are carried out. In 1998 the OSPAR Commission (see p. 329) agreed rules for the disposal of offshore installations at sea. There is now a presumption that all installations will be removed for re-use, recycling or final disposal on land. Derogations, however, are possible for concrete platforms and for the footings of steel installations with a jacket weight above 10,000 tonnes. All installations put in place after 9 February 1999 must be completely removed.

Offshore Safety

Offshore health and safety are the responsibility of the Health and Safety Executive (HSE—see p. 160). Aberdeen University's Petroleum and Economic Consultants Ltd has evaluated the offshore health and safety regime and will recommend how it should be developed over the period up to 2010.

Suppliers of Goods and Services

The oil and gas industry supply chain has been seriously affected by the downturn in investment in the UKCS, with the worst hit sector—the fabrication industry—reducing employment from about 20,000 jobs in the early 1990s to nearer 1,000 towards the end of 2000. Many companies have needed to seek work in other sectors and overseas, and the Oil and Gas Industry Development Directorate of the Department of Trade and Industry (DTI) has worked with the PILOT initiatives and by other direct action to help the industry realign to the changed market circumstances.

DOWNSTREAM OIL

Oil Consumption

Deliveries of petroleum products for inland consumption (excluding refinery consumption) in 1999 included 21.5 million tonnes of petrol for motor vehicles, 15.2 million tonnes of DERV (diesel-engined road vehicles) fuel, 9.7 million tonnes of aviation turbine fuel, 6.8 million tonnes of gas oil (distilled from petroleum) and 2.2 million tonnes of fuel oils (blends of heavy petroleum).

Oil Refineries

In 1999 the UK's 13 refineries processed 88.3 million tonnes of crude and process oils, a decrease of 6 per cent on 1998. About 80 per cent of output by weight is in the form of lighter, higher-value products, such as gasoline, DERV and jet kerosene. The UK is much more geared towards petrol production than its European counterparts; this accounts for about a third of each barrel of crude oil, compared with a European average of just over a fifth.

Trade

In 1999, UK exports of refined petroleum products (see p. 493) were worth £892 million. Virtually all exports went to its partners in the EU and in the IEA, especially France and Germany, and the United States.

Exports of UKCS gas were more than 2.6 times higher in 1999 than in 1998. Some 7.6 billion cubic metres went to the Netherlands, from the British share of the Markham transboundary field and the neighbouring Windermere field, to the Irish Republic and to Belgium through the UK–Belgium interconnector. About 1.2 billion cubic metres were imported from Norway, and from Belgium via the interconnector, representing 1.3 per cent of total supplies in 1999, compared with 1.1 per cent in 1998.

GAS SUPPLY INDUSTRY

Structure of the Industry

The holder of a public gas transporter's licence may not also hold licences for supply or shipping in a fully competitive market.[3] Of the two entirely separate companies formed from the demerged British Gas, the supply business is now part of the holding company Centrica plc (which still trades under the British Gas brand name in the UK), while the pipeline and storage businesses, most exploration and production, and R&D have been retained within British Gas plc, renamed BG plc. In March 2000 BG announced that the regulated pipeline business and the R&D side would be demerged to form a separate company listed on the Stock Exchange.

The national and regional gas pipeline network is owned by Transco, part of BG plc, which retains responsibility for dealing with leaks and emergencies, and also has a current monopoly in gas metering, which the energy regulator (see p. 499) plans to open to competition. New gas trading arrangements introduced in October 1999 involve a screen-based on-the-day commodity market for trading in wholesale supplies of gas; auctions for the allocation of entry capacity into the high-pressure national transmission system; and commercial incentives for Transco to operate and balance the system efficiently.

Competition

Since 1994 independent suppliers have captured 83 per cent of the industrial and commercial gas market. Some 60 companies are licensed to sell gas to the commercial sector and 26 to domestic customers.

By December 1999 over 5.3 million (out of 20 million) domestic customers had switched from British Gas, which still has just over 70 per cent of the household market, to one of about 25 other companies now in it, and also between these other companies. In 1999 the changes were estimated to have brought each standard credit customer average savings of £53 a year on a gas bill.

Only companies which have been granted a supplier's licence are allowed to sell gas. Licence conditions include providing gas to anyone who requests it and is connected to the mains gas supply. Special services must be made available for elderly, disabled and chronically sick people. Suppliers must offer customers a range of payment options; they are able to set their own charges, but have to publish their prices and other terms so that customers can make an informed choice.

The Director General of Ofgem (Office of Gas and Electricity Markets) has powers to set price controls for British Gas Trading and Transco, to set and enforce standards of performance, and to see that competitive practices continue. In April 2000, Ofgem introduced a one-year price control on BG which is expected to reduce by £10 the typical annual bill of a customer not paying by direct debit.

Consumption

Natural gas consumption, at an estimated 994.6 terawatt[4] hours (TWh) in 1999 (compared with 541.8 TWh in 1989), was up 6.7 per cent on 1998, with gas supplied for electricity generation (amounting to 313.4 TWh) up 18 per cent. Sales to industry (204.3 TWh) were 6.9 per cent up and to the commercial sector (121 TWh) 2.3 per cent up, while domestic sales (356 TWh) were broadly the same as in 1998. In 1999 UK industrial gas prices were the lowest among the EU countries. Between 1986 (when British Gas

[3] Suppliers sell piped gas to consumers; public gas transporters (PGTs) operate the pipeline system through which gas will normally be delivered; shippers arrange with PGTs for appropriate amounts of gas to go through the pipeline system.

[4] 1 TW = 1,000 gigawatts (GW). 1 GW = 1,000 megawatts (MW). 1 MW = 1,000 kilowatts (kW).

was privatised) and 1999 average industrial gas prices fell by 62 per cent in real terms; domestic prices were reduced by 31 per cent (including VAT). In Great Britain a typical standard credit household's annual gas bill fell in real terms from £399 in 1986 to £271 in 1999.

COAL

The UK coal industry is entirely in the private sector. The main deep-mine operators in the UK are RJB Mining plc (in England); Mining Scotland Ltd; Tower (a pit at Hirwaun in south Wales); Hatfield Colliery in South Yorkshire; and Betws, also in south Wales. RJB Mining, Mining Scotland Ltd and Celtic Energy, which operates in Wales, are the main opencast operators. In August 2000 there were 29 underground mines in production, including 17 major deep mines, employing 8,372 workers and 48 opencast sites, owned by various companies throughout the UK, employing 2,647. Opencast accounts for most of the relatively low sulphur coal mined in Scotland and south Wales, and contributes towards improving the average quality and cost of coal supplies.

Market for Coal

In 1999 inland consumption of coal, at 56 million tonnes, was down 12 per cent on 1998. About 73 per cent was used by the electricity generators, 15 per cent by coke ovens and blast furnaces, 1 per cent by other fuel producers, 6 per cent by industry and 5 per cent by domestic consumers. Exports were 762,000 tonnes, while imports amounted to 20.8 million tonnes—mainly of steam coal for electricity generation and coking coal. Total production from British deep mines fell by 16 per cent, from 25 million tonnes in 1998 to 21 million tonnes in 1999. Opencast output remained at 15 million tonnes.

In April 2000, the Government announced that it would be lifting the stricter gas consents policy (in operation since 1998) when the new electricity trading arrangements were in place. Recognising that this would create much uncertainty for the UK coal market and that it would provide new challenges for the coal industry, the Government also announced that it would be seeking European Commission approval for a subsidy scheme. This is expected to provide short-term transitional help to those parts of the UK coal industry that are considered to have a viable future, but that would face the risk of premature closure in the next few years without government support.

Clean Coal

Cleaner coal technologies reduce the environmental impact of coal used for power and industrial applications by increasing the efficiency of converting it to energy and reducing harmful emissions of particulates, oxides of nitrogen and sulphur, which are the cause of acid rain. Improvements in the efficiency of coal-fired power stations lead directly to reductions of CO_2, a major contributor to climate change. The DTI contribution of £12 million during 1999–2000 to 2001–02 to the cleaner coal R&D programme aims to encourage collaboration between UK industry and universities in the development of the technologies and expertise. The Coal Authority (see below) has started work on developing a sub-commercial underground coal gasification project to meet government criteria on cleaner coal.

The Coal Authority

The Coal Authority is a public body sponsored by the DTI. It has five main responsibilities: licensing coal-mining operations; repairing coal subsidence damage; managing coalfield property; managing minewater pollution and other environmental problems of coal mining; and providing information to house buyers about mining activity near property.

ELECTRICITY

England and Wales

In December 1999, some 70 companies held generation licences in England and Wales. The major power producers are National

Power, PowerGen, AES Electric, British Energy, TXU Europe (which has taken over Energy Group, which includes Eastern Electricity), Edison Mission Energy, and British Nuclear Fuels' (BNFL) Magnox Generation Group. They have sold electricity to suppliers through a marketing mechanism known as the 'Pool'. The National Grid (NGC) owns and operates the transmission system, and is responsible for calling up generation plant to meet demand.

Distribution—transfer of electricity from the national grid to consumers via local networks—is carried out by the 12 regional electricity companies (RECs) in England and Wales. Supply—the purchase of electricity from generators and its sale to consumers—is fully open to competition; since June 1999 all consumers in Great Britain, including 24 million homes and 2 million small businesses, have been able to choose from whom they can buy electricity.

Cross-border acquisitions and takeovers have become a feature of the European power market and eight of the 12 RECs are owned by overseas companies. All the main UK generators are being vertically integrated through ownership of supply businesses. British electricity companies continue to invest overseas. In early 2000, for example, PowerGen bought LG&E, the Kentucky-based electricity company, for $3.22 billion and National Power has split its international and UK power businesses.

In 1999–2000, 7.8 GW of coal-fired plant was sold by major generators to other concerns. A further 2 GW was sold in March 2000. Coal-fired plant is now owned by five unrelated companies and the total market shares in generation of National Power and PowerGen have fallen to 17 and 15 per cent respectively.

Reform of Electricity Trading

New wholesale electricity trading arrangements (NETA) will replace the Pool in March 2001. NETA introduces greater competition into electricity trading which should ensure downward pressure on prices. Generators, suppliers, traders and customers are encouraged to enter into bilateral contracts in forwards and futures markets and short-term power exchanges. Participants are free to trade electricity until 3½ hours ahead of real time for any half-hour period. From that point until real time, the market will be operated through a balancing mechanism run by the NGC—because of the need to balance the system on a second-by-second basis. NETA will take effect through new conditions inserted into generation, supply and transmission licences. These have been designated by the Secretary of State for Trade and Industry under the Utilities Act 2000.

> In June 2000 the UK Power Exchange (UKPX) launched the country's first online trading of power contracts. Although this is a core feature of NETA, DTI and Ofgem have left the development of power exchanges to market forces. In addition to UKPX, a number of other companies are developing power exchanges.

Scotland

ScottishPower plc and Scottish and Southern Energy plc generate, transmit, distribute and supply electricity within their respective franchise areas. They are also contracted to buy all the output from British Energy's two Scottish nuclear power stations (Hunterston B and Torness), until 2005. The over-100 kWh market in Scotland comprises about 6,750 customers and accounts for about 45 per cent of all electricity consumed. ScottishPower and Scottish and Southern Energy have second-tier licences which allow them to compete in each other's area. In 1999–2000, 29.5 per cent of customers in the over-100-kWh market obtained their power from holders of second-tier supply licences. In 1999 Ofgem proposed reforms (for implementation by 2002) to the Scottish electricity market which would include cutting distribution charges (by 13 per cent by ScottishPower and 5 per cent by Scottish and Southern Energy), separation of generation, supply, transmission and distribution interests to provide greater transparency and reduce the potential for market abuse, and increasing competition by giving English and Welsh companies greater access to the interconnector between England and Scotland.

Northern Ireland

Three private companies, Nigen, Premier Power and Coolkeeragh Power, generate electricity from four power stations. They are obliged to sell to Northern Ireland Electricity plc (NIE), which has a monopoly of transmission and distribution, and a right to supply. From July 1999 supply to leading industrial users (25 per cent of the total market) has been open to outside competition. Northern Ireland's Energy Action Plan (Vision 2010) envisages an all-Ireland energy market which would widen the scale and remove the relative isolation of a system in which standard domestic consumers paid an average 25 per cent more for electricity than their counterparts in Great Britain in 1999. Expansion of the cross-border power link agreed in December 1999 is to be furthered by enhancement of the capacity of the north–south interconnector and of the two stand-by links with the Irish Republic.

The Province has a power surplus, with a peak demand of 1,500 MWh. The energy regulator for Northern Ireland combines responsibilities for electricity and gas.

Regulation and Other Functions

In June 1999, the Office of Gas Supply and the Office of Electricity Regulation were merged to form Ofgem. The Utilities Act 2000 has created a new legal structure for Ofgem, which means that the statutory responsibilities under the Gas Act 1986, the Electricity Act 1989 and the Utilities Act 2000 will fall to an authority rather than (as has until recently been the case) to an individual. Ofgem's principal objective is to protect the interests of gas and electricity customers, wherever appropriate, by promoting effective competition. Other duties and objectives include the need to maintain security of supply and to ensure that electricity and gas licensees are able to finance their statutory obligations. Ofgem will be responsible for setting performance standards for gas and electricity companies, and price regulation of companies where competition has not yet fully emerged or where there is a natural monopoly.

Consumption

In 1999 sales of electricity through the distribution system in the UK amounted to 308.1 TWh. Domestic users took 36 per cent of the total, industry 32 per cent, and commercial and other users the remainder.

In 1999 the average industrial electricity price was lower in real terms than for any year since 1970. UK prices have fallen in real terms by 19 per cent for domestic customers and by 46 per cent for large industrial users since privatisation in 1990. In 1999 an annual electricity bill for a typical standard credit household was £264. Average UK domestic electricity prices, including taxes, in 1998 were the fourth lowest within the EU and industrial prices the tenth lowest.

Generation

The shares of generating capacity during 1998–2000 are shown in Table 29.3.

Table 29.3: Shares of Generating Capacity in England and Wales

Per cent

	Winter 1998–99	Winter 1999–2000
National Power	25.2	18.7
PowerGen	24.0	16.1
British Energy	11.5	11.3
Eastern Electricity	10.5	10.3
Edison Mission Energy	3.3	9.2
AES	0.6	7.3
BNFL/Magnox	5.1	5.2
Interconnectors	5.0	4.9
Others	14.9	17.1
Total	**100.0**	**100.0**
Total (GW)	63,999	65,330

Source: *The Energy Report 1999* (DTI)

Table 29.4: Generation by and Capacity of Power Stations Owned by the Major Power Producers in the UK

	Electricity generated (GWh)[1]			%	Output capacity
	1989	1994	1999	1999	(MW)[2]
Nuclear plant	66,740	83,944	96,202	29	12,956
Other conventional steam plant	219,714	175,362	118,916	35	35,427
Gas turbines and oil engines	542	244	203	—	1,333
Pumped storage plant	2,067	1,463	2,902	—	2,788
Natural flow hydro-electric plant	3,845	4,317	4,422	1	1,327
CCGTs	—	36,971	113,772	34	16,143
Renewables other than hydro	1	506	646	—	117
Total	**297,890**	**302,807**	**337,142**	**100**	**70,091**
Electricity supplied (net)	276,003	284,835	317,186	—	—

[1] Electricity generated less electricity used at power stations (both electricity used on works and that used for pumping at pumped-storage stations).
[2] At end December 1999.
Source: Department of Trade and Industry

Non-nuclear power stations owned by the UK's major power producers consumed 49.7 million tonnes of oil equivalent in 1999, of which coal and natural gas accounted for 48.6 per cent each and oil and hydro 2.4 per cent. Other power companies (for which gas is the most widely used fuel), and over 2,000 small autogenerators (which produce power for their own use), have equal access with the major generators to the grid transmission and local distribution systems. A ten-year programme to control emissions of oxides of nitrogen (NO_X) through the installation of low-NO_X burners at 12 major power stations in England and Wales is in progress. ScottishPower has fitted low-NO_X burners at Longannet power station.

Combined Cycle Gas Turbines (CCGT)

In 1999, CCGT stations accounted for 34 per cent of the electricity generated by major power producers, compared with 16 per cent in 1995. This increase has been balanced by a fall in coal- and oil-fired generation. CCGT stations, favoured by the smaller, independent producers and using natural gas, offer cheap generation, and give out almost no sulphur dioxide and some 55 per cent less CO_2 than coal-fired plant per unit of electricity. At the end of March 2000, 33 such stations in the UK (with a total registered capacity of 21.7 GW) were generating power. The Government has indicated that restrictions on the building of new CCGTs will be lifted with the introduction of NETA (see p. 498).

Combined Heat and Power

Combined Heat and Power (CHP) plants are designed to produce both electricity and usable heat. They convert about 80 per cent of fuel input into useful energy, compared with conventional generation which wastes at least half the energy content of the fuel and emits considerably more CO_2. CHP thus benefits the environment by reducing emissions of greenhouse gases. It is also used for cooling and chilling.

CHP can be fuelled by a variety of energy sources. It offers particular benefits in applications where there is a regular need for heat as well as electricity—such as hospitals, leisure centres and housing developments—and can be provided on a local scale. About 83 per cent of CHP plants are less than 1 MW capacity; large-scale plant (above 10 MW) represents just over 80 per cent of total CHP capacity. In 1999 over 1,300 CHP schemes supplied more than 4,250 MW of generating capacity, 5.5 per cent of the UK's total electricity (and 15 per cent of that used by industry), with some 1,080 MW under development; the Government aims to have at least 10,000 MW by 2010. EU strategy is to double CHP's share of the electricity market from 9 per cent to 18 per cent by the same year.

The Government is promoting CHP by developing and administering a quality assurance programme under the EEBPP—to assess CHP schemes for exemption from the climate change levy and for other benefits.

Trade

The NGC and Electricité de France run a 2,000 MW cross-Channel cable link, allowing transmission of electricity between the two countries. The link has generally been used to supply 'baseload' power—which needs to be generated and available round the clock—from France to England. Imports met just over 4 per cent of the UK's electricity needs in 1999.

Scotland has a peak winter demand of under 6 GW and generating capacity of over 9 GW. This additional available capacity (see p. 498) is used to supply England and Wales through transmission lines linking the Scottish and English grid systems. This interconnector's capacity is now 1,600 MW, with plans to increase it to 2,200 MW. Construction of a 60-km (37.5-mile) 500 MW undersea interconnector between Scotland and Northern Ireland will allow further exports of power from Scotland, with 125 MW supplied to NIE at less than the Great Britain Pool price, by 2001.

Nuclear Power

Nuclear power generates about one-sixth of the world's energy and over a third of Europe's. It substantially reduces the use of fossil fuels which would otherwise be needed for generation. In the UK nuclear stations generated 96.3 TWh in 1999 and contributed 26 per cent of total electricity generation.

The private sector company British Energy owns and operates seven advanced gas-cooled reactors (AGRs) and the pressurised water reactor (PWR) at Sizewell B. British Energy's reactors have a rated output of 7,130 MW in England and 2,440 MW in Scotland. British Nuclear Fuels (BNFL; see below) and Magnox Electric, which merged in 1998, operate seven magnox power stations, together with a further four magnox stations that are being decommissioned.

In the absence of nuclear generation, emissions of CO_2 in 1998 would have been some 12 to 24 mtc higher in the UK, depending on the mix of generation used to replace it. However, there are currently no proposals for new nuclear power stations in the UK, principally because the cost, compared to new generation from other sources, is not currently competitive. Concerns about radioactive waste disposal and public acceptability are also likely to be contributory factors. These issues are common to many countries, including some with an existing nuclear generation industry.

British Nuclear Fuels

BNFL is Britain's primary provider of nuclear products and services to both UK and international customers. The company's turnover in 1999–2000 was just over £2 billion, of which about a third came from reprocessing spent nuclear fuel at its Thorp plant at Sellafield (Cumbria). In September 1999 the Nuclear Installations Inspectorate (NII) began an investigation after quality checks on mixed oxide fuel (MO_X) manufactured at Sellafield were found to have been falsified. In early 2000 both Japan and Germany, two of BNFL's biggest customers, put contracts to buy large quantities of MO_X on hold. The Government has ordered BNFL to make improvements and has delayed consideration of a proposal to introduce a Public-Private Partnership into the company until at least 2002. BNFL has responded to two NII reports into working practices at the Sellafield site and made changes to management structures and safety procedures.

United Kingdom Atomic Energy Authority

UKAEA's main function is to maintain and decommission safely and cost effectively its redundant nuclear facilities used for the UK's nuclear R&D programme. UKAEA owns the sites at Dounreay (Caithness), Culham and Harwell (Oxfordshire), Windscale (Cumbria) and Winfrith (Dorset), and is also responsible for Britain's fusion programme (see below).

Fusion Research

Nuclear fusion in the UK is funded by the DTI and Euratom (75 per cent and 25 per cent respectively). The Government spends £15 million a year on fusion research, of which the main focus is magnetic confinement, based at Culham science centre, where Britain's own nuclear fusion research is carried out. The UK also operates the experimental JET (Joint European Torus) project, also at Culham. Through the EU the Euratom/UKAEA Fusion Association contributes to the international effort to demonstrate the principle of power production from fusion, currently embodied in ITER (International Thermonuclear Experimental Reactor).

Nuclear Safety

Responsibility for ensuring the safety of nuclear installations falls to nuclear operators within a system of regulatory control enforced by the HSE.

The International Convention on Nuclear Safety, in force since 1996, has been ratified by 46 countries, including the UK, and each has reported on how it has progressed towards meeting its nuclear safety obligations. The UK's main contribution to the international effort to improve safety in Central and Eastern Europe and in the former Soviet republics is channelled through the EU PHARE and TACIS nuclear safety programmes.

NEW AND RENEWABLE SOURCES OF ENERGY

R&D expenditure on renewables increased to £14 million in 2000–01. Renewables play a vital role in enabling the UK to meet its environmental targets of reducing greenhouse gases by 12.5 per cent by 2012 and CO_2 emissions by 20 per cent by 2010. The Government's targets are for renewable energy to provide 5 per cent of UK electricity supplies by 2003 and 10 per cent by 2010, subject to the cost being acceptable to consumers. Over 700 British companies are involved in renewables, directly employing some 3,500 people. UK renewables exports are estimated to have risen to about £100 million in 1999–2000. The Government's new and renewable energy R&D programme covers biofuels (including wastes), fuel cells, hydro, solar, wave and wind. These accounted for 2.6 per cent of all electricity generating capacity in Britain in 1999; natural flow hydro schemes provided about three-quarters of this total.

The Government has announced that the new Renewables Obligation will replace the Non-Fossil Fuel Obligation (NFFO) and will require all licensed electricity suppliers to buy from renewable sources. The NFFO has supported renewables-sourced power at above the market price for conventionally generated electricity, the difference being reimbursed through the fossil fuel levy, paid by all

Britain's coastal waters are the windiest areas in Europe. It has the potential to generate more than three times its electricity consumption through offshore wind turbines. The UK's first offshore wind farm, a 2 MW scheme off the Northumberland coast, developed at a cost of £4 million by Royal/Dutch Shell and PowerGen under NFFO-4 and an EU THERMIE grant, will generate enough power to satisfy 3,000 homes. National Power has spent £1 million rebuilding the Croesor hydro plant at Blaencwm in Snowdonia, built in the late 19th century to serve slate quarries, but disused since the early 1950s. It supplies 500 kW, enough to power 500 homes. In 1999, Unit Energy, the UK's first independent power trader to deal exclusively in green electricity, launched its service to sell electricity to domestic consumers and small businesses.

Electricity produced by Renewable Sources of Energy, UK, 1999

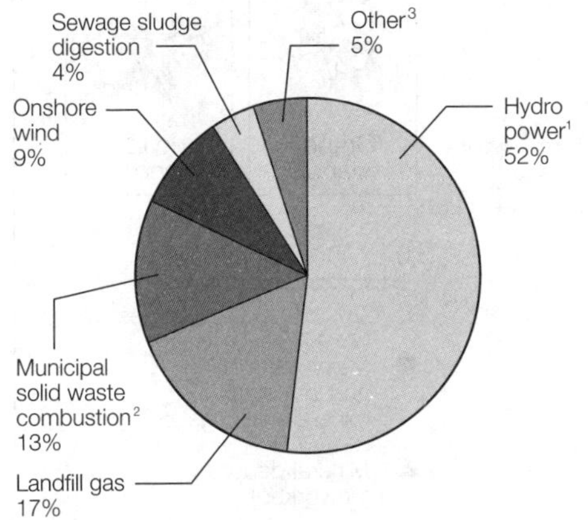

[1] Excluding pumped storage stations.

[2] Includes combustion of refuse-derived fuel pellets.

[3] Includes the use of farm waste digestion, waste tyre combustion, poultry litter combustion and solar photovoltaics.

Source: Department of Trade and Industry

electricity consumers through their bills. Since 1990 the NFFO has provided over £600 million of support for renewables. In Scotland an associated Renewables (Scotland) Obligation will replace the Scottish Renewables Obligation.

At 31 March 2000, under five Renewables Orders for England and Wales, three for Scotland and two for Northern Ireland, 933 projects have been contracted, with a declared net capacity of 3,639 MW; 317 of these were 'live' and generating 762 MW. The cost of renewable energy under successive Orders has fallen significantly—from 6.4 pence a kilowatt hour under NFFO-1 to an average 2.73 p/kWh under NFFO-5.

Non-energy Minerals

Output of non-energy minerals in 1998 came to 310 million tonnes, valued at £2,394 million. The total number of employees in the extractive industry was about 25,000.

Table 29.5: Production of Some of the Main Non-energy Minerals in the UK

	1993	1998	Production value 1998 (£ million)
	(million tonnes)		
Sand and gravel	100.0	98.3	549
Silica sand	3.6	4.7	62
Igneous rock	57.7	45.9	276
Limestone and dolomite	111.7	104.9	703
Chalk[1]	9.1	9.9	59
Sandstone	16.1	20.1	115
Gypsum and anhydrite	2.5	2.0	14
Salt, comprising rock salt, salt in brine and salt from brine	6.6	5.5	174
Common clay and shale[1]	10.9	12.2	20
China clay[2]	2.5	2.4	237
Ball clay	0.7	1.0	45
Fireclay[1]	0.5	0.6	2
Potash	0.9	1.0	91
Fluorspar	0.1	0.1	7
Fuller's earth	0.2	0.1	9
Slate	0.5	0.4	27

[1] Great Britain only.

[2] Moisture-free basis.

Source: British Geological Survey, *United Kingdom Minerals Yearbook*

Some Minerals Produced in Britain

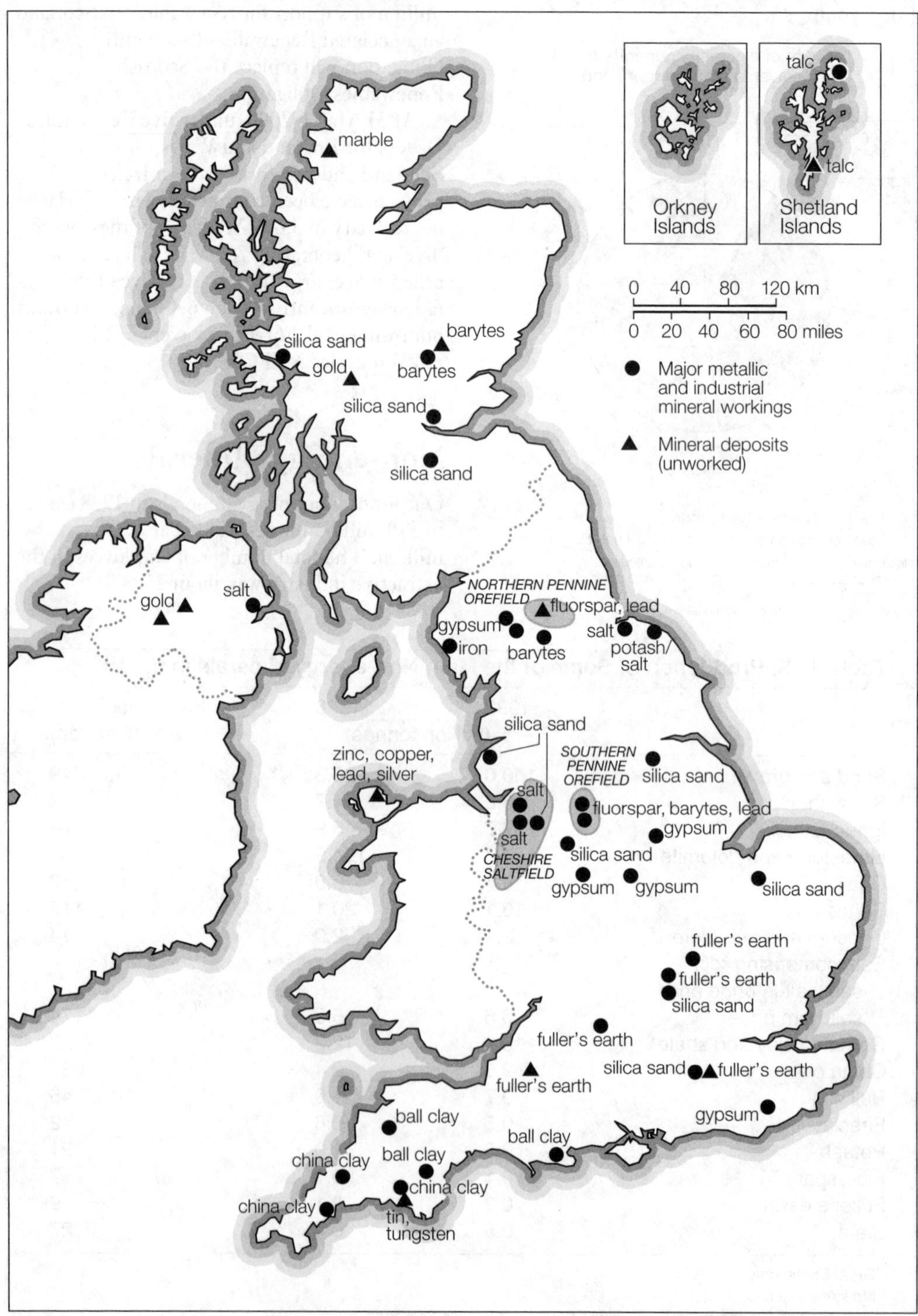

Value of UK Minerals Production, 1998

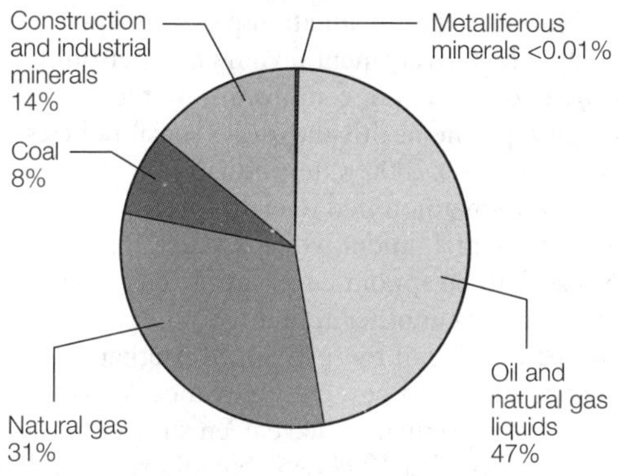

Source: British Geological Survey, *United Kingdom Minerals Yearbook 1999*

The UK is virtually self-sufficient in construction minerals, and produces and exports several industrial minerals, notably china clay, ball clay, potash and salt. The Boulby potash mine in north-east England is the UK's most important non-energy mineral operation. Production in 1998 was down from a record 1.03 million tonnes in 1996 to 1.01 million tonnes, of which 57 per cent was exported. Sales of china clay (or kaolin), the largest export, increased by 1.4 per cent to 2.4 million tonnes, of which 88 per cent of output was exported.

The largest non-energy mineral imports are metals (ores, concentrates and scrap—valued at £1.5 billion in 1998), refined non-ferrous metals (£3.8 billion) and non-metallic mineral products (£4.5 billion, of which rough diamonds account for £2.6 billion).

Water Supply

About 75 per cent of the UK's water supplies are obtained from mountain lakes, reservoirs and river intakes; and about 25 per cent from underground sources (stored in layers of porous rock). South-east England and East Anglia are more dependent on groundwater than any other parts of the UK. Scotland and Wales have a relative abundance of unpolluted water from upland sources. Northern Ireland also has plentiful supplies for domestic use and for industry.

Water put into the public supply system (including industrial and other uses) in England and Wales averaged 15,144 megalitres a day (Ml/d) in 1998–99, of which average daily consumption per head was about 160 litres. An average of 2,165 Ml/d was supplied in Scotland in 1998–99. In Northern Ireland the figure was 692 Ml/d.

Some 35,144 Ml/d were abstracted from surface waters (for example, rivers and reservoirs) in England and Wales in 1998, of which public water supplies accounted for 11,723 Ml/d. The electricity supply industry took 15,955 Ml/d; fish farming 5,182 Ml/d; and agriculture 11 Ml/d, with spray irrigation accounting for a further 144 Ml/d.

England and Wales

Water Companies

There are currently 25 water companies across England and Wales with statutory responsibilities for public water supply, including quality and sufficiency. Ten of these companies are also responsible for public sewerage and sewage treatment.

The Water Industry Act 1999 prohibited water companies from disconnecting households, as well as other premises vital to the community. It also introduced regulations to protect water customers vulnerable to hardship owing to high-measured water bills. These groups have been defined as those with meters who are in receipt of tax credits or benefits and who have certain medical conditions requiring high water use or have three or more children under 16. Since 1989 water bills have risen by more than a third in real terms. The Government also plans to introduce a Water Bill which would comprise provisions to encourage the efficient use of water, including changes to the licensing system for water abstraction, and provisions to improve the regulation of the water industry and promote the interests of consumers.

Over the next five years the Government will require the water companies to pay for a capital investment programme costing an estimated £15 billion,[5] including £7.4 billion on improving water quality and on meeting new UK and EU environmental standards up to 2005. It also wants to ensure that customers do not have to face unreasonably high bills.

The Director General of Water Services, who heads Ofwat (Office of Water Services), the industry's regulatory body, determined that the companies' efficiency improvements would fund the investments specified and offer average price cuts in real terms of 12.3 per cent from April 2000.

About 17 per cent of households and 87 per cent of commercial and industrial customers are charged for water on the basis of consumption measured by meter. Most homes are charged according to the rateable value of their property. The Government has given customers increased choice over whether or not to be charged according to a water meter. As a result, all water companies now supply free meters to households on request. Average water and sewerage bills for households without a meter, at £268 in 1999–2000, are expected to be £18 lower in real terms by 2005.

Of some 2.8 million tests on drinking water in England and Wales in 1999, 99.82 per cent met standards that are in some cases stricter than those in the 1980 EC Drinking Water Directive. A new EC Directive, adopted in 1998, requires member states to meet a number of even more stringent standards, for example an obligation to ensure maximum concentrations of lead in water of 25 microgrammes per litre within five years and 10 µg/l within 15 years.

The Drinking Water Inspectorate (DWI) checks that water companies meet the drinking water quality regulations. Enforcement action is taken when there are infringements of standards. The DWI also investigates incidents and consumer complaints about quality, and initiates prosecution if water unfit for human consumption has been supplied.

[5] The programme includes dismantling what remains of Victorian sewerage systems; tanks to prevent sewage overflows; removal of lead from supply pipes; and replacement of iron water mains, which cause discoloration. The Government has accepted the conclusions of a review on the provision of new sewers.

Competition

The Government has been undertaking a review of the scope for extending competition in the water industry in England and Wales and published a consultation paper in April 2000. The Government favours competition, provided it does not compromise water quality, public health and wider social policies. By September 2000 water industry competition amounted to eight 'inset appointments', under which a water company can seek to be appointed to supply customers in the area of another appointed water company. Five of these involved Anglian Water, and one a new entrant. Since April 2000 water companies have been subject to the Competition Act 1998, which could result in others using their pipe networks to supply customers. In August 2000 the Government lowered the 'inset' threshold allowing customers to seek alternative suppliers from users of 250 million litres a year to 100 million litres. This means that some hospitals and universities, for example, could go to another supplier.

Ensuring Supplies

The Director General of Water Services set the companies mandatory targets to reduce an average leakage of some 200 million gallons a day by 26 per cent between 1996 and 2000. The industry spent £816 million on leakage repair and £1.7 billion on mains rehabilitation and replacement over 1998–2000.

Scotland

Responsibility for the provision of water and sewerage services rests with three public bodies—the North, West and East of Scotland Water Authorities. The Water Industry Commissioner for Scotland promotes customer interests and advises the Scottish Executive about the level of the authorities' charges. Water Industry Consultative Committees for each of the authorities advise the Commissioner about customer interests.

Modernisation of the water industry is in progress, with the authorities investing some £1.8 billion over 1999–2002, including projects worth about £700 million in partnership with the private sector. New water treatment plants are being built and all major towns are expected to benefit from new waste water treatment works by the end of 2000. Prices for water services depend on the type of consumer: domestic consumers presently pay amounts based on their council tax band (see p. 412) or in very few cases metered charges; and non-domestic consumers pay non-domestic water rates, or metered charges and trade effluent charges.

Northern Ireland

The Northern Ireland Executive envisages expenditure of up to £2.5 billion over 15–20 years to bring water and sewerage services up to standard and to meet increasing demand. (Some of the main sewers of Belfast date from Victorian times and may be at risk of collapse.) An extra 10 per cent in water rates bills would be necessary to pay for these improvements.

Further Reading

Annual Publications

Digest of Environmental Statistics. Department of the Environment, Transport and the Regions. The Stationery Office.

Digest of United Kingdom Energy Statistics. Department of Trade and Industry. The Stationery Office.

Energy Report (the Blue Book). Department of Trade and Industry. The Stationery Office.

Oil and Gas Resources of the United Kingdom (the Brown Book). Department of Trade and Industry. The Stationery Office.

United Kingdom Minerals Yearbook. British Geological Survey.

Water Quality and Standards Paper. Scottish Executive.

Websites

Department of Trade and Industry: www.dti.gov.uk

Department of the Environment, Transport and the Regions: www.environment.detr.gov.uk

Northern Ireland Executive: www.nio.gov.uk

Scottish Executive: www.scotland.gov.uk

Ofwat: www.open.gov.uk/ofwat

Water Conservation Research Database: www.databases.detr.gov.uk/water/index.htm

British Geological Survey Minerals UK: www.mineralsUK.com

30 Finance and Other Service Industries

The service sector in the United Kingdom is continuing to grow and now contributes over 70 per cent of gross value added at current basic prices and 75 per cent of employment. Over 21 million people had jobs in the service sector at the end of 1999, a rise of nearly 800,000 in two years.

Financial services make a major contribution to the UK economy, and London is by far the largest international financial centre in Europe. Technological change is having a significant impact in many areas, for example, in the spread of telephone-based services and the growing use of the Internet. New Internet banking services are being established, and share-dealing over the Internet has become much more widespread.

As a result of rising real incomes, consumer spending on financial, personal and leisure services has increased considerably. Travel, hotel and restaurant services in the UK are among those to have benefited from the growth in tourism, and the UK is one of the world's leading tourist destinations. Computer activities and business services are among the non-financial sectors which experienced strong growth in turnover in 1999 (see Table 30.1).

Financial Services

The UK's financial services sector accounts for over 6 per cent of gross domestic product (GDP) and employs more than 1 million people. Net overseas earnings have risen substantially, reaching a record £31.2 billion in 1999.

Historically, the heart of the industry has been in the 'Square Mile' in the City of London, and this remains broadly the case. Among the major financial institutions and markets in the City are the Bank of England, the London Stock Exchange and Lloyd's insurance market. The City is one of the world's three leading financial centres, along with Tokyo and New York. An important feature is the size of its international activities. It is noted for having:

Table 30.1: Turnover in Selected Services, 1999

	£ million	% increase on 1998
Motor trades	122,948	0.8
Hotels and restaurants	51,148	7.5
Renting	15,845	11.6
Computer and related activities	36,224	19.5
Research and development	4,930	–3.6
Business services	140,351	9.6
Education[1]	21,636	4.7
Sewage and refuse disposal, etc	7,519	14.4
Recreation[2]	22,566	4.2

[1] Excludes public sector activities.
[2] Excludes sporting, betting and gaming activities.
Source: Office for National Statistics—annual data derived from short-term turnover inquiries

- more overseas banks than any other financial centre;
- the biggest market in the world for trading foreign equities, accounting for 58 per cent of global turnover;
- by far the world's biggest foreign exchange market, actively trading the largest range of currencies;
- the largest fund management centre;
- the leading international insurance centre;
- the major international centre for primary and secondary dealing in the Euromarket; and
- the most important centre in the world for advice on privatisation.

Scotland (Edinburgh and Glasgow) is the fifth largest financial centre in the EU, in terms of institutional equity funds managed. Manchester, Cardiff, Liverpool and Leeds are also important financial centres.

BI (British Invisibles) promotes the international activities of UK-based financial institutions and related business services. It also seeks to raise awareness of the UK's leading role in international financial markets and of the major contribution of financial services to the UK economy. In April 2000 a review of the role of BI, including its relationship with other City organisations, was launched.

London has a full range of ancillary and support services, including legal, accountancy and management services. A report by BI in December 1999 confirmed London's position as a leading centre for international legal services. Of the world's 50 largest legal firms, ten were based in London, more than in any other centre. City firms have established themselves as leading advisers in international financial markets, taking advantage of the growth in international bond and equity issues, and in mergers and acquisitions. Overseas earnings of UK legal firms were £791 million in 1998, over 50 per cent higher than in 1995. Legal services account for 1 per cent of UK national output and grew by 5 per cent a year in real terms between 1992 and 1998.

REGULATION

In 1997 the Government announced major reforms of the regulation of financial services, including the creation of the Financial Services Authority (FSA). In 1998 responsibility for banking supervision was transferred to the FSA from the Bank of England. The Financial Services and Markets Act 2000 provides for the formal establishment of the FSA, bringing together the regulation of investment business, banks, building societies and insurance companies previously handled by nine regulatory bodies. New compensation arrangements and a single Financial Ombudsman are being set up. The new regulatory regime is expected to be fully operational by summer 2001.

FSA Objectives and Functions

The FSA's statutory objectives are maintaining confidence in the UK financial system and promoting public understanding of it, protecting consumers and reducing financial crime. In delivering these objectives, the FSA has to be efficient and economic, facilitate innovation in financial services, take account of the international nature of financial services business and minimise any adverse effects of regulation on competition.

The FSA is currently supplying regulatory and other services under contract to several of the regulatory bodies which it will replace when the Act is fully implemented, including the Building Societies Commission, the Friendly Societies Commission, the Investment Management Regulatory Organisation, the Securities and Futures Authority, and the Personal Investment Authority. It is also supplying services to HM Treasury in its regulation of insurance business, including regulatory oversight of the Lloyd's market (see p. 518). In the light of the development of electronic trading systems and greater competition between exchanges, the FSA is reviewing its regulatory approach to investment exchanges and clearing houses—it supervises the UK's seven recognised investment exchanges (including the London Stock Exchange) and two recognised clearing houses, and will be taking over responsibility from HM Treasury for supervising the nine overseas investment exchanges which wish to be recognised in the UK. In May 2000 the FSA acquired responsibility from the London Stock Exchange for acting as the competent authority for listing companies in the UK, determining the rules for companies that wish to be listed.

The FSA will also become responsible for statutory regulation of key aspects of mortgage lending, which will take effect in 2001 as part of the Government's plans to reform the selling of mortgages (see p. 346), and a new statutory system for regulating credit unions (see p. 517).

Banking Supervision

Banks are required to meet minimum standards on the integrity and competence of directors and management, the adequacy of capital and cash flow, and the systems and controls to deal with the risks they experience. If a bank fails to meet the criteria, its activities may be restricted, or it may be closed. These arrangements are intended to strengthen, but not guarantee, the protection of bank depositors, thereby increasing confidence in the banking system as a whole. The FSA is consulting on proposed changes to the international agreement governing the adequacy of capital, which are designed to link this more closely to the degree of risk taken.

> In January 2000 the FSA announced a new risk-based strategy for the regulation of financial services designed to help the Authority achieve its statutory objectives. This new framework, which will come fully into operation in 2001–02, will aim to identify and address the most important risks to firms, markets and consumers, with less routine monitoring for well-run firms. Each year the FSA will identify key regulatory themes for priority attention by managers and regulators.

Consumer Education

The FSA is to publish comparative information on costs and charges in savings, insurance and pensions products, so that consumers will be better able to assess the products available. It is working with the Department for Education and Employment and the Qualifications and Curriculum Authority on preparing guidelines for personal finance education, which are being included in the National Curriculum in England from September 2000.

Compensation

A single Financial Services Compensation Scheme is being set up for the protection of consumers in cases where authorised firms are unable to meet their liabilities. It will replace a number of schemes, including the Investors Compensation Scheme, for private investors; the Deposit Protection Scheme, for bank customers; and the Building Societies Investor Protection Scheme.

Financial Ombudsman Service

A new Financial Ombudsman Service is being set up as a one-stop service for dealing with complaints about financial services, and will have an annual budget of around £20 million. It will replace eight schemes, including those covering banks, building societies, insurers and firms conducting investment business. All firms authorised by the FSA will be subject to the Ombudsman's procedures, but will be required to attempt to resolve complaints themselves in the first instance. Firms not authorised by the FSA will be able to join the scheme on a voluntary basis.

International Agreements

The UK plays a major role in international efforts to maintain global prosperity and prevent financial crises. The Group of Seven (G7) leading industrialised countries agreed in 1998 on measures to reform the international financial architecture, including enhanced global supervision and strengthened co-operation between regulatory authorities. A new Financial Stability Forum (FSF) was set up in early 1999, bringing together senior representatives of G7 national governments, central banks and statutory regulators, together with international financial institutions and the key global financial regulatory standard-setting agencies.

In March 2000 the FSF produced papers with significant regulatory and other recommendations on hedge funds, capital flows and offshore financial centres. These were aimed at improving standards and strengthening stability, particularly in vulnerable areas. The FSF has also contributed views on programmes for assessing regulatory standards in offshore centres. Several UK Overseas Territories have important financial services sectors, and the UK and relevant Overseas Territories governments have commissioned a review by independent regulatory experts, due to be published later in 2000.

HM Treasury represents the UK in negotiating EC Directives on the financial services sector, co-ordinating as necessary with the FSA and other bodies.

BANK OF ENGLAND

The Bank of England was established in 1694 by Act of Parliament and Royal Charter as a corporate body. Its capital stock was acquired by the Government in 1946. Fundamental changes to the Bank's role took effect under the Bank of England Act 1998, in particular the acquisition of operational responsibility for setting interest rates.

As the UK's central bank, the Bank's overriding objective is to maintain a stable and efficient monetary and financial framework for the effective operation of the economy. In pursuing this goal, it has three main purposes:

- maintaining the integrity and value of the currency;
- maintaining the stability of the financial system; and
- seeking to ensure the effectiveness of the financial services sector.

Monetary Policy Framework

The Bank's monetary policy objective is to maintain price stability and to support the Government's economic policy, including growth and employment objectives. Price stability is defined in terms of the Government's inflation target (see p. 388). The responsibility for meeting this target rests with the Bank's Monetary Policy Committee, which comprises the Governor, the two Deputy Governors and six other members. The Committee meets every month and interest rate decisions are announced as soon as is practicable after the meeting. The Committee is accountable to the Bank's Court of Directors as regards its procedures and to Parliament.

Financial Stability

Under the Memorandum of Understanding between the Bank, HM Treasury and the FSA, the Bank is responsible for the overall stability of the financial system, and its Financial Stability Committee oversees the Bank's work in this area. In exceptional circumstances, it may provide financial support as a last resort to prevent problems affecting one financial institution from spreading to other parts of the financial system. The Bank also oversees the effectiveness of the financial sector in meeting the needs of customers and in maintaining the sector's international competitiveness.

Other Main Functions

The Bank's money market operations are designed to steer short-term market interest rates to levels required to implement monetary policy. Through its daily operations in the money market, the Bank supplies the funds which the banking system as a whole needs to achieve balance by the end of each settlement day. It also acts as the Treasury's agent in managing the Government's reserves of gold and foreign exchange and its foreign currency borrowing.

The Bank provides banking services to its customers, principally the Government, the banking system and other central banks. It plays a key role in payment and settlement systems, and has sole right in England and Wales to issue banknotes, which are backed by government and other securities. The profit from the note issue is paid directly to the Government. Three Scottish and four Northern Ireland banks may also issue notes, but these have to be fully backed by Bank of England notes.

Court of Directors

The Court of Directors is responsible for managing the affairs of the Bank other than the formulation of monetary policy. It comprises the Governor, the two Deputy Governors and 16 Directors. The Directors form a sub-committee; functions include reviewing the Bank's performance in relation to its objectives and strategy, and the internal procedures of the Monetary Policy Committee. The Court is required to report annually to the Chancellor of the Exchequer.

BANKING SERVICES

At the end of March 2000, there were 315 banks authorised to accept deposits in the UK under the Banking Act 1987. In addition, 103 branches of European-authorised institutions were entitled to accept deposits in the UK. With around 20 per cent of cross-border bank lending, the UK is the world's largest single market for international banking. Banks from around 80 countries have subsidiaries, branches or representative offices in London.

'Retail' banking primarily caters for personal customers and small businesses, offering services including current accounts, savings accounts, loan arrangements, credit and debit cards, mortgages, insurance, investment products and share-dealing services. Nearly all banks engage in some 'wholesale' activities, which involve taking larger deposits, deploying funds in money-market instruments, and making corporate loans and investments, while some concentrate on wholesale business. Many dealings are conducted on the inter-bank market, among banks themselves.

Around 85 per cent of households have at least one member with a bank or building society current account (see Table 30.2).

Retail Banks and Banking Groups

The 'big four' banks are HSBC, Lloyds TSB, Royal Bank of Scotland (following its acquisition of National Westminster in February 2000) and Barclays. They have a significant share of current accounts, credit cards and personal loans (see Table 30.3). Other large-scale banks include Halifax, Abbey National, Bank of Scotland, Woolwich (which is being acquired by Barclays), Alliance & Leicester and Northern Rock. Standard Chartered, which mainly operates overseas, has a network of around 740 offices in more than 55 countries, notably in Asia, Africa and the Middle East.

Several large building societies have joined the banking sector, and Bradford & Bingley is due to convert to a bank by the end of 2000. Other businesses, notably insurance companies and supermarkets (see p. 524), have also entered the sector, although relatively few

Table 30.2: Households[1] with Different Types of Account or Savings in Great Britain 1998–99

	Per cent of households
Accounts	
Current account	85
Post Office account	11
TESSA[2]	14
Other bank or building society accounts excluding current accounts and TESSAs	64
Other savings	
Stocks and shares	28
Unit trusts or investment trusts	6
Personal Equity Plans	15
Gilt-edged stock	1
Premium bonds	27
National Savings	8
Save as you earn	2

1 Households in which at least one member has an account.
2 Tax Exempt Special Savings Account.
Source: Family Resources Survey, Department of Social Security

offer current accounts, while several US banks have entered the market for issuing credit cards.

Traditionally, the major banks have operated through their branches, but the number of branches is falling, as banks have taken steps to cut costs, such as through centralising 'back office' processing operations, to take account of fewer customers in some instances and as more customers are using telephone and Internet banking (see box).

Review of UK Banking Services

A major independent review of banking services, *Competition in UK Banking: A Report to the Chancellor of the Exchequer*, published in March 2000, found that, although the UK had a stable financial system and one of the most open regulatory regimes in the world, a more competitive policy framework was needed. The main recommendations included:

- a stronger policy framework for the Government's approach to banking services, which would aim to increase transparency in banking supervision, deliver effective competition scrutiny, eliminate regulatory distortions and prevent anti-competitive mergers in the banking industry;
- the establishment of a new payments system commission (PayCom), which would supervise a licensing regime for banks' payments systems, such as those used for debit and credit cards;
- an investigation of the existence or possible existence of a monopoly position in the supply of banking services to small businesses;
- better information to help customers make the most from developing competition in the banking sector;

Table 30.3: Market Shares[1] for Various Banking Products 1998 *Per cent*

	'Big four'[2] banks	Other established banks	Converted building societies	Building societies	Others
Current accounts	68	13	14	4	1
Savings accounts	19	5	42	27	7[3]
Credit cards	61	17	6	1	15[3]
Personal loans	46	13	16	1	24[3]
Mortgages	17	5	48	19	11

1 Figures refer to the share of the number of accounts or of the products issued rather than the value.
2 Barclays, HSBC, Lloyds TSB and National Westminster (as it was before its acquisition by the Royal Bank of Scotland).
3 New entrants—financial firms which had entered the activity in the past ten years—accounted for 1 per cent of savings accounts, 5 per cent of personal loans outstanding and 13 per cent of credit cards issued.
Source: *Competition in UK Banking: A Report to the Chancellor of the Exchequer*

Technological developments, such as the growing use of telephone banking and of automated teller machines for dispensing and depositing money, are having a major impact on banking. Over 8 million people used telephone and/or personal computer (PC)/Internet banking services in 1999, of whom around 2 million used PC/Internet banking. Most customers use these services to view balances and transactions or to transfer funds between accounts, with only a small proportion using them for making payments. Banking services using the Internet are becoming much more widely available. Most major banks are introducing Internet banking, either as an additional option for customers or as a separate stand-alone facility. Several are planning to introduce Internet banking with access through mobile telephones and/or digital television.

- an opportunity for everyone, especially those on low incomes, to have access to affordable basic banking services; and
- better procedures for handling complaints about banking services.

The report also recommended that the Government should review the impact of the Financial Services and Markets Act 2000 on competition in banking two years after its implementation, with particular emphasis on the governance of the FSA and the impact of regulation on competition.

Government Response

On publication of the report, the Government announced that it would implement two of the key recommendations through:

- referring to the Competition Commission the supply of banking services to small businesses by clearing banks; and
- announcing that it would legislate to open up access to payment systems and to oversee access charges.

In its formal response to the report, published in August 2000, the Government announced a number of new measures designed to improve competition in UK banking markets and to deliver benefits to consumers, including:

- reviewing self-regulatory redress mechanisms, with the aim of ensuring that they deliver sufficient consumer benefits;
- encouraging the provision of comparative information on banking products;
- agreeing to a review of the effect of the Financial Services and Markets Act 2000 on competition after two years; and
- reforming the Treasury's objectives on promoting competition in financial services.

Investment Banks

Investment banks offer a range of professional financial services, including corporate finance and asset management. A major activity is the provision of advice and financial services to companies, especially in respect of mergers, takeovers and other forms of corporate reorganisation. Investment banks have considerable expertise in advising governments on privatisation. Many UK-owned investment banks have been acquired by overseas concerns, the most recent example being the acquisition in 2000 of Robert Fleming by Chase Manhattan of the United States.

Building Societies

Building societies are mutual institutions, owned by their savers and borrowers. As well as their retail deposit-taking services, they specialise in housing finance, making long-term mortgage loans against the security of property—usually private dwellings purchased for owner-occupation. Some of the larger societies provide a full range of personal banking services. According to the Building Societies Association, about 17 million adults have building society savings accounts, and some 3 million adults are buying their homes through mortgage loans from a building society. The chief requirements for societies are that:

- their principal purpose is making loans which are secured on residential property and are funded substantially by their members;
- at least 75 per cent of lending has to be on the security of housing; and
- a minimum of 50 per cent of funds must be in the form of deposits made by individual members.

There are 68 authorised building societies, all of which are members of the Building Societies Association, with total assets of around £160 billion. The largest is the Nationwide, with assets of £64 billion.

The number of societies has fallen substantially as a result of mergers and the decision by several large societies to give up their mutual status and become banks. In July 2000 members of the Bradford & Bingley (the second biggest society) voted to convert the society to a bank. Many of the remaining societies have taken steps to defend their mutual status, for example, by requiring new members to assign to charity any 'windfall' payments arising from a conversion.

Payment Systems

Apart from credit and debit card arrangements, the main payment systems are run by three separate companies operating under an umbrella organisation, the Association for Payment Clearing Services (APACS). One system covers bulk paper clearings—cheques and credit transfers. A second, CHAPS (Clearing House Automated Payment System), is a nationwide electronic transfer service dealing with high-value clearings for same-day settlement. A third covers bulk electronic clearing for direct credits, standing orders and direct debits. A total of 29 banks and building societies are members of one or more clearing companies, while several hundred others obtain access to APACS clearing through agency arrangements with one of the members.

Trends in Financial Transactions

Major changes in the nature of financial transactions have included the rapid growth in the use of plastic cards (which first appeared in 1966) and of automated teller machines (ATMs). According to APACS, there were around 3.5 billion plastic transactions in the UK in 1999 when 118 million plastic cards were in circulation, with 86 per cent of adults holding one or more cards. Most non-regular payments are still made by cash, but the trend is away from cash and cheques towards greater use of plastic cards (see Table 30.4).

Consumers now acquire more than half their cash through withdrawals from ATMs. The number of ATMs has risen by three-quarters in the last ten years, to 28,300 at the end of 1999. There were 1,968 million cash withdrawals from ATMs in 1999. About three-fifths of adults use ATMs regularly, making on average 67 withdrawals a year.

Plastic Cards

The main types of plastic card are debit cards, credit/charge cards, cash cards and cheque guarantee cards, although individual cards frequently cover more than one use. Charge cards are similar to credit cards, but are designed to be paid off in full each month and are usually available only to those with relatively high income or assets. Several major retailers issue store cards for use within their own outlets. Electronic purse cards are being tested: cards are 'charged' with money from the card holder's bank account, and can be used to purchase goods or services at retailers through electronic tills.

There are nearly 45 million credit cards (including charge cards) in use in the UK, and 52 per cent of adults have at least one credit card. Most credit cards are affiliated to one of the two major international organisations, Visa and MasterCard. Competition has increased, with new providers entering the market and particularly rapid growth in the number of 'affinity' cards, where the card is linked to an organisation such as a charity or trade union.

Debit cards, where payments are deducted directly from the purchaser's bank or building society account, were first issued in 1987. Purchases using debit cards are rising rapidly, with the volume of debit card payments up by nearly 19 per cent in 1999. Over 46 million cards have been issued, and around four-fifths

Table 30.4: Transaction Trends in the UK				Million
	1989	1994	1998	1999
Plastic card purchases	774	1,723	3,094	3,537
of which:				
Debit card	*68*	*808*	*1,736*	*2,062*
Credit and charge card	*650*	*815*	*1,224*	*1,344*
Store card[1]	*56*	*100*	*134*	*131*
Plastic card withdrawals at ATMs and counters	918	1,372	1,917	2,025
Direct debits, standing orders, direct credits and CHAPS	1,556	2,196	3,056	3,255
Cheques	3,900	3,430	2,986	2,854
of which:				
For payment	*3,453*	*3,074*	*2,757*	*2,641*
For cash acquisition	*447*	*356*	*229*	*213*
Total non-cash transactions	**7,148**	**8,721**	**11,053**	**11,672**
Cash payments[1]	28,122	26,179	25,309	25,596
Post Office Order Book payments and passbook withdrawals	1,030	1,127	1,017	962
Total transactions	**36,300**	**36,026**	**37,379**	**38,230**

[1] Estimated figures.
Source: APACS

of adults in the UK hold a debit card, often combined with cheque guarantee and ATM facilities in a single card.

Banks have been concerned at the rising level of fraud on plastic cards, with losses of £189 million in 1999 being 40 per cent higher than in 1998. They are investing in the replacement of cards with a magnetic strip by 'smart' cards, in which information is contained on a microchip embedded in the card. These are very difficult to counterfeit and can also store securely much more information than was previously possible.

National Savings

National Savings, an executive agency of the Chancellor of the Exchequer, is a source of finance for government borrowing and offers personal savers a range of investments. Its operational services—including its three main sites in Blackpool, Durham and Glasgow—are now run under a 15-year partnership agreement with Siemens Business Services, with National Savings retaining responsibility for policy and marketing. In March 2000, £62.5 billion was invested in National Savings. Sales of National Savings products totalled £10.2 billion in 1999–2000.

Premium Bonds are held by 23 million people and are entered in a monthly draw, with tax-free prizes ranging from £50 to a single top prize of £1 million. Other savings products include Savings Certificates (both Fixed Interest and Index-linked), Pensioners' Bonds, Children's Bonus Bonds and Ordinary and Investment Accounts (where deposits and withdrawals can be made at post offices). New products were launched during 1999–2000, including a cash mini ISA (Individual Savings Account—see p. 520) and a new Fixed Rate Savings Bond.

Friendly Societies

Friendly societies have traditionally been unincorporated societies of individuals, offering their members a limited range of financial and insurance services, such as small-scale savings products, life insurance and provision against loss of income through sickness or unemployment. The Friendly Societies Act 1992 enabled societies to incorporate, take on new powers and provide a wider range of financial services through subsidiaries. Under the Financial Services and Markets Act 2000, the Government has removed the remaining restrictions on the activities of friendly society subsidiaries.

There are around 250 friendly societies, with total funds of £15 billion and an estimated membership of over 5 million. The largest society is the Liverpool Victoria, which has over 1 million members and manages some £5 billion of funds.

Credit Unions

Credit unions are mutually owned financial co-operatives. They are less widespread in the UK than in some other countries, but grew rapidly during the 1990s. There were 666 credit unions registered in Great Britain in September 1999. At the end of 1998 credit union membership amounted to 256,000 and assets totalled just under £148 million.

In November 1999 a report by a Treasury taskforce found that credit unions could provide safe, low-cost loans of particular help to those in disadvantaged communities who have difficulty in obtaining credit. Following the report, as part of its measures to deal with financial exclusion, the Government announced a bigger role for credit unions, including more flexibility in their operations, an increase in the maximum repayment period for loans and a proposed new central services organisation to spread best practice. Under the Financial Services and Markets Act 2000, the statutory basis for the regulation of credit unions will be strengthened, including the introduction of a protection scheme similar to that for bank and building society customers. The FSA will be responsible for regulation.

Venture Capital

Venture capital companies offer medium- and long-term equity financing for new and developing businesses, management buy-outs and buy-ins, and company rescues. The UK sector is the largest and most developed in Europe. The British Venture Capital Association has 131 full members, which represent a large majority of private equity and venture capital sources in the UK. During 1999 UK venture capital companies invested a record £7.8 billion worldwide in 1,358 businesses, 60 per cent more than in 1998. Investment in the UK was up by 63 per cent to £6.2 billion. The Government is encouraging the further development of venture capital, particularly for smaller firms, and is working with the Regional Development Agencies to establish new regional venture capital funds.

Other Credit and Financial Services

Finance houses and leasing companies provide consumer credit, business finance and leasing, and motor finance. The 92 full members of the Finance and Leasing Association undertook new business worth £67 billion in 1999.

Factoring comprises a range of financial services, including credit management and finance in exchange for outstanding invoices. The industry provides working capital to more than 27,000 businesses a year. Member companies of the Factors & Discounters Association handled business worth £64 billion in 1999, 13 per cent higher than in 1998.

INSURANCE

London is one of the biggest centres for insurance business, handling 24 per cent of world marine insurance and 37 per cent of aviation insurance business in 1998. It is also the largest global centre for reinsurance.

Main Types of Insurance

There are two broad categories of insurance: long-term (such as life insurance), where contracts may be for periods of many years; and general, where contracts are for a year or less. Most insurance companies reinsure their risks; this performs an important function in spreading losses and in helping insurance companies to manage their businesses.

Long-term Insurance

Around 230 companies handle long-term insurance. In addition to providing life cover, life insurance is a vehicle for saving and investment as premiums are invested in securities and other assets. About 63 per cent of households have life insurance cover. Total long-term insurance assets under management by companies in 1998 were £739 billion on behalf of their worldwide operations. Total long-term premium income by companies in 1998 was £87 billion.

General Insurance

General insurance business is undertaken by insurance companies and by underwriters at Lloyd's. It includes fire, accident, general liability, motor, marine, aviation and other transport risks. Competition has intensified in areas like motor and household insurance, particularly with the growth of insurers offering telephone-based services. Total worldwide premium income of members of the Association of British Insurers (ABI) in 1998 was £41 billion, of which £27 billion was earned in the UK.

Structure of the Industry

At the end of 1999, around 800 companies were authorised to carry on one or more classes of insurance business in the UK. Over 420 companies belong to the ABI.

The industry, which includes both public limited companies and mutual institutions (companies owned by their policyholders), has seen considerable restructuring in recent years. In 2000 two of the biggest concerns, CGU and Norwich Union, merged to form CGNU, which is now the largest insurance group in the UK; it controls over £200 billion in funds under management and has more than 25 million customers worldwide. The mutually owned sector is gradually contracting—Scottish Widows has been acquired by the banking group Lloyds TSB, Scottish Provident is being acquired by Abbey National, and Friends Provident and Equitable Life have announced their intention to abandon their mutual status. However, in June 2000 members of Standard Life, the largest mutual insurer in Europe, rejected resolutions put forward in a campaign to convert the insurer to a public limited company.

Lloyd's

Lloyd's is an incorporated society of private insurers in London. It is not a company but a market for insurance administered by the Council of Lloyd's and Lloyd's Regulatory and Market Boards.

The net premium income of the market in 1997 was £4.7 billion. For 2000 the market has a total projected allocated capacity of £10.0 billion, of which some £8.0 billion will be capacity provided by 853 limited liability members, representing both companies and individuals who have converted to limited liability. The number of individual 'Names'—wealthy individuals who accept insurance risks for their own profit or loss, with unlimited liability—was 3,296 in 2000. Members underwrite through 123 syndicates. Each syndicate is managed by an underwriting agent responsible for appointing a professional underwriter to accept insurance risks and manage claims on behalf of the members.

Insurance may currently only be placed through 127 active Lloyd's brokers and one 'umbrella' broker, which negotiate with Lloyd's syndicates on behalf of the insured. However, in May 2000 Lloyd's announced that it would open up the market from January 2001 when other UK and overseas brokers would be able to have access, subject to meeting certain technical and customer service standards. Reinsurance constitutes a large part of Lloyd's business—around 3 per cent of the world's reinsurance is placed at Lloyd's. Around one-sixth of Lloyd's current work is in its traditional marine market, and it has a significant share of the UK motor insurance market. Lloyd's is a major insurer of aviation and satellite risks, and underwrites in other areas of insurance except long-term life insurance.

Under the Financial Services and Markets Act 2000, the FSA will have regulatory oversight of Lloyd's. The FSA's primary concern will be protecting the interests of Lloyd's policyholders.

Insurance Brokers and Intermediaries

Medium to large insurance brokers almost exclusively handle commercial matters, with the biggest dealing in worldwide risks. Smaller brokers deal mainly with personal lines, such as motor, household and holiday insurance, or specialise in a particular type of commercial insurance. Some brokers specialise in reinsurance business. Under the Financial Services and Markets Act 2000, the statutory regime of professional standards governing insurance brokers will be abolished and replaced by a new self-regulating regime for intermediaries arranging general insurance business, which will operate under the General Insurance Standards Council. For intermediaries arranging life insurance constituting an investment (such as a personal pension), regulation will be by the FSA.

INVESTMENT

The UK has considerable expertise in fund management, which involves managing funds on behalf of investors, or advising them how best to invest their funds. The main types of investment fund include pension schemes, life insurance, unit trusts, open-ended investment companies and investment trusts. According to BI, identified assets under management in the UK totalled £2,500 billion at the end of 1998, one-third more than at the end of 1995, and overseas service earnings of the fund management industry were £540 million in 1999.

Pension funds are major investors in securities markets, holding around 22 per cent of securities listed on the London Stock Exchange. Funds are managed mainly by the investment management houses.

Unit Trusts

Over 1,800 authorised unit trusts and open-ended investment companies (oeics) pool investors' money, and divide funds into units or shares of equal size, enabling people with relatively small amounts of money to benefit from diversified and managed portfolios. In April 2000 total funds under management were £254 billion, 21 per cent higher than a year earlier; £58 billion represented funds in Personal Equity Plans and £12 billion in Individual Savings Accounts (ISAs), with over 4 million ISA accounts taken out in 1999–2000. Most unit trusts are general funds, investing in a wide variety of UK or international securities, but there are also many specialist funds.

There are over 150 unit trust management groups, of which 61 had total fund values exceeding £1 billion in April 2000. Unit trust management groups are represented by the Association of Unit Trusts and Investment Funds (AUTIF). According to AUTIF, the four largest groups are Fidelity, Schroders, M & G and Threadneedle, all with fund values exceeding £10 billion.

Oeics are similar to unit trusts, but investors buy shares in the fund rather than units. They were set up in 1997 to enable UK companies to compete on an equal footing with similar schemes operating elsewhere in the EU. By April 2000, 381 oeics had been set up by 43 management groups.

Investment Trusts

Investment trust companies are listed on the London Stock Exchange and their shares can be bought and sold in the same way as other companies. Like unit trusts, they offer the opportunity to diversify risk on a relatively small lump-sum investment or through regular savings; investments can be made through private investor plans administered by their managements. Investment trusts are exempt from tax on gains realised within the funds and invest principally in the shares and securities of other companies. Assets are purchased mainly out of shareholders' funds, although investment trusts are also allowed to borrow money for investment.

There are about 350 investment trusts, which form the largest listed sector of the London Stock Exchange. Around 40 per cent of their shares by value are held by private investors. Over 300 listed trust companies are members of the Association of Investment Trust Companies. At the end of April 2000 the industry had £80 billion of assets under management and a stock market capitalisation of £65 billion. The three largest trusts by market capitalisation are the venture capital company 3i Group, Foreign & Colonial Investment Trust and Witan Investment Trust.

Share Ownership

Financial institutions hold the bulk of equities. At the end of 1999 UK financial institutions held ordinary shares valued at £917 billion (51 per cent of the total market value of £1,807 billion), with insurance companies holding £390 billion and pension funds £354 billion. Holders from outside the UK had £530 billion. The value of holdings of UK individual shareholders was £276 billion (15 per cent). About 28 per cent of households have at least one person owning shares (see Table 30.2).

According to ProShare (an independent organisation encouraging share ownership), the number of investment clubs—groups of individuals, usually about 15 to 20 people, who regularly invest in shares—has risen to around 8,000. The conversion of a number of building societies to banks, privatisation, employee share schemes and measures to increase tax-free savings have led to increased share ownership by individuals. The spread of low-cost share dealing facilities has also facilitated the growth in share ownership. Initially these were available on an execution-only basis primarily by post and telephone, but recently there has been a rapid rise in share-dealing and other personal finance services available over the Internet.

Tax-free Savings

The main method of tax-free saving is now the Individual Savings Account (ISA). The Government introduced ISAs in April 1999 to help encourage savings, especially among those on more modest incomes, and to distribute the tax relief on savings more fairly. They succeeded Personal Equity Plans (PEPs), which allowed tax-free investment in shares, unit trusts and certain corporate bonds, and TESSAs (Tax Exempt Special Savings Accounts, of which 5.7 million were held in March 1999). Between 1987 and April 1999 some £70 billion were subscribed to 17 million PEPs.

ISAs allow tax-free saving of up to £5,000 a year (£7,000 in 1999–2000 and 2000–01). There are three main elements of an ISA:

- cash—up to an annual total of £1,000 (£3,000 in 1999–2000 and 2000–01)—such as in a bank or building society ISA account;
- stocks and shares—up to a maximum of £5,000 a year (£7,000 in 1999–2000 and 2000–01); and
- life insurance—up to £1,000 a year.

There are two main types of ISA: a maxi ISA, which can include all three elements in a single ISA with one manager; and mini ISAs—an individual can have three mini ISAs each year, from different managers, for cash, stocks and shares, and life insurance, but is not allowed to take out both a mini ISA and a maxi ISA in the same tax year.

In 1999–2000 over 9.3 million ISAs were opened, attracting nearly £28.4 billion, about a third more than the sum put into PEPs and TESSAs combined in 1998–99.

FINANCIAL MARKETS

London Stock Exchange

The London Stock Exchange is one of the world's leading exchanges. In August 2000, 1,911 UK and 504 international companies were listed on the main market, with a market capitalisation of £1,968 billion and £3,831 billion respectively. A further 460 companies, with a total capitalisation of £17.3 billion, were listed on AIM, the Alternative Investment Market, primarily for small, young and growing companies. In November 1999 the London Stock Exchange launched 'techMARK', a market which brings together 190 of the listed companies engaged in technology or related sectors. CREST, a computerised settlement system for shares and other company securities, handles the settlement of all company securities traded in the UK.

The value and volume of equity business on the Exchange reached record levels in 1999. Turnover in international equities was 10 per cent higher than in 1998, at £2,403 billion, while turnover in UK equities was up by 36 per cent, to £1,406 billion.

Several other products for raising capital are handled, including Eurobonds (see below), warrants, depositary receipts and gilt-edged stock (see p. 405). The London Stock

Exchange provides a secondary or trading market where investors can buy or sell gilts.

Other Equity Exchanges

Three other markets in the City of London for trading equities are Tradepoint, OM London, and Ofex (a lightly regulated exchange run by market maker J. P. Jenkins). Tradepoint has developed a pan-European electronic trading facility with the backing of a group of investment banks, and in July 2000 agreed a merger of its facilities with those of the Swiss stock exchange to form a new exchange, Virt-X, which should be fully operational by early 2001.

Euromarket

The Euromarket began with Eurodollars—US dollars lent outside the United States—and has developed into a major market in a variety of currencies lent outside their domestic markets. London is at the centre of the Euromarket and houses most of the leading international banks and securities firms. Its share of trading in the two main types of international bonds—Eurobonds and foreign bonds—is around 70 per cent. Coredeal, the most recently recognised UK investment exchange, started operations in May 2000 and acts as an exchange for transactions involving such bonds.

Foreign Exchange Market

London is the world's biggest centre for foreign exchange trading, accounting for about 30 per cent of global net daily turnover in foreign exchange. A survey by the Bank of England in 1998 found that daily turnover in the UK was US$637 billion. Dealing is conducted through telephone and electronic links between the banks, other financial institutions and a number of firms of foreign exchange brokers which act as intermediaries. The institutions keep close contact with financial centres abroad and quote buying and selling rates throughout the day for both immediate ('spot') and forward transactions in many currencies. Foreign exchange trading has declined globally following the introduction of the euro in 1999 (see p. 79), but trading in London has declined less than in financial centres in the euro area.

LIFFE

The London International Financial Futures and Options Exchange (LIFFE) handles financial derivatives (including 'futures' and 'options'), which offer a means of protection against changes in prices, exchange rates and interest rates. It also handles trade in commodities, such as coffee, cocoa and sugar. LIFFE has 214 members, including many of the world's leading financial institutions. LIFFE handled 117 million futures and options contracts in 1999, and currently is handling an average of nearly 624,000 contracts a day, with a nominal average value of over £300 billion.

All LIFFE's financial futures and options contracts are now trading on the LIFFE Connect electronic trading system, and the commodity contracts will move to this system in November 2000. In June 2000 LIFFE announced its intention to work with technology and venture capital partners to accelerate the development of its exchange business using the Connect system and to exploit the opportunities available in the rapidly growing e-commerce business-to-business markets.

Other Exchanges

Other important City exchanges include:

- the *London bullion market*—around 60 banks and other financial trading companies participate in the London gold and silver markets;
- the *London Metal Exchange (LME)*—the primary base metals market in the world, trading contracts in aluminium, aluminium alloy, copper, lead, nickel, tin and zinc;
- the *International Petroleum Exchange (IPE)*; and
- the *Baltic Exchange*—the world's leading international shipping market.

Table 30.5: Wholesale and Retail Enterprises in the UK, 2000

Number of enterprises

Annual turnover (£'000)	Wholesale Total	*of which:* Sole proprietors	Partner-ships	Retail Total	*of which:* Sole proprietors	Partner-ships
1–49	18,345	9,095	2,670	20,770	12,435	4,795
50–99	17,215	7,630	2,985	49,690	29,380	14,465
100–249	23,225	7,520	4,430	71,025	31,130	28,465
250–499	15,025	2,875	2,935	33,165	9,990	14,345
500–999	13,045	1,365	2,065	15,815	3,160	5,615
1,000+	26,035	835	1,785	10,330	895	2,085
of which:						
1,000–1,999	*10,290*	*n.a.*	*n.a.*	*6,305*	*n.a.*	*n.a.*
2,000–4,999	*8,535*	*n.a.*	*n.a.*	*2,525*	*n.a.*	*n.a.*
5,000–9,999	*3,500*	*n.a.*	*n.a.*	*695*	*n.a.*	*n.a.*
10,000–49,999	*3,010*	*n.a.*	*n.a.*	*580*	*n.a.*	*n.a.*
50,000+	*700*	*n.a.*	*n.a.*	*225*	*n.a.*	*n.a.*
Total	**112,890**	**29,320**	**16,865**	**200,795**	**86,995**	**69,770**

n.a. = not available.
Turnover relates mainly to a 12-month period ending in spring 1999.
Source: Office for National Statistics. *Size Analysis of UK Businesses 2000*. Business Monitor PA1003

The London Clearing House (LCH) clears and settles business at LIFFE, LME, IPE and Tradepoint.

Other Services

The distribution of goods, including food and drink, to their point of sale is a major economic activity. The large wholesalers and retailers of food and drink operate extensive distribution networks, either directly or through contractors.

WHOLESALING

In 2000 there were almost 113,000 enterprises (see Table 30.5) engaged in wholesaling in the UK; 26 per cent were sole proprietors and 15 per cent partnerships. There were 1,120,000 employee jobs in the UK in this sector in December 1999 and turnover in 1999 amounted to £328 billion, 0.4 per cent lower than in 1998.

In the food and drink trade almost all large retailers have their own buying and central distribution operations. Many small wholesalers and independent grocery retailers belong to voluntary 'symbol' groups, which provide access to central purchasing facilities and co-ordinated promotions. This has helped smaller retailers to remain relatively competitive; many local and convenience stores and village shops would not otherwise be able to stay in business. London's wholesale markets play a significant part in the distribution of fresh foodstuffs. New Covent Garden is the main market for fruit and vegetables, London Central Markets for meat and Billingsgate for fish.

In April 2000 Co-operative Wholesale Society (CWS) and Co-operative Retail Services (CRS) merged, integrating separate food retailing, funerals and motor businesses. The merger has created the UK's largest mutual retail group, with an annual turnover of £4.7 billion, 1,135 stores and more than 50,000 employees.

CWS has been the principal supplier of goods and services to the Co-operative Movement and was a founder member of the Co-operative Retail Trading Group (CRTG). The latter was formed in 1993 to act as a central marketing, buying and distribution partnership for retail co-operative societies.

The CRTG now accounts for around 90 per cent of Co-op food trade. CWS is also the largest co-operative retailer in Europe, with stores located in Scotland, Northern Ireland, Wales, Cumbria, Nottingham, south Midlands and the south-west, south-east and north-east of England. Retail co-operative societies are voluntary organisations controlled by their members, membership being open to anyone paying a small deposit on a minimum share. The Co-operative Movement, which comprises 44 independent societies, has around 2,560 stores.

RETAILING

The retail sector accounts for 40 per cent of all consumer expenditure and employs one in 11 of the workforce. In 2000 there were nearly 201,000 retail enterprises in the UK (see Table 30.5); 43 per cent were sole proprietors and 35 per cent partnerships. In December 1999 there were 2,528,000 employee jobs in the UK in this sector. Total turnover in the retail trade sector (including repair of personal and household goods) in 1998 amounted to £199 billion, over 6 per cent higher than in 1997. Businesses range from national supermarket and other retail chains to independent corner grocery shops, hardware stores, chemists, newsagents and a host of other types of retailer. The large multiple retailers have grown considerably, tending to increase outlet size until relatively recently and to diversify product ranges. Some also operate overseas, through either subsidiaries or franchise agreements. Small independent retail businesses and co-operative societies have been in decline for some time. Sunday trading laws have been relaxed to allow retailers to open for specified periods on Sundays. To help their competitive position, smaller retailers can open for longer hours than the larger supermarkets and department stores, which are restricted to six hours, except in Scotland. Some main supermarket chains are experimenting with 24-hour opening on six days a week.

The volume of retail sales rose by about 25 per cent between 1989 and 1999 (see Table 30.6). Growth in non-food stores (28 per cent) has been slightly higher than predominantly food stores (26 per cent), with the most significant increase in household goods stores, 48 per cent higher than in 1989.

The four biggest supermarket chains by sales value are Tesco (with about 600 stores), J. Sainsbury (400, excluding 12 Savacentre stores), Asda (230, excluding Dales) and Safeway (480, excluding Presto and Wellworths). They accounted for 45 per cent of total grocery sales, worth £96.6 billion in 1999. Asda was taken over by US discount giant Wal-Mart in 1999. Other significant food retailers are Somerfield, Marks & Spencer, Waitrose, Iceland and Morrisons which account for 16 per cent of grocery sales. Alcoholic drinks are sold mainly in specialist 'off licences' and in supermarkets.

The leading mixed retail chains are found in high streets nationwide. Competition with lower-priced outlets and discount chains is squeezing some of the more traditional suppliers selling a range of items. Several chains of DIY (Do-It-Yourself) stores and superstores cater for people carrying out their own repairs and improvements to their homes and gardens; they stock tools, decorating and building materials, kitchen and bathroom

As part of its inquiry into the supply of groceries from multiple stores, the Competition Commission (see p. 397) considered a range of issues including price competition, competition for services and sites, relationships with suppliers and whether local monopolies exist. The results of the inquiry, announced in October 2000, found that the big supermarket chains were broadly competitive and did not charge excessive prices or earn excessive profits. The report cited a number of concerns over a lack of supermarket competition in local areas and below-cost pricing, and highlighted concerns over retailers' relationships with suppliers. It also recommended that those with more than 8 per cent of the £90 billion a year food industry—the top five retailers, Tesco, J. Sainsbury, Asda, Safeway and Somerfield—should be legally required to comply with an industry code of practice.

Table 30.6: Volume of Retail Sales in the UK 1995 =100

	1989	1994	1998	1999
Predominantly food stores	88.0	98.1	108.8	110.8
Predominantly non-food stores				
Non-specialised stores	94.0	99.0	111.5	114.7
Textile, clothing and footwear stores	88.5	97.5	112.0	117.1
Household goods stores	91.3	97.3	125.2	135.2
Other stores	100.9	100.1	109.2	113.2
Total	93.5	98.4	114.3	119.9
Non-store retailing and repair	111.8	106.1	111.6	115.2
All retailing	**92.4**	**98.8**	**111.7**	**115.6**

Source: Office for National Statistics—annual data derived from short-term turnover inquiries

fittings, and garden products. Specialist shops such as those selling mobile telephones have shown substantial growth.

The large multiple groups have broadened their range of goods and services. Large food retailers are also placing greater emphasis on selling own-label groceries (which now account for over half of sales) and environmentally friendly products (including organic produce), together with household wares and clothing. In-store pharmacies, post offices, customer cafeterias and dry-cleaners are now a feature of large supermarkets, which also sell books, magazines, newspapers, pre-recorded videos, cassettes, compact discs and electrical goods. 'Stores within stores' are common; for example, sportswear and sports goods retailers are found in several of the big mixed department stores. The major supermarket chains have their own petrol stations at some of their bigger outlets (see p. 525). Several large retailers offer personal finance facilities in an attempt to encourage sales, particularly of high-value goods, while others have diversified into financial services. Some supermarkets now offer banking facilities (see also p. 512). 'Loyalty' cards were introduced in the mid-1990s by supermarket and other retail groups, giving regular customers cash discounts related to the size of their purchases and providing the stores with detailed information on shoppers' buying habits.

A survey by NatWest and the British Franchise Association (BFA) in March 2000 estimated that there were 642 fully-fledged business-format franchises, with around 35,000 outlets, accounting for 316,000 direct jobs in Britain and with annual turnover of £8.9 billion. Franchising is a business in which a company owning the rights to a particular form of trading licenses them to franchisees, usually by means of an initial payment with continuing royalties. Franchised activities operate in many areas, including cleaning services, film processing, print shops, fitness centres, courier delivery, car rental, engine tuning and servicing, and fast food retailing. About 300 franchisers are members of the BFA.

Vehicle, Vehicle Parts and Petrol Retailing

In December 1999 there were 551,000 employee jobs in the UK in retailing motor vehicles and parts, and in petrol stations. Turnover in the motor trades industry in 1999 amounted to almost £123 billion, 1 per cent higher than in 1998 (see Table 30.7).

Most businesses selling new vehicles are franchised by the motor manufacturers. Vehicle components are available for sale at garages which undertake servicing and repair work and also at retail chains and at independent retailers. Drive-in fitting centres sell tyres, exhaust systems, batteries, clutches and other vehicle parts. According to the Retail Motor Industry Federation, there were 12,850 retail outlets for petrol at the end of 1999, with the top three companies accounting for about one-third of the total. The number of petrol stations has declined by about 35 per cent between 1989 and 1999, reflecting intense competition in the sector, relatively low profit margins and consolidation among operators. This is particularly so in rural areas. Petrol stations have increasingly offered other retail services, such as shops, car washes and fast food outlets, with the aim of attracting more business. Over one-quarter of petrol sold in the UK comes from the 1,050 supermarket forecourts operated at the end of 1999.

Shopping Facilities

Government policy is to focus new retail development in existing centres. This is to ensure that everyone has easy access to a range of shops and services, whether they have a car or not; and to enable businesses of all sizes and types to prosper. Many smaller and middle-range retailers traditionally concentrated in high streets have experienced high costs, with a result that many have closed down. The Government aims to revitalise town centres by focusing new shopping, leisure and other facilities in these centres. One of the most significant trends in retailing has been the spread of superstores, many of which were built away from urban centres until recently. Since 1996, social, economic and environmental considerations have led the Government and local planning authorities to limit new retail developments outside town centres, as these had undermined the vitality and viability of existing town and district centres, were not always readily accessible by those without a car and encouraged greater car use.

All new retail development requires planning permission from the local planning authority, which must consult central government before granting permission for most retail developments of 2,500 sq m (27,000 sq ft) or more. Retailers' attentions are now being turned back to town centres, redeveloping existing stores and building smaller outlets. Almost 50 new small (1,000 sq m) stores have been opened by two of the major supermarket chains so far and up to 50 smaller (300 sq m) stores are planned over the next two years.

Regional out-of-town shopping centres, of which there are eight, are located on sites offering good road access and ample parking facilities. The latest is the Bluewater shopping centre near Dartford, Kent, which opened in 1999. It is the largest out-of-town retail development in Europe, covering 160,000 sq m (1.7 million sq ft), and has created some 7,000 jobs. It has 320 shops and parking for 13,000 cars, and attracted 28 million shoppers in its first year of opening. It is likely to be the last such out-of-town centre. The other out-of-town regional shopping centres are: the Metro Centre at Gateshead in Tyne and Wear; Meadowhall near Sheffield; Trafford Centre in Manchester; Merry Hill at Dudley in the West Midlands; Cribbs Causeway at Bristol; Lakeside at Thurrock in Essex, and Braehead, near Glasgow. About half of total food sales are accounted for by superstores away from town centres, compared with a fifth at the beginning of the 1980s.

Retailers of non-food goods, such as DIY products, toys, furniture and electrical appliances, sportswear, and office and computer products, have also built outlets away from urban centres. There was a trend in the 1990s towards grouping retail warehouses

Table 30.7: Turnover in the Motor Trades Industry

	1998	1999	% change
Sale of motor vehicles	87,030	86,319	–0.8
Maintenance and repair of motor vehicles	8,946	8,749	–2.2
Sale of motor vehicle parts and accessories	10,182	11,424	12.2
Sale, maintenance and repair of motorcycles and related parts and accessories	1,621	1,629	0.5
Retail sale of automotive fuel	14,182	14,829	4.6
Total	**121,961**	**122,948**	**0.8**

Source: Office for National Statistics—annual data derived from short-term turnover inquiries

into retail parks, often with food and other facilities, although planning controls now limit approvals for new retail warehouse parks.

Computers monitor stock levels and record sales figures through electronic point-of-sale (EPOS) systems by means of product bar codes. Techniques such as 'just-in-time' ordering, in which products arrive at the store at the last possible moment before sale, have become widespread as a result. Electronic data interchange (EDI) systems enable retailers' and suppliers' computers to communicate and transmit orders and invoices electronically, so reducing errors and saving time. 'Superscan' technology—where customers use an electronic scanning device to calculate their own bills—is undergoing trials in a number of supermarkets.

Home Shopping

Traditionally, all kinds of goods and services have been, and can still be, purchased through mail order catalogues. In 1998 sales by direct and agency mail order totalled £8.15 billion. The largest-selling items are clothing, footwear, furniture, household textiles and domestic electrical appliances. More recently introduced have been electronic home shopping, using a television and telephone, and 'online' shopping, where personal computers are linked to databases—this 'e-commerce' is growing rapidly. Supermarkets are looking closely at different forms of home shopping (by telephone, fax and Internet) and delivery.

CONSUMER PROTECTION

The Government aims to maintain and develop a clear and fair regulatory framework that gives confidence to consumers and contributes to the competitiveness of business. It works closely with outside bodies that have expert knowledge of consumer issues to develop policies and legislation. In July 1999, the Government issued a White Paper, *Modern Markets: Confident Consumers*, setting out a range of initiatives to improve protection for consumers. The main proposals include: a hallmark for consumers identifying companies signed up to a code of practice and a digital hallmark for Internet traders abiding by codes guaranteeing security of payment and privacy of information; increased powers to deal with dishonest traders; new advice networks, including a consumer 'gateway' on the Internet; new measures to ensure information is accurate, comprehensive and easy to understand; a review of consumer protection legislation; and a review by the Director General of Fair Trading of his consumer protection functions.

Consumer Legislation

The Sale of Goods Act 1979 (as amended in 1994) ensures that consumers are entitled to receive goods which fit their description and are of satisfactory quality. The Trade Descriptions Act 1968 prohibits misdescriptions of goods and services, and enables regulations to be made requiring information or instructions relating to goods to be marked on, or to accompany, the goods or to be included in advertisements.

Misleading indications about prices of goods are covered by the Consumer Protection Act 1987. This Act also makes it a criminal offence to supply unsafe products, and provides product liability rights for consumers. The regulatory framework to control product safety is a mixture of European and UK legislation, voluntary safety standards and industry codes of practice. The Department of Trade and Industry (DTI) runs a programme of safety awareness initiatives. This aims to reduce accidents by increasing consumer awareness of potential hazards in the home and by encouraging consumers to change their behaviour.[1]

The marking and accuracy of quantities are regulated by weights and measures legislation. Another law provides for the control of medical products, and certain other substances and articles, through a system of licences and certificates. New regulations have been introduced to strengthen the protection of consumers from unscrupulous doorstep sellers.

---

[1] DTI's Home Accident Surveillance System shows that, every year, there are just under 4,000 deaths and nearly 3 million medically treated injuries as a result of home accidents.

The Director General of Fair Trading promotes good trading practices and acts against malpractice. Under the Fair Trading Act 1973, the Director General can recommend legislative or other changes to stop practices adversely affecting consumers' economic interests; encourage trade associations to develop codes of practice promoting consumers' interests; and disseminate consumer information and guidance. The Director General can also demand assurances as to future conduct from traders who persistently breach the law to the detriment of consumers.

The Consumer Credit Act 1974 is intended to protect consumers in their dealings with credit businesses. Most businesses connected with the consumer credit or hire industry or which supply ancillary credit services—for example, credit brokers, debt collectors, debt counsellors and credit reference agencies—require a consumer credit licence. The Director General is responsible for administering the licensing system, including refusing or revoking licences of those unfit to hold them. The Director General also has powers to prohibit unfit people from carrying out estate agency work; to take court action to prevent the publication of misleading advertisements; and to stop traders using unfair terms in standard contracts with consumers.

The EU's consumer programme covers activities such as health and safety, protection of the consumer's economic interests, promotion of consumer education and strengthening the representation of consumers. The views of British consumer organisations on EU matters are represented by a number of organisations including the National Consumers Council and the Consumers in Europe Group (UK).

Consumer Advice and Information

Citizens Advice Bureaux deal with over 60 million problems a year, providing advice on a wide range of subjects at around 770 bureaux in the UK. Their work is co-ordinated by a national association linked to the bureaux by local and regional committees (Scotland has its own Association). Similar assistance is provided by trading standards and consumer protection departments of local authorities in Great Britain and, in some areas, by specialist consumer advice centres.

The National Consumer Council (and associated councils for Scotland and Wales), which receives government finance, gives its view to government, industry and others on consumer issues. The General Consumer Council for Northern Ireland has wide-ranging duties in consumer affairs in general.

Consumer bodies for privatised utilities investigate questions of concern to the consumer. Some trade associations have set up codes of practice. In addition, several organisations work to further consumer interests by representing the consumer's view to government, industry and other bodies. The largest is the Consumers' Association, funded by the subscriptions of approximately 1 million members to its various *Which?* magazines.

HOTELS, RESTAURANTS AND CATERING

The hotel and restaurant trades, which include public houses (pubs), wine bars and other licensed bars in addition to all kinds of businesses offering accommodation and prepared food, had 1,371,000 employee jobs in the UK in December 1999. Total turnover in 1999 amounted to £51 billion, 7 per cent higher than in 1998. There are estimated to be over 60,000 hotels and guest houses in the UK, ranging from major hotel groups to small guest houses, individually owned. Holiday centres, including holiday camps with full board, self-catering centres and caravan parks, are run by several companies.

In 1999 there were around 44,420 restaurants, cafés and take-away food shops in the UK, with a total turnover of £15 billion, 10 per cent higher than in 1998. An analysis of the UK restaurant market—including fast food outlets and takeaways as well as eat-in restaurants and cafés—showed sales of £14.17 billion in 1999, 5.3 per cent higher than in 1998. Excluding sales not generated in sit-down eating outlets, such as sandwich shops, the total market was estimated at £10.15 billion in 1999. Burger restaurants accounted for 16.1 per cent of the total, public house restaurants 12.7 per cent, pizza and pasta restaurants 7.4 per cent, roadside restaurants 5.6 per cent, and other restaurants—ranging from small cafés and bars, and ethnic food outlets, through to expensive restaurants, as well as many chicken outlets and some fish and chip outlets—58.2 per cent.

Restaurants offer cuisine from virtually every country in the world, and several of the highest-quality ones have international reputations. Chinese, Indian, Thai, Italian, French and Greek restaurants are very popular. 'Fast food' restaurants are widespread, many of which are franchised. They specialise in selling hamburgers, chicken, pizza and a variety of other foods, to be eaten on the premises or taken away. Traditional fish and chip shops are another main provider of cooked take-away food. Sandwich bars are common in towns and cities, typically in areas with high concentrations of office workers.

There were an estimated 50,500 pubs in the UK in 2000, a decline of over 6 per cent since 1990. They account for 58 per cent of all fully-licensed premises, compared with 65 per cent in 1990. Estimated sales in 1999 were £13.75 billion, averaging £270,000 per pub. Pubs sell alcoholic drinks (beer, wines and spirits) to adults for consumption on the premises, with non-alcoholic (soft) drinks and hot and cold food a growing part of their trade. Many pubs are owned by the large brewing companies which either provide managers to run them or offer tenancy agreements; these pubs tend to sell just their own brands of beer, although some also offer 'guest' beers. Others, called 'free houses', are independently owned and managed, and frequently serve a variety of different branded beers. Wine bars are normally smaller than pubs and tend to specialise in wine and food. 'Themed' pubs, for example Irish bars, are becoming increasingly popular.

TRAVEL AGENTS

Most British holidaymakers travelling overseas buy 'package holidays' from travel agencies, where the cost covers both transport and accommodation. Popular package holiday destinations include Spain and France. Long-haul holidays to places like North America, the Caribbean, Australia and New Zealand have gained in popularity as air fares have come down. Some people prefer to travel more independently, and there are travel firms that will make just travel arrangements for customers.

Around 85 per cent of high street travel agencies are members of the Association of British Travel Agents (ABTA). Although most are small businesses, a few large firms have hundreds of branches. Nearly 830 tour operators are members of ABTA; about half are both retail agents and tour operators. In 1999 turnover in the travel agency and tour operator businesses amounted to £16 billion, 3 per cent higher than in 1998. ABTA operates financial protection schemes to safeguard its members' customers and maintains codes of conduct drawn up with the Office of Fair Trading. It also offers a free consumer affairs service to help resolve complaints against members, and a low-cost independent arbitration scheme for members' customers. The British Incoming Tour Operators' Association is the leading body representing tour operators engaged in incoming tourism to the UK.

TOURISM AND LEISURE

Tourism is one of the UK's key long-term growth sectors, with total spending in 1999 estimated at £64 billion. In Great Britain there were around 1.8 million jobs in tourism and related activities in 1999; of these, around 155,000 are self-employed. About 126,000 businesses, mainly independent small ones—hotels and guest houses, restaurants, holiday homes, caravan and camping parks and so on—are responsible for providing the bulk of tourism services; about 8 per cent of small businesses are engaged in tourism.

The number of overseas visitors to the UK fell slightly by 1 per cent in 1999 to reach an estimated 25.4 million, spending £12.5 billion. The UK's share of world tourism earnings reached 4.5 per cent. The number of visitors from Western Europe fell by 3 per cent to 16.1 million but there were increases of 1 per cent

Table 30.8: Top UK Tourist Attractions Charging Admission

Million

	1998	1999
Alton Towers, Staffordshire	2.78	2.65
Madame Tussaud's, London	2.77	2.64
Tower of London	2.55	2.42
Natural History Museum, London	1.90	1.74
Legoland, Windsor	1.51	1.62
Chessington World of Adventures, Surrey	1.65	1.55
Science Museum, London	1.60	1.48
Royal Academy, London	0.91	1.39
Canterbury Cathedral	1.50	1.35
Windsor Castle, Berkshire	1.50	1.28
Westminster Abbey, London	n.a.	1.27
Edinburgh Castle	1.22	1.22
Flamingo Land Theme Park, North Yorkshire	1.11	1.20
Drayton Manor Park, Staffordshire	1.00	1.17
Windermere Lake Cruises, Cumbria	1.06	1.14

n.a. = not available on a comparable basis.
Source: British Tourist Authority

in the number from North America, at 4.6 million, and 4 per cent in the number from other areas, at 4.7 million. The highest proportion from a single country was the United States (15 per cent). Business travel accounts for about £4.0 billion, 31 per cent of all overseas tourism revenue. London's Heathrow and Gatwick airports, the seaport of Dover and the Channel Tunnel are the main points of entry.

Some 54 per cent of overseas tourists spend all or most of their visit in London, while others venture further afield to see the many attractions in the English regions as well as to Scotland, Wales and Northern Ireland.

Domestic tourism generated approximately £48.2 billion in 1999. Of British residents opting to take their main holiday in the UK, 23 per cent choose a traditional seaside destination, such as Blackpool (Lancashire), Bournemouth (Dorset), Great Yarmouth (Norfolk) and resorts in Devon and Cornwall. Short holiday breaks (up to three nights), valued at £3.5 billion in 1999, make up an increasing part of the market.

The UK's historic towns and cities and its scenic rural and coastal areas continue to have great appeal for British and overseas tourists alike. There is a growing interest in heritage, arts and culture; attractions include museums, art galleries, historic buildings and monuments, and theatres, as well as shopping, sports and business facilities. Domestic and foreign tourists play an increasingly important role in supporting the UK's national heritage and creative arts, in addition to the large financial contribution they make to hotels, restaurants, cafés and bars, and public transport.

Business travel, which accounts for a growing share of the tourism market, includes attendance at conferences, exhibitions, trade fairs and other business sites. Activity holidays—based on walking, canoeing, mountain climbing, or artistic activities, for example—are becoming more popular. The Youth Hostel Association operates a comprehensive network of hostels offering young people and families a range of facilities, including self-catering.

'Leisure parks' attract over 35 million visitors a year. Alton Towers (Staffordshire) was the biggest in terms of visitor numbers in 1999 (see Table 30.8). Attractions in these parks include spectacular 'white knuckle' rides and overhead cable cars and railways, while some parks also feature domesticated and wild animals. The Millennium Dome in Greenwich, London, which opened in January 2000, attracted some 3.7 million visitors in its first six months. The largest tourist attraction with free admission is Blackpool Pleasure Beach in Lancashire (see also Table 30.9).

Tourism Promotion

The Department for Culture, Media and Sport is responsible for tourism in England, and the Scottish Parliament, Welsh Assembly and Northern Ireland Assembly have

Table 30.9: Top UK Free Tourist Attractions, 1999 *Million*

	Million
Blackpool Pleasure Beach	7.2[1]
British Museum, London	5.5
National Gallery, London	5.0
Palace Pier, Brighton	3.7[1]
Segaworld, The Trocadero, London	3.5
Eastbourne Pier	2.8[1]
Pleasureland, Southport	2.5[1]
Peter Pan's Adventure Island, Southend	2.0[1]
Tate Gallery, London	1.8
York Minster	1.8[1]
Pleasure Beach, Great Yarmouth	1.5[1]
Hampton Court Gardens, London	1.2[1]
Kelvingrove Art Gallery and Museum, Glasgow	1.1
Chester Cathedral	1.0[1]
National Portrait Galley, London	1.0

[1] Estimated visitor numbers.
Source: British Tourist Authority

responsibility for tourism in their respective countries. The government-supported British Tourist Authority (BTA)—which is receiving an estimated £37 million in grant in 2000–01—boosts tourism spending in Britain by focusing its marketing resources on 27 key markets worldwide (which in total generate 89 per cent of all visitors to Britain) and encourages the development of tourist facilities in the UK to meet the needs of overseas visitors. The tourist bodies for England, Scotland, Wales and Northern Ireland, which also receive government finance, support domestic tourism and work with the BTA to promote Britain overseas. In 1999 the English Tourism Council (ETC) replaced the English Tourist Board. The ETC is responsible for developing and promoting a sustainable and competitive industry in England, and in July 2000 additional funding of £4.5 million over two years was announced.

The Government is working with the tourism industry to raise standards of accommodation and service, and to address certain key issues facing the industry. These include improving visitor attractions; boosting business tourism; encouraging best practice for the development of workforce skills; and government-industry communication. The Government is also considering how best to support tourism growth which is economically, socially and environmentally sustainable. The BTA and the national tourist boards inform and advise the Government on issues of concern to the industry. They also help businesses and other organisations to plan by researching and publicising trends affecting the industry. The national tourist boards work closely with regional tourist boards, on which local government and business interests are represented. There are about 560 local Tourist Information Centres in England. The national tourist boards, in conjunction with motoring organisations, operate accommodation classification and quality grading schemes.

EXHIBITION AND CONFERENCE CENTRES

The UK is one of the world's three leading countries for international conferences—along with the United States and France. London and Paris are the two most popular conference cities. Other British towns and cities—including several traditional seaside holiday resorts diversifying to take advantage of the growing business tourism market—have conference and exhibition facilities.

Among the most modern purpose-built centres are the National Exhibition and International Conference Centres in Birmingham; the Queen Elizabeth II and Olympia Conference Centres, both in London; Cardiff International Arena; and the Belfast Waterfront Hall. In Scotland, Edinburgh, Glasgow and Aberdeen have major exhibition and conference centres. Brighton (East Sussex), Harrogate (North Yorkshire), Bournemouth (Dorset), Manchester, Nottingham and Torquay (Devon) all have exhibition and conference centres. Other important exhibition facilities in London are at the Barbican, Earls Court, Alexandra Palace and Wembley Arena. A new exhibition and conference centre, Excel, will open in London Docklands in autumn 2000.

RENTAL SERVICES

A varied range of rental services, many franchised, are available throughout the UK. These include hire of cars and other vehicles; televisions, video recorders and camcorders; household appliances such as washing machines; tools and heavy decorating equipment (such as ladders and floor sanders); and video films and computer games. Retailing of many types of service is dominated by chains, although independent operators are still to be found in most fields. In addition, there is a thriving sector renting to businesses—all sorts of machinery and other types of equipment, together with computers and other office appliances. In December 1999 there were 158,000 employee jobs in the UK in the rental sector. Turnover in 1999 amounted to £16 billion, 12 per cent higher than in 1998.

COMPUTING SERVICES

The computing services industry comprises businesses engaged in software development; systems integration; IT consultancy; IT 'outsourcing'; processing services; and the provision of complete computer systems. It also includes companies that provide IT education and training; independent maintenance; support, contingency planning and recruitment; and contract staff. In December 1999 there were 448,000 employee jobs in the UK in computer and related activities. Turnover of companies in this sector amounted to £36 billion in 1999, 20 per cent higher than in 1998. British firms and universities have established strong reputations in software R&D. A number of international IT conglomerates have set up R&D operations in the UK. US software company Computer Associates is building a new £100 million European headquarters at Datchet, near Heathrow Airport, and Microsoft has made a major R&D investment at Cambridge. Academic expertise is especially evident in such areas as artificial intelligence, neural networks, formal programming for safety critical systems, and parallel programming systems.

Software firms have developed strengths in sector-specific applications, including systems for retailing, banking, finance and accounting, the medical and dental industries, and the travel and entertainment industries. Specialist 'niche' markets in which UK software producers are active include artificial intelligence, scientific and engineering software (especially computer-aided design), mathematical software, geographical information systems, and data visualisation packages. Some firms specialise in devising multimedia software. Distance learning, 'virtual reality' and computer animation all benefit from a large pool of creative talent.

One of the biggest users of software is the telecommunications industry. The provision of almost all new telecommunications services, including switching and transmission, is dependent on software.

OTHER BUSINESS ACTIVITIES

In December 1999 a total of 188,000 employee jobs in Great Britain were in market research, business and management consultancy activities.

Market Research

The UK's market research profession has grown strongly in the last five years and there are now over 800 companies, with a total UK revenue of over £1 billion a year. UK-owned market research companies include the largest international customised market research specialists.

Management Consultancy

The UK's 37,000 management consultants supply techncal assistance and advice to business and government clients. The 36 members of the Management Consultancies Association account for more than half of management consultancy work carried out in the UK. In 1999 member firms earned £2.5 billion in the UK and £6 billion abroad.

Advertising and Public Relations

The UK is a major centre for creative advertising, and multinational corporations

Table 30.10: Top Ten Advertisers in the UK in 1999

Advertiser	Total expenditure (£ million)
Procter and Gamble	165.4
COI—Central Office of Information	92.5
Renault UK	84.5
BT—British Telecom	84.4
Vauxhall	83.9
L'Oréal Golden	67.1
Mars	63.7
Ford	57.3
Kellogg's (GB)	53.1
Van den Bergh	52.7

Source: *Advertising Statistics Yearbook 2000*—ACNeilsen-MMS

often use advertising created in the UK for marketing their products globally. British agencies have strong foreign links through overseas ownership and associate networks. Advertising turnover in the UK increased by 14 per cent to £18 billion in 1999. The press accounted for 52 per cent of the total, television for 28 per cent, direct mail for 12 per cent, and posters, transport, commercial radio and cinema for the rest. The largest advertising expenditure is on food, household durables, cosmetics, office equipment, motor vehicles and financial services. The top ten spenders in 1999 are shown in Table 30.10. British television advertising receives many international awards.

Campaigns are planned by around 1,100 advertising agencies. In addition to their creative, production and media-buying roles, some agencies offer integrated marketing services, including consumer research and public relations. Many agencies have sponsorship departments, which arrange for businesses to sponsor products and events, including artistic, sporting and charitable events. Government advertising campaigns—on crime prevention, health promotion, armed services recruitment and so on—are often organised by the Central Office of Information, an executive agency of the Government.

The UK's public relations industry has developed rapidly, and there are now many small specialist firms as well as some quite large ones. About 11 per cent of the earnings of UK public relations firms represents overseas work.

Business Support Services

One of the major growth areas in the services sector is in support services, reflecting the trend among more and more firms to 'outsource' non-core operations. Initially, operating areas that were outsourced or contracted out were in cleaning, security and catering. However, firms are now outsourcing other activities, such as IT and personnel support services. A study for the DTI in 1996 found that the annual turnover of business support services in the UK was around £10 billion, and the sector employed 675,000 people.

Further Reading

Competition in UK Banking: A Report to the Chancellor of the Exchequer. HM Treasury. The Stationery Office, 2000.

Modern Markets: Confident Consumers. Cm 4410. The Stationery Office, 1999.

Bank of England Annual Report.

Financial Services Authority Annual Report.

London Stock Exchange *Fact File* (annual).

Websites

Bank of England: www.bankofengland.co.uk

Financial Services Authority: www.fsa.gov.uk

Appendix 1: Government Departments and Agencies

An outline of the principal functions of the main government departments and a list of their executive agencies is given below. Departments headed by Cabinet ministers are indicated by an asterisk. Executive agencies are normally listed under the relevant department, although in some cases they are included within the description of the department's responsibilities.

The principal address, telephone, fax number and website of each department are given.

More detailed information, including e-mail addresses and the addresses of executive agencies and the Government Offices for the Regions, can be found in the annual *Civil Service Year Book*. The websites of many departments and agencies can be accessed via the website www.open.gov.uk. UK online—a new single point of entry to government information and services using the Internet—is being developed. The website address is: www.ukonline.gov.uk.

The work of many of the departments and agencies covers the United Kingdom as a whole and is indicated by (UK). Where this is not the case, the abbreviations used are (GB) for functions covering England, Wales and Scotland; (E, W & NI) for those covering England, Wales and Northern Ireland; (E & W) for those covering England and Wales; and (E) for those concerned with England only.

*Cabinet Office

70 Whitehall, London SW1A 2AS
Tel: 020 7270 3000 Fax: 020 7270 0618
Website: www.cabinet-office.gov.uk
The responsibilities of the Cabinet Office are described on p. 55.

Executive Agency

Government Car and Despatch Agency

*Prime Minister's Office

10 Downing Street, London SW1A 2AA
Tel: 020 7930 4433
Website: www.number-10.gov.uk
See p. 54 for further information.

UK TERRITORIAL DEPARTMENTS

*Northern Ireland Office

Castle Buildings, Stormont, Belfast BT4 3ST
Tel: 028 9052 0700 Fax: 028 9052 8473
Website: www.nics.gov.uk
11 Millbank, London SW1P 4QE
Tel: 020 7210 3000 Fax: 020 7210 8254
Website: www.nio.gov.uk
The Secretary of State for Northern Ireland is the Cabinet minister responsible for Northern Ireland. Through the Northern Ireland Office, the Secretary of State has direct responsibility for political and constitutional matters, law and order, security, and electoral matters.

Executive Agencies

Compensation Agency
Forensic Science Agency of Northern Ireland
Northern Ireland Prison Service

*Scotland Office

Dover House, Whitehall, London SW1A 2AU
Tel: 020 7270 3000 Fax: 020 7270 6812
Represents Scottish interests within the UK Government.

*Wales Office (Office of the Secretary of State for Wales)

Gwydyr House, Whitehall, London SW1A 2ER
Tel: 020 7270 0534 Fax: 020 7270 0561
The Secretary of State for Wales is the member of the UK Cabinet who takes the lead in matters connected with the Government of Wales Act. The

Secretary of State is responsible for consulting the Assembly on the Government's legislative programme.

ECONOMIC AFFAIRS

*Ministry of Agriculture, Fisheries and Food

Nobel House, 17 Smith Square, London SW1P 3JR Tel: 020 7238 3000 Fax: 020 7238 6591
Website: www.maff.gov.uk
Policies on agriculture, horticulture and fisheries; responsibilities for related environmental and rural issues (E); food policies (UK).

Executive Agencies

Central Science Laboratory
Centre for Environment, Fisheries and Aquaculture Science
Farming and Rural Conservation Agency
Intervention Board[1]
Pesticides Safety Directorate
Veterinary Laboratories Agency
Veterinary Medicines Directorate

*Department of Trade and Industry

1 Victoria Street, London SW1H 0ET
Tel: 020 7215 5000 Fax: 020 7222 0612
Website: www.dti.gov.uk
Competitiveness; enterprise, innovation and productivity; science, engineering and technology; markets; the legal and regulatory framework for business and consumers. Specific responsibilities include innovation policy; regional industrial policy (E); small business (E); spread of management best practice; business/education links (E); employment relations; international trade policy; energy policy; company law; insolvency; radio regulation; patents and copyright protection (GB); relations with specific business sectors (UK).

Executive Agencies

Companies House
Employment Tribunals Service
Insolvency Service
National Weights and Measures Laboratory
Patent Office
Radiocommunications Agency
Small Business Service

British Trade International (whose main responsibilities are inward investment and promotion of British business abroad) is a body jointly funded by DTI and the Foreign & Commonwealth Office.

*HM Treasury

Parliament Street, London SW1P 3AG
Tel: 020 7270 5000 Fax: 020 7270 5653
Website: www.hm-treasury.gov.uk
Oversight of the framework for monetary policy; tax policy; planning and control of public spending; government accounting; the quality of public services; international financial relations; the regime for supervision of financial services, management of central government debt and supply of notes and coins (UK).

HM Customs and Excise

New King's Beam House, 22 Upper Ground, London SE1 9PJ Tel: 020 7620 1313
Website: www.hmce.gov.uk
A department reporting to the Chancellor of the Exchequer. Responsible for collecting and accounting for Customs and Excise revenues, including VAT (value added tax); agency functions, including controlling certain imports and exports, policing prohibited goods, and compiling trade statistics (UK).

ECGD (Export Credits Guarantee Department)

PO Box 2200, 2 Exchange Tower, Harbour Exchange Square, London E14 9GS
Tel: 020 7512 7000 Fax: 020 7512 7649
Website: www.ecgd.gov.uk
A department reporting to the Secretary of State for Trade and Industry. Access to bank finance and provision of insurance for UK project and capital goods exporters against the risk of not being paid for goods and services; political risk insurance cover for UK investment overseas (UK).

Office of Fair Trading

Fleetbank House, 2–6 Salisbury Square, London EC4Y 8JX Tel: 020 7211 8000 Fax: 020 7211 8800
Website: www.oft.gov.uk
A non-ministerial department, headed by the Director General of Fair Trading. Administers a

[1] The Intervention Board is a department in its own right as well as an executive agency. Responsibility for it is shared jointly by the four agriculture ministers in the UK.

wide range of competition and consumer protection legislation, with the overall aim of protecting the economic welfare of consumers and enforcing UK competition policy (UK).

Regional Co-ordination Unit

Regional Co-ordination Unit (Operations)

2nd Floor, Riverwalk House, 157–161 Millbank, London SW1P 4RR Tel: 020 7217 3595
Fax: 020 7217 3590
Website: www.detr.gov.uk
Resources, personnel policy, planning and administration for the nine Government Offices for the Regions (see pp. 10–11) (E).

Inland Revenue

Somerset House, Strand, London WC2R 1LB
Tel: 020 7438 6622 Fax: 020 7438 6971
Website: www.inlandrevenue.gov.uk
A department, reporting to the Chancellor of the Exchequer, responsible for the administration and collection of direct taxes; valuation of property (GB).

Executive Agencies

National Insurance Contributions Office
Valuation Office

National Savings

Charles House, 375 Kensington High Street, London W14 8SD Tel: 020 7605 9300
Fax: 020 7605 9438
Website: www.nationalsavings.co.uk
A department in its own right and an executive agency, reporting to the Chancellor of the Exchequer. Aims to raise funds for the Government by selling a range of investments to personal savers (UK).

Royal Mint

Llantrisant, Pontyclun CF72 8YT
Tel: 01443 222111 Fax: 01443 623190
Website: www.royalmint.com
The Royal Mint is responsible for the production of coin for the United Kingdom and for overseas customers. It also produces military and civil decorations and medals, commemorative medals, royal and official seals.

LEGAL AFFAIRS

*Lord Chancellor's Department

Selborne House, 54–60 Victoria Street, London SW1E 6QW Tel: 020 7210 8500
Website: www.open.gov.uk/lcd
Responsibility for procedure of the civil courts and for the administration of the Supreme Court and county courts and a number of tribunals under the Court Service; overseeing the locally administered magistrates' courts and the Official Solicitor's Department; work relating to judicial appointments; overall responsibility for the Community Legal Service and criminal legal aid and for the promotion of general reforms in the civil law (E & W). Sponsor department for the Children and Family Court Advisory and Support Service (CAFCASS). The Lord Chancellor also has responsibility for the Northern Ireland Court Service.

Executive Agencies

Court Service
Public Trust Office[2]

Two further agencies—HM Land Registry and the Public Record Office—report to the Lord Chancellor but are departments in their own right and not part of the Lord Chancellor's Department (see p. 539).

Legal Secretariat to the Law Officers

Attorney-General's Chambers, 9 Buckingham Gate, London SW1E 6JP Tel: 020 7271 2400
Fax: 020 7271 2430
Website: www.lslo.gov.uk
Supporting the Law Officers of the Crown (Attorney-General and Solicitor-General) in their functions as the Government's principal legal advisers (E, W & NI).

Treasury Solicitor's Department

Queen Anne's Chambers, 28 Broadway, London SW1H 9JS Tel: 020 7210 3000
Fax: 020 7210 3004
Website: www.open.gov.uk/tsd
A department in its own right and an executive agency reporting to the Attorney-General. Provides legal services to most government departments,

[2] Will cease to exist as a separate executive agency from 1 April 2001.

agencies, and public and quasi-public bodies. Services include litigation; giving general advice on interpreting and applying the law; instructing Parliamentary Counsel (part of the Cabinet Office) on Bills and drafting subordinate legislation; and providing conveyancing services and property-related legal work (E & W).

Crown Prosecution Service

50 Ludgate Hill, London EC4M 7EX
Tel: 020 7976 8000 Fax: 020 7976 8651
Website: www.cps.gov.uk
Responsible for deciding independently whether criminal proceedings begun by the police should be continued, and for prosecuting those cases it decides to continue (E & W). The CPS is headed by the Director of Public Prosecutions, who is accountable to Parliament through the Attorney-General.

Serious Fraud Office

Elm House, 10–16 Elm Street, London WC1X 0BJ
Tel: 020 7239 7272 Fax: 020 7837 1689
Website: www.sfo.gov.uk
Investigating and prosecuting serious and complex fraud. The Director of the SFO is accountable to Parliament through the Attorney-General (E, W & NI).

The Crown Office and Procurator Fiscal Service (see p. 542)

EXTERNAL AFFAIRS AND DEFENCE

***Ministry of Defence**

Main Building, Horseguards Avenue, London SW1A 2HB Tel: 020 7218 9000
Fax: 020 7218 6460
Website: www.mod.uk
Defence policy and control and administration of the Armed Services (UK).

Defence Agencies

Armed Forces Personnel Administration Agency
Army Base Repair Organisation
Army Personnel Centre
Army Technical Support Agency
Army Training and Recruiting Agency
British Forces Post Office
Defence Analytical Services Agency
Defence Aviation Repair Agency
Defence Bills Agency
Defence Clothing and Textiles Agency
Defence Communication Services Agency
Defence Dental Agency
Defence Estates
Defence Evaluation and Research Agency
Defence Geographic and Imagery Intelligence Agency
Defence Housing Executive
Defence Intelligence and Security Centre
Defence Medical Training Organisation
Defence Procurement Agency
Defence Secondary Care Agency
Defence Storage and Distribution Agency
Defence Transport and Movements Agency
Defence Vetting Agency
Disposal Sales Agency
Duke of York's Royal Military School
Hydrographic Office
Joint Air Reconnaissance Intelligence Centre
Logistic Information Systems Agency
Medical Supply Agency
Meteorological Office
Ministry of Defence Police
Naval Bases and Supply Agency[3]
Naval Manning Agency
Naval Recruiting and Training Agency
Pay and Personnel Agency
Queen Victoria School
RAF Logistics Support Services
RAF Personnel Management Agency
RAF Signals Engineering Establishment
RAF Training Group Defence Agency
Service Children's Education
Ships Support Agency[3]

***Foreign & Commonwealth Office**

King Charles Street, London SW1A 2AH
Tel: 020 7270 3000
Website: www.fco.gov.uk
Conduct of the UK's overseas relations, including advising on policy, negotiating with overseas governments and conducting business in international organisations; promoting British exports and investment into the UK; presenting British ideas and policies to the people of overseas countries; administering the remaining Overseas Territories; and protecting British interests abroad, including the welfare of British citizens (UK).

[3] Planned to merge in April 2001 to form the Warship Support Agency.

Executive Agency

Wiston House Conference Centre (Wilton Park)

***Department for International Development**

94 Victoria Street, London SW1E 5JL
Tel: 020 7917 7000 Fax: 020 7917 0019
Website: www.dfid.gov.uk
Responsibility for promoting international development and the reduction of extreme poverty globally; managing the UK's programme of assistance to poorer countries and for ensuring that government policies which affect developing countries, including the environment, trade, investment and agricultural policies, take account of developing countries' issues.

SOCIAL AFFAIRS, THE ENVIRONMENT AND CULTURE

***Department for Culture, Media and Sport**

2–4 Cockspur Street, London SW1Y 5DH
Tel: 020 7211 6200 Fax: 020 7211 6032
Website: www.culture.gov.uk
For national museums and galleries, tourism and sport the Department has UK-wide responsibility. The devolved administrations have delegated responsibilities for these in their parts of the UK. Areas in which the Department has an overall interest are: the arts; public libraries; museums and galleries; tourism; sport; the built heritage (E); broadcasting; press regulation; film industry; cultural property; music industry; the National Lottery (UK).

Executive Agencies

Historic Royal Palaces
Royal Parks

***Department for Education and Employment**

Sanctuary Buildings, Great Smith Street, London SW1P 3BT Tel: 020 7925 5000
Fax: 020 7925 6000
Website: www.dfee.gov.uk
Overall responsibility for school, college and university education (E); student support (E & W); the Careers Service (E); Employment Service (GB); youth and adult training policy and programmes (E); sponsorship of Training and Enterprise Councils (E); European social policies and programmes and equal opportunities issues in employment (GB).

Executive Agency

Employment Service

***Department of the Environment, Transport and the Regions**

Eland House, Bressenden Place, London SW1E 5DU Tel: 020 7944 3000 Fax: 020 7944 6589
Website: www.detr.gov.uk
Policies for environmental protection; planning; housing; construction; regeneration; the countryside; local and regional government; roads; local transport (E); aviation (UK); shipping (E); railways (GB) and the Civil Aviation Authority (UK). Also responsible for sponsoring 33 executive non-departmental public bodies, including the Environment Agency (E & W), the Countryside Agency (E), and the Health and Safety Executive and Commission (GB).

Executive Agencies

Driver and Vehicle Licensing Agency
Driving Standards Agency
Highways Agency
Maritime and Coastguard Agency
Planning Inspectorate
Queen Elizabeth II Conference Centre
Rent Service
Vehicle Certification Agency
Vehicle Inspectorate

***Department of Health**

Richmond House, 79 Whitehall, London SW1A 2NS Tel: 020 7210 3000 Fax: 020 7210 5661
Website: www.doh.gov.uk
National Health Service; personal social services provided by local authorities; and all other health issues, including public health matters and the health consequences of environmental and food issues (E). Represents UK health policy interests in the EU and the World Health Organisation.

Executive Agencies

Food Standards Agency
Medical Devices Agency
Medicines Control Agency
NHS Estates
NHS Pensions Agency

***Home Office**

50 Queen Anne's Gate, London SW1H 9AT
Tel: 020 7273 4000 Fax: 020 7273 2190

Website: www.homeoffice.gov.uk
Administration of justice; criminal law; treatment of offenders, including probation and the prison service; the police; crime prevention; fire service and emergency planning; licensing laws; regulation of firearms and dangerous drugs; the voluntary sector; electoral matters; and local legislation (E & W). Gaming (GB). Passports, immigration and nationality; race relations; royal matters (UK). Responsibilities relating to the Channel Islands and the Isle of Man.

Executive Agencies

Fire Service College
Forensic Science Service
HM Prison Service
United Kingdom Passport Agency

*Department of Social Security

Richmond House, 79 Whitehall, London SW1A 2NS Tel: 020 7238 0800 Fax: 020 7238 0831
Website: www.dss.gov.uk
The social security system (GB).

Executive Agencies

Benefits Agency
Child Support Agency
War Pensions Agency

REGULATORY BODIES

Financial Services Authority

25 The North Colonnade, Canary Wharf, London E14 5HS Tel: 020 7676 1000 Fax: 020 7676 1099
Website: www.fsa.gov.uk
New regulatory body for the whole of the financial services industry (see pp. 509–11) (UK).

National Lottery Commission

Ashley House, 2 Monck Street, London SW1P 2BQ Tel: 020 7227 2000 Fax: 020 7227 2005
Website: www.natlotcomm.gov.uk
Responsible for the grant, variation and enforcement of licences to run the National Lottery; protecting players' interests; ensuring propriety and that net proceeds for good causes are as great as possible.

Office of Gas and Electricity Markets (Ofgem)

9 Millbank, London SW1P 3GE
Tel: 020 7901 7000 Fax: 020 7901 7066
Website: www.ofgem.gov.uk
Ofgem is the office of the gas and electricity regulator. It works to bring choice and value to all customers by promoting competition and regulating monopolies.

Shadow Strategic Rail Authority (SSRA)

55 Victoria Street, London SW1H 0EU
Tel: 020 7654 6000 Fax: 020 7654 6010
Website: www.sra.gov.uk
See p. 367.

Office of the Rail Regulator (ORR)

1 Waterhouse Square, 138–142 Holborn, London EC1N 2TQ Tel: 020 7282 2000 Fax: 020 7282 2040
Website: www.rail-reg.gov.uk
See p. 367.

Office for Standards in Education (OFSTED)

Alexandra House, 33 Kingsway, London WC2B 6SE Tel: 020 7421 6800 Fax: 020 7421 6707
Website: www.ofsted.gov.uk
Responsible for arranging the regular inspection of schools, nursery education providers, teacher training colleges and local education authority central services, and for making such reports public. From September 2001 OFSTED will also be responsible for the registration, regulation and inspection of childminders and the inspection of all educational provision for 16–19 year olds. Providing advice to government and those in education (E).

Office of Telecommunications (OFTEL)

50 Ludgate Hill, London EC4M 7JJ
Tel: 020 7634 8700 Fax: 020 7634 8943
Website: www.oftel.gov.uk
Protecting the interests of customers; promoting competition in fixed and mobile telephony markets; ensuring that telephone and cable companies meet their licence obligations; and regulating access to digital television services (UK).

Office of Water Services (OFWAT)

Centre City Tower, 7 Hill Street, Birmingham B5 4UA Tel: 0121 625 1300 Fax: 0121 625 1400
Website: www.open.gov.uk/ofwat

Monitors the activities of companies appointed as water and sewerage undertakers; regulates prices, promotes economy and efficiency, protects customers' interests and facilitates competition (E & W).

OTHER OFFICES AND AGENCIES

Central Office of Information

Hercules Road, London SE1 7DU
Tel: 020 7928 2345 Fax: 020 7928 5037
Website: www.coi.gov.uk
A department in its own right and an executive agency reporting to the Minister for the Cabinet Office. Main responsibilities are procuring publicity material and other information services on behalf of government departments, agencies and other public sector clients (UK).

Office of the Data Protection Commissioner

Wycliffe House, Water Lane, Wilmslow, Cheshire SK9 5AF Tel: 01625 545745 Fax: 01625 524510
Website: www.dataprotection.gov.uk
The Data Protection Act 1998 sets rules for processing personal information and applies to some paper records as well as those held on computers. It is the Commissioner's duty to compile and maintain the register of data controllers and provide facilities for members of the public to examine the register; promote observance of the data protection principles; and disseminate information to the public about the Act. The Commissioner also has the power to produce codes of practice.

HM Land Registry

Lincoln's Inn Fields, London WC2A 3PH
Tel: 020 7917 8888 Fax: 020 7955 0110
Website: www.landreg.gov.uk
An executive agency responsible to the Lord Chancellor. Main purpose is to register title to land in England and Wales, and to record dealings once the land is registered. It grants guaranteed title to interests in land for 17 million registered titles, providing a system for the transfer and mortgage of land and access to up-to-date and authoritative information (E & W).

Office for National Statistics

1 Drummond Gate, London SW1V 2QQ
Tel: 020 7533 5888 Fax: 01633 652747
Website: www.statistics.gov.uk
An executive agency accountable to the Chancellor of the Exchequer. Collects, compiles and provides a range of statistical information and population estimates and projections, and carries out research on behalf of government departments concerned with social and economic issues. Also responsible for the administration of the marriage laws and local registration of births, marriages and deaths; and taking the ten-yearly Census of Population (E & W).

Ordnance Survey

Romsey Road, Southampton SO16 4GU
Tel: 023 80 792000 Fax: 023 80 792452
Website: www.ordnancesurvey.co.uk
An executive agency, which reports to the Secretary of State for the Environment, Transport and the Regions, providing official surveying, mapping and associated scientific work covering Great Britain and some overseas countries (GB).

Public Record Office

Ruskin Avenue, Kew, Richmond, Surrey TW9 4DU Tel: 020 8876 3444
Fax: 020 8878 8905
Website:www.pro.gov.uk
The National Archives: a department in its own right and an executive agency reporting to the Lord Chancellor. Responsible for the records of the central government and courts of law dating from the 11th century. Advises government departments on the selection of records for preservation and makes records available to the public (UK).

NORTHERN IRELAND EXECUTIVE

Office of the First Minister and Deputy First Minister

Castle Buildings, Stormont Estate, Belfast BT4 3SR Tel: 028 9052 8400
Economic policy; equality; liaison with the North/South Ministerial Council, British-Irish Council, British-Irish Intergovernmental Conference; Civic Forum and the Secretary of State for Northern Ireland; European affairs; international matters; liaison with the International Fund for Ireland; the Information Service; community relations; public appointments policy; honours; freedom of information; victims; Nolan standards; women's issues; policy innovation; public service improvement.

Department of Agriculture and Rural Development

Dundonald House, Upper Newtownards Road, Belfast BT4 3SB Tel: 028 9052 0100

Food; farming and environment policy; agri-food development; veterinary matters; Science Service; rural development; forestry; sea fisheries; rivers.

Executive Agencies

Forest Service and Agency
Rivers Agency

Department of Enterprise, Trade and Investment

Netherleigh House, Massey Avenue, Belfast BT4 2JP Tel: 028 9052 9900
Economic development policy; industry; research and development, tourism; Health and Safety Executive; Employment Medical Advisory Service; company regulation; consumer affairs; energy policy; Minerals and Petroleum Unit; NICO; company training grants schemes, Company Development Programme and Explorers.

Executive Agencies

Industrial Research and Technology Unit

Department of Education

Rathgael House, Balloo Road, Bangor, County Down BT19 7PR Tel: 028 9127 9279
Control of the five education and library boards and education from nursery to secondary education; youth services; and the development of community relations within and between schools.

Department of the Environment

Clarence Court, 10–18 Adelaide Street, Belfast BT2 8GB Tel: 028 9054 0540
Most of the Department's functions are carried out by executive agencies. These include: planning; protection and conservation of the natural and built environment; and driver and vehicle testing and licensing. Core departmental functions include: the improvement and promotion of road safety and supporting a system of local government which meets the needs of citizens and taxpayers.

Executive Agencies

Driver and Vehicle Licensing (Northern Ireland)
Driver and Vehicle Testing Agency
Environment and Heritage Service
Planning Service

Department of Finance and Personnel

Rathgael House, Balloo Road, Bangor, County Down BT19 7NA Tel: 028 9127 9657
Control of public expenditure; personnel management of the Northern Ireland Civil Service; provision of central services and advice.

Executive Agencies

Business Development Service
Construction Service
Government Purchasing Agency
Land Registers of Northern Ireland
Northern Ireland Statistics and Research Agency
Rates Collection Agency
Valuation and Lands Agency

Department of Health, Social Services and Public Safety

Castle Buildings, Stormont, Belfast BT4 3SJ
Tel: 028 9052 0500
Health and personal social services; public health and public safety.

Executive Agencies

Health Estates Agency
Health Promotion Agency

Department of Higher and Further Education, Training and Employment

39–49 Adelaide House, Adelaide Street, Belfast BT2 8FD Tel: 028 9025 7777
Higher education; further education; vocational training; employment services; employment law and labour relations; teacher training and teacher education; student support and postgraduate awards; training grants.

Executive Agency

Training and Employment Agency

Department for Regional Development

Clarence Court, 10–18 Adelaide Street, Belfast BT2 8GB Tel: 028 9054 0540
Main functions include: strategic planning; transport strategy; transport policy and support including rail and bus services, ports and airports

policy; provision and maintenance of roads; and the provision and maintenance of water and sewerage services.

Executive Agencies

Roads Service
Water Service

Department for Social Development

Churchill House, Victoria Square, Belfast
BT1 4SD Tel: 028 9056 9100 Fax: 028 9056 9240
Departmental functions include: urban regeneration; voluntary and community sector; housing; social policy and legislation; social security; child support; state, occupational and personal pensions; policy and legislation.

Executive Agencies:

Northern Ireland Child Support Agency
Northern Ireland Social Security Agency

SCOTTISH EXECUTIVE

The Scottish Executive

St Andrew's House, Edinburgh EH1 3DG
Tel: 0131 556 8400 Fax: 0131 244 8240
(for all departments)
Website: www.scotland.gov.uk
The Scottish ministers and Scottish Executive are responsible in Scotland for a wide range of statutory functions. These are administered by six main departments: the Scottish Executive Rural Affairs Department, the Scottish Executive Education Department, the Scottish Executive Enterprise and Lifelong Learning Department, the Scottish Executive Development Department, the Scottish Executive Justice Department and the Scottish Executive Health Department. These departments (plus Corporate Services, Finance Group and Executive Secretariat) are collectively known as the Scottish Executive. In addition, there are a number of other Scottish departments for which the Scottish ministers have some degree of responsibility; the department of the Registrar General for Scotland (the General Register Office), the National Archives of Scotland and the department of the Registers of Scotland. Other government departments with significant Scottish responsibilities have offices in Scotland and work closely with the Scottish Executive.

Scottish Executive Rural Affairs Department

Pentland House, 47 Robbs Loan, Edinburgh
EH14 1TY
The promotion and regulation of agriculture: safeguarding public food, plant and animal health and welfare; land use and forestry; livestock subsidies and commodities. Co-ordination of the Executive's policy on the promotion of rural development and overall responsibility for land reform. Environment, including environmental protection, nature conservation and the countryside; water and sewerage services; sustainable development. Promotion and the regulation of fisheries and aquaculture; protection of the marine environment; research on, and monitoring of, fish stocks; enforcement of fisheries laws and regulations. Funding of the agricultural and biological science base.

Executive Agencies

Scottish Agricultural Science Agency
Scottish Fisheries Protection Agency
Scottish Fisheries Research Services

Scottish Executive Development Department

Victoria Quay, Edinburgh EH6 6QQ
Housing and area regeneration, social inclusion, local government organisation and finance; transport and local roads, National Roads Directorate, co-ordination of Scottish Executive European structural funds; land-use planning; building control.

Scottish Executive Education Department

Victoria Quay, Edinburgh EH6 6QQ
Administration of public education; science and technology; youth and community services; the arts; libraries; museums; galleries; Gaelic; broadcasting; and sport. Protection and presentation to the public of historic buildings and ancient monuments.

Executive Agencies

Historic Scotland
Scottish Public Pensions Agency
The Student Awards Agency for Scotland

Scottish Executive Enterprise and Lifelong Learning Department

Meridian Court, Cadogan Street, Glasgow G2 7AB and Europa Building, 450 Argyle Street, Glasgow G2 8LG

Industrial and economic development: responsibility for selective financial and regional development grant assistance to industry; for the promotion of industrial development and for matters relating to energy policy; urban regeneration; and training policy. The Department is also responsible for policy in relation to Scottish Enterprise, Highlands and Islands Enterprise and the Scottish Tourist Board.
Lifelong learning: further and higher education; sponsorship of the Scottish Further Education Funding Council and the Scottish Higher Education Funding Council; student support; youth and adult training; transitions to work; development of the Scottish University for Industry (learndirect scotland) and individual learning accounts; science.

Scottish Executive Health Department

St Andrew's House, Regent Road, Edinburgh EH1 3DG
National Health Service; Chief Scientist's Office; and public health.

Scottish Executive Justice Department

Saughton House, Broomhouse Drive, Edinburgh EH11 3XD
Central administration of law and order (including police service, criminal justice and licensing, legal aid and the Scottish Prison Service); civil law, fire, home defence and civil emergency services.

Executive Agency

Scottish Prison Service

The Crown Office and Procurator Fiscal Service

25 Chambers Street, Edinburgh EH1 1LA
Tel: 0131 226 2626 Fax: 0131 226 6910
Website: www.crownoffice.gov.uk
The Crown Office and Procurator Fiscal Service provides Scotland's independent public prosecution and deaths investigation service. It is a Department of the Scottish Executive and is headed by the Lord Advocate.

Corporate Services

Corporate services to the six Executive Departments. Directorate of Administrative Service, Finance and Personnel Groups.

Executive Secretariat

Matters relating to powers and functions of the Scottish Parliament and Executive; constitutional policy, Scottish Parliament elections; Information Directorate and the Office of the Solicitor to the First Minister.

NATIONAL ASSEMBLY FOR WALES

National Assembly for Wales (Cynulliad Cenedlaethol Cymru)

Cathays Park, Cardiff CF10 3NQ and Cardiff Bay, Cardiff CF99 1NA
Tel: 029 2082 5111 Fax: 029 2082 3807
Website: www.wales.gov.uk neu (yn Gymraeg) www.cymru.gov.uk
The National Assembly for Wales (see p. 28) is responsible for many aspects of Welsh affairs, including agriculture, forestry and fisheries; education; health and personal social services; local government; Welsh language and culture, including the arts, museums and libraries. Also responsible for housing; water and sewerage; environmental protection; the countryside and nature conservation; sport; land use, including town and country planning; transport issues; tourism; training and enterprise; economic development, business support and regional selective assistance to industry. The Assembly is also responsible for over 50 public bodies which discharge functions in these areas in Wales.

Executive Agencies

Cadw: Welsh Historic Monuments
Welsh European Funding Office

Appendix 2: Obituaries

Marquess of Abergavenny, KG, OBE
(John Henry Guy Nevill; 5th marquess)
Chancellor of the Order of the Garter and former Lord Lieutenant of East Sussex (1974–89)
Born 1914, died February 2000

Janet Adam Smith, OBE
Literary editor, author, mountaineer
Born 1905, died September 1999

Major Derek Allhusen, CVO
Olympic gold medallist (equitation) and former president of British Horse Society
Born 1914, died April 2000

Marjorie Anderson
Broadcaster
Born 1913, died December 1999

John Aspinall
Zoo owner and casino proprietor
Born 1926, died June 2000

Edith Atkins
Cyclist
Born 1920, died August 1999

Vera Atkins, CBE
Security officer in SOE during Second World War, reputed inspirer of James Bond's Miss Moneypenny
Born 1908, died June 2000

Kenny Baker
Jazz trumpeter and bandleader
Born 1921, died December 1999

Ian Bannen
Actor
Born 1928, died November 1999

Dame Josephine Barnes, DBE
Obstetrician and gynaecologist
Born 1912, died December 1999

Kevin Barry, OBE
Engineer, prominent in North Sea oil and gas industry
Born 1930, died September 1999

Philip Bate
Authority on wind instruments, broadcaster and scholar
Born 1909, died November 1999

Patricia Beer
Poet
Born 1919, died August 1999

Frank Berni
Restaurateur
Born 1903, died July 2000

Professor Charles Boxer, FBA
Historian
Born 1904, died April 2000

June Brae
Ballerina
Born 1917, died January 2000

Lord Braine of Wheatley (Bernard)
Former Conservative MP and Father of the House of Commons, 1987–92
Born 1914, died January 2000

Sir Nigel Broakes
Chairman of Trafalgar House, 1969–92, and property tycoon
Born 1934, died September 1999

Vice-Admiral Sir Ronald Brockman, KCB, CSI, CIE, CVO, CBE
Secretary to Earl Mountbatten of Burma, 1943–59
Born 1909, died September 1999

Dominic Bruce
Former prisoner in Colditz, who escaped 17 times from the Germans
Born 1915, died February 2000

Lord Butterfield, OBE (William John Hughes)
Medical researcher and former Master of Downing College, Cambridge, 1978–87
Born 1920, died July 2000

Dame Barbara Cartland, DBE
Romantic novelist
Born 1901, died May 2000

Sir Hugh Casson, CH, KCVO
Architect
Born 1910, died August 1999

Lord Charteris of Amisfield, GCB, GCVO, OBE, QSO (NZ), PC (Martin)
Private Secretary to the Queen, 1972–77; formerly Provost of Eton
Born 1913, died December 1999

Rt Hon Alan Clark, MP
Conservative MP for Plymouth Sutton, 1974–92 and Kensington and Chelsea, 1997–99, former Minister of State for Defence, 1989–92
Born 1928, died September 1999

Prunella Clough
Painter
Born 1919, died December 1999

Most Reverend and Rt Hon Lord Coggan (Donald)
Archbishop of Canterbury, 1974–80
Born 1909, died May 2000

Michael Colvin, MP
Conservative MP, 1979–2000
Born 1932, died February 2000

Alex Comfort
Physician and writer
Born 1920, died March 2000

Jill Craigie
Film director and writer
Born 1914, died December 1999

Charles Crichton
Film director
Born 1910, died September 1999

Sir Francis Dashwood
11th baronet—premier baronet of Great Britain
Born 1925, died March 2000

Donald Davies, CBE, FRS
Computer pioneer
Born 1924, died May 2000

Sir Robin Day
TV journalist
Born 1923, died August 2000

Rt Hon Edmund Dell
Secretary of State for Trade, 1976–78; Labour MP for Birkenhead, 1964–79
Born 1921, died November 1999

André Deutsch, CBE
Publisher
Born 1917, died April 2000

Paddy Devlin, CBE
Northern Ireland politician, and co-founder of SDLP
Born 1925, died August 1999

Robert Dougall, MBE
Radio and TV newsreader
Born 1913, died December 1999

Joey Dunlop
Motorcyclist
Born 1952, died July 2000

Frankie Durr
Jockey
Born 1925, died January 2000

Ian Dury
Singer, songwriter and actor
Born 1942, died March 2000

Professor John Emery
Paediatric pathologist and researcher into cot deaths
Born 1915, died May 2000

Andrew Faulds
Actor and former Labour MP
Born 1923, died May 2000

Penelope Fitzgerald
Novelist
Born 1916, died April 2000

Meriel Forbes (Lady [Ralph] Richardson)
Actress
Born 1913, died April 2000

Clifford Forsythe
Ulster Unionist MP, 1983–2000
Born 1929, died April 2000

Eileen Fowler, MBE
Keep-fit instructor
Born 1906, died March 2000

Sir John Gielgud, OM, CH
Actor
Born 1904, died May 2000

Sir William Glock, CBE
Controller of Music, BBC, 1959–72
Born 1908, died June 2000

Bernie Grant, MP
Labour MP for Tottenham, 1987–2000
Born 1944, died April 2000

Charles Gray
Actor
Born 1928, died February 2000

Sir Alec Guinness
Actor
Born 1914, died August 2000

Deryck Guyler
Actor
Born 1914, died October 1999

Greta Gynt (Margrethe Woxholt)
Actress
Born 1916, died April 2000

Sir John Hale, FBA
Historian
Born 1923, died August 1999

Kathleen Hale, OBE
Artist and writer (*Orlando the Marmalade Cat*)
Born 1898, died January 2000

Sir Arnold Hall, FRS
Former chairman of the Hawker Siddeley group
Born 1915, died January 2000

William Hamilton
Former Labour MP for West Fife, 1950–74; Fife Central, 1974–87
Born 1917, died January 2000

William Donald Hamilton, FRS
Biologist
Born 1936, died March 2000

Doris Hare, MBE
Actress
Born 1905, died May 2000

Ruth Harrison, OBE
Animal welfare campaigner
Born 1920, died June 2000

Sir Rupert Hart-Davis
Publisher
Born 1907, died December 1999

Francis Haskell, FBA
Art historian
Born 1928, died January 2000

Lionel Haworth, OBE, FRS
Aero-engine designer
Born 1912, died April 2000

Alastair Hetherington
Editor of *The Guardian*, 1956–75
Born 1919, died October 1999

Terence Hodgkinson, CBE
Art historian and curator
Born 1913, died October 1999

Lord Jakobovits (Immanuel)
Chief Rabbi, 1967–91
Born 1921, died October 1999

Clive Jenkins
Trade union leader, former general secretary of ASTMS
Born 1926, died September 1999

Noel Johnson
Actor, BBC radio's first Dick Barton
Born 1916, died October 1999

Sir Emrys Jones
Agricultural adviser and Principal of the Royal Agricultural College, 1973–78
Born 1915, died June 2000

Peter Jones
Actor and comedian
Born 1920, died April 2000

Mary Kerridge
Actress
Born 1914, died July 1999

Dorothy Laird
Royal biographer and racing journalist
Born 1912, died January 2000

Viscount Leverhulme, KG, TD (Philip William Bryce Lever; 3rd viscount)
Racehorse owner; Lord Lieutenant of Cheshire, 1949–90
Born 1915, died July 2000

Peter Levi
Professor of Poetry, University of Oxford, 1984–2000 and former Jesuit
Born 1931, died February 2000

Desmond Llewellyn
Actor
Born 1914, died December 1999

Cliff Lloyd, OBE
Secretary of the Professional Footballers' Association, 1953–81
Born 1916, died January 2000

Ernest Lough
Former boy chorister
Born 1911, died February 2000

James MacGibbon
Publisher
Born 1912, died February 2000

Lord MacLehose of Beoch, KT, GBE, KCMG, KCVO (Crawford Murray)
Governor of Hong Kong, 1971–82
Born 1917, died May 2000

Wilf Mannion
Footballer
Born 1918, died April 2000

Sir Eric Mansforth
Aeronautical engineer
Born 1905, died February 2000

Colin Matthew
Professor of History, University of Oxford; editor of *New Dictionary of National Biography*
Born 1941, died October 1999

Sir Stanley Matthews, CBE
Footballer
Born 1915, died February 2000

Sir Harry Melville, KCB, FRS
Chemist and former principal of Queen Mary College, University of London
Born 1908, died June 2000

Jean Metcalfe
Broadcaster
Born 1923, died January 2000

Penelope Mortimer
Novelist and biographer
Born 1918, died October 1999

Don Mosey
Cricket journalist and broadcaster
Born 1924, died August 1999

Dame Anne Mueller, DCB
Highest-ranking woman civil servant—at Cabinet Office and Treasury, 1984–90
Born 1930, died July 2000

Eva Neurath
Publisher
Born 1908, died January 2000

Patrick O'Brian
Novelist
Born 1914, died January 2000

Robert Parry
Labour MP for Liverpool constituencies, 1970–74, 1983–2000
Born 1933, died March 2000

Jennifer Paterson
Cook, one-half of the TV 'Two Fat Ladies'
Born 1928, died August 1999

Charles Pick
Publisher
Born 1917, died January 2000

Thea Porter
Fashion designer
Born 1927, died July 2000

Sir Anthony Powell, CH, CBE
Novelist
Born 1905, died March 2000

Alan Pryce-Jones
Man of letters
Born 1908, died January 2000

Sir Leon Radzinowicz
Criminologist
Born 1906, died January 2000

Sir Patrick Reilly, GCMG, OBE
British ambassador to Moscow, 1957–60; to Paris, 1965–68
Born 1909, died October 1999

Helen Rollason
TV sports presenter
Born 1956, died August 1999

Most Reverend and Rt Hon Lord Runcie, MC (Robert Alexander Kennedy)
Archbishop of Canterbury, 1980–91
Born 1921, died July 2000

Sir Robert Sainsbury
Former chairman of J. Sainsbury and arts benefactor
Born 1906, died April 2000

Lionel Salter
Musical writer, performer and critic
Born 1914, died March 2000

Lady Sayer (Sylvia)
Conservationist, defender of Dartmoor
Born 1904, died January 2000

Hardiman Scott
Former political editor of the BBC
Born 1920, died September 1999

Robin Scott
Launched BBC Radio 1 and Radio 2 in 1967
Born 1920, died February 2000

Air Vice-Marshal David Scott-Malden DSO, DFC
Wartime fighter ace and classical scholar
Born 1919, died March 2000

Fr Brocard Sewell, ODC
Carmelite friar and writer
Born 1912, died April 2000

Sir Giles Shaw
Conservative MP for Pudsey, 1974–97
Born 1931, died April 2000

John Skelton, MBE
Sculptor
Born 1923, died November 1999

David Spanier
Journalist and author
Born 1932, died August 2000

David Stafford-Clark
Psychiatrist
Born 1916, died September 1999

Brian Statham, CBE
Lancashire and England cricketer
Born 1930, died June 2000

E. W. Swanton
Cricket writer and commentator
Born 1907, died January 2000

Nora Swinburne
Actress
Born 1902, died May 2000

John W. R. Taylor, OBE
Editor *Jane's All the World's Aircraft*, 1959–89
Born 1922, died December 1999

Sir Adam Thomson, CBE
Aviation entrepreneur, founder and chairman of British Caledonian, 1976–88
Born 1926, died May 2000

Professor Hugh Tinker
Historian and former Director of the Institute of Race Relations, 1970–72
Born 1921, died April 2000

David Tomlinson
Actor
Born 1917, died June 2000

Carl Toms
Theatrical designer
Born 1927, died August 1999

David Treharne
Nurseryman
Born 1908, died April 2000

Meriol Trevor
Novelist and biographer
Born 1919, died January 2000

Frankie Vaughan, CBE
Entertainer
Born 1928, died September 1999

Very Rev. Derrick Walters, OBE
Dean of Liverpool, 1983–99
Born 1932, died April 2000

John Wells
Artist—one of the first of the St Ives Group
Born 1907, died July 2000

Rt Rev. William Westwood
Bishop of Peterborough, 1984–95
Born 1925, died September 1999

Baroness White (Eirene)
Former Labour MP and Foreign Office and Welsh Office minister
Born 1909, died December 1999

Elsie Widdowson, CH, CBE, FRS
Nutritionist
Born 1906, died June 2000

Sir John Wilson, CBE
Campaigner for the blind
Born 1919, died November 1999

Philip Windsor
International relations specialist
Born 1935, died June 2000

Charles Wintour, CBE
Editor of London *Evening Standard*, 1959–76
Born 1917, died November 1999

Alexander Young
Tenor
Born 1920, died March 2000

Lena Zavaroni
Entertainer
Born 1964, died October 1999

Appendix 3: Principal Abbreviations

ACAS: Advisory, Conciliation and Arbitration Service

ACE: Arts Council of England

ACW: Arts Council of Wales

AIDS: Acquired Immune Deficiency Syndrome

AMAs: Advanced Modern Apprenticeships

AONB: Area of Outstanding Natural Beauty

ASA: Advertising Standards Authority

ASEM: Asia-Europe Meeting

ASSI: Area of Special Scientific Interest

ATMs: Automated teller machines

BA: Benefits Agency

BAFTA: British Academy of Film and Television Arts

BBC: British Broadcasting Corporation

BBSRC: Biotechnology and Biological Sciences Research Council

bfi: British Film Institute

BL: British Library

BNFL: British Nuclear Fuels

BSC: Broadcasting Standards Commission

BSE: Bovine spongiform encephalopathy

BT: British Telecom

CAA: Civil Aviation Authority

CAF: Charities Aid Foundation

CAP: Common Agricultural Policy

CBI: Confederation of British Industry

CCGT: Combined cycle gas turbine

CCLRC: Council for the Central Laboratory of the Research Councils

CCW: Countryside Council for Wales

CFCs: Chlorofluorocarbons

CFP: Common Fisheries Policy

CFSP: Common Foreign and Security Policy

CHP: Combined heat and power

CITES: Convention on International Trade in Endangered Species

CJD: Creutzfeldt-Jakob disease

CO_2: Carbon dioxide

CPS: Crown Prosecution Service

CRE: Commission for Racial Equality

CSA: Child Support Agency

DCMS: Department for Culture, Media and Sport

DARD: Department of Agriculture and Rural Development (Northern Ireland)

DERA: Defence Evaluation and Research Agency

DETI: Department of Enterprise, Trade and Investment (Northern Ireland)

DETR: Department of the Environment, Transport and the Regions

DfEE: Department for Education and Employment

DFID: Department for International Development

DH: Department of Health

DHFETE: Department of Higher and Further Education, Training and Employment (Northern Ireland)

DNA: Deoxyribonucleic acid

DOE: Department of the Environment (Northern Ireland)

DPP: Director of Public Prosecutions

DRD: Department for Regional Development (Northern Ireland)

DSD: Department for Social Development (Northern Ireland)

DSS: Department of Social Security

DTI: Department of Trade and Industry

EAGGF: European Agricultural Guidance and Guarantee Fund

EAZ: Education Action Zone

EC: European Community

ECGD: Export Credits Guarantee Department

EEA: European Economic Area

EMU: Economic and monetary union

ENO: English National Opera

EOC: Equal Opportunities Commission

EP: English Partnerships

EPSRC: Engineering and Physical Sciences Research Council

ERDF: European Regional Development Fund

ESA: Environmentally Sensitive Area; European Space Agency

ESRC: Economic and Social Research Council

EU: European Union

FA: Football Association

FC: Film Council

FCO: Foreign & Commonwealth Office

FHE: Further and higher education

FMAs: Foundation Modern Apprenticeships

FSA: Financial Services Authority; Food Standards Agency

G7: Group of seven leading industrial countries

G8: Group of eight leading industrial countries (the G7 members plus Russia)

GCE: General Certificate of Education

GCSE: General Certificate of Secondary Education

GDP: Gross domestic product

GLA: Greater London Authority

GM: Genetically modified

GMOs: Genetically modified organisms

GNP: Gross national product

GNVQ: General National Vocational Qualification

GOs/GORs: Government Offices (for the Regions)

GP: General Practitioner

HSC: Health and Safety Commission

HSE: Health and Safety Executive

ICT: Information and communications technology

IEA: International Energy Agency

ILA: Individual learning account

ILO: International Labour Organisation

IMF: International Monetary Fund

IPC: Integrated pollution control

ISA: Individual savings account

ISP: Internet service provider

ISO: International Organisation for Standardisation

IT: Information technology

ITC: Independent Television Commission

JNCC: Joint Nature Conservation Committee

JSA: Jobseeker's Allowance

km/h: Kilometres per hour

kW: Kilowatt

LEA: Local education authority

LEC: Local enterprise company

LFA: Less favoured area

LFS: Labour Force Survey

LPG: Liquefied petroleum gas

m (mm, km): Metre (millimetre, kilometre)

MAFF: Ministry of Agriculture, Fisheries and Food

MEP: Member of the European Parliament

Ml: Megalitre

MoD: Ministry of Defence

MP: Member of Parliament

mph: Miles per hour

MRC: Medical Research Council

MSP: Member of the Scottish Parliament

mtc: Million tonnes of carbon

MW: Megawatt

NAfW: National Assembly for Wales

NATO: North Atlantic Treaty Organisation

NDPBs: Non-departmental public bodies

NERC: Natural Environment Research Council

NETA: New electricity trading arrangements

NFFO: Non-fossil fuel obligation

NGC: National Grid (Company)

NGLs: Natural gas liquids

NHS: National Health Service

NI: Northern Ireland; National Insurance

NIE: Northern Ireland Electricity

NOx: Oxides of nitrogen

NTOs: National Training Organisations

nvCJD: new variant Creutzfeldt-Jakob disease (now more commonly known as vCJD)

NVQ: National Vocational Qualification

OECD: Organisation for Economic Co-operation and Development

OFSTED: Office for Standards in Education

OFTEL: Office of Telecommunications

ONS: Office for National Statistics

OSCE: Organisation for Security and Co-operation in Europe

OST: Office of Science and Technology

PEP: Personal Equity Plan

PFI: Private Finance Initiative

plc: Public limited company

PM_{10}: Particulate matter

PPARC: Particle Physics and Astronomy Research Council

R&D: Research and development

RABs: Regional Arts Boards

RAF: Royal Air Force

RDAs: Regional development agencies

RECs: Regional electricity companies

RNT: Royal National Theatre

RPG: Regional Planning Guidance

RPI: Retail Prices Index

RPI(X): Retail Prices Index (*ex*cluding mortgage interest payments)

RSC: Royal Shakespeare Company

RSL: Registered social landlord

RSPB: Royal Society for the Protection of Birds

RUC: Royal Ulster Constabulary

SAC: Scottish Arts Council

SAT: Standardised assessment task

SE: Scottish Executive

SEN: Special educational needs

SEPA: Scottish Environment Protection Agency

SERAD: Scottish Executive Rural Affairs Department

SERPS: State earnings-related pension scheme

SET: Science, engineering and technology

SIP: Social inclusion partnership

SMEs: Small and medium-sized enterprises

SNH: Scottish Natural Heritage

SO_2: Sulphur dioxide

sq km: Square kilometre

SRA: Strategic Rail Authority

SRB: Single Regeneration Budget

SRM: Specified risk material

SSRA: Shadow Strategic Rail Authority

SSSI: Site of Special Scientific Interest

SVQ: Scottish Vocational Qualification

TA: Territorial Army

TAC: Total allowable catch

TEC: Training and Enterprise Council

TUC: Trades Union Congress

UDP: Unitary development plan

UfI: University for Industry

UK: United Kingdom of Great Britain and Northern Ireland

UKCS: United Kingdom Continental Shelf

UKSI: United Kingdom Sports Institute

UN: United Nations

US: United States

VAT: Value added tax

V&A: Victoria and Albert Museum

VED: Vehicle excise duty

WDA: Welsh Development Agency

WEU: Western European Union

WNO: Welsh National Opera

WTO: World Trade Organisation

Appendix 4: Public Holidays, 2001

Monday 1 January	New Year Holiday	UK
Tuesday 2 January	Public holiday	Scotland only[1]
Monday 19 March	St Patrick's Day	Northern Ireland only
Friday 13 April	Good Friday	UK
Monday 16 April	Easter Monday	UK[2]
Monday 7 May	May Day Bank Holiday	UK
Monday 28 May	Spring Bank Holiday	UK
Thursday 12 July	Orangemen's Day	Northern Ireland only
Monday 6 August	Public holiday	Scotland only[1]
Monday 27 August	Summer Bank Holiday	UK[2]
Tuesday 25 December	Christmas Day	UK
Wednesday 26 December	Boxing Day	UK

[1] Subject to regional and institutional variations.
[2] Subject to regional and institutional variations in Scotland.

Appendix 5: Calendar of Main Arts Events in the UK, 2001

January: London International Mime Festival.

January: London Book Fair.

January: Celtic Connections, in Glasgow.

February–March: Bath Literary Festival.

February–May: Royal Shakespeare Company (RSC) London season, at the Barbican.

March: Bradford Film Festival.

March: London Handel Festival.

March–October: RSC Summer Festival, at Stratford-upon-Avon.

April and September: Chelsea Antiques Fair, in London.

April: Chelsea Art Fair, in London.

May: Bath Festival, including Clerical Medical Jazz Weekend (European jazz) and Bath Contemporary Music Weekend.

May: Brighton Festival. The largest mixed arts festival in England, including theatre, music, opera, street arts, etc.

May: Bishopstock Blues Festival (Devon).

May–June: Urdd National Eisteddfod. Europe's largest youth arts festival, at Lampeter (Dyfed).

May–June: Salisbury Festival (Wiltshire). Various events, including sculpture and street arts.

May–June: Covent Garden Festival, in London. Opera and music theatre.

May–August: Glyndebourne Festival. Opera.

May–September: Shakespeare summer season at the Globe (London).

May–September: Shakespeare at the Open Air Theatre in Regent's Park (London).

May–September: Chichester Festival. Theatre.

June: Singer of the World competition in Cardiff.

June: St Magnus Festival (Orkney). Music.

June: Aldeburgh Festival (Suffolk). Music, visual arts, film.

June: Spitalfields Festival, in London. Music.

June: Glastonbury Festival (Somerset). Pop and rock.

June: Hampton Court Festival. Music.

June–July: City of London Festival. Concerts in churches, livery halls and open spaces.

June–July: Lufthansa Festival of Baroque Music, in London.

June–July: Opera at Garsington (Oxfordshire).

June–July: Opera at Longborough (Gloucestershire).

June–July: Opera at Grange Park (Hampshire).

July: Buxton Festival (Derbyshire). Opera, music and theatre.

July: International Music Eisteddfod at Llangollen (Denbighshire).

July: Cheltenham International Festival. Modern British music.

July: Fishguard International Music Festival (Pembrokeshire).

July: World of Music and Dance at Reading (Berkshire). Festival of world music and dance.

July–August: Edinburgh International Jazz and Blues Festival.

July–September: BBC Henry Wood Promenade Concerts ('the Proms') at the Royal Albert Hall (London).

August: Brecon Jazz Festival (Powys).

August: Machynlleth Festival (Powys). Music.

August: Three Choirs Festival. Rotates between Hereford, Gloucester and Worcester. Founded in 1724, the oldest choral festival in Europe.

August: Royal National Eisteddfod, alternating each year in south and north Wales.

August: Edinburgh International Book Festival.

August: Edinburgh International Film Festival.

August–September: Edinburgh International Festival. Opera, dance, theatre, music, and the famous Fringe.

September: North Wales International Music Festival at St Asaph (Denbighshire).

September: Leeds International Pianoforte Competition.

September–October: Windsor Festival of Music (Berkshire).

October: Royal National Mod (Am Mod Naiseanta Rioghail). At a different venue each year in the Highlands. Music, dance, drama and literature.

October: Canterbury Festival. Various art forms.

October: Malvern Festival (Worcestershire). Exhibitions, music, literature, drama and film.

October: Cheltenham Festival of Literature.

October: Chelsea Crafts Fair, in London.

October–December: Glyndebourne Touring Opera, at various places in England.

November: Oris London Jazz Festival.

November: London Film Festival, hosted by the British Film Institute (*bfi*), which shows some 250 new international films.

November–December: Huddersfield Festival (West Yorkshire). Contemporary music.

Index

A

B

C

D

E

F

G

H

I

O

P

Q

R

S

T

U

V

W

Y

Z

Gas and Oil Production in the UK

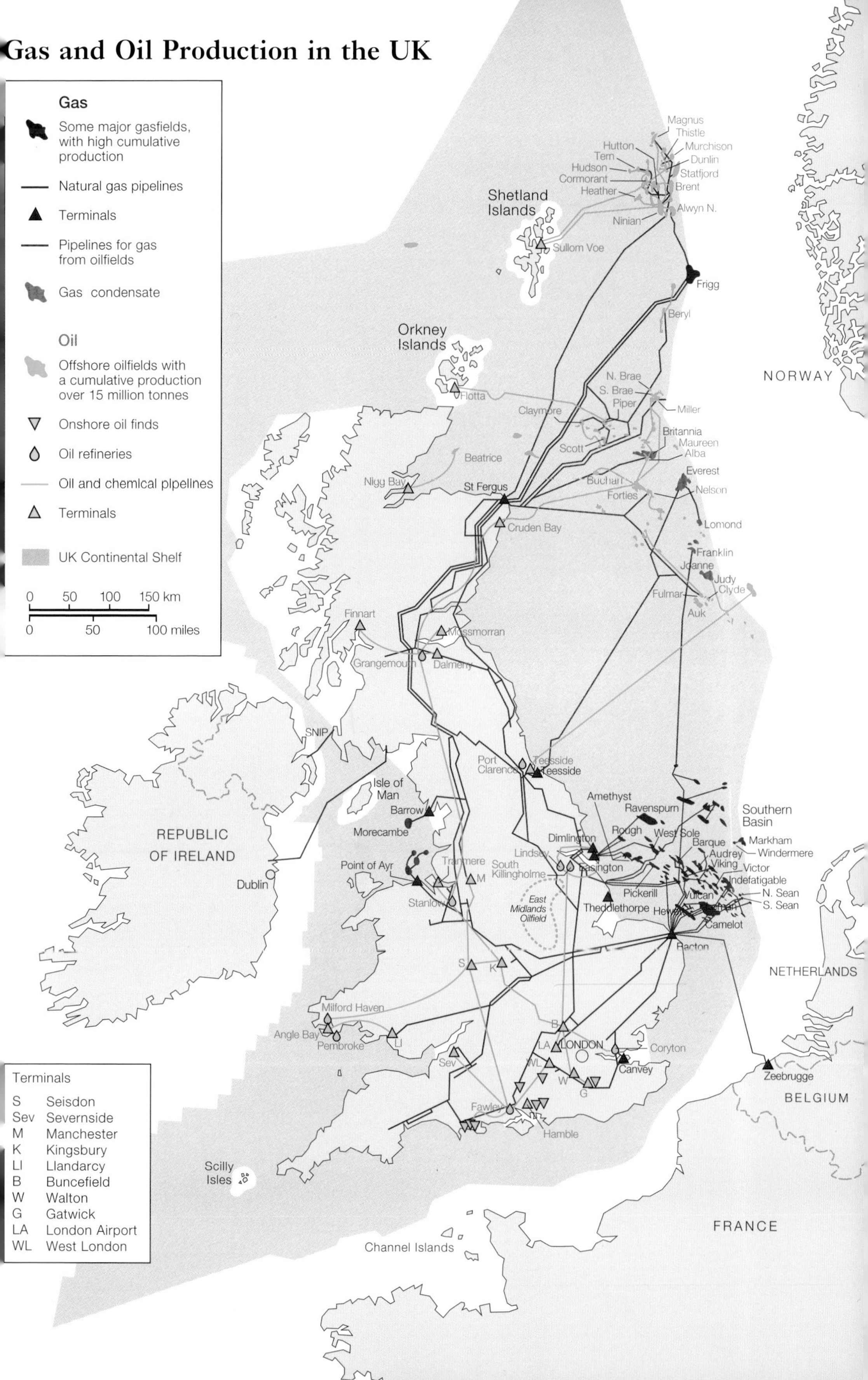

Gas
Some major gasfields, with high cumulative production
Natural gas pipelines
Terminals
Pipelines for gas from oilfields
Gas condensate
Oil
Offshore oilfields with a cumulative production over 15 million tonnes
Onshore oil finds
Oil refineries
Oil and chemical pipelines
Terminals
UK Continental Shelf
0 50 100 150 km
0 50 100 miles
Terminals
S Seisdon
Sev Severnside
M Manchester
K Kingsbury
Ll Llandarcy
B Buncefield
W Walton
G Gatwick
LA London Airport
WL West London
Shetland Islands
Sullom Voe
Magnus
Thistle
Murchison
Dunlin
Statfjord
Brent
Alwyn N.
Hutton
Tern
Hudson
Cormorant
Heather
Ninian
Frigg
Beryl
Orkney Islands
Flotta
NORWAY
N. Brae
S. Brae
Piper
Miller
Claymore
Britannia
Maureen
Alba
Scott
Beatrice
Everest
Nelson
Nigg Bay
St Fergus
Buchan
Forties
Cruden Bay
Lomond
Franklin
Joanne
Judy
Clyde
Fulmar
Auk
Finnart
Mossmorran
Grangemouth
Dalmeny
SNIP
Port Clarence
Teesside
Teesside
Isle of Man
Barrow
Morecambe
Amethyst
Ravenspurn
Southern Basin
Rough
West Sole
Markham
Windermere
Barque
Audrey
Victor
Viking
Indefatigable
REPUBLIC OF IRELAND
Dublin
Dimlington
Easington
Lindsey
South Killingholme
Tranmere
Point of Ayr
Stanlow
East Midlands Oilfield
Pickerill
Theddlethorpe
Vulcan
Hewett
N. Sean
S. Sean
Camelot
Bacton
NETHERLANDS
Milford Haven
Angle Bay
Pembroke
LONDON
Coryton
Canvey
Zeebrugge
BELGIUM
Fawley
Hamble
Scilly Isles
FRANCE
Channel Islands

Passenger Railway Network in the UK

Orkney Islands
Shetland Islands
Wick
Inverness
Kyle of Lochalsh
Aberdeen
SCOTLAND
Mallaig
Fort William
Dundee
Perth
Oban
Stirling
Glasgow
Edinburgh
0 40 80 120 km
0 20 40 60 80 miles
Londonderry
NORTHERN IRELAND
Belfast
Stranraer
Newcastle upon Tyne
Sunderland
Hartlepool
Carlisle
Darlington
Middlesbrough
Scarborough
Harrogate
York
Hull
Leeds
Bradford
Blackpool
Preston
Bolton
Grimsby
Manchester
Doncaster
Sheffield
Liverpool
REPUBLIC OF IRELAND
Holyhead
Retford
Lincoln
Chester
Newark
Crewe
Stoke-on-Trent
Nottingham
Grantham
King's Lynn
Norwich
Shrewsbury
Leicester
Peterborough
Wolverhampton
Birmingham
Rugby
Kettering
Coventry
ENGLAND
Worcester
Northampton
Cambridge
WALES
Hereford
Fishguard
Milton Keynes
Cheltenham
Harwich
Gloucester
Stansted
Colchester
Oxford
London
Southend
Swindon
Newport
Swansea
Reading
Margate
Bristol
Cardiff
Bath
Canterbury
Ashford
Dover
Gatwick
Folkestone
Taunton
Salisbury
Southampton
Hastings
Bournemouth
Eastbourne
Brighton
Portsmouth
Exeter
Weymouth
Newton Abbot
Plymouth
Penzance
France